Schriften zum Internationalen und Europäischen Strafrecht

Edited by

Professor Dr. Martin Heger, Humboldt-Universität zu Berlin
Professor Dr. Florian Jeßberger, Universität Hamburg
Professor Dr. Frank Neubacher, M.A., Universität zu Köln
Professor Dr. Helmut Satzger, LMU München
Professor Dr. Gerhard Werle, Humboldt-Universität zu Berlin

Vol. 11

Sarah Raveling

Self-Representation Before International Criminal Tribunals

Nomos

Stämpfli Verlag

The views expressed herein are those of the author alone and do not necessarily reflect the views of the International Tribunal or the United Nations in general.

Die Deutsche Nationalbibliothek lists this publication in the Deutsche Nationalbibliografie; detailed bibliographic data is available in the Internet at http://dnb.d-nb.de.

a.t.: Berlin, Humboldt-Univ., Diss., 2013

ISBN 978-3-8487-0875-8 (Nomos Verlagsgesellschaft, Baden-Baden)

ISBN 978-3-7272-7741-2 (Stämpfli Verlag, Bern)

1. Edition 2014

"Of course, I'm defending myself here,
but it is a fact that the importance of this trial goes beyond
the importance of a single individual."

Prosecutor v. Radovan Karadžić,
Case No. IT-95-5/18-T,
Hearing, 19 May 2010, T.2380.

Preface/Vorwort

The right to defend oneself in person touches upon fundamental issues with regard to rights of accused before international criminal tribunals. At the same time, it significantly influences the day-to-day trial management of major war crimes trials. This work tries to approach the topic of self-representation before international criminal tribunals from a practical perspective which hopes to shed light on the reasons for which the current system is in need for change.

Die folgende Arbeit wurde im Wintersemester 2012/2013 von der Juristischen Fakultät der Humboldt-Universität zu Berlin als Dissertation angenommen. Text und Nachweise befinden sich auf dem Stand von Oktober 2012. Dadurch sind spätere Entwicklungen wie das erstinstanzliche Urteil im Verfahren gegen Zdravko Tolimir nicht mehr besprochen.

Ganz herzlich bedanken möchte ich mich bei Herrn Professor Dr. Gerhard Werle für seine aufgeschlossene Bereitschaft, mich dieses Thema in der vorliegenden Art bearbeiten zu lassen, seine geduldige Begleitung bei der Entstehung der Arbeit und die Übernahme des Erstgutachtens. Herrn Professor Dr. Florian Jeßberger danke ich für die Übernahme und rasche Erstellung des Zweitgutachtens.

Mein besonderer Dank gilt meinen Eltern, die mich ausnahmlos in meinen Unternehmungen unterstützen und mit ihrem Glauben an meine Fähigkeiten die Entstehung dieser Arbeit, wie so vieles andere, erst ermöglicht haben. Ihnen ist diese Arbeit gewidmet.

Den Haag, Dezember 2013 — Sarah Raveling

Contents

CHAPTER ONE. Background

A. Introduction: Subject and methodology

More than fifteen years after the creation of the *ad hoc* tribunals for the former Yugoslavia and for Rwanda, and over ten years after the signature of the Rome Statute of the International Criminal Court (ICC), the right to self-representation before international criminal tribunals remains a debated issue. The topic continues to give rise to dispute and discussions despite years during which jurisprudence and practice developed in the context of proceedings with accused presenting their defence in person.

This dissertation will examine the origins of the right to self-representation before international criminal tribunals[1] and highlight the problems, issues and developments which could be observed over the past years. To be looked at in the course of this enquiry are the potential lessons to be drawn for the future work of the ICC as a permanent institution occupied with international criminal procedure. In conclusion, it will be argued that the right to defend oneself in person will have to be approached and implemented differently in future international criminal proceedings in order to adequately address the realities of major criminal trials.

This study is set to examine the nature, scope and implications of the right to self-representation before international criminal tribunals.[2] The dissertation will focus on the exercise of the right to self-representation in international criminal proceedings as well as the theoretical and practical repercussions on the conduct of international criminal trials. On the basis of an analysis of the existing jurisprudence and developments in the international criminal legal system, an assessment will be made of the possible future dealing with the right to self-representation in international criminal institutions such as

1 The term "international criminal tribunals" is meant to encompass all international and internationalised (hybrid) tribunals and courts dealing with international criminal law, whether of an *ad hoc* or permanent nature.

2 Any decisions, jurisprudence or other official texts with authoritative versions in English or French will be referred to in the language of the authoritative text, respectively. The use of but the last names of persons will occur for ease of writing and reading solely. If the last name of an accused before a tribunal or court is written in *italics*, the reference regards the proceedings in that case in general.

the International Criminal Court. It will have to be analysed in this context whether the right to self-representation as currently acknowledged and practiced at international criminal tribunals is a model to be adopted in the future or whether the International Criminal Court could and should draw from the experiences of other international criminal tribunals in order to rectify identified complications.

At the outset, the foundation for the exercise of the right to self-representation before international criminal tribunals will be established. While it has been argued that the right to defend oneself should be seen as a privilege rather than a right,[3] the review of the pertinent jurisprudence will show that international criminal tribunals in general consider the right to self-representation as fundamental right which forms part of the overarching right to a fair trial. Having determined this position, this dissertation will examine whether the practical implications of the exercise of the right to conduct one's defence in person still allow for this prominent status. A review of the potential and actual practical repercussions of the exercise of the right to self-representation in international criminal proceedings thus far will lead to the conclusion that the interests of all participants, from the accused in particular to the international community in general, may be better served with an appropriately amended understanding of the right as a right to defend oneself in person in a broader sense, rather than a right to self-representation as currently recognised before international criminal tribunals.

Therefore, it will be argued in the course of this dissertation that it will be necessary for upcoming international criminal proceedings to modify the application of the right to self-representation in order to address well-known and often criticised complications. An adapted model of a right to defend oneself in person will be more capable of striking the required balance between fundamental concepts such as the right to self-representation – as recognised thus far in international criminal tribunals – and the public interests in the delivery of justice in an encompassing sense.[4]

---

3 *Cf.* Mark Ellis, Self-Representation is a Privilege, Not a Right, 23 (42) *Lawyer* 6 (2009). *See also* Alexander Zahar, Legal Aid, Self-Representation, and the Crisis at the Hague Tribunal, 19 *Criminal Law Forum* 241 (2008), at 247, 249.

4 *See* Joanne Williams, Slobodan Milosevic and the Guarantee of Self-Representation, 32 *Brooklyn Journal of International Law* 553 (2007), at 555; Rachel K. Jones, Untangling the Right to Self-Representation in the International Criminal Tribunal for the Former Yugoslavia, 43 *Georgia Law Review* 1285 (2009), at 1287; *Anthony Pasquall Faretta v. State of California* (U.S. Supreme Court), 422 U.S. 806, 30 June

A modified approach to the exercise of a right to defend oneself in person in international criminal proceedings may be of particular significance for upcoming cases before the International Criminal Court, as they may involve additional and distinct complexities such as the possibility of victim participation in the proceedings. With victim communities potentially being an additional party to the proceedings, their interests need to be taken into account even more as regards procedural aspects of a case than in ordinary international criminal proceedings. Therefore, additional interests will weigh in the balance considering the exercise of the right to defend oneself in person. In light of the model which will be favoured in this dissertation which places an emphasis on active participation by an accused rather than the conduct of the entire defence as one's own counsel, it may be feasible to create solutions which adequately address the concerns of all parties and participants to the proceedings, including participating victims.

This dissertation will outline the pertinent statutory provisions on the right to defend oneself in person, as can be found in statutes, rules of procedure and evidence, and practice directions of international criminal tribunals, in order to provide the basis which has been interpreted and applied in the course of international criminal proceedings.

Subsequently, the main focus of this dissertation will be on the review and analysis of the relevant jurisprudence and practice of international criminal tribunals thus far which shape the exercise of the right to self-representation. This review and analysis will include decisions, filings of all participants as well as transcripts of hearings which equally reflect the interpretation and application of the relevant provisions. Views expressed in literature and academic publications will be examined as a supplement in order to question and argue own concepts or underline certain positions advanced in this dissertation with regard to the interpretation and application of the law by international criminal tribunals. However, the predominant emphasis of this dissertation will be on the practical aspects of the right to self-representation before international criminal tribunals, as this practice provides the main contribution to the development and changes in the interpretation and exercise of this right.

Cases that will be examined in this dissertation derive primarily from the International Criminal Tribunal for the Former Yugoslavia (ICTY), namely

---

1975, Dissenting Opinion Chief Justice Burger, joined by Justices Blackmun and Rehnquist, at 839-840.

the proceedings involving Slobodan Milošević, Radovan Karadžić, Vojislav Šešelj, Zdravko Tolimir and Momčilo Krajišnik. In addition, the relevant jurisprudence from the International Criminal Tribunal for Rwanda (ICTR) as well as the Special Court for Sierra Leone (SCSL) will be analysed. The research will highlight the consistencies and divergences in the approaches adopted, and include examination of cases in which accused invoked their right to defend themselves in person without ultimately exercising it (*cf.* Samuel Hinga Norman before the SCSL), as well as a case in which the defendant successfully invoked his right to self-represent only at the appeals – but not the trial – stage of the proceedings (*cf.* Momčilo Krajišnik before the ICTY).

Even though future proceedings, for example at the International Criminal Court, are likely to be faced with similar scenarios as those to be analysed in this dissertation in case accused request to exercise the right to conduct their defence in person, it may be sufficient for upcoming international criminal trials to interpret and develop the practices which have been shaped in the course of international criminal proceedings over years with the adequate flexibility to allow for new approaches. Therefore, this dissertation will not necessarily argue that the statutory provisions of international criminal tribunals inevitably have to be amended in order to address the practical implications of the exercise of the right to self-representation.

In conclusion, this dissertation will adopt the position that the right to defend oneself in person in international criminal proceedings should be given a new meaning which places the emphasis on active participation of accused whenever so requested and determined to be feasible, in conjunction with professional representation by counsel, rather than the exercise of a right to self-representation which has given rise to complications and criticism in a number of international criminal trials. This modified model will be capable of addressing the concerns and interests of all participants to the proceedings – above all and including the accused – and is adapted to the specific nature of international criminal proceedings.

B. The right to self-representation in national and regional jurisdictions

In order to determine the scope of the right to self-representation in the context of international criminal trials and its theoretical as well as practical impact on international criminal proceedings, this dissertation will first examine the origins and developments of such a right, to be followed by a description and examination of the *status quo*. Before addressing the provisions as found in regional, supranational and international instruments, a succinct discussion of selected national practices is in order to provide a rough background of the development of a right to self-representation before international criminal tribunals. While the provisions adopted at international criminal tribunals can be traced back to the wording of the International Covenant on Civil and Political Rights, to be discussed later, the interpretation and application of the specific right to self-representation in practice mostly draws from experiences in national and regional jurisdictions.

I. National jurisdictions

1. Common law systems: The example of *Faretta v. California*

The following part of the dissertation will provide a concise overview of the origins of the right to self-representation in common law systems, taking the specific example of the jurisprudence of the United States Supreme Court on the matter. In general it can be noted that the purpose of allowing self-representation in early jury trials was to favour self-incrimination of an accused that necessarily did not possess the knowledge required to mount an effective defence.[5] Yet, time favoured the development of rights to be granted to defendants in the courtroom, taking into account the necessity to offer a certain degree of protection to accused, thereby creating the basis for fair trial rights such as the right to counsel.[6]

One important decision to be examined as an indication of a specific common law position on the right to self-representation is the decision of the United States Supreme Court of 1975 in *Faretta v. California*.[7] In this

---

5 Eugene Cerruti, Self-Representation in the International Arena: Removing a False Right to Spectacle, 40 *Georgetown Journal of International Law* 919 (2009), at 923, 927-928.

6 Sharon Finegan, Pro Se Criminal Trials and the Merging of Inquisitorial and Adversarial Systems of Justice, 58 *Catholic University Law Review* 445 (2009), at 449-450; Eugene Cerruti, Self-Representation in the International Arena: Removing a False Right to Spectacle, 40 *Georgetown Journal of International Law* 919 (2009), at 931-940. *See also Powell et al. v. State of Alabama* (U.S. Supreme Court), 287 U.S. 45, 07 November 1932.

7 *Anthony Pasquall Faretta v. State of California* (U.S. Supreme Court), 422 U.S. 806, 30 June 1975.

decision, the U.S. Supreme Court recognised a right to self-representation stemming from the Sixth and Fourteenth Amendments to the U.S. Constitution, with a status equal to the right to counsel explicitly safeguarded in the Sixth Amendment. The decision will need to be discussed in further detail given that international criminal tribunals took this particular decision as primary guideline for solutions to the right of self-representation in the context of international criminal proceedings.

Justice Stewart, writing the majority opinion of the U.S. Supreme Court which acknowledged a constitutional right to self-representation,[8] based his analysis on the reading of the Sixth Amendment by federal U.S. courts[9] and on the historic roots of the Amendment in English legal history.[10] The majority opinion saw a constitutional right of self-representation "necessarily implied by the structure of the Amendment", despite the fact that it was not named as such in the text.[11] In the majority's view, it would not accord with the right to a fair trial to impose a lawyer on an unwilling defendant who would consequently not get the defence of his choice.[12] Justice Stewart focused on the personal nature of the choice of a defendant whether to present his own defence and of the consequences to be borne eventually by the defendant and not counsel or state.[13] While emphasising the fundamental importance of the right to self-representation, Justice Stewart did concede that there must be a possibility to assign counsel to a *pro se* defendant in case of

---

8 *Anthony Pasquall Faretta v. State of California* (U.S. Supreme Court), 422 U.S. 806, 30 June 1975, at 817.

9 *Anthony Pasquall Faretta v. State of California* (U.S. Supreme Court), 422 U.S. 806, 30 June 1975, at 812, 813. The text of the Sixth Amendment reads: "In all criminal prosecutions, the accused shall enjoy the right to a speedy and public trial, by an impartial jury of the state and district wherein the crime shall have been committed, which district shall have been previously ascertained by law, and to be informed of the nature and form of the accusation; to be confronted with the witnesses against him; to have compulsory process for obtaining witnesses in his favour, and to have the assistance of counsel for his defence." Available for example at http://www.archives.gov/exhibits/charters/bill_of_rights_transcript.html (last accessed 13 October 2012).

10 *Anthony Pasquall Faretta v. State of California* (U.S. Supreme Court), 422 U.S. 806, 30 June 1975, at 818.

11 *Anthony Pasquall Faretta v. State of California* (U.S. Supreme Court), 422 U.S. 806, 30 June 1975, at 819-820, 821.

12 *Anthony Pasquall Faretta v. State of California* (U.S. Supreme Court), 422 U.S. 806, 30 June 1975, at 832-833, 834.

13 *Anthony Pasquall Faretta v. State of California* (U.S. Supreme Court), 422 U.S. 806, 30 June 1975, at 834.

disruption of the proceedings.[14] It was further made clear that a self-represented accused could, due to his choice, not benefit from the same advantages as represented accused,[15] a view later to be found in the ICTY jurisprudence. Therefore, in light of its consequences, this choice would need to be an informed and voluntary one.[16]

However, the decision of the U.S. Supreme Court was not unanimous: two dissenting opinions heavily criticised the approach taken by the majority. The first dissent of Chief Justice Burger did not see a constitutional basis for a right to self-representation[17] and considered it undesirable to provide any accused, independent of any potential background in education or experience, the possibility to conduct his or her own defence.[18] At least in most cases it would not be of advantage for an accused to represent him- or herself.[19] Additionally, the role of prosecution and judges to serve justice in a wider sense and preserve the criminal justice system would be jeopardised.[20] Consequently, it would need to be determined by the trial judge whether a defendant wishing to act *pro se* would actually be in a position to and capable of doing so.[21]

The remainder of the first dissent of Chief Justice Burger, as well as the second dissenting opinion of Justice Blackmun, criticised the majority's attempt to base its conclusions on a historical analysis of the matter or on se-

---

14 *Anthony Pasquall Faretta v. State of California* (U.S. Supreme Court), 422 U.S. 806, 30 June 1975, at 834 fn.46.

15 *Anthony Pasquall Faretta v. State of California* (U.S. Supreme Court), 422 U.S. 806, 30 June 1975, at 835.

16 *Anthony Pasquall Faretta v. State of California* (U.S. Supreme Court), 422 U.S. 806, 30 June 1975, at 807, 835.

17 *Anthony Pasquall Faretta v. State of California* (U.S. Supreme Court), 422 U.S. 806, 30 June 1975, Dissenting Opinion Chief Justice Burger, joined by Justices Blackmun and Rehnquist, at 837.

18 *Anthony Pasquall Faretta v. State of California* (U.S. Supreme Court), 422 U.S. 806, 30 June 1975, Dissenting Opinion Chief Justice Burger, joined by Justices Blackmun and Rehnquist, at 836.

19 *Anthony Pasquall Faretta v. State of California* (U.S. Supreme Court), 422 U.S. 806, 30 June 1975, Dissenting Opinion Chief Justice Burger, joined by Justices Blackmun and Rehnquist, at 838.

20 *Anthony Pasquall Faretta v. State of California* (U.S. Supreme Court), 422 U.S. 806, 30 June 1975, Dissenting Opinion Chief Justice Burger, joined by Justices Blackmun and Rehnquist, at 839-840.

21 *Anthony Pasquall Faretta v. State of California* (U.S. Supreme Court), 422 U.S. 806, 30 June 1975, Dissenting Opinion Chief Justice Burger, joined by Justices Blackmun and Rehnquist, at 840.

lected extracts of case law.[22] It is of particular interest for purposes of this dissertation that the dissent of Justice Blackmun alluded to procedural problems which would inevitably arise in the context of trials with self-represented accused[23] – problems which will be subject of discussion later in this dissertation. Justice Blackmun concluded that "[i]f there is any truth to the old proverb that 'one who is his own lawyer has a fool for a client', the Court by its opinion today now bestows a constitutional right on one to make a fool of himself".[24]

As formulated by Justice Stewart, the Supreme Court was concerned with the question whether a *constitutional* right to self-representation exists.[25] The question was thus not whether there is such a right at all, but rather whether it was also guaranteed by the U.S. Constitution and whether, in consequence, states would be constitutionally prohibited from imposing a lawyer on defendants that had expressed the wish to conduct their own defence. The majority's review of the state's jurisprudence, including decisions of the court of appeals, led to a finding of a "consensus not easily ignored".[26] Chief Justice Burger in his dissent did not show himself convinced by the reading of the jurisprudence as brought forward by the majority and attempted to show that the "consensus" detected in the decision was not as crystal clear

---

22 *Anthony Pasquall Faretta v. State of California* (U.S. Supreme Court), 422 U.S. 806, 30 June 1975, Dissenting Opinion Chief Justice Burger, joined by Justices Blackmun and Rehnquist, at 840-846; Dissenting Opinion Justice Blackmun, joined by Justices Burger and Rehnquist, at 846-852.

23 *Anthony Pasquall Faretta v. State of California* (U.S. Supreme Court), 422 U.S. 806, 30 June 1975, Dissenting Opinion Justice Blackmun, joined by Justices Burger and Rehnquist, at 852: "Must every defendant be advised of his right to proceed pro se? If so, when must that notice be given? Since the right to assistance of counsel and the right to self-representation are mutually exclusive, how is the waiver of each right to be measured? If a defendant has elected to exercise his right to proceed pro se, does he still have a constitutional right to assistance of standby counsel? How soon in the criminal proceeding must a defendant decide between proceeding by counsel or pro se? Must he be allowed to switch in midtrial? May a violation of the right to self-representation ever be harmless error? Must the trial court treat the pro se defendant differently than it would professional counsel?".

24 *Anthony Pasquall Faretta v. State of California* (U.S. Supreme Court), 422 U.S. 806, 30 June 1975, Dissenting Opinion Justice Blackmun, joined by Justices Burger and Rehnquist, at 852.

25 *Anthony Pasquall Faretta v. State of California* (U.S. Supreme Court), 422 U.S. 806, 30 June 1975, at 807.

26 *Anthony Pasquall Faretta v. State of California* (U.S. Supreme Court), 422 U.S. 806, 30 June 1975, at 817.

as portrayed.[27] Indeed, it appears that the decisions relied upon by the majority are not necessarily as unambiguous and to the point as found by the Supreme Court.[28] Of note in this context is one early decision of the Supreme Court which explicitly refers to a "recognized privilege" of self-representation.[29] The later statement by Justice Stewart that a right to self-representation would be "necessarily implied by the structure of the [Sixth] Amendment"[30] equally needs to be questioned. It is interesting that the majority opinion seemed to see a need to find support for its conclusions in the English and colonial legal history, which leads to the question whether this was warranted for want of other clear indications of a constitutional basis of the right. Such reference to foreign law by the U.S. Supreme Court is of note insofar as the practice of resorting to comparative law is not uncontroversial in the context of determining constitutional questions by U.S. courts.[31]

---

27 *Anthony Pasquall Faretta v. State of California* (U.S. Supreme Court), 422 U.S. 806, 30 June 1975, Dissenting Opinion Chief Justice Burger, joined by Justices Blackmun and Rehnquist, at 840-843.

28 *Cf. Adams v. U.S. ex rel. McCann* (U.S. Supreme Court), 317 U.S. 269, 21 December 1942; *Carter v. People of State of Illinois* (U.S. Supreme Court), 329 U.S. 173, 09 December 1946.

29 *Price v. Johnston* (U.S. Supreme Court), 334 U.S. 266, 24 May 1948, at 285-286, overruled on other grounds by *Warren McCleskey v. Walter D. Zant* (U.S. Supreme Court), 499 U.S. 467, 16 April 1991.

30 *Anthony Pasquall Faretta v. State of California* (U.S. Supreme Court), 422 U.S. 806, 30 June 1975, at 819. *See also* at 820, 821.

31 Cheryl Saunders, The Use and Misuse of Comparative Constitutional Law, 13 *Indiana Journal of Global Legal Studies* 37 (2006), at 39; Luke Nikas, Rethinking the Use of Foreign Law and Public Consensus: The U.S. Supreme Court's Inconsistent Methods for Defining Constitutional Rights, 13 *Lewis & Clark Law Review* 1007 (2009), at 1008; Ganesh Sitarama, The Use and Abuse of Foreign Law in Constitutional Interpretation, 32 *Harvard Journal of Law and Public Policy* 653 (2009), at 655; Jacob Foster, The Use of Foreign Law in Constitutional Interpretation: Lessons from South Africa, 45 *University of San Francisco Law Review* 79 (2010), at 79. *See also Jay Printz v. Richard Mack* (U.S. Supreme Court), 521 U.S. 898, 27 June 1997, Dissenting Opinion Justice Breyer, joined by Justice Stevens, at 977 (emphasising the "empirical value" of a comparative exercise); *Donald P. Roper v. Christopher Simmons* (U.S. Supreme Court), 543 U.S. 551, 01 March 2005, at 578 ("It does not lessen our fidelity to the Constitution or our pride in its origins to acknowledge that the express affirmation of certain fundamental rights by other nations and peoples simply underscores the centrality of those same rights within our own heritage of freedom."); but also *Donald P. Roper v. Christopher Simmons* (U.S. Supreme Court), 543 U.S. 551, 01 March 2005, Dissenting Opinion Justice Scalia, joined by Chief Justice Rehnquist and Justice Thomas, at 627: "To invoke alien law when it

In addition, it appears rather extraordinary that despite the emphasis placed on the constitutional nature of the right to self-representation by the majority opinion, it only takes a footnote to hold that such right may be restricted by the trial judge in cases of obstruction.[32] This leaves the impression that establishing a basis for restrictions was significantly easier than finding the right itself rooted in the U.S. Constitution to begin with. In any event, the majority decision is probably best considered keeping in mind that the emphasis seems to be on safeguarding a defendant's free choice whether to be represented by counsel. This transpires from the majority opinion which made clear that it is the accused who will eventually have to bear the consequences of his or her defence,[33] and that if he or she does indeed elect to self-represent, there is no room to later complain about the results of such a defence.[34] In a similar vein, the majority opinion held that a defendant electing to proceed *pro se* would not enjoy the advantages of representation by counsel.[35] For purposes of this dissertation, it should be borne in mind that the conclusion reached by the majority in *Faretta* was not uncontroversial, which might have an impact on the examination of the application of the decision in subsequent international criminal jurisprudence. At the same time, it is also important to be aware of the caveats which the U.S. Supreme Court provided in the majority decision. These caveats include that a decision to defend oneself in person needs to be made knowingly and intelligently; that a self-represented accused does not enjoy the privileges and advantages of represented defendants; and that the former cannot subsequently make the potentially poor quality of his or her defence subject of a complaint. It will be shown that the jurisprudence at international criminal tribunals based its recognition and application of the right to self-representation on similar considerations.

Almost twenty years after *Faretta*, the U.S. Supreme Court went even further in its recognition of the right to defend oneself in person in finding

agrees with one's own thinking, and ignore it otherwise, is not reasoned decisionmaking, but sophistry."

32 *Anthony Pasquall Faretta v. State of California* (U.S. Supreme Court), 422 U.S. 806, 30 June 1975, at 834 fn.46.

33 *Anthony Pasquall Faretta v. State of California* (U.S. Supreme Court), 422 U.S. 806, 30 June 1975, at 834.

34 *Anthony Pasquall Faretta v. State of California* (U.S. Supreme Court), 422 U.S. 806, 30 June 1975, at 834 fn.46.

35 *Anthony Pasquall Faretta v. State of California* (U.S. Supreme Court), 422 U.S. 806, 30 June 1975, at 835.

that the competency standard required to waive one's right to counsel and thus proceed *pro se* was the same as for competency to stand trial.[36] According to the U.S. Supreme Court, there was already a "heightened" standard for waiving the right to counsel insofar as the waiver had to be knowing and voluntary.[37] Justice Blackmun in his dissenting opinion disagreed with the majority opinion in that "a defendant who is utterly incapable of conducting his own defense cannot be considered 'competent' to make such a decision, any more than a person who chooses to leap out of a window in the belief that he can fly can be considered 'competent' to make such a choice."[38] However, a more recent decision by the U.S. Supreme Court opened the door for states to deny the invoked right to self-represent if the defendant's mental capacity might allow him or her to stand trial, but not necessarily enable the accused to conduct the defence in person, thereby expressly acknowledging a competency limitation for the exercise of self-representation.[39] At the same time, the U.S. Supreme Court declined to overrule *Faretta* on the basis of "recent empirical research" which would suggest that trials with *pro se* defendants are not necessarily less fair.[40] The dissenting opinion of Justice Scalia rejected the idea of any constitutional room for states to substitute even a mentally ill defendant's choice for the sake of fairness.[41]

---

36 *Godinez v. Moran* (U.S. Supreme Court), 509 U.S. 389, 24 June 1993, at 399-400. The court held that "the competence that is required of a defendant seeking to waive his right to counsel is the competence to *waive the right*, not the competence to represent himself." *Ibid.*, at 399 (emphasis in the original).

37 *Godinez v. Moran* (U.S. Supreme Court), 509 U.S. 389, 24 June 1993, at 400-402.

38 *Godinez v. Moran* (U.S. Supreme Court), 509 U.S. 389, 24 June 1993, Dissenting Opinion Justice Blackmun, joined by Justice Stevens, at 416. *See also* John F. Decker, The Sixth Amendment Right to Shoot Oneself in the Foot: An Assessment of the Guarantee of Self-Representation Twenty Years After Faretta, 6 *Seton Hall Constitutional Law Journal* 483 (1996), at 517-523.

39 *Indiana v. Ahmad Edwards* (U.S. Supreme Court), 554 U.S. 164, 19 June 2008, at 174-176.

40 *Indiana v. Ahmad Edwards* (U.S. Supreme Court), 554 U.S. 164, 19 June 2008, at 178, referring to Erica J. Hashimoto, Defending the Right of Self-Representation: An Empirical Look at the Pro Se Felony Defendant, 85 *North Carolina Law Review* 423 (2007), at 427-428, 447.

41 *Indiana v. Ahmad Edwards* (U.S. Supreme Court), 554 U.S. 164, 19 June 2008, Dissenting Opinion Justice Scalia, joined by Justice Thomas, at 180: "In my view the Constitution does not permit a State to substitute its own perception of fairness for the defendant's right to make his own case before the jury – a specific right long understood as essential to a fair trial." For a critique of the decision see also: Jaime Kristine Richards, Shots, Shoes, and Self-Representation: Indiana v. Edwards and

When the U.S. Court of Appeals for the Ninth Circuit had to decide on whether a defendant had waived his right to counsel in an informed, intelligent and voluntary manner, Judge Reinhardt wrote a specially concurring opinion in which he argued that the fundamental right to a fair trial in case of conflict with the right to self-representation would have to prevail.[42] It was argued that the U.S. Supreme Court should acknowledge this conflict created by *Faretta* and reconsider the repercussions of that decision,[43] especially the question whether an accused may at all waive his or her right to a fair trial.[44]

In the same vein, critics have argued in recent years that the practical implications of a right to defend oneself in person endanger the guarantee of a fair trial.[45] Similarly, as maintained in the later discussion in particular by proponents of a restriction of a right to self-representation in the international sphere, certain common law systems equally know limitations to that right. To be mentioned in this context are proceedings with disruptive defendants, case in which already the *Faretta* court recognised the possibility to impose counsel on an accused.[46] Additionally, a further concept which can be found in U.S. case law and of relevance to this dissertation is the idea of "hybrid representation", which gives the defendant the possibility – but not the right – to actively participate in his or her trial when validly waiving the right to counsel, while however still retaining professional defence counsel.[47]

---

the New Limitation on the Sixth Amendment Right of Self-Representation, 60 *Mercer Law Review* 1509 (2009), at 1524-1526.

42 *United States of America v. Kashani Farhad* (U.S. Court of Appeals Ninth Circuit), 190 F.3d 1097, 13 September 1999, Judge Reinhardt specially concurring, at 1102. The judge argued that "[…] elevating a Sixth Amendment procedural right over the fundamental right to a fair trial, as *Faretta* implicitly does, impermissibly elevates form over substance." *Ibid.*, at 1105.

43 *United States of America v. Kashani Farhad* (U.S. Court of Appeals Ninth Circuit), 190 F.3d 1097, 13 September 1999, Judge Reinhardt specially concurring, at 1102, 1106.

44 *United States of America v. Kashani Farhad* (U.S. Court of Appeals Ninth Circuit), 190 F.3d 1097, 13 September 1999, Judge Reinhardt specially concurring, at 1107-1108.

45 Martin Sabelli/Stacey Leyton, Train Wrecks and Freeway Crashes: An Argument for Fairness and Against Self Representation in the Criminal Justice System, 91 *Journal of Criminal Law and Criminology* 161 (2000), at 165.

46 *Anthony Pasquall Faretta v. State of California* (U.S. Supreme Court), 422 U.S. 806, 30 June 1975, at 834 fn.46.

47 John F. Decker, The Sixth Amendment Right to Shoot Oneself in the Foot: An Assessment of the Guarantee of Self-Representation Twenty Years After Faretta, 6

Finally, as will be discussed further below, the right is not equally recognised for example in U.S. courts at trial and appellate stages of the proceedings and jurisprudence has established criteria for the imposition of and role to be played by standby counsel.

Considering the status of the right to self-representation for example in the United Kingdom, it appears that the practice of self-representation has a long history and nowadays takes a stance similar to the U.S. acknowledgement,[48] as do other legal systems adopting a primarily common law approach in criminal proceedings.[49] One decision to be noted in the context of this dissertation is *Woodward*: a defendant had counsel assigned to him under the Poor Prisoners' Defence Act 1930, yet counsel handed his mandate over to another counsel who did not have the opportunity to meet with his client before trial.[50] The accused then asked to conduct his own defence but was refused to do so.[51] The court found that "no person charged with a criminal offence ought to have counsel forced on him against his will."[52] This was, however, restricted insofar as was held that if counsel had already started to represent the accused, the latter could then not midway express his wish to conduct the case in person.[53] Additionally of interest is the decision in *Lyons* which upheld the decision of the trial judge to refuse the defendant's request

---

Seton Hall Constitutional Law Journal 483 (1996), at 537-544; Joshua L. Howard, Hybrid Representation and Standby Counsel: Let's Clear the Air for the Attorneys of South Carolina, 52 *South Carolina Law Review* 851 (2001), at 857-865.

48 *Cf. Anthony Pasquall Faretta v. State of California* (U.S. Supreme Court), 422 U.S. 806, 30 June 1975, at 821-826. *See also* Shawn A. Carter, The Pro Se Dilemma: Can Too Many Rights Make a Wrong?, 62 *Louisiana Law Review* 1299 (2002), at 1306; Eugene Cerruti, Self-Representation in the International Arena: Removing a False Right to Spectacle, 40 *Georgetown Journal of International Law* 919 (2009), at 926-932.

49 *Cf.* Jona Goldschmidt, Judicial Assistance to Self-Represented Litigants: Lessons from the Canadian Experience, 17 *Michigan State Journal of International Law* 601 (2008-2009), at 611; Rachel K. Jones, Untangling the Right to Self-Representation in the International Criminal Tribunal for the Former Yugoslavia, 43 *Georgia Law Review* 1285 (2009), at 1296.

50 *R. v Ernest Isaac Woodward*, (1944) 29 Cr. App. R. 159, 08 December 1943, at 160.

51 *R. v Ernest Isaac Woodward*, (1944) 29 Cr. App. R. 159, 08 December 1943, at 160-161.

52 *R. v Ernest Isaac Woodward*, (1944) 29 Cr. App. R. 159, 08 December 1943, at 161.

53 *R. v Ernest Isaac Woodward*, (1944) 29 Cr. App. R. 159, 08 December 1943, at 161.

to take over his defence towards the end of the case, and further clarified that this kind of decision fell within the discretion of the trial judge.[54]

In general it has to be kept in mind for purposes of this dissertation, however, that case and statutory law have developed restrictions on the practical exercise of the right to self-representation in order to protect *e.g.* victims in rape cases from being cross-examined by the alleged perpetrator.[55]

2. Civil law / Other legal systems: Review of legislation[56]

Examining specific examples of positions adopted in some civil law systems, it can be said from the outset that, contrary to the widespread recognition as discussed above, civil law countries do not place such an emphasis on the recognition of the free choice of an individual as expression of his or her autonomy,[57] but rather on the protection of that individual against inference

54 *R. v Desmond Francis Lyons*, (1979) 68 Cr. App. R. 104, 10-11 July 1978, at 107-108.

55 *See e.g.* England and Wales Youth Justice and Criminal Evidence Act 1999, section 38; Sexual Offences (Procedure and Evidence) (Scotland) Act 2002 and Sexual Offences (Procedure and Evidence) (Scotland) Act 2002 Explanatory Notes. *See also* Canada Criminal Code (R.S., 1985, c. C-46), act current to 02 December 2010, available at http://laws.justice.gc.ca/eng/C-46/FullText.html (last accessed 17 November 2012), sect.486.3.

56 By characterising the systems under review to include civil law and "other" legal systems, this dissertation attempts to avoid additional generalisations by summarising all reviewed countries under the civil law model, as – similar to the broad characterisation of common law – no generally homogeneous civil law system can be said to exist. *Cf.* Vladimir Tochilovsky, Legal Systems and Cultures in the International Criminal Court: The Experience from the International Criminal Tribunal for the Former Yugoslavia, in: Horst Fischer/Claus Kreß/Sascha Rolf Lüder (eds), *International and National Prosecution of Crimes Under International Law. Current Developments* (Berlin: Berlin Verlag Arno Spitz GmbH) 2001, p.627-644, at 630. *See also* Kensie Kim, Mixed Systems in Legal Origin Analysis, 83 *Southern California Law Review* 693 (2010), at 701; Salvatore Mancuso, The New African Law: Beyond the Difference Between Common Law and Civil Law, 14 *Annual Survey of International and Comparative Law* 39 (2008), at 42-43.

57 *Cf.* Erica J. Hashimoto, Resurrecting Autonomy: The Criminal Defendant's Right to Control the Case, 90 *Boston University Law Review* 1147 (2010), at 1156. *See*, however, Eugene Cerruti, Self-Representation in the International Arena: Removing a False Right to Spectacle, 40 *Georgetown Journal of International Law* 919 (2009), at 925: "Self-Representation is not an inherent guarantee of individual autonomy essential to the philosophy of the adversarial system."

by state authorities.[58] While this is necessarily a generalisation adopting rather broad dividing lines, it ought to suffice as plain basis for the discussions to follow.[59]

In the context relevant for this dissertation, this approach may lead to mandatory representation by counsel for example in cases of a certain gravity, in order to safeguard the fair trial rights of all participants – even if this might go against the express waiver by an accused of his or her right to counsel and, potentially, right to fair proceedings. However, to be noted in this regard is the Italian system which, after the adoption of a reformed code of criminal procedure, is generally said to have attempted to incorporate substantive adversarial characteristics into its criminal procedure.[60] Yet, as affirmed by the country's constitutional court, an accused does not have any possibility to defend him- or herself in court and is required to engage counsel in order to represent his or her interests – on the basis that *because* of the adversarial nature of the system, meant to safeguard a right to fair trial, equality of arms between the parties would need to be guaranteed.[61] Thus, the specific Italian context provides a particularly interesting and unique illustration of the fact that a legal interpretation which in most common law, adversarial-type systems leads to a broad recognition of an accused's autonomous choice to self-

---

58 *Cf.* Stefan Trechsel, *Human Rights in Criminal Proceedings* (Oxford: Oxford University Press) 2005, p.263, speaking of the "liberal" and the "social" approach to the administration of criminal justice. *See also* Eugene Cerruti, Self-Representation in the International Arena: Removing a False Right to Spectacle, 40 *Georgetown Journal of International Law* 919 (2009), at 970-971.

59 For a more detailed discussion of the two approaches which the author calls "reactive state" and "activist state", and the respective procedural models which the author subsequently labels "conflict-solving" and "policy-implementing" justice, *see* Mirjan R. Damaška, *The Faces of Justice and State Authority. A Comparative Approach to the Legal Process* (New Haven/London: Yale University Press) 1986, p.71-88.

60 Mario Chiavario, Some Considerations on Faces of Justice by a 'Non-Specialist', 6 *Journal of International Criminal Justice* 69 (2008), at 70-71. *See also* William T. Pizzi/Luca Marafioti, The New Italian Code of Criminal Procedure: The Difficulties of Building an Adversarial System on a Civil Law Foundation, 17 *Yale Journal of International Law* 1 (1992), at 10-15; and critical of the results of the reform: Elisabetta Grande, Italian Criminal Justice: Borrowing and Resistance, 48 *American Journal of Comparative Law* 227 (2000), at 249-251.

61 Mario Chiavario, Some Considerations on Faces of Justice by a 'Non-Specialist', 6 *Journal of International Criminal Justice* 69 (2008), at 79-81. For a further discussion of the Italian system in this context *see* Boris Petersdorf, *Eigenverteidigung und aufgedrängte Pflichtverteidigung im formellen Völkerstrafrecht* (Baden-Baden: Nomos Verlagsgesellschaft) 2010, p.190-193.

represent can in contrast equally entail an implicit restriction of the right to self-representation.[62] This is of interest for this dissertation as in some discussions on the nature and scope of the right to self-representation before international criminal tribunals, the argument is made that the allegedly predominantly adversarial nature of international criminal proceedings would necessarily compel a full-blown recognition of a right to self-representation of the same nature as in national common law systems.[63] The Italian example indicates that this does not have to be the only valid conclusion.

For purposes of this dissertation, a cursory review of the statutory provisions of some selected countries will be sufficient. In light of the fact that the ICC will most likely be the next international criminal institution after the *ad hoc* tribunals which will have to consider the issue of the right to self-representation, potentially also drawing from the national experiences of its member states,[64] a selection has been made among countries which are states parties to the ICC Rome Statute. An analysis of the codifications of some selected examples provides indication of a wide range of approaches with regard to the right to defend oneself in person, with the two main positions being either recognition of the right to self-representation in its full form without qualifications or the incorporation of specific conditions and restrictions on the exercise of a right to defend oneself in person.

Of interest for current purposes is the observation that even though there are models which incorporate a wider recognition of a right to defend oneself

---

62 Mario Chiavario, Some Considerations on Faces of Justice by a 'Non-Specialist', 6 *Journal of International Criminal Justice* 69 (2008), at 81-84.

63 *See, e.g.*, Constantinos Hotis, A 'Fair and Expeditious' Trial: A Reappraisal of Slobodan Milosevic's Right to Self-Representation Before the International Criminal Tribunal for the Former Yugoslavia, 6 *Chicago Journal of International Law* 775 (2006), at 787-788. Note, however, that it has also been argued that the right of a criminal defendant to proceed *pro se* in fact conflicts with the nature of adversarial proceedings: Sharon Finegan, Pro Se Criminal Trials and the Merging of Inquisitorial and Adversarial Systems of Justice, 58 *Catholic University Law Review* 445 (2009), at 447.

64 *Cf.* Article 21(1)(c) of the Rome Statute: "1. The Court shall apply [...] (c) Failing that, general principles of law derived by the Court from national laws of legal systems of the world including, *as appropriate, the national laws of States that would normally exercise jurisdiction over the crime*, provided that those principles are not inconsistent with this Statute and with international law and internationally recognized norms and standards." (emphasis added).

in person,[65] there are equally numerous examples of national legal systems which recognise a general right to defend oneself in person while at the same time, however, placing more or less strict conditions on the exercise of the right to self-representation and provide for mandatory representation by counsel under certain circumstances, usually in the context of alleged serious crimes. Countries implementing variations of this specific model include Albania;[66] Austria;[67] Bosnia and Herzegovina;[68] Bulgaria;[69] Estonia;[70] Finland;[71] Former Yugoslav Republic of Macedonia;[72] France;[73] Germany;[74]

---

65 *See e.g.* Slovakia: Code of Criminal Procedure (amended), 18 August 1994, available at http://www.legal-tools.org/en (last accessed 17 November 2012), sect.13, 14.

66 Criminal Procedure Code of the Republic of Albania, as of 29 June 1999, available at http://legislationline.org/documents/section/criminal-codes (last accessed 17 November 2012), art.6, 49.

67 Strafprozeßordnung 1975, BGBl. Nr. 631/1975 zuletzt geändert durch BGBl. I Nr. 108/2010, 24 December 2010, available at http://www.ris.bka.gv.at/Bundesrecht/ (last accessed 17 November 2012), § 61.

68 Criminal Procedure Code of the Federation of Bosnia and Herzegovina, "Official Gazette" 35/03, available at http://legislationline.org/documents/section/criminal-codes (last accessed 17 November 2012), art.7, 59. Similar provisions can be found in art.7, 45 Criminal Procedure Code of Bosnia and Herzegovina, "Official Gazette" of Bosnia and Herzegovina, 3/03, 32/03, 36/03, 26/04, 63/04, 13/05, 48/05, December 2006; and art.7, 53 Republika Srpska Criminal Procedure Code, 01 July 2003.

69 Criminal Procedure Code, State Gazette No. 86/28.10.2006, amended, SG No. 46/12.06.2007, effective 1.01.2008, available at http://legislationline.org/documents/section/criminal-codes (last accessed 17 November 2012), art.15, 55, 94.

70 Code of Criminal Procedure, 12 February 2003 (as amended), available at http://www.legal-tools.org/doc/3d6027/ (last accessed 17 November 2012), § 8 (1), § 45.

71 Criminal Procedure Act (689/1997; Amendments up to 260/2002 included), available at http://www.legal-tools.org/doc/76a9e6/ (last accessed 17 November 2012), chapter 2 sec.1.

72 Code of Criminal Procedure, Official Gazette No. 15/2005 and Amendments from 2008 and 2009, available at http://legislationline.org/documents/section/criminal-codes (last accessed 17 November 2012), art.4, 66.

73 Code de Procédure Pénale, Version consolidée au 07 janvier 2011, available at http://www.legifrance.gouv.fr/affichCode.do?cidTexte=LEGITEXT000006071154&dateTexte=20110110 (last accessed 17 November 2012), art.274, 317.

74 § 140 Strafprozessordnung ("StPO").

Japan;[75] Liechtenstein;[76] Montenegro;[77] Norway;[78] Poland;[79] Romania;[80] Serbia;[81] Sweden;[82] and Switzerland.[83]

To mention merely a small number of these countries, for example Albania in general acknowledges the right to "self-defense", but provides for mandatory representation by counsel in case the accused is less than eighteen years of age or with psychological or physical limitations which do not allow the defendant to exercise the right to self-representation.[84] Bosnia and Herzegovina provides for the assignment of counsel by the court *inter alia*

---

75 The Code of Criminal Procedure, Law No. 131, 10 July 1948 (as amended), available at http://www.legal-tools.org/doc/a417e0/ (last accessed 17 November 2012), art.30, 37.

76 Strafprozessordnung (StPO), Liechtensteinisches Landesgesetzblatt, Jahrgang 1988 Nr. 62, 18 Oktober 1988, available at http://www.gesetze.li/get_pdf.jsp?PDF=1988062.pdf (last accessed 17 November 2012), § 26 Abs. 3.

77 Republic of Montenegro Criminal Procedure Code, "Official Gazette of the Republic of Montenegro", no. 79/2003 and no.7/2004 – Correction, available at http://legislationline.org/documents/section/criminal-codes (last accessed 17 November 2012), art.13, 69.

78 Criminal Procedure Act, Act of 22 May 1981 No. 25, latest amendments by Act of 30 June 2006 No.53, available at http://www.ub.uio.no/ujur/ulovdata/lov-19810522-025-eng.pdf (last accessed 17 November 2012), sect.94, 96, 98, 99, 313.

79 Code of Criminal Procedure, Act of 06 June 1997, available at http://www.legal-tools.org/doc/43b23e/ (last accessed 17 November 2012), art.6, 79, 80, 81.

80 Criminal Procedure Code, available at http://www.legal-tools.org/doc/d70ff1/ (last accessed 17 November 2012), art.6, 171.

81 The Criminal Procedure Code, Official Gazette of the Republic of Serbia, No. 46/2006, November 2006, available at http://legislationline.org/documents/section/criminal-codes (last accessed 17 November 2012), art.5, 71. *See also* Belgrade Centre for Human Rights, *Human Rights in Serbia and Montenegro 2005. Legal Provisions, Practice and Awareness in the State Union of Serbia and Montenegro Compared to International Human Rights Standards* (Belgrade: The Belgrade Centre for Human Rights) 2006, p.145-146; Belgrade Centre for Human Rights, *Human Rights in Serbia 2006. Legal Provisions and Practice Compared to International Human Rights Standards* (Belgrade: The Belgrade Centre for Human Rights) 2007, p.94-95.

82 The Swedish Code of Judicial Procedure, 01 January 1948 (as amended), available at www.sweden.gov.se/content/1/c4/15/40/472970fc.pdf (last accessed 17 November 2012), chapter 21, sect.1, 3, 3a, 4.

83 Schweizerische Strafprozessordnung, 05. Oktober 2007 (Stand am 01. Januar 2011), available at http://www.admin.ch/ch/d/sr/3/312.0.de.pdf (last accessed 17 November 2012), Art. 130-132.

84 Criminal Procedure Code of the Republic of Albania, as of 29 June 1999, available at http://legislationline.org/documents/section/criminal-codes (last accessed 17 November 2012), art.6, 49.

in case a person is suspected of a crime which mandates imposition of a long-term sentence of imprisonment, or if the court finds the assignment of counsel required in light of the complexity of the case or for other reasons.[85] It is of interest to note for the discussion to follow that in case defence counsel is assigned to a suspect or accused, the latter shall be permitted to select assigned counsel, only failing which the court will select the defence attorney.[86] Estonia provides for the mandatory representation by counsel *inter alia* if life imprisonment may be imposed for the offence of which someone is suspected or accused,[87] which is comparable to the provisions found for the Former Yugoslav Republic of Macedonia[88] and Montenegro.[89] Finland leaves room for assignment of defence counsel by court if the suspect or accused is determined to be incapable of conducting the defence in person or if there are other reasons to assign counsel.[90] Mandatory representation by counsel is more restrictive in Austria, which in particular provides for the assignment of counsel to indigent accused under a number of circumstances, including in case of legally or factually complex proceedings.[91]

For purposes of this dissertation, it is important to bear in mind that systems which limit the possibility of full-fledged self-representation in criminal

---

85 Criminal Procedure Code of Bosnia and Herzegovina, "Official Gazette" of Bosnia and Herzegovina, 3/03, 32/03, 36/03, 26/04, 63/04, 13/05, 48/05, December 2006, available at http://legislationline.org/documents/section/criminal-codes (last accessed 17 November 2012), art.7, 45. *See also* Republika Srpska Criminal Procedure Code, 01 July 2003, art.7, 53.

86 Criminal Procedure Code of Bosnia and Herzegovina, art.45(6).

87 Code of Criminal Procedure, 12 February 2003 (as amended), available at http://www.legal-tools.org/doc/3d6027/ (last accessed 17 November 2012), § 8 (1), § 45.

88 Code of Criminal Procedure, Official Gazette No. 15/2005 and Amendments from 2008 and 2009, available at http://legislationline.org/documents/section/criminal-codes (last accessed 17 November 2012), art.4, 66.

89 Republic of Montenegro Criminal Procedure Code, "Official Gazette of the Republic of Montenegro", no. 79/2003 and no.7/2004 – Correction, available at http://legislationline.org/documents/section/criminal-codes (last accessed 17 November 2012), art.13, 69.

90 Criminal Procedure Act (689/1997; Amendments up to 260/2002 included), available at http://www.legal-tools.org/doc/76a9e6/ (last accessed 17 November 2012), chapter 2 sec.1.

91 Strafprozeßordnung 1975, BGBl. Nr. 631/1975 zuletzt geändert durch BGBl. I Nr. 108/2010, 24 December 2010, available at http://www.ris.bka.gv.at/Bundesrecht/ (last accessed 17 November 2012), § 61.

proceedings will often provide for other opportunities of the accused to participate in their case and thus ensure the personal involvement of the defendant in different ways. This can be seen for example in the German system which allows for an accused to address the chamber with regard to the charges in the indictment[92] as well as at other stages of the proceedings even if represented by counsel.[93] Comparable to this model, the Swiss system provides for the questioning of an accused at the beginning of the evidentiary phase,[94] as well as the opportunity of the defendant to address the court after the closing arguments of the parties.[95] Before the *Cour d'Assises* in France, the presiding judge can question the accused,[96] who at this instance is to be represented by defence counsel.[97] A defendant has furthermore the possibility to put questions to witnesses through the presiding judge.[98] Similar to the German and Swiss procedures, the accused (or his counsel) will have the opportunity of the last word in the proceedings.[99] These examples indicate that while there might be restrictions on the right to self-representation as practiced before international criminal tribunals, a broader right to a personal

---

92 § 243(5) StPO.

93 §§ 257(1), 258 StPO.

94 Schweizerische Strafprozessordnung, 05. Oktober 2007 (Stand am 01. Januar 2011), available at http://www.admin.ch/ch/d/sr/3/312.0.de.pdf (last accessed 17 November 2012), Art. 341(3).

95 Schweizerische Strafprozessordnung, 05. Oktober 2007 (Stand am 01. Januar 2011), available at http://www.admin.ch/ch/d/sr/3/312.0.de.pdf (last accessed 17 November 2012), Art. 347(1).

96 Code de Procédure Pénale, Version consolidée au 07 janvier 2011, available at http://www.legifrance.gouv.fr/affichCode.do?cidTexte=LEGITEXT000006071154&dateTexte=20110110 (last accessed 17 November 2012), art.328, 339.

97 Code de Procédure Pénale, Version consolidée au 07 janvier 2011, available at http://www.legifrance.gouv.fr/affichCode.do?cidTexte=LEGITEXT000006071154&dateTexte=20110110 (last accessed 17 November 2012), Article 274: « L'accusé est ensuite invité à choisir un avocat pour l'assister dans sa défense. Si l'accusé ne choisit pas son avocat, le président ou son délégué lui en désigne un d'office. Cette désignation est non avenue si, par la suite, l'accusé choisit un avocat. »; Article 317: « À l'audience, la présence d'un défenseur auprès de l'accusé est obligatoire. Si le défenseur choisi ou désigné conformément à l'article 274 ne se présente pas, le président en commet un d'office. ».

98 Code de Procédure Pénale, Version consolidée au 07 janvier 2011, available at http://www.legifrance.gouv.fr/affichCode.do?cidTexte=LEGITEXT000006071154&dateTexte=20110110 (last accessed 17 November 2012), art.312, 332.

99 Code de Procédure Pénale, Version consolidée au 07 janvier 2011, available at http://www.legifrance.gouv.fr/affichCode.do?cidTexte=LEGITEXT000006071154&dateTexte=20110110 (last accessed 17 November 2012), art.346.

defence can be argued to exist by giving an accused the opportunity to present his or her views on the charges and evidence throughout the proceedings.[100]

As noted above, the comparison of the broad approaches adopted in common law and in civil law countries indicates that the underlying reasoning in the two systems places significance on distinct values to be safe-guarded.[101] The understanding of this difference is necessary for the easier comprehension of part of the discussion to be found and issues addressed in the sphere of international criminal proceedings. What is important to note despite this divergence, however, is that both tendencies appear to attempt safeguarding a defendant's right to a fair trial as well as providing an opportunity for accused to present a defence in line with their personal ideas.[102] If this is accepted to be the motivating principle, the goal likely aimed at when initially recognising a right to self-representation before international criminal tribunals will be equally – and even better – attained in the future when opting for a right to defend oneself in person as argued in this dissertation.

Thus, having reviewed some of the arguments, international criminal tribunals like the ICC in the future will arguably need to depart from the notion that their system exclusively leans to either one of the two legal currents outlined above.[103] In order to overcome at least a number of the problems encountered thus far by international criminal courts, the idea that international criminal law encompasses a legal system of its own[104] would

---

100 The distinct approaches have been argued to relate to a difference in "substantive" and "procedural" defence: "substantive" when the accused is "self-represented" insofar as he is given the opportunity to actively participate in the proceedings alongside defence counsel; "procedural" when the accused in fact presents his defence in person. *See* Boris Petersdorf, *Eigenverteidigung und aufgedrängte Pflichtverteidigung im formellen Völkerstrafrecht* (Baden-Baden: Nomos Verlagsgesellschaft) 2010, p.195 (discussing the concept of "materielle Verteidigung" and "formelle Verteidigung").

101 *Cf.* Stefan Trechsel, *Human Rights in Criminal Proceedings* (Oxford: Oxford University Press) 2005, p.263, 266.

102 *Cf.* for some general discussions Karsten Gaede, *Fairness als Teilhabe – Das Recht auf konkrete und wirksame Teilhabe durch Verteidigung gemäß Art. 6 EMRK* (Berlin: Duncker & Humblot GmbH) 2007, p.468-486, 617, 618-621; Boris Petersdorf, *Eigenverteidigung und aufgedrängte Pflichtverteidigung im formellen Völkerstrafrecht* (Baden-Baden: Nomos Verlagsgesellschaft) 2010, p.195, 205.

103 Kai Ambos, International criminal procedure: "adversarial", "inquisitorial" or mixed?, 3 *International Criminal Law Review* 1 (2003), at 7, 34-35, 37.

104 *Prosecutor v. Dražen Erdemović*, Case No. IT-96-22-A, Judgement, 07 October 1997, Separate and Dissenting Opinion of Judge Cassese, para.4; Patrick L. Robinson, Ensuring Fair and Expeditious Trials at the International Criminal Tribunal

assist in concentrating on solutions apposite for the international context rather than looking at national considerations which have historic roots and might work well in the respective systems, but are ill-suited for application in international criminal proceedings.

II. Regional jurisdictions

1. Existing provisions

Turning to the examination of international and regional instruments which are not primarily concerned with international criminal proceedings but rather with the general protection of human rights, the International Covenant on Civil and Political Rights (ICCPR) contains with Article 14(3)(d) a provision which should later be mirrored by the statutes of international criminal tribunals. The article provides for minimum guarantees that are to be safeguarded in any criminal proceedings, including the right of the accused

> "to be tried in his presence, and *to defend himself in person* or through legal assistance of his own choosing."[105]

The Body of Principles for the Protection of All Persons Under Any Form of Detention or Imprisonment is an additional indication for the recognition of a right to defend oneself in person on the international human rights level.[106]

---

for the Former Yugoslavia, 11 *European Journal of International Law* 569 (2000), at 579-580. *See also* Salvatore Zappalà, *Human Rights in International Criminal Proceedings* (Oxford: Oxford University Press) 2005, p.22.

105 International Covenant on Civil and Political Rights, GA Res. 2200A (XXI), 16 December 1966 ("ICCPR"), Article 14(3)(d): "In the determination of any criminal charge against him, everyone shall be entitled to the following minimum guarantees, in full equality: [...] (d) to be tried in his presence, and *to defend himself in person or through legal assistance of his own choosing*; to be informed, if he does not have legal assistance, of this right; and to have legal assistance assigned to him, in any case where the interests of justice so require, and without payment by him in any such case if he does not have sufficient means to pay for it; [...]" (emphasis added).

106 Body of Principles for the Protection of All Persons Under Any Form of Detention or Imprisonment, adopted by General Assembly Resolution 43/173 of 09 December 1988, Principle 11(1): "A detained person shall not be kept in detention without being given effective opportunity to be heard promptly by a judicial or other authority. *A detained person shall have the right to defend himself or to be assisted by counsel as prescribed by law.*" (emphasis added).

On the regional level, Article 6(3)(c) of the European Convention for Human Rights (ECHR)[107] and Article 8(2)(d) of the American Convention for Human Rights (AmCHR)[108] contain language which is similar to that found in Article 14(3)(d) of the ICCPR.

At first sight, this preliminary review appears to indicate that the texts of the international and regional instruments like ICCPR, ECHR or AmCHR seem to be unequivocal in guaranteeing a right to self-representation to any person charged in criminal proceedings. Yet, the Inter-American Court of Human Rights noted in an Advisory Opinion that while an accused could defend him- or herself personally, this would only be possible where provided for under domestic law.[109] In addition, it read Article 8 of the AmHCR "to require legal counsel only when that is necessary for a fair hearing".[110] This implies, *a contrario*, that it is equally feasible not to provide for self-representation without violating the American Convention and to demand mandatory legal representation if required to safeguard a fair trial.

Similarly, as will be indicated by the review of some of the pertinent jurisprudence before the Human Rights Committee and the European Court of Human Rights, it will have to be examined whether this right to self-representation is not more adequately seen as a right to a personal defence. This

---

107 Convention for the Protection of Human Rights and Fundamental Freedoms, as amended by Protocol Nos. 11 and 14, 01 June 2010 ("ECHR"), Article 6(3)(c): "Everyone charged with a criminal offence has the following minimum rights: […] (c) *to defend himself in person or through legal assistance of his own choosing* or, if he has not sufficient means to pay for legal assistance, to be given it free when the interests of justice so require; […]" (emphasis added).

108 American Convention on Human Rights, O.A.S Treaty Series No. 36, 1144 U.N.T.S. 123, OEA/Ser.L.V/II.82 doc.6 rev. 1 at 25 (1992), Article 8(2)(d): "Every person accused of a criminal offense has the right to be presumed innocent so long as his guilt has not been proven according to law. During the proceedings, every person is entitled, with full equality, to the following minimum guarantees: […] d. *the right of the accused to defend himself personally or to be assisted by legal counsel of his own choosing*, and to communicate freely and privately with his counsel; […]" (emphasis added).

109 Inter-American Court of Human Rights, Advisory Opinion OC-11/90, Exceptions to the Exhaustion of Domestic Remedies (Art. 46(1), 46(2)(a) and 46(2)(b) American Convention on Human Rights), 10 August 1990, para.25: "Thus, a defendant may defend himself personally, but it is important to bear in mind that this would only be possible where permitted under domestic law."

110 Inter-American Court of Human Rights, Advisory Opinion OC-11/90, Exceptions to the Exhaustion of Domestic Remedies (Art. 46(1), 46(2)(a) and 46(2)(b) American Convention on Human Rights), 10 August 1990, para.26.

notion would reconcile the different approaches in divergent national jurisdictions which, for example, might fall under the same human rights considerations within the framework of the ECHR. This meaning, which places an emphasis on the active participation of an accused rather than his or her acting as defence counsel throughout the proceedings, is arguably also more fitting for international specifics and thereby might further the delivery of international criminal justice. The analysis of practical implications in the context of this dissertation will highlight the reasons for which the international sphere, in general concerned with the alleged commission of crimes on a large scale, might not be the best suitable arena for the unqualified exercise of a right to self-representation as interpreted thus far.

This approach is underscored by the observation that the apparent consensus on a full right to self-representation is probably not as internationally recognised as it seems, which is revealed by a look at the African Charter on Human and Peoples' Rights (ACHPR). The ACHPR does not explicitly provide for a right to self-representation. Rather, Article 7(1)(c) of the ACHPR enshrines more generally the right to a defence, as well as a right to be defended by counsel of one's own choosing.[111] While this provision has been interpreted to "possibly" guarantee self-representation,[112] it has at the same time explicitly been considered to incorporate the right to defend oneself in person.[113] The formulation of this provision does indicate, at least, that what appears to have been the focus in the mind of the drafters was a right of accused to be given the opportunity to effectively defend against criminal charges – if necessary with the assistance of counsel –, rather than the way in which this right might be implemented procedurally.

An additional instrument which adopts an approach comparable to that formulated in the ACHPR, albeit on the supranational level and in a more general context than merely criminal proceedings, is the Charter of Funda-

---

111 African (Banjul) Charter on Human and Peoples' Rights, 1981, OAU Doc. CAB/LEG/67/3 rev. 5, 21 I.L.M 58 (1982), Article 7(1)(c): "Every individual shall have the right to have his cause heard. This comprises: […] (c) the right to defence, including the right to be defended by counsel of his choice; […]".

112 M. Cherif Bassiouni, Human Rights in the Context of Criminal Justice: Identifying International Procedural Protections and Equivalent Protections in National Constitutions, 3 *Duke Journal of Comparative and International Law* 235 (1993), at 283.

113 Valère Eteka Yemet, *La Charte Africaine des Droits de l'Homme et des Peuples* (Paris: L'Harmattan) 1996, p.85. Less clear in the interpretation is U. Oji Umozurike, *The African Charter on Human and Peoples' Rights* (The Hague/Boston/London: Martinus Nijhoff Publishers) 1997, p.32.

mental Rights of the European Union, the text of which does not explicitly mention any right to defend oneself in person, but rather guarantees a more generic right to defence.[114] It has to be observed in this context that – as indicated by the review of national approaches before – the national jurisdictions of European Union member states encompass a variety of legal systems[115] which have to be reconciled not only from a human rights perspective. Therefore, it will not come as a surprise that the Charter remains vague in its determination of the specific nature of a right to defend oneself in person. In a similar vein, all members of the European Union[116] are equally members to the Council of Europe[117] and thus subject to the guarantees spelled out in the ECHR.[118] Both factors favour the argument that a right to a personal defence has to be found which reconciles the different approaches in an effort to safeguard the position of accused as the subject of criminal proceedings.[119]

---

114 Charter of Fundamental Rights of the European Union, 2000/C 364/01, 07 December 2000, Article 47: "[...] Everyone is entitled to a fair and public hearing within a reasonable time by an independent and impartial tribunal previously established by law. *Everyone shall have the possibility of being advised, defended and represented.*"; Article 48(2): "Respect for the right of the defence of anyone who has been charged shall be guaranteed." (emphasis added).

115 Kai Ambos, International criminal procedure: "adversarial", "inquisitorial" or mixed?, 3 *International Criminal Law Review* 1 (2003), at 4-5.

116 *See* list of EU member states: http://europa.eu/about-eu/member-countries/index_en.htm (last accessed 17 November 2012).

117 *See* list of Council of Europe member states: www.coe.int/aboutCoe/index.asp?page=47pays1europe&l=en (last accessed 17 November 2012).

118 *See* in particular also Article 6 of the Consolidated Versions of the Treaty on European Union and the Treaty on the Functioning of the European Union (2010/C 83/01): "[...] 3. Fundamental rights, as guaranteed by the European Convention for the Protection of Human Rights and Fundamental Freedoms and as they result from the constitutional traditions common to the Member States, shall constitute general principles of the Union's law."

119 *Cf.* Stefan Trechsel, *Human Rights in Criminal Proceedings* (Oxford: Oxford University Press) 2005, p.247. *See also* Kai Ambos, International criminal procedure: "adversarial", "inquisitorial" or mixed?, 3 *International Criminal Law Review* 1 (2003), at 18-19.

2. Human Rights Committee and European Court of Human Rights

Turning to the concrete interpretation and application of the right to self-representation by regional and supranational institutions, additional case law concerns national legislation and its treatment of a right to self-representation and the compatibility with international human rights standards. In light of the fact that these decisions are frequently referred to in the jurisprudence of international criminal tribunals, the pertinent case law will be discussed at this stage in order to provide some foundation for the later comprehension of the case law of international criminal tribunals.

The Human Rights Committee in its initial general comment on Article 14 of the ICCPR appeared to recognise a general right to self-representation protected by the Covenant, alongside the other right enshrined in the same subparagraph, *i.e.* assistance by counsel of one's own choosing.[120] However, in its General Comment No. 32, replacing the earlier comment on Article 14 of the ICCPR,[121] the Human Rights Committee stated unequivocally that the two distinct rights enshrined in that article, *i.e.* the right to defend oneself in person and the right to be assisted by professional counsel, are "*not* mutually exclusive".[122] In part relaying word-for-word the jurisprudence of the *ad hoc* tribunals to be discussed *infra*, the Human Rights Committee expressed its recommendation that domestic legislation "should avoid any absolute bar against the right to defend oneself in criminal proceedings without the assistance of counsel".[123]

---

120 Human Rights Committee, General Comment No. 13, 13 April 1984, para.11: "Not all reports have dealt with all aspects of the right of defence as defined in subparagraph 3 (d). The Committee has not always received sufficient information concerning the protection of the right of the accused to be present during the determination of any charge against him nor how the legal system assures his right either to defend himself in person or to be assisted by counsel of his own choosing, or what arrangements are made if a person does not have sufficient means to pay for legal assistance. The accused or his lawyer must have the right to act diligently and fearlessly in pursuing all available defences and the right to challenge the conduct of the case if they believe it to be unfair. When exceptionally for justified reasons trials in absentia are held, strict observance of the rights of the defence is all the more necessary."

121 Human Rights Committee, General Comment No. 32, CCPR/C/GC/32, 23 August 2007, para.1.

122 Human Rights Committee, General Comment No. 32, CCPR/C/GC/32, 23 August 2007, para.37 (emphasis added).

123 Human Rights Committee, General Comment No. 32, CCPR/C/GC/32, 23 August 2007, para.37.

The first case to be mentioned is *Hill v. Spain* before the Human Rights Committee (HRC).[124] In this case, two British citizens were charged before a Spanish court with alleged arson and damage to private property. Having been unsatisfied with the services of both legal aid and privately engaged counsel, one of the defendants eventually decided to proceed *pro se*, but was denied that choice in trial and subsequent appellate proceedings. Following their conviction, the applicants complained, *inter alia*, of a violation of Article 14(3)(d) of the ICCPR, guaranteeing the right to defend oneself in person.[125] Without providing any further analysis, the HRC found a violation of Article 14(3)(d) of the ICCPR on the basis that Spanish legislation did not provide for self-representation.[126]

While this decision by the HRC does indicate that there is a right to self-representation recognised under the ICCPR, it does not provide any legal analysis of the matter and thus gives no indication on the scope of the right or under which circumstances, if at all, limitations could be imposed.[127] Therefore, this decision does not appear to provide significant assistance for a number of issues to be discussed in the context of the practical exercise of the right to follow. Moreover, the HRC rendered decisions on the inadmissibility of communications regarding domestic requirements to be represented by counsel in certain appellate proceedings, which indicate that it did not

124 *Michael and Brian Hill v. Spain*, Human Rights Committee, Communication No. 526/1993, U.N. Doc. CCPR/C/59/D/526/1993, 02 April 1997.

125 *Michael and Brian Hill v. Spain*, Human Rights Committee, Communication No. 526/1993, U.N. Doc. CCPR/C/59/D/526/1993, 02 April 1997, para.2.1-4.4.

126 *Michael and Brian Hill v. Spain*, Human Rights Committee, Communication No. 526/1993, U.N. Doc. CCPR/C/59/D/526/1993, 02 April 1997, para.14.2: "The Committee recalls that Michael Hill insists that he wanted to defend himself, through an interpreter, and that court denied this request. The State party has answered that the records of the hearing do not show such a request, and that Spain recognized the rights of 'auto defence' pursuant to the Covenant and the European Convention of Human Rights, but that 'such defence should take place by competent counsel, which is paid by the State when necessary', thereby conceding that its legislation does not allow an accused person to defend himself in person, as provided for under the Covenant. The Committee accordingly concludes that Michael Hill's right to defend himself was not respected, contrary to article 14, paragraph 3(d), of the Covenant."

127 *Cf.* Michael P. Scharf/Christopher M. Rassi, Do Former Leaders have an International Right to Self-Representation in War Crimes Trials?, 20 *Ohio State Journal on Dispute Resolution* 3 (2005), at 16-17; Boris Petersdorf, *Eigenverteidigung und aufgedrängte Pflichtverteidigung im formellen Völkerstrafrecht* (Baden-Baden: Nomos Verlagsgesellschaft) 2010, p.216.

from the outset reject the possibility of such requirements without violating Article 14 of the ICCPR.[128] However, it needs to be borne in mind that these communications did not concern criminal proceedings, did thus not invoke Article 14(3)(d) but rather Article 14(1) of the ICCPR, and were not decided on the merits.

The second decision to be addressed is the case of *Croissant v. Germany*[129] before the European Court of Human Rights (ECtHR) in Strasbourg. In this case, the applicant, a lawyer himself, was charged in criminal proceedings before the regional court (*Landgericht*) in Stuttgart. In addition to the two lawyers he had engaged himself, the court later appointed a third one with office in Stuttgart. The applicant objected to that appointment in general as well as in light of the political affiliations of the third counsel which, in his opinion, would not allow him to build the relationship of trust necessary for his representation. The appointed lawyer also objected to his assignment.[130] After conviction, the applicant objected on the basis of Article 6(3)(c) of the ECHR to the calculations of his contributions for legal assistance rendered by the regional court, and in particular against him having to pay the charges of the third lawyer appointed against his will. The federal constitutional court (*Bundesverfassungsgericht*) eventually dismissed his appeal, finding that although Article 6(3)(c) of the ECHR would provide for legal aid, it would not necessarily mean that legal assistance would always be accorded completely free of charge. It further upheld the appointment of the third lawyer by the regional court.[131] The applicant lodged an application with the European Court, arguing a violation of Article 6(3)(c) in conjunction with Article 6(1) of the ECHR due to his held obligation to pay the charges of his counsel, including of the court appointed lawyer, and arguing that his right to counsel of his own choice had not been respected in the context of the assignment of the third lawyer.[132] The ECtHR first found that section 140 of the German Code of Criminal Procedure, which demands representa-

---

128 *Marina Torregrosa Lafuente et al. v. Spain*, Human Rights Committee, Communication No. 866/1999, U.N. Doc. CCPR/C/72/D/866/1999, 16 July 2001, para.6.3; *Concepción Sánchez González v. Spain*, Human Rights Committee, Communication No.1005/2001, U.N. Doc. CCPR/C/74/D/1005/2001, 21 March 2002, para.4.3.

129 *Croissant c. Allemagne*, Requête n° 13611/88, Arrêt, 25 septembre 1992.

130 *Croissant c. Allemagne*, Requête n° 13611/88, Arrêt, 25 septembre 1992, para.6-11.

131 *Croissant c. Allemagne*, Requête n° 13611/88, Arrêt, 25 septembre 1992, para.12-19.

132 *Croissant c. Allemagne*, Requête n° 13611/88, Arrêt, 25 septembre 1992, para.25.

tion by counsel *e.g.* in all cases in the first instance before (higher) regional courts,[133] could not be considered to be incompatible with the ECHR.[134] In the view of the ECtHR, in case counsel was appointed by a court, it was found to be necessary that the accused concerned first be heard as to the number of lawyers wanted, especially in case the defendant would have to bear the costs in case of conviction.[135] However, the Court equally held that although Article 6(3)(c) of the ECHR would recognise the right to counsel of one's own choosing, this right was not absolute and could be subject to limitations despite the importance of a relationship of trust between counsel and client, in particular when concerned with legal aid regimes and in case counsel was appointed by court "in the interests of justice".[136]

As can be seen from the factual background to the decision, the case was not concerned with a self-represented accused.[137] Instead, the pertinent part

---

133 Section 140 of the Code of Criminal Procedure (*Strafprozessordnung*) reads: "(1) Die Mitwirkung eines Verteidigers ist notwendig, wenn 1. die Hauptverhandlung im ersten Rechtszug vor dem Oberlandesgericht oder dem Landgericht stattfindet; 2. dem Beschuldigten ein Verbrechen zur Last gelegt wird; [...] (2) In anderen Fällen bestellt der Vorsitzende auf Antrag oder von Amts wegen einen Verteidiger, wenn wegen der Schwere der Tat oder wegen der Schwierigkeit der Sach- oder Rechtslage die Mitwirkung eines Verteidigers geboten erscheint oder wenn ersichtlich ist, daß sich der Beschuldigte nicht selbst verteidigen kann – namentlich, weil dem Verletzten nach den §§ 397a und 406g Abs. 3 und 4 ein Rechtsanwalt beigeordnet worden ist. Dem Antrag eines hör- oder sprachbehinderten Beschuldigten ist zu entsprechen."

134 *Croissant c. Allemagne*, Requête n° 13611/88, Arrêt, 25 septembre 1992, para.27: « La règle – dont on rencontre l'équivalent dans la législation d'autres États contractants – imposant à un accusé l'assistance d'un conseil à tous les stades de l'instance devant le tribunal régional (article 140 du code de procédure pénale; paragraphe 20 ci-dessus) ne saurait, aux yeux de la Cour, passer pour incompatible avec la Convention. »

135 *Croissant c. Allemagne*, Requête n° 13611/88, Arrêt, 25 septembre 1992, para.27.

136 *Croissant c. Allemagne*, Requête n° 13611/88, Arrêt, 25 septembre 1992, para.29: « À la vérité, l'article 6 par. 3 c) (art. 6-3-c) reconnaît à tout accusé le droit à l'assistance d'un défenseur de son choix (arrêt Pakelli c. Allemagne du 25 avril 1983, série A n° 64, p. 15, par. 31). Néanmoins, et malgré l'importance de relations confiantes entre avocat et client, on ne saurait prêter à ce droit un caractère absolu. Il est forcément sujet à certaines limitations en matière d'assistance judiciaire gratuite et lorsque, comme en l'espèce, il appartient aux tribunaux de décider si les intérêts de la justice exigent de doter l'accusé d'un défenseur d'office. »

137 In the same vein, *see* Nicolas A.J. Croquet, The Right to Self-Representation under the European Convention on Human Rights: What Role for the Limitation Analysis?, 3 *European Human Rights Law Review* 292 (2012), at 298-299.

regarded the issue whether counsel could be appointed by a court even against a defendant's will, holding only on a very generic level that such could be the case without violating Article 6(3)(c) of the ECHR, which also enshrines the right to represent oneself in person. Furthermore, the question was addressed whether the accused in question had a right to select such court-appointed counsel. Interestingly enough, the case does not appear to have been considered in any of the legal aid cases to be discussed *infra*, whereas it seems to be rather applicable to these than to the question of potential restrictions on the right to self-representation.

When the Commission in an early case considered the meaning of Article 6(3)(c) of the ECHR, it interpreted this provision to lay down a guarantee for an accused to have an "adequate representation of the case of the defence, but does not give an accused person the right to decide himself in what manner his defence should be assured".[138] When the European Court later interpreted the same provision, it found that it enshrined three distinctive rights, namely to defend oneself in person, to defend oneself through legal assistance of one's own choosing, and, under certain conditions, to be accorded legal assistance free of charge.[139] In a more recent decision, the ECtHR noted not only that the guarantees as specified in paragraph 3 of Article 6 of the ECHR form part of a general right to a fair trial,[140] but also that Article 6 of the ECHR enshrines a guarantee to effective participation in a criminal trial.[141] Similarly, the Court found already at an earlier occasion that an applicant should have been given the possibility to participate in appeals pro-

---

138 *X. v. Austria*, Application no. 7138/75 (Commission), Decision, 05 July 1977, p.51-52.

139 *Pakelli c. Allemagne*, Requête n° 8398/78, Arrêt, 05 avril 1983, para.31. *See also* Ben Emmerson/Andrew Ashworth, *Human Rights and Criminal Justice* (London: Sweet & Maxwell) 1st edition 2001, at 2-35, 14-25; Karsten Gaede, *Fairness als Teilhabe – Das Recht auf konkrete und wirksame Teilhabe durch Verteidigung gemäß Art. 6 EMRK* (Berlin: Duncker & Humblot GmbH) 2007, p.252.

140 *Lagerblom v. Sweden*, Application no. 26891/95, Judgment, 14 April 2003, para.48.

141 *Lagerblom v. Sweden*, Application no. 26891/95, Judgment, 14 April 2003, para.49. The ECtHR further defined "effective participation" in *Grigoryevskikh v. Russia*, Application no. 22/03, Judgment, 09 July 2009, para.78. *See also Timergaliyev v. Russia*, Application no. 40631/02, Judgment, 14 January 2009, para.51; *Moiseyev v. Russia*, Application no. 62936/00, Judgment, 06 April 2009, para.214; *Güveç v. Turkey*, Application no. 70337/01, Judgment, 20 April 2009, para.123-124, 128.

ceedings "together with his counsel" in light of the significance of the questions to be determined.[142]

In addition, referring to *Croissant*, the ECtHR reiterated that a "legal requirement that an accused be assisted by counsel in criminal proceedings cannot be deemed incompatible with the Convention",[143] indicating deference to national assessment of the question whether the interests of justice would require legal assistance.[144] According to the ECtHR, the way in which it would interpret and apply Article 6(1) and 6(3) of the ECHR with regard to questions arising from appellate proceedings would depend on the respective domestic legal system at stake.[145] Similarly, reiterating the earlier jurisprudence that the safeguard of an adequate defence presentation would not confer on defendants a right to decide how to assure it, the European Court found that the possibility of choice between self-representation, representation by counsel or defence counsel appointed by the court would depend on the applicable legislation and rules of court.[146]

The ECtHR jurisprudence on the right to self-representation in general has been criticised insofar as it has been argued that the inconsistent approach in the recognition and/or limitations of this right leaves individuals with a number of uncertainties concerning the extent of the right itself and any potential restrictions that could be imposed on the national level.[147]

One case of particular interest for the purposes of this dissertation is the case of *Correia de Matos v. Portugal.* The complainant, a lawyer himself, submitted the matter to both the Human Rights Committee and the European Court of Human Rights, alleging a violation of his right to self-representation enshrined in Article 14(3)(d) of the ICCPR and Article 6(3)(c) of the ECHR, respectively. It is of note that while interpreting virtually identical legal

---

142 *Kremzow v. Austria*, Application no. 12350/86, Judgment, 21 September 1993, para.67. *See also Zana v. Turkey* [GC], Application no. 18954/91, Judgment, 25 November 1997, para.71-73.

143 *Lagerblom v. Sweden*, Application no. 26891/95, Judgment, 14 April 2003, para.50.

144 *Lagerblom v. Sweden*, Application no. 26891/95, Judgment, 14 April 2003, para.53.

145 *Shulepov v. Russia*, Application no. 15435/03, Judgment, 01 December 2008, para.32.

146 *Mayzit v. Russia*, Application no. 63378/00, Judgment, 06 July 2005, para.65.

147 Nicolas A.J. Croquet, The Right to Self-Representation under the European Convention on Human Rights: What Role for the Limitation Analysis?, 3 *European Human Rights Law Review* 292 (2012), at 292-293.

provisions with regard to the same facts of a case, the two different bodies reached opposing conclusions.[148]

The ECtHR, the first institution seised of the issue, initially declared the application to be inadmissible in part[149] and subsequently found no violation of the ECHR.[150] The European Court argued that states parties enjoyed a margin of appreciation to determine in which cases representation by counsel might be required, even against the express wishes of an accused.[151] According to the ECtHR, the assignment of counsel over the objection of an accused might be in the interests of the accused to ensure an effective defence.[152] The European Court did not see any reason to amend this conclusion in case the accused was a lawyer himself.[153]

In contrast, the Human Rights Committee subsequently found a violation of Article 14(3)(d) of the ICCPR:[154] the HRC first determined that the two rights enshrined in the article at stake – to defend oneself in person or to be represented by counsel of one's own choice – were not mutually exclusive.[155] At the same time, it considered that the imposition of counsel against the wishes of an accused might deprive the accused of mounting an effective defence and could thus lead to a violation of the right to a personal defence, a cornerstone of justice.[156] However, the HRC did accept that the right to

---

148 Wolfgang Schomburg, Development of Human Rights Before International Criminal Tribunals. A European Perspective, 17(2) *Croatian Annual of Criminal Law and Practice* 909 (2010), at 924 fn.75; Wolfgang Schomburg, Some Reflections on the Right to Self-Representation Before International Tribunals, 12 *ERA Forum* 189 (2011), at 194.

149 *Carlos Correia de Matos c. Portugal*, Requête n° 48188/99, Décision partielle, 14 septembre 2000.

150 *Carlos Correia de Matos c. Portugal*, Requête n° 48188/99, Décision, 15 novembre 2001.

151 *Carlos Correia de Matos c. Portugal*, Requête n° 48188/99, Décision, 15 novembre 2001, p.6.

152 *Carlos Correia de Matos c. Portugal*, Requête n° 48188/99, Décision, 15 novembre 2001, p.7.

153 *Carlos Correia de Matos c. Portugal*, Requête n° 48188/99, Décision, 15 novembre 2001, p.7.

154 *Carlos Correia de Matos c. Portugal*, Comité des droits de l'homme, Communication No. 1123/2002, U.N. Doc. CCPR/C/86/D/1123/2002, 26 mars 2006, para.7.5.

155 *Carlos Correia de Matos c. Portugal*, Comité des droits de l'homme, Communication No. 1123/2002, U.N. Doc. CCPR/C/86/D/1123/2002, 26 mars 2006, para.7.3.

156 *Carlos Correia de Matos c. Portugal*, Comité des droits de l'homme, Communication No. 1123/2002, U.N. Doc. CCPR/C/86/D/1123/2002, 26 mars 2006, para.7.3.

self-representation was not absolute and could be restricted under certain circumstances.[157]

These two decisions illustrate the potential divergences which may arise when interpreting the currently existing provisions on the right to self-representation. It has been argued that the difference in conclusion is based on the ECtHR considering the general – more objective – fairness of the proceedings, whereas the HRC is more focused on the subjective perception of fairness from the point of view of the accused.[158] The least that becomes clear in reading the decisions is that the ECtHR leaves the ECHR member states with considerable discretion in the practical organisation of proceedings, while the HRC obviously underwent a change in its approach away from an uncompromised recognition of a right to self-representation. As will be illustrated below, similar difficulties in finding a consistently applicable solution should be replicated in the jurisprudence of international criminal tribunals.

III. Influence of national and regional interpretations of the right to self-representation on the international criminal legal system

Having examined the approaches taken in national systems, as well as at the international and regional human rights level, it will be convenient at this stage to further detail the relationship between these solutions adopted in national and human rights contexts, and the systems in international criminal proceedings to be found at the *ad hoc* tribunals as well as at the ICC.

On a general level, the sources to be referred to by international criminal tribunals in the determination of matters raised in the course of proceedings will be similar to those drawn upon in international law in general as outlined in Article 38 of the Statute of the International Court of Justice, and will include written provisions, customary international law and general principles

---

157 *Carlos Correia de Matos c. Portugal*, Comité des droits de l'homme, Communication No. 1123/2002, U.N. Doc. CCPR/C/86/D/1123/2002, 26 mars 2006, para.7.4.

158 Boris Petersdorf, *Eigenverteidigung und aufgedrängte Pflichtverteidigung im formellen Völkerstrafrecht* (Baden-Baden: Nomos Verlagsgesellschaft) 2010, p.221. *See also* Karsten Gaede, *Fairness als Teilhabe – Das Recht auf konkrete und wirksame Teilhabe durch Verteidigung gemäß Art. 6 EMRK* (Berlin: Duncker & Humblot GmbH) 2007, p.433-436.

of law.[159] Apart from these generic sources of international law, international criminal tribunals especially in the beginning did not have an established body of case law and practice to draw upon in their litigations. Thus, in particular the *ad hoc* tribunals had to find supplemental sources of international law for the interpretation and application of their respective statutes and rules. In one of the early judgements at the ICTY, the trial chamber in *Furundžija* stated that in case of identified lacunae in the applicable law and lack of uniformity in national approaches, it would be appropriate to resort to general principles of international criminal law and international law.[160]

The approach of attempting to isolate general principles of law has been criticised on the basis that the *ad hoc* tribunals never established a uniform methodology of how to arrive at such general principles but rather utilised an "arbitrary procedure".[161] On the other hand, it has been acknowledged that there are different ways in which international tribunals could refer to national laws, namely in an approach which recognises the "*pre-eminence* of international law with respect to national law" on the one hand, and the approach of applying national legal solutions directly to issues arising in the

159 *See* Statute of the International Court of Justice, Article 38: "1. The Court, whose function is to decide in accordance with international law such disputes as are submitted to it, shall apply: a. international conventions, whether general or particular, establishing rules expressly recognised by the contesting states; b. international custom, as evidence of a general practice accepted as law; c. the general principles of law recognized by civilized nations; d. subject to the provisions of Article 59, judicial decisions and the teachings of the most highly qualified publicists of the various nations, as subsidiary means for the determination of rules of law." For a general overview of sources and interpretation in international criminal law *see* Gerhard Werle, *Principles of International Criminal Law* (The Hague: TMC Asser Press) 2nd edition 2009, para.135-182.

160 *Prosecutor v. Anto Furundžija*, Case No. IT-95-17/1-T, Judgement, 10 December 1998, para.182. *See also* Gideon Boas, Self-Representation Before the ICTY. A Case for Reform, 9 *Journal of International Criminal Justice* 53 (2011), at 76-77. Critical of the trial chamber's approach is Ilias Bantekas, Reflections on Some Sources and Methods of International Criminal and Humanitarian Law, 6 *International Criminal Law Review* 121 (2006), at 126-127, 136.

161 Ilias Bantekas, Reflections on Some Sources and Methods of International Criminal and Humanitarian Law, 6 *International Criminal Law Review* 121 (2006), at 129: "The ordinary working method is accumulating a random number of provisions or case law from particular criminal justice systems and making up their minds on this basis."

context of international criminal law on the other.[162] However, in this context one has to bear in mind the argument that international and national legal systems constitute distinct frameworks within which similar rules may be interpreted and applied differently.[163]

After long years of practical experience, the *ad hoc* tribunals have established a solid body of collective jurisprudence and practice on international criminal procedure in general, and on the question of the exercise of the right to self-representation more specifically. The import of national and regional interpretations of this right is therefore by now less significant than in the beginning and may rather become of interests in case novel questions of a fundamental nature arise.

In contrast, the systems outlined above are potential sources for the ICC when the Court will eventually have to manage proceedings with self-represented accused. While the ICTY and ICTR, as well as other international and hybrid criminal tribunals, have established a body of jurisprudence and practice in years of operation, this does not necessarily exclude the ICC from referring to other non-international bodies having dealt with relevant issues. Of interest to note is the argument underscoring the significance and relevance of reference to decisions for example of the ECtHR given that this court is equally an international body applying international law, and thus on a level more comparable to international criminal courts than any national legal system could be.[164] In the more specific context of the interpretation and application of rights of the accused, it has even been submitted that the ICC deferred to a considerable extent to the jurisprudence of the ECtHR, some-

---

162 Antonio Cassese, The Influence of the European Court of Human Rights on International Criminal Tribunals – Some Methodological Remarks, in: Morten Bergsmo (ed.), *Human Rights and Criminal Justice for the Downtrodden. Essays in Honour of Asbjørn Eide* (Leiden/Boston: Martinus Nijhoff Publishers) 2003, p.19-52, at 21. *See also* Alexander K.A. Greenawalt, The Pluralism of International Criminal Law, 86 *Indiana Law Journal* 1063 (2011), at 1078-1079.

163 *Cf.* Althea Alexis, The Convergence of the Common Law and Inquisitorial Systems in International Criminal Law, in: Emmanuel Decaux *et al.* (eds), *From Human Rights to International Criminal Law: Studies in Honour of an African Jurist, the Late Judge Lairy Kama* (Leiden/Boston: Martinus Nijhoff Publishers) 2007, p.461-481, at 464-465.

164 Antonio Cassese, The Influence of the European Court of Human Rights on International Criminal Tribunals – Some Methodological Remarks, in: Morten Bergsmo (ed.), *Human Rights and Criminal Justice for the Downtrodden. Essays in Honour of Asbjørn Eide* (Leiden/Boston: Martinus Nijhoff Publishers) 2003, p.19-52, at 24.

times without even considering views adopted by further international human rights bodies.[165]

While the statutes of ICTY and ICTR do not include any provisions on specific legal systems or provisions that might be considered in addition to the tribunals' own legislation,[166] the Rome Statute of the ICC contains with Article 21 a specific rule clarifying the sources upon which the chambers of the ICC might rely.[167] In the first place, this will be the ICC's legislation proper,[168] followed "where appropriate" by "applicable treaties and the principles and rules of international law, including the established principles of the international law of armed conflict".[169] In addition, the Rome Statute explicitly refers to the possibility, failing previously mentioned sources, of taking into account "general principles of law derived by the Court from national laws of legal systems of the world including, as appropriate, the national laws of States that would normally exercise jurisdiction over the crime, provided that those principles are not inconsistent with this Statute and with international law and internationally recognised norms and standards".[170] It is further specified that the "application and interpretation of law pursuant to this article must be consistent with internationally recognised human rights".[171]

---

165 Nicolas A.J. Croquet, The International Criminal Court and the Treatment of Defence Rights: A Mirror of the European Court of Human Rights' Jurisprudence?, 11 *Human Rights Law Review* 91 (2011), at 92, 108-109.

166 Patrick L. Robinson, Fair but Expeditious Trials, in: Hirad Abtahi/Gideon Boas (eds), *The Dynamics of International Criminal Justice. Essays in Honour of Sir Richard May* (Leiden/Boston: Martinus Nijhoff Publishers) 2006, p.169-192, at 172; Margaret McAuliffe deGuzman, Article 21, in: Otto Triffterer (ed.), *Commentary on the Rome Statute of the International Criminal Court. Observers' Notes, Article by Article* (Munich: Verlag C.H. Beck) 2nd edition 2008, p.701-712, at note 6; Nicolas A.J. Croquet, The International Criminal Court and the Treatment of Defence Rights: A Mirror of the European Court of Human Rights' Jurisprudence?, 11 *Human Rights Law Review* 91 (2011), at 97.

167 It has been argued that in essence, there is no difference between the applicable law for the *ad hoc* tribunals and the ICC: Patrick L. Robinson, Rough Edges in the Alignment of Legal Systems in the Proceedings at the ICTY, 3 *Journal of International Criminal Justice* 1037 (2005), at 1038-1039.

168 Article 21(1)(a) Rome Statute: "1. The Court shall apply (a) In the first place, this Statute, Elements of Crimes and its Rules of Procedure and Evidence; (…)".

169 Article 21(1)(b) Rome Statute.

170 Article 21(1)(c) Rome Statute.

171 Article 21(3) Rome Statute: "The application and interpretation of law pursuant to this article must be consistent with internationally recognized human rights, and be

It has been stated that this article "derives generally from the sources enumerated in article 38 of the ICJ Statute".[172] It appears that in light of the drafting history of Article 21 of the Rome Statute, the provision provides for the application of principles drawn from domestic systems as deemed appropriate by the chambers of the ICC.[173] While creating a hierarchy of sources,[174] it seems that Article 21 of the ICC Statute equally leaves room for references to national legal systems in case this is determined to be necessary. Thus, it is possible that the general approach with regard to the establishment of the applicable law as found for example at the *ad hoc* tribunals might not necessarily change substantially in practice. However, it has been pointed out with regard to the analysis of domestic laws in order to derive general principles that a certain danger of inconsistency exists.[175] More importantly for purposes of this dissertation, it has been argued that Article 21 of the Rome Statute is "clear" in not providing for any direct application of domestic legal provisions.[176] A similar argument considers that the process as laid out in Article 21(1)(c) of the ICC Statute "require[s] a triple mental operation: a comparison between national systems, the search for common 'principles', and their transposition to the international sphere".[177] Considering specifically the subject matter of this dissertation, this interpretation

---

without any adverse distinction founded on grounds such as gender as defined in article 7, paragraph 3, age, race, colour, language, religion or belief, political or other opinion, national, ethnic or social origin, wealth, birth or other status."

172 Margaret McAuliffe deGuzman, Article 21, in: Otto Triffterer (ed.), *Commentary on the Rome Statute of the International Criminal Court. Observers' Notes, Article by Article* (Munich: Verlag C.H. Beck) 2nd edition 2008, p.701-712, at note 1.

173 Margaret McAuliffe deGuzman, Article 21, in: Otto Triffterer (ed.), *Commentary on the Rome Statute of the International Criminal Court. Observers' Notes, Article by Article* (Munich: Verlag C.H. Beck) 2nd edition 2008, p.701-712, at note 7.

174 Margaret McAuliffe deGuzman, Article 21, in: Otto Triffterer (ed.), *Commentary on the Rome Statute of the International Criminal Court. Observers' Notes, Article by Article* (Munich: Verlag C.H. Beck) 2nd edition 2008, p.701-712, at note 1.

175 Margaret McAuliffe deGuzman, Article 21, in: Otto Triffterer (ed.), *Commentary on the Rome Statute of the International Criminal Court. Observers' Notes, Article by Article* (Munich: Verlag C.H. Beck) 2nd edition 2008, p.701-712, at note 14.

176 Margaret McAuliffe deGuzman, Article 21, in: Otto Triffterer (ed.), *Commentary on the Rome Statute of the International Criminal Court. Observers' Notes, Article by Article* (Munich: Verlag C.H. Beck) 2nd edition 2008, p.701-712, at note 15.

177 Alain Pellet, Chapter 25. Applicable Law, in: Antonio Cassese/Paola Gaeta/John R.W.D. Jones (eds), *The Rome Statute of the International Criminal Court: A Commentary (Volume II)* (Oxford: Oxford University Press) 2002, p.1051-1084, at 1073.

would indicate that it would not be possible for a trial chamber of the ICC to refer for example to merely one specific domestic procedural model,[178] without this selected model reflecting a general consensus across a wide majority of national legal systems.

Article 21 of the Rome Statute indicates that the ICC is likely to refer to an amalgamation of sources in its interpretation and application of the ICC Statute and its RPE. In light of this possibility, it becomes clear why it is necessary to take into account the respective approaches taken by national, regional, supranational and human rights institutions with regard to the exercise of the right to self-representation. While concerns have been expressed with regard to a mechanical importation of national legal concepts into the international context,[179] it has also been made clear that in a *sui generis* legal system as can be found at international criminal tribunals, interpretation and application of specific notions mirrored from national systems requires an understanding "as to how it operated in its domestic jurisdiction".[180] Going even further, it has been argued that if international criminal procedure is determined as placeholder for national systems incapable of functioning due to conflict, the international framework should – at least to a certain extent – refer more distinctly to the domestic procedures at stake instead of applying one model of international criminal procedure to every situation.[181] From a methodological point of view, comparative law has been suggested to provide the means to both "cross-fertilise" and "harmonise" international criminal law and domestic legal systems.[182]

---

178 *Cf.* Alain Pellet, Chapter 25. Applicable Law, in: Antonio Cassese/Paola Gaeta/John R.W.D. Jones (eds), *The Rome Statute of the International Criminal Court: A Commentary (Volume II)* (Oxford: Oxford University Press) 2002, p.1051-1084, at 1076: "Thus there is never any question of purely and simply applying the law of any State; […]".

179 *Prosecutor v. Dražen Erdemović*, Case No. IT-96-22-A, Judgement, 07 October 1997, Separate and Dissenting Opinion of Judge Cassese, para.2.

180 Patrick L. Robinson, Fair but Expeditious Trials, in: Hirad Abtahi/Gideon Boas (eds), *The Dynamics of International Criminal Justice. Essays in Honour of Sir Richard May* (Leiden/Boston: Martinus Nijhoff Publishers) 2006, p.169-192, at 174.

181 Jens David Ohlin, A Meta-Theory of International Criminal Procedure: Vindicating the Rule of Law, 14 *UCLA Journal of International Law and Foreign Affairs* 77 (2009), at 112-115.

182 Mireille Delmas-Marty, The Contribution of Comparative Law to a Pluralist Conception of International Criminal Law, 1 *Journal of International Criminal Justice* 13 (2003).

At the same time, however, an understanding has started to develop that the international criminal justice system has grown into a framework separate of national legal foundations, arguing that the underlying theories for international criminal law themselves have to be reconsidered.[183] This line of thought considers international criminal procedure to be a separate system which is tailored to the specific circumstances of international criminal trials.[184] In light of this view, it may have to be deliberated to which extent international criminal procedure can and should build upon national legal notions for its own specific interpretations and applications.[185] In the context of the ICC, it has been argued that the procedural system established by the Rome Statute embodies a "blend of different legal traditions",[186] and, more importantly, exists within a framework which is still to be filled by developing jurisprudence.[187] In fleshing out this body of jurisprudence, however, it is likely that reference will be made to other international, regional and national systems which may provide guidelines for the interpretation and application of international criminal law, whether substantive or procedural.[188] Importantly, it has been pointed out that eventually, the origin of a measure which might have been derived from domestic legal inspirations is not of issue, but

183 Noah Weisbord/Matthew A. Smith, The Reason Behind the Rules: From Description to Normativity in International Criminal Procedure, 36 *North Carolina Journal of International Law and Commercial Regulation* 255 (2011), at 256-257.

184 Jens David Ohlin, A Meta-Theory of International Criminal Procedure: Vindicating the Rule of Law, 14 *UCLA Journal of International Law and Foreign Affairs* 77 (2009), at 81-82.

185 Noah Weisbord/Matthew A. Smith, The Reason Behind the Rules: From Description to Normativity in International Criminal Procedure, 36 *North Carolina Journal of International Law and Commercial Regulation* 255 (2011), at 269-270.

186 Fatou Bensouda, The ICC Statute – An Insider's Perspective on a Sui Generis System for Global Justice, 36 *North Carolina Journal of International Law and Commercial Regulation* 277 (2011), at 279.

187 Fatou Bensouda, The ICC Statute – An Insider's Perspective on a Sui Generis System for Global Justice, 36 *North Carolina Journal of International Law and Commercial Regulation* 277 (2011), at 281.

188 *Cf.* Margaret McAuliffe deGuzman, Article 21, in: Otto Triffterer (ed.), *Commentary on the Rome Statute of the International Criminal Court. Observers' Notes, Article by Article* (Munich: Verlag C.H. Beck) 2nd edition 2008, p.701-712, at note 16: "As a developing body of law, international criminal law does not currently contain answers to every legal question likely to arise in a criminal trial."

rather "whether its incorporation in the law of the Tribunal produces a result that is consistent with international standards of fairness".[189]

C. *Preliminary observations*

This first examination of approaches to the exercise of the right to self-representation in national, regional and international human rights systems indicates that the matter is not uniformly or consistently dealt with.

While the right to defend oneself in person is at times given a prominent status and rarely restricted, other systems recognise the exercise of the right to self-representation merely to a limited extent. As will be demonstrated in the following, this divergence dependent on different legislative frameworks informs the interpretation and application of the right to defend oneself in person in the context of international criminal legal systems. Therefore, it is apposite to bear in mind the diverse picture illustrated in the first chapter, in order to properly assess the relevant case law in international criminal proceedings, which provide the flexibility of drawing upon a multitude of resources.

This review furthermore prompts the question whether a right to self-representation as interpreted and applied before international criminal tribunals is in fact established within the human rights framework on an internationally recognised level. On the one hand it could be argued that no such full right to self-representation is safeguarded by international human rights conventions in light of the opposed views taken in different national legal systems. On the other hand, however, it seems more apt to conclude, especially in light of General Comment No. 32 of the Human Rights Committee mentioned above,[190] that while there is in fact a right to a *personal defence* widely recognised in the international sphere, the interpretation and application of such a right is more diverse depending on the jurisdictional system involved. In essence, this would lead to the conclusion that the subject matter at the heart of the discussion is the role of the accused to be played in his or her own proceedings, with a focus on the defendant's right to a fair

---

189 Patrick L. Robinson, Rough Edges in the Alignment of Legal Systems in the Proceedings at the ICTY, 3 *Journal of International Criminal Justice* 1037 (2005), at 1056.

190 Human Rights Committee, General Comment No. 32, CCPR/C/GC/32, 23 August 2007.

trial. This assumption would serve to reconcile the different attitudes towards the nature and scope of active participation of defendants in their own proceedings and appropriately place the emphasis on the necessity to ensure that the accused is seen as the subject of the proceedings, rather than as their object.

Especially the ICC might potentially refer to divergent national legislations depending on the situation country concerned. Unless a consistent solution taking into account the specifics of international criminal proceedings is adopted from the start, this approach could lead to divergent and even contradictory jurisprudence. The discrepancy in dealing with a right to defend oneself in person that can be observed in the context of national and regional jurisdictions indicates that a direct reliance on any specific solution adopted by the national or regional courts could lead to further complications in the context of international criminal proceedings. While national solutions might be capable of providing useful guidelines, it is argued that it will be necessary to depart from previous approaches of overly exclusive reliance on such models in order to avoid the direct import of practices which were not designed and are in fact illsuited for purposes of international criminal legal systems.

As will be outlined in the following chapter, the exercise of the right to self-representation in the context of international criminal trials brings with it complexities and complications which are inherent in the conduct of international criminal proceedings. National and regional approaches are unlikely to provide adequate solutions to address these implications. Therefore, it is suggested that international criminal tribunals, in particular the ICC, in the future will have to adopt solutions with respect to the exercise of a right to defend oneself in person which are specifically tailored to the particularities of international criminal proceedings.

CHAPTER TWO. The right to self-representation in international criminal proceedings

A. Statutory provisions on the right to defend oneself in person

In order to provide a basis for the discussion of the right to self-representation before international criminal tribunals which is to follow, relevant codifications of international criminal procedure will be described below.

The first pertinent legislative instrument to be mentioned is the Nuremberg Charter, which in its Article 16(d) provided in a language similar to subsequent human rights conventions for the right of a defendant to conduct his own defence or be assisted by counsel.[191] It does not appear that any of the accused before the Nuremberg Tribunal specifically invoked their right to defend themselves in person. When Hermann Goering at the pleading stage tried to address the court personally in more detail, he was advised by the bench that he would not be able to do so unless later on called as witness in his own case.[192] While this "precedent" is not of much significance for purposes of this dissertation as the Nuremberg Tribunal did not have to deal with *pro se* defendants,[193] it nevertheless appears to indicate that its proceedings were influenced by the adversarial system. However, given that the decision of the U.S. Supreme Court in *Faretta*, as discussed before, should be rendered only some 30 years later, one can only speculate to which extent the judges in Nuremberg would have permitted the exercise of the right to

191 Charter of the International Military Tribunal – Annex to the Agreement for the Prosecution and Punishment of the Major War Criminals of the European Axis ("London Agreement"), 08 August 1945, available at: http://www.unhcr.org/refworld/docid/3ae6b39614.html (last accessed 17 November 2012), Article 16(d): "In order to ensure fair trial for the Defendants, the following procedure shall be followed: [...] (d) A Defendant shall have the right to conduct his own defense before the Tribunal or to have the assistance of counsel".

192 International Military Tribunal Hearing, 21 November 1945, available at http://avalon.law.yale.edu/imt/11-21-45.asp (last accessed 17 November 2012), at 96-97.

193 *See* Eugene Cerruti, Self-Representation in the International Arena: Removing a False Right to Spectacle, 40 *Georgetown Journal of International Law* 919 (2009), at 965.

self-representation and which restrictions, if any, would have been considered feasible to be imposed in this specific context.

As alluded to before, the statutes of international and hybrid criminal tribunals and courts essentially mirror the language of international human rights instruments.[194] Of relevance and to be referred to in more detail in the following are Article 21(4)(d) of the ICTY Statute[195] and Article 20(4)(d) of the ICTR Statute;[196] as well as Article 17(4)(d) of the SCSL Statute;[197] Article 16(4)(d) of the Statute of the Special Tribunal for Lebanon (STL

---

194 *See, e.g.*, the direct reference to Article 14 of the ICCPR in the report of the Secretary-General on the draft ICTY statute: Report of the Secretary-General Pursuant to Paragraph 2 of Security Council Resolution 808 (1993), S/25704, 03 May 1993, para.106.

195 Updated Statute of the International Criminal Tribunal for the Former Yugoslavia (as amended 07 July 2009 by Resolution 1877) ("ICTY Statute"), Article 21(4)(d): "In the determination of any charge against the accused pursuant to the present Statute, the accused shall be entitled to the following minimum guarantees, in full equality: [...] (d) to be tried in his presence, and *to defend himself in person or through legal assistance of his own choosing*; to be informed, if he does not have legal assistance, of this right; and to have legal assistance assigned to him, in any case where the interests of justice so require, and without payment by him in any such case if he does not have sufficient means to pay for it; [...]" (emphasis added).

196 Statute of the International Criminal Tribunal for Rwanda, 31 January 2010 (as amended) ("ICTR Statute"), Article 20(4)(d): "In the determination of any charge against the accused pursuant to the present Statute, the accused shall be entitled to the following minimum guarantees, in full equality: [...] (d) to be tried in his or her presence, and *to defend himself or herself in person or through legal assistance of his or her own choosing*; to be informed, if he or she does not have legal assistance, of this right; and to have legal assistance assigned to him or her, in any case where the interests of justice so require, and without payment by him or her in any such case if he or she does not have sufficient means to pay for it; [...]" (emphasis added).

197 Statute of the Special Court for Sierra Leone, annexed to the Agreement between the United Nations and the Government of Sierra Leone on the Establishment of a Special Court for Sierra Leone, 16 January 2002 ("SCSL Statute"), Article 17(4)(d): "In the determination of any charge against the accused pursuant to the present Statute, he or she shall be entitled to the following minimum guarantees, in full equality: [...] d. To be tried in his or her presence, and *to defend himself or herself in person or through legal assistance of his or her own choosing*; to be informed, if he or she does not have legal assistance, of this right; and to have legal assistance assigned to him or her, in any case where the interests of justice so require, and without payment by him or her in any such case if he or she does not have sufficient means to pay for it; [...]" (emphasis added).

Statute);[198] Article 35 new of the law governing the procedure of the Extraordinary Chambers in the Courts of Cambodia (ECCC);[199] and eventually Article 67(1)(d) of the Rome Statute of the ICC.[200]

It is of note that the Statute of the Iraqi Special Tribunal (IST)[201] initially contained a provision with language similar to the formulations found in the basic texts of international criminal tribunals cited *supra*, but later amended

---

198 Statute of the Special Tribunal for Lebanon, S/RES/1757 (2007), Attachment, 30 May 2007 ("STL Statute"), Article 16(4)(d): "In the determination of any charge against the accused pursuant to this Statute, he or she shall be entitled to the following minimum guarantees, in full equality: […] (d) Subject to the provisions of article 22, to be tried in his or her presence, *and to defend himself or herself in person or through legal assistance of his or her own choosing*; to be informed, if he or she does not have legal assistance, of this right; and to have legal assistance assigned to him or her, in any case where the interests of justice so require and without payment by him or her in any such case if he or she does not have sufficient means to pay for it; […]" (emphasis added).

199 Law on the Establishment of the Extraordinary Chambers, with inclusion of amendments as promulgated on 27 October 2004 (NS/RKM/1004/006) ("ECCC Law"), Article 35 new: "In determining charges against the accused, the accused shall be equally entitled to the following minimum guarantees, in accordance with Article 14 of the International Covenant on Civil and Political Rights. […] d. to be tried in their own presence and *to defend themselves in person or with the assistance of counsel of their own choosing*, to be informed of this right and to have legal assistance assigned to them free of charge if they do not have sufficient means to pay for it; […]" (emphasis added).

200 Rome Statute for the International Criminal Court, A/CONF.183/9, 17 July 1998 ("Rome Statute", "ICC Statute"), Article 67(1)(d): "In the determination of any charge, the accused shall be entitled to a public hearing, having regard to the provisions of the Statute, to a fair hearing conducted impartially, and to the following minimum guarantees, in full equality: […] (d) Subject to article 63, paragraph 2, to be present at the trial, *to conduct the defence in person or through legal assistance of the accused's choosing*, to be informed, if the accused does not have legal assistance, of this right and to have legal assistance assigned by the Court in any case where the interests of justice so require, and without payment if the accused lacks sufficient means to pay for it; […]" (emphasis added).

201 Iraqi High Criminal Court Law, No. 4006, 18 October 2005, Article 19 Fourth D: "In directing any charge against the accused pursuant to the present Law, the accused shall be entitled to a just fair trial in accordance with the following minimum guarantees: […] D. To be tried in his presence, *and to use a lawyer of his choosing, and to be informed of his right assistance of his own choosing*; to be informed, if he does not have legal assistance, of this right; and to have legal assistance and to have the right to request such aid to appoint a lawyer without paying the fees, case if he does not have sufficient means to pay for it; if he does not have the financial ability to do so." (emphasis added).

the statue in order to remove the possibility of self-representation.[202] It had been argued already earlier that in drafting the statute of the Iraqi tribunal, the "pitfalls of the Milošević fiasco" could be avoided by providing for mandatory representation by counsel.[203]

A number of commentaries that address the drafting history of the ICC Statute provide certain indications that the text of the relevant provisions in the Rome Statute do not, in view of the drafters, provide for any solutions with regard to issues arising from the exercise of the right to self-representation.[204] Consequently, judges at the ICC will have to draw from the experience gained at other international criminal tribunals over the last few years, if and when such a situation occurs during proceedings before the ICC.

A commentary analysing the drafting history of the Rome Statute submits that significant parts of Article 67 of the ICC Statute are based on Article 14 of the ICCPR and the provisions of the *ad hoc* tribunals.[205] This would suggest that the basic assumption at the ICC is to be seen in the recognition of a full and factual right to self-representation, as initially adopted before the *ad hoc* tribunals.

Another commentary on the Rome Statute considers the existing case law to be inconsistent and, referring to a decision by a trial chamber of the SCSL in *Norman*, states that such a situation was not contemplated in the Rome

---

202 Kevin Jon Heller, A Poisoned Chalice: The Substantive and Procedural Defects of the Iraqi High Tribunal, 39 *Case Western Reserve Journal of International Law* 261 (2007), at 288-289; Philipp Ambach, Selbstvertretung im internationalen Strafprozess – Grundlagen, Kritik und ein Lösungsansatz für die prozessuale Handhabung in der Zukunft, 6 *Zeitschrift für Internationale Strafrechtsdogmatik* 286 (2009), at 286 fn.4. *See also* Michael P. Scharf/Christopher M. Rassi, Do Former Leaders have an International Right to Self-Representation in War Crimes Trials?, 20 *Ohio State Journal on Dispute Resolution* 3 (2005), at 37; and only a little later Nina H.B. Jørgensen, The Problem of Self-Representation at International Criminal Tribunals. Striking a Balance Between Fairness and Effectiveness, 4 *Journal of International Criminal Justice* 64 (2006), at 76-77.

203 Michael P. Scharf, Is It International Enough? A Critique of the Iraqi Special Tribunal in Light of the Goals of International Criminal Justice, 2 *Journal of International Criminal Justice* 330 (2004), at 337.

204 *Cf.* also Stuart Beresford/Hafida Lahiouel, The Right to be Defended in Person or Through Legal Assistance and the International Criminal Court, 13 *Leiden Journal of International Law* 949 (2000), at 966.

205 Håkan Friman, Chapter IV. Rights of Persons Suspected or Accused of a Crime, in: Roy S. Lee (ed.), *The International Criminal Court. The Making of the Rome Statute. Issues, Negotiations, Results* (The Hague/London/Boston: Kluwer Law International) 2002, p.247-262, at 248, 262.

Statute, probably because it had not yet arisen before ICTY or ICTR.[206] If it is indeed the case that the drafters of the Rome Statute did not envisage specific procedures to be applied to a right to self-representation, it will be interesting to see what the ICC will make of the sometimes unclear and even contradictory jurisprudence of the *ad hoc* tribunals. While the late years in the operation of the *ad hoc* tribunals have seen an accumulation of issues surrounding the exercise of the right to self-representation that needed to be resolved and in this way provided for clarification in a number of matters, this dissertation will attempt to highlight some of the problems neither addressed nor solved by international criminal tribunals thus far. It will eventually seek to suggest an improved procedure which could be considered for future proceedings before the ICC and which is based on a more generic right to a personal defence.

In addition to the statutory provisions mentioned above, further regulations to be referred to as background for the following analysis are those that can be found in the respective procedural and evidentiary rules of international criminal tribunals, as they supplement the provisions in the respective statutes and equally influence the interpretation of the right to self-representation and, even more importantly, the practical exercise of the right. Pertinent provisions include Rule 45(F)[207] and 45*ter*[208] of the Rules of Procedure and Evidence of the ICTY (ICTY RPE), with the same language to be found in Rule 45(F) and 45*quater* of the Rules of Procedure and Evidence of the ICTR (ICTR RPE),[209] respectively, as well as Rule 21(4) of the Rules of Procedure

---

206 William A. Schabas, Article 67, in: Otto Triffterer (ed.), *Commentary on the Rome Statute of the International Criminal Court. Observers' Notes, Article by Article* (Munich: Verlag C.H. Beck) 2nd edition 2008, p.1247-1274, at note 3.

207 Rules of Procedure and Evidence, IT/32/Rev. 47, 28 August 2012 ("ICTY RPE"), Rule 45(F): "A suspect or an accused electing to conduct his or her own defence shall so notify the Registrar in writing at the first opportunity."

208 Rule 45*ter* ICTY RPE: "The Trial Chamber may, if it decides that it is in the interests of justice, instruct the Registrar to assign a counsel to represent the interests of the accused."

209 Rules of Procedure and Evidence, adopted on 29 June 1995, as amended on 01 October 2009 ("ICTR RPE").

and Evidence of the ICC[210] and Regulation 76(1) of the Regulations of the Court for the ICC.[211]

Regulation 76(1) of the ICC Regulations further develops Article 67 of the Rome Statute and provides for a chamber of the Court to appoint counsel, and specifically refers to the possibility to appoint standby counsel.[212] The language regarding appointment of counsel in the "interests of justice" is similar to the one found in Rule 45*ter* of the ICTY RPE and Rule 45*quater* of the ICTR RPE.[213] It seems that the provision of the ICC Regulations is not only referring to the assignment of legal assistance to indigent accused, which would be the scenario already envisaged under Article 67 of the Rome Statute, but equally, similar to Rule 45*ter* of the ICTY RPE, to the assignment of counsel to *pro se* defendants if deemed necessary by the chamber. This argument is underscored by the fact that the specific reference to the possibility to assign standby counsel was not included in the initial regulations adopted in 2004.[214] It may have been the case that following the developments at other international criminal courts such as the ICTY, the ICC judges saw a necessity to provide for the assignment of counsel to self-represented accused. On the other hand, bearing in mind that an equivalent providing for assignment of counsel in the interests of justice had been included in the ICTR RPE already in 2002, and the first version of the regulations of the ICC was adopted in 2004, one might wonder why no such provision was

---

210 Rule 21(4) of the Rules of Procedure and Evidence, ICC-ASP/1/3, 10 September 2002: "A person choosing to represent himself or herself shall so notify the Registrar in writing at the first opportunity."

211 Regulation 76(1) of the Regulations of the Court, ICC-BD/01-03-11 (as amended), 02 November 2011 ("ICC Court Regulations"): "A Chamber, following consultation with the Registrar and, when appropriate, after hearing from the person entitled to legal assistance, may appoint counsel in the circumstances specified in the Statute, Rules and these Regulations or where the interests of justice so require. This may include the appointment of standby counsel, if appropriate."

212 Regulation 76(1) of the ICC Court Regulations.

213 Rule 45*quater* ICTR RPE and Rule 45*ter* ICTY RPE contain the same language: "The Trial Chamber may, if it decides that it is in the interests of justice, instruct the Registrar to assign a counsel to represent the interests of the accused."

214 Regulation 76(1) of the Regulations of the Court, ICC-BD/01-01-04, 26 May 2004, reads: "1. A Chamber, following consultation with the Registrar, may appoint counsel in the circumstances specified in the Statute and the Rules or where the interests of justice so require." The different versions are available at http://icc-cpi.int/Menus/ICC/Legal+Texts+and+Tools/Official+Journal/Regulations+of+the+Court.htm (last accessed 13 October 2012).

included in the initial regulations from the start. However, the ICTY RPE would see a similar amendment only in 2008, development which might also have prompted reconsideration of the regulations applicable at the ICC.

Considering on a more general level the formulation of some provisions which relate to the assignment of counsel "in the interests of justice", *e.g.* Rules 45*ter* and 45*quater* of the ICTY and ICTR RPE, it has been argued that the phrase "interests of justice" does not merely apply to the question of legal aid to indigent accused, as can be seen from the analysis of the trial chamber in *Norman*, which took this part of Article 17(4)(d) of the SCSL Statute as indication that the right to self-representation was not absolute, but qualified.[215] The SCSL appeals chamber took a similar position several months later in *Sesay* when it found that Article 17(4)(d) of the SCSL Statute contained three rights, two of which were open to choice by the accused, while the third, namely assignment of counsel in the interests of justice, was not.[216]

Similarly, the trial chamber in *Blagojević & Jokić* adopted the view that the right to be represented by counsel in general was linked to the concept of interests of justice, independently of the context of indigent accused.[217] Furthermore, it has been commented that, in contrast to most of the texts the language of which appears to be rather ambiguous,[218] the ECHR is the only instrument which explicitly links the notion of "interests of justice" to the provision of legal aid.[219] Yet, when examining for example the STL RPE, it appears that the concept in that context is equally linked to the assignment

---

215 *Prosecutor v. Samuel Hinga Norman et al.*, Case No. SCSL-04-14-T, Decision on the Application of Samuel Hinga Norman for Self-Representation Under Article 17(4)(d) of the Statute of the Special Court, 08 June 2004, para.8-9.

216 *Prosecutor v. Issa Hassan Sesay et al.*, Case No. SCSL-04-15-AR73, Gbao – Decision on Appeal Against Decision on Withdrawal of Counsel, 23 November 2004, para.57-58.

217 *Prosecutor v. Blagojević & Jokić*, Case No. IT-02-60-T, Decision on Independent Counsel for Vidoje Blagojević's Motion to Instruct the Registrar to Appoint New Lead and Co-Counsel, 03 July 2003, para.73.

218 *Cf.* M. Cherif Bassiouni/Peter Manikas, *The Law of the International Criminal Tribunal for the Former Yugoslavia* (New York: Transnational Publishers, Inc.) 1996, p.967.

219 Nina H.B. Jørgensen, The Right of the Accused to Self-Representation Before International Criminal Tribunals, 98 *The American Journal of International Law* 711 (2004), at 713. *See also Pakelli c. Allemagne*, Requête n° 8398/78, Arrêt, 05 avril 1983, para.31.

of counsel to indigent accused.[220] The same holds true for the directive on the assignment of counsel drafted for the SCSL.[221] In a similar vein, it has been considered for the ICCPR, and in consequence the Rome Statute, that the right to legal aid for indigent accused is linked to the notion of interests of justice, while this however would be fulfilled in all cases before the ICC.[222]

Further of note and to be discussed later in this dissertation is Regulation 74(2),[223] which appears to open the door for more inventive legal assistance and participation models before the ICC. In addition, it has been argued that Regulation 77(4), concerning "general support and assistance" to be provided for the defence by the Office of Public Counsel to defence counsel as well as "to the person entitled to legal assistance"[224] is equally applicable to self-represented accused.[225] However, considering that this regulation is included in the section on "defence through counsel", it appears more reasonable to assume that the regulation in fact refers to an accused who is established to be entitled to receive legal assistance and who is appointed counsel on this basis, rather than a self-represented accused who might need assistance in the presentation of his or her defence case. Yet, the same argument then might hold true for the regulation providing for assignment of standby counsel, in particular since that provision specifically refers to "the person entitled to legal assistance".[226]

Another interpretative issue relates to the ECCC: while Article 35 new of the ECCC law as mentioned above is a word-for-word replication of Article 14 of the ICCPR, Rule 21 of the Internal Rules of the ECCC only mentions the right to counsel of one's own choice, but not the possibility to

---

220 Rule 59(A) STL RPE.

221 Directive on the Assignment of Counsel, 03 October 2003, Article 3.

222 William A. Schabas, *An Introduction to the International Criminal Court* (Cambridge: Cambridge University Press) 3rd edition 2007, p.292.

223 Regulation 74(2) of the Court Regulations reads: "Whenever represented by defence counsel, the person entitled to legal assistance shall, subject to article 67, paragraph 1 (h), act before the Court through his or her counsel, *unless otherwise authorised by the Chamber*." (emphasis added).

224 Regulation 77 of the Court Regulations provides for establishment of an Office of Public Counsel for the defence and specifies some of its tasks.

225 G. Mettraux/A. Cengic, The Role of a Defence Office – Some Lessons from Recent and not so Recent War Crimes Precedents, in: Michael Bohlander (ed.), *International Criminal Justice. A Critical Analysis of Institutions and Procedures* (London: Cameron May Ltd) 2007, p.391-428, at 413 fn.86, 418-419.

226 Regulation 76(1) of the ICC Court Regulations.

present the defence in person.[227] It is possible that this rule is the reason for which the procedural rules do not include any provision which is equivalent to Rules 45*ter* and 45*quater* of the ICTY and ICTR RPE. The only rule providing for assignment of counsel by the court deals with the removal of the accused from the courtroom and subsequent conduct of the proceedings without his or her presence.[228] However, it then would still have to be asked how Rule 21 of the ECCC Internal Rules was envisaged to be reconciled with Article 35 of the ECCC law. Neither Article 35 of the ECCC law nor Rule 21 of the ECCC Internal Rules provides any indication whether this omission might have been erroneous or based on specific reasons. Similarly, the agreement concluded between the United Nations and the Cambodian government on the establishment of the Extraordinary Courts on the one hand specifically provides for the rights of accused to be derived from Articles 14 and 15 of the ICCPR, but in particular merely mentions the right to engage counsel of choice.[229]

---

227 Extraordinary Chambers in the Courts of Cambodia, Internal Rules (Rev. 8), as revised on 03 August 2011 ("ECCC IR"), Rule 21: "[…] d) Every person suspected or prosecuted shall be presumed innocent as long as his/her guilt has not been established. Any such person has the right to be informed of any charges brought against him/her, *to be defended by a lawyer of his/her own choice*, and at every stage of the proceedings shall be informed of his/her right to remain silent." (emphasis added).

228 ECCC IR, Rule 81(4): "If the Accused, following an initial appearance and having been duly summoned to the subsequent hearing, continues to refuse or fails to attend the proceedings, or is expelled from them in accordance with these IRs, the proceedings may continue in his or her absence. In such cases, the Accused may be defended during the proceedings either by his or her lawyer. Where the Accused refuses to choose a lawyer, the Chamber shall order that the accused be represented by a lawyer and request the Defence Support Section to assign him or her a lawyer, from the lists mentioned at Rule 11."

229 Agreement between the United Nations and the Royal Government of Cambodia Concerning the Prosecution Under Cambodian Law of Crimes Committed During the Period of Democratic Kampuchea, available at http://www.eccc.gov.kh/sites/default/files/legal-documents/Agreement_between_UN_and_RGC.pdf(last accessed 17 November 2012), Article 13 (Rights of the Accused): "1. The rights of the accused enshrined in Articles 14 and 15 of the 1966 International Covenant on Civil and Political Rights shall be respected throughout the trial process. Such rights shall, in particular, include the right: […] to engage a counsel of his or her choice; […] to have counsel provided if he or she does not have sufficient means to pay for it; […] 2. The United Nations and the Royal Government of Cambodia agree that the provisions on the right to defence counsel in the Law on the Establishment of Extraordinary Chambers mean that the accused has the right to engage counsel of his

It appears that Cambodian criminal procedure provides for a limited right to defend oneself in person.[230] The French criminal procedure, which served as model upon which the Cambodian legislation is drawn,[231] at a higher instance (before the *Cour d'Assises*) provides for mandatory counsel to be assigned by the judge in case the accused does not choose one.[232] The potential divergence in the criminal procedure in Cambodian national courts and the ECCC is of specific concern insofar as the ECCC is a hybrid tribunal which combines elements of national and international criminal procedure. An obvious deviation in ECCC proceedings might impact the potential influence of these procedures on the national system in an attempt of improvement. This might be even more so considering that the initial agreement on the establishment of the ECCC, mentioned above, is considered to apply as law within the Cambodian national system.[233] However, any potential difference appears to be a rather hypothetical scenario given that none of the defendants currently still to be tried before the ECCC ever indicated that they would prefer to conduct their own defence. Therefore, it cannot be assessed how the ECCC might have dealt with the apparent contradiction in its legislation. In addition, due to the significant health issues of all accused, it might be unproblematic for a trial chamber to reject any request for self-representation, especially in light of the *Milošević* jurisprudence with regard to "unintention-

---

or her own choosing as guaranteed by the International Covenant on Civil and Political Rights."

230 Kram on Criminal Procedure, 08 February 1993, available at www.bigpond.com.kh/Council_of_Jurists/Penal/pen002g.htm (last accessed 17 November 2012), Articles 76, 108.

231 Rupert Skilbeck, Frankenstein's Monster. Creating a New International Procedure, 8 *Journal of International Criminal Justice* 451 (2010), at 455; Robert Petit/Anees Ahmed, A Review of the Jurisprudence of the Khmer Rouge Tribunal, 8 *Northwestern University Journal of International Human Rights* 165 (2010), para.12.

232 Code de Procédure Pénale, Version consolidée au 07 janvier 2011, available at http://www.legifrance.gouv.fr/affichCode.do?cidTexte=LEGITEXT000006071154&dateTexte=20110110 (last accessed 17 November 2012), Article 274; Article 317.

233 Agreement between the United Nations and the Royal Government of Cambodia Concerning the Prosecution Under Cambodian Law of Crimes Committed During the Period of Democratic Kampuchea, available at http://www.eccc.gov.kh/sites/default/files/legal-documents/Agreement_between_UN_and_RGC.pdf (last accessed 17 November 2012), Article 31 (Application within Cambodia): "The present Agreement shall apply as law within the Kingdom of Cambodia following its ratification in accordance with the relevant provisions of the internal law of the Kingdom of Cambodia regarding competence to conclude treaties."

al" obstruction of proceedings by a defendant's ill-health, as to be discussed *infra*.

While there have been no cases of self-represented accused before the ECCC, the office of co-prosecutors at the ECCC considered the jurisprudence on the right to defend oneself in person in the context of a civil party's submission[234] and argued "that the Pre-trial Chamber view the legal principles governing the defendant's right to self-representation as instructive in its determination of the rights of the civil parties in the proceedings before it".[235] However, there is no indication as to the potential position of the judges on the matter, since the pre-trial chamber did not further discuss this particular submission of the co-prosecutors.[236]

To be kept in mind are also the Rules of Procedure and Evidence of the Special Tribunal for Lebanon (STL RPE), which explicitly provide for the assignment of counsel in the interests of justice and to safeguard the right to a fair and expeditious trial, and at the same time leave open the possibility for defendants to continue their active participation in the proceedings.[237] In his explanatory memorandum accompanying the STL RPE, the President of the Tribunal explained the reasoning behind the adoption of Rule 59(F) of the STL RPE and in this context the interpretation to be given to Article 16(4)(d) of the STL Statute. Outlining the reasons for which a provision such as Rule 59(F) of the STL RPE was considered to be necessary,[238] the memorandum clarified that the drafters of the STL Statute deemed it appro-

---

234 Case File No. 002/19-09-2007-ECCC/OCIJ (PTC 03), C22/I/61, Co-Prosecutor's Response to an Application for Reconsideration of the Pre-trial Chamber's Decision Regarding a Civil Party's Right of Audience, 17 July 2008, para.7-14.

235 Case File No. 002/19-09-2007-ECCC/OCIJ (PTC 03), C22/I/61, Co-Prosecutor's Response to an Application for Reconsideration of the Pre-trial Chamber's Decision Regarding a Civil Party's Right of Audience, 17 July 2008, para.15.

236 Case File No. 002/19-09-2007-ECCC/OCIJ (PTC 03), C22/I/68, Decision on Application for Reconsideration of Civil Party's Right to Address Pre-trial Chamber in Person, 28 August 2008.

237 Rules of Procedure and Evidence, STL/BD/2009/01/Rev. 4 (amended on 08 February 2012) ("STL RPE"), Rule 59(F): "A suspect or an accused electing to conduct his own defence shall so notify, in writing, the Pre-trial Judge or a Chamber of his election. The Pre-trial Judge or a Chamber may impose counsel to represent *or otherwise assist* the accused in accordance with international criminal law and international human rights law *where this is deemed necessary in the interests of justice and to ensure a fair and expeditious trial.*" (emphasis added).

238 Rules of Procedure and Evidence (as of 25 November 2010). Explanatory Memorandum by the Tribunal's President, para.33.

priate, "[i]n light of recent unfortunate experience at the ICTY", to interpret the right to self-representation in Article 16 of the STL Statute

> "as the right of the accused to ask questions, call witnesses or examine or cross-examine witnesses either himself – or whenever required by the interests of justice – with the assistance of defence counsel."[239]

The explanation continued that

> "the complexity of international criminal proceedings is such that it is almost inconceivable that an accused, in order to fully ensure his defence, will not need the assistance of experienced defence counsel."[240]

To be taken into account in any balance of interests that might have to be conducted in the context of the right to self-representation, the memorandum adopted the position that

> "the interests of justice clearly include, *inter alia*, the interest of the international community and of the Lebanese people to a fair and expeditious trial of the accused in question and of any other accused [...], the effective presentation of evidence, the orderly administration of justice, the truth-searching mission of the Tribunal, and the protection and interests of victims and witnesses."[241]

This is a remarkable position and explanation insofar as the STL is the first international criminal tribunal which explicitly embraces the experiences made at the *ad hoc* tribunals and attempts to provide remedies for flaws detected in the course of their proceedings. Thus, the STL Statute and RPE, read together with the explanatory memorandum, appear to contain the most advanced provisions with regard to the right to self-representation.[242]

As can be seen from the outline of statutory provisions for international criminal tribunals, the general consensus can be found in offering a basis for the recognition of the right to *defend oneself in person*. At the same time, rules regulating the actual procedure before international criminal tribunals have recently come to incorporate acknowledgement of the fact that there may be situations which require adaptation of a previously accepted right to

---

239 Rules of Procedure and Evidence (as of 25 November 2010). Explanatory Memorandum by the Tribunal's President, para.32.

240 Rules of Procedure and Evidence (as of 25 November 2010). Explanatory Memorandum by the Tribunal's President, para.32.

241 Rules of Procedure and Evidence (as of 25 November 2010). Explanatory Memorandum by the Tribunal's President, para.32.

242 *Cf.* Wolfgang Schomburg, The Role of International Criminal Tribunals in Promoting Respect for Fair Trial Rights, 8 *Northwestern University Journal of International Human Rights* 1 (2009), fn.143.

self-representation to the specific nature of international criminal proceedings. Thus, while it is generally recognised that accused before international criminal tribunals may have a vested interest in actively participating in presenting their defence, more pragmatic approaches are being developed in order to provide for a system that – while taking into account interests of other participants in the proceedings as well as the interests of justice in general – at the same time safeguards accused's right to a fair and expeditious trial and their plausible interest to remain the subject of their own case through presenting a personal defence.

B. Judicial interpretation of the right to self-representation

A significant part of this dissertation will be concerned with the meticulous reading of the interpretation and application of the existing provisions on the right to self-representation by international criminal tribunals. This will form the foundation for an examination of the problems encountered by the participants involved, *i.e.* accused, prosecution, chambers and registry, before international criminal tribunals such as the ICTY, ICTR or SCSL, as well as of the developments in the course of proceedings before these tribunals. This analysis will provide a framework to discuss potential issues to be resolved and lessons to be learnt in particular by the ICC in possible future trials with *pro se* defendants in order to prevent misuse and abuse of the right to self-representation. This section will include, *inter alia*, a discussion of the question whether the exercise of the right to self-representation is treated differently at distinct stages of the proceedings, namely pre-trial, trial and appeals phase. In this context to be examined is a decision of the ICTY appeals chamber in *Krajišnik* alongside the appended fundamentally dissenting opinion.[243]

The following examination of international criminal jurisprudence will first focus on the question under which circumstances and to which extent international criminal tribunals, above all the ICTY, initially acknowledged the right to self-representation. The extent to which a right to defend oneself

243 *Prosecutor v. Momčilo Krajišnik*, Case No. IT-00-39-A, Decision on Momčilo Krajišnik's Request to Self-Represent, on Counsel's Motion in Relation to Appointment of *Amicus Curiae*, and on the Prosecution Motion of 16 February 2007, 11 May 2007, and Fundamentally Dissenting Opinion of Judge Schomburg on the Right to Self-Representation.

in person during international criminal proceedings is recognised and exercised is not uncontroversial. Accordingly, the views adopted in the discussions of the pertinent case law, either approving the maximum extent of self-representation possible or favouring limitations on the exercise of the right to defend oneself in person, will be set out below.

Furthermore, as will become clear in the course of the review of the different approaches adopted in separate cases, a continuous concern informing judges' considerations of the exercise of self-representation relates to safeguarding the accused's fundamental right to fair and expeditious proceedings. Therefore, a short section will address the particular issue of any potential impact of self-representation on the right to a fair trial. This is of import insofar as one recalls the underlying premise mentioned previously which is sought to be attained by permitting an accused to actively participate in proceedings: that the defendants are in fact treated as subjects in their own case.

In light of the fact that the international criminal tribunals' case law is likely to be the first point of reference for the ICC when dealing with the right to self-representation, the analysis of the existing and developing jurisprudence and practice of the *ad hoc* tribunals will be applied to the general situation before the ICC. It will be necessary to examine in which way the ICC could and should draw from the experiences before other international criminal tribunals and address problems that emerged in the course of various proceedings in the past.

I. The initial recognition of the right to self-representation

1. The case of Slobodan Milošević

The era of the right to self-representation before international criminal tribunals can be said to have really begun in the case against former Serbian president Slobodan Milošević. With him being the first accused in international criminal proceedings to indeed demand[244] and be granted the exercise of his right to self-representation, the jurisprudence arising from his case and its special circumstances continue to have decisive impact on subsequent international criminal proceedings with self-represented accused. It will

244 *Prosecutor v. Slobodan Milošević*, Case No. IT-99-37-I, Initial Appearance, 03 July 2001, T.2.

therefore be necessary to consider the case law in this particular case in a preliminary review in order to grasp the considerations and concerns that surfaced in later proceedings, and to illustrate progress made in other international criminal trials.

In the first status conference in *Milošević*, the trial chamber recognised the accused's right to represent himself[245] and even found that this was mandated under "customary international law".[246] This characterisation needs to be questioned.[247] While it could be argued that it is internationally recognised that a defendant must be granted a, albeit not absolute, right to self-representation, it is of doubt whether this would indeed form part of customary international law,[248] given that especially civil law systems frequently recognise the need to impose counsel on accused even against their will.[249]

The trial chamber subsequently provided the accused with the possibility of privileged communications with two legal associates who would assist

245 *Prosecutor v. Slobodan Milošević*, Case No. IT-99-37-PT, Status Conference, 30 August 2001, T.6-7.

246 *Prosecutor v. Slobodan Milošević*, Case No. IT-99-37-PT, Status Conference, 30 August 2001, T.16-18: "However, I do not consider it appropriate for the Chamber to impose counsel upon the accused. We have to act in accordance with the Statute and our Rules, which, in any event, reflect the position under customary international law, which is that the accused has a right to counsel, but he also has a right not to have counsel. He has a right to defend himself, and it is quite clear that he has chosen to defend himself. He has made that abundantly clear. … but I stress that it would be wrong for the Chamber to impose counsel on the accused, because that would be in breach with the position under customary international law."

247 In the same vein, *see* Boris Petersdorf, *Eigenverteidigung und aufgedrängte Pflichtverteidigung im formellen Völkerstrafrecht* (Baden-Baden: Nomos Verlagsgesellschaft) 2010, p.96.

248 *Cf.* Statute of the International Court of Justice, Article 38.1.b: "[…] international custom, as evidence of a *general practice accepted as law*; […]" (emphasis added).

249 Michael P. Scharf/Christopher M. Rassi, Do Former Leaders have an International Right to Self-Representation in War Crimes Trials?, 20 *Ohio State Journal on Dispute Resolution* 3 (2005), at 14-15; Philipp Ambach, Selbstvertretung im internationalen Strafprozess – Grundlagen, Kritik und ein Lösungsansatz für die prozessuale Handhabung in der Zukunft, 6 *Zeitschrift für Internationale Strafrechtsdogmatik* 286 (2009), at 304 fn.177; Patricia M. Wald, *Tyrants on Trial. Keeping Order in the Courtroom* (New York: Open Society Justice Institute) 2009, p.40; Gideon Boas, Self-Representation Before the ICTY. A Case for Reform, 9 *Journal of International Criminal Justice* 53 (2011), at 58-59, 76.

the accused with legal advice.[250] However, in order to safeguard additional interests involved, the trial chamber at the same time appointed *amicus curiae*, setting out the specific tasks *amicus* would assume in order to assist the trial chamber in the course of the case.[251]

At a later stage of the trial, the prosecution sought to have counsel imposed on the accused, not the least because of the defendant's increasing health problems which significantly impacted upon the conduct of the proceedings.[252] Yet, the trial chamber denied the prosecution's motion, affirming the accused's "right to defend himself in person".[253] In its decision on the matter, the trial chamber found that a "plain reading" of Article 21(4)(d) of the ICTY Statute indicated that there existed a right to self-representation and rejected the proposition that counsel could be assigned against the will of the accused[254] on the basis of the "essentially adversarial" proceedings before the ICTY.[255] The trial chamber drew a distinction between the investigative role of judges in civil law systems and the responsibility placed on the parties in adversarial systems, and concluded accordingly that "in an adversarial system, the imposition of defence counsel on an unwilling accused

---

250 *Prosecutor v. Slobodan Milošević*, Case No. IT-99-37-PT & IT-01-50-PT, Order, 15 November 2001, p.3; *Prosecutor v. Slobodan Milošević*, Case No. IT-02-54-T, Order, 16 April 2002, p.3.

251 *Prosecutor v. Slobodan Milošević*, Case No. IT-99-37-PT, Status Conference, 30 August 2001, T.6-7; Order Inviting Designation of *Amicus Curiae*, 30 August 2001, p.2; Order Concerning *Amici Curiae*, 11 January 2002. *See also Prosecutor v. Slobodan Milošević*, Case No. IT-02-54-T, Reasons for the Decision on the Prosecution Motion Concerning Assignment of Counsel, 04 April 2003, para.3.

252 *Prosecutor v. Slobodan Milošević*, Case No. IT-02-54-T, Submission from the Office of the Prosecutor on the Future Conduct of the Case in the Light of the State of the Accused's Health and the Length and Complexity of the Case, 08 November 2002, para.14 *et seq*.

253 *Prosecutor v. Slobodan Milošević*, Case No. IT-02-54-T, Reasons for Decision on the Prosecution Motion Concerning Assignment of Counsel, 04 April 2003, para.42. *See also* Oral Ruling, 18 December 2002, T.14574.

254 *Prosecutor v. Slobodan Milošević*, Case No. IT-02-54-T, Reasons for Decision on the Prosecution Motion Concerning Assignment of Counsel, 04 April 2003, para.18. *See also* para.25.

255 *Prosecutor v. Slobodan Milošević*, Case No. IT-02-54-T, Reasons for Decision on the Prosecution Motion Concerning Assignment of Counsel, 04 April 2003, para.20. *See also Prosecutor v. Slobodan Milošević*, Case No. IT-02-54-T, Submission from the Office of the Prosecutor on the Future Conduct of the Case in the Light of the State of the Accused's Health and the Length and Complexity of the Case, 08 November 2002, para.21.

would effectively deprive that accused of the possibility of putting forward a defence" and that in this regard Article 21(4)(d) of the ICTY Statute could be seen as "reflective of the common law position".[256] According to the bench, counsel that was not instructed by his or her client would not be capable of putting the defence's case as foreseen by Rule 90(H) of the ICTY RPE.[257] However, the trial chamber concluded its decision with the remark that the right to self-representation was not absolute and that "there may be circumstances [...] where it is in the interests of justice to appoint counsel".[258]

The reasoning of the *Milošević* trial chamber in this decision is open to debate. The judges did not provide any further basis for their conclusion that the imposition of counsel on a potentially uncooperative accused would deprive the defendant of effectively arguing his case. Ethical implications for counsel imposed by a chamber will be addressed at a later stage in this dissertation. However, the trial chamber's decision failed to clarify or even address the question why counsel imposed against an accused's will might not be capable of presenting a defence case even if the client in question did not provide specific instructions to counsel. Moreover, the trial chamber in its decision omitted to mention that even the U.S. Supreme Court in *Faretta* – decision repeatedly referred to by the *Milošević* trial chamber[259] – left room for the possibility to terminate self-representation of obstructive defendants and assign counsel; the majority of the U.S. Supreme Court did not appear to detect a problem in that case of having counsel imposed upon – presumably – unwilling accused whose right to conduct their defence in person might be restricted.

256 *Prosecutor v. Slobodan Milošević*, Case No. IT-02-54-T, Reasons for Decision on the Prosecution Motion Concerning Assignment of Counsel, 04 April 2003, para.24.

257 *Prosecutor v. Slobodan Milošević*, Case No. IT-02-54-T, Reasons for Decision on the Prosecution Motion Concerning Assignment of Counsel, 04 April 2003, para.25.

258 *Prosecutor v. Slobodan Milošević*, Case No. IT-02-54-T, Reasons for Decision on the Prosecution Motion Concerning Assignment of Counsel, 04 April 2003, para.40. The trial chamber gave the example of Rule 80(B) of the ICTY RPE which provides for removal of a disruptive accused from the courtroom. According to the bench, "an accused whose behaviour has resulted in his removal from the courtroom pursuant to Rule 80(B) of the Rules, has also relinquished his right to defend himself in person."

259 *Cf. Prosecutor v. Slobodan Milošević*, Case No. IT-02-54-T, Reasons for Decision on the Prosecution Motion Concerning Assignment of Counsel, 04 April 2003, para.22-23, 39.

The argument might have been more convincing if the procedural system of the ICTY was indeed purely adversarial – an assumption which at least at the time of the decision of the *Milošević* trial chamber in 2003 cannot be considered to have still been valid.[260] Going even further, if adopting the position that the fair trial provisions of the ICTY Statute are in fact heavily inspired by provisions of the ICCPR[261] which applies to a variety of legal systems of both common and civil law orientation, it has to be asked why the fair trial rights as guaranteed before the ICTY should necessarily be interpreted in a way which favours a solution adopted in one of the systems, thereby excluding consideration of the other.

In addition, the position rejecting the proposition that counsel would be capable of putting a case to the opposing party even without any detailed instructions from the accused would prove to be invalid in light of subsequent (appeals chamber) jurisprudence which maintained that counsel should be competent of doing just that.

The trial chamber furthermore relied upon the ICCPR and interpretation of its relevant provisions by the Human Rights Committee, which, in view of the trial chamber, recognised a right to self-representation and "rejects the imposition of defence counsel on an unwilling accused".[262] Considering the position of the Human Rights Committee at the time with regard to Article 14(3)(d) of the ICCPR as outlined above, the first part of the argument concerning the recognition of a right to self-representation does indeed seem reasonable. However, the trial chamber in *Milošević* did not provide any basis for the subsequent assertion that the imposition of counsel on an unwilling accused would equally be rejected by the Human Rights Committee as a necessary consequence flowing from the initial position. In the opinion

---

260 *See*, considering the ICTY to be *sui generis*: Michael P. Scharf/Christopher M. Rassi, Do Former Leaders have an International Right to Self-Representation in War Crimes Trials?, 20 *Ohio State Journal on Dispute Resolution* 3 (2005), at 15. In the same vein, *see* Gideon Boas, Moving on From Milošević, 75 *European Lawyer* 54 (2008), at 54. *See also* Salvatore Zappalà, *Human Rights in International Criminal Proceedings* (Oxford: Oxford University Press) 2005, p.22; Daryl A. Mundis, From 'Common Law' Towards 'Civil Law': The Evolution of the ICTY Rules of Procedure and Evidence, 14 *Leiden Journal of International Law* 367 (2001), at 368, 382.

261 *Cf.* Report of the Secretary-General Pursuant to Paragraph 2 of Security Council Resolution 808 (1993), S/25704, 03 May 1993, para.106.

262 *Prosecutor v. Slobodan Milošević*, Case No. IT-02-54-T, Reasons for Decision on the Prosecution Motion Concerning Assignment of Counsel, 04 April 2003, para.37.

referred to by the *Milošević* trial chamber, the Human Rights Committee found a violation of the right to self-representation in light of the fact that the national legislation at issue did not provide for any self-representation.[263] The *Milošević* trial chamber did not give any reason for the position that this otherwise unreasoned decision by the Human Rights Committee would also extend to situations in which national laws might provide for a right to self-representation, but subsequently recognise restrictions of that right for example through the imposition of counsel – this rather appeared to be the situation under consideration by the trial chamber in *Milošević*.

On a related note, it may be asked for which reasons the trial chamber in *Milošević* did not consider it apt to examine other possible interpretations of a right to defend oneself in person, *i.e.* why the bench did not examine opportunities for active participation by an accused for example in the form of statements to the court without having to forego the assistance of professional defence counsel. This is of note insofar as the trial chamber, while denying to impose counsel in December 2002, only one month earlier in related discussions did in fact suggest that the accused should reflect on possibilities at least to engage help, for example by way of having his legal associates present in the courtroom in order to assist during (cross-) examination of witnesses.[264] The prosecution took this opportunity to point to the common law concept of the "McKenzie friend",[265] which the accused countered with referring to the *Faretta* decision.[266] In the course of this discussion, the presiding judge considered that there was a conflict between the civil law and the common law approach to self-representation and that there was "no clear-cut legal answer to the issue that has been raised".[267] This would indicate that the trial chamber might have been in a position to adopt an equally

---

263 *Michael and Brian Hill v. Spain*, Human Rights Committee, Communication No. 526/1993, U.N. Doc. CCPR/C/59/D/526/1993, 02 April 1997, para.14.2.

264 *Prosecutor v. Slobodan Milošević*, Case No. IT-02-54-T, Hearing, 11 November 2002, T.12836-12839.

265 *Prosecutor v. Slobodan Milošević*, Case No. IT-02-54-T, Hearing, 11 November 2002, T.12839. *See also Prosecutor v. Slobodan Milošević*, Case No. IT-02-54-T, Attachment "A" to Prosecution Submissions in Response to the Trial Chamber's 19 July 2004 "Further Order on Future Conduct of the Trial", 26 July 2004, para.58-59.

266 *Prosecutor v. Slobodan Milošević*, Case No. IT-02-54-T, Hearing, 11 November 2002, T.12840.

267 *Prosecutor v. Slobodan Milošević*, Case No. IT-02-54-T, Hearing, 11 November 2002, T.12840-12841.

differentiated approach in reasoned decisions to be rendered, or at least consider additional arrangements for the practical exercise of a right to defend oneself in person.

The concept of the "McKenzie friend" goes back to a decision of the English Court of Appeals rendered in 1970.[268] The court found in this case that a *pro se* litigant was allowed to be accompanied in court by a person assisting in the arguing of his or her case without however being directly involved in the proceedings.[269] It needs to be analysed to which extent the exact concept is applicable to criminal proceedings, as the Court of Appeals was seised of a civil litigation. In civil litigation cases, the right to defend oneself is often recognised to a wider extent and indeed practiced on a broader level.[270] Yet, this would indicate that accused in criminal proceedings could be even more entitled to ask for such assistance when appearing before court and analogies could be drawn from this concept.

Another attempt of the prosecution to have counsel assigned followed almost one year later in September 2003, above all due to the delays caused by the health problems of the accused, and arguably worsened by the strains put on him by representing himself.[271] The *amici curiae* opposed the proposition to impose counsel upon the accused, arguing that a fair trial was not possible if counsel was to act without instructions from or communication with an uncooperative defendant.[272] The trial chamber decided to extend the role of *amici curiae* and authorised them to receive communications from

268 *McKenzie v McKenzie* (Court of Appeal), [1971] P. 33, 12 June 1970.

269 *McKenzie v McKenzie* (Court of Appeal), [1971] P. 33, 12 June 1970, at 37, 42: "It is moreover always, to my mind, in the public interest that litigants should be seen to have all available aid in conducting cases in court surroundings, which must of their nature to them seem both difficult and strange."

270 *Cf.* Beverly W. Snukals/Glen H. Sturtevant Jr., Pro Se Litigation: Best Practices from a Judge's Perspective, 42 *University of Richmond Law Review* 93 (2007), p.93.

271 *Prosecutor v. Slobodan Milošević*, Case No. IT-02-54-T, Prosecution's Submission on the Implications of the Accused's Recurring Ill-Health and the Future Conduct of the Case – Corrected Version, 30 September 2003, para.5, 13-18.

272 *Prosecutor v. Slobodan Milošević*, Case No. IT-02-54-T, *Amici Curiae* Submission in Response to the Order of the Trial Chamber Concerning the Implications of the Accused's Health Dated 24 September 2003, 27 September 2003, para.11. *See also* Motion Hearing, 30 September 2003, T.27049-27050.

the accused and "to act in any way to protect and further the interests of his Defence".[273]

a. Discussion of the *Milošević* approach

Having seen the degree to which the right to self-representation was recognised in the *Milošević* proceedings, a look will be taken at the voices critical with regard to granting this right to self-representation in the context of international criminal proceedings.

The right to self-representation has been characterised as a "spreading problem in international criminal law",[274] a problem which was considered to be based on the recognition of "an outmoded and dysfunctional privilege".[275] Reasons that have been expressed which militate against any extensive recognition of a right to self-representation include the potential inability of an accused to take objective (and strategic) defence decisions, in light of the necessarily deep personal involvement with the charges,[276] or the inability to effectively digest the often substantial amounts of material.[277]

The practical repercussions of an assertion to defend oneself in person, as well as the potential room for abuse, suggest that the right to self-representation is indeed a problematic issue to be dealt with in the sphere of international criminal proceedings. It ought to be examined whether the interests usually motivating an accused to defend him- or herself in person could and should not better be met by other means of active participation in their pro-

---

273 *Prosecutor v. Slobodan Milošević*, Case No. IT-02-54-T, Order of Further Instruction to the Amici Curiae, 06 October 2003, p.3.

274 Gideon Boas, Moving on From Milošević, 75 *European Lawyer* 54 (2008), at 55.

275 Eugene Cerruti, Self-Representation in the International Arena: Removing a False Right to Spectacle, 40 *Georgetown Journal of International Law* 919 (2009), at 965.

276 *Cf.* Stefan Trechsel, *Human Rights in Criminal Proceedings* (Oxford: Oxford University Press) 2005, p.245-246.

277 Iain Bonomy, The Reality of Conducting a War Crimes Trial, 5 *Journal of International Criminal Justice* 348 (2007), at 356: "[…] (1) personal hobby horses are not normally the best forensic points; (2) the court may be abused as a political platform; (3) failure of accused to have a clear objective view of the case to be met – 'failing to see the wood for the trees' – means trial not conducted in his best forensic or legal interests; (4) accused may not be able to cope with the volume of material; (5) any sanctions imposed for breaches of orders may have adverse side effects on the conduct of the trial."

ceedings. It is argued that there may be forms of participation which could strike the necessary balance between the interests involved. On the one hand, a certain extent of participation would provide the defendant with an opportunity to present his or her personal views concerning the case and sometimes significantly contribute with regard to factual matters, thereby paying heed to an accused's personal dignity.[278] At the same time, however, this type of active participation without the entire defence presentation being conducted by the accused in person would prevent the proceedings from being hijacked by a misuse of the right to self-representation and from becoming engulfed in procedural problems which merely prolong the trial and divert from the content of the proceedings as well as factual assertions that are to be adjudicated.

An examination of the relevant provisions for international criminal tribunals shows that for example the ICTY RPE explicitly envisage only a rather limited participation of an accused who has decided to be represented by counsel, namely by way of giving an unsworn statement before the court[279] or by testifying as witness in their own case.[280] The Rome Statute of the ICC does not explicitly address the question of an accused appearing as witness in his or her own case,[281] but provides for the possibility of making an unsworn statement orally or in writing as part of the fair trial guarantees in Article 67.[282] As such, it has been considered to be a "genuine innovation"

---

278 Stefan Trechsel, *Human Rights in Criminal Proceedings* (Oxford: Oxford University Press) 2005, p.247. *See also* Wolfgang Schomburg, The Role of International Criminal Tribunals in Promoting Respect for Fair Trial Rights, 8 *Northwestern University Journal of International Human Rights* 1 (2009), at 51.

279 Rule 84*bis* ICTY RPE reads: "(A) After the opening statement of the parties or, if the defence elects to defer its opening statement pursuant to Rule 84, after the opening statement of the Prosecutor, if any, the accused, if he or she so wishes, and the Trial Chamber so decides, make a statement under the control of the Trial Chamber. The accused shall not be compelled to make a solemn declaration and shall not be examined about the content of the statement. (B) The Trial Chamber shall decide on the probative value, if any, of the statement."

280 Rule 85(C) ICTY and ICTR RPE; Rule 85(C) SCSL RPE.

281 Claus Kreß, Witnesses in Proceedings Before the International Criminal Court: An Analysis in the Light of Comparative Criminal Procedure, in: Horst Fischer/Claus Kreß/Sascha Rolf Lüder (eds), *International and National Prosecution of Crimes Under International Law. Current Developments* (Berlin: Berlin Verlag Arno Spitz GmbH) 2001, p.309-383, at 322.

282 Article 67(1)(h) Rome Statute reads: "To make an unsworn oral or written statement in his or her defence; [...]".

in the international sphere.[283] This kind of recognition of an opportunity for the accused to address the court without having to take a solemn declaration seems to be a certain development. The step could be considered as a sign for an increased acknowledgement of growing participation by represented defendants in their proceedings at the international level. Such a view is underscored by the argument that the ICC provision, in contrast to the equivalent ICTY rule, does not limit the possibility of such an unsworn statement to a specific point in time in the case.[284]

However, neither of these two options – unsworn statement or testimony under oath – might appear sufficient for accused who in fact wish to participate more actively in the proceedings in which they are tried. Given that defendants in international criminal proceedings might indeed be able to make useful contributions especially with regard to factual matters, an obvious need exists to be open towards additional approaches which take into account the different interests involved. The STL RPE appear to be more advanced than similar provisions in this context, in light of the fact that they provide for an accused to make relevant statements to the court at any stage of the proceedings,[285] for questioning of the accused during the course of trial and still allow for the possibility of a defendant testifying as witness in his or her own case.[286] In addition, an accused can make a final statement relevant to the case after the closing arguments of the parties.[287] These provisions recognise an accused's legitimate interest in a defence that is personal, without inevitably requiring them to act as their own counsel.

It has to be kept in mind, however, that at the same time, as is readily apparent from proceedings before the ICTY, even accused conducting their defence in person may still elect to give an unsworn statement, as did the defendant in *Šešelj*,[288] or – as in *Karadžić* – take the opportunity to provide

283 William A. Schabas, Article 67, in: Otto Triffterer (ed.), *Commentary on the Rome Statute of the International Criminal Court. Observers' Notes, Article by Article* (Munich: Verlag C.H.Beck) 2nd ed. 2008, p.1247-1274, at note 48.

284 Salvatore Zappalà, *Human Rights in International Criminal Proceedings* (Oxford: Oxford University Press) 2005, p.142.

285 Article 16(5) STL Statute reads: "The accused may make statements in court at any stage of the proceedings, provided such statements are relevant to the case at issue. The Chambers shall decide on the probative value, if any, of such statements."

286 Rule 144 STL RPE.

287 Rule 147 STL RPE.

288 *Prosecutor v. Vojislav Šešelj*, Case No. IT-03-67-T, Statement of the Accused, 08 November 2007, T.1857-1947.

an opening statement pursuant to Rule 84 of the ICTY RPE at the beginning of the trial proceedings,[289] then be given the chance to give a second opening statement before the start of the defence case,[290] request instead to be permitted to give an unsworn statement pursuant to Rule 84*bis* of the ICTY RPE,[291] and still leave open the possibility to testify as witness in their own case.[292]

Already at a time when the issues arising before international criminal tribunals could not yet have been foreseen, doubt has been expressed as regards an absolute right to self-representation. This right was rather considered to be complementary to the right to counsel, seeing a duty on the court to ensure that any self-representation is effective, which would include the appointment of counsel if deemed necessary to safeguard the fair trial guarantee.[293]

In addition, certain doctrine heavily criticises the initial approach of the trial chamber in *Milošević* allowing the exercise of his right to self-representation. It has been questioned on a more general level, as it appears *inter alia* for policy reasons, whether former leaders should be given the possibility to proceed *pro se* in international criminal trials, and it has been argued that waiting for disruptive behaviour of the accused in order to then restrict the right to self-representation would make the decision too late.[294] According to this argument, the complex nature of international criminal proceedings as well as the need to ensure a fair and expeditious trial calls for limitations

289 *Prosecutor v. Radovan Karadžić*, Case No. IT-95-5/18-T, Defence Opening Statement, 01 March 2010, T.808-903; 02 March 2010, T.904-993.

290 *Prosecutor v. Radovan Karadžić*, Case No. IT-95-5/18-T, Scheduling Order on Close of the Prosecution Case, Rule 98 *bis* Submissions, and Start of the Defence Case, 26 April 2012, para.13, 28.

291 *Prosecutor v. Radovan Karadžić*, Case No. IT-95-5/18-T, Defence Submission Pursuant to Rule 65 *ter* and Related Motions, 27 August 2012, para.22. The Trial Chamber granted the requested, but limited the statement to 1.5 hours: *see* Status Conference, 03 September 2012, T.28789; Defence Rule 84*bis* Statement, 16 October 2012, T.28849-28881.

292 *Prosecutor v. Radovan Karadžić*, Case No. IT-95-5/18-T, Defence Submission Pursuant to Rule 65 *ter* and Related Motions, 27 August 2012, para.14.

293 M. Cherif Bassiouni, Human Rights in the Context of Criminal Justice: Identifying International Procedural Protections and Equivalent Protections in National Constitutions, 3 *Duke Journal of Comparative and International Law* 235 (1993), at 283-284.

294 Michael P. Scharf/Christopher M. Rassi, Do Former Leaders have an International Right to Self-Representation in War Crimes Trials?, 20 *Ohio State Journal on Dispute Resolution* 3 (2005), at 20-21.

of the right to self-representation.[295] In the same vein, it has been suggested that the assignment of counsel to Slobodan Milošević, instead of employing the *amicus curiae* model, would have duly taken into account the political (and thus wider) implications of trials of former political leaders, which should form part of the balance.[296] The precedent of *Milošević* was considered to have "become the Faretta of international law", a "seminal case that was generously but foolishly decided and [...] has immediately spawned a humiliating spectacle of its own design".[297]

It cannot be denied that trials of former (political) leaders include particular political aspects and can and often do have wider implications in the political arena. However, it needs to be questioned whether such concerns should indeed factor into the balance of the interests at stake. In light of the fact that the balancing exercise is to be conducted between an overarching right to a fair trial – to be further discussed below –, the interest of an accused to conduct his or her defence in person and the right to a fair and expeditious trial, the inclusion of political implications might become a problematic issue. It seems that fundamental matters such as fair trial rights of a defendant should be abstracted from potential political concerns.

b. Confirmation and modification of the *Milošević* approach

Following the end of the prosecution case and shortly before the start of the presentation of the defence case, the trial chamber in *Milošević* eventually decided to assign counsel to the accused in light of his health problems.[298]

---

295 Michael P. Scharf/Christopher M. Rassi, Do Former Leaders have an International Right to Self-Representation in War Crimes Trials?, 20 *Ohio State Journal on Dispute Resolution* 3 (2005), at 21-26.

296 Tom Dannenbaum, The Milošević Trial: Lessons for the Conduct of International Criminal Proceedings (Review of Gideon Boas), 33 *Yale Journal of International Law* 513 (2008), at 515-516.

297 Eugene Cerruti, Self-Representation in the International Arena: Removing a False Right to Spectacle, 40 *Georgetown Journal of International Law* 919 (2009), at 982.

298 *Prosecutor v. Slobodan Milošević*, Case No. IT-02-54-T, Oral Ruling, 02 September 2004, T.32357-32359; Order on the Modalities to be Followed by Court Assigned Counsel, 03 September 2004; Reasons for Decision on Assignment of Defence Counsel, 22 September 2004.

This decision was appealed by the assigned counsel.[299] In the final decision on the matter, the appeals chamber provided its own analysis of the right to self-representation as enshrined in the ICTY Statute. The judges considered Article 21 of the ICTY Statute to be a guarantee of the right to self-representation and even went as far as designating it as "presumptive right" which was an "indispensable cornerstone of justice":

> "[...] This is a straightforward proposition: given the *text's binary opposition* between representation 'through legal assistance' and representation 'in person', the Appeals Chamber sees no reasonable way to interpret Article 21 except as a guarantee of the right to self-representation. Nor should this right be taken lightly. The drafters of the Statute clearly viewed the right to self-representation as an *indispensable cornerstone of justice,* placing it on a structural par with defendants' right to remain silent, to confront witnesses against them, to a speedy trial, and even to demand a court-appointed attorney if they cannot afford one themselves. [...] Defendants before this Tribunal, then, have the *presumptive right to represent themselves notwithstanding a Trial Chamber's judgement that they would be better off if represented by counsel.*"[300]

It is of note that the appeals chamber in this aspect appears to follow the reasoning in *Faretta,* decision in which the U.S. Supreme Court majority equally remarked that it might often not even be in an accused's interest to exercise his or her right to self-representation, but that given the fundamental nature of that right, it would need to be safeguarded by chambers even against better knowledge.[301]

Although the choice to represent oneself has to be made in an informed and voluntary manner, the position taken by the appeals chamber in *Milošević* raises the issue whether a defendant who might not be fully aware of the consequences such a choice entails should that easily be allowed to waive his or her right to a fair trial or rather to an effective defence. The problem becomes especially significant at least in the U.S. national context when bearing in mind the restriction that the U.S. Supreme Court placed in *Faretta*

---

299 *Prosecutor v. Slobodan Milošević,* Case No. IT-02-54-AR73.7, Appeal Against the Trial Chamber's Decision on Assignment of Defence Counsel, 29 September 2004.

300 *Prosecutor v. Slobodan Milošević,* Case No. IT-02-54-AR73.7, Decision on Interlocutory Appeal of the Trial Chamber's Decision on the Assignment of Defence Counsel, 01 November 2004, para.11 (internal footnotes omitted) (emphasis added).

301 *Cf. Anthony Pasquall Faretta v. State of California* (U.S. Supreme Court), 422 U.S. 806, 30 June 1975, at 834.

on appealing a conviction on the basis of ineffective defence for self-represented accused.[302]

Even more significant for this dissertation is the fact that the appeals chamber in *Milošević* spelled out its position that the right to self-representation on the one side, and the right to assistance by counsel on the other, as guaranteed by Article 21 of the Statute, were mutually exclusive. It is of interest in this context that the notion of the two rights being "mutually exclusive" is not new. Justice Blackmun of the U.S. Supreme Court alluded already in *Faretta* to many of the procedural problems that would be faced in proceedings with self-represented accused and consequently discussed in this dissertation, including the alleged exclusivity of choice between these two rights.[303]

Keeping in mind the position of the appeals chamber taken in *Milošević*, it has to be mentioned that one and a half years earlier, the pre-trial chamber in *Šešelj* had taken a diametrically opposed view with regard to the question whether the notions of either self-representation or assistance by counsel of one's own choosing indeed stand in binary opposition:

> "The right to self-representation and the appointment of standby counsel do not exclude the right of the Accused to obtain legal advice from counsel of his own choosing. The human rights referred to earlier in this Decision are by their nature only minimum rights. *It would be a misunderstanding of the word 'or' in the phrase 'to defend himself in person or through legal assistance of his own choosing' to conclude that self-representation excludes the appointment of counsel to assist the Accused or vice versa.* The Accused may file a power of attorney under Rule 44(A) if he wishes to have additional assistance from counsel meeting the necessary requirements under that Rule. Such counsel would enjoy counsel-client privilege while being bound by all the obligations of counsel working with the Tribunal."[304]

---

302 *Anthony Pasquall Faretta v. State of California* (U.S. Supreme Court), 422 U.S. 806, 30 June 1975, at 834 fn.46. *See also* Sarah Livingstone Allen, Faretta: Self-Representation, or Legal-Misrepresentation?, 90 *Iowa Law Review* 1553 (2005), at 1564.

303 *See Anthony Pasquall Faretta v. State of California* (U.S. Supreme Court), 422 U.S. 806, 30 June 1975, Dissenting Opinion Justice Blackmun, joined by Justices Burger and Rehnquist, at 852: "[…] Since the right to assistance of counsel and the right to self-representation are mutually exclusive, how is the waiver of each right to be measured? If a defendant has elected to exercise his right to proceed pro se, does he still have a constitutional right to assistance of standby counsel? […]".

304 *Prosecutor v. Vojislav Šešelj*, Case No. IT-03-67-PT, Decision on Prosecution's Motion for Order Appointing Counsel to Assist Vojislav Šešelj with his Defence, 09 May 2003, para.29 (emphasis added).

This remark by the pre-trial chamber is of note insofar as the appeals chamber in *Milošević* did not seem to have considered the position expressed by the pre-trial chamber in *Šešelj* at all.[305] One has to wonder whether any reference, even if only in a footnote, was omitted on purpose, or whether the "binary opposite" position of the pre-trial chamber was not considered as being relevant by the appeals chamber. The latter would be surprising given that the pre-trial chamber expressed a different view on the same issue. A more complete review of the matter appears to ask for at least reference to, and in case, distinction of, such divergent opinions, especially in light of the repercussions an interpretation in one way or another will have on future proceedings before this and other international criminal tribunals. On a side note, the approach of the pre-trial chamber might not come as a surprise in view of the fact that the presiding judge of the pre-trial chamber rendering the decision in *Šešelj* would afterwards express a similar view in his fundamentally dissenting opinion to an appeals chamber decision in *Krajišnik*. At the same time, this position is even more interesting if one takes into account subsequent jurisprudence from both trial chambers and appeals chamber which keeps emphasising the binary opposition of the two rights enshrined in Article 21(4)(d) of the ICTY Statute, as expressed by the appeals chamber in *Milošević*.

Further on the question whether a right to defend oneself in person and the right to counsel are in fact mutually exclusive, it has been held in *Karadžić* that an accused who is in fact exercising his chosen right to self-representation is not concurrently in a position to argue a right to select imposed counsel.[306] In a similar vein, it has subsequently been submitted that once an accused exercises his right to choose between self-representation on the one hand and legal assistance of his own choosing on the other, the guarantees of Article 21(4)(d) of the ICTY Statute have been exhausted.[307] The appeals chamber eventually confirmed the initial position adopted by the trial

---

305 *See*, however, also reference to this position in discussions with the *Milošević* trial chamber: *Prosecutor v. Slobodan Milošević*, Motion Hearing, 30 September 2003, T.27050-27051.

306 *Prosecutor v. Radovan Karadžić*, Case No. IT-95-5/18-T, Decision on the Accused's Motion to Vacate Appointment of Richard Harvey, 23 December 2009, para.26.

307 *Prosecutor v. Radovan Karadžić*, Case No. IT-95-5/18-AR73.6, Prosecution's Response to Karadžić's Appeal from Decision on Motion to Vacate Appointment of Richard Harvey, 29 January 2010, para.7-9.

chamber.[308] Thus, following this jurisprudence, an accused actively exercising his right to self-representation cannot argue to have a right to choose counsel appointed to him, or be granted legal aid for that appointed counsel. Rather, a *pro se* defendant may have legal associates in his defence team, recognised by the registry, for which he may also apply for financial aid.[309] Yet, as has been submitted, this practice would not include, as of right, the possibility to select counsel imposed on the accused by a trial chamber.[310]

On the other hand, the appeals chamber allowed in *Krajišnik* that a counsel may represent the interests of the accused exercising his right to self-representation with regard to the discrete legal issue of joint criminal enterprise: the judges thus permitted a sort of "partial self-representation", considering that although the rights in Article 21(4)(d) of the ICTY Statute stand in opposition, this would not exclude the possibility of a *pro se* defendant to engage counsel for specific parts of his defence case.[311] Given that numerous other decisions reiterate the earlier notion of the appeals chamber in *Milošević* on the "binary opposition", this decision of the appeals chamber in *Krajišnik* could be seen as only one of numerous incongruent positions that can be found in the jurisprudence. It is even more unsatisfactory insofar as the appeals chamber in *Krajišnik* does not provide any detailed analysis of the matter and above all does not explain how it can uphold the notion of mutual exclusion while at the same time restricting the application of that notion to situations as it sees fit.

The appeals chamber in *Milošević*, however, did continue in its decision with providing a qualification for the exercise of the right to self-representation in view of the existing national and international jurisprudence, and made clear that the right is not absolute, despite its earlier sweeping and far-reaching valuation of a right to self-representation in the same case:

---

308 *Prosecutor v. Radovan Karadžić*, Case No. IT-95-5/18-AR73.6, Decision on Radovan Karadžić's Appeal from Decision on Motion to Vacate Appointment of Richard Harvey, 12 February 2010, para.26.

309 *See Prosecutor v. Radovan Karadžić*, Case No. IT-95-5/18-T, Decision on the Accused's Motion to Vacate Appointment of Richard Harvey, 23 December 2009, para.26.

310 *Prosecutor v. Radovan Karadžić*, Case No. IT-95-5/18-AR73.6, Prosecution's Response to Karadžić's Appeal from Decision on Motion to Vacate Appointment of Richard Harvey, 29 January 2010, para.10.

311 *Prosecutor v. Momčilo Krajišnik*, Case No. IT-00-39-A, Decision on Momčilo Krajišnik's Motion to Reschedule Status Conference and Permit Alan Dershowitz to Appear, 28 February 2008, para.6-8.

> "While this right to self-representation is indisputable, jurisdictions around the world recognize that it is not categorically inviolable. [...] And while this Appellate Chamber has not previously passed on the question, *existing precedent from contemporary war crimes tribunals is unanimous in concluding that the right to self-representation 'is a qualified and not an absolute right'*."[312]

The appeals chamber considered it viable to restrict the right to self-representation, "under the appropriate circumstances", and subject to the condition

> "that a defendant's self-representation is substantially and persistently obstructing the proper and expeditious conduct of his trial."[313]

This decision of the appeals chamber in *Milošević*, including this specific test which it established for any potential limitation of the right to self-representation, proved to have significant impact on the future dealing of trial and appeals chambers with the right to self-representation. Therefore, a more detailed analysis of the decision is in order to uncover the underlying reasoning and potential flaws which may be incorporated in this particular determination.

The approach of the appeals chamber to only briefly refer to national jurisprudence differing from its own characterisation, while at the same time confirming a right to self-representation as a "cornerstone of justice", appears questionable. The appeals chamber did use the contradicting case law in order to justify potential restrictions of any right to self-representation, without however discussing the question whether there might not be a possibility to give the right to defend oneself in person a different interpretation to begin with, rather than insisting on a binary opposition of self-representation and representation through counsel. Given the stage of the proceedings and in light of the lack of the jurisprudence on the matter at the time the decision was rendered, one might ask whether it would not have been possible to assert the right to a defence in person in other ways, at least for the beginning, thereby leaving open the possibility to work with the right and its repercussions on the proceedings as necessary in any given situation. Taking into account the divergent national practice in this field, it would arguably have been possible to allow for an exercise of the right to defend oneself in person

---

312 *Prosecutor v. Slobodan Milošević*, Case No. IT-02-54-AR73.7, Decision on Interlocutory Appeal of the Trial Chamber's Decision on the Assignment of Defense Counsel, 01 November 2004, para.12 (internal footnotes omitted) (emphasis added).

313 *Prosecutor v. Slobodan Milošević*, Case No. IT-02-54-AR73.7, Decision on Interlocutory Appeal of the Trial Chamber's Decision on the Assignment of Defense Counsel, 01 November 2004, para.13.

under a different premise, thereby giving a right to self-representation in the sense as understood by the appeals chamber an exceptional status – rather than recognising it and then qualifying its exercise as a rule. With the precedent created in the decision by the appeals chamber in *Milošević*, the implications and concerns judges have to deal with in order to reconcile jurisprudence on the one hand with practical and pragmatic considerations on the other are still perceptible. In light of the far-reaching conclusion by the ICTY appeals chamber at the time, subsequent jurisprudence on the matter frequently appears to endeavour correction of the scope of a right to self-representation, usually in order to limit its exercise. Yet, this necessarily gives rise to objections from the side of *pro se* defendants who consider a "fundamental" fair trial right to be unduly restricted, and leaves chambers oftentimes at pains to justify restrictive decisions that usually illustrate an attempt to adjust an accused's theoretical wishes with reality.

2. Models differing from the *Milošević* approach

The system's potential to embrace different tactics to dealing with the right to defend oneself in person than the one proclaimed by the *Milošević* appeals chamber is epitomised by other decisions issued by separate chambers at the ICTY.

For example, one trial chamber denied an accused's request to proceed self-represented and based its decision on several factors: referring to the U.S. Supreme Court's decision in *Faretta*, the bench in *Janković & Stanković* recalled the necessity to make the choice to self-represent in a voluntary, unequivocal and intelligent manner. According to the bench, the reason for applying this standard was "to ensure that a defendant is protected to the fullest extent possible".[314] As opposed to the U.S. Supreme Court decision in *Faretta*, the underlying rationale of the trial chamber's decision in this case therefore appears not to be the protection of the autonomy of an accused in his or her choices, but rather protection of the accused from such choices in the interest of ensuring his or her trial to be fair in a more encompassing

314 *Prosecutor v. Janković & Stanković*, Case No. IT-96-23/2-PT, Decision Following Registrar's Notification of Radovan Stanković's Request for Self-Representation, 19 August 2005, para.9.

sense.[315] After the trial chamber had analysed several in its view pertinent factors, the accused's request was denied on the basis of his previous behaviour.[316]

At other tribunals, there have been similar instances when judges had to consider the requests of accused to defend themselves in person.

In the *Norman* proceedings before the SCSL, it is especially interesting that the trial chamber considered that the right to self-representation could only be exercised with assistance of counsel.[317] It is equally of interest to consider the justification given by the trial chamber in *Norman* for granting the accused only a "qualified right to self-representation":[318] its reasons included the fact that the defendant was tried with two co-accused; the timing of the request – a factor also considered in the context of the first *Krajišnik* request –; as well as, of even more significance, the complexity of the case and the interest in its fair and expeditious conclusion.[319] While the trial chamber did not specify which role counsel was to assume in the first decision, it subsequently issued a decision on the assignment and role of standby counsel.[320] The right of the accused to conduct his defence in person was eventually revoked and counsel assigned to fully represent the defendant based on the accused's behaviour.[321]

---

315 *See also* Boris Petersdorf, *Eigenverteidigung und aufgedrängte Pflichtverteidigung im formellen Völkerstrafrecht* (Baden-Baden: Nomos Verlagsgesellschaft) 2010, p.93-94.

316 *Prosecutor v. Janković & Stanković*, Case No. IT-96-23/2-PT, Decision Following Registrar's Notification of Radovan Stanković's Request for Self-Representation, 19 August 2005, para.22, 23.

317 *Prosecutor v. Samuel Hinga Norman et al.*, Case No. SCSL-04-14-T, Decision on the Application of Samuel Hinga Norman for Self Representation Under Article 17(4)(d) of the Statute of the Special Court, 08 June 2004, para.32.

318 *See Prosecutor v. Samuel Hinga Norman et al.*, Case No. SCSL-04-14-T, Decision on the Application of Samuel Hinga Norman for Self Representation Under Article 17(4)(d) of the Statute of the Special Court, 08 June 2004, para.27, 30.

319 *Prosecutor v. Samuel Hinga Norman et al.*, Case No. SCSL-04-14-T, Decision on the Application of Samuel Hinga Norman for Self Representation Under Article 17(4)(d) of the Statute of the Special Court, 08 June 2004, para.26.

320 Nina H.B. Jørgensen, The Problem of Self-Representation at International Criminal Tribunals. Striking a Balance Between Fairness and Effectiveness, 4 *Journal of International Criminal Justice* 64 (2006), at 68.

321 *Prosecutor v. Samuel Hinga Norman et al.*, Case No. SCSL-04-14-T, Ruling on the Issue of Non-Appearance of the First Accused Samuel Hinga Norman, the Second Accused Moinina Fofana, and the Third Accused, Allieu Kondewa at the Trial Proceedings, 01 October 2004, para.23.

It has been argued that the approach taken by the trial chamber in *Norman* to allow the exercise of the right to self-representation merely alongside assistance by counsel is a contradiction in terms.[322] Furthermore, the decision has been criticised for reducing the right to defend oneself in person "to an ineffective platitude".[323] According to this opinion, the unconvincing reasoning of the decision would make the trial chamber appear as if "they simply found the whole business of self-representation to be a big inconvenience".[324]

Yet, this criticism appears to be based on the assumption that a right to defend oneself and the right to the assistance of counsel of one's own choosing are indeed mutually exclusive. This coincides with the position adopted for example by chambers at the ICTY. At the same time, however, it can be argued that the two rights in question do not necessarily have to exclude each other.[325] Rather, as will be demonstrated in the course of this dissertation, it can be viably envisaged – at least for future proceedings – that an accused enjoys representation by qualified counsel and may still be permitted to actively participate in the proceedings. Against this background, the decision of the *Norman* trial chamber would not have to be seen as contradiction.

Another example from the SCSL illustrates a more general position taken by trial chambers at the Special Court with regard to representation of accused: one SCSL trial chamber – interpreting Rule 45(E) of the SCSL RPE[326]

---

322 William A. Schabas, *The UN International Criminal Tribunals. The Former Yugoslavia, Rwanda and Sierra Leone* (Cambridge: Cambridge University Press) 2006, p.531.

323 William A. Schabas, *The UN International Criminal Tribunals. The Former Yugoslavia, Rwanda and Sierra Leone* (Cambridge: Cambridge University Press) 2006, p.531.

324 William A. Schabas, *The UN International Criminal Tribunals. The Former Yugoslavia, Rwanda and Sierra Leone* (Cambridge: Cambridge University Press) 2006, p.531.

325 *Cf.* Wolfgang Schomburg, The Role of International Criminal Tribunals in Promoting Respect for Fair Trial Rights, 8 *Northwestern University Journal of International Human Rights* 1 (2009), at 51.

326 Rule 45(E) SCSL RPE reads: "Subject to any order of a Chamber, Counsel will represent the accused and conduct the case to finality. Failure to do so, absent just cause approved by the Chamber, may result in forfeiture of fees in whole or in part. In such circumstances the Chamber may make an order accordingly. Counsel shall only be permitted to withdraw from the case to which he has been assigned in the most exceptional circumstances. In the event of such withdrawal the Principal Defender shall assign other Counsel who may be a member of the Defence Office, to the indigent accused."

– held that the accused's assertion that he did not recognise the legitimacy of the SCSL did not constitute "exceptional circumstances" that would justify the withdrawal of counsel.[327] The trial chamber considered it appropriate not to permit the accused to appear unrepresented before the court in order to "safeguard the rights of the accused and the integrity of the proceedings", and specifically held that "an accused person cannot waive his right to a fair and expeditious trial whatever the circumstances".[328] When deciding on the appeal of the decision, the appeals chamber found that the issue at hand was not one of self-representation, but rather of refusal to participate on the part of the accused.[329] In the appeals chamber's view, Article 17(4)(d) of the SCSL Statute provided for three rights, two of which depended on the choice of the accused, while the third – assignment of counsel in the interests of justice – did not. The appeals chamber considered that the SCSL Statute "does not recognise a right 'not to have counsel assigned' to an accused who has refused to exercise the choice available".[330]

The proceedings against Charles Taylor would pose similar questions: before the start of the evidentiary phase in *Taylor*, some issues surfaced with regard to the formation of a defence team.[331] In addition, the question arose whether the accused would be allowed to give an unsworn statement after the opening arguments, despite the lack of a specific rule in this regard in the SCSL provisions.[332] When the trial chamber ruled that the defendant would not be permitted to give such a statement,[333] and in light of the continuing issues with regard to his defence team, the accused boycotted the

327 *Prosecutor v. Issa Hassan Sesay et al.*, Case No. SCSL-04-15-T, Gbao – Decision on Application to Withdraw Counsel, 06 July 2004, para.11, 13.

328 *Prosecutor v. Issa Hassan Sesay et al.*, Case No. SCSL-04-15-T, Gbao – Decision on Application to Withdraw Counsel, 06 July 2004, para.15.

329 *Prosecutor v. Issa Hassan Sesay et al.*, Case No. SCSL-04-15-AR73, Gbao – Decision on Appeal Against Decision on Withdrawal of Counsel, 23 November 2004, para.47.

330 *Prosecutor v. Issa Hassan Sesay et al.*, Case No. SCSL-04-15-AR73, Gbao – Decision on Appeal Against Decision on Withdrawal of Counsel, 23 November 2004, para.57-58.

331 *Prosecutor v. Charles Ghankay Taylor*, Case No. SCSL-03-01-PT, Pre-trial Conference, 07 May 2007, p.8-10, 62.

332 *Prosecutor v. Charles Ghankay Taylor*, Case No. SCSL-03-01-PT, Pre-trial Conference, 07 May 2007, p.23.

333 *Prosecutor v. Charles Ghankay Taylor*, Case No. SCSL-03-01-PT, Decision on Urgent and Public Defence Motion Requesting Leave for Charles Ghankay Taylor to Give an Un-Sworn Statement from the Dock, 29 May 2007.

start of the trial and did not appear for the prosecution's opening statement. In a letter to the bench, the accused explained that without being given the time and resources he needed to prepare for trial, he did not see himself in a position to attend.[334] The defendant therefore terminated the mandate of his counsel and notified the registrar that he would represent himself as he deemed fit.[335] When the trial chamber directed counsel to continue to represent the defendant for purposes of the opening statement in the accused's absence,[336] counsel fiercely protested on the basis of the code of conduct to be adhered to in his view, objection which the trial chamber did not accept.[337] The defendant continued to absent himself from the proceedings at the next session.[338] Presenting the views of the accused, the principal defender, as head of the defence office mandated to ensure that the fair trial rights of accused before the SCSL are observed,[339] indicated that the defendant was perceptive of the idea that presenting his defence personally in a case of the magnitude at hand would not be to his advantage.[340] The prosecution submitted that the issue at hand was one of boycott of the proceedings, rather than self-representation,[341] view which seemed to be shared by the bench.[342] The trial chamber eventually held that the absence of the accused was in contradiction to his alleged right to self-representation and amounted to a boycott of the trial.[343] It interpreted the earlier submissions to indicate that the defendant no longer wished to conduct his defence personally and would accept

334 *Prosecutor v. Charles Ghankay Taylor*, Case No. SCSL-03-01-T, Prosecution Opening Statement, 04 June 2007, p.243-251.

335 *Prosecutor v. Charles Ghankay Taylor*, Case No. SCSL-03-01-T, Prosecution Opening Statement, 04 June 2007, p.251.

336 *Prosecutor v. Charles Ghankay Taylor*, Case No. SCSL-03-01-T, Prosecution Opening Statement, 04 June 2007, p.259.

337 *Prosecutor v. Charles Ghankay Taylor*, Case No. SCSL-03-01-T, Prosecution Opening Statement, 04 June 2007, p.259-267.

338 *Prosecutor v. Charles Ghankay Taylor*, Case No. SCSL-03-01-T, Hearing, 25 June 2007, p.341-342.

339 Rule 45 SCSL RPE.

340 *Prosecutor v. Charles Ghankay Taylor*, Case No. SCSL-03-01-T, Hearing, 25 June 2007, p.344-345, 372-373.

341 *Prosecutor v. Charles Ghankay Taylor*, Case No. SCSL-03-01-T, Hearing, 25 June 2007, p.370-371.

342 *Prosecutor v. Charles Ghankay Taylor*, Case No. SCSL-03-01-T, Hearing, 25 June 2007, p.373-374.

343 *Prosecutor v. Charles Ghankay Taylor*, Case No. SCSL-03-01-T, Hearing, 25 June 2007, p.380-381.

assigned counsel.[344] The chamber further instructed duty counsel to represent the interests of the accused until such time a new defence team was formed.[345] The start of the evidentiary phase was subsequently postponed for a period of four months to give the newly formed defence team time to prepare for trial.[346]

The examples from both ICTY and SCSL illustrate that rather than accepting an accused's assertion of the right to self-representation at face value without considering further consequences, trial chambers may reach different conclusions as to the feasibility of the exercise of this right depending on the circumstances of each case. Such careful consideration of the specifics at issue is of particular significance insofar as the question whether an accused in fact voluntarily chooses to conduct his or her defence in person or rather attempts to use the right to self-representation as a threat and last resort in disputes surrounding the choice of counsel is not always easily solved. The underlying rationale may be of importance for a chamber's final determination as it can raise issues concerning the accused's (and others') right to a fair trial. The case of *Taylor* before the SCSL, in addition to the initial arguments presented in *Krajišnik* before the ICTY, seems to be a particularly illustrative example that trial chambers have to attentively assess the facts of the case to be able to determine whether an accused genuinely wishes to exercise his or her right to self-representation.

II. Recognition of the right to self-representation at different stages of the proceedings

The previous section has shown that, in principle, an extensive right to self-representation is recognised before international criminal tribunals. This prompts the question as to whether this right to self-representation is acknowledged and granted at all stages of international criminal proceedings or if there might be differences in the practical exercise of this right depending on whether the pre-trial, trial or appeals stage of a case is concerned.

---

344 *Prosecutor v. Charles Ghankay Taylor*, Case No. SCSL-03-01-T, Hearing, 25 June 2007, p.381. *See also* Status Conference, 20 August 2007, p.406-407.

345 *Prosecutor v. Charles Ghankay Taylor*, Case No. SCSL-03-01-T, Hearing, 25 June 2007, p.383-384, 388.

346 *Prosecutor v. Charles Ghankay Taylor*, Case No. SCSL-03-01-T, Status Conference, 20 August 2007, p.435-436.

When examining specific examples of relevant national jurisprudence, in this case a decision of the U.S. Supreme Court rendered after *Faretta*, it appears that a distinction is drawn at least between the trial and the appellate stage of proceedings. The U.S. Supreme Court held in the more recent case of *Martinez v. Court of Appeal of California*[347] that *Faretta* did not require the recognition of a right to self-representation on appeal. In the context of trial proceedings, the U.S. Supreme Court considered that "the government's interest in ensuring the integrity and efficiency of the trial at times outweighs the defendant's interest in acting as his own lawyer".[348] Turning to the appellate stage, the U.S. Supreme Court found the governmental interests to prevail[349] and the "autonomy interests [...] less compelling".[350] It did however leave open the possibility for state courts to provide for a right to defend oneself during the appeals stage of a case.[351] It is of interest to note that the three judges writing concurring opinions to the decision, amongst them especially Justice Scalia, appeared to be at pains to underscore the continuing validity of the U.S. Supreme Court's decision in *Faretta*.[352]

At the same time, a decision by the European Court of Human Rights in Strasbourg has been interpreted as recognising a right to self-representation at all stages of the proceedings, without difference.[353] In *Belziuk*, the ECtHR held that the fair trial guarantees enshrined in Article 6(3) of the ECHR were

---

347 *Martinez v. Court of Appeal of California, Fourth Appellate District* (U.S. Supreme Court), 528 U.S. 152 (2000), 12 January 2000.

348 *Martinez v. Court of Appeal of California, Fourth Appellate District* (U.S. Supreme Court), 528 U.S. 152 (2000), 12 January 2000, at 162.

349 *Martinez v. Court of Appeal of California, Fourth Appellate District* (U.S. Supreme Court), 528 U.S. 152 (2000), 12 January 2000, at 162.

350 *Martinez v. Court of Appeal of California, Fourth Appellate District* (U.S. Supreme Court), 528 U.S. 152 (2000), 12 January 2000, at 163.

351 *Martinez v. Court of Appeal of California, Fourth Appellate District* (U.S. Supreme Court), 528 U.S. 152 (2000), 12 January 2000, at 163.

352 *Martinez v. Court of Appeal of California, Fourth Appellate District* (U.S. Supreme Court), 528 U.S. 152 (2000), 12 January 2000, Concurring opinions of Justices Kennedy, Breyer, and Scalia, at 164-166. *See* in particular at 165: "Our system of laws generally presumes that the criminal defendant, after being fully informed, knows his own best interests and does not need them dictated by the State. Any other approach is unworthy of a free people."

353 *Prosecutor v. Momčilo Krajišnik*, Case No. IT-00-39-A, Decision on Momčilo Krajišnik's Request to Self-Represent, on Counsel's Motions in Relation to Appointment of *Amicus Curiae*, and on the Prosecution Motion of 16 February 2007, Separate Opinion of Judge Shahabuddeen, 11 May 2007, para.15-16.

applicable to all instances of the proceedings.[354] On the facts of the case, the European Court found a violation of Article 6(1) in conjunction with Article 6(3)(c) of the ECHR on the basis that the applicant was denied the right to be present at the appeals hearing and defend himself in person.[355]

Turning to the relevant decisions issued by chambers of international criminal tribunals, it appears that in approaching the right to self-representation, indeed a distinction is drawn on the basis of the timing of an accused's request to proceed *pro se*. While Slobodan Milošević, Vojislav Šešelj, Radovan Karadžić and Zdravko Tolimir before the ICTY expressed their will to represent themselves from the start, Samuel Hinga Norman before the SCSL did so at the first day of trial, whereas Momčilo Krajišnik, again before the ICTY, for the first time only requested to be granted such right in the middle of trial proceedings. This first request was rejected by the trial chamber, based *inter alia* on considerations of its timing. When Momčilo Krajišnik subsequently asked to represent himself for the duration of the appeals proceedings, the appeals chamber granted his request to exercise his right to self-representation in a much discussed decision.

The difference in granting, and thereafter potentially restricting, the right to self-representation depending on the stage of proceedings at which the exercise of such right is requested was alluded to in the case against Vojislav Šešelj. Examining the issue of restriction of the right to self-representation, the appeals chamber held in this case that "at the pre-trial stage, the Trial Chamber should satisfy itself that the accused's pre-trial behaviour, when considered as a whole, provides a strong indication that continued self-representation *would* substantially and persistently obstruct the proper and expeditious conduct of the trial proceedings".[356] In the appeals chamber's view, "a Trial Chamber should have a high degree of certainty before exceptionally placing a restriction on the right to self-representation pre-emptively at the pre-trial stage before an accused has had the opportunity to conduct his own defence at trial".[357]

---

354 *Belziuk v. Poland*, Application no. 23103/93, Judgment, 25 March 1998, para.37(i).

355 *Belziuk v. Poland*, Application no. 23103/93, Judgment, 25 March 1998, para.38, 40.

356 *Prosecutor v. Vojislav Šešelj*, Case No. IT-03-67-AR73.3, Decision on Appeal Against the Trial Chamber's Decision on Assignment of Counsel, 20 October 2006, para.28 (emphasis in the original).

357 *Prosecutor v. Vojislav Šešelj*, Case No. IT-03-67-AR73.3, Decision on Appeal Against the Trial Chamber's Decision on Assignment of Counsel, 20 October 2006, para.28.

This indicates that the appeals chamber differentiated between the considerations to be satisfied at pre-trial stage and in the trial phase with regard to restrictions of the right to self-representation. The approach of the appeals chamber appears to be reasonable insofar as the issues to be dealt with during the pre-trial and trial phases of proceedings are distinctly different, especially when it comes to the time spent in court by the defendant. Arguably, behaviour such as extended political speeches or direct harassing of witnesses during cross-examination in court by the self-represented accused could be considered more disruptive of the proceedings than "merely" insulting language in pre-trial filings. Thus, within the currently existing framework of self-representation, a higher standard to be met when restricting self-representation before the start of the trial stage appears to be justifiable.

1. The case of Momčilo Krajišnik: Trial phase

The case against Momčilo Krajišnik depicted a longer history of dealing with the issue of the right to self-representation.

The accused requested to defend himself in person for the first time in the course of the trial proceedings in May 2005. It appears that at a certain point in the course of the evidentiary proceedings, the defendant adopted the view that his defence team "is unable to assist [him] in establishing the truth" and thus decided "very unwillingly" to assume a more active role in the case.[358] As a consequence, defence counsel took the position to no longer represent the interests of the accused.[359]

Yet, with reference to the decision of the appeals chamber in *Milošević*, the trial chamber in *Krajišnik* considered the right to self-representation not to be absolute, but subject to limitations in certain circumstances.[360] In a provisional oral decision, the trial chamber clarified that an application for self-representation had to be made "knowingly and intelligently".[361] However, according to the bench, the accused had made his decision "unwillingly",

358 *Prosecutor v. Momčilo Krajišnik*, Case No. IT-00-39-T, Hearing, 25 May 2005, T.13399.

359 *Prosecutor v. Momčilo Krajišnik*, Case No. IT-00-39-T, Hearing, 25 May 2005, T.13402, 13405-13406.

360 *Prosecutor v. Momčilo Krajišnik*, Case No. IT-00-39-T, Hearing, 25 May 2005, T.13404, 13410, 13412.

361 *Prosecutor v. Momčilo Krajišnik*, Case No. IT-00-39-T, Procedural Hearing, 26 May 2005, T.13416.

which led the judges to conclude that they were "unable at this moment to recognise Mr. Krajišnik's application to represent himself as being made validly".[362] As a result, the trial chamber found that "Mr. Krajišnik continues to be represented by counsel appointed by the Registrar".[363]

Whereas the accused reiterated his decision to conduct his own defence,[364] he further explained that he had asked the bench in general already "on a number of occasions for the opportunity to address the Trial Chamber" and "for the opportunity to put questions and submit documents to a certain number of witnesses".[365] The defendant argued that the issue at hand was that he did not want to take over his defence, but rather that he would simply like to be able to present information to the trial chamber.[366] In light of these demands made by the accused, and pending a decision on his request to proceed *pro se*, the trial chamber allowed the accused, "as an experiment", "to put supplementary questions, following cross-examination by counsel, to each witness".[367] In permitting this, the trial chamber made clear that the accused would be bound by the rules and explicitly warned him that his "lack of legal experience means that there is a serious risk" for him to damage his position and that if he "inadvertently" did so when examining witnesses, he would have to bear the consequences.[368] Yet, the trial chamber subsequently extended the "experimental phase when Mr. Krajišnik was allowed to participate in examining witnesses"[369] in the context of the instructions given before the start of the presentation of the defence case.[370] At the same time, the trial

---

362 *Prosecutor v. Momčilo Krajišnik*, Case No. IT-00-39-T, Procedural Hearing, 26 May 2005, T.13416.

363 *Prosecutor v. Momčilo Krajišnik*, Case No. IT-00-39-T, Procedural Hearing, 26 May 2005, T.13416.

364 *Prosecutor v. Momčilo Krajišnik*, Case No. IT-00-39-T, Procedural Hearing, 26 May 2005, T.13418.

365 *Prosecutor v. Momčilo Krajišnik*, Case No. IT-00-39-T, Procedural Hearing, 26 May 2005, T.13419-13420.

366 *Prosecutor v. Momčilo Krajišnik*, Case No. IT-00-39-T, Procedural Hearing, 26 May 2005, T.13420.

367 *Prosecutor v. Momčilo Krajišnik*, Case No. IT-00-39-T, Procedural Hearing, 26 May 2005, T.13439.

368 *Prosecutor v. Momčilo Krajišnik*, Case No. IT-00-39-T, Procedural Hearing, 26 May 2005, T.13440.

369 *Prosecutor v. Momčilo Krajišnik*, Case No. IT-00-39-T, Hearing, 28 September 2005, T.17205.

370 *Prosecutor v. Momčilo Krajišnik*, Case No. IT-00-39-T, Hearing, 28 September 2005, T.17205-17208.

chamber reiterated its concern whether the accused would be capable of following the applicable rules and reserved itself the possibility to cut the defendant's examination at any time and reconsider its approach of allowing him to put additional questions to witnesses.[371]

This initial method adopted by the trial chamber is of significance insofar as it provided for the possibility of the accused to actively participate in the proceedings while however at the same time not requiring him to present his case entirely on his own. This indicates that despite the position of the appeals chamber taken earlier in *Milošević* that self-representation and representation by counsel were mutually exclusive, the trial chamber in *Krajišnik* still saw room for the accused playing a role in his case that might fall in between the two extremes.

A few days after the initial determination of the trial chamber to allow the accused to put additional questions to witnesses, a further hearing was held in *Krajišnik* to give the parties the opportunity to elaborate on their respective positions with regard to the defendant's request.[372] In addition to the oral arguments it presented, the prosecution submitted in writing that while an accused would have a qualified right to self-represent, it might be prudent to assign defence counsel as standby counsel if the defendant's request to proceed *pro se* was granted.[373] The ICTY registry took the view that while the right to self-representation was to be decided upon by the trial chamber, it was linked to the question of withdrawal of counsel, which falls within the competence of the ICTY registry, and that therefore the first should be decided before the latter could be properly addressed.[374] It further opined that it would not be in a position to assign or remunerate any legal assistance

371 *Prosecutor v. Momčilo Krajišnik*, Case No. IT-00-39-T, Hearing, 28 September 2005, T.17206.

372 *Prosecutor v. Momčilo Krajišnik*, Case No. IT-00-39-T, Special Hearing on Self-Representation, 31 May 2005, T.13690-13740.

373 *Prosecutor v. Momčilo Krajišnik*, Case No. IT-00-39-T, Prosecution's Submissions on Self-Representation, 31 May 2005, para.3-4, 18-19.

374 *Prosecutor v. Momčilo Krajišnik*, Case No. IT-00-39-T, Registrar's Notification Pursuant to Rule 33(B) of the Rules of Procedure and Evidence Regarding Momčilo Krajišnik's Legal Representation, 31 May 2005, para.11-13. A similar position was taken in a filing in *Janković & Stanković* on the same day: *Prosecutor v. Janković & Stanković*, Case No. IT-96-23/2-PT, Registrar's Notification Pursuant to Rule 33(B) of the Rules of Procedure and Evidence Regarding Radovan Stanković's Legal Representation, 31 May 2005, para.8-10.

in case the accused was to conduct his defence in person.[375] Defence counsel submitted that the accused had made an informed and intelligent choice.[376] Yet, due to the timing of the request, it would fall within the discretion of the chamber to in fact grant it.[377]

Eventually, the denial of the trial chamber of the accused's request was based on the fact that it did not consider the request by the defendant to represent himself to have been made in an unequivocal manner.[378] In the alternative, the trial chamber considered whether the request, if it was to be determined unequivocal, would have been made in a timely manner, given that a late request to proceed *pro se* would bring with it more potential to disrupt the proceedings,[379] which would give the chamber more discretion in denying such a request.[380] Furthermore, the bench observed that the defendant was likely to mount a comparably ineffective defence if he was to attempt it without assistance, which might negatively impact on the integrity of the proceedings.[381] In view of the trial chamber, the problems invoked by the accused when requesting to exercise his right to self-representation could

---

375 *Prosecutor v. Momčilo Krajišnik*, Case No. IT-00-39-T, Registrar's Submission Pursuant to Rule 33(B) of the Rules of Procedure and Evidence Regarding the Resources that Can be Made Available to Momčilo Krajišnik if He is to Represent Himself, 03 June 2005, para.19.

376 *Prosecutor v. Momčilo Krajišnik*, Case No. IT-00-39-T, Defence Submissions: Summary of Current Position on Self-Representation by Mr Krajišnik, 08 June 2005, para.2.

377 *Prosecutor v. Momčilo Krajišnik*, Case No. IT-00-39-T, Defence Submissions: Summary of Current Position on Self-Representation by Mr Krajišnik, 08 June 2005, para.8, 10.

378 *Prosecutor v. Momčilo Krajišnik*, Case No. IT-00-39-T, Reasons for Oral Decision Denying Mr. Krajišnik's Request to Proceed Unrepresented by Counsel, 18 August 2005, para.7, 10, 20-21. *See also* Oral Decision, 22 July 2005, T.17048.

379 *Prosecutor v. Momčilo Krajišnik*, Case No. IT-00-39-T, Reasons for Oral Decision Denying Mr. Krajišnik's Request to Proceed Unrepresented by Counsel, 18 August 2005, para.31.

380 *Prosecutor v. Momčilo Krajišnik*, Case No. IT-00-39-T, Reasons for Oral Decision Denying Mr. Krajišnik's Request to Proceed Unrepresented by Counsel, 18 August 2005, para.24, 32.

381 *Prosecutor v. Momčilo Krajišnik*, Case No. IT-00-39-T, Reasons for Oral Decision Denying Mr. Krajišnik's Request to Proceed Unrepresented by Counsel, 18 August 2005, para.34.

be solved in a manner different from granting the defendant's request to defend himself in person.[382]

The issue of whether a request to exercise the right to self-representation was indeed made in an unequivocal manner also appeared to arise in the course of the appeal proceedings in *Akayesu* before the ICTR. When rendering its judgement in this case, the appeals chamber took the view that while the accused apparently had asked to defend himself on numerous occasions, his behaviour in other respects did not allow the conclusion that he indeed desired to proceed *pro se*.[383] In a similar vein, the accused in *Kambanda* seemed to have alleged his right to self-representation merely in the context of choosing defence counsel to be assigned, without however indicating any serious intention to defend himself personally.[384]

The appeals chamber in its judgement in *Krajišnik* eventually upheld the decision of the trial chamber to deny the request of the accused to proceed self-represented at a late stage of the trial proceedings, expressly rejecting the suggestion that "a request to self-represent must always be honoured in the absence of persistent obstructionist conduct".[385] The appeals chamber further held that in the circumstances of the case, it did not amount to an unfair trial if an accused who is represented by counsel was allowed, in certain situations, to put questions to witnesses in addition to those asked by counsel.[386] This appears to be in line with the suggestion advanced by the prosecution at an early stage in *Milošević*, when it argued that more innovative solutions for participation of the accused, despite being represented, should be considered.[387]

---

382 *Prosecutor v. Momčilo Krajišnik*, Case No. IT-00-39-T, Reasons for Oral Decision Denying Mr. Krajišnik's Request to Proceed Unrepresented by Counsel, 18 August 2005, para.35.

383 *Prosecutor v. Jean-Paul Akayesu*, Case No. ICTR-96-4-A, Judgment, 01 June 2001, para.65-66.

384 *Prosecutor v. Jean Kambanda*, Case No. ICTR-97-23-A, Judgement, 19 October 2000, para.16 *et seq.*

385 *Prosecutor v. Momčilo Krajišnik*, Case No. IT-00-39-A, Judgement, 17 March 2009, para.118.

386 *Prosecutor v. Momčilo Krajišnik*, Case No. IT-00-39-A, Judgement, 17 March 2009, para.119.

387 *See Prosecutor v. Slobodan Milošević*, Case No. IT-02-54-T, Submission from the Office of the Prosecutor on the Future Conduct of the Case in the Light of the State of the Accused's Health and the Length and Complexity of the Case, 08 November 2002, para.21.

2. The case of Momčilo Krajišnik: Appeals phase

a. The majority opinion recognising self-representation on appeal

In May 2007, the appeals chamber issued its decision in *Krajišnik* on the request of the accused to continue self-represented in the appeals proceedings of his case.

According to the appeals chamber, it was to consider "the core question [...] whether individuals possess a right to self-representation before this Tribunal during appeals from judgement".[388] Initially examining Article 21(4)(d) of the ICTY Statute, the appeals chamber first observed that the provision itself does not distinguish between the different stages of proceedings.[389] The appeals chamber furthermore found that "there is no obvious reason why self-representation at trial is so different in character from self-representation on appeal as to require an *a priori* distinction between the two".[390] While it conceded that "[s]elf-representation on appeal may be a complex and tricky business", the appeals chamber did not think it to be more difficult than self-representation at trial since at both stages complicated issues would be involved.[391] Using the terms of the earlier decision in *Milošević*, the appeals chamber stated that "[i]t may never be in an individual's interests to represent himself, either at trial or at appeal, but he nonetheless has a 'cornerstone' right to make his own case to the Tribunal".[392]

---

388 *Prosecutor v. Momčilo Krajišnik*, Case No. IT-00-39-A, Decision on Momčilo Krajišnik's Request to Self-Represent, on Counsel's Motions in Relation to Appointment of *Amicus Curiae*, and on the Prosecution Motion of 16 February 2007, 11 May 2007, para.10.

389 *Prosecutor v. Momčilo Krajišnik*, Case No. IT-00-39-A, Decision on Momčilo Krajišnik's Request to Self-Represent, on Counsel's Motions in Relation to Appointment of *Amicus Curiae*, and on the Prosecution Motion of 16 February 2007, 11 May 2007, para.11.

390 *Prosecutor v. Momčilo Krajišnik*, Case No. IT-00-39-A, Decision on Momčilo Krajišnik's Request to Self-Represent, on Counsel's Motions in Relation to Appointment of *Amicus Curiae*, and on the Prosecution Motion of 16 February 2007, 11 May 2007, para.11.

391 *Prosecutor v. Momčilo Krajišnik*, Case No. IT-00-39-A, Decision on Momčilo Krajišnik's Request to Self-Represent, on Counsel's Motions in Relation to Appointment of *Amicus Curiae*, and on the Prosecution Motion of 16 February 2007, 11 May 2007, para.11.

392 *Prosecutor v. Momčilo Krajišnik*, Case No. IT-00-39-A, Decision on Momčilo Krajišnik's Request to Self-Represent, on Counsel's Motions in Relation to Appoint-

The appeals chamber, having succinctly referred to the "review of the case law of domestic jurisdictions" without, however, giving specific sources, found no support for the distinction of the right to self-representation between trial and appeal phases of a case.[393] The appeals judges concluded that therefore the accused had the right to represent himself during the appeals proceedings of his case.[394] However, the appeals chamber did clarify at the same time that as at trial, "this right is not unqualified".[395] The appeals chamber found that in case the accused's "self-representation substantially and persistently obstruct[s] the proper and expeditious conduct of his appeal, then counsel may be imposed upon him".[396] Therefore, the appeals chamber deemed it "prudent to appoint *amicus curiae* to keep an eye on [the accused's] interests"[397] and "invite[d] the participation of a particular *amicus curiae* to assist the Appeals Chamber by arguing in favour of [his] interests" who at the same time, however, was "to work independently from Mr. Krajišnik".[398]

It becomes clear when going back to the origins upon which the recognition of a right to self-representation is based within the international criminal

---

ment of *Amicus Curiae*, and on the Prosecution Motion of 16 February 2007, 11 May 2007, para.11.

393 *Prosecutor v. Momčilo Krajišnik*, Case No. IT-00-39-A, Decision on Momčilo Krajišnik's Request to Self-Represent, on Counsel's Motions in Relation to Appointment of *Amicus Curiae*, and on the Prosecution Motion of 16 February 2007, 11 May 2007, para.12.

394 *Prosecutor v. Momčilo Krajišnik*, Case No. IT-00-39-A, Decision on Momčilo Krajišnik's Request to Self-Represent, on Counsel's Motions in Relation to Appointment of *Amicus Curiae*, and on the Prosecution Motion of 16 February 2007, 11 May 2007, para.13.

395 *Prosecutor v. Momčilo Krajišnik*, Case No. IT-00-39-A, Decision on Momčilo Krajišnik's Request to Self-Represent, on Counsel's Motions in Relation to Appointment of *Amicus Curiae*, and on the Prosecution Motion of 16 February 2007, 11 May 2007, para.13.

396 *Prosecutor v. Momčilo Krajišnik*, Case No. IT-00-39-A, Decision on Momčilo Krajišnik's Request to Self-Represent, on Counsel's Motions in Relation to Appointment of *Amicus Curiae*, and on the Prosecution Motion of 16 February 2007, 11 May 2007, para.13.

397 *Prosecutor v. Momčilo Krajišnik*, Case No. IT-00-39-A, Decision on Momčilo Krajišnik's Request to Self-Represent, on Counsel's Motions in Relation to Appointment of *Amicus Curiae*, and on the Prosecution Motion of 16 February 2007, 11 May 2007, para.18.

398 *Prosecutor v. Momčilo Krajišnik*, Case No. IT-00-39-A, Decision on Momčilo Krajišnik's Request to Self-Represent, on Counsel's Motions in Relation to Appointment of *Amicus Curiae*, and on the Prosecution Motion of 16 February 2007, 11 May 2007, para.19.

law context, *i.e.* the U.S. Supreme Court's decision in *Faretta*, that the idea of appointing *amicus curiae* in order to mitigate potential harmful consequences of the exercise of the right to self-represent is not new: in his dissenting opinion to the U.S. Supreme Court's decision, Chief Justice Burger mentioned the possibility of this method and opined that the majority's decision did not exclude such a measure.[399]

One separate opinion to the appeals chamber decision in *Krajišnik* agreed with the majority recognising a right to self-representation on appeal, and provided further arguments in support of its conclusion.[400]

A further opinion dissented from the majority with regard to the appointment of *amicus curiae*, noting "that there is nothing in our Statute or Rules of Procedure and Evidence that allows for the appointment of *amicus curiae* to a trial or appeal proceeding to act as a *de facto* counsel".[401] There have been further critical receptions of the use of the concept of *amicus curiae* especially in the context of the assignment in *Milošević* which will be addressed further below.

b. The fundamental dissent opposing self-representation

An additional, "fundamentally dissenting opinion", proclaimed to be "deeply convinced that international criminal tribunals dealing with mega crimes can only carry out their important task of balancing the interests of victims with the interests of an accused by requiring the latter to be assisted by counsel

---

399 *Anthony Pasquall Faretta v. State of California* (U.S. Supreme Court), 422 U.S. 806, 30 June 1975, Dissenting Opinion Chief Justice Burger, joined by Justices Blackmun and Rehnquist, at 846 fn.7: "Some of the damage we can anticipate from a defendant's ill-advised insistence on conducting his own defense may be mitigated by appointing a qualified lawyer to sit in the case as the traditional 'friend of the court'. The Court does not foreclose this option."

400 *Prosecutor v. Momčilo Krajišnik*, Case No. IT-00-39-A, Decision on Momčilo Krajišnik's Request to Self-Represent, on Counsel's Motions in Relation to Appointment of *Amicus Curiae*, and on the Prosecution Motion of 16 February 2007, Separate Opinion of Judge Shahabuddeen, 11 May 2007.

401 *Prosecutor v. Momčilo Krajišnik*, Case No. IT-00-39-A, Decision on Momčilo Krajišnik's Request to Self-Represent, on Counsel's Motions in Relation to Appointment of *Amicus Curiae*, and on the Prosecution Motion of 16 February 2007, Dissenting Opinion of Judge Pocar, 11 May 2007, para.1.

for his own benefit".[402] The opinion considered the appeals chamber's jurisprudence in this regard to be "based on a false dichotomy which assumes that the right to defend oneself negates the right to be assisted by counsel".[403] In this view, the "fundamental misunderstanding that both rights are mutually exclusive adversely affects the fairness of the proceedings" and there is "no fair procedure before international tribunals without public legal assistance".[404]

The dissent reiterated the position that "in serious cases like those before international criminal tribunals it is impossible for an accused to defend himself",[405] and took issue with the succinct discussion by the appeals chamber of the differences between pre-trial, trial and appeals stage of a case.[406] The opinion continued with a detailed outline of national and supranational jurisprudence, which led *inter alia* to the conclusion that under the European Convention for Human Rights, "an accused does not have an

---

402 *Prosecutor v. Momčilo Krajišnik*, Case No. IT-00-39-A, Decision on Momčilo Krajišnik's Request to Self-Represent, on Counsel's Motions in Relation to Appointment of *Amicus Curiae*, and on the Prosecution Motion of 16 February 2007, Fundamentally Dissenting Opinion of Judge Schomburg on the Right to Self-Representation, 11 May 2007, para.2. *See*, however, an earlier article alluding to the position that "arguably", the "or" in the provisions is to be read "either or": Wolfgang Schomburg/Tobias Wild, The Defence Rights in the Practice of the International Criminal Tribunals, 4 *ERA Forum* 533 (2004), at 539.

403 *Prosecutor v. Momčilo Krajišnik*, Case No. IT-00-39-A, Decision on Momčilo Krajišnik's Request to Self-Represent, on Counsel's Motions in Relation to Appointment of *Amicus Curiae*, and on the Prosecution Motion of 16 February 2007, Fundamentally Dissenting Opinion of Judge Schomburg on the Right to Self-Representation, 11 May 2007, para.2.

404 *Prosecutor v. Momčilo Krajišnik*, Case No. IT-00-39-A, Decision on Momčilo Krajišnik's Request to Self-Represent, on Counsel's Motions in Relation to Appointment of *Amicus Curiae*, and on the Prosecution Motion of 16 February 2007, Fundamentally Dissenting Opinion of Judge Schomburg on the Right to Self-Representation, 11 May 2007, para.2.

405 *Prosecutor v. Momčilo Krajišnik*, Case No. IT-00-39-A, Decision on Momčilo Krajišnik's Request to Self-Represent, on Counsel's Motions in Relation to Appointment of *Amicus Curiae*, and on the Prosecution Motion of 16 February 2007, Fundamentally Dissenting Opinion of Judge Schomburg on the Right to Self-Representation, 11 May 2007, para.3.

406 *Prosecutor v. Momčilo Krajišnik*, Case No. IT-00-39-A, Decision on Momčilo Krajišnik's Request to Self-Represent, on Counsel's Motions in Relation to Appointment of *Amicus Curiae*, and on the Prosecution Motion of 16 February 2007, Fundamentally Dissenting Opinion of Judge Schomburg on the Right to Self-Representation, 11 May 2007, para.10.

absolute right to represent himself either at trial or, as in this case, on appeal".[407] In this analysis, the dissent referred to decisions of the ECtHR that recognise the possibility of imposing mandatory counsel,[408] as well as to decisions which emphasise the difference of the nature of proceedings in the (pre-) trial and appellate stage.[409]

The opinion considered the rights to fair and to expeditious appellate proceedings to be "intertwined" so that an assessment would be necessary whether granting the right to self-representation on appeal "would benefit an appellant by ensuring his fundamental right to be the subject, not the object, of a fair and expeditious appeals process" since "[a]n accused cannot waive his right to fair proceedings, under whatever circumstances".[410]

In light of a general proportionality principle, the dissenting opinion proceeded to assess the effects of self-representation and fairness of the proceedings upon each other.[411] The position was taken that at the appellate level "there are circumstances other than obstructive behaviour by an appellant that allow for the assignment of counsel, if need be even against the will of an appellant in his well-understood own interests".[412] Furthermore, concern

407 *Prosecutor v. Momčilo Krajišnik*, Case No. IT-00-39-A, Decision on Momčilo Krajišnik's Request to Self-Represent, on Counsel's Motions in Relation to Appointment of *Amicus Curiae*, and on the Prosecution Motion of 16 February 2007, Fundamentally Dissenting Opinion of Judge Schomburg on the Right to Self-Representation, 11 May 2007, para.25.

408 *Croissant c. Allemagne*, Requête n° 13611/88, Arrêt, 25 septembre 1992; *Lagerblom v. Sweden*, Application no. 26891/95, Judgment, 14 April 2003; *Mayzit v. Russia*, Application no. 63378/00, Judgment, 06 July 2005, para.64-71.

409 *Monnell and Morris v. United Kingdom*, Application no. 9562/81 & 9819/82, Judgment, 02 March 1987, para.56; *Tripodi v. Italy*, Application no. 13743/88, Judgment, 22 February 1994, para.27.

410 *Prosecutor v. Momčilo Krajišnik*, Case No. IT-00-39-A, Decision on Momčilo Krajišnik's Request to Self-Represent, on Counsel's Motions in Relation to Appointment of *Amicus Curiae*, and on the Prosecution Motion of 16 February 2007, Fundamentally Dissenting Opinion of Judge Schomburg on the Right to Self-Representation, 11 May 2007, para.68.

411 *Prosecutor v. Momčilo Krajišnik*, Case No. IT-00-39-A, Decision on Momčilo Krajišnik's Request to Self-Represent, on Counsel's Motions in Relation to Appointment of *Amicus Curiae*, and on the Prosecution Motion of 16 February 2007, Fundamentally Dissenting Opinion of Judge Schomburg on the Right to Self-Representation, 11 May 2007, para.70.

412 *Prosecutor v. Momčilo Krajišnik*, Case No. IT-00-39-A, Decision on Momčilo Krajišnik's Request to Self-Represent, on Counsel's Motions in Relation to Appointment of *Amicus Curiae*, and on the Prosecution Motion of 16 February 2007, Fun-

was expressed with regard to the delays to be expected in appeal proceedings if the appellant was allowed to present his defence in person.[413] In this view, it was "predictable that there will be a significant disruption of the appeal proceedings […], endangering the integrity of the proceedings, rendering them fundamentally unfair from the outset and in all likelihood provoking a miscarriage of justice".[414] In conclusion, it was submitted that "[w]hen it conflicts with the overarching right to a fair, public and expeditious trial, the right to self-representation must yield".[415]

3. Discussion of the *Krajišnik* positions

a. Views expressed in the trial proceedings

A first matter of potential concern may be the position taken by the trial chamber when it allowed the accused to put additional questions to witnesses, while at the same time warning that it would not be inclined to grant leeway in case the defendant put himself in a disadvantageous position by doing so. If the right to self-representation is, on the one hand, presumed to be a right of a level comparable to other fair trial rights, the reasons for which a trial chamber appeared to explicitly warn the accused that he would be held to the same, or at least similar, standards as qualified defence counsel, seem questionable. A defendant may be disinclined to exercise the possibility

---

damentally Dissenting Opinion of Judge Schomburg on the Right to Self-Representation, 11 May 2007, para.70.

413 *Prosecutor v. Momčilo Krajišnik*, Case No. IT-00-39-A, Decision on Momčilo Krajišnik's Request to Self-Represent, on Counsel's Motions in Relation to Appointment of *Amicus Curiae*, and on the Prosecution Motion of 16 February 2007, Fundamentally Dissenting Opinion of Judge Schomburg on the Right to Self-Representation, 11 May 2007, para.74.

414 *Prosecutor v. Momčilo Krajišnik*, Case No. IT-00-39-A, Decision on Momčilo Krajišnik's Request to Self-Represent, on Counsel's Motions in Relation to Appointment of *Amicus Curiae*, and on the Prosecution Motion of 16 February 2007, Fundamentally Dissenting Opinion of Judge Schomburg on the Right to Self-Representation, 11 May 2007, para.75.

415 *Prosecutor v. Momčilo Krajišnik*, Case No. IT-00-39-A, Decision on Momčilo Krajišnik's Request to Self-Represent, on Counsel's Motions in Relation to Appointment of *Amicus Curiae*, and on the Prosecution Motion of 16 February 2007, Fundamentally Dissenting Opinion of Judge Schomburg on the Right to Self-Representation, 11 May 2007, para.83.

given by the trial chamber out of fear of damaging his own case, thereby reversing the intentions of the trial chamber to grant this possibility in order to provide for active participation of the accused in the first place.

Taking this to the next level of the practical exercise of the right to self-representation, the choice to defend oneself in person is acknowledged to require an informed decision, *i.e.* the accused has to be aware of the potential consequences and must be willing to take the risk. The question then arises if, and to which extent, *pro se* defendants can and should be held to the same standards as qualified defence lawyers in preparing and presenting their own case. This situation creates an obvious conflict between permitting the exercise of the right to self-representation by accused who accept potential negative consequences on the one side, and the need to allow for some latitude with defendants who are not experienced in running international criminal proceedings on the other.

Thus, a balance has to be struck between the right to a fair and expeditious trial not only for the accused, but also taking into account other participants to the proceedings. An additional factor to be kept in mind in this balance is the underlying idea that international criminal proceedings should ideally further the delivery of international justice. This notion could be jeopardised if the international community as such and affected communities in particular do not perceive justice done in proceedings which, from the outside, seem to be primarily dominated by an accused who portrays him- or herself as victim of a sort of international community's witch-hunt in the name of victor's justice. This counterproductive effect might even be enhanced if a self-represented accused originates from a national judicial system which does not recognise self-representation at all or not at the level of serious crimes. However, this consideration has to be approached carefully as the past has shown that even the accused concerned use similar hypotheses in order to argue for additional rights to be granted in the respective cases, as to be discussed later in this dissertation.

Turning to another example for discussion, the written decision of the trial chamber rejecting the defendant's request should be mentioned: in its August 2005 reasoned decision, the *Krajišnik* trial chamber took the reliance of the appeals chamber in *Milošević* on the decision of the U.S. Supreme Court in *Faretta* as a reason that "US case-law must feature unusually prominently in any derogation by this Tribunal from the right to self-representation".[416]

It has to be questioned whether the fact that the appeals chamber in one case relied heavily on one specific national case is sufficient justification for a similar reliance on U.S. jurisprudence by a trial chamber in a different case with different factual circumstances. Considering that the trial chamber referred to an "unusually" prominent role of domestic jurisprudence, this concern appears to have been in the minds of the trial judges.[417] At least, one has to ask whether in the context of an international criminal tribunal which deals with crimes committed in the territories of civil law jurisdictions, common law jurisprudence should play such a significant role in the resolution of fundamental procedural matters.[418] The argument has been made previously that the approach of directly applying national legal solutions to issues arising in international criminal trials "does not appear to be justified by any legal principles or logic, because it does not take account of the facts, (1) that international tribunals belong to a *totally distinct legal system from that of national courts*, a legal sphere with its own rules, time-frame and institutions, [...]".[419] Thus, it ought to be questioned whether it is advisable to rely on one specific jurisdiction, while other jurisdictions have different systems and take divergent approaches with regard to the right to self-repre-

---

416 *Prosecutor v. Momčilo Krajišnik*, Case No. IT-00-39-T, Reasons for Oral Decision Denying Mr. Krajišnik's Request to Proceed Unrepresented by Counsel, 18 August 2005, para.23.

417 *See* in this regard Nina H.B. Jørgensen, The Problem of Self-Representation at International Criminal Tribunals. Striking a Balance Between Fairness and Effectiveness, 4 *Journal of International Criminal Justice* 64 (2006), at 67, who notes the bench referred to U.S. case law "somewhat reluctantly".

418 *Cf.* Patricia M. Wald, *Tyrants on Trial. Keeping Order in the Courtroom* (New York: Open Society Justice Institute) 2009, p.41. *See also* Mirjan Damaška, Reflections on Fairness in International Criminal Justice, 10 *Journal of International Criminal Justice* 611 (2012), at 617: "[...] international criminal courts must be capable of absorbing a variety of influences and accommodate a considerable ideological diversity. After all, if Anglo-American legal culture was not so influential in the drafting of human rights documents, even an outright denial of self-representation in the processing of core international crimes could hardly be regarded as fundamentally unfair."

419 Antonio Cassese, The Influence of the European Court of Human Rights on International Criminal Tribunals – Some Methodological Remarks, in: Morten Bergsmo (ed.), *Human Rights and Criminal Justice for the Downtrodden. Essays in Honour of Asbjørn Eide* (Leiden/Boston: Martinus Nijhoff Publishers) 2003, p.19-52, at 21 (emphasis in the original).

sentation, including the countries which are directly concerned by the work of the ICTY and which would not provide for a right to self-representation in cases of such magnitude in their national courts. After all, proceedings before the ICTY supposedly are to promote closure and reconciliation in the region.[420] It needs to be questioned how these goals can be achieved or even only furthered if the ICTY incorporates procedural complexities which are incomprehensible to people on the ground who perceive self-represented accused to "run the show".[421] It is open to doubt whether an approach causing such results is still serving the interests of international criminal justice, especially keeping in mind the initial consideration by the Security Council when deciding on the establishment of the ICTY that the tribunal "would contribute to the restoration and maintenance of peace".[422] Distinct examples to be mentioned in this regard are witnesses cross-examined by self-represented accused who feel the accused to dominate the courtroom. For the uninformed individual not versed in the workings of international criminal proceedings, admonishing interventions by judges in the questioning of a *pro se* defendant might be insufficient to counter that impression.

b. Position of the appeals chamber majority

In view of the effects of the majority opinion of the appeals chamber in *Krajišnik*, it has to be asked whether the appeals chamber should not have spent time on a more detailed analysis of the issue. This would appear to have been worthwhile, considering potential implications of the exercise of the right to self-representation in the context of international criminal pro-

---

420 Laurel E. Fletcher/Harvey M. Weinstein, Violence and Social Repair: Rethinking the Contribution of Justice to Reconciliation, 24 *Human Rights Quarterly* 573 (2002), at 586, 597-601.

421 *See e.g.*, considering the example of the Saddam Hussein trial, Michael P. Scharf/Christopher M. Rassi, Do Former Leaders have an International Right to Self-Representation in War Crimes Trials?, 20 *Ohio State Journal on Dispute Resolution* 3 (2005), at 6-7, and generally at 28-29; Marko Milanović, The Arrest and Impending Trial of Radovan Karadžić, 58 *International and Comparative Law Quarterly* 212 (2009), at 217.

422 United Nations Security Council, Resolution 808 (1993), S/RES/808 (1993), 22 February 1993, para.9: "Convinced that in the particular circumstances of the former Yugoslavia the establishment of an international tribunal would enable this aim to be achieved and would contribute to the restoration and maintenance of peace, [...]".

ceedings. Although it is less difficult to analyse decisions *a posteriori* and in view of subsequent developments, the appeals chamber does not seem to have contemplated the full extent and power of impact of its findings and reasoning at the time.

It has to be examined why the appeals chamber bestowed such a prominent status upon the right to self-representation even though it appeared to concede concomitantly that in most cases it will not necessarily benefit the defendant to actually exercise this right. Against the backdrop of an examination of the criteria that are employed in order to determine whether an accused is in fact capable of taking a voluntary and informed decision to exercise his or her right to self-representation – for which indications can be found in the discussion on the competency standard in the U.S. system –, the question arises whether the existing focus on an exclusivity of choice is (still) compatible with the notion of the right to a fair trial and the need to protect the rights of accused. Any misgivings in this regard will only intensify in the context of international criminal proceedings which are habitually scrutinised on an international level, and even more so in the regions which used to be the scenes of events under consideration in these proceedings. Yet, if international criminal trials are to achieve any of their presumed objectives,[423] the aspirations to attain and preserve the highest standards of fair trial and international justice should be even more resilient.

The facts of the case in *Krajišnik* are of particular interest insofar as the defendant's request to conduct his defence in person was denied in the trial proceedings, while he was permitted to exercise his right to self-representation during the appeals phase of the case. The permissive attitude of the appeals chamber in this regard may in part have been based on the fact that the accused presented his second request at the beginning of the appeals case, as opposed to some point in mid-trial as had happened previously. More significantly, the accused had been allowed to question witnesses alongside defence counsel during trial, which could have been used as argument that the

---

423 *See, e.g.*, Antonio Cassese, Reflections on International Criminal Justice, 6(1) *The Modern Law Review* 1 (1998), at 6; Mark Findlay/Clare McLean, Emerging International Criminal Justice, 18(3) *Current Issues in Criminal Justice* 457 (2007), at 460-462; Bert Swart, Damaska and the Faces of International Criminal Justice, 6 *Journal of International Criminal Justice* 87 (2008), at 100-103. *See also* Martti Koskenniemi, Between Impunity and Show Trials, 6 *Max Planck Yearbook of United Nations Law* 1 (2002).

defendant was already familiar with the specific techniques of witness examination and the conduct of the proceedings.

This could hypothetically be taken further in case a defendant did in fact present his own defence in the course of trial proceedings, and wished to continue to do so during appeal. It would not seem reasonable, indeed not consistent with the "fundamental" nature of the right, to allow an accused to represent him- or herself during the course of pre-trial and/or trial proceedings and then end his or her self-representation once a case enters the appeals stage of the case, without any further showing of obstruction or similar obstacles on the part of the accused. The appellant could argue that he or she already conducted, probably years of, trial proceedings as *pro se* defendant, and is therefore intimately familiar with the procedural and factual issues at hand. Although an appellant would most likely engage legal assistance to write the appeals brief, this would not necessarily change his or her position with regard to appeals hearings.

On the other hand, the appeals chamber could take the position that, in particular due to the difference in nature of trial and appeals proceedings, the appellant should be disallowed to continue self-represented, for example in light of the accused's conduct during trial proceedings. However, this would then arguably have to be based for example on obstructive behaviour of the appellant, which for its part is likely to have been subject to previous litigation in the course of trial. It seems more probable the appeals chamber would need to give the appellant at least the possibility at the beginning of the appeals stage to show that he or she is able to continue self-represented and could only terminate self-representation in case disruptive behaviour of the appellant is established. Considering the scope of appellate proceedings, this would likely be based on the nature of written submission from the defence. Even if one takes the position argued in the dissenting opinion in *Krajišnik* that due to the nature of appellate proceedings, circumstances other than obstructive behaviour could justify the imposition of defence counsel, the right to self-representation and other general fair trial principles would need to be carefully balanced.

In case counsel is appointed, the chamber concerned would need to consider with due care who could act as counsel for a previously self-represented accused. A defence counsel unfamiliar with the case would be unable to take over immediately and it could be difficult to justify any delay to allow counsel to familiarise him- or herself with the case to contribute to the appeals brief, especially given that the appellant most probably already spent several years in custody since the start of the proceedings. However, any counsel having previously acted as legal advisor to the appellant could justifiably refuse to then appear as appointed counsel since this would be against the expressed will of his or her client and therefore could create a delicate ethical situation for counsel.

A flip side of this problem might surface if an accused who conducted his or her own defence during trial proceedings wishes to be represented by counsel in the appeals stage of his or her case. Bearing in mind the position taken thus far that accused at the level of international criminal proceedings should be significantly assisted by professional counsel in the first place, such change in attitude could only be encouraged. However, one also needs to take into account the realities of the problem. Although unlikely, it could be the case that an accused concluded the presentation of the defence at the trial stage without assistance of professional counsel in the form of a legal advisor. In case she or he then requests the assistance of qualified defence counsel for the appeals stage, it might surface that no counsel sufficiently familiar with the proceedings is available to assume the duties of defence counsel without further ado. Any counsel chosen by the accused or appointed by the chamber would then have to be given more time than other counsel in order to be able to familiarise him- or herself with the facts of the case to be able to conduct the appeals proceedings. Such familiarisation will be even more important for drafting an appeals brief as counsel would have to possess intimate knowledge of the evidence presented at trial and the legal implications involved in order to submit a valid brief.[424] It could be argued on the one hand that once an accused chooses to conduct his or her own defence this should be continued until the final conclusion of the case. Yet, the contrary argument that counsel should take over the presentation of the defence during the appellate proceedings would coincide with the difference between the stages of proceedings, as argued by some. Bearing in mind the view that the appeals stage of a case would be much more complex and legalistic to conduct for an unqualified self-represented accused, any choice of counsel for this important part of the case could only be encouraged. Such an approach would also appropriately protect the right of all parties to a fair and expeditious trial.

Of interest in this context is the approach adopted by the appeals chamber in *Krajišnik* when it allowed the accused, in addition to the court-appointed

424 *See e.g.* Rules 108, 111 ICTY RPE; Rules 108, 111 ICTR RPE; Rules 177(C), 182 STL RPE.

amici curiae, to be represented by professional counsel with regard to representations to be made on the distinct question of joint criminal enterprise.[425] This decision is of significance insofar as it granted the defendant's request to be represented by counsel with regard to specific issues despite his recognised status as self-represented accused.

In its decision on the matter, the appeals chamber adopted the position that the issue of "binary opposition" of self-representation and representation by counsel was concerned with potential "mix-and-match" attempts by self-represented accused, but did not exclude the possibility of "partial self-representation".[426] In the view of the appeals chamber, the choice between either self-representation or representation by counsel would need to be taken "only with respect to each issue", considering that there was "no fundamental reason why a defendant may not make different choices – self-representing or engaging legal counsel – with regard to different issues".[427]

This approach needs to be seriously questioned. The appeals chamber failed to define these "issues" in respect to which an accused would be permitted to again choose between proceeding *pro se* and being represented by counsel. In addition, the opinion is not in any way compatible with other jurisprudence on the matter. While from a pragmatic point of view, the permission of a maximum extent of professional legal assistance for self-represented accused is commendable, this decision of the appeals chamber is unpersuasive as it does not adopt either approach of the different views outlined earlier and falls short of unravelling the matter which the appeals chamber itself identified as "conundrum".[428] Apart from briefly referring to the question of legal aid, the decision does not provide any further explanation of the alleged distinction between mixing "elements" of self-representation

---

425 *Prosecutor v. Momčilo Krajišnik*, Case No. IT-00-39-A, Decision on Momčilo Krajišnik's Motion to Reschedule Status Conference and Permit Alan Dershowitz to Appear, 28 February 2008.

426 *Prosecutor v. Momčilo Krajišnik*, Case No. IT-00-39-A, Decision on Momčilo Krajišnik's Motion to Reschedule Status Conference and Permit Alan Dershowitz to Appear, 28 February 2008, para.8.

427 *Prosecutor v. Momčilo Krajišnik*, Case No. IT-00-39-A, Decision on Momčilo Krajišnik's Motion to Reschedule Status Conference and Permit Alan Dershowitz to Appear, 28 February 2008, para.8.

428 *See Prosecutor v. Momčilo Krajišnik*, Case No. IT-00-39-A, Decision on Momčilo Krajišnik's Motion to Reschedule Status Conference and Permit Alan Dershowitz to Appear, 28 February 2008, para.6.

and legal representation, and the assumed possibility of "partial self-representation" with regard to different "issues".[429]

Similarly, bearing in mind the initial appeals chamber decision on the defendant's request to self-represent during appeal in which the majority found that the request should be granted on the basis of the assumption that the nature of trial and appellate proceedings are not so different after all,[430] this approach is astounding, to say the least. The decision seems to implicitly concede that during appeal proceedings legal questions may arise which cannot possibly be dealt with by a lay self-represented accused.

It has to be examined which scope the appeals chamber intended for this decision's impact. The appeals chamber does not provide any indication as to whether the decision was supposed to be limited to "discrete" issues *e.g.* arising at the appeals stage of a case like in *Krajišnik* where counsel was permitted to file a brief on the issue of joint criminal enterprise, *i.e.* only concerning complex legal matters as opposed to general factual matters, or whether it envisaged the decision to extend to *e.g.* the evidentiary phase of a case, so that an accused could choose to defend himself in person for one factual component of the case, while having legal representation for another. Taking it one step further, one could ask whether the appeals chamber intended this reasoning to apply to situations where a *pro se* defendant would argue that he would cross-examine one expert witness, but not the following, since the latter's field of expertise was of a different nature than the former testified to. In the latter cases, the contradiction with the jurisprudence would be even more extreme and similarly incomprehensible. Although it does not seem likely that the appeals chamber did indeed intend its decision to encompass such scenarios, considering that it explicitly would not allow for what it called a "mix-and-match" approach, more guidance on the scope of the reasoning would then have been in order. This holds especially true in view of the participation granted by another trial chamber of the ICTY which included examination of witnesses by the accused falling into his specific field of

429 *Prosecutor v. Momčilo Krajišnik*, Case No. IT-00-39-A, Decision on Momčilo Krajišnik's Motion to Reschedule Status Conference and Permit Alan Dershowitz to Appear, 28 February 2008, para.8.

430 *Prosecutor v. Momčilo Krajišnik*, Case No. IT-00-39-A, Decision on Momčilo Krajišnik's Request to Self-Represent, on Counsel's Motions in Relation to Appointment of *Amicus Curiae*, and on the Prosecution Motion of 16 February 2007, 11 May 2007, para.11.

expertise.[431] If it is argued that active participation rather than single-handed presentation of the defence by accused should be encouraged, this approach appears to be reasonable, even though inconsistent with previous jurisprudence on the matter. Yet, the appeals chamber should then have taken a clear position to this effect. In light of the fact that this is not the only divergence in the long list of discussion topics in the context of the right to self-representation, the approach of the ICTY in this regard does indeed seem, to speak with one commentator, rather "improvised".[432]

When the prosecution sought clarification of the matter,[433] the appeals chamber rejected the argument that in the instant case, the accused benefited not only from the briefs filed in his interest by *amicus curiae*, but additionally from the brief permitted by the appeals chamber to be filed by legal counsel: according to the appeals chamber, the argument did not hold stand given that the *amicus'* mandate was to assist the appeals chamber, not the accused.[434] The further decision did not address any other concerns, but reiterated that the representation by counsel was limited to the issue of joint criminal enterprise.[435]

---

431 *See Prosecutor v. Prlić et al.*, Case No. IT-04-74-T, Decision Adopting Guidelines on Conduct of Trial Proceedings, 26 April 2006, II.c); *Procureur c/ Prlić et consorts*, Affaire n° IT-04-74-T, Décision Portant sur les Modalités de l'Interrogatoire des Témoins, 10 mai 2007; *Prosecutor v. Prlić et al.*, Case No. IT-04-74-AR73.5, Decision on Praljak's Appeal of the Trial Chamber's 10 May 2007 Decision on the Mode of Interrogating Witnesses, 24 August 2007; *Procureur c/ Prlić et consorts*, Affaire n° IT-04-74-T, Décision Portant sur une Demande de Réexamen Présentée par la Défense Praljak, 26 juin 2008; *Prosecutor v. Prlić et al.*, Case No. IT-04-74-AR73.11, Decision on Slobodan Praljak's Appeal of the Trial Chamber's Decision on the Direct Examination of Witnesses Dated 26 June 2008, 11 September 2008.

432 William A. Schabas, Article 67, in: Otto Triffterer (ed.), *Commentary on the Rome Statute of the International Criminal Court. Observers' Notes, Article by Article* (Munich: Verlag C.H. Beck) 2nd edition 2008, p.1247-1274, at note 30.

433 *Prosecutor v. Momčilo Krajišnik*, Case No. IT-00-39-A, Prosecution Motion for Clarification and Reconsideration of the Appeal Chamber's "Decision on Momčilo Krajišnik's Motion to Reschedule Status Conference and Permit Alan Dershowitz to Appear", 29 February 2008.

434 *Prosecutor v. Momčilo Krajišnik*, Case No. IT-00-39-A, Decision on Prosecution's Motion for Clarification and Reconsideration of the Decision of 28 February 2008, 11 March 2008, para.8.

435 *Prosecutor v. Momčilo Krajišnik*, Case No. IT-00-39-A, Decision on Prosecution's Motion for Clarification and Reconsideration of the Decision of 28 February 2008, 11 March 2008, para.9. The appeals chamber reiterated at para.9: "In short, because

This second decision does not help to clarify any of the issues raised above. In addition, the view that *amicus curiae*'s task was to assist the appeals chamber nothing but highlights the problems associated with engaging this concept in the context of self-represented accused. The appeals chamber itself initially incorporated the complexities in one sentence when providing for "*amicus curiae* to assist the Appeals Chamber by arguing in favour of Mr. Krajišnik's interests".[436] This implicates that the *amicus curiae*, while as "friend of the court" in the original meaning of the term not supposed to take sides or even an actual part in proceedings,[437] was ordered to do just that by the appeals chamber, albeit not on the face of it. Thus, the argument submitted by the appeals chamber that the accused did not benefit equally from the submissions of *amicus curiae* does not withstand further examination.

The issues in *Krajišnik* with the accused being self-represented on appeal developed further with regard to requests by the defendant concerning implementation of the decision on his self-representation during appeal proceedings[438] and the subsequent decision,[439] which will be addressed later in this dissertation in the context of the discussion of the role of legal advisors to *pro se* defendants and the question of financial aid for self-represented accused.

c. Opinion of the fundamental dissent

Analysing the fundamentally dissenting opinion to the *Krajišnik* appeals chamber decision, it ought to be questioned whether the approach adopted

---

Mr. Dershowitz will be acting as counsel for Mr. Krajišnik, at least in a limited capacity, the two must speak with a single voice."

436 *Prosecutor v. Momčilo Krajišnik*, Case No. IT-00-39-A, Decision on Momčilo Krajišnik's Request to Self-Represent, on Counsel's Motion in Relation to Appointment of *Amicus Curiae*, and on the Prosecution Motion of 16 February 2007, 11 May 2007, para.19.

437 *See* Rule 74 of the ICTY RPE, which provides: "A Chamber may, if it considers it desirable for the proper determination of the case, invite or grant leave to a State, organization or person to appear before it and make submissions on any issue specified by the Chamber."

438 *Prosecutor v. Momčilo Krajišnik*, Case No. IT-00-39-A, Request to Provide Conditions to Work and to Reverse the Decision of the Registry of 07 June 2007, 10 June 2007 (filed: 18 June 2007).

439 *Prosecutor v. Momčilo Krajišnik*, Case No. IT-00-39-A, Decision on Krajišnik Request and on Prosecution Motion, 11 September 2007.

in the dissent is indeed a viable option to be argued or whether it might not be too heavily influenced by the generic approach of civil law systems without taking due account of the divergent common law notion of the right to self-representation.

For the sake of argument, the position may be adopted that international criminal proceedings need to be seen as operating in a framework distinct of national and regional approaches, and as a system which should refer to these practices only by way of analogy. Consequently, the right to defend oneself in person as guaranteed and exercised in the international sphere could be seen as a right to actively participate in the proceedings, without however necessarily having to waive the right to be assisted by counsel, rather than a right which automatically excludes to draw on such qualified assistance.

Then, the underlying argument as expressed by the fundamental dissent in *Krajišnik*, that the right to defend oneself and the right to assistance by counsel should not be mutually exclusive, could serve as starting point for future developments. The author of the fundamental dissent should later re-iterate the view that the allegedly wrongly understood dichotomy in Article 14(3)(d) of the ICCPR should be amended accordingly.[440]

In order to alleviate the problems encountered thus far in this context, it is argued that a departure from the initial concepts which place the system of international criminal proceedings closer to the adversarial model of common law countries is necessary. This might have been accurate at the moment of the foundation of the *ad hoc* tribunals[441] as first institutions to address the most serious crimes on an international level after the Nuremberg proceedings. Yet, by now, after over a decade of developing jurisprudence on substantive and procedural law in the field of international crimes, it might better be seen as truly *sui generis* system[442] which may draw inspiration

---

440 Wolfgang Schomburg, Development of Human Rights Before International Criminal Tribunals. A European Perspective, 17(2) *Croatian Annual of Criminal Law and Practice* 909 (2010), at 920.

441 *Cf.* Vladimir Tochilovsky, Legal Systems and Cultures in the International Criminal Court: The Experience from the International Criminal Tribunal for the Former Yugoslavia, in: Horst Fischer/Claus Kreß/Sascha Rolf Lüder (eds), *International and National Prosecution of Crimes Under International Law. Current Developments* (Berlin: Berlin Verlag Arno Spitz GmbH) 2001, p.627-644, at 629.

442 Patrick L. Robinson, Ensuring Fair and Expeditious Trials at the International Criminal Tribunal for the Former Yugoslavia, 11 *European Journal of International Law* 569 (2000), at 588.

from national, transnational and supranational practice, but not over-emphasise its importance. This approach would seem to be even more viable in the context of interpretation of the Rome Statute, given that the ICC, according to Article 21 of its Statute, is to apply first and foremost the legislation of the Rome system, before looking for guidance in international law principles, and, potentially, national legal systems. Bearing in mind this background for interpretation and application in particular of the right to self-representation, it would be possible to provide for proceedings which acknowledge an active role to be played by the defendant in his or her own trial, without however leaving full-fledged self-representation as the only option and render complications inevitable from the very moment an accused elects to present his or her defence in person.

III. The impact of self-representation on the right to a fair trial

1. Interests of the accused

The discussions in the context of the appeals chamber decision in *Krajišnik* in particular raise the demur of compatibility of the exercise of the right to self-representation with the fundamental right to a fair trial. It is clear from the standards applied throughout that an accused has to make an informed choice when deciding to conduct his or her defence in person. At the same time, as becomes obvious from the discussion of the recognition of a right to self-representation before international criminal tribunals, chambers appear to be mindful of the significant number of factors to be considered when it comes to the exercise of self-representation, including the right to fair and expeditious proceedings. In particular in light of the position expressed by an SCSL trial chamber in the context of assignment of counsel that a defendant cannot waive the right to a fair trial,[443] as well as the concern expressed in the dissent of the *Krajišnik* appeals chamber decision,[444] the question has

443 *Prosecutor v. Issa Hassan Sesay et al.*, Case No. SCSL-04-15-T, Gbao – Decision on Application to Withdraw Counsel, 06 July 2004, para.15.

444 *Prosecutor v. Momčilo Krajišnik*, Case No. IT-00-39-A, Decision on Momčilo Krajišnik's Request to Self-Represent, on Counsel's Motions in Relation to Appointment of *Amicus Curiae*, and on the Prosecution Motion of 16 February 2007, Fundamentally Dissenting Opinion of Judge Schomburg on the Right to Self-Representation, 11 May 2007, para.2: "There is no fair procedure before international tribunals without public legal assistance."

to be raised whether the initial recognition and eventual practical exercise of the right to self-representation could effectively amount to a waiver of the overall right to a fair trial.

Since the right to self-representation is considered to form part of this overarching right to a fair trial, conflicting interests will have to be balanced.[445] Assuming that any balance of interests is indeed permissible to begin with,[446] the question of the extent to which a balancing exercise will have to be conducted in order to safeguard the different interests involved, including the right of defendants to fair and expeditious proceedings, will be developed further below. It has to be questioned whether an accused, how intelligent and educated he or she may be, is in fact in the position to make an informed decision as to whether he or she will be capable of conducting their own defence without foregoing the chances of an effective – and professional – defence, and thereby more generally of a fair trial. This concern appears to be reflected in the discussions on the recognition of the right to self-representation before international criminal tribunals.[447]

Especially bearing in mind the distinct approaches of different chambers to dealing with fundamental questions on self-representation, it becomes obvious that, in fact, the deeper roots of the conflicting views on the notion of waiver of the right to a fair trial may rest once more in the disputed determination of the question whether the autonomy of an accused should be respected in absolute terms, or whether the protection of an individual – potentially even against his or her own wishes, if it is obvious that these wishes

---

445 *Cf.* Joanne Williams, Slobodan Milosevic and the Guarantee of Self-Representation, 32 *Brooklyn Journal of International Law* 553 (2007), at 572-574.

446 Arguing to the contrary: Guénaël Mettraux, Foreword, 8 *Journal of International Criminal Justice* 75 (2010), at 77; Salvatore Zappalà, The Rights of Victims v. the Rights of the Accused, 8 *Journal of International Criminal Justice* 137 (2010), at 149. *See also* Mirjan Damaška, The Competing Visions of Fairness: The Basic Choice for International Criminal Tribunals, 36 *North Carolina Journal of International Law and Commercial Regulation* 365 (2011), at 378-380.

447 *See, e.g., Prosecutor v. Janković & Stanković*, Case No. IT-96-23/2-PT, Decision Following Registrar's Notification of Radovan Stanković's Request for Self-Representation, 19 August 2005, para.9: "[…] The rationale behind this qualified exercise is to ensure that a defendant is protected to the fullest extent possible."; para.10: "Secondly, this Tribunal as well as other international courts have consistently held that there may be circumstances where it is appropriate and the Chamber is competent to insist that the defence is presented by counsel and not by the accused in person [fn. omitted] in order to ensure that the exercise of the right to self-representation does not in effect obstruct the conduct of a fair trial [fn. omitted]."

are detrimental – should prevail.[448] According to one view, the difference in outcome depending on the approach adopted by a chamber arises from an underlying tension between the accused's autonomous choice to conduct his or her defence in person, and the general interest in a fair and expeditious conduct of the proceedings.[449] Similarly, it has been mentioned earlier that the conflict between the right to a fair trial and the recognition of a right to defend oneself has been acknowledged in U.S. courts, without however the U.S. Supreme Court ever addressing the matter or appeal courts following up on an alleged violation of the right to a fair trial.[450]

Considering the possibility of waiving fair trial guarantees within the framework of the ECHR, the European Court of Human Rights found that "[n]either the letter nor the spirit of Article 6 of the Convention prevents a person from waiving of his own free will, either expressly or tacitly, the entitlement to the guarantees of a fair trial".[451] Yet, any such waiver, in the

---

448 *Cf.* Mirjan Damaška, The Competing Visions of Fairness: The Basic Choice for International Criminal Tribunals, 36 *North Carolina Journal of International Law and Commercial Regulation* 365 (2011), at 382; Mirjan Damaška, Assignment of Counsel and Perceptions of Fairness, 3 *Journal of International Criminal Justice* 3 (2005), at 5. *See also* Frédéric Mégret, Beyond "Fairness": Understanding the Determinants of International Criminal Procedure, 14 *UCLA Journal of International Law and Foreign Affairs* 37 (2009), at 46; Nina H.B. Jørgensen, The Problem of Self-Representation at International Criminal Tribunals. Striking a Balance Between Fairness and Effectiveness, 4 *Journal of International Criminal Justice* 64 (2006), at 69-70. For a more general overview of the paternalism discussion *see* Danny Scoccia, In Defence of Hard Paternalism, 27(4) *Law & Philosophy* 351 (2008), and Gerald Dworkin in Stanford Encyclopaedia of Philosophy, available at http://plato.stanford.edu/entries/paternalism/ (last accessed 17 November 2012).

449 Boris Petersdorf, *Eigenverteidigung und aufgedrängte Pflichtverteidigung im formellen Völkerstrafrecht* (Baden-Baden: Nomos Verlagsgesellschaft) 2010, p.93-94.

450 *Cf. United States of America v. William Stewart McDowell* (U.S. Court of Appeals Sixth Circuit), 814 F.2d 245, 16 March 1987, at 251; *United States of America v. Rigoberto Moya-Gomez* (U.S. Court of Appeals Seventh Circuit), 860 F.2d 706, 30 September 1988, at 740-741 (referring to *McDowell*); *United States of America v. Kashani Farhad* (U.S. Court of Appeals Ninth Circuit), 190 F.3d 1097, 13 September 1999, Judge Reinhardt specially concurring, at 1107-1109.

451 *Sejdovic v. Italy* [GC], Application no. 56581/00, Judgment, 01 March 2006, para.86. *See also Padalov c. Bulgarie*, Requête n° 54784/00, Arrêt, 10 novembre 2006, para.47; *Shulepov v. Russia*, Application no. 15435/03, Judgment, 01 December 2008, para.33; *Seyithan Demir v. Turkey*, Application no. 25381/02, Judgment, 28 October 2009, para.38; *Sakhnovskiy v. Russia* [GC], Application no. 21272/03, Judgment, 02 November 2010, para.90.

instant case an alleged waiver of the right to be present at trial, would have to be "established in an unequivocal manner and be attended by minimum safeguards commensurate to its importance".[452] In addition, the waiver of a fair trial guarantee is not to be contrary to any other overriding public interest and it would have to be shown that the defendant was capable of adequately foreseeing the consequences of such waiver.[453] In the case at hand, the European Court did not think that the applicant, without vocational training and of modest background, could have been considered to be able to grasp the implications of any choice to waive the right to counsel in a case that might lead to a death sentence.[454] In a similar vein, the ECtHR considered that a lay person without formal legal training could not be expected to make specific procedural claims and thus the failure to formulate any requests with the necessary specificity could not be interpreted as waiver of a fair trial guarantee.[455]

These decisions indicate a more protective approach adopted before the ECtHR and might provide some indication as to how similar situations could be dealt with before international criminal tribunals. The practical experience in proceedings with self-represented accused for example before the ICTY already indicates that chambers in fact do attempt to strike a proper balance of potentially conflicting rights in order for the issue of a waiver of the right to a fair trial not to arise to begin with.

The implications of the exercise of the right to self-representation which are most often linked to the insufficient mastering of the conduct of international criminal proceedings by *pro se* defendants may endanger the defen-

---

452 *Sejdovic v. Italy* [GC], Application no. 56581/00, Judgment, 01 March 2006, para.86. *See also Galstyan v. Armenia*, Application no. 26986/03, Judgment, 15 February 2008, para.90-91. Note that in the latter decision, the court was split in its not finding a violation of Article 6(3)(c) in conjunction with Article 6(1) of the ECHR: disagreeing with the majority on the basis of doubts as to whether the applicant's waiver was voluntary, and considering the right to legal assistance to form part of the right against self-incrimination, *see* Partly dissenting opinion of Judge Fura-Sandström joined by Judge Zupančič.

453 *Talat Tunç c. Turquie*, Requête n° 32432/96, Arrêt, 27 juin 2007, para.59. *See also Seyithan Demir v. Turkey*, Application no. 25381/02, Judgment, 28 October 2009, para.38; *Sakhnovskiy v. Russia* [GC], Application no. 21272/03, Judgment, 02 November 2010, para.90.

454 *Talat Tunç c. Turquie*, Requête n° 32432/96, Arrêt, 27 juin 2007, para.60.

455 *Sakhnovskiy v. Russia* [GC], Application no. 21272/03, Judgment, 02 November 2010, para.91-92.

dants' right to a trial which is both fair and expeditious.[456] Therefore, it may be necessary to provide accused with the opportunity to contribute to and participate in the preparation and presentation of their defence case without however being driven to endanger their overarching right to a fair trial by exercising the currently recognised right to self-representation. Experience indicates that the decision to exercise the right to self-representation entails a plethora of consequences that are at times substantial and may impact on the right to a fair trial, and are not to be dismissed by mere reference to a conscientious decision of a defendant to exercise this right.[457]

Future proceedings will enable trial and appeals chambers, for example at the ICC, to interpret said right to defend oneself in person in a way which takes due account of both the general fair trial right of an accused and the pitfalls related to the exercise of the right to self-representation. As has been pointed out, this is likely to even enhance the perception of overall fairness of the proceedings:

> "Is it not probable that many consumers of international criminal justice would find it inappropriate to let a psychologically burdened and forensically unskilled accused wage a court room battle with a powerful international prosecutor? Disregarding the insistence of the accused on such a lopsided contest would be regarded in many quarters as perfectly appropriate – especially where the 'equality of arms' between the prosecution and the defence is taken seriously."[458]

2. Interests of other participants in the proceedings

An additional, though not undisputed, factor to be considered in the weighing of interests concerning due process is the question of a right to a fair trial

---

456 Gideon Boas, Self-Representation Before the ICTY. A Case for Reform, 9 *Journal of International Criminal Justice* 53 (2011), at 77-82. For the discussion of the cumulative nature of fair *and* expeditious proceedings *see* Patrick L. Robinson, Ensuring Fair and Expeditious Trials at the International Criminal Tribunal for the Former Yugoslavia, 11(3) *European Journal of International Law* 569 (2000), at 583.

457 *See*, however, Göran Sluiter, 'Fairness and the Interests of Justice'. Illusive Concepts in the *Milošević* Case, 3 *Journal of International Criminal Justice* 9 (2003), at 11 (with regard to the *Milošević* proceedings): "No human-rights violation occurs if an individual of sound mind is offered all tools, but fails – of his own choice – to put up the most effective defence."

458 Mirjan Damaška, Reflections on Fairness in International Criminal Justice, 10 *Journal of International Criminal Justice* 611 (2012), at 619.

enjoyed by the prosecution.[459] In this regard, one must take into account the consideration of the ICTY appeals chamber in the *Omarska camp* case, in which it stated that

> "[p]rocedural equality requires that the concept of a fair trial be applied taking into account the interests of both parties. The Prosecution acts on behalf of and in the interests of the international community [fn. omitted]. Thus, as the international community has an interest in the enforcement of such guarantee, it cannot be deprived of it by the mere circumstance that the Appellant would like to waive his own entitlement to a fair trial."[460]

The appeals chamber itself referred to a decision in the case against Zlatko Aleksovski, in which the ICTY appeals chamber considered that

> "[t]his application of the concept of a fair trial in favour of both parties is understandable because the Prosecution acts on behalf of and in the interests of the community, including the interests of the victims of the offence charged (in cases before the tribunal the Prosecutor acts on behalf of the international community). This principle of equality of arms does not affect the fundamental protections given by the general law or Statute to the accused, [fn. omitted] and the trial proceeds against the background of those fundamental protections. Seen in this way, it is difficult to see how a trial could ever be considered to be fair where the accused is favoured at the expense of the Prosecution beyond a strict compliance with those fundamental protections."[461]

The statement of the appeals chamber in the *Omarska camp* case is of equal importance in the context of the question whether a waiver by the accused of any or all of his or her fair trial rights is, and if so, should, be possible, considering the importance of the safeguard of such rights for the international community. In addition, it is interesting to note that the appeals chamber in *Aleksovski* explicitly referred to the prosecution acting in the interests of, *inter alia*, the victim community.

---

459 *See also* Gideon Boas, The Right to Self-Representation in International and Domestic Criminal Law – Limitations and Qualifications on that Right, in: Hirad Abtahi/Gideon Boas (eds), *The Dynamics of International Criminal Justice. Essays in Honour of Sir Richard May* (Leiden/Boston: Martinus Nijhoff Publishers) 2006, p.39-93, at 88-89.

460 *Prosecutor v. Kvočka et al.*, Case No. IT-98-30/1-AR73.5, Decision on Interlocutory Appeal by the Accused Zoran Žigić Against the Decision of Trial Chamber I dated 5 December 2000, 25 May 2001, para.21.

461 *Prosecutor v. Zlatko Aleksovski,* Case No. IT-95-14/1-AR73, Decision on Prosecutor's Appeal on Admissibility of Evidence, 16 February 1999, para.25.

However, it has to be borne in mind that there are equally arguments to the contrary which reject the claim of a right to a fair trial enjoyed by the prosecution as such or as representative of the international community.[462]

In addition to the factors mentioned above, the ICC is the first international criminal court to provide for an elaborate system of victim participation,[463] concept according to which victim representatives can participate as *de facto* parties to the proceedings, albeit with limited possibilities of direct participation,[464] and only to such an extent as the rights of the defendant and "a fair and impartial trial" are not prejudiced.[465] While similar modes of participation had already been envisaged before hybrid tribunals,[466] before the ICC, with the potential likelihood of facing cases with accused defending themselves, this system adds one more factor to be taken into account in the balancing exercise in case the right of the accused to present his or her defence in person and the interests of justice or rights of other participants are in conflict.[467]

---

462 Salvatore Zappalà, The Rights of Victims v. the Rights of the Accused, 8 *Journal of International Criminal Justice* 137 (2010), at 149: "Despite some perplexing claims according to which the right to a fair trial is seen as a sort of general public interest – which would imply that the proceedings must be fair towards the Prosecution or society at large – it is important to stress that *only the accused has a right to a fair trial.*" (emphasis in the original). *See also*, calling the notion of a fair trial right of the prosecution "eminently contestable": Frédéric Mégret, Beyond "Fairness": Understanding the Determinants of International Criminal Procedure, 14 *UCLA Journal of International Law and Foreign Affairs* 37 (2009), at 39 fn.6.

463 *See* William A. Schabas, *An Introduction to the International Criminal Court* (Cambridge: Cambridge University Press) 3rd edition 2007, p.327, 328.

464 Article 68(3) Rome Statute; Rules 89-93 ICC RPE.

465 Article 68(3) of the Rome Statute reads in full: "Where the personal interests of the victims are affected, the Court shall permit their views and concerns to be presented and considered *at stages of the proceedings determined to be appropriate by the Court and in a manner which is not prejudicial to or inconsistent with the rights of the accused and a fair and impartial tria*l. Such views and concerns may be presented by the legal representatives of the victims where the Court considers it appropriate, in accordance with the Rules of Procedure and Evidence." (emphasis added).

466 *Cf.* the concept of "civil parties", comparable to the "parties civiles" in French proceedings, before the ECCC: Rules 23-23*quinquies* ECCC IR. *See also* Article 17 STL Statute; Rules 86-87 STL RPE.

467 *See*, however – warning that in any such balance important rights of the accused might be "balanced away" – Mirjan Damaška, Reflections on Fairness in International Criminal Justice, 10 *Journal of International Criminal Justice* 611 (2012), at 615: "For this reason, I think, the traditional liberal tilt in favour of defendants' interests should continue in international criminal procedure. The ghost of the inno-

Chambers at the ICC have determined that the requirement of procedural fairness benefits not only the accused, but all participants of the proceedings, *i.e.* also the prosecution and potentially participating victims.[468] However, it has been questioned whether it is even possible to safeguard the rights of the defendant and at the same time take into account interests of victims.[469]

As mentioned above, the appeals chamber at the ICTY found a basis for a right to a fair trial enjoyed by the prosecution in the fact that it acted in the interests of the international and victims' communities. This consideration may become invalid in light of active participation of victims in proceedings for example before the ICC, representing their own interests themselves. Arguably, in this context the prosecution may lose certain protective entitlements as it is less acting for the victims' community than it would be at other tribunals which do not provide for such extensive victim participation. However, the number of victims in fact participating in proceedings will necessarily be limited and is subject to review of specific applications. Therefore, it can be argued that even though victims might be specifically represented at international criminal tribunals in more recent proceedings, the prosecution continues to act also in their name as well as in the interests of the international community.

The preceding discussion shows that judges in international criminal proceedings do in fact consider the potential implications of the exercise of

---

cent men convicted must continue to hover over international criminal justice just as it hovers over domestic criminal law enforcement. It is for good reasons that in enumerating 'fair trial' rights, international human rights documents mention only rights belonging to persons charged with criminal offences." *See also* Mugambi Jouet, Reconciling the Conflicting Rights of Victims and Defendants at the International Criminal Court, 26 *Saint Louis University Public Law Review* 249 (2007), at 250, 279.

468 Situation in Uganda, No. ICC-02/04-01/05, Decision on Prosecutor's Application for Leave to Appeal in part Pre-trial Chamber II's Decision on the Prosecutor's Applications for Warrants of Arrest under Article 58, 19 August 2005, para.31; Situation in Uganda, No. ICC-02/04-01/05, Decision on Prosecutor's Applications for Leave to Appeal dated the 15th day of March and to Suspend or Stay Consideration of Leave to Appeal dated the 11th day of May 2006, 10 July 2006, para.24.

469 Mirjan Damaška, The Competing Visions of Fairness: The Basic Choice for International Criminal Tribunals, 36 *North Carolina Journal of International Law and Commercial Regulation* 365 (2011), at 373. *See also* Brianne N. McGonigle, Bridging the Divides in International Criminal Proceedings: An Examination into the Victim Participation Endeavor of the International Criminal Court, 21 *Florida Journal of International Law* 93 (2009), at 141-142.

the right to self-representation on the overarching right to a fair trial. While no general and preliminary balancing exercise can be detected, trial chambers for example at the ICTY or the SCSL have expressed concerns that an accused, by exercising a choice provided for as part of the overall fair trial guarantee, might thereby endanger a more general notion of that right. Similarly, judges seem to be aware that in addition to the defendant's rights, criminal proceedings of international import equally implicate interests of other participants. While this concern does not justify on its own an outright denial or restriction of the right to self-representation, it informs judicial consideration of requests to exercise this right. Notwithstanding, it does lead back to the arguably underlying concern of presenting accused with the opportunity to actively participate in their proceedings in order to achieve a double-sided purpose: ensure fair proceedings which appreciate defendants to be their subject.

C. Potential pitfalls and actual repercussions of self-representation in the practice of international criminal proceedings

Having examined the tendentially more theoretical judicial interpretations of the nature and scope of the right to self-representation which stand at the beginning of any exercise of this right, the following section will address both concrete and conceivable problems that are being or might be encountered in practice in the course of proceedings with accused presenting their defence in person. The analysis will include matters that could be observed in actual proceedings as well as issues that are likely to arise. An initial examination of the manner in which self-represented defendants are to deal with any and all consequences resulting from their status will be followed by an inquiry into more routine issues to be dealt with, such as language and translation problems; procedural complexities faced by legally inexperienced accused; and more fundamental matters evolving around the question of adequate time and facilities for *pro se* defendants to present their case. The section will serve to illustrate the panoply of complications that – potentially and actually – stem from the exercise of the right to self-representation in international criminal tribunals, thereby laying the groundwork for the argument that a practical implementation of the right to self-representation as interpreted up until now is not realistically feasible without jeopardising the interests of all participants, including above all the accused.

In particular to be assessed at the start of any such inquiry are the actual and hypothetical differences in the treatment of the situation of accused represented by counsel and accused presenting their defence in person. A first matter of discussion is the issue as to whether defendants are and should be held to the same or similar standards as professional defence counsel appearing before international criminal tribunals. This will be of particular interest bearing in mind the hypothesis that the exercise of the right to self-representation without any qualifications and adjustments should potentially not have been accorded the status it currently enjoys to begin with.

The initial decision to analyse will be the clarification provided by the ICTY appeals chamber in *Milošević* that accused who invoke their right to self-representation would have to cope with all – including negative – consequences resulting from this choice.[470]

As mentioned *supra*, the appeals chamber in its decision in *Milošević* did in fact make reference to national practice with regard to the recognition of the right to self-representation and the need for any accused to accept the consequences of the choice to defend oneself, *inter alia* to the U.S. Supreme Court's decision in *Martinez*[471] mentioned above:

> "There is no doubt that, by choosing to conduct his own defence, the Accused deprived himself of resources a well-equipped legal defence team could have provided. *A defendant who decides to represent himself relinquishes many of the benefits associated with representation by counsel.* The legal system's respect for a defendant's decision to forgo assistance of counsel must be reciprocated by the acceptance of responsibility for the disadvantages this choice may bring

---

470 *Prosecutor v. Slobodan Milošević*, Case No. IT-02-54-AR73.6, Decision on the Interlocutory Appeal by the *Amici Curiae* Against the Trial Chamber Order Concerning the Presentation and Preparation of the Defence Case, 20 January 2004, para.19.

471 *Martinez v. Court of Appeal of California, Fourth Appellate District* (U.S. Supreme Court), 528 U.S. 152 (2000), 12 January 2000, at 162: "Additionally, the trial judge is under no duty to provide personal instruction on courtroom procedure or to perform any legal 'chores' for the defendant that counsel would normally carry out."; referring to *McKaskle v. Wiggins* (U.S. Supreme Court), 465 U.S. 168 (1984), 23 January 1984, at 183-184: "A defendant does not have a constitutional right to receive personal instruction from the trial judge on courtroom procedure. Nor does the Constitution require judges to take over chores for a *pro se* defendant that would normally be attended to by trained counsel as a matter of course. *Faretta* recognized as much."

> [fn. omitted]. Where an accused elects self-representation, the concerns about the fairness of the proceedings are, of course, heightened and a Trial Chamber must be particularly attentive to its duty of ensuring that the trial be fair."[472]

Already earlier in the proceedings the presiding judge of the trial chamber had mentioned that the defendant's choice to proceed *pro se* could not be taken as basis to accord him any particular advantages in the preparation of his defence case.[473]

This approach needs to be examined in detail. It indicates that at the time the appeals chamber adopted the position that although, on the one hand, the right to self-representation ought not to be neglected at the level of international criminal proceedings due to its recognition in the national sphere of at least some jurisdictions, the exercise of this right has two sides which any accused choosing it has to be aware of. In some way a "give-and-take" approach, the appeals chamber expressed the view that while an accused is free to conduct his or her own defence, the choice to do so equally means that he or she needs to be reconciled with any disadvantages that may flow from this right and might be inherent in its exercise. Consequently, the reasoning of the appeals chamber that a *pro se* defendant would "relinquish many of the benefits associated with representation by counsel"[474] is frequently referred to in the context of the issue of adequate time and facilities for the preparation and presentation of the defence case.

With this reasoning applied in *Milošević*, the appeals chamber left no doubt that a *pro se* defendant could not expect to be granted any particular privileges in comparison with represented accused, but rather that he or she had to make an informed choice in such respect that he or she would be aware of each and every consequence.

At the same time, however, and in line with the initial concerns regarding the overarching right to a fair trial as discussed before, the appeals chamber was obviously wary of the necessity for chambers to be particularly attentive

---

472 *Prosecutor v. Slobodan Milošević*, Case No. IT-02-54-AR73.6, Decision on the Interlocutory Appeal by the *Amici Curiae* Against the Trial Chamber Order Concerning the Presentation and Preparation of the Defence Case, 20 January 2004, para.19 and fn.45 (emphasis added).

473 *Prosecutor v. Slobodan Milošević*, Case No. IT-02-54-T, Pre-Defence Conference, 02 September 2003, T.25959.

474 *Prosecutor v. Slobodan Milošević*, Case No. IT-02-54-AR73.6, Decision on the Interlocutory Appeal by the *Amici Curiae* Against the Trial Chamber Order Concerning the Presentation and Preparation of the Defence Case, 20 January 2004, para.19.

with regard to safeguarding this right for self-represented accused. Thus, it seems that while *pro se* defendants from a practical point of view are assumed to accept disadvantages in their case presentation, this assumption does not relieve the judges from their overall duty to guarantee fair and expeditious proceedings. This underlying concern is of significance for the subsequent discussion regarding potential limitations of the right to self-representation.

The question of taking responsibility for all, even negative, consequences in case an accused chooses for self-representation, reflects the position taken by the U.S. Supreme Court in *Faretta*. In a similar vein, the judge presiding over the initial appearance of the accused in *Karadžić* made clear that "[i]f an accused would elect to represent himself, then he also should accept responsibility for disadvantages which result from self-representation in the absence of qualified counsel" and that an "accused who represents himself is not given special treatment".[475] The presiding judge ensured recalling this position when the accused complained about the organisation of proofing defence witnesses.[476]

In addition, a differently composed appeals chamber would later in *Karadžić* dismiss the accused's appeal in the context of funding for his legal associates, stating that even though the possibilities offered to the accused to be assisted in the preparation of his defence may not be exactly the same as those available to defence teams of accused represented by counsel, the finding of the chamber in *Milošević* would have to be borne in mind.[477] Subsequently, the appeals chamber in the same case again referred to the decision of the appeals chamber in *Milošević* when it dismissed the defendant's appeal against a trial chamber decision setting a date for the start of trial proceedings.[478]

---

475 *Prosecutor v. Radovan Karadžić*, Case No. IT-95-5/18-I, Initial Appearance, 31 July 2008, T.19.

476 *Prosecutor v. Radovan Karadžić*, Case No. IT-95-5/18-T, Hearing, 12 November 2012, T.30106: "[...] just simply speaking for myself, you have to accept some consequences of your decision to represent yourself, and it's absolutely not necessary for you to proof every and each witness."

477 *Prosecutor v. Radovan Karadžić*, Case No. IT-95-5/18-AR73.2, Decision on Interlocutory Appeal of the Trial Chamber's Decision on Adequate Facilities, 07 May 2009, para.27.

478 *Prosecutor v. Radovan Karadžić*, Case No. IT-95-5/18-AR73.5, Decision on Radovan Karadžić's Appeal of the Decision on Commencement of Trial, 13 October 2009, para.24.

Another illustrative example in the context of the appeals chamber's decision in *Milošević* is the remark of the presiding judge during the pre-trial conference in the case against Zdravko Tolimir. While the trial chamber did not find reasons to terminate the accused's self-representation and appoint counsel at that point in time,[479] the presiding judge explained to the defendant that "[a]s a self-represented accused, you will be held on the same standards as any counsel practising before this Tribunal".[480] Therefore, the accused "must be prepared to address issues as they arise, whether in the context of cross-examination, objections from the opposing party, or questions from the Bench", while the chamber would "closely monitor [his] conduct in this trial and any impact it may have on the progress of this trial", in light of Rule 45*ter* of the ICTY RPE.[481] This latter part is of interest insofar as it refers to the possibility of the trial chamber to appoint counsel to the accused in case it determines this step to be in the interests of justice, as provided for by Rule 45*ter* of the ICTY RPE.

The position of the trial chamber in *Tolimir* appears to go even further than the appeal chamber's decision in *Milošević* since it purports to hold the accused to the same standards as professional defence counsel, not merely that he would not enjoy the same benefits as represented accused flowing from representation by professional counsel. Yet, it appears that the trial judges in *Tolimir* in the course of the proceedings did in fact take into account the accused's lack in legal training, *e.g.* by approaching his conduct of cross-examinations with a certain degree of leeway.[482]

The approach adopted in different cases as outlined above is in line with the initial requirement of making the choice to self-represent "knowingly

---

479 *Prosecutor v. Zdravko Tolimir*, Case No. IT-05-88/2-T, Pre-trial Conference, 25 February 2010, T.317.

480 *Prosecutor v. Zdravko Tolimir*, Case No. IT-05-88/2-T, Pre-trial Conference, 25 February 2010, T.317.

481 *Prosecutor v. Zdravko Tolimir*, Case No. IT-05-88/2-T, Pre-trial Conference, 25 February 2010, T.317-318.

482 *See e.g. Prosecutor v. Zdravko Tolimir*, Case No. IT-05-88/2-T, Hearing, 29 March 2009, T.926; Hearing, 26 April 2010, T.1357; Hearing, 24 June 2010, T.3219; Hearing, 01 July 2010, T.3416; Hearing, 06 July 2010, T.3492; Hearing, 09 July 2010, T.3753; Hearing, 23 August 2010, T.4309; Hearing, 15 September 2010, T.5417-5418; Hearing, 20 September 2010, T.5580-5582; Hearing, 08 October 2010, T.6385-6386; Hearing, 26 October 2010, T.6812-6813; Hearing, 04 November 2010, T.7294-7295; Hearing, 09 November 2010, T.7508; Hearing, 29 November 2010, T.8141; Hearing, 16 December 2010, T.9063. *See also* Hearing, 09 June 2010, T.2611.

and intelligently".[483] At the same time, however, it begs the question of whether an accused ordinarily not proficient in international criminal law and procedure can indeed be held to the same standards as defence counsel who will usually enjoy significant experience in the relevant field. In practice it appears that while chambers are determined to remind defendants that the choice of self-representation does not automatically include an option for more preferential treatment by the bench, at least in the beginning of proceedings more latitude is granted in order to give an accused the time and opportunity necessary for familiarisation with the relevant rules and jurisprudence.

II. Risk of self-incrimination

The discussion above indicates that trial and appeals chambers might exhibit certain latitude with regard to the standards applied in the course of trials with *pro se* defendants. Yet, while this may accommodate a number of concerns, the actual exercise of the right to self-representation still involves potential for abuse and a variety of procedural problems.

One prominent example to be mentioned is the danger that an accused who acts *pro se* might, albeit inadvertently, incriminate him- or herself.[484] For example, the fact of acting as one's own defence counsel will *inter alia* require cross-examination of witnesses, which includes the necessity to put the defence case to the witness in order to establish a foundation for questions.[485] Inevitably, this will often involve factual statements by the party cross-examining the witness, which in case of a self-represented accused could amount to and be interpreted as admissions which the prosecution in pleadings and even judges in their consideration of the evidence might take into account.[486] Thus, the right to remain silent or not to incriminate oneself

---

483 *Cf. Anthony Pasquall Faretta v. State of California* (U.S. Supreme Court), 422 U.S. 806, 30 June 1975, at 835. *See also* for the ECHR: *Melin v. France*, Application no. 12914/87, Judgement, 22 June 1993, para.25: "[…] As he had deliberately waived his right to be assisted by a lawyer, he was under a duty to show diligence himself. […]".

484 *Cf.* Alexander Zahar, Legal Aid, Self-Representation, and the Crisis at the Hague Tribunal, 19 *Criminal Law Forum* 241 (2008), at 246.

485 *See e.g.* Rule 90(H)(ii) ICTY RPE; Rule 90(G)(ii) ICTR RPE; Rule 150(J) STL RPE.

486 *See e.g. Prosecutor v. Vojislav Šešelj*, Case No. IT-03-67-PT, Status Conference, 30 May 2005, T.378: "Mr. Šešelj, I would suggest to you to keep your mouth shut.

needs to be reconciled in practice with the actual requirements of self-representation. In order to strike a careful balance, it has to be addressed in which way potentially self-incriminatory remarks made by an accused in the course of trial ought or ought not be considered. For example, it may have to be clarified whether the prosecution would be in a position to use such statements as evidentiary material or admissions to certain facts, and, if so, which weight could be given to such remarks by the trial chamber subsequently.

In the past, the position has been taken that an accused who exercises the right to self-representation would have to be made aware of the abovementioned complications, even though not all trial chambers necessarily adopted the same approach in actually providing such a warning.[487] In addition, even if a self-represented accused is given such a warning, the exact impact of any such caution is still to be assessed, in light of the fact that no judgement has thus far been rendered in any case with *pro se* defendants.

In *Milošević*, the trial chamber took the initiative of notifying the accused of his right to remain silent and advised him of the possibility that factual statements made by him in court despite the express caution by the bench might be used by the judges in their consideration of the evidence.[488] Sub-

---

Don't jump the gun. Wait until you receive whatever documentation you receive and then if – whatever you have to say, say it after you've taken advice, because sometimes you open your mouth and you do more harm to yourself than you can imagine." *See also Prosecutor v. Radovan Karadžić*, Case No. IT-95-5/18-T, Hearing, 15 April 2010, T.1186; 08 June 2010, T.3519-3520.

487 *Prosecutor v. Slobodan Milošević*, Case No. IT-02-54-T, Order, 19 February 2002, Annex A (d). *See also Prosecutor v. Slobodan Milošević*, Case No. IT-02-54-T, Prosecution Opening Statement, 13 February 2002, T.215-216; *Prosecutor v. Zdravko Tolimir*, Case No. IT-05-88/2-T, Pre-trial Conference, 25 February 2010, T.317-318, T.321-322; *Prosecutor v. Radovan Karadžić*, Case No. IT-95-5/18-T, Prosecution Motion for an Instruction Regarding the Admissibility of Submissions and Statements of the Accused, 23 February 2010.

488 *Prosecutor v. Slobodan Milošević*, Case No. IT-02-54-T, Order, 19 February 2002, Annex A (d): "Other than when giving evidence, you are not obliged to answer questions about the facts of the case, but should be aware that if you make statements about the facts during submissions to the court, such statements may be part of the material considered by the Trial Chamber in reaching its decision on the case." *See also* Prosecution Opening Statement, 13 February 2002, T.215-216; Hearing, 19 February 2002, T.542.

sequently, the prosecution filed similar requests for a warning to be issued to the accused in *Karadžić*[489] and *Tolimir*,[490] respectively.

The difference in the approach taken by the trial chambers is illustrative of the divergence in solutions applied at the ICTY in cases with self-represented accused to be observed in a number of instances: the trial chamber in *Tolimir* read a warning to the accused with the same formulation as employed in the *Milošević* proceedings already at the beginning of the pre-trial conference.[491] In contrast, the trial chamber in *Karadžić* did not discuss the prosecution's request in any further detail until the first evidentiary hearing, *i.e.* after the opening statement by the accused,[492] and gave a similar warning only in an abbreviated form which did not refer to the possibility of the trial chamber to consider any factual statements made by the defendant in court.[493] While the bench in *Karadžić* appeared to see a need to prevent the accused from making statements and comments during the cross-examination of witnesses,[494] the judges clarified at the same time that any statements of the accused made in the course of the proceedings would not be considered as evidence.[495] The trial chamber appeared to be conscious of the fact and its implications that the accused was acting in a double role of both indicted

489 *Prosecutor v. Radovan Karadžić*, Case No. IT-95-5/18-T, Prosecution Motion for an Instruction Regarding the Admissibility of Submissions and Statements of the Accused, 23 February 2010.

490 *Prosecutor v. Zdravko Tolimir*, Case No. IT-05-88/2-PT, Prosecution Motion for an Instruction Regarding the Admissibility of Submissions and Statements of the Accused, 23 February 2010.

491 *Prosecutor v. Zdravko Tolimir*, Case No. IT-05-88/2-T, Pre-trial Conference, 25 February 2010, T.322.

492 *Prosecutor v. Radovan Karadžić*, Case No. IT-95-5/18-T, Defence Opening Statement, 01 March 2010, T.808-903; Defence Opening Statement, 02 March 2002, T.904-993.

493 *Prosecutor v. Radovan Karadžić*, Case No. IT-95-5/18-T, Hearing, 13 April 2010, T.999-1000.

494 *Prosecutor v. Radovan Karadžić*, Case No. IT-95-5/18-T, Hearing, 13 April 2010, T.1084-1085; Hearing, 14 April 2010, T.1115; Hearing, 03 June 2010, T.3294; Hearing, 08 June 2010, T.3519-3520; Hearing, 10 June 2010, T.3645; Hearing, 08 July 2010, T.4954; Hearing, 06 September 2010, T.6207; Hearing, 09 December 2010, T.9480-9481; Hearing, 16 December 2010, T.10012; Hearing, 14 January 2011, T.10234; Hearing, 18 January 2011, T.10470, 10482, 10494; Hearing, 20 January 2011, T.10621-10622.

495 *Prosecutor v. Radovan Karadžić*, Case No. IT-95-5/18-T, Hearing, 03 June 2010, T.3318; Hearing, 15 September 2010, T.6775; Hearing, 16 December 2010, T.10012; Hearing, 18 January 2011, T.10470; Hearing, 10 February 2011, T.11562-11563.

individual and defence counsel.[496] In contrast, it was made clear to the accused in *Šešelj* on more than one occasion that whatever he might say in court could be used against him.[497]

In light of this need to balance the accused's right to self-representation – as part of the overarching right to a fair trial – with the right against self-incrimination, it ought to be questioned how the notion of having to accept all consequences of the choice to defend oneself can be reconciled with the "heightened concern" with regard to a trial being fair as expressed by the appeals chamber in *Milošević*.

On the one hand chambers deem it necessary to caution defendants for example with regard to the right to remain silent, thereby taking a protective and proactive role in order to safeguard the accused's rights. Nevertheless, judges often leave no doubt from the very beginning of the proceedings that accused, having consciously elected to conduct their defence in person, would be held to the same standards as professional counsel. This may consequently also involve the obligation for a defendant to regularly make factual assertions in the context of cross-examinations.

This potential double role to be played by the trial chamber leads to the question how far a bench can and should go in either direction without endangering its role of an impartial arbiter in the proceedings. As will be discussed *infra*, the question arises whether judges should give detailed instructions to *pro se* defendants for example with regard to the manner in which a cross-examination is to be conducted, or whether, in case the accused is assisted by professional legal advisors, the bench should limit itself to referring the defendant to receive adequate advice from his or her legal associates. Despite the warning at times given to self-represented defendants that they would be held to the same standards as professional defence attorneys, it does not seem feasible for a chamber not to monitor closely an accused's conduct during the proceedings, and caution him or her as to the potential

496 *Prosecutor v. Radovan Karadžić*, Case No. IT-95-5/18-T, Hearing, 01 November 2011, T.20685, 20686-20687: "[…] I don't think you have to take the rather schizophrenic view of actually dividing yourself into defendant and lawyer in the – in your language. We understand both."

497 *Prosecutor v. Vojislav Šešelj*, Case No. IT-03-67-PT, Initial Appearance, T.4: "But I have to warn you at the same time, everything you may say in courtroom may be used even against you in evidence."; *Prosecutor v. Vojislav Šešelj*, Case No. IT-03-67-T, Hearing, 11 December 2007, T.2020: "[…] He knows this very well. He knows that everything he is saying can be used. He knows this."

consequences whenever necessary in order to safe-guard the overarching fair trial guarantee.

III. Complexity of proceedings and (lack of) legal knowledge

1. Use of legal framework by self-represented accused

Additional potential problems that might surface in cases with self-represented accused revolve around the lack of knowledge regarding the manner in which to conduct proceedings in case a defendant is not legally trained. The subject matter and legal questions arising in international criminal proceedings are often of a complex nature.[498] Not only the procedure in court and for filings needs to be mastered, but also the elements of the crimes at stake digested and analysed in order to counter allegations put forward by the prosecution. The volume and quality of work involved is likely to present problems even for accused who are in fact legally trained – for instance Slobodan Milošević and Vojislav Šešelj –, not to mention accused who see themselves confronted with the legal and factual complexities of their own trials for the first time in detention when preparing for and in the course of the proceedings. For both categories of accused, the procedure might further create difficulties insofar as even if they are familiar with one legal system, they would most likely not be conversant in the *sui generis* mechanisms observed before international criminal tribunals which developed over years of operation.[499] In practice, this concern even provoked the argument that a self-represented accused would in fact require more financial aid to engage legal advisors than accused represented by counsel, since any assisting team would have to include experts on both common and civil law systems.[500]

Apart from the undisputed factual and legal volume which is to be processed in the course of international criminal proceedings, self-represented accused, even if lawyers by training in their respective national systems,

---

498 *See* Gideon Boas, Self-Representation Before the ICTY. A Case for Reform, 9 *Journal of International Criminal Justice* 53 (2011), at 79-81.

499 *See e.g.* remark by accused in *Prosecutor v. Radovan Karadžić*, Case No. IT-95-5/18-T, Status Conference, 28 January 2010, T.722.

500 *Prosecutor v. Radovan Karadžić*, Case No. IT-95-5/18, Status Conference, 19 January 2009, T.93.

might not be familiar with the procedures to be observed.[501] This further relates to the potential difficulties with which *pro se* defendants will be confronted, and the need to accommodate the accused in the course of the proceedings accordingly.[502]

However, less consideration has been given to more recent cases which seem to support the idea that self-represented accused are not only well-advised as to the meaning and significance of the procedural system and the manner to work with it, but that they also do indeed utilise the procedural framework of international criminal trials in their own manner.

For example in the *Karadžić* proceedings, one could observe an extensive use of requests by the accused pursuant to Rule 66(B)[503] of the ICTY RPE,[504] as well as numerous requests under Rule 54*bis* of the ICTY RPE, concerned with orders directed to states for the production of documents. Within merely a few months and subsequently on a continuing basis throughout the proceedings, more than 20 motions for binding orders to be issued to governments and international organisations like NATO were filed by the accused,[505]

---

501 *Cf.* Mark S. Ellis, The Evolution of Defense Counsel Appearing Before the International Criminal Tribunal for the Former Yugoslavia, 37 *New England Law Review* 949 (2003), at 957; Patricia M. Wald, *Tyrants on Trial. Keeping Order in the Courtroom* (New York: Open Society Justice Institute) 2009, at 37-38. *See also* Mirjan Damaška, What is the Point of International Criminal Justice, 83 *Chicago-Kent Law Review* 329 (2008), at 338.

502 *Cf.* Patricia M. Wald, *Tyrants on Trial. Keeping Order in the Courtroom* (New York: Open Society Justice Institute) 2009, at 54; Eugene Cerruti, Self-Representation in the International Arena: Removing a False Right to Spectacle, 40 *Georgetown Journal of International Law* 919 (2009), at 974, 978. *See also* Human Rights Watch, *The Balkans: Weighing the Evidence. Lessons from the Milosevic Trial*, Volume 18, No.10(D), December 2006, at 60-61.

503 Rule 66(B) ICTY RPE reads: "The Prosecutor shall, on request, permit the defence to inspect any books, documents, photographs and tangible objects in the Prosecutor's custody or control, which are material to the preparation of the defence, or are intended for use by the Prosecutor as evidence at trial or were obtained from or belonged to the accused."

504 *See Prosecutor v. Radovan Karadžić*, Case No. IT-95-5/18-T, Prosecution's Further Response to Karadžić's Motion for Postponement of Trial Pursuant to Trial Chamber's Order of 03 February 2010 with Confidential Appendices A-F, 09 February 2010, para.5-16; Submission Pursuant to Trial Chamber's Order Setting Deadlines for Further Submissions, 22 February 2010, para.3; Prosecution Request for Reconsideration of Trial Chamber's 11 November 2010 Decision, 01 December 2010, para.13 fn.11 and Appendix A.

505 *Prosecutor v. Radovan Karadžić*, Case No. IT-95-5/18-PT, Motion for Binding Order: Government of Norway, 08 July 2009; Motion for Binding Order: Govern-

many of which were withdrawn once the respective governments provided documents or other material according to the requests, or notified the defence that it did not possess any of the requested information.[506] It is of note that

ment of Belgium, 20 July 2009; Motion for Binding Order to NATO, 22 July 2009; Motion for Binding Order: Government of Austria, 03 August 2009; Motion for Binding Order: Government of Italy, 03 August 2009; Motion for Binding Order: Government of Bangladesh, 05 August 2009; Motion for Binding Order: Government of Malta, 05 August 2009; Motion for Binding Order: Government of Malaysia, 03 August 2009 (filed: 10 August 2009); Motion for Binding Order: Government of Pakistan, 10 August 2009; Motion for Binding Order: Government of Germany, 12 August 2009; Motion for Binding Order: Government of Poland, 12 August 2009; Motion for Binding Order: Government of Egypt, 14 August 2009; Motion for Binding Order: Government of Jordan, 14 August 2009; Motion for Binding Order: Government of Turkey, 24 August 2009; Motion for Binding Order: Government of France, 24 August 2009; Motion for Binding Order: Government of Iran, 26 August 2009; Motion for Binding Order: Government of Bosnia, 31 August 2009; Motion for Binding Order: Government of Denmark, 02 September 2009; Motion for Binding Order: Government of Sweden, 04 September 2009; Motion for Binding Order: Government of Croatia, 11 September 2009; Motion for Binding Order: Government of The Netherlands, 11 September 2009; Motion for Binding Order: Government of the United Kingdom, 11 September 2009; Motion for Binding Order: Government of the United States of America, 11 September 2009; Motion for Binding Order: Government of Greece, 28 September 2009; *Prosecutor v. Radovan Karadžić*, Case No. IT-95-5/18-T, Motion for Binding Order: Government of Belgium, 16 August 2010 (filed: 17 August 2010); Motion for Binding Order: European Union, 19 October 2010; Motion for Binding Order: Government of Venezuela, 01 November 2010; Motion for Binding Order: United Nations, 01 November 2010; Motion for Binding Order: United Nations and NATO, 29 November 2010; Second Motion for Binding Order: Government of Iran, 07 December 2010; Second Motion for Binding Order: United States of America, 07 December 2010; Motion for Binding Order: United Arab Emirates, 18 January 2011; Motion for Binding Order: Saudi Arabia, 18 January 2011; Third Motion for Binding Order: United States of America, 24 January 2011; Third Motion for Binding Order: Government of Bosnia, 05 April 2011; Fourth Motion for Binding Order: United States of America, 12 April 2011; Fourth Motion for Binding Order: Government of Bosnia, 07 June 2011.

506 *Prosecutor v. Radovan Karadžić*, Case No. IT-95-5/18-PT, Withdrawal of Motion for Binding Order to NATO, 10 August 2009; Withdrawal of Motion for Binding Order to Bangladesh, 24 August 2009; Withdrawal of Motion for Binding Order: Government of Jordan, 04 September 2009; Withdrawal of Motion for Binding Order: Government of Malta, 22 September 2009; Withdrawal of Motion for Binding Order: Government of Malaysia, 28 September 2009; Withdrawal of Motion for Binding Order: Government of Sweden, 30 September 2009; Withdrawal of Motion for Binding Order: Government of the United Kingdom, 14 October 2009;

only few governments objected to a specific request on legal grounds,[507] while most of the governments and institutions partly provided documents falling under any specific request or merely notified the defence team that they had no such material in their possession. Several hearings were held in this context, with representatives of selected governments invited to be present, in order to discuss the (non-) cooperation by states and clarify any potential issues.[508]

As is illustrated by a decision of the trial chamber in *Karadžić* considering the matter in the context of adequate time and facilities for the defence

---

Withdrawal of Motion for Binding Order: Government of Denmark, 21 October 2009; *Prosecutor v. Radovan Karadžić*, Case No. IT-95-5/18-T, Withdrawal of Motion for Binding Order: Government of Egypt, 02 November 2009; Withdrawal of Motion for Binding Order: Government of Greece, 02 November 2009; Withdrawal of Motion for Binding Order: Government of Turkey, 02 November 2009; Withdrawal of Motion for Binding Order: Government of Austria, 04 November 2009; Withdrawal of Motion for Binding Order: Government of Belgium, 30 November 2009; Withdrawal of Motion for Binding Order: Government of Norway, 30 November 2009; Withdrawal of Motion for Binding Order: Government of Poland, 01 December 2009; Withdrawal of Motion for Binding Order: Government of Pakistan, 27 January 2010; Withdrawal of Motion for Binding Order: Government of Italy, 19 March 2010; Withdrawal of Motion for Binding Order: Government of The Netherlands, 13 April 2010; Withdrawal of Second Motion for Binding Order: Government of Belgium, 10 September 2010; Withdrawal of Motion for Binding Order: Government of Canada, 06 January 2011; Withdrawal of Motion for Binding Order: European Union, 24 February 2011; Withdrawal of Second Motion for Binding Order: Government of Denmark, 05 April 2011; Withdrawal of Second Motion for Binding Order: Government of Bosnia, 11 April 2011; Withdrawal of Fourth Motion for Binding Order: United States of America, 02 May 2011; Withdrawal of Motion for Binding Order: United Arab Emirates, 18 May 2011.

507 *Prosecutor v. Radovan Karadžić*, Case No. IT-95-5/18-PT, Answer to the Request for Motion for a Binding Order to be Issued to the Government of the Federal Republic of Germany for the Production of Documents Pursuant to Rule 54*bis*, 25 September 2009; Response of the United States of America to the Trial Chamber's 13 April 2011 "Invitation to the United States of America", 28 April 2011. In response to the filing from the U.S., the accused withdrew his motion, *see* Withdrawal of Fourth Motion for Binding Order: United States of America, 02 May 2011, even though maintaining that the existence of the material concerned was "beyond question" and that "[a]n apology, rather than an attack, would have been a more appropriate response", *cf.* para.3.

508 *Prosecutor v. Radovan Karadžić*, Case No. IT-95-5/18-T, Rule 54 *bis* Hearing, 15 February 2010, T.743-804; Rule 54 *bis* Hearing, 15 October 2010, T.7961-7988; Rule 54 *bis* Hearing, 10 May 2011, T.13862-13878.

preparation,[509] this example is not to suggest that an accused would not be entitled to make such requests, since it will be his choice to determine the potential relevance of material for his defence case. Rather, the example is intended to illustrate that an accused who is indeed making use of the ICTY's procedural framework should on the other hand not complain about the scarcity of resources accorded to the defence preparation, *i.e.* he or she should not lose sight of the relevant proportions. Deciding on a motion filed by the accused in *Karadžić* requesting postponement of the trial,[510] *inter alia* in order to analyse material disclosed by the prosecution,[511] the chamber determined that the "overwhelming proportion" of the material disclosed to the accused in the course of the relevant period concerned requests pursuant to Rule 66(B) of the ICTY RPE.[512] The bench considered that an accused "cannot be penalised for exercising in a reasonable way this entitlement provided for under the Rules" and that the chamber has the duty to balance the accused's right with the need to ensure a fair and expeditious trial.[513] In addition, the trial chamber determined that, in light of the fact that the defence could make such requests at any time of the proceedings, a deadline for the related disclosure could not be set, since otherwise the defence would be able to control the start of trial by deferring requests to the last minute and simply demanding more time for review of disclosed material.[514] This conclusion suggests that the trial chamber was well aware of the potential leverage on the side of the self-represented – but obviously well advised – accused.

There are further examples which indicate that in practice, self-represented accused are well aware of the opportunities created by using the relevant statutes, rules of procedure and evidence, jurisprudence and legal concepts.

509 *Prosecutor v. Radovan Karadžić*, Case No. IT-95-5/18-T, Decision on the Accused's Motion for Postponement of Trial, 26 February 2010.

510 *Prosecutor v. Radovan Karadžić*, Case No. IT-95-5/18-T, Motion for Postponement of Trial, 01 February 2010.

511 *Prosecutor v. Radovan Karadžić*, Case No. IT-95-5/18-T, Supplemental Submission on Motion for Postponement of Trial Following President's Decision, 22 February 2010, para.3.

512 *Prosecutor v. Radovan Karadžić*, Case No. IT-95-5/18-T, Decision on the Accused's Motion for Postponement of Trial, 26 February 2010, para.34.

513 *Prosecutor v. Radovan Karadžić*, Case No. IT-95-5/18-T, Decision on the Accused's Motion for Postponement of Trial, 26 February 2010, para.37.

514 *Prosecutor v. Radovan Karadžić*, Case No. IT-95-5/18-T, Decision on the Accused's Motion for Postponement of Trial, 26 February 2010, para.37.

The unprecedented use of Rule 66(B) of the ICTY RPE and requests to governments or international organisations by the accused in *Karadžić* thus far are only one example. Further illustration of this hypothesis can be found in written submissions by the defence the purpose of which might not necessarily be self-explanatory at first sight.

For example, the defence in *Karadžić* once attempted to utilise the common law concept of collateral estoppel in order to have one scheduled incident stricken from the indictment.[515] The trial chamber observed that the filing was influenced by the accused's legal advisor and refused to acknowledge the applicability of this specific concept in the context of procedure before the ICTY in a rather unmistakable decision.[516]

In another motion, the accused requested a stay of the proceedings arguing a violation of the burden of proof and presumption of innocence in light of the use of judicial notice of adjudicated facts and admission of evidence pursuant to Rules 92*bis* and 92*quater* of the ICTY RPE.[517] However, the trial chamber again did not consider the arguments of the defendant to be valid, and found them to be repetitive of arguments dismissed earlier.[518]

Another significant and long-lasting topic that was to involve significant resources on all sides concerned the matter of disclosure and alleged disclosure violations by the prosecution. The defence in *Karadžić* submitted a considerable number of motions requesting the trial chamber to find violations of disclosure obligations, with 74 of such motions presented between May 2010[519] and October 2012.[520]

---

515 *Prosecutor v. Radovan Karadžić*, Case No. IT-95-5/18-T, Motion to Strike Allegation G9 on Grounds of Collateral Estoppel, 04 March 2010.

516 *Prosecutor v. Radovan Karadžić*, Case No. IT-95-5/18-T, Decision on Accused's Motion to Strike Scheduled Shelling Incident on Grounds of Collateral Estoppel, 31 March 2010, para.9.

517 *Prosecutor v. Radovan Karadžić*, Case No. IT-95-5/18-T, Motion for Stay of Proceedings: Violation of Burden of Proof and Presumption of Innocence, 01 April 2010.

518 *Prosecutor v. Radovan Karadžić*, Case No. IT-95-5/18-T, Decision on Motion for Stay of Proceedings, 08 April 2010, para.5, 6.

519 *Prosecutor v. Radovan Karadžić*, Case No. IT-95-5/18-T, Second Motion for Finding of Disclosure Violation and Remedial Measures, 14 May 2010. The first motion was presented orally: Hearing, 22 April 2010, T.1450-1453.

520 *Prosecutor v. Radovan Karadžić*, Case No. IT-95-5/18-T, Motion for Finding of Disclosure Violation and for Remedial Measures -17 *bis*, 25 November 2010; Fifty-Sixth Motion for Finding of Disclosure Violation and for Sanctions: Witness KDZ029, 18 August 2011; 74th Motion for Finding of Disclosure Violation: De-

In light of the numerous litigations concerning alleged disclosure violations by the prosecution which put a significant strain on the resources of all participants, the trial chamber demanded the accused to file motions on the specific matter of alleged disclosure violations on a monthly basis, rather than each time an issue might arise, unless the matter at hand required urgent resolution.[521] While the accused did begin filing consolidated motions on a once-a-month basis,[522] the defence nonetheless equally continued its pattern of submitting similar motions in addition to the monthly filings.[523] Consequently, the bench "reiterate[d] its request that unless a motion seeks an urgent remedy, the Accused should conserve the resources of all parties by filing consolidated disclosure violation motions on a monthly basis".[524]

---

murenko Material, 22 October 2012. The 50th motion was presented orally, and supplemented in writing: *See* Hearing, 03 June 2011, T.14190-14196; Annexes to Fiftieth Motion for Finding of Disclosure Violation and Motion for Seventh Suspension of Proceedings, 03 June 2011; Memorandum in Support of Fiftieth Motion for Finding of Disclosure Violation and Motion for Seventh Suspension of Proceedings, 06 June 2011. The 57th and 60th motion were equally presented orally: *See* Hearing, 02 September 2011, T.18211-18212; Hearing, 20 October 2011, T.20302-20303; Memorandum in Support of Sixtieth Motion for Finding of Disclosure Violation (Ivo Atlija), 21 October 2011. Motions numbered 23, 25, 34 were withdrawn subsequently: Withdrawal of Twenty-Third Motion for Finding of Disclosure Violation and for Remedial Measures, 27 October 2010; Withdrawal of Twenty-Fifth Motion for Finding of Disclosure Violation and for Remedial Measures, 29 October 2010; Withdrawal of Thirty Fourth Disclosure Violation Motion, 07 February 2011.

521 *Prosecutor v. Radovan Karadžić*, Case No. IT-95-5/18-T, Decision on the Accused's Thirty-Second, Thirty-Third, Thirty-Fifth and Thirty-Sixth Disclosure Violation Motions, 24 February 2011, para.23.

522 *Prosecutor v. Radovan Karadžić*, Case No. IT-95-5/18-T, Forty-Third Motion for Finding of Disclosure Violation and for Remedial Measures (February 2011), 02 March 2011.

523 *Prosecutor v. Radovan Karadžić*, Case No. IT-95-5/18-T, Forty-Fourth Motion for Finding of Disclosure Violation and for Admission of Statement of Rajko Koprivica Pursuant to Rule 92 *Quater*, 08 March 2011; Forty-Fifth Motion for Finding of Disclosure Violation and for Remedial Measures (Batch 576), 16 March 2011; Forty-Sixth Motion for Finding of Disclosure Violation and for Sanctions: March 2011 – 66(A)(ii), 05 April 2011; Forty-Seventh Motion for Finding of Disclosure Violation and for Further Suspension of Proceedings (March 2011 – Rule 68), 19 April 2011.

524 *Prosecutor v. Radovan Karadžić*, Case No. IT-95-5/18-T, Decision on Accused's Forty-Third to Forty-Fifth Disclosure Violation Motions, 08 April 2011, para.36.

Remedial measures that were requested in the motions included, *inter alia*, suspension of the proceedings for three months[525] and exclusion of the evidence of witnesses concerned.[526] Eventually, the accused demanded to be granted a new trial as both remedy and sanction to the "cumulative prejudice" he allegedly suffered from the combined disclosure violations.[527]

Having granted a shorter period of suspension earlier,[528] the trial chamber ruled in additional separate decisions that certain witnesses should not be called before a specific date,[529] and furthermore suspended the proceedings for the period of one month towards the end of 2010:[530] rather than granting this suspension on the basis of concrete findings of disclosure violations on the part of the prosecution, the trial chamber found "that the sheer volume of this material is such that it is in the interests of justice to suspend the proceedings temporarily".[531] At the time, the trial chamber showed itself "increasingly troubled by the potential cumulative effect of such late disclosure" and reminded the prosecution that "the size and complexity of this

---

525 *Prosecutor v. Radovan Karadžić*, Case No. IT-95-5/18-T, Twentieth Motion for Finding of Disclosure Violation and for Remedial Measures, 05 October 2010, para.22; Twenty-Third Motion for Finding of Disclosure Violation and for Remedial Measures, 12 October 2010, para.12; Twenty-Fourth Motion for Finding of Disclosure Violation and for Remedial Measures, 13 October 2010, para.18.

526 *Prosecutor v. Radovan Karadžić*, Case No. IT-95-5/18-T, Twenty-Second Motion for Finding of Disclosure Violation and for Remedial Measures, 07 October 2010, para.16.

527 *Prosecutor v. Radovan Karadžić*, Case No. IT-95-5/18-T, Motion for New Trial for Disclosure Violations, 13 August 2012, para.1. The trial chamber dismissed the motion: Decision on Accused's Motion for New Trial for Disclosure Violations, 03 September 2012.

528 *Prosecutor v. Radovan Karadžić*, Case No. IT-95-5/18-T, Oral Ruling, 13 September 2010, T.6592-6594. *See also* Decision on Accused's Seventeenth Motion for Finding of Disclosure Violation and for Remedial Measures, 29 September 2010, para.7.

529 *Prosecutor v. Radovan Karadžić*, Case No. IT-95-5/18-T, Decision on Accused's Eighteenth to Twenty-First Disclosure Violation Motions, 02 November 2010, para.43, 45(a).

530 *Prosecutor v. Radovan Karadžić*, Case No. IT-95-5/18-T, Oral Ruling, 03 November 2010, T.8906-8909. *See also* Decision on Accused's Twenty-Second, Twenty-Fourth and Twenty-Sixth Disclosure Violation Motions, 11 November 2010, para.40-41.

531 *Prosecutor v. Radovan Karadžić*, Case No. IT-95-5/18-T, Oral Ruling, 03 November 2010, T.8907:9-10.

case is not an excuse for its failure to properly organise itself to ensure that disclosure is carried out in accordance with the Rules".[532]

In the course of a previously granted suspension of the proceedings, the accused requested a further adjournment for several months before the start of a new component of the case in order to review potentially exculpatory material.[533] The accused's legal advisor indicated to the trial chamber that the volume and pace of disclosure at that time necessitated deployment of resources and time to complete the necessary review of any disclosed material.[534] Shortly thereafter, the defence moved for a further suspension of the proceedings for three months in order to review and assess the potentially exculpatory material disclosed by the prosecution in early 2011.[535] The material had been disclosed in compliance with an earlier decision by the trial chamber setting certain deadlines for specific categories of disclosure material.[536]

The prosecution argued that a three-month suspension of the proceedings was "excessive"[537] and that "[b]ased on a more realistic estimate of spending an average of ten minutes on each item in order to assess the material as a whole and identify the priority items, seven people could review the 1867 disclosed items within approximately one week."[538]

However, the trial chamber granted the accused a suspension of the proceedings for a period of six weeks in order to conduct the necessary review.[539]

---

532 *Prosecutor v. Radovan Karadžić*, Case No. IT-95-5/18-T, Oral Ruling, 03 November 2010, T.8908:3-7.

533 *Prosecutor v. Radovan Karadžić*, Case No. IT-95-5/18-T, Response to Prosecution Motion for Extension of Rule 68 Deadline, 07 December 2010, para.9.

534 *Prosecutor v. Radovan Karadžić*, Case No. IT-95-5/18-T, Hearing, 28 January 2011, T.10904-10905.

535 *Prosecutor v. Radovan Karadžić*, Case No. IT-95-5/18-T, Motion for Fourth Suspension of the Proceedings, 02 February 2011, para.1.

536 *Prosecutor v. Radovan Karadžić*, Case No. IT-95-5/18-T, Decision on Prosecution's Request for Reconsideration of Trial Chamber's 11 November 2010 Decision, 10 December 2010, para.17(b).

537 *Prosecutor v. Radovan Karadžić*, Case No. IT-95-5/18-T, Prosecution's Response to Karadžić's Motion for Fourth Suspension of Proceedings, 08 February 2011, para.8.

538 *Prosecutor v. Radovan Karadžić*, Case No. IT-95-5/18-T, Prosecution's Response to Karadžić's Motion for Fourth Suspension of Proceedings, 08 February 2011, para.12.

539 *Prosecutor v. Radovan Karadžić*, Case No. IT-95-5/18-T, Oral Ruling, 10 February 2011, T.11474-11476.

Even before the start of the scheduled six-week recess, the defence filed a further motion to extend the granted suspension for another six weeks in light of additional disclosure material to be reviewed by the accused.[540] The trial chamber granted an extension of the six-week period for an additional two weeks, reiterating "its recent observations and concerns about the impact of the Prosecution's inadequate approach to its disclosure obligations on the smooth conduct of this trial" and noted "that this further suspension is the latest product of those failings".[541] Shortly thereafter, during the suspension of the proceedings as granted by the trial chamber, the defendant requested the extension of the suspension for an additional eight weeks,[542] arguing that the documents specifically referred to in his motion were "just the tip of the disclosure violation iceberg".[543]

Eventually, the trial chamber ordered the prosecution to file a detailed report outlining its disclosure practices and measures taken to remedy potential flaws in the system, in order "to satisfy the Chamber that everything has been done to ensure that the smooth conduct of these proceedings will not be affected by continuing issues surrounding disclosure".[544]

In addition to suspensions of the proceedings, the accused requested the trial chamber to not only expressly find a disclosure violation on the part of the prosecution, but also argued that in light of the alleged violation of the trial chamber's disclosure orders, an "adverse inference" should be drawn with regard to the issue of *mens rea* concerning one count of the indictment.[545] Similarly, the defendant submitted that the trial chamber should contemplate reduction of the scope of the case since the "cumulative effect" of the alleged disclosure violations would demonstrate "that the prosecution

---

540 *Prosecutor v. Radovan Karadžić*, Case No. IT-95-5/18-T, Motion for Fifth Suspension of the Proceedings, 08 March 2011, para.1, 11.

541 *Prosecutor v. Radovan Karadžić*, Case No. IT-95-5/18-T, Decision on Accused's Motion for Fifth Suspension of the Proceedings, 17 March 2011, para.9.

542 *Prosecutor v. Radovan Karadžić*, Case No. IT-95-5/18-T, Forty-Seventh Motion for Finding of Disclosure Violation and for Further Suspension of Proceedings (March 2011 – Rule 68), 19 April 2011, para.10.

543 *Prosecutor v. Radovan Karadžić*, Case No. IT-95-5/18-T, Forty-Seventh Motion for Finding of Disclosure Violation and for Further Suspension of Proceedings (March 2011 – Rule 68), 19 April 2011, para.3.

544 *Prosecutor v. Radovan Karadžić*, Case No. IT-95-5/18-T, Decision on Accused's Forty-Ninth and Fiftieth Disclosure Violation Motions, 30 June 2011, para.54.

545 *Prosecutor v. Radovan Karadžić*, Case No. IT-95-5/18-T, Forty-Eighth Motion for Finding of Disclosure Violation and for Sanctions (April 2011), 02 May 2011, para.11.

is unable to manage a case of this scope".[546] According to the accused, this would also reduce the time needed by both prosecution and defence to present their respective cases.[547] Shortly thereafter, the accused suggested that by way of sanction for the alleged disclosure violation, the documents supposedly containing exculpatory material could be admitted into evidence,[548] and submitted that the trial chamber should consider holding a hearing to discuss potential reasons for alleged failure of the prosecution to disclose all exculpatory material.[549]

Similarly, in light of the continued allegations of disclosure violations, the accused suggested that a "special master" be appointed with the task of supervising the prosecution's disclosure, and that the proceedings should be suspended until such time as any disclosure obligations would have been fulfilled.[550] According to the defence, the continuation of the proceedings under the circumstances prevailing at the time would be "unsafe", so that such a measure would be required in order to ensure the trial to be fair.[551]

On a side note, it is to be observed that the concept of a "special master" to oversee the disclosure practices of a party to the proceedings had previously been discussed in proceedings before the ICTR.[552] It will not be surprising

---

546 *Prosecutor v. Radovan Karadžić*, Case No. IT-95-5/18-T, Forty-Eighth Motion for Finding of Disclosure Violation and for Sanctions (April 2011), 02 May 2011, para.12. *See also* Forty-Ninth Motion for Finding of Disclosure Violation and for Sanctions (May 2011), 01 June 2011, para.30.

547 *Prosecutor v. Radovan Karadžić*, Case No. IT-95-5/18-T, Forty-Eighth Motion for Finding of Disclosure Violation and for Sanctions (April 2011), 02 May 2011, para.12.

548 *Prosecutor v. Radovan Karadžić*, Case No. IT-95-5/18-T, Forty-Ninth Motion for Finding of Disclosure Violation and for Sanctions (May 2011), 01 June 2011, para.28.

549 *Prosecutor v. Radovan Karadžić*, Case No. IT-95-5/18-T, Forty-Ninth Motion for Finding of Disclosure Violation and for Sanctions (May 2011), 01 June 2011, para.29.

550 *Prosecutor v. Radovan Karadžić*, Case No. IT-95-5/18-T, Memorandum in Support of Fiftieth Motion for Finding of Disclosure Violation and Motion for Seventh Suspension of Proceedings, 06 June 2011, para.2, 12, 19.

551 *Prosecutor v. Radovan Karadžić*, Case No. IT-95-5/18-T, Memorandum in Support of Fiftieth Motion for Finding of Disclosure Violation and Motion for Seventh Suspension of Proceedings, 06 June 2011, para.13, 19.

552 *See Prosecutor v. Karemera et al.*, Case No. ICTR-98-44-T, Decision on Joseph Nzirorera's Eleventh Notice of Rule 68 Violation and Motion for Stay of Proceedings, 11 September 2008, para.27, 31; Decision on Joseph Nzirorera's 13th, 14th, and 15th Notices of Rule 68 Violation and Motions for Remedial and Punitive

in this context that the defence counsel of the party in the proceedings at the source of such disclosure violation submissions also acted as principal legal advisor to the accused in *Karadžić*.

The requests, litigation and procedures surrounding disclosure that were adopted or imposed in the *Karadžić* proceedings involved the deployment of significant amounts of resources in particular on the side of the prosecution.[553] Presumably, the defence strategy involved forcing the prosecution to concentrate a substantial part of its resources on dealing with alleged disclosure violations, *i.e.* questions of a procedural nature, thereby attempting to distract it from preparing and presenting its case in chief in a way it otherwise might have been able to do. In addition, the tactic of building a continuous record of alleged disclosure violations purportedly impacting the accused's ability to prepare his defence – and thus affecting his right to a fair trial – may have been embarked upon in order to set the scene for future arguments to be advanced during the appeals stage of the case. The delays in the proceedings – initiated in part on the basis of suspensions requested by the accused himself – were probably less of a focus, even though they did give the defence the opportunity to occasionally recalibrate their efforts. However, by turning procedural aspects into the focal point of (public) attention, the substance and factual content of the proceedings as presented by the prosecution were necessarily eclipsed. For an accused who seemed to primarily fight a battle of public opinion,[554] this appears to be an evident defence strategy to choose.

Measures: ZF, Michel Bakuzakundi, and Tharcisse Renzaho, 18 February 2009, para.1, 32; Decision on Prosecutor's Rule 68(D) Application and Joseph Nzirorera's 12th Notice of Rule 68 Violation, 26 March 2009, para.22, 27; Decision on Joseph Nzirorera's 23rd Notice of Rule 66 Violation and Motion for Remedial and Punitive Measures: Witness ALG, 30 March 2009, para.1; Decision on Joseph Nzirorera's 21st Notice of Rule 66 Violation and Motion for Remedial and Punitive Measures: Théophile Urikumwenimana, 22 April 2009, para.6.

553 *See, e.g., Prosecutor v. Radovan Karadžić*, Case No. IT-95-5/18-T, Prosecution's Disclosure Report, 27 July 2011 (filed: 28 July 2011), para.15.

554 *See e.g. Prosecutor v. Radovan Karadžić*, Case No. IT-95-5/18-T, Defence Rule 84*bis* Statement, 16 October 2012, T.28849-28850, 28881. *See also* Mark Lewis, The Trial of Radovan Karadzic: The Accused Takes up his Own Defense, 01 November 2012, available at http://world.time.com/2012/11/01/the-trial-of-radovan-karadzic-the-accused-takes-up-his-own-defense/#ixzz2B3FabTJV (last accessed 02 November 2012): "[…] It also means the former Bosnian Serb leader delays, for as long as possible, the conviction that Robinson says even Karadzic knows is inevitable and his probably lifetime jail sentence."

Given that the above observations on the use of specific rules in the framework of the ICTY Rules of Procedure and Evidence apparently concern in particular proceedings in the most recent cases, the phenomenon might be evidence of a newly appreciated and well-functioning cooperation between self-represented accused and their legal associates, who seem to have ceased being as invisible as they used to be in previous trials. As will be examined in the context of an analysis of the role(s) to be played by legal advisors to *pro se* defendants, a further indication for this more open part adopted by legal associates in the proceedings may be motions filed by the defence which concern overly legalistic questions and do not necessarily seem to have been based on legal strategies of a self-represented accused, but rather on the experience with international criminal trials contributed by their professional legal advisors.[555]

Bearing in mind the continuously valid characterisation of the substantial role to be played by *pro se* defendants in the conduct of their own defence which has been upheld by trial and appeals chambers, the increasingly open influence of legal associates in the proceedings in practice does not appear to reflect the initially advanced theoretical concepts of the right to self-representation. This observation corroborates the argument that the right to self-representation as interpreted thus far in international criminal proceedings does not mirror its practical application and that consequently modification in order to avoid misconceptions and misuse in future proceedings is called for. The all too obvious influence of legal advisors could then be "regularised" with them assuming a legitimate role of professional defence counsel while leaving their clients with the choice whether to actively participate in the presentation of their defence case.

---

555 *See e.g. Prosecutor v. Radovan Karadžić*, Case No. IT-95-5/18-T, Motion to Strike Allegation G9 on Grounds of Collateral Estoppel, 04 March 2010; and Decision on Accused's Motion to Strike Scheduled Shelling Incident on Grounds of Collateral Estoppel, 31 March 2010, para.9: "… The Chamber also notes that the Accused's legal adviser was behind the unsuccessful request in the *Karemera* case referred to above and, thus, would have known how low the likelihood of it succeeding would be here. Yet the Accused was advised to file an almost identical request with this Chamber making, at the same time, a poor attempt at distinguishing the *Karemera* decision. All these factors contribute to the Chamber's view that this Motion is bordering on frivolous, and it advises the Accused, once again, to focus his resources and efforts on his preparations for the hearing of evidence at trial."

2. Impact of lack of legal knowledge on the conduct of proceedings

In contrast to the apparent awareness and use of the procedural framework by self-represented accused discussed above, the potential impact of any unfamiliarity of *pro se* defendants with international criminal substantive and procedural law to be applied is a concern of trial chambers that features already in initial analyses of requests to present a defence case in person.

It has been argued in this context that where a *pro se* defendant is obviously incapable of mounting an objectively effective defence, a chamber would need to consider restricting his or her right to self-representation in order to safeguard the overall interests in a fair conduct of the proceedings.[556]

When the trial chamber in *Janković & Stanković* denied the latter accused's request to defend himself, it took into consideration *inter alia* the nature of the charges and the impact on skills needed for defence. The trial chamber remarked that the "Accused is charged with serious crimes which require particular legal skills".[557] It considered that the "accused before this Tribunal should not be placed at a disadvantageous position compared to the Prosecution which enjoys the assistance of skilled and competent legal expertise".[558] At the same time, however, the bench concluded that "the right of self-representation should not be disregarded *solely* on the basis of the negative effect on the Accused's position caused by his inferior knowledge or skills compared to those of a professional legal counsel".[559]

An analogous approach can be found in the decision taken by the SCSL trial chamber in *Norman*, which denied the request of the accused to conduct his defence in person, *inter alia,* in light of the complexity of the case.[560]

---

556 Philipp Ambach, Selbstvertretung im internationalen Strafprozess – Grundlagen, Kritik und ein Lösungsansatz für die prozessuale Handhabung in der Zukunft, 6 *Zeitschrift für Internationale Strafrechtsdogmatik* 286 (2009), at 297-298.

557 *Prosecutor v. Janković & Stanković*, Case No. IT-96-23/2-PT, Decision Following Registrar's Notification of Radovan Stanković's Request for Self-Representation, 19 August 2005, para.20.

558 *Prosecutor v. Janković & Stanković*, Case No. IT-96-23/2-PT, Decision Following Registrar's Notification of Radovan Stanković's Request for Self-Representation, 19 August 2005, para.20.

559 *Prosecutor v. Janković & Stanković*, Case No. IT-96-23/2-PT, Decision Following Registrar's Notification of Radovan Stanković's Request for Self-Representation, 19 August 2005, para.20 (emphasis added).

560 *Prosecutor v. Samuel Hinga Norman et al.*, Case No. SCSL-04-14-T, Decision on the Application of Samuel Hinga Norman for Self Representation Under Article 17(4)(d) of the Statute of the Special Court, 08 June 2004, para.26.

In a similar vein, the trial chamber in *Krajišnik*, when deciding on the accused's initial request to proceed *pro se* during the trial proceedings, equally referred to the complexity of the case and the impact on preparation and presentation of a defence: it considered that "a criminal case of the present magnitude, which has been experienced as a great strain even by learned defence counsel, would certainly collapse if put into the hands of Mr Krajišnik".[561] The trial chamber seemed to be highly critical of the position that an accused could waive his or her right to be represented by counsel even to his or her own detriment and pointed out that a poor defence mounted by a self-represented accused "would only serve to bring the international criminal process into disrepute".[562]

This stands in obvious contrast with the initial stance adopted by the appeals chamber in *Milošević* when it articulated the position that an accused who decided to conduct his defence in person would have to bear responsibility for any consequences this decision may entail.[563] As discussed before, this arguably implies that an accused who is self-represented might be held to the same or at least similar standards as professional defence counsel.

About two years after the trial chamber's denial of the initial request of Momčilo Krajišnik, the appeals chamber in the same case took the view that in case an accused representing himself is unable to do so effectively and efficiently without legal assistance, the remedy to be sought was restriction of the right to self-representation.[564]

The trial chamber in *Karadžić* later adopted this position, stating that "[s]hould the Accused lack the ability to present his defence efficiently and effectively because of his lack of knowledge of law and legal procedures, or because of the complexities of the case", the solution as envisioned by the appeals chamber in *Krajišnik* was restriction of the right to self-represen-

---

561 *Prosecutor v. Momčilo Krajišnik*, Case No. IT-00-39-T, Reasons for Oral Decision Denying Mr Krajišnik's Request to Proceed Unrepresented by Counsel, 18 August 2005, para.34.

562 *Prosecutor v. Momčilo Krajišnik*, Case No. IT-00-39-T, Reasons for Oral Decision Denying Mr Krajišnik's Request to Proceed Unrepresented by Counsel, 18 August 2005, para.34.

563 *Prosecutor v. Slobodan Milošević*, Case No. IT-02-54-AR73.6, Decision on the Interlocutory Appeal by the *Amici Curiae* Against the Trial Chamber Order Concerning the Presentation and Preparation of the Defence Case, 20 January 2004, para.19.

564 *Prosecutor v. Momčilo Krajišnik*, Case No. IT-00-39-A, Decision on Krajišnik Request and Prosecution Motion, 11 September 2007, para.41.

tation.[565] In contrast, the accused asserted in his appeal of the trial chamber's decision that the appeals chamber never indicated that the lack of legal knowledge could be used as basis for the restriction of the right to self-representation.[566] The appeals chamber did not adopt this interpretation: rather, it concluded that the trial chamber correctly construed the position in the *Krajišnik* decision and specifically linked a potential restriction of the right to self-representation to the lack of legal knowledge of the accused.[567] The appeals chamber stated that it

> "finds no error in the Trial Chamber's interpretation of the *Krajišnik* Appeal Decision to the effect that where an accused lacks the requisite knowledge of the law or legal procedures to the extent that it will substantially and persistently obstruct the proper and expeditious conduct of the trial, the solution is not the funding of highly experienced legal associates, but rather the curtailment of his right to self-representation."[568]

The appeals chamber in *Šešelj* appeared to go even further in a similar context and seemed to take the view that "unfamiliarity with law" might be an unintentional factor that could lead to the assignment of counsel on a footing similar to poor health of an accused: albeit in a footnote, the appeals chamber did state that

> "where an accused's exercise of the right to self-representation is causing disruption to his trial *due to poor health or an unfamiliarity with the law and procedure* of the International Tribunal, an accused may be able to remedy the situation in the former case by changing his diet, exercise or medicinal regime

---

565 *Prosecutor v. Radovan Karadžić*, Case No. IT-95-5/18-PT, Decision on Accused Motion for Adequate Facilities and Equality of Arms: Legal Associates, 28 January 2009, para.31, 36. Note in particular para.36: "[...], then the solution does not lie in the application of the Remuneration Scheme but rather in devising an arrangement for the presentation of his defence that allows him to play an active role while at the same time being represented by counsel."

566 *Prosecutor v. Radovan Karadžić*, Case No. IT-95-5/18-AR73.2, Appeal of the Trial Chamber's Decision on Adequate Facilities, 02 March 2009 (filed: 05 March 2009), para.17, 18.

567 *Prosecutor v. Radovan Karadžić*, Case No. IT-95-5/18-AR73.2, Decision on Interlocutory Appeal of the Trial Chamber's Decision on Adequate Facilities, 07 May 2009, para.13, 14.

568 *Prosecutor v. Radovan Karadžić*, Case No. IT-95-5/18-AR73.2, Decision on Interlocutory Appeal of the Trial Chamber's Decision on Adequate Facilities, 07 May 2009, para.14.

and, in the latter case, by informing himself as to the applicable substantive and procedural law."[569]

In light of the decision of the appeals chamber in *Šešelj*, one could discuss which factors might fall under the notion of "unintentional" as used by the appeals chamber. With regard to the issue of unfamiliarity with the law, it could be argued that an accused opting to conduct his or her defence in person has to make such choice knowingly and voluntarily. He or she being aware of personal qualifications should have known from the start that the own legal skills, if existent at all, might not be sufficient for cases of the magnitude discussed here. Then it could be asked how the lack of legal knowledge, despite its not being receptive to influence on short notice, could be an "unintentional" factor like the health of an accused, even more so in light of the usual warnings a defendant will be provided with when initially voicing the intention to proceed *pro se*.

It can be concluded in light of these decisions that the different chambers were not inclined to take the lack of legal knowledge as an excuse by an accused who knowingly and willingly decided to present his defence in person. This is in line with the position adopted by the U.S. Supreme Court in *Faretta* that an accused choosing self-representation cannot complain at a later stage that the quality of his defence amounted to a denial of effective assistance of counsel.[570] It would also coincide with the position taken by the appeals chamber in *Milošević* when it expressly referred to national jurisprudence on the issue mentioned earlier and the decision in the case against Vojislav Šešelj referred to above, in which the *Šešelj* appeals chamber considered unfamiliarity with the law to be an unintentional factor which could lead to assignment of counsel, *i.e.* to an effective restriction of the exercise of self-representation.[571]

The position which was adopted initially by the trial chamber in *Krajišnik* further indicates that in general a balance exercise has to be performed, weighing the right to self-representation on the one side, and the interests of

---

569 *Prosecutor v. Vojislav Šešelj*, Case No. IT-03-67-AR73.3, Decision on Appeal Against the Trial Chamber's Decision on Assignment of Counsel, 20 October 2006, para.23 fn.62 (emphasis added).

570 *Anthony Pasquall Faretta v. State of California* (U.S. Supreme Court), 422 U.S. 806, 30 June 1975, at 834 fn.46.

571 *Prosecutor v. Vojislav Šešelj*, Case No. IT-03-67-AR73.3, Decision on Appeal Against the Trial Chamber's Decision on Assignment of Counsel, 20 October 2006, para.23 fn.62.

the international community in fair and expeditious proceedings, including an effective defence by professional defence counsel if necessary against the expressed will of the accused, on the other. In light of the importance that was attributed to the right to self-representation in the initial recognition of the right in *Milošević*, it may be the case that any potential and actual interests of the international community may not weigh too heavily in the balance. This will hold true especially in cases, such as the issue at hand, in which fundamental fair trial rights of accused in international criminal proceedings are involved. At the same time, the discussion equally turns around the question whether an accused can, or should be given the opportunity to, effectively waive his or her right to a fair trial by abandoning the possibility of being represented by professional counsel.

A matter of concern in this context is that the positions taken by different chambers outlined above indicate the ambiguous treatment of the practical exercise of the right to self-representation: on the one hand, chambers consider the nature of the charges and the potential legal and factual complexity of proceedings in their determination of requests to conduct a defence in person. On the other hand, accused are expected to make an informed and conscious choice that would put them in a position in which they are to accept the consequences of their choice.

This ambiguity is even more pronounced if these positions are taken further, with chambers having to safeguard the fair trial rights of an accused on the one side, while at the same time allowing for the possibility that accused conduct their defence in person even though there might be an awareness on all sides that this could be to the detriment of the defendants and contrary to their right to fair proceedings.

This issue leads back to the discussion about the nature of the rights at stake in the context of the exercise of the right to self-representation, and their balance against each other. The ambiguity alluded to above arguably creates an uncertainty about potential positions to be adopted by judges, as may be illustrated with two issues raised in the appeal in *Krajišnik* by *amicus curiae*: on the one hand it was argued that the accused should have been granted his right to self-representation despite the late stage of the trial; on the other hand a complaint was submitted that the proceedings had been rendered unfair by the trial chamber's decision to allow the accused to ask questions in addition to counsel.[572]

A further issue to be discussed in this context is whether the approach of the appeals chamber expecting an accused to take responsibility for all consequences flowing from the decision to exercise the right to self-representation may be interpreted differently in cases where the defendant is a qualified lawyer. It can be argued that higher standards should be applicable in this scenario, with the self-represented accused having to satisfy more stringent criteria, for example with regard to determining the preparation time to be granted to the defence. However, in light of the specific nature of proceedings before international criminal tribunals, the fact whether a defendant is a qualified lawyer ought not weigh into the balance.

A more realistic argument focuses on the number of professional legal associates engaged by self-represented accused for assistance in the preparation and presentation of their defence case. Practice indicates that legal advisors to *pro se* defendants often enjoy significant experience in running international criminal proceedings and therefore should be in an ideal position to advise their clients. Rather than having to hide behind their designation as advisors only and having to hold back with that experience for sake of sustaining appearances of self-representation, a more reasonable and genuine approach would resolve the issue by adjusting the interpretation of a right to defend oneself in person that is not based on an exclusivity of personal defence or representation by counsel.

IV. Language barriers influencing the exercise of self-representation

1. *Ad hoc* Tribunals

Language barriers are an additional matter of potential concern that has to be kept in mind in the context of proceedings with *pro se* defendants.

572 *Prosecutor v. Momčilo Krajišnik*, Case No. IT-00-39-A, Public and Redacted *Amicus Curiae*'s Reply to the Prosecution's Response to *Amicus Curiae*'s Appellate Brief, 24 June 2008, para.23-24. *See also Prosecutor v. Momčilo Krajišnik*, Case No. IT-00-39-A, Judgement, 17 March 2009, para.118-119.

For example before the ICTR, the accused are more likely in a position to communicate in either one of the official languages of the tribunal, English or French,[573] which both are among the official languages of Rwanda.

However, the situation is markedly different before the ICTY where defendants will often not have sufficient knowledge of one of these languages in order to conduct their own defence in English or French and will thus require not only simultaneous interpretation during oral proceedings, but also translation of all filings and documents relevant to the case into their own language[574] and *vice versa* to be able to participate. In comparison, defence counsel which are for example assigned to an accused pursuant to Rule 45 of the ICTY RPE in a leading function have to be fluent in one of the working languages.[575] In case counsel is retained by the accused without provision of legal aid, the requirements set by the ICTY registry will usually include the necessity to be fluent in one of the working languages, although this can be waived in case it is determined to be in the interests of justice.[576] Of note in this regard is the much reduced list of requirements to be fulfilled by counsel engaged before the ICTR,[577] mentioning proficiency in any of the ICTR's working languages only in case of assignment to indigent accused.[578] The Rome Statute sets the language requirement more generally for all defence counsel practicing before the Court to be fluent in at least one of the working languages of the Court.[579]

This requirement cannot practically be imposed on self-represented accused who have the right to use their own language in the proceedings.[580] Therefore, in order to preserve well-established rights of defendants, different

573 Rule 3(A) ICTR RPE: "The working languages of the Tribunal shall be English and French."

574 *Cf.* Rule 3(B) ICTY RPE: "An accused shall have the right to use his or her own language."

575 *See Prosecutor v. Zdravko Tolimir*, Case No. IT-05-88/2-PT, Registry Submission Pursuant to Rule 33(B) of the Rules of Procedure and Evidence Regarding the Accused Tolimir's 13 July 2007 Submission on Appointment of Permanent Counsel, 18 July 2007, para.28.

576 Rule 44(A)(ii), (B) ICTY RPE.

577 Rule 44 ICTR RPE.

578 Rule 45(A) ICTR RPE.

579 Rule 22 ICC RPE: "[…] A counsel for the defence shall have an excellent knowledge of and be fluent in at least one of the working languages of the Court. […]".

580 *Cf.* Rule 3(B) ICTY RPE; Rule 3(B) ICTR RPE; Rule 3(B) SCSL RPE; Rule 10(C) STL RPE. *See also* Rule 10(D) STL RPE.

standards have to be applied in the context of working languages in proceedings with *pro se* accused.

Rendering a decision in a case concerning a defendant represented by counsel, an ICTR trial chamber determined, with reference to earlier decisions by both the ICTY[581] and the ICTR,[582] that only basic documents, including the indictment, supporting material and evidence on which a trial chamber relied in reaching its judgement, would have to be translated into a language the accused understands.[583] However, it also held that the prosecution should endeavour to file submissions in French, language of defence counsel of the accused.[584] The ICTY decision referred to by the ICTR trial chamber had additionally clarified that transcripts need not be provided in the language of the accused.[585]

Yet, in the case of self-represented accused who are not proficient in any of the working languages, this will mean that all the material which would in general be provided to counsel has to be translated into a language the accused is able to understand.[586] The need for translation of the entirety of

581 *Prosecutor v. Delalić et al.*, Case No. IT-96-21-T, Decision on Defence Application for Forwarding the Documents in the Language of the Accused, 25 September 1996.

582 *Procureur c. Mika Muhimana*, Affaire n° ICTR-95-1-B-I, Décision Relative à la Requête de la Défense aux Fins de Traduction des Documents de l'Accusation et des Actes de Procédure en Kinyarwanda, Langue de l'Accusé, et en Français, Langue de son Conseil, 06 novembre 2001. This trial chamber somewhat extended the approach adopted by the trial chamber in *Delalić* : « Sur la base de ce qui précède, la Chambre souscrit au principe adopté par la Chambre du TPIY saisie d'une requête similaire dans l'Affaire Delalić et consorts (...) La Chambre ajoute cependant que ce principe doit s'étendre aux déclarations préalables des témoins que le Procureur est tenu de communiquer à l'Accusé en vertu de l'Article 66 A) ii) du Règlement, pour autant que ce dernier entende effectivement les appeler à la barre, et même si ces pièces ne devaient pas être soumises à l'examen de la Chambre de première instance lors du procès » (para.22-23).

583 *Procureur c. Vincent Rutaganira*, Affaire n° ICTR-95-1C-P, Décision Relative à la Requête aux Fins de Transmission des Documents en Versions Française et Kinyarwanda, 06 décembre 2004, para.2.

584 *Procureur c. Vincent Rutaganira*, Affaire n° ICTR-95-1C-P, Décision Relative à la Requête aux Fins de Transmission des Documents en Versions Française et Kinyarwanda, 06 décembre 2004, para.5.

585 *Prosecutor v. Delalić et al.*, Case No. IT-96-21-T, Decision on Defence Application for Forwarding the Documents in the Language of the Accused, 25 September 1996, para.14.

586 Rule 66 ICTY RPE: "(A) Subject to the provisions of Rules 53 and 69, the Prosecutor shall make available to the defence in a language which the accused understands [...]".

materials and filings inevitably brings with it delays in the proceedings, and puts constraints on the resources of international criminal tribunals.[587]

Defendants are without doubt entitled to be served with the disclosure related to their respective cases in a language they do in fact sufficiently understand in order to prepare and present their defence case. On the other hand, this requirement equally tends to become an additional topic to be dealt with exclusively in cases in which an accused exercises the right to self-representation.

Decisions rendered by the ICTY appeals chamber in both *Karadžić* and *Tolimir* clarified a number of issues with regard to the question which language capacity on the part of the accused has to be considered in order to safeguard his or her right under Article 21(4) of the ICTY Statute, including the right to adequate time and facilities for the preparation of the defence.[588] Yet, in case an accused is not determined to possess the relevant language capacities, and *e.g.* filings from the prosecution have to be translated in order for a *pro se* defendant to be able to respond, and *vice versa*, this issue will be another factor contributing to the prolongation of proceedings with self-represented accused, given that deadlines can only run from the moment a version is received in an official language of the ICTY or in a language the accused understands, respectively.[589]

Soon after his initial appearance, the accused in *Karadžić* requested that he be provided with all material, including transcripts of trials not falling

---

587 Patricia M. Wald, *Tyrants on Trial. Keeping Order in the Courtroom* (New York: Open Society Justice Institute) 2009, p.52-53.

588 Article 21(4)(a), (b) ICTY Statute reads: "In the determination of any charges against the accused pursuant to the present Statute, the accused shall be entitled to the following minimum guarantees, in full equality: (a) to be informed promptly and in detail *in a language which he understands* of the nature and cause of the charge against him; (b) to have adequate time and facilities for the preparation of his defence and to communicate with counsel of his own choosing; […]" (emphasis added).

589 *Prosecutor v. Vojislav Šešelj*, Case No. IT-03-67-PT, Order on Translation of Documents, 06 March 2003, p.2; Status Conference, 19 May 2006, T.507; Status Conference, 13 March 2007, T.957; Status Conference, 05 June 2007, T.1202; *Prosecutor v. Zdravko Tolimir*, Case No. IT-05-88/2-PT, Status Conference, 11 December 2007, T.111.

under Rule 66(A) of the ICTY RPE,[590] in Serbian and the Cyrillic script.[591] Yet, the pre-trial judge determined this request to be overly broad and found the prosecution to be only under an obligation to ensure disclosure in Serbo-Croatian ("B/C/S")[592] under Rule 66(A) of the ICTY RPE.[593] It was considered that arrangements could be made in order to assist the accused in working with B/C/S audio material accompanied by English or French transcripts, and the defendant was encouraged to rethink whether he might not want to engage counsel speaking one of the working languages of the ICTY.[594] Furthermore, the fact that the accused voiced a preference for the Cyrillic, instead of Latin, script – rather than submitting an inability to un-

---

590 Rule 66(A) ICTY RPE provides for the disclosure by the prosecution of material supporting the indictment and statements of witnesses to be called by the prosecution. Similar provisions can be found in Rule 66(A) ICTR RPE; Rule 66(A) SCSL RPE; Rule 110(A) STL RPE; Rule 76 ICC RPE.

591 *Prosecutor v. Radovan Karadžić*, Case No. IT-95-5/18-I, Appeal Against the Registry Decision to Provide Me with Transcripts in English Language Only, or as Audio Recordings, 15 August 2008 (filed: 19 August 2008). *See also* Registry Submission Pursuant to Rule 33(B) Regarding the Accused's Representation and the Transmission of Court Documents, 06 August 2008, para.2 and Annex 2 (incl. Notification of self-representation; Request to receive transcripts and other material in Serbian); Submission of the Deputy Registrar Pursuant to Rule 33(B) Regarding Appeal by Mr. Karadžić of 19 August 2008, 27 August 2008; Case No. IT-95-5/18-PT, Prosecution's Response to Karadžić's Submission Regarding the Registry's Provision of Transcripts in the English Language, 02 September 2008.

592 For the use of "Bosnian-Croatian-Serbian" ("B/C/S") at the ICTY, *see Prosecutor v. Zdravko Tolimir*, Case No. IT-05-88/2-AR73.1, Decision on Interlocutory Appeal Against Oral Decision of the Pre-trial Judge of 11 December 2007, 28 March 2008, fn.32; *Prosecutor v. Radovan Karadžić*, Case No. IT-95-5/18-AR73.3, Decision on Interlocutory Appeal of the Trial Chamber's Decision on Prosecution Motion Seeking Determination that the Accused Understands English, 04 June 2009, para.2. *See also Prosecutor v. Zdravko Tolimir*, Case No. IT-05-88/2-PT, Prosecution's Response to Submission by the Accused Dated 25 September 2007, With Appendix, 10 October 2007, para.18; *Prosecutor v. Radovan Karadžić*, Case No. IT-95-5/18-PT, Decision on the Accused's Request that All Materials, Including Transcripts, be Disclosed to Him in Serbian and Cyrillic Script, 25 September 2008, para.10.

593 *Prosecutor v. Radovan Karadžić*, Case No. IT-95-5/18-PT, Decision on the Accused's Request that All Materials, Including Transcripts, be Disclosed to Him in Serbian and Cyrillic Script, 25 September 2008, para.13.

594 *Prosecutor v. Radovan Karadžić*, Case No. IT-95-5/18-PT, Decision on the Accused's Request that All Materials, Including Transcripts, be Disclosed to Him in Serbian and Cyrillic Script, 25 September 2008, para.14.

derstand the Latin script – was not seen as sufficient reason to depart from the standard practice of serving documents in B/C/S and Latin script.[595]

The trial chamber determined at an early stage of the proceedings that the defendant possessed a knowledge of English sufficient for purposes of the procedural rules, more specifically with regard to disclosure pursuant to Rule 66(A) of the ICTY RPE, which removed the burden on the prosecution to disclose such materials translated into the native language of the defendant.[596] On the other hand, the trial chamber showed itself flexible to receive filings by the accused in B/C/S in exceptional circumstances, despite him having numerous assistants capable of drafting in English.[597]

Yet, with regard to documents used by the accused in the course of the proceedings, the trial chamber made abundantly clear that the defence was under an obligation to translate any documents it intended to use in court into English and to ensure that no such translations already existed beforehand in case it planned to request an official translation.[598] Several months into evidentiary hearings, the bench warned the defendant in light of the amount of documents without any English translation used up to that point, that in the future it might repudiate the use of documents without translation in

595 *Prosecutor v. Radovan Karadžić*, Case No. IT-95-5/18-PT, Decision on the Accused's Request that All Materials, Including Transcripts, be Disclosed to Him in Serbian and Cyrillic Script, 25 September 2008, para.15.

596 *Prosecutor v. Radovan Karadžić*, Case No. IT-95-5/18-PT, Decision on Prosecution Motion Seeking Determination that the Accused Understands English for the Purposes of the Statute and the Rules of Procedure and Evidence, 26 March 2009; upheld by the Appeals Chamber: *Prosecutor v. Radovan Karadžić*, Case No. IT-95-5/18-AR73.3, Decision on Interlocutory Appeal of the Trial Chamber's Decision on Prosecution Motion Seeking Determination that the Accused Understands English, 04 June 2009. *See also Prosecutor v. Radovan Karadžić*, Case No. IT-95-5/18-PT, Prosecution Motion Seeking a Determination that the Accused Understands English for the Purposes of the Statute and the Rules of Procedure and Evidence, 17 February 2009; Response to Prosecution Motion Seeking Determination that the Accused Understands English, 20 March 2009; Case No. IT-95-5/18-AR73.3, Appeal of the Trial Chamber's Decision on Languages, 29 April 2009; Prosecution Response to Karadžić's Appeal of Trial Chamber's Decision on Languages, 11 May 2009.

597 *Prosecutor v. Radovan Karadžić*, Case No. IT-95-5/18-PT, Status Conference, 08 September 2009, T.441-445.

598 *Prosecutor v. Radovan Karadžić*, Case No. IT-95-5/18-T, Order in Relation to Exhibits Marked for Identification Pending English Translation, 06 December 2010, para.2-3.

court.[599] The trial chamber later reminded the accused that he needed to translate into English any material he might want to use with witnesses in the course of cross-examination, in order for all participants to be able to follow. The bench warned the defendant that in light of repeated previous reminders in this context,[600] he might not be allowed to use untranslated documents any longer.[601]

The language issue created more substantial obstacles for example in *Šešelj* and *Tolimir*, where both accused not only requested to be provided with all disclosure materials in Serbian, as opposed to B/C/S generally used before the ICTY, but also in Cyrillic script.

In *Šešelj*, the trial chamber determined at an early stage that the accused was capable of understanding B/C/S,[602] and considered his consistent assertion to the contrary as indication of the defendant's obstructionist behaviour.[603] Despite this finding, the accused insisted that any disclosure be served on him in Serbian,[604] and in written form, as opposed to electronic

---

599 *Prosecutor v. Radovan Karadžić*, Case No. IT-95-5/18-T, Order in Relation to Exhibits Marked for Identification Pending English Translation, 06 December 2010, para.3.

600 *See e.g. Prosecutor v. Radovan Karadžić*, Case No. IT-95-5/18-T, Hearing, 03 November 2010, T.8906.

601 *Prosecutor v. Radovan Karadžić*, Case No. IT-95-5/18-T, Hearing, 25 February 2011, T.12428-12429: "[…] You have been repeatedly warned by the Trial Chamber that you must have English translations for all your documents in order to use them in the courtroom. I think we have been very generous in permitting you to make use of untranslated documents thus far. And I also advise you to better organise your team and make use of the Tribunal's translation tracking system, et cetera. Please take this advice to heart. Next time, we may stop you using untranslated documents."; Hearing, 16 September 2011, T.18943. *See also* Hearing, 17 January 2012, T.23142; Hearing, 24 February 2012, T.25203; Hearing, 01 March 2012, T.25590; Hearing, 10 April 2012, T.27269.

602 *Prosecutor v. Vojislav Šešelj*, Case No. IT-03-67-PT, Decision on Prosecution's Motion for Order Appointing Counsel to Assist Vojislav Šešelj with His Defence, 09 May 2003, para.24.

603 *Prosecutor v. Vojislav Šešelj*, Case No. IT-03-67-PT, Decision on Prosecution's Motion for Order Appointing Counsel to Assist Vojislav Šešelj with His Defence, 09 May 2003, para.26.

604 *Prosecutor v. Vojislav Šešelj*, Case No. IT-03-67-PT, Status Conference, 29 October 2003, T.119. *See also* Notification (re defence matters), 25 February 2003 (filed: 26 February 2003); Further Appearance, 25 March 2003, T.58-60; Defence Motion for Provisional Release, 14 June 2004 (filed: 24 June 2004), para.15.1, 15.6.

disclosure.[605] The trial chamber, however, reiterated its finding that B/C/S was to be considered as a language the accused understands.[606]

The defendant subsequently persisted in his requests that documents be disclosed to him in Serbian.[607] These requests formed part of the demands of the accused in the context of his hunger strike at a later stage of the proceedings.[608] The prosecution considered the accused's alleged inability to understand B/C/S to be "absurd",[609] and maintained that from a linguistic point of view, no exclusively distinct language like "Serbian" existed.[610] It further thought the defendant's insistence on written disclosure to be obstruc-

---

605 *Prosecutor v. Vojislav Šešelj*, Case No. IT-03-67-PT, Request of the Accused to Disclose Materials of the Prosecution in Written Form and in Serbian (Submission No. 43), 26 October 2004 (filed: 09 November 2004), p.2-4, 8.

606 *Prosecutor v. Vojislav Šešelj*, Case No. IT-03-67-PT, Decision on Motion Number 28, 19 December 2003, p.2.

607 *Prosecutor v. Vojislav Šešelj*, Case No. IT-03-67-PT, Motion No.30, 27 January 2004 (filed: 26 March 2004); Request of the Accused to Disclose Materials of the Prosecution in Written Form and in Serbian (Submission No. 43), 26 October 2004 (filed: 09 November 2004), p.2-3, 5-7, 8; Submission No.48, 03 November 2004 (filed: 05 November 2004); Submission No.59, 29 November 2004 (filed: 02 December 2004); Submission No.63, 08 December 2004 (filed: 30 December 2004); Submission No.66, 15 December 2004 (filed: 05 January 2005), para.8; Submission No.67, 15 December 2004 (filed: 05 January 2005); Submission No.99, 25 July 2005 (filed: 03 August 2005); Interlocutory Appeal by Professor Vojislav Šešelj Against the Decision on Form of Disclosure Issued by Trial Chamber I on 4 July 2006, 01 February 2007 (filed: 14 February 2007), p.3-4, 6.

608 *Prosecutor v. Vojislav Šešelj*, Case No. IT-03-67-PT, Prosecution Motion for Medical Examination of the Accused and for Consideration of Assignment of Counsel, 16 November 2006, para.2 and Annex A; Status Conference, 22 November 2006, T.780-781. *See also* Professor Vojislav Šešelj's Motion for Review of the Decision on Form of Disclosure Issued by Trial Chamber I on 4 July 2006 (Submission No. 289), 11 May 2007 (filed: 17 May 2007), p.5.

609 *Prosecutor v. Vojislav Šešelj*, Case No. IT-03-67-PT, Prosecution's Response to Accused's Request for Disclosure of Materials in Written Form and in Serbian, 23 November 2004, para.2.

610 *Prosecutor v. Vojislav Šešelj*, Case No. IT-03-67-PT, Prosecution's Response to Accused's Request for Disclosure of Materials in Written Form and in Serbian, 23 November 2004, para.3: "... Any autonomy that does exist between these so called 'different languages' stems from ideological and political values, which, from a scientific, linguistic perspective, are worthless."

tionist[611] and ineffective for purposes of preparation of the defence.[612] In addition, in one decision on a disclosure request by the accused, the trial chamber determined that, as long as a defendant is provided with the necessary relevant training and equipment to effectively use electronic disclosure, no unfairness would ensue.[613] In a later submission, the accused renewed his request to be served with materials in Serbian and hardcopy format.[614]

The ICTY appeals chamber did not find an error in the exercise of discretion by the previous trial chamber with regard to the decision on the form of disclosure.[615] Yet, the pre-trial judge of the newly assigned trial chamber later decided that the accused was entitled to receive material falling under Rule 66(A)(i) and (ii), as well as Rule 68(i) of the ICTY RPE not only in a language he understands, but also in hardcopy.[616]

The matter of languages proved to be particularly problematic in *Tolimir*, case in which the accused persisted in his proclaimed inability to read the Latin script and in his request to be provided with all material in Serbian and Cyrillic script,[617] rejecting to accept documents served not complying with

---

611 *Prosecutor v. Vojislav Šešelj*, Case No. IT-03-67-PT, Prosecution's Response to Accused's Request for Disclosure of Materials in Written Form and in Serbian, 23 November 2004, para.16.

612 *Prosecutor v. Vojislav Šešelj*, Case No. IT-03-67-PT, Prosecution's Response to Accused's Request for Disclosure of Materials in Written Form and in Serbian, 23 November 2004, para.18.

613 *Prosecutor v. Vojislav Šešelj*, Case No. IT-03-67-PT, Decision on Form of Disclosure, 04 July 2006, para.12-13.

614 *Prosecutor v. Vojislav Šešelj*, Case No. IT-03-67-PT, Professor Vojislav Šešelj's Motion for Review of the Decision on Form of Disclosure Issued by Trial Chamber I on 4 July 2006 (Submission No. 289), 11 May 2007 (filed: 17 May 2007), p.4.

615 *Prosecutor v. Vojislav Šešelj*, Case No. IT-03-67-AR73.5, Decision on Vojislav Šešelj's Interlocutory Appeal Against the Trial Chamber's Decision on Form of Disclosure, 17 April 2007. It is of note, however, that the appeals chamber in this decision specifically stated that it would be open to the accused to apply for modification of the decision with the new trial chamber, "which might consider, in its discretion, a different trial management approach than that followed in the Impugned Decision"; *see* para.20.

616 *Procureur c/ Vojislav Šešelj*, Affaire n° IT-03-67-PT, Décision Relative à la Requête 289 Concernant le Mode de Communication de Pièces, 07 juin 2007, para.27-28, 35-36.

617 *See e.g. Prosecutor v. Zdravko Tolimir*, Case No. IT-05-88/2-PT, Submission of the Accused for the Delivery of Documents and Transcripts of the Trial in a Script and Language that He Reads and Writes, 08 July 2007 (filed: 10 July 2007); Submission of the Accused to the Registrar Requesting the Delivery of Files and Documents in Written Form, in the Cyrillic Script and the Serbian Language, which

these criteria.[618] The prosecution did not consider itself to be under any obligation to disclose the relevant material in a particular script, given that it otherwise found it was complying with its disclosure obligations.[619] It also

---

are in Official Use in the Country of the Accused, 02 August 2007 (filed: 10 August 2007); The Accused's Motion to the Pre-trial Chamber to Suspend the Decision on the Filing of Preliminary Motions until the Abduction of the Accused is Resolved, the Prosecution Material Disclosed, and the Decision Made on the Motion by the Accused Concerning the Financing of his Defence in Accordance with Article 21 of the Statute of the International Criminal Tribunal for the Former Yugoslavia, 25 September 2007 (filed: 27 September 2007), para.3-4; Motion to the Pre-trial Chamber and the Registrar Concerning Assistance in Appointing a Legal Advisor, Disclosure of Material in a Language the Accused Understands and Notification of Special Defence on the Charges in the Indictment, 16 November 2007 (filed: 20 November 2007), para.1-3; Submission of the Accused to the Tribunal Concerning the Need for Communication Between the Trial Chamber, Prosecution and Registry With the Accused in his Mother Tongue, Serbian, and Using the Cyrillic Alphabet, which he can Understand, 07 December 2007 (filed: 13 December 2007); The Accused's Submission to the Pre-trial Chamber, Registrar and Prosecution Concerning Disregard by the Tribunal for the Fundamental Rights and Actual Wishes of the Accused Regarding Communication and Appointment of the Accused's Legal Counsel, 03 January 2008 (filed: 10 January 2008); The Accused's Submission to the Registrar and the Pre-trial Chamber Concerning the Submission to the Accused of Documents in a Language and Script the he does not Speak, Read, Write or Understand, 07 January 2008 (filed: 10 January 2008), para.3, 5; Accused's Submission Concerning the Appointment of Legal Advisors and the Need for the Court, Registry and Prosecution to Communicate with the Accused in the Serbian Language, as the only Language he Understands, 03 March 2008 (filed: 05 March 2008), para.6.

618 *See e.g. Prosecutor v. Zdravko Tolimir*, Case No. IT-05-88/2-PT, The Accused's Submission to the Pre-trial Chamber, Registrar and Prosecution Concerning Disregard by the Tribunal for the Fundamental Rights and Actual Wishes of the Accused Regarding Communication and Appointment of the Accused's Legal Counsel, 03 January 2008 (filed: 10 January 2008), para.1; The Accused's Submission to the Registrar and the Pre-trial Chamber Concerning the Submission to the Accused of Documents in a Language and Script the he does not Speak, Read, Write or Understand, 07 January 2008 (filed: 10 January 2008), para.1-2; Submission of the Accused to the Pre-trial Chamber, the Registrar and the Prosecutor Concerning the Need for Communication with the Accused in a Language and Script that he Understands, 23 January 2008 (filed: 25 January 2008).

619 *Prosecutor v. Zdravko Tolimir*, Case No. IT-05-88/2-PT, Prosecution's Response to Submission of Zdravko Tolimir Dated 08 July 2007, 13 July 2007, para.4; Prosecution's Response to Submission by the Accused Dated 25 September 2007, With Appendix, 10 October 2007, para.4, 17; Prosecution Response to the Accused's 16 November 2007 Motion, 04 December 2007, para.4-6; Prosecution's Response to

rejected the claim of the accused that he was incapable of reading the Latin script.[620] The ICTY registry went even further with regard to one of the first requests of the defendant and submitted that transcripts of hearings could only be provided in one of the working languages of the ICTY, as opposed to the audio recordings,[621] and that document translations would be made available in Latin script.[622]

In an initial ruling, the pre-trial judge showed herself satisfied that the accused had been provided with the relevant material in a language which he understands, in order to safeguard his rights, and that the refusal to receive some documents was the choice of the accused.[623] Eventually, the pre-trial judge issued a ruling which ordered the defendant to accept material served in B/C/S, and in Latin script, and warned the accused that his continuing refusal to accept disclosure would necessitate the trial chamber to reconsider his status as self-represented accused.[624]

Subsequently, the defendant seised the appeals chamber of the dispute, arguing that his right to a fair trial had been violated, and seeking the remedy of disclosure by the prosecution in "standard Serbian and the Cyrillic script".[625] Consequently, the accused continued to return to sender documents

---

the Accused's Request for Certification of the Pre-trial Judge's Oral Decision of 11 December 2007, 28 December 2007, para.14-16.

620 *Prosecutor v. Zdravko Tolimir*, Case No. IT-05-88/2-PT, Prosecution's Response to Submission by the Accused Dated 25 September 2007, With Appendix, 10 October 2007, para.8-13; Prosecution's Response to the Accused's Request for Certification of the Pre-trial Judge's Oral Decision of 11 December 2007, 28 December 2007, para.8-12.

621 *Prosecutor v. Zdravko Tolimir*, Case No. IT-05-88/2-PT, Registrar's Submission on "Submission of the Accused for Delivery of Documents and Transcripts of the Trial in a Script and Language that he Reads and Writes", 18 July 2007, para.5.

622 *Prosecutor v. Zdravko Tolimir*, Case No. IT-05-88/2-PT, Registrar's Submission on "Submission of the Accused for Delivery of Documents and Transcripts of the Trial in a Script and Language that he Reads and Writes", 18 July 2007, para.6.

623 *Prosecutor v. Zdravko Tolimir*, Case No. IT-05-88/2-PT, Decision on Submission of Tolimir Requesting Translation of Documents and Transcripts, 20 July 2007, p.4.

624 *Prosecutor v. Zdravko Tolimir*, Case No. IT-05-88/2-PT, Oral Ruling, 11 December 2007, T.113-117. *See also* Decision on Accused's Submission Dated 07 December 2007 and Decision on Certification to Appeal, 15 January 2008; Decision on Motion for Certification to Appeal the 11 December Oral Decision, 15 January 2008.

625 *Prosecutor v. Zdravko Tolimir*, Case No. IT-05-88/2-AR73.1, Appeal by the Accused to the Presiding Judge of Chamber II Against the Verbal Ruling of the Pre-trial Judge Ordering Communication Between the Accused and the International Tribunal

which did not fulfil these requirements.[626] While the appeals chamber dismissed the interlocutory appeal,[627] the defendant continued to express his unwillingness to receive any materials not written in Serbian and Cyrillic script.[628] Although he made arrangements for his legal advisors to receive disclosed documents and transform the script in order for their client to read them,[629] the prosecution expressed doubts as to whether this approach could

---

and the Obligation to Accept Material Accompanying the Indictment in a Language, Script and Form that the Accused does not Understand, 25 January 2008 (filed: 31 January 2008), p.6. *See also* Submission of the Accused to the Presiding Judge of Pre-trial Chamber II for Leave to File an Appeal Against the Oral Ruling of the Pre-trial Judge Ordering Communication Between the Accused and the International Tribunal and Disclosure of Material Supporting the Indictment in a Language, Script and Form that the Accused does not Understand, 17 December 2007 (filed: 19 December 2007).

626 *See e.g. Prosecutor v. Zdravko Tolimir*, Case No. IT-05-88/2-PT, Submission of the Accused to the Trial Chamber, Registrar and Prosecutor for Delivery of Documents in a Language which the Accused does not Understand, 31 January 2008 (filed: 05 February 2008); Submission of the Accused to the Pre-trial Chamber, the Registrar and Prosecutor on the Return of Documents which the Accused does not Understand and the Request that all Communication and Correspondence be carried out in the Serbian Language and Script which the Accused Solely Understands, 01 February 2008 (filed: 05 February 2008); Status Conference, 12 March 2008, T.163.

627 *Prosecutor v. Zdravko Tolimir*, Case No. IT-05-88/2-AR73.1, Decision on Interlocutory Appeal Against Oral Decision of the Pre-trial Judge of 11 December 2007, 28 March 2008. The Appeals Chamber found "that the Appellant has failed to put forward any argument capable of challenging the Pre-trial Judge's factual finding that he is in fact able to read and understand B/C/S and the Latin script." *See* para.22.

628 *Prosecutor v. Zdravko Tolimir*, Case No. IT-05-88/2-PT, Submission by the Accused to the President of the Tribunal, the Registrar and the Pre-trial Chamber, with the Request that the "Decision on Interlocutory Appeal against Oral Decision of the Pre-trial Judge of 11 December 2007" be submitted to him in Serbian, the only Language he Understands, 10 April 2008 (filed: 15 April 2008); Accused's Motion to the President of the Tribunal and Members of the Appeals Chamber to Exercise their Discretionary Powers and Reconsider their Decision on the Appeal Against the Interlocutory Appeal [sic] Against the Oral Decision of the Pre-trial Judge of 11 December 2007, 16 April 2008 (filed: 18 April 2008); Submission of the Accused to the Prosecuting Attorney, the Office of the Prosecutor, the Registry and the Pre-trial Chamber with Request that all Materials from the Indictment be Submitted to him in a Language he that Understands, 21 April 2008 (filed: 25 April 2008), para.3-5; Response by the Accused Zdravko Tolimir to the Question of the Pre-trial Judge Regarding Receipt of Audio and Video Material, 05 June 2008 (filed: 10 June 2008), para.11-12.

629 *Prosecutor v. Zdravko Tolimir*, Case No. IT-05-88/2-PT, Statements in Accordance with the Decision of the Pre-trial Judge of 30 June 2008 Concerning Disclosure,

be maintained in the trial stage of the case.[630] In addition, when the decision of the pre-trial judge regarding the provision of documents in B/C/S was upheld by the appeals chamber and not reconsidered,[631] the accused instructed his legal advisors not to receive any more documents either.[632]

When the accused in *Tolimir* maintained his refusal to receive any disclosure not written in the Cyrillic script, the prosecution applied for counsel to be assigned to represent the interests of the defendant: it argued that the attitude of the accused with regard to receipt of disclosure and use of technical facilities hindered the proper and expeditious conduct of the proceedings.[633] The defendant rejected the allegation that he would refuse to accept materials disclosed to him, on the basis that he was simply not capable of understanding any language other than Serbian in the Cyrillic script and thus could not receive disclosure which did not correspond to these criteria.[634] The prosecution reiterated its submission that the accused was able to read the Latin script,

---

30 June 2008 (filed: 01 July 2008); Submission of the Accused to the Registrar of the Tribunal and the Pre-trial Chamber Pursuant to the Order of the Pre-trial Judge dated 30 June 2008 on Disclosure, 04 July 2008 (filed: 09 July 2008), para.9-10.

630 *Prosecutor v. Zdravko Tolimir*, Case No. IT-05-88/2-PT, Prosecution Submission Regarding 30 July 2008 Status Conference, 25 July 2008, para.3.

631 *Prosecutor v. Zdravko Tolimir*, Case No. IT-05-88/2-AR73.1, Decision on Zdravko Tolimir's Request for Reconsideration of the Appeals Chamber's Decision of 28 March 2008, 18 June 2008. *See also Prosecutor v. Zdravko Tolimir*, Case No. IT-05-88/2-PT, Accused's Motion to the President of the Tribunal and Members of the Appeals Chamber to Exercise their Discretionary Powers and Reconsider their Decision on the Appeal Against the Interlocutory Appeal Against the Oral Decision of the Pre-trial Judge of 11 December 2007, 16 April 2008 (filed: 18 April 2008); Supplement to the Accused Zdravko Tolimir's Motion to the President of the Tribunal and Members of the Appeals Chamber to Review their Decision on the Appeal Against the Decision of the Pre-trial Judge of 11 December 2007, 30 May 2008.

632 *Prosecutor v. Zdravko Tolimir*, Case No. IT-05-88/2-PT, Status Conference, 30 June 2008, T.175.

633 *Prosecutor v. Zdravko Tolimir*, Case No. IT-05-88/2-PT, Prosecution's Motion Requesting Appointment of Permanent Counsel for Accused Tolimir, 29 April 2008, para.21, 40.

634 *Prosecutor v. Zdravko Tolimir*, Case No. IT-05-88/2-PT, Response to the Prosecution's Motion Requesting the Appointment of Permanent Counsel for the Accused Tolimir, 02 June 2008 (filed: 05 June 2008), para.18, 22-23. *See also* Submission of the Accused to the Appeals and Pre-trial Chambers to Dismiss the Legally Unfounded Prosecution Motion Requesting Imposition of Counsel for the Accused Who is Conducting his own Defence, and Request that the Prosecution Withdraw its Motion, 06 May 2008 (filed: 19 May 2008).

should admit to it, and that otherwise counsel should be assigned.[635] In a status conference specifically scheduled for this purpose, the pre-trial judge explicitly admonished the accused that his refusal constituted behaviour substantially and persistently obstructing the proper and expeditious conduct of the trial and that if he did not accept the service of documents in B/C/S, whether written in Latin or Cyrillic, counsel would be imposed.[636] Subsequently, the legal associates to the accused resumed the reception of documents on behalf of the defendant.[637]

The matter arose again in the course of trial proceedings when the accused moved for an order that all transcripts of witness testimonies in previous trials be submitted to him in a language which he understands, instead of English or French, arguing that the work with audio recordings in B/C/S was too time-consuming for defence preparation.[638] The prosecution opposed the request, considering *inter alia* that the accused took an informed choice to defend himself[639] and that he failed to demonstrate any prejudice caused by provision of the audio recordings in B/C/S alongside transcripts in English or French.[640] The prosecution further submitted that, in light of the considerable amount of resources necessary for transcription of all relevant audio recordings of previous proceedings, the defendant should use the resources accorded to him under the legal aid scheme for any such enterprise.[641] In his

---

635 *Prosecutor v. Zdravko Tolimir*, Case No. IT-05-88/2-PT, Prosecution Submission Regarding 30 July 2008 Status Conference, 25 July 2008, para.4. *See also* Response to the Prosecutor's Submission of 25 July 2008, 28 July 2008 (filed: 29 July 2008).

636 *Prosecutor v. Zdravko Tolimir*, Case No. IT-05-88/2-PT, Status Conference, 30 June 2008, T.176-177.

637 *Prosecutor v. Zdravko Tolimir*, Case No. IT-05-88/2-PT, Status Conference, 30 July 2008, T.185. *See also* Statements in Accordance with the Decision of the Pre-trial Judge of 30 June 2008 Concerning Disclosure, 30 June 2008.

638 *Prosecutor v. Zdravko Tolimir*, Case No. IT-05-88/2-T, Zdravko Tolimir's Request for Transcripts in a Language which he Understands, 09 July 2010 (filed: 12 July 2010).

639 *Prosecutor v. Zdravko Tolimir*, Case No. IT-05-88/2-T, Prosecution's Response to Zdravko Tolimir's Request for Transcripts in a Language which he Understands, 23 July 2010, para.9.

640 *Prosecutor v. Zdravko Tolimir*, Case No. IT-05-88/2-T, Prosecution's Response to Zdravko Tolimir's Request for Transcripts in a Language which he Understands, 23 July 2010, para.9-10.

641 *Prosecutor v. Zdravko Tolimir*, Case No. IT-05-88/2-T, Prosecution's Response to Zdravko Tolimir's Request for Transcripts in a Language which he Understands, 23 July 2010, para.11-14.

reply, the accused additionally moved for the maintenance of the three days per week sitting schedule.[642]

The trial chamber denied the defence motion, as well as the additional request formulated in the defendant's reply, on the basis that the accused had further resources to apply for in order to address the issue and that he had not demonstrated either that the use of the audio recordings up to that point in time impeded his proper preparation or that a sitting schedule of four days per week would create further impediments.[643] In the trial chamber's view, it was under an obligation to equally safeguard the defendant's right to a fair and expeditious trial, which would not be possible if scarce resources were devoted to the transcription of audio recordings or if the number of sitting days was to be reduced.[644]

The accused in *Tolimir* consistently referred to his right to use his "mother tongue" before any court or tribunal, allegedly guaranteed by national and international legislation. However, considering for example the wording of the ICTY Statute, the language to be used in proceedings has to be one the accused understands, which does not necessarily mean that it has to be his or her mother tongue. The appeals chamber in its decision on the interlocutory appeal by the accused in *Tolimir* clarified that the obligation under Article 21(4) of the ICTY Statute required provision of material "in a language which the accused understands sufficiently in order to allow for the effective exercise of his right to conduct his defence".[645] It is obvious from this finding that the language of disclosure does not necessarily have to be the native language of an accused, as long as it is determined that conducting the proceedings in a language other than the defendant's mother tongue does not impede the effective personal presentation of the defence. The appeals chamber in *Karadžić* found no error in the trial chamber's application of the

---

642 *Prosecutor v. Zdravko Tolimir*, Case No. IT-05-88/2-T, Reply to the Responses of the Registrar and the Prosecutor and a Request Regarding the Trial Schedule, 11 August 2010 (filed: 13 August 2010), para.21-27.

643 *Prosecutor v. Zdravko Tolimir*, Case No. IT-05-88/2-T, Decision on Zdravko Tolimir's Request for Transcripts in a Language which he Understands, 27 August 2010, p.7.

644 *Prosecutor v. Zdravko Tolimir*, Case No. IT-05-88/2-T, Decision on Zdravko Tolimir's Request for Transcripts in a Language which he Understands, 27 August 2010, p.7-8.

645 *Prosecutor v. Zdravko Tolimir*, Case No. IT-05-88/2-AR73.1, Decision on Interlocutory Appeal Against Oral Decision of the Pre-trial Judge of 11 December 2007, 28 March 2008, para.15.

same standard as established by the appeals chamber in *Tolimir*.[646] Furthermore, the appeals chamber adopted the position that the volume of disclosure under Rule 66(A) of the ICTY RPE or the implications of comparing English transcripts to B/C/S recordings would not influence a determination of an accused's understanding of English for the purposes of the ICTY RPE.[647]

The approach of the trial chamber in *Tolimir* prompts the question whether provision of audio recordings together with transcripts in a language the accused does not understand can indeed be sufficient to safeguard the right to a fair trial. Preparation of a defence case, especially in combination with regular sitting days in court, involves rigours that call for stringent time and resource management. Yet, listening to audio recordings and in the following having a second person compare the references to such recordings with transcripts in another language in order to be able to effectively cross-examine prosecution witnesses amounts to tying up considerable resources which might otherwise be used for further – and more efficient as well as effective – preparation of the defence case. The argument that the defendant by choosing to represent himself at least implicitly conceded into enduring such disadvantages should not weigh too heavily in the balance against the fair trial right of the accused in this instance. This would be different to some extent only in cases where it is determined that a *pro se* defendant possesses language capabilities sufficient in order to understand transcripts in one of the official working languages of the international criminal tribunal in question and thus can in fact make efficient use of these transcripts him- or herself – without first having to resort to other people's assistance.

2. International Criminal Court

The wording adopted in the Rome Statute of the ICC is an additional factor to be noted in the context of potential language issues with regard to the rights of accused, as it is different from the formulations which can be found for example in the ICTY and ICTR Statutes.

---

646 *Prosecutor v. Radovan Karadžić*, Case No. IT-95-5/18-AR73.3, Decision on Interlocutory Appeal of the Trial Chamber's Decision on Prosecution Motion Seeking Determination that the Accused Understands English, 04 June 2009, para.13.

647 *Prosecutor v. Radovan Karadžić*, Case No. IT-95-5/18-AR73.3, Decision on Interlocutory Appeal of the Trial Chamber's Decision on Prosecution Motion Seeking Determination that the Accused Understands English, 04 June 2009, para.17.

Article 67(1)(a) of the ICC Statute provides for information of charges "in a language which the accused *fully* understands *and* speaks".[648] This formulation arguably sets the standard higher for a finding that proceedings can be conducted in a language other than the accused's mother tongue.[649] It seems that the notion was meant to indicate the acceptance of a preference voiced by the defendant.[650] This is in direct contrast to the position adopted *e.g.* in *Tolimir* before the ICTY, that it was not for the defendant to accept material only in a language which he prefers, but rather in a language he can understand.[651]

As a consequence, it is likely that before the ICC considerable resources will have to be deployed in order to ensure disclosure of material in a language which is not only actually understood and spoken, but even preferred, by the accused. Considering the wording of Rule 76(3) of the ICC RPE, such obligation would extend to materials concerning all witnesses to be called by the prosecution, which implies potentially vast amounts of material. However, neither Article 67(2) of the Rome Statute nor Rule 84 of the ICC RPE contain a similar requirement that potentially exculpatory material or additional disclosure before trial would have to be served in a language the accused fully understands and speaks. The only additional prerequisite that guarantees broader rights than the *ad hoc* tribunals can be found in Article

---

648 Emphasis added. *See also* Article 67(1)(f) Rome Statute: "To have, free of any cost, the assistance of a competent interpreter and such translations as are necessary to meet the requirements of fairness, if any of the proceedings of or documents presented to the Court are not in a language which the accused fully understands and speaks; [...]"; Rule 76(3) ICC RPE: "The statements of prosecution witnesses shall be made available in original and in a language which the accused fully understands and speaks."; Rules 144(2)(b), 187 ICC RPE.

649 To be noted is the French version of Article 67(1)(a) of the ICC Statute: « Être informé dans le plus court délai et de façon détaillée de la nature, de la cause et de la teneur des charges dans une langue qu'il comprend et parle *parfaitement* » (emphasis added). It has been submitted that the standard set in the French text is higher than that in the English version: *see Prosecutor v. Germain Katanga*, Case No. ICC-01/04-01/07, Defence Document in Support of Appeal Against "Decision on the Defence Request Concerning Languages", 31 January 2008 (filed: 01 February 2008), para.15.

650 William A Schabas, Article 67, in: Otto Triffterer (ed.), *Commentary on the Rome Statute of the International Criminal Court. Observers' Notes, Article by Article* (Munich: Verlag C.H.Beck) 2nd ed. 2008, p.1247-1274, at note 21.

651 *Prosecutor v. Zdravko Tolimir*, Case No. IT-05-88/2-PT, Status Conference, 11 December 2007, T.114: "[...] the right centres on understanding, not on preference." *See also* Status Conference, 14 September 2007, T.71-73.

67(1)(f) of the Rome Statute, which provides for "translations as are necessary to meet the requirements of fairness".[652]

In terms of interpretation of the Rome Statute, the ICC appeals chamber determined that an "accused fully understands and speaks a language when he or she is completely fluent in the language in ordinary, non-technical conversation".[653] In case of doubt, "the language being requested by the person should be accommodated".[654] The appeals chamber held that the standard set in Article 67 of the Statute had to be interpreted as "very high".[655] Taking into account the indication of the *travaux préparatoires* that good or bad faith would have to be considered in the context of a language request, the appeals chamber found that in case a chamber has reason to believe that the accused fully understands and speaks a working language of the Court, assessment of the situation would need to be made on a case-by-case basis.[656] According to the appeals chamber, in light of the high standard to be met under Article 67 of the Statute, "the language requested should be granted unless it is absolutely clear on the record that the person *fully* understands *and* speaks one of the working languages of the Court and is abusing his or her right under article 67 of the Statute".[657]

---

652 Article 67(1)(f) Rome Statute: "To have, free of any cost, the assistance of a competent interpreter and such translations as are necessary to meet the requirements of fairness, if any of the proceedings of or documents presented to the Court are not in a language which the accused fully understands and speaks; […]". Modelled upon Article 14(3)(f) ICCPR, Articles 21(4)(f) ICTY Statute, 20(4)(f) ICTR Statute, 17(4)(f) SCSL Statute, 16(4)(g) STL Statute, and 35(f) ECCC Law only mentioned "free assistance of an interpreter".

653 *Prosecutor v. Germain Katanga*, Case No. ICC-01/04-01/07, Judgment on the Appeal of Mr. Germain Katanga Against the Decision of Pre-trial Chamber I entitled "Decision on the Defence Request Concerning Languages", 27 May 2008, p.3, para.61.

654 *Prosecutor v. Germain Katanga*, Case No. ICC-01/04-01/07, Judgment on the Appeal of Mr. Germain Katanga Against the Decision of Pre-trial Chamber I entitled "Decision on the Defence Request Concerning Languages", 27 May 2008, p.4, para.61.

655 *Prosecutor v. Germain Katanga*, Case No. ICC-01/04-01/07, Judgment on the Appeal of Mr. Germain Katanga Against the Decision of Pre-trial Chamber I entitled "Decision on the Defence Request Concerning Languages", 27 May 2008, para.40.

656 *Prosecutor v. Germain Katanga*, Case No. ICC-01/04-01/07, Judgment on the Appeal of Mr. Germain Katanga Against the Decision of Pre-trial Chamber I entitled "Decision on the Defence Request Concerning Languages", 27 May 2008, para.60.

657 *Prosecutor v. Germain Katanga*, Case No. ICC-01/04-01/07, Judgment on the Appeal of Mr. Germain Katanga Against the Decision of Pre-trial Chamber I entitled

The scope of a "full" active and passive understanding of a language will still have to be determined on a case-by-case basis. However, it seems to indicate that especially in proceedings with *pro se* defendants, it will have to be established whether an accused's language capabilities do indeed reach a sufficient level of fluency. While the working languages of the Court are, like before the *ad hoc* tribunals, English and French,[658] the official languages furthermore include Arabic, Chinese, Russian and Spanish. The Rules of Procedure and Evidence provide for the possibility to designate these languages as additional working languages if the majority of people involved in a case understand and speak the language in question.[659] While this in general provides for resources necessary to meet any requests with regard to six major languages, in light of the situations dealt with before the ICC, there exists a substantial likelihood that more specific language needs may have to be met in case an accused decides to conduct the defence in person.

In light of the trial chamber's jurisdiction to decide on the relevant disclosure that is to be made, the bench is arguably equally competent to decide on the language in which the material has to be provided. In cases with self-represented accused it is necessary to ensure that all materials related to the proceedings would be available to the accused in some form and in the preferred language. The notion of "requirements of fairness" arguably accords trial chambers a certain margin of appreciation in their determination as to which material concerned with the case need to be translated into a language the defendant indeed fully understands and speaks. From a logistical point of view, this would mean that the ICC would have to engage interpreters, translators and other language assistants on an *ad hoc* basis depending on the language chosen by a self-represented accused for the course of the proceedings.

V. Adequate time and facilities for self-represented accused

A comparison of filings in different cases before international criminal tribunals indicates that one of the most significant questions relates to the

---

"Decision on the Defence Request Concerning Languages", 27 May 2008, para.61 (emphasis in the original).

658 Article 50(2) Rome Statute.

659 Rule 41 ICC RPE.

issue of adequate time and facilities necessary for the preparation of the defence.

In the international human rights context, the Human Rights Committee, commenting on Article 14 of the ICCPR and the question of the content of a right to adequate time and facilities, considered the exact scope of the guarantee to be contingent on the "circumstances of each case".[660]

Article 67 of the Rome Statute provides the right to adequate times and facilities of accused[661] as do the pertinent provisions of other international criminal tribunals.[662] Another relevant provision with regard to specific rules for providing facilities to self-represented accused before the ICC could be Rule 20(1)(e) of the ICC RPE, which includes the generic reference to provision of facilities to "the defence".[663] With regard to the assignment of legal assistance, the procedure is regulated in Rule 21 of the ICC RPE which provides in paragraph 4 that an accused choosing to conduct his or her own defence is to notify the ICC registry in writing of this choice.

The question of equality of arms features prominently among the arguments that are regularly advanced in the context of the provision concerning adequate time and facilities.[664] The matter of potential inequality of arms

---

660 Human Rights Committee, General Comment No. 13, 13 April 1984, para.9; General Comment No. 32, CCPR/C/GC/32, 23 August 2007, para.32.

661 Article 67(1)(b) ICC Statute: "1. In the determination of any charge, the accused shall be entitled to a public hearing, having regard to the provisions of this Statute, to a fair hearing conducted impartially, and to the following minimum guarantees, in full equality: [...] (b) To have adequate time and facilities for the preparation of the defence [...];".

662 Article 21(4)(b) ICTY Statute; Article 20(4)(b) ICTR Statute; Article 17(4)(b) SCSL Statute; Article 16(4)(b) STL Statute; Article 35 new ECCC law.

663 Rule 20(1)(e) ICC RPE reads: "In accordance with article 43, paragraph 1, the Registrar shall organize the staff of the Registry in a manner that promotes the rights of the defence, consistent with the principle of a fair trial as defined in the Statute. For that purpose, the Registrar shall, *inter alia*: [...] (e) Provide the defence with such facilities as may be necessary for the direct performance of the duty of the defence; [...]".

664 *See, e.g., Prosecutor v. Radovan Karadžić*, Case No. IT-95-5/18-PT, Status Conference, 19 January 2009, T.100-101: "[...] I don't know what the Trial Chamber has decided with respect to the equality of arms and the financing of my Defence, but development will depend on that because I won't be able to retain prominent lawyers, very prominent lawyers, and pay them by the hour unless I am given resources to do that, and if I don't have their advice and counsel, then I really will have to self-represent, and this will, of course, have an effect on a fair trial, the semblance of a fair trial."

and any impact on the fairness of the proceedings has even been characterised as "the very crux of the argument about self-representation".[665]

One more recent decision of the ICTR appeals chamber shall be considered in order to give the relevant background for an interpretation of that notion. In *Ngirabatware*, the accused appealed against the trial chamber's decision determining the trial start date,[666] arguing, *inter alia*, that in light of a recent amendment of the indictment and the inequality of arms, he did not have sufficient time to adequately prepare his defence.[667] The appeals chamber in its decision recalled that trial chambers would be accorded a margin of appreciation with regard to trial management issues, including in the context of scheduling trials, discretion which would however be curbed by the need to guarantee fair and expeditious proceedings.[668] The appeals chamber granted the appeal on the basis that the trial chamber failed to consider a number of factors in reaching its conclusion.[669] Notwithstanding, the appeals chamber deemed it impossible to "set a standard of what constitutes adequate time to prepare a defence" given that such an assessment would be subject to different factors, *e.g.* gravity of charges and complexity of the case or the staffing of the defence team.[670] More importantly, considering the argument of the accused that the principle of equality of arms had been violated, the appeals chamber found that this principle "should not be interpreted to mean that the Defence is entitled to exact the same means as the Prosecution".[671]

---

665 Gideon Boas, Self-Representation Before the ICTY. A Case for Reform, 9 *Journal of International Criminal Justice* 53 (2011), at 79.

666 *See Prosecutor v. Augustin Ngirabatware*, ICTR-99-54-T, Decision on Defence Motion to Vary Trial Date, 25 March 2009. *See also* Decision on Defence Motion to Vacate Trial Date of 4 May 2009, 25 February 2009.

667 *Prosecutor v. Augustin Ngirabatware*, ICTR-99-54-T, Decision on Defence Motion to Vacate Trial Date of 4 May 2009, 25 February 2009, para.1-6; Decision on Defence Motion to Vary Trial Date, 25 March 2009, para.6-9, 14-16.

668 *Prosecutor v. Augustin Ngirabatware*, ICTR-99-54-A, Decision on Augustin Ngirabatware's Appeal of Decisions Denying Motions to Vary Trial Date, 12 May 2009, para.22.

669 *Prosecutor v. Augustin Ngirabatware*, ICTR-99-54-A, Decision on Augustin Ngirabatware's Appeal of Decisions Denying Motions to Vary Trial Date, 12 May 2009, para.27.

670 *Prosecutor v. Augustin Ngirabatware*, ICTR-99-54-A, Decision on Augustin Ngirabatware's Appeal of Decisions Denying Motions to Vary Trial Date, 12 May 2009, para.28.

671 *Prosecutor v. Augustin Ngirabatware*, ICTR-99-54-A, Decision on Augustin Ngirabatware's Appeal of Decisions Denying Motions to Vary Trial Date, 12 May 2009, para.28.

A pre-trial chamber at the ICC found equality of arms to depend on the circumstances of each case and, referring to a decision rendered by the European Court of Human Rights,[672] to require that each party be accorded the opportunity to present evidence in support of its case, without being placed at a disadvantage compared to the opposing party.[673]

In the context of self-represented accused, international criminal tribunals like the ICTY endeavoured to set specific standards for the determination of funding matters, for example in the ICTY Remuneration Scheme for Persons Assisting Indigent Self-represented Accused.[674] While this scheme provided a general framework, further amendment was required in light of subsequent decisions, specifically when the pre-trial chamber in *Karadžić* interpreted the position of the appeals chamber in an earlier decision in *Krajišnik* to mean that "it is not for the Registry to fund the provision to a self-represented accused of expensive legal advice"[675] and that it would not be required "to fund experienced high-level lawyers to support a self-represented accused".[676]

This interpretation of the procedural framework in the jurisprudence indicates that while judges are conscious of the need to ensure a fair trial in particular in cases of self-represented accused on the one hand, a position adopted consistently throughout on the other hand leaves no doubt that *pro se* defendants will have to accept certain consequences resulting from their choice to present their defence in person. At the same time, this approach begs the question whether the standards applied to self-represented accused in terms of financial remuneration for legal assistance ought to be different

---

672 *Dombo Beheer B.V. v. The Netherlands*, Application no. 14448/88, Judgement, 27 October 1993, para.33.

673 *Procureur c. Thomas Lubanga Dyilo*, Affaire n° ICC-01/04-01/06, Décision sur la Demande d'Autorisation d'Appel de la Défense Relative à la Transmission des Demandes de Participation des Victimes, 06 novembre 2006, p.7. *See also* Situation in Uganda, No. ICC-02/04-01/05, Decision on Prosecutor's Application for Leave to Appeal in part Pre-trial Chamber II's Decision on the Prosecutor's Applications for Warrants of Arrest under Article 58, 19 August 2005, para.30, fn.50.

674 Remuneration Scheme for Persons Assisting Indigent Self-Represented Accused, 01 April 2010, Rev. 2.

675 *Prosecutor v. Radovan Karadžić*, Case No. IT-95-5/18-PT, Decision on Accused Motion for Adequate Facilities and Equality of Arms: Legal Associates, 28 January 2009, para.31.

676 *Prosecutor v. Radovan Karadžić*, Case No. IT-95-5/18-PT, Decision on Accused Motion for Adequate Facilities and Equality of Arms: Legal Associates, 28 January 2009, para.32.

from those considered to be applicable to defendants represented by qualified legal counsel. Eventually, it will depend on the professional assessment of the bench to ensure that the accused is in a position to effectively prepare and present a defence case with all the assistance required to safeguard his or her fair trial rights, while at the same time making abundantly clear that in accordance with consistent practice, defendants presenting their case in person in fact do act in counsel's stead, thereby eliminating the need to finance a professional defence attorney at a lead counsel rate.

1. Adequate time

Turning to the matter of adequate time for the preparation of the defence case, it appears that trial and appeals chambers do allow for the possibility to grant a self-represented accused more time than a defendant represented by counsel might get.[677] Trial chambers in different cases mentioned for example measures such as suspension or adjournment, as well as extensions of time in the course of trial proceedings in order to give the accused adequate time to prepare.[678]

Such schemes could be envisaged *e.g.* in order to give a defendant the possibility to properly organise the cross-examination of specific witnesses; digest newly discovered material to be used by the prosecution; or adequately respond to motions filed by the opposing party. Yet, it is necessary to take into consideration that any suspensions, adjournments or extensions of time limits form part of the factors that often contribute to delays in proceedings and thus impact on the expeditiousness of the trial.

---

677 *See e.g. Prosecutor v. Slobodan Milošević*, Case No. IT-02-54-AR73.6, Decision on the Interlocutory Appeal by the *Amici Curiae* Against the Trial Chamber Order Concerning the Presentation and Preparation of the Defence Case, 20 January 2004, para.20.

678 *See e.g. Prosecutor v. Radovan Karadžić*, Case No. IT-95-5/18-T, Decision on the Accused's Motion for Postponement of Trial, 26 February 2010, para.40, 42, 47; Decision on Accused's Motion for Suspension of Proceedings, 18 August 2010; *Prosecutor v. Zdravko Tolimir*, Case No. IT-05-88/2-T, Decision on the Accused's Information and Requests for the Trial Chamber, 04 March 2010, para.13. *See*, however, *Prosecutor v. Zdravko Tolimir*, Case No. IT-05-88/2-PT, Decision on Motion for Suspension of Time Limit for Filing of Preliminary Motions, 18 October 2007.

Considering the positions of a number of self-represented accused, however, it appears that defendants themselves are more concerned with being given time which in their view is adequate to prepare, rather than with the expeditious conclusion of their proceedings.[679]

First to be mentioned is the situation in *Tolimir*, case in which the defendant took a proactive step and suggested an approximate date at which the pre-trial conference could be held, having regard to the matters to be dealt with by the accused and his defence team.[680] The prosecution agreed with the suggested timing and start of trial,[681] whereas the pre-trial judge initially anticipated the case to be ready for trial approximately two months before the proposed date.[682] The next time the accused outlined his position with regard to a potential trial start date, he disagreed with the start date set by the trial chamber, in particular in light of the altered composition of the trial chamber, but also taking into consideration outstanding necessary preparations to be carried out by the defence and decisions pending before the trial chamber.[683] The position of the accused in this case is remarkable insofar as he did not seem to ask for excessive amounts of preparation time but rather appeared to give reasonable consideration to the time in fact needed in order to prepare for the presentation of his case in his capacity as *pro se* defendant.

---

679 *See e.g. Prosecutor v. Radovan Karadžić*, Case No. IT-95-5/18-T, Hearing, 04 November 2010, T.8990: "Actually, time is not of the essence; truth is of the essence. And I do not wish these proceedings to be made invalid because of a number of minutes." *See also* Mark Lewis, The Trial of Radovan Karadzic: The Accused Takes up his Own Defense, 01 November 2012, available at http://world.time.com/2012/11/01/the-trial-of-radovan-karadzic-the-accused-takes-up-his-own-defense/#ixzz2B3FabTJV (last accessed 02 November 2012): "The strategy of total denial, as well as Karadzic's insistence that he represents himself, means he will be defending his case until 2014, at least. It also means that former Bosnian Serb leader delays, for as long as possible, the conviction that Robinson says even Karadzic knows is inevitable and his probably lifetime jail sentence."

680 *Prosecutor v. Zdravko Tolimir*, Case No. IT-05-88/2-PT, Notification, 23 June 2009.

681 *Prosecutor v. Zdravko Tolimir*, Case No. IT-05-88/2-PT, Status Conference, 25 June 2009, T.253-254.

682 *Prosecutor v. Zdravko Tolimir*, Case No. IT-05-88/2-PT, Status Conference, 25 June 2009, T.252-253, 254-255.

683 *Prosecutor v. Zdravko Tolimir*, Case No. IT-05-88/2-PT, Notification, 19 October 2009.

In contrast, most self-represented accused appear to ask for as much time for trial preparation as potentially feasible, justifying their demands with the alleged necessity to prepare for presenting their defence in person: Slobodan Milošević made clear at a time the trial had already started that in his estimate, and in light of the scope of the indictment and related material that needed to be reviewed, he would need at a minimum two years in order to prepare his defence, arguing that this would be in keeping with the principle of equality of arms.[684] *Amicus curiae* underscored the arguments in favour of an adequate preparation time for the defence case being given to the accused in light of the scope of the case and the facilities available to the defendant in custody, indicating that cases with lower-level accused often had six months to prepare for their defence cases.[685]

The accused in *Karadžić* submitted repeatedly that he was not given sufficient time to adequately prepare his defence.[686] Providing detailed calculations of the time needed for preparatory works,[687] the defendant argued that the relevant issues had to be dealt with before the commencement of trial.[688]

---

684 *Prosecutor v. Slobodan Milošević*, Case No. IT-02-54-T, Pre-Defence Conference, 02 September 2003, T.25942-25945, T.25963-25964.

685 *Prosecutor v. Slobodan Milošević*, Case No. IT-02-54-T, Pre-Defence Conference, 02 September 2003, T.25948-25951, T.25952-25954.

686 *See e.g. Prosecutor v. Radovan Karadžić*, Case No. IT-95-5/18-PT, Submission on Commencement of Trial, 03 September 2009, para.1 ("Dr Karadžić wishes to alert the Trial Chamber that, should the scope of the trial retain its current or proposed size, he will need an additional 10 months for trial preparation."); *Prosecutor v. Radovan Karadžić*, Case No. IT-95-5/18-AR73.5, Appeal of Decision on Commencement of Trial, 25 September 2009 (*see, e.g.*, para.2: "This is a watershed issue for the fairness of the trial. Dr Karadžić has cooperated fully with the Tribunal during the pre-trial stage of this case. He has been working day and night to prepare for his trial and to bring out the truth of what happened in Bosnia. But he cannot agree to participate in proceedings which will be fundamentally unfair from the beginning."); *Prosecutor v. Radovan Karadžić*, Case No. IT-95-5/18-PT, Submissions on Trial Procedure, 28 September 2009, para.2; Pre-trial Conference, 06 October 2009, T.500; *Prosecutor v. Radovan Karadžić*, Case No. IT-95-5/18-T, Hearing on Trial Proceedings, 03 November 2009, T.676-678, T.697-703; Status Conference, 28 January 2010, T.739.

687 *Prosecutor v. Radovan Karadžić*, Case No. IT-95-5/18-PT, Submission on Commencement of Trial, 03 September 2009, para.16-30.

688 *Prosecutor v. Radovan Karadžić*, Case No. IT-95-5/18-PT, Submission on Commencement of Trial, 03 September 2009, para.15: "All the tasks identified below must be completed before the trial commences. Once the trial begins, there will not be enough time for such tasks."

This led the accused to conclude that over one year after his arrest and transfer to the ICTY, he would need another ten months before the start of trial proceedings in order to commence "adequately prepared" and still fall within the calculated average of pre-trial periods in other cases.[689] The defendant reiterated this position in light of the complexity of the case; the scope of the indictment; the volume of the prosecution's disclosure; the extent of the assistance provided by his defence team; as well as the fact that he was not only self-represented, but also determined to understand English for purposes of the ICTY Statute and RPE, which would increase the time needed by him for reading documents not in his native language.[690] In his filings, the accused made clear that he would consider any trial commencing without adequate time for preparation having been given to him to be unfair, and a trial in which he would not participate.[691] The defendant's firm conviction that he would need more time for preparation and that he could only meaningfully participate in a trial for which he was – in his view – sufficiently prepared, eventually led him to boycott the scheduled trial start, announcing that he would inform the trial chamber and prosecution as soon as he deemed himself ready to proceed.[692] The accused submitted:

> "Resultantly, we have now the worst scenario possible, which should have been avoided at all costs – beginning of a process that is not ready to start: the biggest, most complex, important and sensitive case ever before this Tribunal is about to begin without proper preparation; process that is supposed to reveal the final truth about our conflict and close an old, and turn a new page in our history; process that will determine future relations among the peoples in the region for the following century, perhaps for good; process that will finally determine many destinies, and justify or reverse an enormous injustice done to many individuals, families and even to whole communities; process that is of an undoubtedly great importance for the Tribunal itself, because this process will show the real nature of the Tribunal, what it is and what it should be like in the

---

689 *Prosecutor v. Radovan Karadžić*, Case No. IT-95-5/18-PT, Submission on Commencement of Trial, 03 September 2009, para.34-35.

690 *Prosecutor v. Radovan Karadžić*, Case No. IT-95-5/18-AR73.5, Appeal of Decision on Commencement of Trial, 25 September 2009, para.41-65. *See also* Reply Brief: Appeal of Decision on Commencement of Trial, 12 October 2009, para.13-18.

691 *Prosecutor v. Radovan Karadžić*, Case No. IT-95-5/18-AR73.5, Appeal of Decision on Commencement of Trial, 25 September 2009, para.2; Reply Brief: Appeal of Decision on Commencement of Trial, 12 October 2009, para.37.

692 *Prosecutor v. Radovan Karadžić*, Case No. IT-95-5/18-PT, Submission on the Commencement of Trial, 21 October 2009; Response to the Letter from the Chamber, 24 October 2009 (filed: 26 October 2009); *Prosecutor v. Radovan Karadžić*, Case No. IT-95-5/18-T, Letter to Presiding Judge, 02 November 2009.

future when prospective civil and military leaders of (small) countries are put to trial; and all this is happening in unequal, disproportionate and unjust circumstances, where the defence is deprived of an absolute minimum conditions for the preparations that would make the defence a serious and respectable opponent."[693]

The appeals chamber seised of the appeal against the trial chamber's decision rejecting the accused's submission on commencement of trial showed itself no more convinced of the arguments by the defendant than the trial judges: it found that the trial chamber was aware of the facts and specific circumstances of the case when making its decision that the trial was ready to commence, and that it did not abuse its discretion in weighing the different factors in reaching this conclusion.[694] However, the appeals chamber did acknowledge that the pending filing of a revised version of the indictment by the prosecution would necessitate the accused to be accorded a short time for review, and thus ordered the trial to begin one week after the filing of the marked-up indictment.[695]

At a later stage of the proceedings, the accused filed a motion requiring the suspension of proceedings for one month before the start of the Srebrenica component of the case, in order to have sufficient time to review disclosure material relevant to that specific component.[696] However, the trial chamber denied the motion on the basis that the accused failed to show good cause for a suspension of the proceedings.[697] According to the chamber:

"Given that the Accused has chosen to represent himself, he bears the burden of managing his own case and the resources granted to him. The Chamber finds

693 *Prosecutor v. Radovan Karadžić*, Case No. IT-95-5/18-PT, Submission on the Commencement of Trial, 21 October 2009, p.2 (emphasis in the original).

694 *Prosecutor v. Radovan Karadžić*, Case No. IT-95-5/18-AR73.5, Decision on Radovan Karadžić's Appeal of the Decision on Commencement of Trial, 13 October 2009, para.21-24.

695 *Prosecutor v. Radovan Karadžić*, Case No. IT-95-5/18-AR73.5, Decision on Radovan Karadžić's Appeal of the Decision on Commencement of Trial, 13 October 2009, para.25-27. This decision in fact postponed the initially scheduled start date for no more than one week.

696 *Prosecutor v. Radovan Karadžić*, Case No. IT-95-5/18-T, Motion for Suspension of Proceedings Prior to Srebrenica Evidence, 11 November 2011, para.1, 6; Supplemental Submission: Motion for Suspension of Proceedings Prior to Srebrenica Evidence, 18 November 2011.

697 *Prosecutor v. Radovan Karadžić*, Case No. IT-95-5/18-T, Decision on Accused's Motion for Suspension of Proceedings Prior to Start of Srebrenica Evidence, 22 November 2011, para.23.

it regrettable that the Accused continues to argue in support of his requests the issue of resource-limitations as an obstacle to his ongoing trial preparation."[698]

Less a question of preparation time and more an argument concerned with the equality of arms as mentioned earlier proved to be the discussion regarding the amount of time to be given to the accused in order to present his defence case: when he asked to be granted 600 hours in which to present his view of events[699] – in contrast to the 300 hours allocated to the prosecution[700] – the trial chamber "question[ed] the rationale behind the accused calling all of the witnesses listed in his Rule 65 *ter* list"[701] and eventually decided to give the accused 300 hours to present his case.[702] The accused appealed against the decision, arguing that he needed time to rebut adjudicated facts[703] and also in order to be able to present the "specific nature" of his defence case.[704]

Another specific example concerning the matter of preparation time arose in *Karadžić* after the trial chamber declared its intention to change the sitting schedule from three to four days a week from June 2010 onwards. The accused argued in an oral submission that the defence team "can barely take three days a week, with the resources [it has]".[705] According to him:

"From the point of view of the Defence, this is an opportunity to conduct exemplary hearings at an exemplary trial that will serve the purposes of international

698 *Prosecutor v. Radovan Karadžić*, Case No. IT-95-5/18-T, Decision on Accused's Motion for Suspension of Proceedings Prior to Start of Srebrenica Evidence, 22 November 2011, para.19 (fn. omitted).

699 *Prosecutor v. Radovan Karadžić*, Case No. IT-95-5/18-T, Defence Submission Pursuant to Rule 65 *ter* and Related Motions, 27 August 2012, para.3.

700 *Prosecutor v. Radovan Karadžić*, Case No. IT-95-5/18-T, Pre-trial Conference, 06 October 2009, T.467.

701 *Prosecutor v. Radovan Karadžić*, Case No. IT-95-5/18-T, Status Conference, 03 September 2012, T.28791.

702 *Prosecutor v. Radovan Karadžić*, Case No. IT-95-5/18-T, Decision on Time Allocated to the Accused for the Presentation of his Case, 19 September 2012, para.12, 14.

703 *Prosecutor v. Radovan Karadžić*, Case No. IT-95-5/18-AR73.10, Appeal from Decision on Duration of Defence Case, 11 October 2012 (filed: 12 October 2012), para.19-35.

704 *Prosecutor v. Radovan Karadžić*, Case No. IT-95-5/18-AR73.10, Appeal from Decision on Duration of Defence Case, 11 October 2012 (filed: 12 October 2012), para.42-45.

705 *Prosecutor v. Radovan Karadžić*, Case No. IT-95-5/18-T, Hearing, 19 May 2010, T.2374.

> justice. If that is not the case, we are going to be facing difficulties. We are not going to have a fair trial, we are not going to have an opportunity to present everything that we wish to present and everything that we are supposed to do, in view of everything that the Prosecution is accusing us of."[706]

After having heard from both parties on the matter, the presiding judge merely replied that the accused "will be surprised to hear that the Chamber is minded to sit five days a week from after the recess".[707] Stating that the trial chamber would consider the submissions, the presiding judge concluded that "one potential solution may be to have an exemplary hearing with you being represented, a full team capable of investigating, defending, etc."[708]

In its written decision on this topic, the trial chamber gave some clear indications of its position on the question at hand: it first recalled that the temporary nature of a sitting schedule with three days per week had been known by the accused for several months.[709] The bench then proceeded by dismissing the arguments raised by the defendant with regard to his allegedly limited resources and time needed for preparation of the defence case: given that the accused had been on notice of the witnesses to be called by the prosecution in the first months of the trial for a considerable period, the trial chamber was "convinced that the Accused has had ample time both before the presentation of evidence began and during these last months of trial to prepare his cross-examination".[710] Furthermore, the judges did not agree with the submission that the resources made available to the accused were not sufficient to continue with a sitting schedule in excess of a three-day week, since, in view of the trial chamber, the resources granted by the ICTY President were "comparable to those available to an accused represented by counsel".[711] The bench showed itself "surprised that the Accused continues

---

706 *Prosecutor v. Radovan Karadžić*, Case No. IT-95-5/18, Hearing, 19 May 2010, T.2375.

707 *Prosecutor v. Radovan Karadžić*, Case No. IT-95-5/18, Hearing, 19 May 2010, T.2381.

708 *Prosecutor v. Radovan Karadžić*, Case No. IT-95-5/18, Hearing, 19 May 2010, T.2381.

709 *Prosecutor v. Radovan Karadžić*, Case No. IT-95-5/18-T, Order on the Trial Schedule, 27 May 2010, para.3.

710 *Prosecutor v. Radovan Karadžić*, Case No. IT-95-5/18-T, Order on the Trial Schedule, 27 May 2010, para.4.

711 *Prosecutor v. Radovan Karadžić*, Case No. IT-95-5/18-T, Order on the Trial Schedule, 27 May 2010, para.5.

to raise the issue of resource limitations as a factor in support of any request, particularly the current one".[712] The trial chamber

> "[o]nce again, […] strongly encourage[d] the Accused to use the time and resources that he already has in an effective manner, bearing in mind that his role is simply to create reasonable doubt in the minds of the Judges in relation to the charges in the Indictment."[713]

Finally, the trial chamber considered the argument that an augmented sitting schedule would negatively impact on the health of the accused to be without merit.[714]

After certification to appeal was granted by the bench,[715] which at the same time denied the accused's request for staying the effect of the order,[716] the defendant appealed alleging an incorrect interpretation of the law by the trial chamber by equating his situation with that of defendants represented by counsel.[717] As on other occasions, the defendant considered that such an interpretation would jeopardise the effective exercise of his right to self-representation,[718] *inter alia* since his status as self-represented accused would require him to cross-examine all prosecution witnesses alone, unmanageable for him with an extended sitting schedule.[719] The defendant thought the trial chamber to be resolved to end his self-representation, given that standby counsel had been assigned and in view of the suggestion of the presiding judge to hold an exemplary hearing with the accused being represented by

---

712 *Prosecutor v. Radovan Karadžić*, Case No. IT-95-5/18-T, Order on the Trial Schedule, 27 May 2010, para.5.

713 *Prosecutor v. Radovan Karadžić*, Case No. IT-95-5/18-T, Order on the Trial Schedule, 27 May 2010, para.6.

714 *Prosecutor v. Radovan Karadžić*, Case No. IT-95-5/18-T, Order on the Trial Schedule, 27 May 2010, para.7.

715 *Prosecutor v. Radovan Karadžić*, Case No. IT-95-5/18-T, Decision on Accused's Application for Certification to Appeal the Trial Chamber's Order on Trial Schedule and for Stay, 04 June 2010. *See also* Application for Certification to Appeal Order on Trial Schedule and For Stay Pending Appeal, 31 May 2010.

716 *Prosecutor v. Radovan Karadžić*, Case No. IT-95-5/18-T, Decision on Accused's Application for Certification to Appeal the Trial Chamber's Order on Trial Schedule and for Stay, 04 June 2010, para.8.

717 *Prosecutor v. Radovan Karadžić*, Case No. IT-95-5/18-AR73.8, Appeal from Order on the Trial Schedule, 10 June 2010, para.11.

718 *Prosecutor v. Radovan Karadžić*, Case No. IT-95-5/18-AR73.8, Appeal from Order on the Trial Schedule, 10 June 2010, para.13.

719 *Prosecutor v. Radovan Karadžić*, Case No. IT-95-5/18-AR73.8, Appeal from Order on the Trial Schedule, 10 June 2010, para.14, 20.

counsel.[720] In light of these circumstances, the appellant submitted that the interpretation by the trial chamber was erroneous.[721] In addition, the accused drew parallels of his situation with the cases of three other *pro se* defendants, one of which suffered from health problems and eventually died in the course of trial, while in the other two cases the sitting schedule would amount at most to three days per week.[722] The defendant submitted that:

> "Dr. Karadzic recognises that a Trial Chamber has wide discretion over the conduct and management of a trial. He has stretched his resources and personal strength to the maximum to comply with the arduous requirements of the Trial Chamber since the presentation of evidence began, not missing a day of court nor a single filing deadline. However, he is only human. To require him to do this job alone on a four day a week basis jeopardises not only the fairness of the trial, but his own health."[723]

The appeals chamber dismissed the appeal in its entirety: referring to an earlier decision of the appeals chamber in the same case, the judges reiterated that an accused opting for self-representation would be expected to perform the tasks usually performed by professional counsel, including daily trial preparation.[724] The bench left no doubt that despite the necessity to protect the fair trial rights of *pro se* defendants, such accused would, by virtue of their choice of self-representation, forego many advantages accused represented by counsel might have.[725] The appeals chamber found that the trial chamber committed no error in law in the impugned decision given that it gave due consideration to a number of factors, including the "considerable

---

720 *Prosecutor v. Radovan Karadžić*, Case No. IT-95-5/18-AR73.8, Appeal from Order on the Trial Schedule, 10 June 2010, para.16: "The Trial Chamber seems determined to force Dr. Karadzic into forfeiting his right to self representation."

721 *Prosecutor v. Radovan Karadžić*, Case No. IT-95-5/18-AR73.8, Appeal from Order on the Trial Schedule, 10 June 2010, para.17.

722 *Prosecutor v. Radovan Karadžić*, Case No. IT-95-5/18-AR73.8, Appeal from Order on the Trial Schedule, 10 June 2010, para.18.

723 *Prosecutor v. Radovan Karadžić*, Case No. IT-95-5/18-AR73.8, Appeal from Order on the Trial Schedule, 10 June 2010, para.23.

724 *Prosecutor v. Radovan Karadžić*, Case No. IT-95-5/18-AR73.8, Decision on Appeal from Order on the Trial Schedule, 19 July 2010, para.11, referring to *Prosecutor v. Radovan Karadžić*, Case No. IT-95-5/18-AR73.2, Decision on Interlocutory Appeal of the Trial Chamber's Decision on Adequate Facilities, 07 May 2009, para.23.

725 *Prosecutor v. Radovan Karadžić*, Case No. IT-95-5/18-AR73.8, Decision on Appeal from Order on the Trial Schedule, 19 July 2010, para.11.

resources" at the disposal of the accused.[726] It furthermore considered in passing – mention given merely in a footnote –, to be without merit the arguments regarding alleged inequality of arms and potential ill-health of the accused.[727]

The accused in *Tolimir* would raise comparable issues with regard to the matter of sitting days per week at approximately the same time as in *Karadžić*, albeit with some factual variations. Having started the evidentiary phase with two sitting days per week, the trial chamber scheduled four sitting days per week for the month of June 2010. The accused objected to this planning in a submission in which he detailed that, for a number of reasons, he would not be able to proceed with an increased sitting schedule: he argued that due to the half-hourly checks even at night-time in the detention unit on the basis of medical assessments, he suffered from constant sleep deprivation which rendered his preparation for trial considerably more difficult.[728] Furthermore, in the defendant's view, the extensive use of the procedure under Rule 92*ter* of the ICTY RPE made the defence preparation even more intensive, since the prosecution would not spend much time with direct examination, thereby increasing the pace for the defence,[729] which additionally also had to cope with language barriers[730] and issues with regard to the number of defence team members.[731] The accused submitted that the probable importance of witnesses called pursuant to Rule 92*ter* would ask for even more intensive

726 *Prosecutor v. Radovan Karadžić*, Case No. IT-95-5/18-AR73.8, Decision on Appeal from Order on the Trial Schedule, 19 July 2010, para.12.

727 *Prosecutor v. Radovan Karadžić*, Case No. IT-95-5/18-AR73.8, Decision on Appeal from Order on the Trial Schedule, 19 July 2010, para.12 fn.32.

728 *Prosecutor v. Zdravko Tolimir*, Case No. IT-05-88/2-T, Zdravko Tolimir's Submission Concerning the Possible Trial Schedule for June, 10 May 2010 (filed: 13 May 2010), para.3.

729 *Prosecutor v. Zdravko Tolimir*, Case No. IT-05-88/2-T, Zdravko Tolimir's Submission Concerning the Possible Trial Schedule for June, 10 May 2010 (filed: 13 May 2010), para.4. *See also* para.9.

730 *Prosecutor v. Zdravko Tolimir*, Case No. IT-05-88/2-T, Zdravko Tolimir's Submission Concerning the Possible Trial Schedule for June, 10 May 2010 (filed: 13 May 2010), para.5.

731 *Prosecutor v. Zdravko Tolimir*, Case No. IT-05-88/2-T, Zdravko Tolimir's Submission Concerning the Possible Trial Schedule for June, 10 May 2010 (filed: 13 May 2010), para.12.

preparations of their cross-examination.[732] One specific argument concerned the voluminous disclosure by the prosecution only shortly before the filing, including material of recently completed cases and items which might potentially be of importance to the defence strategy.[733] Similarly, the accused argued that the at the time impending judgement in the *Popović* case would in light of the close connection of the two cases require time and resources in order to be analysed carefully.[734] Finally, the defendant drew a comparison to the other cases with self-represented accused and concluded that the particular circumstances in his own case would call for a sitting schedule of two days per week.[735]

The trial chamber in *Tolimir* granted the accused's request in part and decided to schedule three sitting days per week until the summer court recess, notifying, however, the parties of its intention to increase the number of sitting days per week after the break.[736]

Of particular interest is the remark of the bench that any determination of the pace of proceedings would need to be based on the circumstances of the specific case, and should not be influenced by the approach taken in other proceedings with *pro se* defendants.[737] While this view on the one hand appears to be reasonable insofar as especially the scheduling of trials lies within the discretion of the respective trial chamber[738] due to its "organic

---

732 *Prosecutor v. Zdravko Tolimir*, Case No. IT-05-88/2-T, Zdravko Tolimir's Submission Concerning the Possible Trial Schedule for June, 10 May 2010 (filed: 13 May 2010), para.13.

733 *Prosecutor v. Zdravko Tolimir*, Case No. IT-05-88/2-T, Zdravko Tolimir's Submission Concerning the Possible Trial Schedule for June, 10 May 2010 (filed: 13 May 2010), para.6, 7.

734 *Prosecutor v. Zdravko Tolimir*, Case No. IT-05-88/2-T, Zdravko Tolimir's Submission Concerning the Possible Trial Schedule for June, 10 May 2010 (filed: 13 May 2010), para.10.

735 *Prosecutor v. Zdravko Tolimir*, Case No. IT-05-88/2-T, Zdravko Tolimir's Submission Concerning the Possible Trial Schedule for June, 10 May 2010 (filed: 13 May 2010), para.11.

736 *Prosecutor v. Zdravko Tolimir*, Case No. IT-05-88/2-T, Decision on Zdravko Tolimir's Submission Concerning the Possible Trial Schedule for June, 26 May 2010, p.2, 3.

737 *Prosecutor v. Zdravko Tolimir*, Case No. IT-05-88/2-T, Decision on Zdravko Tolimir's Submission Concerning the Possible Trial Schedule for June, 26 May 2010, p.2.

738 *Prosecutor v. Slobodan Milošević*, Case No. IT-02-54-AR73.6, Decision on the Interlocutory Appeal by the *Amici Curiae* Against the Trial Chamber Order Concerning the Presentation and Preparation of the Defence Case, 20 January 2004,

familiarity" with the particular case,[739] it needs to be questioned whether such an exclusive approach is advisable in a setting which necessarily draws from the experience at least within the same institution. The trial chamber based its decision on the alleged need for review of recently disclosed confidential material and of the judgement in the *Popović* case.[740] The increase of sitting days on the other hand was confirmed in light of the scheduling efforts of the Prosecution with regard to its witnesses and given that in the meantime the accused had been assigned an additional defence team member.[741]

As is clear from the defence submissions, accused mostly focus on arguing to be granted more time initially before the start of the evidentiary hearings and presentation of the prosecution case, which is then followed by requests in the course of trial proceedings not to exceed a certain number of court hearing days per week. Overall, defendants are obviously less concerned with a speedy conclusion of the proceedings and more with the issue of being granted sufficient time to prepare and present their own version of events and challenge the prosecution's allegations.

The decisions in general indicate that the judges are attempting to balance the interest of all participants in an expeditious conduct of the proceedings with the increased pressures put on self-represented accused having to divide their time between preparation for and appearance in court. It is obvious that trial chambers are willing to exhibit the necessary flexibility to provide *pro se* defendants with the time they need for the preparation and presentation of their defence. At the same time, however, the judges are equally cognisant of the need not to extend the length of the proceedings beyond anything reasonable. This balancing exercise is only one of the many that have to be

---

para.16, referring to *Prosecutor v. Delalić et al.*, Case No. IT-96-21-A, Appeals Judgement, 20 February 2001, para.291-293.

739 *Prosecutor v. Radovan Karadžić*, Case No. IT-95-5/18-AR73.8, Prosecution Response to Karadžić's Appeal of Order on Trial Schedule, 21 June 2010, para.2, referring to *Prosecutor v. Slobodan Milošević*, Case No. IT-02-54-AR73.7, Decision on Interlocutory Appeal of the Trial Chamber's Decision on the Assignment of Defense Counsel, 01 November 2004, para.9.

740 *Prosecutor v. Zdravko Tolimir*, Case No. IT-05-88/2-T, Decision on Zdravko Tolimir's Submission Concerning the Possible Trial Schedule for June, 26 May 2010, p.2.

741 *Prosecutor v. Zdravko Tolimir*, Case No. IT-05-88/2-T, Decision on Zdravko Tolimir's Submission Concerning the Possible Trial Schedule for June, 26 May 2010, p.2.

conducted in the context of proceedings with self-represented accused. Practice thus far indicates that the path of choice is pragmatism in order to ensure both fair and expeditious proceedings.

2. Adequate facilities

a. Office and assistance facilities

Accused face the additional difficulty of ordinarily being remanded in custody during proceedings, which involves further complications in terms of technical and logistical facilities accessible to them for the preparation and presentation of their defence. For example, *pro se* defendants will need to be provided with storage rooms and potentially cells they can use as office, as well as with the possibility to file submissions, send and receive faxes and other mail or commit time used differently by represented detainees to the work on their defence case.[742]

The ICTY registry in general offered self-represented accused to be provided with a certain number of technical and logistical services that could be made available,[743] including recognition of legal associates for purposes of privileged communication and related access to privileged telephone and facsimile line; privileged sending and receiving of CD / DVD material to and from legal associates; possibility to instruct investigators and legal assistants (not in a privileged manner); access to a storage room at the detention unit for case related material;[744] computers;[745] or privileged visitation facil-

---

742 *Cf. Prosecutor v. Zdravko Tolimir*, Case No. IT-05-88/2-PT, Motion of the Accused for the Pre-trial Chamber and Registrar of the Tribunal to Create Minimum Conditions for the Preparation of his Defence, 06 February 2009 (filed: 10 February 2009).

743 *Prosecutor v. Momčilo Krajišnik*, Case No. IT-00-39-A, Registry Submission on Momčilo Krajišnik's Request to Reverse the Decision of the Registry of 7 June 2007, 19 July 2007, para.52. *See also Prosecutor v. Slobodan Milošević*, Case No. IT-02-54-T, Registry Report on Practical Facilities Available to Accused, 18 March 2002 (filed: 19 March 2002), p.5-7.

744 *Prosecutor v. Momčilo Krajišnik*, Case No. IT-00-39-A, Registry Submission on Momčilo Krajišnik's Request to Reverse the Decision of the Registry of 7 June 2007, 19 July 2007, para.21.

745 *Prosecutor v. Slobodan Milošević*, Case No. IT-02-54-T, Registry Report on Practical Facilities Available to Accused, 18 March 2002 (filed 19 March 2002), p.6; *Prosecutor v. Momčilo Krajišnik*, Case No. IT-00-39-A, Registry Submission on

ities for interviewing witnesses.[746] At the same time, it has been submitted that any facilities provided to *pro se* defendants must not compromise security concerns at the detention unit.[747]

Nevertheless, there has been at least one instance when a self-represented accused complained about the inadequacy of office facilities provided not to himself in detention, but to his assisting defence team: referring to Article 25 of the Remuneration Scheme for Persons Assisting Indigent Self-represented Accused,[748] the defendant in *Karadžić* alleged that the ICTY registry failed to provide adequate office space for his defence team to work from.[749] Drawing a comparison with the resources available to the team working for the standby counsel assigned to his case, the accused submitted that:

Momčilo Krajišnik's Request to Reverse the Decision of the Registry of 7 June 2007, 19 July 2007, fn.37.

746 *Prosecutor v. Vojislav Šešelj*, Case No. IT-03-67-PT, Registry Submission Pursuant to Rule 33(B) on the Facilities and Services that May be Available to Vojišlav [sic] Šešelj to Conduct his Defence, 08 June 2006, para.5 and fn.2. *See also* the list of facilities offered to and in part rejected by the accused: *Prosecutor v. Vojislav Šešelj*, Case No. IT-03-67-PT, Registry Submission Pursuant to Rule 33(B) of the Rules Regarding Vojislav Šešelj's Motion for a Decision by the Trial Chamber on Financing his Defence, 29 June 2007, para.61 fn.24: "The following has been offered to the Accused so far: A *pro se* liaison officer – was rejected by the Accused; payment of a case manager to help the Accused with the preparation of the case and serve as a link between the Accused and the Tribunal; acknowledgement of three legal advisors, with whom he enjoys privileged communication rights; the coverage of travel costs of these advisors (one per month); the rent of an apartment as office/living space for the legal advisors and the case manager; a privileged archive cell as a storage/office room in the UNDU; access to privileged fax and phone; a visiting room at the UNDU to meet with his legal associates and his case manager; provision of Tribunal jurisprudence available in BCS; a desktop computer or a CD/DVD player, plus technical assistance – also rejected by the Accused; basic training on e-court for the Accused's legal advisors; a library system to get video tapes of the hearings through CMSS, plus a video tape player."

747 *Prosecutor v. Slobodan Milošević*, Case No. IT-02-54-T, Registry Report on Practical Facilities Available to Accused, 18 March 2002 (filed: 19 March 2002), p.10; *Prosecutor v. Vojislav Šešelj*, Case No. IT-03-67-PT, Registry Submission Pursuant to Rule 33(B) on the Facilities and Services that May be Available to Vojišlav [sic] Šešelj to Conduct his Defence, 08 June 2006, para.6.

748 Remuneration Scheme for Persons Assisting Indigent Self-Represented Accused, 01 April 2010, Rev. 2, para.25: "The Registrar shall provide office space for defence teams assisting self-represented accused during trial, as determined appropriate by the Registrar."

749 *Prosecutor v. Radovan Karadžić*, Case No. IT-95-5/18-T, Request for Review of Decision on Office Space, 20 December 2011, para.15-18.

> "[i]t is absurd that the Registrar pays the standby team more than 10,295 Euros per month for an office and refuses to provide office space to the defence team of Dr. Karadzic, which is doing all the work."[750]

The president of the ICTY, seised of the accused's request, denied it on the basis that the ICTY registry properly exercised its discretion, and "underscore[d] that by choosing to be self-represented, Karadžić has abjured the broader panoply of support available to represented accused".[751]

Slobodan Milošević invoked the general issue of adequate time and facilities to prepare his defence in an interesting context at the beginning of his case: there was some indication that the accused intended to try to obtain provisional release to be able to properly prepare for the court proceedings, arguing that in detention one would not have the adequate facilities to do so. The accused raised the issue orally during an interlocutory appeal hearing[752] as well as in the course of the proceedings.[753] In addition, *amicus curiae* made oral submissions in this regard[754] and subsequently in the course of a discussion about the implications of his ill-health for the proceedings, the accused himself again referred to the matter.[755]

Yet, the trial chamber had already decided before the latest mentioning by the defendant that there were measures other than provisional release which could serve to safeguard his right to adequate time and facilities for

---

750 *Prosecutor v. Radovan Karadžić*, Case No. IT-95-5/18-T, Request for Review of Decision on Office Space, 20 December 2011, para.20.

751 *Prosecutor v. Radovan Karadžić*, Case No. IT-95-5/18-T, Decision on the Request for Review of Decision on Office Space, 10 February 2012, para.17 (fn. omitted).

752 *Prosecutor v. Slobodan Milošević*, Case No. IT-99-37-AR73/IT-01-50-AR73/IT-01-51-AR73, Interlocutory Appeal Hearing, 30 January 2002, T.349-350/210-211/177-178.

753 *Prosecutor v. Slobodan Milošević*, Case No. IT-02-54-T, Hearing, 26 February 2002, T.1004; Hearing, 27 February 2002, T.1136.

754 *Prosecutor v. Slobodan Milošević*, Case No. IT-02-54-T, Hearing, 27 February 2002, T.1132-1134: "[...] He asked for his own release but not release for the sake of freedom as such but primarily freedom that would make it possible for him to be on a footing of equality with the opposing party. [...]".

755 *Prosecutor v. Slobodan Milošević*, Case No. IT-02-54-T, Hearing, 11 November 2002, T.12835-12836.

preparation of his defence.[756] Based on submissions from the *amici curiae*[757] and on a report from the ICTY registry,[758] the trial chamber determined at a later stage that the accused was provided with all facilities necessary to enable him to conduct his own defence.[759] The trial chamber reiterated its position on the question of provisional release when the accused raised the matter again before the start of the defence case.[760] Referring to the U.S. Supreme Court's decision in *Faretta*, the ICTY registry at the time adopted the view that a self-represented accused was not entitled to exactly the same facilities as counsel representing a defendant would have, but rather only to those that were indispensable for an effective defence.[761]

Vojislav Šešelj advanced a reasoning similar to that found in *Milošević* in his own application for provisional release: the accused considered that, being self-represented, he should be on an equal footing with the prosecution, which could not be the case if he was unable to prepare his defence in detention.[762] The trial chamber did not show itself convinced by any of the arguments brought forward by the accused.[763] Referring to the decision in *Milošević*, the chamber considered that the accused's right to adequate time and facilities to prepare his defence could be guaranteed other than through

---

756 *Prosecutor v. Slobodan Milošević*, Case No. IT-02-54-T, Decision on Accused's Application for Provisional Release, 06 March 2002, p.2: "[...] while recognising the practical difficulties faced by the accused in the preparation of his defence, his right to have adequate time and facilities for the preparation of his defence may be safeguarded by means other than provisional release, [...] the Trial Chamber is not satisfied that the accused, if released, would continue to appear for trial and would not pose a danger to any victim, witness or other person, [...]".

757 *Prosecutor v. Slobodan Milošević*, Case No. IT-02-54-T, Brief on the Provision of Adequate Facilities to Allow the Accused to Prepare his Defence, 05 March 2002 (filed: 06 March 2002). *See also* Hearing, 10 April 2002, T.2787-2792.

758 *Prosecutor v. Slobodan Milošević*, Case No. IT-02-54-T, Registry Report on Practical Facilities Available to Accused, 18 March 2002.

759 *Prosecutor v. Slobodan Milošević*, Case No. IT-02-54-T, Oral Ruling, 24 April 2002, T.3737-3740.

760 *Prosecutor v. Slobodan Milošević*, Case No. IT-02-54-T, Pre-Defence Conference, 02 September 2003, T.25944, 25945-25947.

761 *Prosecutor v. Slobodan Milošević*, Case No. IT-02-54-T, Registry Report on Practical Facilities Available to Accused, 18 March 2002, p.8.

762 *Prosecutor v. Vojislav Šešelj*, Case No. IT-03-67-PT, Defence Motion for Provisional Release, 14 June 2004 (filed: 24 June 2004), para.12-13, 15.2, 15.4.

763 *Prosecutor v. Vojislav Šešelj*, Case No. IT-03-67-PT, Decision on Defence Motion for Provisional Release, 23 July 2004 (filed: 28 July 2004), para.8.

granting provisional release and that in the case at hand, it had not been shown that the defendant could not prepare his defence while in custody.[764]

An interesting matter to be considered in this context is the question which arrangements could be made in case a trial chamber might decide to conduct an onsite visit to locations relevant for the charges in an indictment.[765] In cases with self-represented accused, the defendant might be inclined to demand his or her participation in the visit.[766] However, security and other concerns appear to render arrangements to this effect challenging, if not impossible.[767] Yet, it should be feasible for the accused to appoint a representative for the defence in order to participate in such a visit instead of the defendant.[768] At least one trial chamber determined it to be unnecessary for the accused to participate personally in a site visit in light of the purported objective of any such visit by the trial chamber.[769]

---

764 *Prosecutor v. Vojislav Šešelj*, Case No. IT-03-67-PT, Decision on Defence Motion for Provisional Release, 23 July 2004 (filed: 28 July 2004), para.10. *See also* Prosecution's Response to "Defence Motion for Provisional Release", 07 July 2004 (filed: 20 July 2004), para.36.

765 *Cf. Prosecutor v. Slobodan Milošević*, Case No. IT-02-54-T, Hearing, 28 September 2005, T.44734; *Prosecutor v. Radovan Karadžić*, Case No. IT-95-5/18-T, Hearing, 28 September 2010, T.7073.

766 *Cf. Prosecutor v. Radovan Karadžić*, Case No. IT-95-5/18-T, Submission on Site Visit, 06 October 2010 (made public by subsequent order of the trial chamber: *See* Order Lifting Confidentiality of Decision on Site Visit and Related Pleadings, 24 May 2011); Second Submission on Site Visit, 13 December 2010 (made public by subsequent order of the trial chamber: *See* Order Lifting Confidentiality of Decision on Site Visit and Related Pleadings, 24 May 2011), para.2.

767 *Prosecutor v. Radovan Karadžić*, Case No. IT-95-5/18-T, Registry Submission Pursuant to Rule 33(B) on the Presence of the Accused During a Potential Site Visit, 14 January 2011 (made public by subsequent order of the trial chamber: *See* Order Lifting Confidentiality of Decision on Site Visit and Related Pleadings, 24 May 2011), para.3, 7.

768 *Cf. Prosecutor v. Zdravko Tolimir*, Case No. IT-05-88/2-T, Hearing, 18 October 2010, T.6401.

769 *Prosecutor v. Radovan Karadžić*, Case No. IT-95-5/18-T, Order on Submissions for a Site Visit, 15 November 2010 (made public by subsequent order of the trial chamber: *See* Order Lifting Confidentiality of Decision on Site Visit and Related Pleadings, 24 May 2011), para.6. *See also* Decision on Second Site Visit, 10 February 2012 (made public by subsequent order of the trial chamber: *See* Order Lifting Confidentiality of Decision on Second Site Visit and Related Pleadings, 04 July 2012), para.7: "[…] As such, the site visit will not breach the right of the Accused to be tried in his own presence as envisaged in Article 21(4)(d) of the Statute of the Tribunal."

Similar questions might arise in case the defence requests that hearings be held at locations other than the seat of the Tribunal: in *Karadžić*, the accused requested "that the Trial Chamber hold three one-week trial sessions during his defence case in Sarajevo, Banja Luka, and Belgrade".[770] According to the defendant, such arrangements would have two advantages:

> "First, it will bring the work of the Tribunal directly to the people for whom it is intended to benefit, thus fostering a greater understanding of the work of the Tribunal by people in the former Yugoslavia. And, second, it will be convenient for witnesses, who will not have to make the journey to The Hague to give their testimony, or in the case of incarcerated witnesses, to be transported to The Hague and be housed at the detention unit."[771]

While the accused in this motion did not specifically demand his presence in case such hearings at other locations would be granted, it appears to be implicit in light of the fact that Radovan Karadžić acted as his own counsel and, even more so, considering that the hearings in question would take place during the presentation of the defence case. The transfer, presence, housing and local transfers of the accused in the context of such hearings away from the seat of the Tribunal potentially implicate even greater security concerns than site visits. While site visits are not intended for the gathering of evidence,[772] and therefore the presence of a self-represented accused might not be considered crucial, a similar argument cannot be made with regard to evidentiary sessions scheduled for the purpose of hearing witnesses called by the defence. A potential arrangement that might be envisaged is the participation of the accused in the hearings via video link with at least one of his legal associates being present at the hearings in person. This would on the one hand address the defendant's concern of holding hearings in the re-

---

770 *Prosecutor v. Radovan Karadžić*, Case No. IT-95-5/18-T, Motion for Trial Sessions to be held in the Former Yugoslavia, 07 May 2012, para.1.

771 *Prosecutor v. Radovan Karadžić*, Case No. IT-95-5/18-T, Motion for Trial Sessions to be held in the Former Yugoslavia, 07 May 2012, para.3. *See also Prosecutor v. Radovan Karadžić*, Case No. IT-95-5/18-AR98bis.1, Respondent's Brief, 05 November 2012, para.318-319.

772 *Cf. Prosecutor v. Radovan Karadžić*, Case No. IT-95-5/18-T, Order on Submissions for a Site Visit, 15 November 2010 (made public by subsequent order of the trial chamber: *See* Order Lifting Confidentiality of Decision on Site Visit and Related Pleadings, 24 May 2011), para.6. *See also* Decision on Second Site Visit, 10 February 2012 (made public by subsequent order of the trial chamber: *See* Order Lifting Confidentiality of Decision on Second Site Visit and Related Pleadings, 04 July 2012), para.7.

gion concerned, while on the other hand absolve with any potential security issues that would be raised by the actual presence of the accused himself. In any event, the trial chamber dismissed the motion.[773]

Hypothetically, an accused could argue that due to the insufficiency and inadequacy of facilities provided for in detention, he or she is incapable of preparing adequately for the proceedings. In case such an argument is raised, the point could be made that as long as the defendant was guaranteed assistance on a level comparable to that of other self-represented accused, counsel could be imposed against the will of the accused in question if his or her persistence on requests for more facilities significantly and persistently obstructed the conduct of the proceedings. It is significant to clarify this potential consequence in advance, since otherwise an accused in pre-trial detention might attempt to opt for the exercise of his or her right to self-representation, merely in order to subsequently apply for provisional release or submit other (inordinate) requests for facilities with the argument that the facilities considered necessary for the preparation and presentation of the defence case were inadequate in detention. This scenario leads back to the question of an informed and unequivocal choice to self-represent, which would imply awareness and acceptance of the potential disadvantages associated with the exercise of the right to self-representation. Naturally, it is for a trial chamber to ensure that an accused is tried in a fair and expeditious manner, and to facilitate the possibilities of a *pro se* defendant in detention to prepare for the proceedings as much as possible in light of the circumstances. Yet, at the same time, participants to the proceedings would have to be made aware that the notions of fairness and equality of arms do not necessarily mean, as alluded to above, that all parties are on the exact same footing, but rather that neither of them is at any disadvantage throughout the course of the proceedings.

773 *Prosecutor v. Radovan Karadžić*, Case No. IT-95-5/18-T, Decision on Accused's Motion for Trial Sessions to be Conducted in the Former Yugoslavia and for Invitation to Governments of Bosnia and Herzegovina, Republika Srpska, and Serbia, 04 July 2012.

b. Financial aid

Other than issues regarding more technical facilities for *pro se* defendants, a recurrent theme in virtually all proceedings with self-represented accused is the question of legal aid – if any – to be provided to the defendants.

The Pre-trial and Trial Legal Aid Policies issued by the ICTY registry establish criteria according to which legal aid can be provided, *inter alia*, to self-represented accused.[774] The matter did not arise in the first proceedings with a self-represented accused before the ICTY since Slobodan Milošević did not claim indigence in order to ask for financial compensation of his defence.[775]

According to the ICTY registry, as of June 2011 out of 133 accused before the ICTY, 79 received full legal aid; 37 received partial legal aid; 6 were under financial means inquiry; 1 was found to be able to pay for his defence; and 10 did not request legal aid.[776]

i. The cases of Momčilo Krajišnik and Vojislav Šešelj

The discussions regarding which financial aid, if any, to be provided to self-represented accused would present some significant overlap at least for the initial considerations of the matter in the cases of Momčilo Krajišnik and Vojislav Šešelj. Therefore, these arguments will be considered together, and then followed by an overview of the litigation in the *Karadžić* proceedings which would subsequently raise some additional questions.

The first discussions on the extent of legal aid arose in the case against Momčilo Krajišnik. At the time of the accused's first request to proceed unrepresented for the remainder of the trial proceedings, the ICTY registry adopted the subsequently repeated view that it was not in a position to provide legal aid to a defendant without counsel having been appointed: considering

---

774 ICTY: Defence Counsel – Pre-trial Legal Aid Policy, 01 May 2006; Defence Counsel – Trial Legal Aid Policy, 01 November 2009.

775 *Prosecutor v. Momčilo Krajišnik*, Case No. IT-00-39-T, Registrar's Submission Pursuant to Rule 33(B) of the Rules of Procedure and Evidence Regarding the Resources that Can be Made Available to Momčilo Krajišnik if he is to Represent Himself, 03 June 2005, para.9.

776 *See* ICTY Legal Aid Tool, http://www.icty.org/sid/163 (last accessed 24 October 2012).

that neither *Milošević* nor *Šešelj* provided any guidance on the matter,[777] it submitted that in light of the applicable provisions, primarily the French text of Article 21(4)(d) of the ICTY Statute,[778] as well as the ICTY RPE, it was neither authorised to assign support staff independent of lead counsel, nor to assign support staff to self-represented accused without intermediary, nor to provide funding directly to self-represented accused.[779] In the instant case, the accused's request to proceed *pro se* was not granted as discussed above,[780] reason for which the discussion of provision of legal aid to a self-represented accused was not further pursued at that point.

The question surfaced the next time when the appeals chamber granted the accused's request to represent himself in the appeals proceedings of his case,[781] shortly after which the defendant filed a request demanding that his legal advisors be reimbursed by the ICTY.[782]

---

777 *Prosecutor v. Momčilo Krajišnik*, Case No. IT-00-39-T, Registrar's Submission Pursuant to Rule 33(B) of the Rules of Procedure and Evidence Regarding the Resources that Can be Made Available to Momčilo Krajišnik if he is to Represent Himself, 03 June 2005, para.9.

778 Article 21(4)(d) of the ICTY Statute reads in French as follows: « Toute personne contre laquelle une accusation est portée en vertu du présent statut a droit, en pleine égalité, au moins aux garanties suivantes: [...] (d) à être présent au procès et à se défendre elle-même ou à avoir l'assistance d'un défenseur de son choix; si elle n'a pas de défenseur, à être informée de son droit d'en avoir un, et, chaque fois que l'intérêt de la justice l'exige, à se voir attribuer d'office un défenseur, sans frais, si elle n'a pas les moyens de le rémunérer [...] ».

779 *Prosecutor v. Momčilo Krajišnik*, Case No. IT-00-39-T, Registrar's Submission Pursuant to Rule 33(B) of the Rules of Procedure and Evidence Regarding the Resources that Can be Made Available to Momčilo Krajišnik if he is to Represent Himself, 03 June 2005, para.12-17.

780 *Prosecutor v. Momčilo Krajišnik*, Case No. IT-00-39-T, Reasons for Oral Decision Denying Mr Krajišnik's Request to Proceed Unrepresented by Counsel, 18 August 2005.

781 *Prosecutor v. Momčilo Krajišnik*, Case No. IT-00-39-A, Decision on Momčilo Krajišnik's Request to Self-Represent, On Counsel's Motion in Relation to Appointment of *Amicus Curiae*, and on the Prosecution Motion of 16 February 2007, 11 May 2007.

782 *Prosecutor v. Momčilo Krajišnik*, Case No. IT-00-39-A, Request to Provide Conditions to Work and to Reverse the Decision of the Registry of 07 June 2007, 10 June 2007 (filed: 18 June 2007).

The accused in *Šešelj* requested the ICTY to finance his defence already in October 2003,[783] and submitted the first written request detailing allegedly incurred defence costs in January 2006.[784] The accused's submissions would later be linked to Article 21(4)(d) of the ICTY Statute[785] and refute the ICTY registry's position that the provision of legal funds depended on the assignment of counsel,[786] arguing that he was entitled to receive legal aid for his "expert team" under the principle of equality of arms and in light of the fact that his right to self-representation had been reinstated twice.[787] The accused submitted that an obligation to provide legal aid was linked to the presumption of innocence,[788] and argued that an effective exercise of the right to self-representation would necessitate provision of legal aid.[789]

---

783 *Prosecutor v. Vojislav Šešelj*, Case No. IT-03-67-PT, Registry Submission Pursuant to Rule 33(B) of the Rules Regarding Vojislav Šešelj's Motion for a Decision by the Trial Chamber on Financing his Defence, 29 June 2007, para.7.

784 *Prosecutor v. Vojislav Šešelj*, Case No. IT-03-67-PT, Request of Dr Vojislav Šešelj for the Issuing of an Order to Approve the Payment of Expenses for Preparation of his Defence (Submission No. 124), 03 January 2006 (filed: 16 January 2006), p.5, in which the accused submitted that the expenses for preparation of his defence by his "expert team" counting 25 members amounted to US$ 2,339,400 up to that point.

785 *Prosecutor v. Vojislav Šešelj*, Case No. IT-03-67-PT, Professor Vojislav Šešelj's Motion for a Decision by Trial Chamber III on Financing his Defence in Accordance with the Statute (Submission No. 294), 04 June 2007 (filed: 14 June 2007), p.5. This submission set the amount of reimbursement requested at 6,395,000 Euros for the period 2003-2006 (*see* p.3).

786 *Prosecutor v. Vojislav Šešelj*, Case No. IT-03-67-PT, Professor Vojislav Šešelj's Motion for a Decision by Trial Chamber III on Financing his Defence in Accordance with the Statute (Submission No. 294), 04 June 2007 (filed: 14 June 2007), p.5.

787 *Prosecutor v. Vojislav Šešelj*, Case No. IT-03-67-PT, Professor Vojislav Šešelj's Motion for a Decision by Trial Chamber III on Financing his Defence in Accordance with the Statute (Submission No. 294), 04 June 2007 (filed: 14 June 2007), p.5, 6.

788 *Prosecutor v. Vojislav Šešelj*, Case No. IT-03-67-PT, Professor Vojislav Šešelj's Motion for a Decision by Trial Chamber III on Financing his Defence in Accordance with the Statute (Submission No. 294), 04 June 2007 (filed: 14 June 2007), p.8.

789 *Prosecutor v. Vojislav Šešelj*, Case No. IT-03-67-PT, Professor Vojislav Šešelj's Motion for a Decision by Trial Chamber III on Financing his Defence in Accordance with the Statute (Submission No. 294), 04 June 2007 (filed: 14 June 2007), p.13.

The ICTY registry submitted an outline of the facilities provided to both the accused in *Krajišnik*[790] and in *Šešelj*.[791] Despite the approach to supply the defendant with working facilities in order to implement the appeals chamber's decision in *Krajišnik*, it reiterated that it did not have the "authority to allocate money to a self-represented accused",[792] arguing that there was no legal basis for legal aid to be provided to self-represented accused aside the existing legal aid scheme.[793] The ICTY registry submitted that the ICTY legal framework did not provide for legal aid to be given to a self-represented accused independent of the assignment of counsel.[794] It argued that the decision to grant legal aid to a *pro se* defendant amounted to a policy decision that could only be taken by the U.N. Security Council with an amendment to the ICTY Statute.[795] According to the ICTY registry, the choice to exercise the right to self-representation implied an acceptance of all potential consequences,[796] and this choice could not serve as basis to argue inequality of

---

790 *Prosecutor v. Momčilo Krajišnik*, Case No. IT-00-39-A, Registry Submission on Momčilo Krajišnik's Request to Reverse the Decision of the Registry of 07 June 2007, 19 July 2007, para.21.

791 *Prosecutor v. Vojislav Šešelj*, Case No. IT-03-67-PT, Registry Submission Pursuant to Rule 33(B) of the Rules Regarding Vojislav Šešelj's Motion for a Decision by the Trial Chamber on Financing his Defence, 29 June 2007, para.61, fn.24.

792 *Prosecutor v. Momčilo Krajišnik*, Case No. IT-00-39-A, Registry Submission on Momčilo Krajišnik's Request to Reverse the Decision of the Registry of 07 June 2007, 19 July 2007, para.33.

793 *Prosecutor v. Vojislav Šešelj*, Case No. IT-03-67-PT, Registry Submission Pursuant to Rule 33(B) of the Rules Regarding Vojislav Šešelj's Motion for a Decision by the Trial Chamber on Financing his Defence, 29 June 2007, para.43, 70.

794 *Prosecutor v. Vojislav Šešelj*, Case No. IT-03-67-PT, Registry Submission Pursuant to Rule 33(B) of the Rules Regarding Vojislav Šešelj's Motion for a Decision by the Trial Chamber on Financing his Defence, 29 June 2007, para.49-57. *See* para.57: "... a decision to disburse public funds without assigning counsel would be contrary to the Statute, the legislative intent of the Tribunal's legal aid scheme, and the relevant national and international legislation and practice. As such, it would be *ultra vires* the Registrar's authority."; *Prosecutor v. Momčilo Krajišnik*, Case No. IT-00-39-A, Registry Submission on Momčilo Krajišnik's Request to Reverse the Decision of the Registry of 07 June 2007, 19 July 2007, para.40.

795 *Prosecutor v. Vojislav Šešelj*, Case No. IT-03-67-PT, Registry Submission Pursuant to Rule 33(B) of the Rules Regarding Vojislav Šešelj's Motion for a Decision by the Trial Chamber on Financing his Defence, 29 June 2007, para.57.

796 *Prosecutor v. Vojislav Šešelj*, Case No. IT-03-67-PT, Registry Submission Pursuant to Rule 33(B) of the Rules Regarding Vojislav Šešelj's Motion for a Decision by the Trial Chamber on Financing his Defence, 29 June 2007, para.60.

arms.[797] The ICTY registry did acknowledge that "exceptionally", Article 21(4)(b) of the ICTY Statute would require the ICTY to pay expenses for self-represented accused to a certain extent, without however paying for substantial legal advice.[798] With regard to financial assistance to the accused to provide for legal advisors, the ICTY registry took the clear position that "[w]hilst the Tribunal will be required to facilitate the self-represented accused's communication with such persons, it cannot be expected to pay them".[799] In essence, the position was adopted that in case the defendant wanted to receive funding for legal advice in the preparation of his defence, he would need to have counsel assigned,[800] in particular referring to a decision of the pre-trial chamber in the same case four years earlier which did not find the appointment of standby counsel to be in contradiction with the exercise of the right to self-representation.[801]

The prosecution submitted that any decision in *Šešelj* should be postponed awaiting resolution of the issue in *Krajišnik*.[802] It argued that a potential right to legal aid had been exhausted by the defendant's choice to conduct

797 *Prosecutor v. Vojislav Šešelj*, Case No. IT-03-67-PT, Registry Submission Pursuant to Rule 33(B) of the Rules Regarding Vojislav Šešelj's Motion for a Decision by the Trial Chamber on Financing his Defence, 29 June 2007, para.68.

798 *Prosecutor v. Vojislav Šešelj*, Case No. IT-03-67-PT, Registry Submission Pursuant to Rule 33(B) of the Rules Regarding Vojislav Šešelj's Motion for a Decision by the Trial Chamber on Financing his Defence, 29 June 2007, para.63.

799 *Prosecutor v. Momčilo Krajišnik*, Case No. IT-00-39-A, Registry Submission on Momčilo Krajišnik's Request to Reverse the Decision of the Registry of 07 June 2007, 19 July 2007, para.53, 63.

800 *Prosecutor v. Vojislav Šešelj*, Case No. IT-03-67-PT, Registry Submission Pursuant to Rule 33(B) of the Rules Regarding Vojislav Šešelj's Motion for a Decision by the Trial Chamber on Financing his Defence, 29 June 2007, para.53 ("Legal aid equals the assignment of counsel."), 75, 77. *See also* Alexander Zahar, Legal Aid, Self-Representation, and the Crisis at the Hague Tribunal, 19 *Criminal Law Forum* 241 (2008), p.246.

801 *Prosecutor v. Vojislav Šešelj*, Case No. IT-03-67-PT, Registry Submission Pursuant to Rule 33(B) of the Rules Regarding Vojislav Šešelj's Motion for a Decision by the Trial Chamber on Financing his Defence, 29 June 2007, para.76; referring to *Prosecutor v. Vojislav Šešelj*, Case No. IT-03-67-PT, Decision on Prosecution's Motion for Order to Appoint Counsel to Assist Vojislav Šešelj with his Defence, 09 May 2003, para.29.

802 *Prosecutor v. Vojislav Šešelj*, Case No. IT-03-67-PT, Prosecution's Response to the Accused's Motion for a Decision by Trial Chamber III on Financing his Defence in Accordance with the Statute (Number 294), 28 June 2007, para.2.

his defence in person,[803] and stated that any entitlement to legal funds was linked to assignment of counsel.[804] Further, it argued that the applicable provision was Article 21(4)(b) of the ICTY Statute on adequate time and facilities,[805] not to be confused with equality of resources.[806] According to the prosecution, the right to adequate time and facilities should not be equated with provision of financial aid to self-represented accused[807] and, in any event, the defendant failed to show his indigence or inability to pay for his defence team outside the legal aid scheme.[808] Referring to the appeals chamber decision in *Milošević*, it was argued that by choosing to conduct his defence in person, the accused ought to accept any disadvantages resulting from that choice.[809]

Litigation of the arguments was eventually rendered moot with the issuance of the appeals chamber decision in *Krajišnik* discussed *infra*, pursuant to which the ICTY registry adopted a "Remuneration Scheme for Persons Assisting Indigent Self-represented Accused".[810] According to the ICTY registry, the scheme was "established to facilitate the participation of a detained, self-represented accused in proceedings against him in accordance with

803 *Prosecutor v. Vojislav Šešelj*, Case No. IT-03-67-PT, Prosecution's Response to the Accused's Motion for a Decision by Trial Chamber III on Financing his Defence in Accordance with the Statute (Number 294), 28 June 2007, para.11.

804 *Prosecutor v. Vojislav Šešelj*, Case No. IT-03-67-PT, Prosecution's Response to the Accused's Motion for a Decision by Trial Chamber III on Financing his Defence in Accordance with the Statute (Number 294), 28 June 2007, para.12-15.

805 *Prosecutor v. Vojislav Šešelj*, Case No. IT-03-67-PT, Prosecution's Response to the Accused's Motion for a Decision by Trial Chamber III on Financing his Defence in Accordance with the Statute (Number 294), 28 June 2007, para.16.

806 *Prosecutor v. Vojislav Šešelj*, Case No. IT-03-67-PT, Prosecution's Response to the Accused's Motion for a Decision by Trial Chamber III on Financing his Defence in Accordance with the Statute (Number 294), 28 June 2007, para.17, 18.

807 *Prosecutor v. Vojislav Šešelj*, Case No. IT-03-67-PT, Prosecution's Response to the Accused's Motion for a Decision by Trial Chamber III on Financing his Defence in Accordance with the Statute (Number 294), 28 June 2007, para.19.

808 *Prosecutor v. Vojislav Šešelj*, Case No. IT-03-67-PT, Prosecution's Response to the Accused's Motion for a Decision by Trial Chamber III on Financing his Defence in Accordance with the Statute (Number 294), 28 June 2007, para.20.

809 *Prosecutor v. Vojislav Šešelj*, Case No. IT-03-67-PT, Prosecution's Response to the Accused's Motion for a Decision by Trial Chamber III on Financing his Defence in Accordance with the Statute (Number 294), 28 June 2007, para.21.

810 Remuneration Scheme for Persons Assisting Indigent Self-Represented Accused, 01 April 2010, Rev. 2, para.2.

Article 21(4)(b) of the Statute [...]".[811] The scheme would subsequently be revised to take into account a decision issued by the ICTY president in *Karadžić* in 2010.[812]

The appeals chamber in its decision in *Krajišnik* appeared to concur with the ICTY registry's approach concerning the provision of working facilities.[813] Addressing the question of funding, the appeals chamber recalled its position in *Milošević*, when it held that the rights in Article 21(4)(d) of the ICTY Statute stand in binary opposition.[814] Against this background, it saw no support for the suggestion that a self-represented accused would be entitled to legal aid.[815] It clarified that when choosing to proceed *pro se*, an accused asserted "his ability to conduct his case without legal assistance and thus Tribunal funding for legal aid for him can be presumed to be unnecessary to the conduct of a fair trial".[816] The appeals chamber found:

> "[t]o the extent that the accused lacks the ability to conduct his own case and his self-representation is thus 'substantially and persistently obstructing the proper and expeditious conduct of his trial', then the remedy is restriction of his right to self-representation."[817]

It further made clear that:

> "[t]o allow an accused to self-represent and yet also to receive full legal aid funding from Tribunal would, as the saying goes, let him have his cake and eat it too."[818]

However, the appeals chamber qualified this at first sight rigorous position by adopting the view that it would in fact be appropriate to provide the de-

---

811 Remuneration Scheme for Persons Assisting Indigent Self-Represented Accused, 01 April 2010, Rev. 2, para.1.

812 Remuneration Scheme for Persons Assisting Indigent Self-Represented Accused, 01 April 2010, Rev. 2, fn.2.

813 *Prosecutor v. Momčilo Krajišnik*, IT-00-39-A, Decision on Krajišnik Request and Prosecution Motion, 11 September 2007, para.41.

814 *Prosecutor v. Momčilo Krajišnik*, IT-00-39-A, Decision on Krajišnik Request and Prosecution Motion, 11 September 2007, para.40.

815 *Prosecutor v. Momčilo Krajišnik*, IT-00-39-A, Decision on Krajišnik Request and Prosecution Motion, 11 September 2007, para.40.

816 *Prosecutor v. Momčilo Krajišnik*, IT-00-39-A, Decision on Krajišnik Request and Prosecution Motion, 11 September 2007, para.41.

817 *Prosecutor v. Momčilo Krajišnik*, IT-00-39-A, Decision on Krajišnik Request and Prosecution Motion, 11 September 2007, para.41 (fn. omitted).

818 *Prosecutor v. Momčilo Krajišnik*, IT-00-39-A, Decision on Krajišnik Request and Prosecution Motion, 11 September 2007, para.41.

fence with some funding in case indigent self-represented accused are assisted by legal advisors. While such funding should, according to the appeals chamber, not be comparable to any amount paid to counsel for represented accused, it "nonetheless should adequately reimburse the legal associates for their coordinating work and for related legal consultation".[819]

With this decision, the appeals chamber apparently intended to leave trial chambers with a margin of appreciation in the interpretation and application of notions such as "adequate" remuneration, the nature of "coordination work" and "related legal consultation". Yet, it has to be noted that such an allowance leaves potential room for insecurity about the position and argument, as should be illustrated later in related litigations in the *Karadžić* proceedings.

In parallel to the litigation in both *Krajišnik* and *Šešelj*, the pre-trial judge newly assigned to the latter case addressed the matter independently of the ongoing discussions and took the unambiguous position that the accused would be entitled to legal aid and that his associates should be paid by the ICTY even before its litigation in that case[820] or the pre-trial judge's official decision.[821] Eventually, the pre-trial judge concluded that:

> « […] un accusé qui se défend seul sans l'assistance d'un avocat devant une juridiction internationale a le droit d'avoir des collaborateurs rétribués par ladite juridiction internationale, sous certaines conditions. »[822]

The pre-trial judge reiterated the important status accorded to the right to self-representation as one of the fair trial rights,[823] and identified in his ana-

---

819 *Prosecutor v. Momčilo Krajišnik*, IT-00-39-A, Decision on Krajišnik Request and Prosecution Motion, 11 September 2007, para.42. In the related footnote (fn.105), the appeals chamber remarked: "The Appeals Chamber considers that this conclusion, combined with the observations made in the next paragraph, are not necessarily incompatible with the point made in a United Nations Office of Legal Affairs memorandum and quoted in the *Šešelj* Decision at para.50 and fn.71. The Appeals Chamber further observes that the quoted portions of this memorandum nowhere suggest that this funding should be comparable to that provided for a represented accused."

820 *Prosecutor v. Vojislav Šešelj*, Case No. IT-03-67-PT, Status Conference, 13 March 2007, T.929. *See also* Status Conference, 22 May 2007, T.1147-1149.

821 *Prosecutor v. Vojislav Šešelj*, Case No. IT-03-67-PT, Status Conference, 04 July 2007, T.1283-1286.

822 *Procureur c/ Vojislav Šešelj*, Affaire nº IT-03-67-PT, Décision Relative au Financement de la Défense de l'Accusé, 30 juillet 2007, para.45.

823 *Procureur c/ Vojislav Šešelj*, Affaire nº IT-03-67-PT, Décision Relative au Financement de la Défense de l'Accusé, 30 juillet 2007, para.28, 39, 40.

lysis of the applicable law a legal void due the lack of explicit provisions in the ICTY Statute or the ICTY RPE regulating the provision of legal aid to self-represented accused.[824] The judge considered it necessary to fill this void in order to guarantee the effective exercise of the right to self-representation in case a defendant acting *pro se* declared himself indigent.[825]

The approach which followed this initial determination is interesting insofar as the pre-trial judge turned to provisions of the ICC: the judge argued that since in the course of drafting the regulations for the ICC registry, the wording indicated the possibility of providing legal aid to self-represented accused, the provision eventually adopted could be interpreted in the same way, despite it not explicitly regulating the issue.[826] It should be noted that the ICTY registry in an earlier submission on the matter reached the opposite conclusion considering the same draft provision discussed for the ICC.[827]

While the appeals chamber in *Krajišnik* took note of the pre-trial judge's decision in *Šešelj*, it did not provide any evaluation as to its contents.[828] Yet, the appeals chamber did not contemplate the application of the official legal aid scheme to self-represented accused.[829] The prosecution submitted that the appeals chamber issued a solution contrary to that found by the pre-trial judge which accordingly would have to be reconsidered in light of the findings in *Krajišnik*.[830]

---

824 *Procureur c/ Vojislav Šešelj*, Affaire nº IT-03-67-PT, Décision Relative au Financement de la Défense de l'Accusé, 30 juillet 2007, para.41.

825 *Procureur c/ Vojislav Šešelj*, Affaire nº IT-03-67-PT, Décision Relative au Financement de la Défense de l'Accusé, 30 juillet 2007, para.42.

826 *Procureur c/ Vojislav Šešelj*, Affaire nº IT-03-67-PT, Décision Relative au Financement de la Défense de l'Accusé, 30 juillet 2007, para.43.

827 *Prosecutor v. Vojislav Šešelj*, Case No. IT-03-67-PT, Registrar's Submission Pursuant to the Trial Chamber's Request for Further Information on the Request by Vojislav Šešelj for Payment of Expenses for the Preparation of his Defence, 21 September 2006, para.25 fn.6.

828 *Prosecutor v. Momčilo Krajišnik*, IT-00-39-A, Decision on Krajišnik Request and Prosecution Motion, 11 September 2007, para.39.

829 *Prosecutor v. Momčilo Krajišnik*, IT-00-39-A, Decision on Krajišnik Request and Prosecution Motion, 11 September 2007, para.40.

830 *Prosecutor v. Vojislav Šešelj*, Case No. IT-03-67-PT, Status Conference, 27 September 2007, T.1531. See also immediate reaction of the pre-trial judge (T.1531): "The decision of the Appeals Chamber, I know it just as well as you do, and certainly better than you do. Secondly, I have been extremely clear. Never, ever will I reconsider the decision which I have made. Never. So there's no need even to talk about this, discuss this."

Even though the appeals chamber decision in *Krajišnik* as well as the procedure developed by the ICTY registry in response to the judges' directions would appear to mark the end of any further more substantial discussions, the matter would continue to pose significant challenges to the continuance of proceedings in *Šešelj*.

The accused was repeatedly invited to provide requisite information for an indigency determination to the ICTY registry,[831] a necessary step in the legal aid procedure. Yet, the defendant eventually claimed that he had fulfilled all requirements – while at the same time refusing to provide certain information[832] – and insisted on being provided figures regarding payments to defence teams in other cases.[833] While he announced that there would be no defence case if the tribunal did not fund his team,[834] he interestingly listed no less than 30 members of an "expert team assisting the defence"[835] in a subsequent request for legal aid[836] prompted by the presiding judge's suggestion.[837]

The ICTY registry submitted that any obstacle to the provision of funding resulted from the accused's non-adherence to established procedures[838] and that in light of the defendant's non-cooperation, it had no other possibility but to deny the accused's request. [839]

---

831 *Procureur c/ Vojislav Šešelj*, Affaire nº IT-03-67-PT, Décision Relative à la Mise En Œuvre du Financement de la Défense, 30 octobre 2007.

832 *See also Prosecutor v. Vojislav Šešelj*, Case No. IT-03-67-T, Hearing, 22 April 2008, T.6357-6363.

833 *Prosecutor v. Vojislav Šešelj*, Case No. IT-03-67-T, Hearing, 11 March 2008, T.4706-4709.

834 *Prosecutor v. Vojislav Šešelj*, Case No. IT-03-67-T, Hearing, 08 January 2009, T.13013.

835 *Prosecutor v. Vojislav Šešelj*, Case No. IT-03-67-T, Request for the Trial Chamber to Secure the Financing of Professor Vojislav Šešelj's Defence (Submission No. 411), 15 January 2009 (filed: 03 February 2009), p.1 (cover page).

836 *Prosecutor v. Vojislav Šešelj*, Case No. IT-03-67-T, Request for the Trial Chamber to Secure the Financing of Professor Vojislav Šešelj's Defence (Submission No. 411), 15 January 2009 (filed: 03 February 2009).

837 *Prosecutor v. Vojislav Šešelj*, Case No. IT-03-67-T, Hearing, 08 January 2009, T.13016.

838 *Prosecutor v. Vojislav Šešelj*, Case No. IT-03-67-T, Registry Third Submission Pursuant to Rule 33(B) of the Rules Regarding the Financing of the Accused's Defence, 16 March 2009, para.23.

839 *Prosecutor v. Vojislav Šešelj*, Case No. IT-03-67-T, Registry Third Submission Pursuant to Rule 33(B) of the Rules Regarding the Financing of the Accused's Defence, 16 March 2009, para.28.

Being somewhat stricter than the pre-trial judge initially, the trial chamber rejected the accused's unqualified demands and invited him to finally provide the required information to the ICTY registry.[840] It found, *inter alia*:

> « [...] que l'Accusé ne démontre pas qu'il a soumis au Greffe tous les justificatifs permettant d'établir qu'il n'a pas les moyens d'assurer financièrement sa défense et d'obtenir en conséquence une aide financière du Tribunal, et elle estime par conséquent que tant que les renseignements requis dans la Lettre du 28 septembre 2007 ne seront pas fournis, la Chambre ne peut instruire le Greffe d'octroyer le financement demandé par l'Accusé pour préparer sa défense. »[841]

Eventually, the ICTY registry denied the request of the accused pursuant to Article 8(C) of the Directive on the Assignment of Defence Counsel,[842] and based on the argument that after several years and repeated demands from the side of the ICTY registry to provide the necessary documentation, with the accused still failing to present the required information even after the respective decision of the trial chamber, it did not see itself in a position to establish whether the accused was indeed indigent.[843]

It appears rather obvious that over a period of more than three years, the accused was given ample opportunity to provide the ICTY registry with the requested information. One might be tempted to consider this approach too lenient in light of the general attitude of the defendant towards the entire proceedings and considering the fact that he was aware for several years which facts needed to be given to the ICTY registry in order to determine his indigence and potential eligibility for legal aid from the ICTY.

However, while the ICTY registry decision at first sight appears to end the matter, the trial chamber showed itself ready to intervene yet again in

---

840 *Procureur c/ Vojislav Šešelj*, Affaire n° IT-03-67-T, Décision Relative au Financement de la Défense de l'Accusé, 23 avril 2009, para.27.

841 *Procureur c/ Vojislav Šešelj*, Affaire n° IT-03-67-T, Décision Relative au Financement de la Défense de l'Accusé, 23 avril 2009, para.23.

842 Directive on the Assignment of Defence Counsel (Directive No. 1/94), as amended on 29 June 2006 (IT/73/Rev. 11), Article 8(C): "Where a suspect or accused fails to comply with his obligations under Articles 8(A) and (B) to the extent that the Registrar is unable to properly assess the suspect or accused's ability to remunerate counsel, the Registrar may deny the request for the assignment of counsel after warning the suspect or accused and giving him an opportunity to respond."

843 *Prosecutor v. Vojislav Šešelj*, Case No. IT-03-67-T, Decision of the Deputy Registrar, 05 July 2010, p.3-4. *See also* Registry Submission Pursuant to Rule 33(B) of the Rules Regarding the Registry's Indigency Investigation of the Accused Vojislav Šešelj, 25 June 2010, para.3.

order to secure resources for the defence.[844] It ordered the ICTY registry to cover the defence costs up to an amount of fifty per cent of the funding provided to indigent accused, including financing of three privileged legal associates, one case manager and one investigator.[845] Early remarks by the presiding judge had already indicated that the trial chamber intended to see to it that financial means for the preparation and presentation of the defence case would be secured.[846]

The jurisdictional basis assumed for issuing this decision despite the determination by the ICTY registry that it could not decide on provision of funding to the accused due to his failure to proof his indigence is unclear. The trial chamber referred in the decision *inter alia* to Article 13 of the directive, which provides for a remedy against a decision by the ICTY registry concerning legal aid.[847] The disposition, however, refers to Articles 21(4)(b) of the ICTY Statute and Rule 54 of the ICTY RPE.[848] According to the trial

---

844 *Prosecutor v. Vojislav Šešelj*, Case No. IT-03-67-T, Hearing, 21 September 2010, T.16378.

845 *Prosecutor v. Vojislav Šešelj*, Case No. IT-03-67-T, Administrative Hearing, 02 November 2010, T.16424-16425; *Procureur c/ Vojislav Šešelj*, Affaire n° IT-03-67-T, Version Expurgée de la « Décision Relative au Financement de la Défense » Enregistrée le 29 octobre 2010, 02 novembre 2010, p.5 (dispositif).

846 *See e.g. Prosecutor v. Vojislav Šešelj*, Case No. IT-03-67-PT, Status Conference, 13 March 2007, T.929; Status Conference, 22 May 2007, T.1146-1149, T.1151-1153; Status Conference, 04 July 2007, T.1282-1283; Status Conference, 17 August 2007, T.1374-1375; *Prosecutor v. Vojislav Šešelj*, Case No. IT-03-67-T, Hearing, 07 February 2008, T.3301 ("Rest assured the Trial Chamber is fully committed to doing its utmost for you to have the assistance of your associates. [...] But you also have the administration services, and that's the problem."); Hearing, 13 February 2008, T.3503-3504; Hearing, 07 July 2010, T.16348-16349; Hearing, 05 May 2011, T.17001-17003.

847 *Procureur c/ Vojislav Šešelj*, Affaire n° IT-03-67-T, Version Expurgée de la « Décision Relative au Financement de la Défense » Enregistrée le 29 octobre 2010, 02 novembre 2010, para.19. The decision refers to Article 13(A) of the directive. However, the proper reference appears to be Article 13(B), which reads in the relevant part: "The accused whose request for assignment of counsel has been denied or who has been found to have sufficient means to remunerate counsel in part, may within fifteen days from the date upon which he is notified of that decision, file a motion to the Chamber before which he is due to appear for review of the Registrar's decision. The Chamber may: [...] (iii) direct the Registrar to reconsider the extent to which the accused is able to remunerate counsel."

848 *Procureur c/ Vojislav Šešelj*, Affaire n° IT-03-67-T, Version Expurgée de la « Décision Relative au Financement de la Défense » Enregistrée le 29 octobre 2010, 02 novembre 2010, p.5 (dispositif).

chamber it seised itself *proprio motu* of the matter[849] in order to prevent any negative impact of the unsettled question of funding for the defence on the proceedings.[850]

Of note is the reaction of the accused to the trial chamber's decision who stated that he would not accept any payment for future work if there was no reimbursement for assistance allegedly provided in the past.[851]

The ICTY registry submitted that the trial chamber erred in assuming jurisdiction in this matter[852] and wrongly applied Article 13 of the directive which arguably did not vest the trial chamber with a review power of the initial ICTY registry's decision to the extent presumed by the bench.[853] It argued that Articles 20 and 21 of the ICTY Statute could not provide any such basis either, in view of the fact that the right of the accused to adequate time and facilities for defence preparation was safeguarded by the provision of facilities and, in case of indigence, remuneration of recognised legal advisors.[854] It was submitted that even if the trial chamber's jurisdiction were to be acknowledged,[855] it had misinterpreted applicable law and jurispru-

---

849 *Procureur c/ Vojislav Šešelj*, Affaire n° IT-03-67-T, Version Expurgée de la « Décision Relative au Financement de la Défense » Enregistrée le 29 octobre 2010, 02 novembre 2010, para.27.

850 *Procureur c/ Vojislav Šešelj*, Affaire n° IT-03-67-T, Version Expurgée de la « Décision Relative au Financement de la Défense » Enregistrée le 29 octobre 2010, 02 novembre 2010, para.26.

851 *Prosecutor v. Vojislav Šešelj*, Case No. IT-03-67-T, Administrative Hearing, 02 November 2010, T.16450-16452.

852 *Prosecutor v. Vojislav Šešelj*, Case No. IT-03-67-R33B, Registry Submission Pursuant to Rule 33(B) Following the Trial Chamber's Decision on Financing of Defence Dated 29 October 2010, 18 November 2010, para.9-10.

853 *Prosecutor v. Vojislav Šešelj*, Case No. IT-03-67-R33B, Registry Submission Pursuant to Rule 33(B) Following the Trial Chamber's Decision on Financing of Defence Dated 29 October 2010, 18 November 2010, para.11-22.

854 *Prosecutor v. Vojislav Šešelj*, Case No. IT-03-67-R33B, Registry Submission Pursuant to Rule 33(B) Following the Trial Chamber's Decision on Financing of Defence Dated 29 October 2010, 18 November 2010, para.26-28.

855 *Prosecutor v. Vojislav Šešelj*, Case No. IT-03-67-R33B, Registry Submission Pursuant to Rule 33(B) Following the Trial Chamber's Decision on Financing of Defence Dated 29 October 2010, 18 November 2010, para.40.

dence, considering burden of proof[856] and scope of the indigence determination.[857]

Interestingly, the appeals chamber determined the trial chamber's dealing not to be "unreasonable" since

> "[t]he issue of the legal assistance provided to a self-represented accused is not just an administrative matter, but may also impact the substantive rights of an accused to a fair and expedient trial."[858]

According to the appeals chamber, the trial chamber did not interfere with the registry's jurisdiction, but rather issued a substituting decision which did not prevent the ICTY registry from reaching a separate conclusion as to the indigence of the accused.[859] It found the allocation of funds by the trial chamber to be "simply an interim measure" which would leave room for the possibility "to recover the allocated funds from the Accused, if it becomes apparent that he has sufficient means to remunerate his legal associates".[860]

Two judges of the appeals chamber dissented: while the first dissent agreed in general with the intervention of the trial chamber in the matter based on the fair trial principle,[861] it disagreed with the extent of the trial chamber's decision and argued that the appeals chamber should have referred the matter

---

856 *Prosecutor v. Vojislav Šešelj*, Case No. IT-03-67-R33B, Registry Submission Pursuant to Rule 33(B) Following the Trial Chamber's Decision on Financing of Defence Dated 29 October 2010, 18 November 2010, para.42-45.

857 *Prosecutor v. Vojislav Šešelj*, Case No. IT-03-67-R33B, Registry Submission Pursuant to Rule 33(B) Following the Trial Chamber's Decision on Financing of Defence Dated 29 October 2010, 18 November 2010, para.46-49.

858 *Prosecutor v. Vojislav Šešelj*, Case No. IT-03-67-R33B, Public Redacted Version of the "Decision on the Registry Submission Pursuant to Rule 33(B) Regarding the Trial Chamber's Decision on Financing the Defence" Rendered on 8 April 2011, 17 May 2011, para.20 (internal footnotes omitted).

859 *Prosecutor v. Vojislav Šešelj*, Case No. IT-03-67-R33B, Public Redacted Version of the "Decision on the Registry Submission Pursuant to Rule 33(B) Regarding the Trial Chamber's Decision on Financing the Defence" Rendered on 8 April 2011, 17 May 2011, para.23.

860 *Prosecutor v. Vojislav Šešelj*, Case No. IT-03-67-R33B, Public Redacted Version of the "Decision on the Registry Submission Pursuant to Rule 33(B) Regarding the Trial Chamber's Decision on Financing the Defence" Rendered on 8 April 2011, 17 May 2011, para.28.

861 *Prosecutor v. Vojislav Šešelj*, Case No. IT-03-67-R33B, Public Redacted Version of the "Decision on the Registry Submission Pursuant to Rule 33(B) Regarding the Trial Chamber's Decision on Financing the Defence" Rendered on 8 April 2011, 17 May 2011, Partially Dissenting Opinion of Judge Güney, para.2.

back to the ICTY registry in order for it to determine which amount of financial aid should be granted to the accused.[862] In contrast, the second dissent "strongly disagree[d] that the Trial Chamber had jurisdiction to rule on the issue of financing Šešelj defence team"[863] since this "effectively reversed the burden of proof" and "set a very dangerous precedent".[864] With regard to the determination by the appeals chamber majority that any allocated funds could be recovered if necessary, the opinion stated that

> "it is naïve to believe that an accused, who refused to collaborate with the Registry to prove his indigence, will reimburse the allocated funds if he is ultimately proved not indigent."[865]

Even after this decision of the appeals chamber, the accused persisted in his request of retroactive payment of any expenses incurred by his defence team members, starting from the time of his arrest in 2003.[866] The trial chamber rejected this request on the basis that the accused did not provide any arguments which would justify reconsideration of its earlier decision,[867] while clarifying that its previous decision on financing of the defence had not been

---

862 *Prosecutor v. Vojislav Šešelj*, Case No. IT-03-67-R33B, Public Redacted Version of the "Decision on the Registry Submission Pursuant to Rule 33(B) Regarding the Trial Chamber's Decision on Financing the Defence" Rendered on 8 April 2011, 17 May 2011, Partially Dissenting Opinion of Judge Güney, para.5.

863 *Prosecutor v. Vojislav Šešelj*, Case No. IT-03-67-R33B, Public Redacted Version of the "Decision on the Registry Submission Pursuant to Rule 33(B) Regarding the Trial Chamber's Decision on Financing the Defence" Rendered on 8 April 2011, 17 May 2011, Dissenting Opinion of Judge Pocar, para.6.

864 *Prosecutor v. Vojislav Šešelj*, Case No. IT-03-67-R33B, Public Redacted Version of the "Decision on the Registry Submission Pursuant to Rule 33(B) Regarding the Trial Chamber's Decision on Financing the Defence" Rendered on 8 April 2011, 17 May 2011, Dissenting Opinion of Judge Pocar, para.8.

865 *Prosecutor v. Vojislav Šešelj*, Case No. IT-03-67-R33B, Public Redacted Version of the "Decision on the Registry Submission Pursuant to Rule 33(B) Regarding the Trial Chamber's Decision on Financing the Defence" Rendered on 8 April 2011, 17 May 2011, Dissenting Opinion of Judge Pocar, para.10.

866 *Procureur c/ Vojislav Šešelj*, Affaire n° IT-03-67-T, Audience de la Règle 98 bis Jugement, 05 mai 2011, T.16991-16992 (French transcript).

867 *Procureur c/ Vojislav Šešelj*, Affaire n° IT-03-67-T, Décision Consolidée Relative aux Requêtes Orales de l'Accusé en Relation avec la Présentation de sa Défense, 09 juin 2011, para.46-47.

rendered on the basis of an indigence determination, but rather in order to ensure the rights of the defence and forestall any palsy of the proceedings.[868]

The ICTY registry resorted to requesting an order from the trial chamber to national jurisdictions for provision of information relevant to an indigency determination.[869] In separate contempt proceedings against the accused, it made clear that absent an indigence determination and without any order from the trial chamber, "it would be inappropriate to disburse public funds for the defence of the Accused in the instant case".[870]

ii. The case of Radovan Karadžić

In *Karadžić*, the judge presiding over the initial appearance of the accused clarified that "there is no provision for legal aid to be given to self-represented accused" and that "some funding may be allowed for assistance by legal associates [...], but the right to privileged access to such legal associates cannot be guaranteed".[871]

Subsequently, challenges to decisions of the ICTY registry and of the Office for Legal Aid and Detention Matters (OLAD) were a recurrent scheme.

The defendant requested the trial chamber to order the ICTY registry to provide adequate facilities by being provided with the assistance of adequately qualified and experienced legal advisors who were to receive appropriate remuneration,[872] reiterating that

---

868 *Procureur c/ Vojislav Šešelj*, Affaire n° IT-03-67-T, Décision Consolidée Relative aux Requêtes Orales de l'Accusé en Relation avec la Présentation de sa Défense, 09 juin 2011, para.44.

869 *Prosecutor v. Vojislav Šešelj*, Case No. IT-03-67-T, Registry Submission Pursuant to Rule 33(B) Further to the Decision on Financing of the Defence, 21 June 2011 (filed: 22 June 2011), para.4.

870 *Prosecutor v. Vojislav Šešelj*, Case No. IT-03-67-R77.4, Registry Submission Pursuant to Rule 33(B) Regarding the Application of the Decision on Financing, 11 July 2011 (filed: 12 July 2011), para.7.

871 *Prosecutor v. Radovan Karadžić*, Case No. IT-95-5/18-PT, Initial Appearance, 31 July 2008, T.19.

872 *Prosecutor v. Radovan Karadžić*, Case No. IT-95-5/18-PT, Motion for Adequate Facilities and Equality of Arms: Legal Associates, 24 November 2008 (filed: 25 November 2008), para.1. *See also* para.15-17.

> "[w]hile he insists on self-representation, he recognizes that to defend himself professionally, he needs assistance from legal professionals."[873]

Criticising the compensation scheme and its application by the ICTY registry,[874] the accused submitted that:

> "self-representation at the Tribunal is reduced to an illusion granted under conditions in which it cannot effectively be exercised and then taken away when the accused collapses from the burdens of doing the impossible."[875]

The trial chamber considered the *Krajišnik* appeals chamber to be clear in not foreseeing "expensive legal advice", but rather "modest financial support" to assist in the defence case presentation.[876] It observed "a clear distinction between the purpose of the legal aid scheme for representation through counsel under the Directive and what the Appeals Chamber saw as the purpose of support to self-represented accused".[877] Following the appeals chamber in *Krajišnik*, the trial chamber concluded that:

> "[i]f [...] his principal concern is that his case is exceptionally complex and that he requires, or may require, special assistance in performing various aspects of the work involved, including general advice, drafting, and relief from making submissions in court, then the solution does not lie in the application of the Remuneration Scheme but rather in devising an *arrangement for the presentation of his defence that allows him to play an active role while at the same time being represented by counsel*."[878]

---

873 *Prosecutor v. Radovan Karadžić*, Case No. IT-95-5/18-PT, Motion for Adequate Facilities and Equality of Arms: Legal Associates, 24 November 2008 (filed: 25 November 2008), para.2.

874 *Prosecutor v. Radovan Karadžić*, Case No. IT-95-5/18-PT, Motion for Adequate Facilities and Equality of Arms: Legal Associates, 24 November 2008 (filed: 25 November 2008), para.19. *See also* para.31.

875 *Prosecutor v. Radovan Karadžić*, Case No. IT-95-5/18-PT, Motion for Adequate Facilities and Equality of Arms: Legal Associates, 24 November 2008 (filed: 25 November 2008), para.19.

876 *Prosecutor v. Radovan Karadžić*, Case No. IT-95-5/18-PT, Decision on Accused Motion for Adequate Facilities and Equality of Arms: Legal Associates, 28 January 2009, para.31.

877 *Prosecutor v. Radovan Karadžić*, Case No. IT-95-5/18-PT, Decision on Accused Motion for Adequate Facilities and Equality of Arms: Legal Associates, 28 January 2009, para.31.

878 *Prosecutor v. Radovan Karadžić*, Case No. IT-95-5/18-PT, Decision on Accused Motion for Adequate Facilities and Equality of Arms: Legal Associates, 28 January 2009, para.36 (emphasis added).

In his appeal against this decision, the accused interpreted the position of the appeals chamber in *Krajišnik* on a potential restriction of the right to self-representation to concern the level of disruption.[879] The defence submitted that it

> "would do nothing for the reputation of the ICTY if it were known that it had been decided at the highest level of the Tribunal that those entrusted with giving him legal advice and assistance, and ensuring that he receives a competent and professional defence, were being funded only at the level of support staff."[880]

However, when reading paragraph 41 of the *Krajišnik* appeals decision[881] in context, it is rather unambiguous that the level of disruption was not the sole concern of the appeals chamber. Thus, the interpretation of the *Karadžić* defence does not withstand scrutiny when properly contextualising the relevant parts of the decision.[882] The language in the pertinent portion of the

---

879 *Prosecutor v. Radovan Karadžić*, Case No. IT-95-5/18-AR73.2, Appeal of the Trial Chamber's Decision on Adequate Facilities, 02 March 2009 (filed: 05 March 2009), para.18.

880 *Prosecutor v. Radovan Karadžić*, Case No. IT-95-5/18-AR73.2, Appeal of the Trial Chamber's Decision on Adequate Facilities, 02 March 2009 (filed: 05 March 2009), para.45.

881 *Prosecutor v. Momčilo Krajišnik*, IT-00-39-A, Decision on Krajišnik Request and Prosecution Motion, 11 September 2007, para.41: "The question nonetheless remains whether some other provision of the Statute or source of law requires the Registry to provide an indigent self-representing accused with funded legal aid. Mr. Krajišnik suggests that the principle of equality referenced in Article 21(1) of the Statute and the fair trial rights referenced in Article 21(2) of the Statute have this effect [fn. omitted]. The Appeals Chamber does not find these arguments convincing. While Article 21(1) may require that accused in similar circumstances receive roughly comparable treatment, it does not require that an accused who opts for self-representation receive all the benefits held by an accused who opts for counsel. To the contrary, as 'part of the choice to self-represent, Mr. Krajišnik must accept responsibility for the disadvantages this choice may bring' [fn. omitted]. Moreover, the Appeals Chamber considers that where an accused elects to self-represent, he is asserting his ability to conduct his case without legal assistance and thus Tribunal funding for legal aid for him can be presumed to be unnecessary to the conduct of a fair trial. To the extent that the accused lacks the ability to conduct his own case and his self-representation is thus 'substantially and persistently obstructing the proper and expeditious conduct of his trial', then the remedy is restriction of his right to self-representation [fn. omitted]. To allow an accused to self-represent and yet also to receive full legal aid funding from the Tribunal would, as the saying goes, let him have his cake and eat it too."

882 *See Prosecutor v. Radovan Karadžić*, Case No. IT-95-5/18-AR73.2, Prosecution's Response to Karadžić's Appeal of the Trial Chamber's Decision on Adequate Fa-

decision leaves no doubt that, rather than standing alone, the level of disruption was linked by the appeals chamber to the potential inability of a self-represented defendant to conduct his or her own case. Placed into this context, it is viable to interpret the paragraph so as to mean that in case any such inability leads to a substantial and persistent obstruction of the proceedings, the correct remedy to revert to would be restriction of the right to self-representation. Therefore, the interpretation of the trial chamber in *Karadžić* appears to correctly apply this part of the *Krajišnik* decision.

The appeals chamber found that the *Krajišnik* decision did in fact address an accused's ability to conduct proceedings, rather than issues of misconduct or ill health.[883] It did not see any error in the trial chamber's interpretation and specifically stated that if the lack of knowledge amounted to a significant and persistent obstruction of the proceedings, resolution was to be found in the "curtailment of his right to self-representation".[884] The appeals chamber made clear that legal consultation "is not to be equated with the comprehensive work of counsel which is to be undertaken by the accused himself",[885] and that "in general a self-represented accused is expected to undertake himself all the tasks normally assumed by counsel".[886]

The matter of financial aid, however, would not end with the appeals chamber decision. Challenging an OLAD decision concerning pre-trial funds, the defendant submitted that additional hours would have to be allocated to review significant amounts of disclosure,[887] though obviously at the same

cilities, 13 March 2009, para.7-8; Registrar's Submission Pursuant to Rule 33 (B) Regarding Radovan Karadžić's Appeal of the Trial Chamber's Decision on Adequate Facilities, 30 March 2009, para.23 *et seq.*

883 *Prosecutor v. Radovan Karadžić*, Case No. IT-95-5/18-AR73.2, Decision on Interlocutory Appeal of the Trial Chamber's Decision on Adequate Facilities, 07 May 2009, para.13.

884 *Prosecutor v. Radovan Karadžić*, Case No. IT-95-5/18-AR73.2, Decision on Interlocutory Appeal of the Trial Chamber's Decision on Adequate Facilities, 07 May 2009, para.14.

885 *Prosecutor v. Radovan Karadžić*, Case No. IT-95-5/18-AR73.2, Decision on Interlocutory Appeal of the Trial Chamber's Decision on Adequate Facilities, 07 May 2009, para.16.

886 *Prosecutor v. Radovan Karadžić*, Case No. IT-95-5/18-AR73.2, Decision on Interlocutory Appeal of the Trial Chamber's Decision on Adequate Facilities, 07 May 2009, para.23.

887 *Prosecutor v. Radovan Karadžić*, Case No. IT-95-5/18-T, Appeal of OLAD Decision in Relation to Additional Pre-trial Funds, 10 November 2009, para.7, 13.

time being wary of the *Krajišnik* decision.[888] In a similar challenge to the funding allocated for trial, the accused argued that it was not possible to conduct the defence with the resources provided; that the OLAD decision turned the right to self-representation "in to [sic] an illusion"; and that a "fair trial under these circumstances is absolutely unattainable".[889] Submitting that OLAD failed to appreciate the significance of tasks to be assumed by a self-represented accused which would necessitate engagement of support staff just as in case of represented accused,[890] the motion concluded that:

> "Dr. Karadžić is ready to defend himself at this Tribunal in an exemplary manner if given the resources to do so. The decisions of OLAD are not only unreasonable, they are absurd. No civilized country would force an accused to participate in a trial of such unequal proportions. Those that did could not expect the outcome of such a trial to be respected. The President of this institution should not allow the bureaucrats of this Tribunal to foul its legacy."[891]

Far into the trial proceedings, the accused again applied for additional funds, arguing that OLAD either wrongly interpreted the Remuneration Scheme, or that the scheme as such violated his right to adequate facilities as guaranteed in Article 21(4)(b) of the ICTY Statute.[892] According to the defendant, "[h]is team simply cannot keep its head above water absent additional resources".[893] It subsequently appeared as if the defence team was intent on leaving no doubt as to the impact of the alleged resource limitations pending a further decision.[894]

---

888 *Prosecutor v. Radovan Karadžić*, Case No. IT-95-5/18-T, Appeal of OLAD Decision in Relation to Additional Pre-trial Funds, 10 November 2009, para.15.

889 *Prosecutor v. Radovan Karadžić*, Case No. IT-95-5/18-T, Request for Review of OLAD Decision on Trial Phase Remuneration, 14 January 2010, para.20.

890 *Prosecutor v. Radovan Karadžić*, Case No. IT-95-5/18-T, Request for Review of OLAD Decision on Trial Phase Remuneration, 14 January 2010, para.26.

891 *Prosecutor v. Radovan Karadžić*, Case No. IT-95-5/18-T, Request for Review of OLAD Decision on Trial Phase Remuneration, 14 January 2010, para.46.

892 *Prosecutor v. Radovan Karadžić*, Case No. IT-95-5/18-T, Request for Review of Decision on Defence Team Funding, 22 August 2011, para.9, 20, 22.

893 *Prosecutor v. Radovan Karadžić*, Case No. IT-95-5/18-T, Request for Review of Decision on Defence Team Funding, 22 August 2011, para.16.

894 *See e.g. Prosecutor v. Radovan Karadžić*, Case No. IT-95-5/18-T, Hearing, 31 October 2011, T.20641-20642: "I don't know whether this part was translated; it should have maybe. But Excellency, really, we are under such pressure that the Defence feels disabled in many ways. Everybody admits that this is a mega-trial but nothing else is mega. Everything else is average; the number of people working on this case, the resources that I have, so if it's a mega-trial then there should be a mega-defence."; Motion for Interviews of Prosecution Witnesses or an Order Re-

Having reviewed the amount of disclosure at issue, as well as in light of "the particular circumstances of the case",[895] the ICTY president in fact found the OLAD funding decision to be unreasonable[896] and ordered the ICTY registry to allocate a significantly higher amount of remunerable hours to the defence team for the entire pre-trial phase.[897] Similarly, when the amount of trial funds was challenged, the ICTY president found the determination of funds to be erroneous,[898] granted additional resources to the accused,[899] and also allocated a payment raise to the accused's legal advisor.[900] At the same time, the ICTY president clarified that such decisions had to be made on a case-by-case basis and should not be considered as entitling all self-represented accused to the same remuneration.[901] The ICTY president subsequently granted another increase in funding,[902] finding that the initial

---

quiring Prosecution to Proof their Witnesses by Telephone, 31 October 2011 (para.1: "[...] if Dr. Karadzic is not allowed to interview prosecution witnesses in person, he requests that the Chamber issue an order that the prosecution counsel may only proof its witnesses by telephone in order to ensure equality of arms."); Motion for Reconsideration of Decision on Ninth Suspension of Proceedings: Witness KDZ456, 31 October 2011, para.5. *See also* Registrar's Submission Pursuant to Rule 33(B) of the Rules Regarding Radovan Karadžić's Motion for Interviews of Prosecution Witnesses or an Order Requiring Prosecution to Proof their Witnesses by Telephone, 31 October 2011. *See also* Reply Brief: Request for Review of Decision on Defence Team Funding, 08 September 2011, para.8.

895 *Prosecutor v. Radovan Karadžić*, Case No. IT-95-5/18-T, Decision on Appeal of OLAD Decision in Relation to Additional Pre-trial Funds, 17 December 2009, para.23.

896 *Prosecutor v. Radovan Karadžić*, Case No. IT-95-5/18-T, Decision on Appeal of OLAD Decision in Relation to Additional Pre-trial Funds, 17 December 2009, para.25. *See also* para.29.

897 *Prosecutor v. Radovan Karadžić*, Case No. IT-95-5/18-T, Decision on Appeal of OLAD Decision in Relation to Additional Pre-trial Funds, 17 December 2009, para.30. *See also* para.5, 8.

898 *Prosecutor v. Radovan Karadžić*, Case No. IT-95-5/18-T, Decision on Request for Review of OLAD Decision on Trial Phase Remuneration, 19 February 2010, para.39, 43.

899 *Prosecutor v. Radovan Karadžić*, Case No. IT-95-5/18-T, Decision on Request for Review of OLAD Decision on Trial Phase Remuneration, 19 February 2010, para.45-46.

900 *Prosecutor v. Radovan Karadžić*, Case No. IT-95-5/18-T, Decision on Request for Review of OLAD Decision on Trial Phase Remuneration, 19 February 2010, para.53.

901 *Prosecutor v. Radovan Karadžić*, Case No. IT-95-5/18-T, Decision on Request for Review of OLAD Decision on Trial Phase Remuneration, 19 February 2010, para.47.

902 *Prosecutor v. Radovan Karadžić*, Case No. IT-95-5/18-T, Decision on Request for Review of Decision on Defence Team Funding, 31 January 2012, para.45.

decision on remuneration "did not sufficiently consider the scope and complexity of Karadžić's trial".[903] However, the ICTY president did dismiss the defence argument with regard to alleged incompatibility of the Remuneration Scheme with the right to a fair trial.[904]

While the ICTY registry took the position that the accused failed to show unforeseeable circumstances which would justify an increase in funding,[905] it did amend its Remuneration Scheme[906] in order to ensure its consistency with the rights of *pro se* defendants as determined in the relevant jurisprudence, and that all accused receive the same treatment.[907]

It is of interest that the accused used the revocation of the initial OLAD remuneration decision to argue for an additional 3 ¾ months time period for trial preparation with a full defence team.[908] The defendant went as far as stating that the decision of the ICTY president "led him to decide to participate in his trial".[909] Subsequently, the accused applied for certification and asked for a stay of the proceedings pending final determination of the matter.[910] The trial chamber consequently adjourned the hearing of evidence

---

903 *Prosecutor v. Radovan Karadžić*, Case No. IT-95-5/18-T, Decision on Request for Review of Decision on Defence Team Funding, 31 January 2012, para.44.

904 *Prosecutor v. Radovan Karadžić*, Case No. IT-95-5/18-T, Decision on Request for Review of Decision on Defence Team Funding, 31 January 2012, para.23-24.

905 *Prosecutor v. Radovan Karadžić*, Case No. IT-95-5/18-T, Registrar's Submission Pursuant to Rule 33 (B) Regarding Radovan Karadžić's Request for Review of Decision on Defence Team Funding, 05 September 2011, para.40.

906 *Prosecutor v. Radovan Karadžić*, Case No. IT-95-5/18-T, Registrar's Submission Pursuant to Rule 33(B) Regarding Radovan Karadžić's Request for Review of Decision on Defence Team Funding, 05 September 2011, para.20. *See also* Remuneration Scheme for Persons Assisting Indigent Self-Represented Accused, 01 April 2010, Rev. 2, para.12(iii).

907 *Prosecutor v. Radovan Karadžić*, Case No. IT-95-5/18-T, Registrar's Submission Pursuant to Rule 33(B) Regarding Radovan Karadžić's Request for Review of Decision on Defence Team Funding, 05 September 2011, para.21.

908 *Prosecutor v. Radovan Karadžić*, Case No. IT-95-5/18-T, Supplemental Submission on Motion for Postponement of Trial Following President's Decision, 22 February 2010, para.5.

909 *Prosecutor v. Radovan Karadžić*, Case No. IT-95-5/18-T, Request for Review of Decision on Defence Team Funding, 22 August 2011, para.2.

910 *Prosecutor v. Radovan Karadžić*, Case No. IT-95-5/18-T, Application for Certification to Appeal and for Stay Pending Appeal of Decision on Commencement of Evidence, 01 March 2010, para.35. *See also* Prosecution's Response to Application for Certification to Appeal and for Stay Pending Appeal of Decision on Commencement of Evidence, 01 March 2010, which did not object to a certification of appeal, but did reject the request for stay of the proceedings.

sine die.[911] The defence argued that the decision on funding of the ICTY president was to be seen as "remedy" which the trial chamber "made [...] impossible to implement",[912] thereby "exceed[ing] its authority" and "invad[ing] the province of the President".[913] According to the accused, his right to adequate time and facilities had been jeopardised by the trial chamber's decision, necessitating another three months suspension.[914]

In response, it was argued that the accused had been determined ready for trial already before the issue of defence team funding arose[915] and that he failed to show how his readiness would have regressed in the time period since that determination.[916] Additionally, it was submitted that it was for the trial chamber to assess the commencement of trial independently of the president's funding decision,[917] which in any case would be separate of and not be binding on the trial chamber in determining the time needed for trial preparation.[918] It was argued that the president's decision was falsely interpreted as remedy,[919] and submitted that the amount of legal assistance available to the accused in the relevant time period was pertinent with regard to allegedly suffered disadvantages.[920]

---

911 *Prosecutor v. Radovan Karadžić*, Case No. IT-95-5/18-T, Oral Decision, 02 March 2010, T.993-995.

912 *Prosecutor v. Radovan Karadžić*, Case No. IT-95-5/18-AR73.7, Appeal from Decision on Commencement of Evidence, 09 March 2010, para.24, 25, 29, 45.

913 *Prosecutor v. Radovan Karadžić*, Case No. IT-95-5/18-AR73.7, Appeal from Decision on Commencement of Evidence, 09 March 2010, para.25, 34, 35.

914 *Prosecutor v. Radovan Karadžić*, Case No. IT-95-5/18-AR73.7, Appeal from Decision on Commencement of Evidence, 09 March 2010, para.50-51.

915 *Prosecutor v. Radovan Karadžić*, Case No. IT-95-5/18-T, Prosecution's Response to Karadžić's Motion for Postponement of Trial, 03 February 2010, para.2.

916 *Prosecutor v. Radovan Karadžić*, Case No. IT-95-5/18-T, Prosecution's Response to Karadžić's Motion for Postponement of Trial, 03 February 2010, para.5.

917 *Prosecutor v. Radovan Karadžić*, Case No. IT-95-5/18-AR73.7, Prosecution Response to Karadžić's Appeal of Decision on Postponement of Trial, 17 March 2010, para.5-7.

918 *Prosecutor v. Radovan Karadžić*, Case No. IT-95-5/18-AR73.7, Prosecution Response to Karadžić's Appeal of Decision on Postponement of Trial, 17 March 2010, para.7, para.10-11.

919 *Prosecutor v. Radovan Karadžić*, Case No. IT-95-5/18-AR73.7, Prosecution Response to Karadžić's Appeal of Decision on Postponement of Trial, 17 March 2010, para.12-14.

920 *Prosecutor v. Radovan Karadžić*, Case No. IT-95-5/18-AR73.7, Prosecution Response to Karadžić's Appeal of Decision on Postponement of Trial, 17 March 2010, para.21, fn.54.

The trial chamber did not consider the decision of the ICTY president on remuneration of the defence team to be relevant for the determination of any potential postponement of the evidentiary phase, matter falling within its proper discretion.[921] Conducting a detailed review of the amount and nature of disclosure material,[922] the trial chamber clarified that in light of ongoing disclosure obligations, the accused could not expect to have reviewed the entirety of disclosure before the start of trial, or have completed other "typical" obligations related to the conduct of proceedings.[923] Thus, according to the bench, a further delay merely based on recent disclosure was not justified,[924] since it would "be a drastic measure that would, concurrently, have real repercussions for the parties' rights to a fair and expeditious trial".[925] At the same time, the trial chamber left open the possibility to request additional funding and to be granted more time for example for the preparation of cross-examinations.[926]

The appeals chamber limited its own review to the issue whether the trial chamber had committed a "discernible error" in the exercise of its discretion,[927] and clarified that the ICTY president had no authority to issue decisions binding a trial chamber, authority solely accorded to the appeals chamber.[928] According to the appeals chamber, the president's determination was limited to the issue of defence funding, without interfering with the trial chamber's considerations on issues of trial scheduling.[929] While the president's determination could be taken into account by the trial chamber, it

---

921 *Prosecutor v. Radovan Karadžić*, Case No. IT-95-5/18-T, Decision on Accused's Motion for Postponement of Trial, 26 February 2010, para.23.

922 *Prosecutor v. Radovan Karadžić*, Case No. IT-95-5/18-T, Decision on Accused's Motion for Postponement of Trial, 26 February 2010, para.24-40.

923 *Prosecutor v. Radovan Karadžić*, Case No. IT-95-5/18-T, Decision on Accused's Motion for Postponement of Trial, 26 February 2010, para.38.

924 *Prosecutor v. Radovan Karadžić*, Case No. IT-95-5/18-T, Decision on Accused's Motion for Postponement of Trial, 26 February 2010, para.38.

925 *Prosecutor v. Radovan Karadžić*, Case No. IT-95-5/18-T, Decision on Accused's Motion for Postponement of Trial, 26 February 2010, para.39.

926 *Prosecutor v. Radovan Karadžić*, Case No. IT-95-5/18-T, Decision on Accused's Motion for Postponement of Trial, 26 February 2010, para.40.

927 *Prosecutor v. Radovan Karadžić*, Case No. IT-95-5/18-AR73.7, Decision on Appeal from Decision on Motion for Further Postponement of Trial, 31 March 2010, para.13.

928 *Prosecutor v. Radovan Karadžić*, Case No. IT-95-5/18-AR73.7, Decision on Appeal from Decision on Motion for Further Postponement of Trial, 31 March 2010, para.19.

929 *Prosecutor v. Radovan Karadžić*, Case No. IT-95-5/18-AR73.7, Decision on Appeal from Decision on Motion for Further Postponement of Trial, 31 March 2010, para.20.

would not necessarily lead to a further postponement.[930] The appeals chamber found the argument of it being a remedy to be "based on the misconception of both the law and the Impugned Decision",[931] and dismissed the appeal.[932]

The observation of the trial chamber concerning the "parties' rights"[933] is interesting insofar as it indicates the necessity to conduct a balancing exercise in the course of which chambers will not only be required to safeguard the rights of self-represented accused, thereby implicitly recognising a right also of the prosecution to a fair and expeditious trial. At the same time, however, it ought to be questioned whether the trial chamber's decision properly drew a distinction between the president's decision on the funding of the defence team during the adjournment period on the one hand, and the issue of further postponement of the evidentiary phase on the other. Especially paragraphs 40[934] and 43[935] of the decision seem to take the matter rather lightly, assuming that an application by the accused to the ICTY registry for

930 *Prosecutor v. Radovan Karadžić*, Case No. IT-95-5/18-AR73.7, Decision on Appeal from Decision on Motion for Further Postponement of Trial, 31 March 2010, para.21.

931 *Prosecutor v. Radovan Karadžić*, Case No. IT-95-5/18-AR73.7, Decision on Appeal from Decision on Motion for Further Postponement of Trial, 31 March 2010, para.22.

932 *Prosecutor v. Radovan Karadžić*, Case No. IT-95-5/18-AR73.7, Decision on Appeal from Decision on Motion for Further Postponement of Trial, 31 March 2010, para.28, 29.

933 *Prosecutor v. Radovan Karadžić*, Case No. IT-95-5/18-T, Decision on Accused's Motion for Postponement of Trial, 26 February 2010, para.39.

934 *Prosecutor v. Radovan Karadžić*, Case No. IT-95-5/18-T, Decision on Accused's Motion for Postponement of Trial, 26 February 2010, para.40: "[...] Furthermore, in light of the fact that the President's Decision, finding that the Accused should have benefited from the assistance of a full defence team of eight people during the adjournment period, was only issued one week prior to the end of the adjournment period, the Trial Chamber notes that it is open to the Accused to make a reasoned request to the Registry for remuneration for all eight of his defence team members during the first few weeks of the resumed trial, in order for them to be able to regain some of the time 'lost' during the adjournment period, and to make progress in the review of the provided Rule 66(B) material [fn. omitted]."

935 *Prosecutor v. Radovan Karadžić*, Case No. IT-95-5/18-T, Decision on Accused's Motion for Postponement of Trial, 26 February 2010, para.43: "[...] In this regard, the Chamber notes that, following the President's Decision, the eight defence team members will be funded for the adjournment period. While the President envisaged that, once the trial resumes, this number could be somewhat reduced, as the Chamber has noted above, the Accused could make a reasoned request to the Registry for the continued funding of all eight members of his defence team for a certain period following the resumption of trial in order to complete certain specific tasks."

more funding would be sufficient to remedy the alleged disadvantageous situation. One would need to question whether the president's decision was indeed irrelevant to the determination of the issue of which the trial chamber was seised.

With regard to the arguments raised by the accused, it has to be mentioned that the ICTY president never stated that as a necessary consequence of his decision, the defendant would have to be accorded more time for the preparation, which refutes the allegation that the trial chamber without authority "overruled" the president's decision. Secondly, the appeal failed to provide any basis for the argument that the trial chamber's decision made the president's determination impossible to implement, not to speak of the questionable assumption that the president's decision was in effect a "remedy" to be accorded to the defendant. The reference to the ICTY Directive on the Assignment of Defence Counsel[936] does not appear to be a sufficient basis for the submission that the president's determination was binding on the trial chamber. Moreover, the president's finding did not in any way indicate that the matter of funding would impact on the scheduling of trial proceedings, a matter which, in any case, falls within the discretion of the trial chamber. The defendant did not provide any convincing basis or source for his allegation that the trial chamber's discretion to schedule resumption of hearings "cannot be exercised in a manner which overrules a decision of the President".[937] In addition, the reference to the decision on the trial date in *Ngirabatware*[938] does not appear to be conclusive insofar as the situation is not comparable[939] and the accused could not possibly argue at that stage of the

---

936 Directive on the Assignment of Defence Counsel (Directive No. 1/94), as amended 29 June 2006 (IT/73/Rev. 11), Article 31(C): "Where the dispute involves a sum greater than €4,999, an aggrieved party may file a request for review with the Registrar, who shall refer the matter to the President for his determination. Before making a determination the President shall request submissions from the aggrieved party and the respondent. The President's determination shall be final and binding upon the parties."

937 *Prosecutor v. Radovan Karadžić*, Case No. IT-95-5/18-AR73.7, Appeal from Decision on Commencement of Evidence, 09 March 2010, para.35.

938 *Prosecutor v. Radovan Karadžić*, Case No. IT-95-5/18-AR73.7, Appeal from Decision on Commencement of Evidence, 09 March 2010, para.41.

939 The accused in that case was not self-represented and did not argue lack of preparation time in light of funding issues which impacted on the work of his defence team, but rather more generally a lack of adequate time of preparation for the proceedings: *see Prosecutor v. Augustin Ngirabatware*, Case No. ICTR-99-54-A, Decision on

proceedings that his defence team had not been in place long enough to be able to adequately prepare for trial.

It is of note that the ICTY registry, having concluded its indigency investigation, determined that the accused was to pay for part of his defence costs.[940]

c. Discussion

As can be seen from the discussion of the relevant litigation in different cases before the ICTY, the issue of financing legal and other support of self-represented accused has undergone significant developments. While initially the position was presented by both prosecution and the ICTY registry that any legal aid would be subject to the assignment of defence counsel, subsequent jurisprudence by both appeals and trial chambers made clear that indigent self-represented accused should in fact receive at least part of the defence costs provided for by the tribunal. It has been made clear that in line with the overall position that a self-represented accused in fact acts as his or her own defence counsel, such financial aid would not necessarily be the same as that provided to professional defence teams.

At the same time, the abundance of jurisprudence leads to a number of issues to be discussed, in particular in light of the fact that depending on which part of an institution deals with the matter – registry, separate chambers, individual judges – different approaches appear to have been adopted.

On a general note, the question needs to be asked which reasons might underlie the initial and apparently continuing reluctance of the ICTY registry to actually provide legal aid to self-represented accused, especially considering the argument that a higher complexity of proceedings would not be sufficient justification for provision of legal aid.[941] From an accountability point of view, it is understandable that financial aid is provided only in compliance with strict guidelines, as the ICTY registry is responsible for the disbursement

---

Augustin Ngirabatware's Appeal of Decisions Denying Motions to Vary Trial Date, 12 May 2009, para.2-7.

940 *Prosecutor v. Radovan Karadžić*, Case No. IT-95-5/18-T, Decision of the Registrar, 10 October 2012 (filed: 11 October 2012), p.4: "[…] Decides […] that the Accused shall contribute €146,501.00 to the cost of his defence […]".

941 *Prosecutor v. Vojislav Šešelj*, Case No. IT-03-67-PT, Registry Submission Pursuant to Rule 33(B) of the Rules Regarding Vojislav Šešelj's Motion for a Decision by the Trial Chamber on Financing his Defence, 29 June 2007, para.57 fn.20.

of public funds and thus has to be able to account for everything spent in the context of legal aid before the ICTY. From a pragmatic point of view, however, a *pro se* defendant should be granted as much assistance as possible, including financial aid upon showing indigence, to exhaust all possibilities for ensuring smooth and efficient proceedings. More importantly, indigent self-represented accused who are provided with funding for legal associates, investigators and case managers would be able to prepare a potentially more solid defence case, which could serve as a guarantee that, despite the exercise of the right to self-representation in international criminal proceedings, the accused would get a fair trial with the possibility to actually challenge the prosecution case. This is of particular significance in cases with a high level of complexity. Such meaningful conduct of the defence case would also be perceived to be more equitable by outstanding observers and thus contribute to the integrity of the proceedings and of the international criminal justice system in general.

This is even more so since in practice, assigned or chosen defence counsel acting as attorney on behalf of an accused would not prepare the defence case on their own either, but rather rely on legal teams which include other lawyers, investigators and other support staff. While the exercise of the right to self-representation entails that no defence counsel should act on behalf of the accused for the entirety of the proceedings, it would need to be reconsidered whether it equally has to involve the denial of legal aid. The argument could be made that the restriction of financial aid for self-represented accused may amount to a punishment of defendants exclusively based on their choice to exercise their right to self-representation. It is difficult to see how this is supposed to be reconciled with the position adopted by various chambers at the ICTY that the right to self-representation is a cornerstone of the international criminal justice system. If a right is regarded as part of the overall fair trial guarantee of accused and awarded such a prominent status, in consequence arguably the necessary means should be provided so that this right can in fact be exercised.[942]

On the other hand, and from a purely financial point of view, it might have created lower costs not to permit the exercise of the right to self-representation in the current form, and rather provide for mandatory lead counsel

942 *Cf. Prosecutor v. Radovan Karadžić*, Case No. IT-95-5/18-PT, Motion for Adequate Facilities and Equality of Arms: Legal Associates, 24 November 2008 (filed: 25 November 2008), para.19; *Prosecutor v. Radovan Karadžić*, Case No. IT-95-5/18-T, Submission on Trial Schedule, 20 May 2010, para.3.

from the start. This would arguably have contributed to avoiding situations as in the *Karadžić* proceedings, in which ICTY funds were used to at least partially finance the defence team of the self-represented accused, and at the same time for the payment of standby counsel which had been assigned by the trial chamber, *i.e.* the ICTY funded two attorneys and their respective defence teams at the rate of (lead) counsel due to the implications of the accused's decision to present his defence in person.

It is of interest that the ICTY registry appears to initially have adopted the position that the right to defend oneself and the right to counsel of choice are *not* necessarily mutually exclusive, expressly referring to the pre-trial chamber's decision in *Šešelj* and the fundamental dissent in *Krajišnik*.[943] The prosecution had argued the interpretation submitted in *Šešelj* already several years earlier when advocating the imposition of counsel against the will of the accused in *Milošević*.[944] Yet, only a few months after arguing this position, the ICTY registry in a different case submitted that by choosing to present his defence in person, the accused exhausted his rights enshrined in Article 21(4)(d) of the ICTY Statute,[945] thus repeating the arguments formulated by the prosecution earlier. One might wonder about the reasons for which the ICTY registry at first conceded that accused defending themselves could be assigned counsel, thereby triggering the application of the legal aid scheme and potentially establishing a basis for the entitlement to the (partial) funding of the defence, while on the other hand arguing that a *pro se* defendant could not engage such counsel as legal associate and nevertheless claim legal aid, at least to some extent. Given that the effect of both solutions is essentially the same, namely that a self-represented accused will have professional advice financed by the ICTY, it appears peculiar that both arrangements were supported and rejected, respectively, in the same submission.

The reality of the matter has apparently also been recognised by self-represented accused: the accused in *Karadžić* for example insisted on presenting

943 *Prosecutor v. Vojislav Šešelj*, Case No. IT-03-67-PT, Registry Submission Pursuant to Rule 33(B) of the Rules Regarding Vojislav Šešelj's Motion for a Decision by the Trial Chamber on Financing his Defence, 29 June 2007, para.76.

944 *Prosecutor v. Slobodan Milošević*, Case No. IT-02-54-T, Prosecution Submissions in Response to the Trial Chamber's 19 July 2004 "Further Order on Future Conduct of the Trial", 26 July 2004, para.37; Attachment "A" to Prosecution Submissions in Response to the Trial Chamber's 19 July 2004 "Further Order on Future Conduct of the Trial", 26 July 2004, para.15.

945 *Prosecutor v. Zdravko Tolimir,* Case No. IT-05-88/2-PT, Registrar's Submission on the Accused's Motion Dated 16 November 2007, 07 December 2007, para.9.

his defence in person while at the same time admitting that he was in fact incapable of running his case without the assistance of professional defence counsel. This could have been an opportunity for the trial chamber to determine the accused's effective ability to self-represent, issue the bench alluded to itself,[946] in particular in light of the earlier position of the *Krajišnik* trial chamber that, even though not considering this point in detail, an accused's inability to run a criminal defence case may factor into the balance when deciding whether to grant a request to self-represent.[947]

While the position of the accused that his legal advisor should occasionally relieve him in the execution of his tasks as his own counsel[948] seems to be at least partially justified, it could be argued that the role of a legal associate to self-represented accused does not encompass "relieving" the defendant in the course of trial proceedings. Opting for exercising the right to self-representation does not, at least under the scheme currently acknowledged, entitle the accused to pick and choose when to exercise this right during the case, thereby in effect having both self-representation and defence counsel acting on his behalf. The mood of the defendant should not be allowed to determine the procedural nature of his defence. To base this view on the right to equality of arms does not withstand scrutiny if the accused is still provided with adequate time and facilities to prepare and present his or her case. The general underlying rationale in the particular context of self-represented accused also appears to have been adopted in other proceedings.[949]

---

946 *Prosecutor v. Radovan Karadžić*, Case No. IT-95-5/18-PT, Decision on Accused Motion for Adequate Facilities and Equality of Arms: Legal Associates, 28 January 2009, para.36.

947 *Prosecutor v. Momčilo Krajišnik*, IT-00-39-T, Reasons for Oral Decision Denying Mr Krajišnik's Request to Proceed Unrepresented by Counsel, 18 August 2005, para.34: "Our silence on this point is not to be taken as a concession that the integrity of international criminal proceedings should not be given greater weight than in certain domestic jurisdictions."

948 *Prosecutor v. Radovan Karadžić*, Case No. IT-95-5/18-PT, Motion for Adequate Facilities and Equality of Arms: Legal Associates, 24 November 2008 (filed: 25 November 2008), para.28.

949 *Cf.* in general for example *Procureur c/ Vojislav Šešelj*, Affaire n° IT-03-67-T, Opinion Individuelle Concordante du Président de la Chambre Relative à la Décision Consolidée de la Chambre Relative aux Requêtes Orales de l'Accusé en Relation avec la Présentation de sa Défense, 09 juin 2011, p.1 : « Le fait de se défendre seul, s'il amène des avantages, présente également des inconvénients qui peuvent être importants, compte tenu de la complexité de la procédure suivie devant ce Tribunal. [...] L'Accusé doit en supporter lui-même les conséquences et non les faire supporter

After all, the choice to conduct one's own defence has to be an informed one, and it has been made clear that an accused not only has to bear the consequences of this choice, but also that he or she cannot resort to the potentially limited quality of defence as an excuse at a later stage in the proceedings.

This seems to be the position taken by the trial chamber in its decision on the motion in *Karadžić*, which, at first sight, appears to adopt a pragmatic approach undertaking to remind the accused of the fact that with his choice to conduct his own defence, he also accepted all consequences, whether positive or negative, of this choice, at least according to the theory of the jurisprudence, and supposedly implicitly so. Similarly, the appeals chamber decision reaffirmed the position that an accused representing his own interests would be treated like any other professional defence counsel acting for a represented accused. This stance is underscored by the appeals chamber's view that a self-represented accused would have to assume all tasks usually performed by defence counsel. At least, this standpoint does not exclude the possibility for *pro se* defendants to be assisted by defence team members other than lead counsel – as a professional defence attorney would be. The position further corresponds with the view adopted by the appeals chamber in *Krajišnik*.[950]

While the arguments presented above favour a flexible approach to resolving financing issues of self-represented accused, the independent and separately followed approach of the pre-trial judge in *Šešelj* has been heavily criticised. It was argued that, although *pro se* defendants in general should receive legal aid, self-represented accused like Vojislav Šešelj should not, in light of the circumstances of the proceedings which would show that the defendant should have lost the privilege to conduct his own defence and that "therefore the legal aid budget must not be used to fund such a misassigned privilege".[951]

---

par les autres. » *See also Prosecutor v. Slobodan Milošević*, Case No. IT-02-54-AR73.6, Decision on the Interlocutory Appeal by the *Amici Curiae* Against the Trial Chamber Order Concerning the Presentation and Preparation of the Defence Case, 20 January 2004, para.19.

950 *Prosecutor v. Momčilo Krajišnik*, IT-00-39-A, Decision on Krajišnik Request and Prosecution Motion, 11 September 2007, para.41.

951 Alexander Zahar, Legal Aid, Self-Representation, and the Crisis at the Hague Tribunal, 19 *Criminal Law Forum* 241 (2008), at 262.

In contrast, it ought to be questioned whether there is any viable justification to restrict the possibilities provided to an accused to conduct his defence in person merely because of the (mis-) apprehension of the right to self-representation by a trial or appeals chamber, even if at hindsight the exercise of this right should not have been granted to begin with. In case the right to proceed *pro se* has been upheld throughout different instances and on numerous occasions, it does not seem valid to argue that the conduct of the accused should have any direct impact on the provision of legal funds in case he or she is indigent. If the defendant's conduct during the proceedings is indeed unbearable, rather than denying legal aid, the exercise of his right to self-representation should be restricted on the basis of the test established by the appeals chamber, *i.e.* on the basis of a determination of behaviour which substantially and persistently obstructs the proper and expeditious conduct of proceedings. The digression from pertinent jurisprudence, which itself is already subject to numerous interpretations, would further endanger the application of clear and objective criteria, thereby opening the door for criticism as to alleged arbitrary treatment of *pro se* defendants.

In general, it can be seen from the existing jurisprudence that while a specific system to provide self-represented accused with any financial means potentially necessary to safeguard their right to present an effective defence has developed over the years, any eventual practical solution depends on the specific participants involved. While this is sufficiently flexible to be able to address the particular circumstances of each case, it also brings with it procedural uncertainties which, as could be seen in *Šešelj*, may raise important accountability questions.

The defendant's motion in *Karadžić* supports the argument advanced in this dissertation that an accused might wish to engage actively in his or her own proceedings while however being cognisant of the fact that it would be difficult, if not impossible, to conduct the entire defence case without professional assistance. One might thus ask for which reasons the position has been adopted at an early stage at the ICTY that the exercise of the right to self-representation on the one side, and representation by counsel in court on the other, have to be mutually exclusive. A *pro se* defendant cooperating and working together with legal associates, cooperation which might include a reasonable distribution of tasks, could be compared to a defence team consisting of professional defence attorneys in which at times a number of lawyers and support staff contribute to the work of the defence, and distribute tasks including (cross-) examination of and preparation for different witnesses among them. There does not seem to be an apparent reason why this approach thus far appears to lack acceptance. As noted before, in light of the importance awarded to the right of self-representation in the international criminal sphere up to this point, any accused opting to conduct the defence in person should, from a pragmatic point of view, be provided with as much assistance as possible. This model would safeguard the rights of the defendant to a fair and expeditious trial and at the same time equally ensure the integrity of the proceedings and thereby serve the interests of the international community in a smooth delivery of justice.

3. Use of resources by self-represented accused

a. Notion of "waste" of resources

Having established under which conditions and to which extent *pro se* defendants are provided with time and facilities to prepare and present their case, an additional matter of interest is the question in which manner these allocated resources are in practice used by self-represented accused.

The provision of funds to indigent self-represented accused is closely related to the prominently present issue of a reasonable use of the resources that are in fact made available. There are numerous examples which illustrate how (pre-) trial chambers, presiding judges and others participants to the proceedings remind *pro se* defendants of the necessity to effectively manage the allotted resources and to avoid their waste on unnecessary matters. The concepts of "waste" and "unnecessary" might at first sight appear to be rather subjective and prone to divergent readings. At the same time, however, in interpreting such concepts, trial chambers operate within certain limits: a balance has to be struck between, on the one hand, giving self-represented accused the opportunity to conduct their defence in person with all the resources required to do so effectively, and safeguarding through appropriate trial management the right of defendants to an expeditious trial as well as rights of other participants to the proceedings on the other.

It has been argued that the completion strategy with which both ICTY and ICTR are confronted is the "primary driving force" motivating chambers before the ICTY to invoke the right to an expeditious trial in order to justify innovations of the procedural framework.[952] However, as will be outlined

952 Gideon Boas, Self-Representation Before the ICTY. A Case for Reform, 9 *Journal of International Criminal Justice* 53 (2011), at 81. *See also* Gregory P. Lombardi,

infra, it has been made clear that aspects of the completion strategy can never trump the necessity to safeguard the overarching right to a fair trial. In addition, some examples indicate that *pro se* defendants indeed tend to assign their resources to patently irrelevant issues, thereby likely exhausting the patience of the bench, approach which at times might also not necessarily be advisable from a strategic point of view.

There are plenty concrete examples that illustrate the different ways in which resources were (not) used by self-represented accused. For instance, the defendant in *Šešelj* in general filed submissions with the court which were handwritten,[953] since the accused refused to use a computer for his work.[954] In addition, the defendant's motions or submissions were often excessive in length, and made repetitive arguments that were not necessarily to the point of the matter in question.[955] As acknowledged by the trial chamber, this put an additional burden on the resources of the ICTY,[956] *e.g.* with regard to motions which would have to be translated in order for the parties even only to be in a position to consider them.[957] In the course of the

---

Legitimacy and the Expanding Power of the ICTY, 37 *New England Law Review* 887 (2003), at 895-899.

953 *See e.g. Prosecutor v. Vojislav Šešelj*, Case No. IT-03-67-PT, Submission No. 115, 24 October 2005 (filed: 01 November 2005).

954 *Prosecutor v. Vojislav Šešelj*, Case No. IT-03-67-PT, Status Conference, 25 March 2003, T.66 ("I would like neither a laptop nor a typewriter because I am afraid of receiving an electric shock."); Status Conference, 29 October 2003, T.155-157; Status Conference, 14 June 2004, T.237; Status Conference, 08 November 2006, T.760-761; Status Conference, 02 May 2007, T.1065-1066, T.1080-1081.

955 *See e.g. Prosecutor v. Vojislav Šešelj*, Case No. IT-03-67-PT, Decision on Prosecution's Motion for Order Appointing Counsel to Assist Vojislav Šešelj With His Defence, 09 May 2003, para.7 fn.7 ("The remainder of the Accused's Response amounted to a frivolous abuse of the Tribunal's Translation Unit."), para.23; Status Conference, 19 May 2006, T.491, 493; *Prosecutor v. Vojislav Šešelj*, Case No. IT-03-67-AR72.1, Decision on Motion for Reconsideration of the "Decision on the Interlocutory Appeal Concerning Jurisdiction" Dated 31 August 2004, 15 June 2006, para.10; *Prosecutor v. Vojislav Šešelj*, Case No. IT-03-67-PT, Decision on Filing of Motions, 19 June 2006. *See also Prosecutor v. Vojislav Šešelj*, Case No. IT-03-67-PT, Status Conference, 29 October 2003, T.126-128.

956 *Prosecutor v. Vojislav Šešelj*, Case No. IT-03-67-PT, Decision on Filing of Motions, 19 June 2006, p.3; Decision on Assignment of Counsel, 21 August 2006, para.37, 75; Status Conference, 13 March 2007, T.931-932. *See also Prosecutor v. Vojislav Šešelj*, Case No. IT-03-67-AR73.3, Decision on Appeal Against the Trial Chamber's Decision on Assignment of Counsel, 20 October 2006, para.29.

957 *Prosecutor v. Vojislav Šešelj*, Case No. IT-03-67-PT, Status Conference, 22 November 2006, T.815.

proceedings, the accused's tendency to file submissions which were considered to be frivolous and vexatious formed part of his behaviour which would later be determined as obstructionist,[958] or, in the context of the first contempt proceedings, as "aimed at disturbing the fair and expeditious conduct of the trial".[959] The ICTY Bureau[960] made clear at an earlier occasion that an accused was not to make "abusive and insulting" statements in submissions to the ICTY on the basis that Rule 46(C) of the ICTY RPE[961] and similar sanctions would be applicable to self-represented accused filing frivolous or procedurally abusive motions.[962] Throughout the proceedings, the defendant in *Šešelj* continued to submit frivolous and vexatious motions that caused the respective chambers to reprimand him accordingly.[963]

958 *Prosecutor v. Vojislav Šešelj*, Case No. IT-03-67-PT, Decision on Prosecution's Motion for Order Appointing Counsel to Assist Vojislav Šešelj With His Defence, 09 May 2003, para.23, 26; Decision on Assignment of Counsel, 21 August 2006, para.75-77; *Prosecutor v. Vojislav Šešelj*, Case No. IT-03-67-AR73.3, Decision on Appeal Against the Trial Chamber's Decision on Assignment of Counsel, 20 October 2006, para.29; *Prosecutor v. Vojislav Šešelj*, Case No. IT-03-67-PT, Status Conference, 22 November 2006, T.802-804.

959 *Prosecutor v. Vojislav Šešelj*, Case No. IT-03-67-R77.2-A, Decision on Motion for Disqualification of Judges Fausto Pocar and Theodor Meron From the Appeals Proceedings, 02 December 2009, para.19.

960 Rule 23(A) ICTY RPE reads as follows: "The Bureau shall be composed of the President, the Vice-President and the Presiding Judges of the Trial Chambers." The Bureau is a body concerned with the internal functioning of the ICTY, *cf.* Rule 23(B) ICTY RPE.

961 The Bureau in its decision refers to Rule 46(C) of the ICTY RPE. However, the applicable rule rather seems to be Rule 46(A) of the ICTY RPE, which reads: "If a Judge or a Chamber finds that the conduct of a counsel is offensive, abusive or otherwise obstructs the proper conduct of the proceedings, or that counsel is negligent or otherwise fails to meet the standard of professional competence and ethics in the performance of his duties, the Chamber many, after giving counsel due warning: (i) refuse audience to that counsel; and/or (ii) determine, after giving counsel and opportunity to be heard, that counsel is no longer eligible to represent a suspect or an accused before the Tribunal pursuant to Rule 44 and 45."

962 *Prosecutor v. Vojislav Šešelj*, Case No. IT-03-67-PT, Decision on Motion for Disqualification, 10 June 2003 (filed: 11 June 2003), para.5-6.

963 *See Prosecutor v. Vojislav Šešelj*, Case No. IT-03-67-PT, Status Conference, 03 July 2003, T.83; Decision on Motion Number 28, 19 December 2003 (filed: 22 December 2003), p.3; Decision on "Request of the Accused Asking President of the Tribunal Theodor Meron to Reverse the Decision of the Deputy Registrar Prohibiting Dr Vojislav Šešelj From Communicating With Anyone and Receiving Visits for at least 60 Days", 21 September 2005, para.3; Status Conference, 19 May 2006, T.522-523; *Prosecutor v. Vojislav Šešelj*, Case No. IT-03-67-AR72.1, Decision

Nonetheless, with a new trial chamber having been appointed, the presiding judge appeared to be determined to change the previous course and turn a page in the trial proceedings.[964]

In the context of other trials, submissions were considered to be frivolous in case of repetitive arguments that had been decided upon before,[965] or for obvious lack of foundation.[966]

In *Karadžić*, it was made clear to the accused more than once that an effective and efficient use of resources would be required and contribute to a meaningful preparation of the defence for the trial proceedings:[967] while warning the accused to be realistic in his approach with regard to challenging certain parts of the prosecution case,[968] the importance to concentrate on evidence which was in fact to be presented in the course of trial was emphasised,[969] as was the need to convince the bench that the issue for which re-

---

on Motion for Reconsideration of the "Decision on the Interlocutory Appeal Concerning Jurisdiction" Dated 31 August 2004, 15 June 2006, para.11, 22, 28; *Prosecutor v. Vojislav Šešelj*, Case No. IT-03-67-PT, Status Conference, 04 July 2006, T.564-565.

964 *Prosecutor v. Vojislav Šešelj*, Case No. IT-03-67-PT, Status Conference, 02 May 2007, T.1106: "[…] Now we move on. This is behind us. You have a new Trial Chamber, you have a new Prosecution team, […]".

965 *Prosecutor v. Zdravko Tolimir*, Case No. IT-05-88/2-AR73.1, Decision on Interlocutory Appeal Against Oral Decision of the Pre-trial Judge of 11 December 2007, 28 March 2008, para.26.

966 *Prosecutor v. Zdravko Tolimir*, Case No. IT-05-88/2-T, Decision on the Accused's Submission of 18 August 2008, 02 September 2008.

967 *Prosecutor v. Radovan Karadžić*, Case No. IT-95-5/18-PT, Status Conference, 03 June 2009, T.270-271, T.275; Rule 65*ter* Conference (Closed session – confidentiality partially lifted by later order of the Chamber), 15 June 2009, T.100; *Prosecutor v. Radovan Karadžić*, Case No. IT-95-5/18-T, Status Conference, 08 September 2009, T.455; Hearing on Trial Proceedings, 03 November 2009, T.679.

968 *Prosecutor v. Radovan Karadžić*, Case No. IT-95-5/18-PT, Status Conference, 03 June 2009, T.270-271.

969 *Prosecutor v. Radovan Karadžić*, Case No. IT-95-5/18-PT, Status Conference, 03 June 2009, T.275: "[…] Now, I know that you can't be faulted for the hours that you and your many helpers put in this case, but I can't at the moment gauge just how much of it is being spent in preparation, direct preparation, for the trial. But it is important to emphasise now that your concentration ought to be very specifically on dealing with the evidence that the Prosecution allege they are going to present and focusing for the Trial Chamber the issues in relation to the evidence."; *Prosecutor v. Radovan Karadžić*, Case No. IT-95-5/18-T, Hearing on Trial Proceedings, 03 November 2009, T.679: "[…] The Chamber appreciates that you are preparing your trial very hard and appreciate your efforts; but at the same time, I note that

sources were spent in fact contributed to the preparation of the defence.[970] Thus, the issue of provision of resources was specifically linked to the manner in which they were used, in particular bearing in mind the significant amount of assistance the defendant enjoyed in the preparation of his case.[971] The trial chamber subsequently found clear words for its view on the (mis-) allocation of resources by the accused, determining one motion to be "bordering on frivolous", and "advise[d] the Accused, once again, to focus his resources and efforts on his preparations for the hearing of evidence at trial".[972]

---

you were reminded and advised by the former Pre-trial Judge Lord Bonomy, as you referred to, on more than one occasion that you should be devoting your resources to and concentrating your efforts on preparation for the trial itself. So at the end of the day, I again remind you that it is in your best interest to attend and participate fully in the trial so that justice can be done."

970 *Prosecutor v. Radovan Karadžić*, Case No. IT-95-5/18-PT, Rule 65*ter* Conference (Closed session – confidentiality partially lifted by later order of the Chamber), 15 June 2009, T.100: "[...] So there is a status conference in a couple of weeks, or just over. I think I would like you to give some thought, between now and then, to whether we can't find a way of satisfying the Chamber, at least, that these measures are still appropriate at this stage without necessarily spending much-needed resources on checking something which doesn't go to the root of the matter just at the moment."

971 *Prosecutor v. Radovan Karadžić*, Case No. IT-95-5/18-T, Status Conference, 08 September 2009, T.455: "[...] Putting those aside, I must say that the Chamber is not convinced by a number of assertions and claims that you make in your submission, or that the period of extension that you claim you need would be warranted even if the size of the trial were to remain the same. [...] The Registry has been very flexible and accommodating in paying for a number of your assistants and investigators, that is greater than that envisaged by remuneration scheme for self-represented accused. The fact of how many assistants you receive has been continuously demonstrated throughout the pre-trial period by the volume of motions and requests that you have filed, which I am confident in saying has exceeded what is normally the case. I'm not suggesting that you do not have the right to make any submissions or applications you deem appropriate, but merely that you are clearly well assisted by many hard-working people and are yourself actively engaged in your defence. I'm also aware that Judge Bonomy has urged you on several occasions to devote your resources to actual preparation for trial and trust you have done so."

972 *Prosecutor v. Radovan Karadžić*, Case No. IT-95-5/18-T, Decision on Accused's Motion to Strike Scheduled Shelling Incident on Grounds of Collateral Estoppel, 31 March 2010, para.9.

In a decision dealing with a motion filed by the accused requesting the exclusion of the testimony of a former war correspondent,[973] the trial chamber unambiguously expressed its position on the use of resources, agreeing with the prosecution[974] that "the Accused is essentially repeating the same meritless arguments" and that the motion "is also frivolous and vexatious":[975]

> "Once again, the Chamber expresses its concern about the manner in which the Accused is employing his resources, while continuing to mention resource-limitations as an obstacle to his ongoing trial preparation. Filing the present Motion, in light of the settled jurisprudence and practice of this Tribunal, as well as the already expressed view of this Chamber on the issue of war correspondents, was a complete waste of the resources available to the Accused, and the Chamber advises him to manage his team in a more productive manner as the trial progresses."[976]

This statement is also to be seen against the backdrop of a decision issued about one year earlier by the pre-trial judge denying a motion to exclude the testimony of war correspondents in general, considering it "is wholly lacking in merit and is a wasteful use of resources".[977] The trial chamber had dismissed a filing determined as bordering on frivolous already earlier, with the pre-trial judge encouraging the accused to better allocate his resources to proper trial preparation.[978]

Considering specific requests for certain additional material which had been submitted by the defence, the trial chamber reiterated that the accused could not complain about the alleged lack of resources which could be used for the review and analysis of disclosure material, while at the same time

973 *Prosecutor v. Radovan Karadžić*, Case No. IT-95-5/18-T, Motion to Exclude Testimony of Aernout van Lynden, 14 May 2010.

974 *Prosecutor v. Radovan Karadžić*, Case No. IT-95-5/18-T, Prosecution's Response to Accused's Motion to Exclude Testimony of Aernout van Lynden, 17 May 2010, para.1, 3.

975 *Prosecutor v. Radovan Karadžić*, Case No. IT-95-5/18-T, Decision on the Accused's Motion to Exclude Testimony of Aernout van Lynden, 17 May 2010, para.4.

976 *Prosecutor v. Radovan Karadžić*, Case No. IT-95-5/18-T, Decision on the Accused's Motion to Exclude Testimony of Aernout van Lynden, 17 May 2010, para.6.

977 *Prosecutor v. Radovan Karadžić*, Case No. IT-95-5/18-PT, Decision on Motion to Exclude Testimony of War Correspondents, 20 May 2009, para.3.

978 *Prosecutor v. Radovan Karadžić*, Case No. IT-95-5/18-PT, Status Conference, 06 May 2009, T.228-229.

deploying the considerable resources the defence in fact did have on matters which might not be as significant as portrayed by the accused.[979]

The ICTY registry for its part drew the attention of the trial chamber in *Karadžić* to the issue of resources that had to be made available in order to meet requests by the defendant which he thought to be necessary for the preparation of his defence case, more specifically outlining the facilities required in order to accommodate the request of the accused to personally interview prosecution witnesses in the detention unit.[980]

These specific examples show that trial chambers are not willing to entertain clearly frivolous motions by self-represented accused, in particular if the defendant at the same time complains about allegedly limited resources. Arguably, judges will be stricter in such assessments when they expect recognised legal associates of *pro se* defendants to be well versed in the workings of international criminal proceedings – less leeway is likely to be granted in cases where the legal advisor should have known better.[981] The

---

979 *Prosecutor v. Radovan Karadžić*, Case No. IT-95-5/18-T, Hearing, 08 February 2011, T.11294-11295: "The Chamber has previously advised you that there comes a point in every case where responsible Defence has to focus on the evidence and material before it and its position, rather than constantly searching for more information that may be of marginal importance. We understand that you feel that you must have it in your possession, every document bearing the slightest connection to your case, and that it may be a feature of your self-represented status that you do not fully appreciate that there is no Defence or Prosecution team at this Tribunal or in any domestic jurisdiction in the world that can have access to or to have analysed all such material. While at the same time complaining over and over again that you don't have sufficient resources to analyse the material disclosed to you by the Prosecution, Mr. Karadzic, you keep using the substantial resources that you have; so to speak, seven Defence team members remunerated by the Tribunal, in addition to your pro bono associates and interns, to pursue additional material that, in the end, may not be of much use to you. Therefore, I suggest that you take heed of this advice, speak to the experienced Defence counsel who are available to you, who know how the trial process runs, and think carefully about your strategy in this case [...]".

980 *Prosecutor v. Radovan Karadžić*, Case No. IT-95-5/18-PT, Status Conference, 20 August 2009, T.408-409.

981 *See, e.g., Prosecutor v. Radovan Karadžić*, Case No. IT-95-5/18-T, Status Conference, 03 September 2012, T.28789: "For Mr. Karadzic not to know this is one thing, but for you, Mr. Robinson, and the rest of the legal team, to me it is unacceptable."; Addendum to Order in Relation to Accused's Notice of Request of Protective Measures for Witnesses Issued on 8 October 2012, 09 October 2012, p.2: "Noting first that having had the experience of the Prosecution's case during the course of which numerous requests for protective measures were filed by the Prosecution on

examples illustrate an awareness on the part of chambers that while self-represented accused should be provided with all facilities necessary to conduct their defence in person, the defendants equally have to responsibly manage these resources, just as any professional defence counsel would have to.

b. Time management and delays

One issue relating to the subject matter of allocation to and use of resources by *pro se* defendants is that of time management and potential consequences of delays in the proceedings. Such delays might impact not only the accused and his or her right to a fair and expeditious trial, but also other participants involved, including victims and witnesses who are concerned with the proceedings.

The time aspect plays an important role in international criminal proceedings. Topics which have to be dealt with as illustrated *supra* at times lead to significant interruptions in the course of trials. This can result for example from submissions by accused that in light of their self-representation, they need more time for the preparation of the defence case, even if they enjoy assistance of professional legal advisors.[982] Any undue restriction of the preparation time accorded to the defence could trigger the argument of a violation of the right to adequate time and facilities. However, an accused equally enjoys the right to expeditious proceedings, which forms part of the overall fair trial guarantee and could be infringed upon if the defence is given excessive preparation time. In addition, other participants to the proceedings like the prosecution, victim and witness communities, and the international community in general may have a vested interest in the efficient and expeditious resolution of international criminal trials.[983] Therefore,

---

behalf of its witnesses, the Accused and his legal team should, by now, know the correct procedure for requesting protective measures; […]". *See also* Pre-Defence Conference, 15 October 2012, T.28827-28828.

982 *Prosecutor v. Radovan Karadžić*, Case No. IT-95-5/18-AR73.5, Appeal of Decision on Commencement of Trial, 25 September 2009, para.79-84.

983 *Cf.* for the Special Tribunal for Lebanon: Rules of Procedure and Evidence (as of 25 November 2010). Explanatory Memorandum by the Tribunal's President, para.32: "[…] In the context of the STL, the interests of justice clearly include, *inter alia*, the interest of the international community and of the Lebanese people to a fair and expeditious trial of the accused in question and of any other accused (whether they are being tried jointly or separately), the effective presentation of evidence, the or-

chambers have to be cognisant of both the need to ensure the defendants are provided with adequate time to prepare and present their defence, as well as the necessity to safeguard the accused's right to expeditious proceedings.

Delays in the course of trial proceedings and evidentiary hearings are usually caused by a number of different factors. One of these factors relates to the manner in which self-represented accused conduct their (cross-) examination of witnesses, interrogation which often includes irrelevant, repetitive and argumentative questions.

Before examining the actual conduct of accused in the course of witness examination, it has to be kept in mind that the procedural rules of a number international criminal tribunals explicitly bestow upon trial chambers the power to intervene in witness examinations with a view to ascertain effective questioning and avoid waste of time: while judges at the ICTY, ICTR and SCSL enjoy a general competence in this matter,[984] the STL allows such intervention merely upon objection to the questioning by one of the parties.[985]

As for specific examples of situations which bear the potential of delaying proceedings with self-represented accused, it is illustrative to familiarise oneself with the transcripts in the respective trials. For instance in *Milošević*, the presiding judge gave a short introduction as to the nature and purpose of cross-examination before the first cross-examination to be conducted by the accused, instructions which were put in writing for the defendant.[986]

---

derly administration of justice, the truth-search mission of the Tribunal, and the protection and interests of victims and witnesses."

984 Rule 90(F) ICTY RPE: "The Trial Chamber shall exercise control over the mode and order of interrogating witnesses and presenting evidence so as to (i) make the interrogation and presentation effective for the ascertainment of the truth; and (ii) avoid needless consumption of time." Similar provisions can be found in Rule 90(F) ICTR RPE and Rule 90(F) SCSL RPE.

985 Rule 150(G) STL RPE: "Upon an objection raised by a Party, the Chamber may exercise control over the mode and order of questioning witnesses and presenting evidence so as to: (i) make the questioning and presentation effective for the ascertainment of the truth; and (ii) avoid needless consumption of time and resources."

986 *Prosecutor v. Slobodan Milošević*, Case No. IT-02-54-T, Hearing, 19 February 2002, T.542: "Since this is the first witness and since you're representing yourself, you should be told about the purpose and limitations of cross-examination. The purpose of cross-examination is to ask questions, to test the witness's evidence and credibility, that is, whether he or she should be believed or not. According to the Tribunal's Rules, it is limited to the subject matter of the evidence in chief, that is the evidence given in answer to questions from the Prosecution and to questions as to credibility. It is also the opportunity to ask questions relating to your case, that is the case which you wish to put forward in your defence. The Trial Chamber may

In addition, both *amici curiae* and prosecution filed submissions which discussed the possible scope of cross-examinations by the accused: *amici* submitted that more leeway should be given to a self-represented accused who is inexperienced in the techniques of cross-examination and necessarily more deeply involved in the substance of the case than professional defence counsel would be.[987] It was argued that the accused should be allowed to develop certain lines of cross-examination beyond any alleged limited knowledge on the part of the witness, in the context of testing the credibility of witnesses and of relevance to the case on a more general level.[988] The prosecution submitted that the defendant should be prevented from making comments in the course of his questioning and be required to put his case,[989] *i.e.* that restraint should be employed to avoid comments, repetition or argument.[990]

Subsequently, the presiding judge repeatedly recalled the need to put questions in fact relevant to the accused's case in order to use the time allocated for cross-examination efficiently and effectively; throughout the proceedings, the defendant had to be prevented from making unnecessary arguments, comments or lengthy speeches during his examinations.[991]

---

permit questions on other matters. Cross-examination is subject to the control of the Trial Chamber in order to make it effective for the ascertainment of the truth and avoid the needless consumption of time. It is restricted to matters relevant to the issues in the trial and must not be used as a way of harassing or intimidating witnesses. Any questions which may reveal the identity of protected witnesses must be asked in closed session. This statement will be put into writing and given to the accused." *See also* Hearing, 26 February 2002, T.1114.

987 *Prosecutor v. Slobodan Milošević*, Case No. IT-02-54-T, *Amici Curiae* Brief on Issues of Cross-Examination by the Accused in Person Including the '*Tu Quoque*' Principle, 05 March 2002 (filed: 06 March 2002), para.3.

988 *Prosecutor v. Slobodan Milošević*, Case No. IT-02-54-T, *Amici Curiae* Brief on Issues of Cross-Examination by the Accused in Person Including the '*Tu Quoque*' Principle, 05 March 2002 (filed: 06 March 2002), para.5-9.

989 *Prosecutor v. Slobodan Milošević*, Case No. IT-02-54-T, Hearing, 26 February 2002, T.1111-1113.

990 *Prosecutor v. Slobodan Milošević*, Case No. IT-02-54-T, Prosecution's Brief Concerning the Scope of Cross-Examination and the "Tu Quoque" Defence, 06 March 2002, para.8, 12.

991 *See e.g. Prosecutor v. Slobodan Milošević*, Case No. IT-02-54-T, Hearing, 14 March 2002, T.2255; Hearing, 15 March 2002, T.2463; Hearing, 26 April 2002, T.3895; Hearing, 01 May 2002, T.4041; Hearing, 06 June 2002, T.6388; Hearing, 03 July 2002, T.7316-7317; Hearing, 04 September 2002, T.9608; Hearing, 07 October 2002, T.11092; Hearing, 11 December 2002, T.14353; Hearing, 30 January 2003,

During the first years of the proceedings, the presiding judge in *Milošević* used a remotely controlled microphone that could be switched off by the bench whenever it found the accused to engage in unnecessary and/or irrelevant arguments and questioning. This is illustrative of the significant control exercised by the chamber over the accused's courtroom behaviour. For example, the first cross-examination conducted by the accused is replete with interferences by the presiding judge reminding above all the accused (but also the witness) to stick to relevant questions and not to engage in unnecessary and irrelevant arguments.[992] The defendant was left in no doubt that he should avoid asking repetitive questions and refrain from making comments while cross-examining witnesses.[993]

Additional specific instances of the microphone being disabled by the presiding judge in the course of cross-examination were identified for March

T.15253; Hearing, 04 February 2003, T.15547; Hearing, 10 March 2003, T.17447; Hearing, 10 April 2003, T.18958; Hearing, 02 May 2003, T.19970; Hearing, 02 June 2003, T.21432; Hearing, 14 July 2003, T.24339; Hearing, 27 August 2003, T.25424-25425; Hearing, 10 September 2003, T.26247; Hearing, 14 October 2003, T.27451; Hearing, 26 November 2003, T.29639; Hearing, 02 December 2003, T.29843; Hearing, 21 January 2004, T.31215; Hearing, 16 February 2005, T.36278-36279; Hearing, 14 April 2005, T.38511; Hearing, 29 June 2005, T.41412; Hearing, 01 September 2005, T.43582; Hearing, 18 October 2005, T.45328-45329; Hearing, 06 December 2005, T.47019; Hearing, 07 February 2006, T.48110; Hearing, 24 February 2006, T.48774-48775. *See also* Decision in Relation to Severance, Extension of Time and Rest, 12 December 2005, para.16 fn.40.

992 *Prosecutor v. Slobodan Milošević*, Case No. IT-02-54-T, Hearing, 19 February 2002, T.558, 560, 564, 568, 571, 597, 603, 605, 606, 614, 618, 620, 622, 625-627, 633, 636, 638, 641, 642.

993 *Prosecutor v. Slobodan Milošević*, Case No. IT-02-54-T, Hearing, 26 February 2002, T.1023: "You have a right to conduct your cross-examination, but we also have a duty to ensure that this trial is concluded expeditiously, and that we will do. Now, you have a right to put your case to the witness. You have a duty to do so. But we note that there's a fair amount of repetition in what you've put and a fair amount of comment. So could you kindly ensure that these – these matters are dealt with as quickly as possible." *See also* T.1008, 1011, 1015, 1026, 1027, 1031-1032, 1039, 1099, 1100.

2002,[994] March,[995] April,[996] May,[997] July,[998] August,[999] October,[1000] and December 2003,[1001] as well as in January 2004.[1002] Yet, on one occasion in

994 *Prosecutor v. Slobodan Milošević*, Case No. IT-02-54-T, Hearing, 15 March 2002, T.2463-2464: "I don't think you should switch off my microphone during the cross-examination, Mr. May. Judge May: It will be switched off if you go on asking irrelevant questions."

995 *Prosecutor v. Slobodan Milošević*, Case No. IT-02-54-T, Hearing, 04 March 2003, T.17377-17378: "Q. Yes. But my question is: […] Judge May: I've stopped the microphone. It's not a relevant question."

996 *Prosecutor v. Slobodan Milošević*, Case No. IT-02-54-T, Hearing, 01 April 2003, T.18318-18319: "I've stopped your microphone because you're going on much too long. There are a series of questions there. We'll go through them one by one."

997 *Prosecutor v. Slobodan Milošević*, Case No. IT-02-54-T, Hearing, 20 May 2003, T.20833-20834: "Mr. May, I see that you keep switching off my microphone. This does not refer to him but it refers to you because you posed the question erroneously. […] Judge May: You have made this point over and over again. There is no point going on. This is a matter which I shall certainly take into account when I come to consider and mention to my colleagues the time which you should have, because I regard your continually going over the same points as a waste of time."

998 *Prosecutor v. Slobodan Milošević*, Case No. IT-02-54-T, Hearing, 11 July 2003, T.24243; Hearing, 16 July 2003, T.24566: "I've stopped the – I've stopped the microphone. You've now had rather more than the quarter of an hour we've promised. We've considered the situation in this case. We will give you another five minutes. We're not going to give you more because of the time that was spent and wasted earlier on on irrelevant cross-examination. You've got five minutes left.";
Hearing, 24 July 2003, T.24875, T.24881; T.24915-24917: "Mr. May – Mr. May, I can only interpret this as violence, because cross-examination makes absolutely no sense if I am not able to go through the entire report. I will not abbreviate my cross-examination. You can turn off my microphone whenever you want. And the fact that Mr. Nice wants to note that I didn't challenge something because you didn't give me enough time is the way you work. I have already said generally that all this is intended to rewrite history. You brought an expert on history here, and you are not allowing me to cross-examine her precisely on the issues which matter. Judge May: It's a matter for us to say, but if you choose, as I've said, with the one historian that we have here, to dwell on events long past as opposed to events that are more recent and relevant, we're not going to stop you, but your time is being limited. And if you challenge the conclusions, particularly those involving yourself, then you should do so in the hour that remains. That's the only point that's being made."

999 *Prosecutor v. Slobodan Milošević*, Case No. IT-02-54-T, Hearing, 25 August 2003, T.25197.

1000 *Prosecutor v. Slobodan Milošević*, Case No. IT-02-54-T, Hearing, 28 October 2003, T.28163: "Q. […] I'm sorry. My microphone was switched off. Judge May: Yes. I'm going to question the relevance of this, […]".

1001 *Prosecutor v. Slobodan Milošević*, Case No. IT-02-54-T, Hearing, 02 December 2003, T.29867; Hearing, 03 December 2003, T.29982: "Judge May: Do you want

January 2004, the accused indicated that this manner of courtroom control would not induce him to adjust his behaviour in court.[1003]

In *Karadžić* a similar incident occurred when the pre-trial judge switched off the microphone of the accused.[1004] Bearing in mind that the pre-trial judge in this case was also a member of the bench in *Milošević* and thus well familiar with this particular technique of cutting the accused short when making unnecessary speeches, this move might not come as a surprise. At a later stage of the proceedings, the presiding judge of the trial chamber equally referred to the possibility of switching off the defendant's microphone and warned the accused that this option might be used if he continued to make unnecessary statements while conducting a cross-examination.[1005]

The presiding judge in *Karadžić* clarified at the beginning of the evidentiary phase that the time required by the defendant for cross-examination would be monitored by the trial chamber and potentially be restricted in case the accused was not "responsible and realistic as to what is reasonable" with regard to the time needed for cross-examining witnesses.[1006] On a side note,

---

to ask another question or not? The Accused: [Interpretation] I want to ask a few more questions unless you turn off my microphone."; Hearing, 15 December 2003, T.30470.

1002 *Prosecutor v. Slobodan Milošević*, Case No. IT-02-54-T, Hearing, 15 January 2004, T.30837-30838: "Please, Mr. May. Would you kindly refrain from switching off my microphone before my sentence is over, because – Judge May: No. I shall cut off your microphone at any occasion when you abuse it, in particular by these lengthy questions which are not allowing witnesses to answer. The witness must have the opportunity to answer your question. You are simply to ask questions, not to make speeches."; T.30902-30903: "What it's matter with the microphone? Judge May: I brought this to an end because it is time for an adjournment, and the witness should certainly have one."

1003 *Prosecutor v. Slobodan Milošević*, Case No. IT-02-54-T, Hearing, 22 January 2004, T.31300: "Well, if you do not waste your time and you are making useful time, we might consider a short addition, but at the moment, that is the current amount that you must follow. The Accused: [Interpretation] Well, you can switch my microphone off any time you like, and it wouldn't be the first time either."

1004 *Prosecutor v. Radovan Karadžić*, Case No. IT-95-5/18-PT, Further Initial Appearance, 03 March 2009, T.133.

1005 *Prosecutor v. Radovan Karadžić*, Case No. IT-95-5/18-T, Hearing, 03 March 2011, T.12903: "I never used this switch to turn microphones off, but next time you're making unnecessary statements, I may use it, Mr. Karadzic."

1006 *Prosecutor v. Radovan Karadžić*, Case No. IT-95-5/18-T, Hearing, 13 April 2010, T.1002: "The Chamber has said that it will not limit – set a time-limit on cross-examination at the present time, while, of course, the cross-examination will be limited to relevant issues. However, the Chamber expects you to be responsible

however, it has to be mentioned that a similar warning with regard to the time estimates for cross-examination of defence witnesses was given to the prosecution at the start of the defence case.[1007] Upon conclusion of the first cross-examination conducted by the accused, another member of the bench endeavoured to explain the manner in which an effective and efficient cross-examination would need to be managed and which type of questions could and should be asked.[1008]

---

and realistic as to what is reasonable. I have to say that we do not consider that the estimate you have given are either of these things. You may certainly need equal time to the Prosecution for your cross-examination. Indeed, given that these witnesses give much of their evidence in writing, you may need double what the Prosecution takes for your cross-examination. And also, there may be exceptional cases where you require even longer. However, do not expect to be granted the kind of time you suggest that you need. In this regard, I would like to remind you that the Prosecution bears the burden of proof in these proceedings. Your role is to challenge the Prosecution's case so as to create reasonable doubt in the minds of the Judges. If you do not take on that role responsibly, the Chamber will have to consider what measures to take, such as imposing time restrictions on your cross-examination of each witness."

1007 *Prosecutor v. Radovan Karadžić*, Case No. IT-95-5/18-T, Decision on Time Allocated to the Accused for the Presentation of his Case, 19 September 2012, para.13; Pre-Defence Conference, 15 October 2012, T.27715-28816, 28820.

1008 *Prosecutor v. Radovan Karadžić*, Case No. IT-95-5/18-T, Hearing, 13 April 2010, T.1084-1086: "Judge Morrison: Dr. Karadzic, obviously until you started cross-examining today, the Bench wasn't aware of how you were going to participate in cross-examination. So what I'm about to say, really, is a suggestion to you that should enable you to be more concise, and, in fact, will not only assist you but will assist the witness, whoever the witness is, and assist the Judges. The first thing that you are inclined to do, and it's been commented on quite rightly by the Prosecution, is that you engage in comment. […] you have to guard against it for three reasons. First of all, comment is not a question; secondly, it's not evidence, what you say in comment is not evidence; and thirdly, because of your duality of the role of an accused and a Defence lawyer, a comment could also be an admission on your part. For instance, if a witness says something and you say, That's right, that's not simply a remark it is actually a comment that may also be an admission that you accept the truth of what that witness is saying, and it can be confusing because it may well be that what you are saying is right relates to only a small portion of what the witness has actually said. So be very cautious about commenting. It wastes time and it doesn't assist the Court. The second point is this: Occasionally in cross-examination, you have to ask non-leading or open questions to elicit information […]. But when you're cross-examining, you have the luxury of being able to ask leading questions. You can put directly to a witness that which you want the witness to say. Obviously you have to be sure of your ground before you say it, but it can save an awful lot of time. […] So think as to whether or not

The *Karadžić* trial chamber initially refrained from imposing any time limits on the defendant's cross-examinations, under the caveat that he would attempt to ask relevant questions.[1009] However, in the course of the proceedings, the accused had to be warned repeatedly as to the use of time during his cross-examinations, requiring him to abstain from making comments or statements or putting irrelevant questions.[1010] The bench eventually considered it indispensable to impose time limits in order to restrict unnecessary use of court time.[1011] Yet, the trial chamber showed itself prepared to extend such imposed time limits in case of demonstrated necessity and if the accused

---

you can put a direct leading question, because if you can, and you are entitled to do so, it can save a lot of time. And it has this very great effect that you are stating your case shortly and a Judge should be able to glean what an advocate's case is within the first 10 or 15 questions that they ask, whether they're prosecuting or defending. And that assists everybody, not least the Judges. So all I'm suggesting to you is that you think carefully about adopting a mode of questioning that does away with comment and, where possible, utilise the great benefit of being able to ask leading questions."

1009 *Prosecutor v. Radovan Karadžić*, Case No. IT-95-5/18-T, Hearing, 23 April 2010, T.1536.

1010 *Prosecutor v. Radovan Karadžić*, Case No. IT-95-5/18-T, Hearing, 22 April 2010, T.1431-1432; Hearing, 27 April 2010, T.1662, 1679; Hearing, 28 April 2010, T.1797; Hearing, 05 May 2010, T.1925; Hearing, 06 May 2010, T.1995; Hearing, 19 May 2010, T.2441; Hearing, 20 May 2010, T.2549; Hearing, 21 May 2010, T.2579; Hearing, 27 May 2010, T.2796; Hearing, 08 June 2010, T.3519-3520; Hearing, 09 June 2010, T.3534-3535; Hearing, 10 June 2010, T.3701; Hearing, 16 June 2010, T.3845; Hearing, 23 June 2010, T.4133; Hearing, 29 June 2010, T.4270; Hearing, 30 June 2010, T.4374, 4377-4378; Hearing, 15 July 2010, T.5255; Hearing, 19 July 2010, T.5430; Hearing, 19 August 2010, T.6010; Hearing, 20 August 2010, T.6087; Hearing, 06 September 2010, T.6199; Hearing, 15 September 2010, T.6773; Hearing, 27 September 2010, T.6986; Hearing, 28 September 2010, T.7024; Hearing, 10 February 2011, T.11558, 11559; Hearing, 28 February 2011, T.12519-12520; Hearing, 14 June 2011, T.14666-14667; Hearing, 15 June 2011, T.14715-14716; Hearing, 29 June 2011, T.15621-15623; Hearing, 23 August 2011, T.17738; Hearing, 06 October 2011, T.20014; Hearing, 24 January 2012, T.23518: "[…] This isn't an exercise in historical revaluation or an attempt to look at every fact and determine every fact." *See also* Hearing, 02 June 2011, T.14186: "[…] Apart from the fact that it's improper, you're acting as counsel and you must behave like counsel. A comment is not for counsel to make, but it also wastes your time."

1011 *Prosecutor v. Radovan Karadžić*, Case No. IT-95-5/18-T, Hearing, 08 June 2010, T.3432-3434; Hearing, 21 June 2010, T.3903-3905.

had used the allocated time efficiently.[1012] While the judges exhibited a certain flexibility with regard to the time given to the accused for his cross-examination, there was some indication that they were not willing to continue warning the accused as to the use of his time without him paying heed to such instructions: one judge remarked that the accused might want to think about having some witnesses cross-examined by his legal advisor rather than doing it himself, without through this arrangement losing his right to defend himself in person.[1013] It had been suggested already before that on an exceptional basis, in the instant case when the accused was not feeling well enough to continue with the proceedings, the legal advisor could assume the task of cross-examining witnesses.[1014] When the accused complained about the alleged inadequacy of the cross-examination times allocated to him, the trial chamber reiterated that there was room to present his case more efficiently and that the accused should take advice from his legal associates on the conduct of cross-examination.[1015]

Depending on the bench sitting in the case, (cross-) examinations by *pro se* defendants might be more or less interfered with. In *Tolimir*, the trial chamber initially appeared to refrain from interfering to any substantial extent

---

1012 *Prosecutor v. Radovan Karadžić*, Case No. IT-95-5/18-T, Hearing, 28 June 2010, T.4167; Hearing, 07 July 2010, T.4859: "Judge Kwon: Let's not waste time anymore, but please bear that in mind, the Chamber will consider how efficiently you have spent your time when there is a request for you for additional time. […] Judge Morrison: And, Dr. Karadzic, as a Freudian, you'll no doubt recall when considering the issue of relevancy, that the first serious academic paper that Dr. Sigmund Freud ever wrote was about the gonads of eels." *See also* Decision on Motion for Admission of Evidence from Bar Table: General Michael Rose, 29 October 2010, para.7.

1013 *Prosecutor v. Radovan Karadžić*, Case No. IT-95-5/18-T, Hearing, 29 October 2010, T.8600-8601. *See also* Hearing, 01 November 2010, T.8701-8702; Hearing, 28 November 2011, T.22001-22002.

1014 *Prosecutor v. Radovan Karadžić*, Case No. IT-95-5/18-T, Hearing, 14 October 2010, T.7935-7938.

1015 *Prosecutor v. Radovan Karadžić*, Case No. IT-95-5/18-T, Hearing, 04 November 2010, T.8989-8993. *See also* Hearing, 02 February 2011, T.11181; Hearing, 12 July 2011, T.16421; Hearing, 24 August 2011, T.17807-17809; Hearing, 13 September 2011, T.18743; Hearing, 15 September 2011, T.18898-18901; Hearing, 21 September 2011, T.19239-19241; Hearing, 01 November 2011, T.20716; Hearing, 18 November 2011, T.21633; Hearing, 17 January 2012, T.23150; Hearing, 18 January 2012, T.23282.

with the accused's manner of cross-examination.[1016] However, with the trial nearing the end of the prosecution case, the presiding judge increasingly took issue with the manner of questioning of the defendant and warned him not to waste any time.[1017] At the same time, however, the accused in *Šešelj* provoked significantly less activity by the trial chamber.[1018]

These specific instances illustrate that at least part of the "day-to-day" or "ordinary" delays in court are caused by the unfamiliarity of self-represented accused with the ordinary procedure of witness examination and cross-examination. Yet, contrasting the manner of questioning in different cases alongside the tendency to intervene by some trial chambers, delays appear to be equally linked to the personality of the accused conducting the cross-examination as well as the willingness on the part of the chamber concerned to take a more or less active approach towards courtroom control. The examples provided above indicate that the behaviour exhibited by an accused does not necessarily have to be obstructionist in the strict sense of the word in order for the judges to step in and bring the proceedings back into course.

The wording and extent of instructions given by trial judges to self-represented accused may give rise to concern. Especially with regard to warnings

---

1016 *Prosecutor v. Zdravko Tolimir*, Case No. IT-05-88/2-T, Hearing, 02 June 2010, T.2417; Hearing, 24 June 2010, T.3168; Hearing, 18 August 2010, T.4074; Hearing, 15 September 2010, T.5439. *See*, however, also Hearing, 24 May 2011, T.14522, T.14523-14524, and T.14528-14529: "Mr. Tolimir, I would like to remind you and to read out to you the legal background for cross-examination, the legal basis, concerning the discussion we had before the break. [...] Mr. Tolimir, the last questions, in my view, went far beyond the scope of the testimony of this witness. If you want to put your case about the reasons – about the reasons of the war or the wars in the former Yugoslavia, you should consider the possibility to call an expert witness during the Defence case, expert witness for history, military background, or political background, and then the Chamber will consider your position. [...] You need evidence in your case, and you should try to get evidence from the witness and not an opinion."

1017 *See e.g. Prosecutor v. Zdravko Tolimir*, Case No. IT-05-88/2-T, Hearing, 06 July 2010, T.3505-3506; Hearing, 18 August 2010, T.4074; Hearing, 08 February 2011, T.9583; Hearing, 16 February 2011, T.10048; Hearing, 23 March 2011, T.11687; Hearing, 24 March 2011, T.11814; Hearing, 19 April 2011, T.13019; Hearing, 19 May 2011, T.14371-14372; Hearing, 02 June 2011, T.15015; Hearing, 04 July 2011, T.16058; Hearing, 20 July 2011, T.16910; Hearing, 12 September 2011, T.17838.

1018 *Prosecutor v. Vojislav Šešelj*, Case No. IT-03-67-T, Hearing, 06 March 2008, T.4575-4576; Hearing, 12 March 2008, T.4788; Hearing, 21 October 2008, T.10889; Hearing, 19 November 2008, T.11859-11860.

as to comments or potential admissions which the accused should be careful about in the course of cross-examinations, one might wonder whether such remarks by the judge still fall under any guidance that could and should reasonably be given to self-represented accused unfamiliar with the procedure in order to ensure a fair trial.[1019] It could be argued that a comment of this nature may exceed the judges' competence, in particular if a defendant is known to enjoy qualified and experienced legal assistance inside and outside the courtroom which should be capable of providing such advice. To be noted for purposes of comparison is a remark of one member of the bench subsequent to further instructions provided during one hearing[1020] that the "advice" given by the judges to the accused as to the conduct of cross-examination was not intended to limit the topics the defendant may want to raise,[1021] as well as the clear expectation that the legal advisor to the accused would appropriately instruct his client.[1022] This approach appears to strike a reasonable compromise between permitting some guidance and initiating such advice to be given to *pro se* defendants as necessary in order to safeguard their fair trial rights on the one side, and ensuring the impartiality of the bench on the other by not overly interfering with the accused's opportunity to challenge witnesses against him.

It might be safe to assume that trial chambers attempt to give accused an opportunity to prove their competences, after guidance by the bench, following which chambers usually started to tighten the leash by expressly warning the accused on his conduct of cross-examinations and use of allocated time, leaving no doubt as to the respective positions in light of the need not to

---

1019 Human Rights Watch, *The Balkans: Weighing the Evidence. Lessons from the Milosevic Trial*, Volume 18, No.10(D), December 2006, p.67-68.

1020 *Prosecutor v. Radovan Karadžić*, Case No. IT-95-5/18-T, Hearing, 04 November 2012, T.8991-8993.

1021 *Prosecutor v. Radovan Karadžić*, Case No. IT-95-5/18-T, Hearing, 04 November 2012, T.9037: "[…] We were offering advice; nothing more, nothing less. This must not be confused in any way as being any sort of restriction that we are imposing on what you should or what you should not cross-examine. Obviously, if you asked a question that is irrelevant, it wouldn't be allowed, but we are not prohibiting you in any way from cross-examining in the manner you see fit. Well, as long, of course, as it is within the bounds of propriety. You have the conduct of your defence. What is your defence, you have, in pectore, and you, and you alone, would decide the form your cross-examination would take." *See also* T.9054-9055.

1022 *Prosecutor v. Radovan Karadžić*, Case No. IT-95-5/18-T, Hearing 02 February 2011, T.11181: "I would expect your role in formulating questions on the part of the Defence, Mr. Robinson."

waste time and resources. This pragmatic approach appears to be practical and considerate of all parties' rights. While recognising the importance of the right to self-representation, trial chambers thus far have equally shown their determination to safeguard the integrity of the proceedings, which seems to take into account the interests of all participants.

In particular the readiness of the *Karadžić* trial chamber to potentially even involve the accused's legal advisor in the (cross-) examination of witnesses is an interesting development insofar as it illustrates a position that a defendant could exercise his right to self-representation while at the same time being assisted by counsel in a more active manner than usually acknowledged. It is to be questioned to which extent such a division of tasks should be recognised, especially after repeated reminders to the accused that due to his choice to defend himself it was for him to assume the ordinary tasks of lead counsel, and in light of previous jurisprudence that it was not for the accused to pick and choose when to exercise his right to self-representation and when to be represented by counsel in the course of proceedings.[1023] However, it can on the other hand considered to be a positive sign by the bench to give the accused the opportunity to enhance effectiveness of his case presentation, bearing in mind his right to a fair trial and effective defence, while at the same time recognising his resolve to speak for himself in the course of trial. This approach leans more towards the idea advanced in this dissertation of according an accused the possibility of actively participating in the proceedings, while at the same time protecting his or her right to a fair trial by providing for professional defence counsel, *i.e.* an approach that does not necessarily view defence in person and assistance by counsel as mutually exclusive.

c. Potential impact of delays

In light of the potential impact of the exercise of the right to self-representation on the expeditiousness of proceedings, it has been suggested that rather

---

1023 *Cf. Prosecutor v. Zdravko Tolimir*, Case No. IT-05-88/2-T, Decision on Accused's Request to the Trial Chamber Concerning Assistance of his Legal Advisor, 28 April 2010 (Public redacted version issued on 27 May 2010. *See* Order Issuing a Public Redacted Version of the "Decision on Accused's Request to the Trial Chamber Concerning Assistance of his Legal Advisor", 27 May 2010), para.27-31.

than other measures taken by international criminal tribunals to expedite trials, a "presumption against self-representation" would be an approach which "could appropriately further its objective of an expeditious trial".[1024] Even though the impact of delays on the accused's right to a fair *and* expeditious trial necessarily arises in the context of proceedings with *pro se* defendants,[1025] the subject matter of the provision of adequate time for self-represented accused as discussed in this dissertation indicates that defendants who conduct their defence in person are less concerned with the length of their trials.[1026]

At this stage, it shall be addressed briefly that delays may have an impact not only on the general conduct of the proceedings and the parties to the case,[1027] but also on other participants which are directly affected by the proceedings, *e.g.* victims and witnesses. In the course of proceedings before the ICTY, the potential influence on witnesses could for example be observed in the reactions of witnesses scheduled to testify in the beginning of proceedings of *Karadžić* who came to the ICTY twice without however being called to the stand due to an adjournment or stay of the proceedings.[1028]

1024 Gideon Boas, Self-Representation Before the ICTY. A Case for Reform, 9 *Journal of International Criminal Justice* 53 (2011), at 81.

1025 *See e.g.* Philipp Ambach, Selbstvertretung im internationalen Strafprozess – Grundlagen, Kritik und ein Lösungsansatz für die prozessuale Handhabung in der Zukunft, 6 *Zeitschrift für Internationale Strafrechtsdogmatik* 286 (2009), at 293. *Cf.* also Constantinos Hotis, A 'Fair and Expeditious' Trial: A Reappraisal of Slobodan Milosevic's Right to Self-Representation Before the International Criminal Tribunal for the Former Yugoslavia, 6 *Chicago Journal of International Law* 775 (2006), at 786-789; Gideon Boas, *The Milošević Trial: Lessons for the Conduct of Complex International Criminal Proceedings* (Cambridge: Cambridge University Press) 2007, at 215.

1026 *See e.g. Prosecutor v. Radovan Karadžić*, Case No. IT-95-5/18-T, Hearing, 04 November 2010, T.8990.

1027 Note, however, that an argument has also been made highlighting the potential advantages of delayed international criminal prosecutions: Alex Whiting, In International Criminal Prosecutions, Justice Delayed can be Justice Delivered, 50 *Harvard International Law Journal* 323 (2009), at 327: "[…] delay can in fact be a necessary component in achieving justice." The author, however, equally outlines the reasons for which in particular victims would benefit from a swift delivery of justice: *Ibid.*, at 331-332, 335.

1028 *Prosecutor v. Radovan Karadžić*, Case No. IT-95-5/18-T, Prosecution's Response to Application for Certification to Appeal and for Stay Pending Appeal of Decision on Commencement of Evidence, 01 March 2010, para.7-8. *See also* Oral Decision, 02 March 2010, T.993-994.

Illuminating in this regard is a statement addressed to the *Karadžić* bench after the end of his testimony by a witness who had to prepare twice without being called to testify and eventually took the witness stand the third time he had travelled to the seat of the ICTY. The statement articulates the concerns of not only victim witnesses:

> "[...] I would, with your allowance, like to make a short statement about the rights of witnesses which I believe have been slightly forgotten. I think a war crimes Tribunal, and I'm specifically referring here to the permanent International Criminal Court that has been set up in The Hague, needs to bear in mind that a witness at a war crimes tribunal is not the same as a witness in a normal civil court. I'm aware that two, at least two victim witnesses were flown twice to The Hague and then flown back again without having been able to give their testimony. I believe that is doing those people a further injustice to the injustices that they've already faced during the wars that they are willing to testify on. [...]"[1029]

Considering this expression of concern of a specific witness, one can only speculate which impact a comparable situation might have on witnesses who were in fact victims of the conflict.[1030] The statement illustrates the importance of interests of victim and witness communities to be taken into account in the context of the interpretation and application of the right to self-representation, as well as with regard to any potential restriction of the right in the "interests of justice".[1031]

This leads to a further matter to be borne in mind, which is the potential impact of delays on witnesses who additionally may have to cope with traumas suffered in the course of conflicts. Witnesses called to testify before international criminal tribunals are likely to face difficulties in the context of re-traumatisation which can be associated with testifying about the sort of events witnesses at international criminal tribunals would usually testify to, especially when it comes to crime base and victim impact witnesses.[1032]

1029 *Prosecutor v. Radovan Karadžić*, Case No. IT-95-5/18-T, Hearing, 31 May 2010, T.3065-3066.

1030 *Cf.* David Tolbert/Frederick Swinnen, The Protection of, and Assistance to, Witnesses at the ICTY, in: Hirad Abtahi/Gideon Boas (eds), *The Dynamics of International Criminal Justice. Essays in Honour of Sir Richard May* (Leiden/Boston: Martinus Nijhoff Publishers) 2006, p.193-229, at 196-197.

1031 *Cf.* for the STL: Rules of Procedure and Evidence (as of 25 November 2010). Explanatory Memorandum by the Tribunal's President, para.32-33.

1032 Suzannah Linton, Putting Cambodia's Extraordinary Chambers Into Context, 11 *Singapore Yearbook of International Law* 195 (2007), at 248; Yael Danieli, Massive Trauma and the Healing Role of Restorative Justice, in: Carla Ferstman/Mariana

The concerns may be heightened when self-represented accused cross-examine these witnesses, situation which might not be able to create the secure environment of testimony victim witnesses might need in order for their testifying being a meaningful experience, or at least not further harm, for them.[1033]

Such issues will not be diminished, not to speak of avoided, when witnesses have to prepare several times to give testimony before the court until they are eventually called to the stand. With regard to the ICC – or for that purpose also the STL which equally provides for victim participation – these concerns might only be heightened. Yet, in case victim participants are represented in the course of proceedings, they arguably might have more possibilities to raise such concerns and potentially obtain adequate remedies than before tribunals such as the ICTY. It is of note that the Rome Statute of the ICC in its provision dealing with the protection of victims and witnesses explicitly refers to the protection of their psychological well-being,[1034] and provides for measures that are to protect (victim) witnesses from potential re-traumatisation due to their testimony before the Court.[1035] However, in proceedings with *pro se* defendants, the implementation of these safeguards would require efforts not only from the bench which controls the proceedings and could potentially restrict the (cross-) examination of self-represented accused in order to protect the witnesses, but equally from the defendants who ought to show respect and sensitivity towards the persons on the witness stand who have already been victimised. Experience indicates that this might not always be the case.[1036]

Goetz/Alan Stephens (eds), *Reparations for Victims of Genocide, War Crimes and Crimes Against Humanity. Systems in Place and Systems in the Making* (Leiden/Boston: Martinus Nijhoff Publishers) 2009, p.41-77, at 66.

1033 *Cf.* Yael Danieli, Massive Trauma and the Healing Role of Restorative Justice, in: Carla Ferstman/Mariana Goetz/Alan Stephens (eds), *Reparations for Victims of Genocide, War Crimes and Crimes Against Humanity. Systems in Place and Systems in the Making* (Leiden/Boston: Martinus Nijhoff Publishers) 2009, p.41-77, at 73.

1034 Article 68(1) Rome Statute reads in the relevant part: "The Court shall take appropriate measures to protect the safety, physical and psychological well-being, dignity and privacy of victims and witnesses. [...]".

1035 M. Cherif Bassiouni, International Recognition of Victims' Rights, 6 *Human Rights Law Review* 203 (2006), at 258. *See also* Rule 112(4) ICC RPE.

1036 *See e.g. Prosecutor v. Radovan Karadžić*, Case No. IT-95-5/18-T, Hearing, 21 April 2010, T.1330-1331, 1357. *See also* Marie-Bénédicte Dembour/Emily Haslam, Silencing Hearing? Victim-Witnesses at War-Crimes Trials, 15 *European Journal*

D. *The role of legal advisors to self-represented accused*

The question of the status of legal advisors to self-represented accused, including their potential role to be played during proceedings, is to be examined particularly in light of the different positions expressed by *pro se* defendants as to the part they imagined their legal associates to assume in the course of their respective cases.

The ICTY registry defined legal advisors or legal associates for purposes of providing adequate facilities as "persons assisting self-represented accused in a support-staff role, as distinct from 'legal representatives' which would refer to an accused's defence counsel".[1037] In *Milošević*, the accused was granted privileged communications with two such legal advisors upon order by the trial chamber.[1038] Yet, neither Slobodan Milošević nor Vojislav Šešelj ever brought their legal advisers to the courtroom or asked for a right of audience for them.

In light of the jurisprudence on the matter that accused who decide to conduct their defence in person thereby take responsibility for the conduct of their case, it is necessary to analyse to which extent the assistance of legal advisors could and should be allowed in the courtroom by the trial chambers concerned. Taking into account the view adopted by the majority of chambers in this regard, a *pro se* defendant must not be left in any doubt about his or her responsibilities. Considering that the exercise of the right to self-representation does in fact mean to act as one's own defence counsel, *i.e.* to assume the duties and tasks professional counsel would normally be responsible for, the accused should be aware that he or she cannot necessarily delegate responsibilities in and outside the courtroom as he or she chooses. From a pragmatic point of view, it is a positive development that judges eventually

---

of International Law 151 (2004), at 171-173; Yael Danieli, Massive Trauma and the Healing Role of Restorative Justice, in: Carla Ferstman/Mariana Goetz/Alan Stephens (eds), *Reparations for Victims of Genocide, War Crimes and Crimes Against Humanity. Systems in Place and Systems in the Making* (Leiden/Boston: Martinus Nijhoff Publishers) 2009, p.41-77, at 70-72.

1037 *Prosecutor v. Vojislav Šešelj*, Case No. IT-03-67-T, Registry Submission Pursuant to Rule 33(B) Regarding the Accused's Submission No. 425, 23 September 2009, para.6 fn.2.

1038 *Prosecutor v. Slobodan Milošević*, Case No. IT-99-37-PT & IT-01-50-PT, Order, 15 November 2001, p.3; *Prosecutor v. Slobodan Milošević*, Case No. IT-02-54-T, Order, 16 April 2002, p.3. *See also* Registry Report on Practical Facilities Available to Accused, 18 March 2002, p.4-5.

acknowledged a more significant role for legal associates in order to ensure fair and expeditious proceedings.

I. The role of legal associates in *Tolimir* and *Karadžić*

In light of the extent to which legal associates or advisors are oftentimes involved in the proceedings of self-represented accused, these advisors might be seen as *de facto* defence counsel, with the only difference lying in their more or less limited active involvement in the court proceedings.[1039] Above all the defendants in *Karadžić* and *Tolimir* relied to a significant extent on their legal associates for legal and practical assistance with regard to submissions, written litigation, and also, even more importantly, concerning active and direct assistance in court proceedings. In particular the main legal advisor in *Karadžić* would assume the role of *de fact*o counsel once the evidentiary hearings had started by dealing with more legalistic issues like objections to prosecution evidence or other matters to be argued on a more legal than factual basis.

The example of the *Tolimir* trial proceedings specifically illustrates a distribution of tasks between self-represented accused and legal advisor which is reminiscent of a lead and co-counsel relationship.[1040] Yet, the defendant attached importance to pointing out that his legal advisors were to be considered as a minimum legal assistance in order to perform tasks which

---

1039 Nina H.B. Jørgensen, The Right of the Accused to Self-Representation Before International Criminal Tribunals, 98 *The American Journal of International Law* 711 (2004), at 721.

1040 *See* comparison drawn by the accused: *Prosecutor v. Zdravko Tolimir*, Case No. IT-05-88/2-T, Request to the Trial Chamber, 01 March 2010 (filed: 03 March 2010), para.4; Request to the Pre-trial Chamber for Leave to File of a Reply and Reply to the Prosecution's Response of 5 March 2010, 08 March 2010 (filed: 10 March 2010), para.7.

could not be carried out by the accused in detention,[1041] rather than as a "replacement of defence counsel".[1042]

The accused in *Tolimir* asked for a legal advisor to be appointed and a defence team formed in order to provide assistance in his personal presentation of the case.[1043] However, the candidate initially put forward did not consent to such appointment under the conditions set by the ICTY registry,[1044] whereas there appeared to be unresolved questions regarding certain qualifications of the next candidate of choice which prevented formal recognition as legal advisor.[1045] The trial chamber which had been seised of the requested review already before found no error in reasoning and upheld the first decision of the ICTY registry.[1046] As a consequence of the rejection of his first

---

1041 *Prosecutor v. Zdravko Tolimir*, Case No. IT-05-88/2-PT, Submission by the Accused to the Trial Chamber, Registry and Prosecution on Depriving the Accused of his Guaranteed Rights, on Creating Conditions for Normal Communication with the Accused and his Legal Advisors, and on Proper Conduct of the Proceedings, 26 March 2008 (filed: 03 April 2008), para.5.

1042 *Prosecutor v. Zdravko Tolimir*, Case No. IT-05-88/2-PT, Response to the Prosecution's Motion Requesting the Appointment of Permanent Counsel for the Accused Tolimir, 02 June 2008 (filed: 05 June 2008), para.8.

1043 *See Prosecutor v. Zdravko Tolimir*, Case No. IT-05-88/2-PT, The Accused's Submission to the Registrar and the Pre-trial Chamber Concerning Status Issues and the Financing of his Defence in Accordance with Article 21 of the Statute of the International Criminal Tribunal for the Former Yugoslavia, 04 September 2007 (filed: 07 September 2007); The Accused's Motion to the Pre-trial Chamber to Suspend the Decision on the Filing of Preliminary Motions Until the Abduction of the Accused is Resolved, the Prosecution Material Disclosed, and the Decision Made on the Motion by the Accused Concerning the Financing of his Defence in Accordance with Article 21 of the Statute of the International Criminal Tribunal for the Former Yugoslavia, 25 September 2007 (filed: 27 September 2007), para.5.

1044 *Prosecutor v. Zdravko Tolimir*, Case No. IT-05-88/2-PT, Registrar's Submission on the Accused's Motion Dated 25 September 2007, 03 October 2007, para.4; Registrar's Submission on the Accused's Motion Dated 16 November 2007, 07 December 2007, para.5.

1045 *Prosecutor v. Zdravko Tolimir*, Case No. IT-05-88/2-PT, Motion to the Pre-trial Chamber and the Registrar Concerning Assistance in Appointing a Legal Advisor, Disclosure of Material in a Language the Accused Understands and Notification of Special Defence on the Charges in the Indictment, 16 November 2007 (filed: 20 November 2007), para.4-5; Registrar's Submission on the Accused's Motion Dated 16 November 2007, 07 December 2007, para.6-8. *See also* Submission by the Accused to the Registrar and the Pre-trial Chamber for Leave to Appoint a Legal Advisor and Defence Team, 10 October 2007 (filed: 23 October 2007).

1046 *Prosecutor v. Zdravko Tolimir*, Case No. IT-05-88/2-PT, Decision on Motion by the Accused for Review of the Registry's Decision of 29 June 2007, 20 July 2007.

choice of permanent counsel, in light of the fact that the candidate put forward did not fulfil the requirements set by the ICTY registry for appointment of counsel,[1047] the accused asserted his right to defend himself in person.[1048] Eventually, two legal assistants were assigned to the accused to form a defence team in order to provide assistance in the presentation of the defence case.[1049] The request of the accused to assign a third person as legal advisor was initially rejected by the ICTY registry,[1050] until the matter was solved by intervention of the pre-trial judge.[1051]

The defendant in *Tolimir* initially indicated that his designated legal advisor for international law would not appear in court, despite his assistance being "essential".[1052] Yet, the accused subsequently moved for his legal advisor to be present in the courtroom, request which was granted by the trial chamber "in the interests of justice".[1053] In the following, the accused submitted a request to grant his legal advisor, after consultation with him, leave

---

1047 *Prosecutor v. Zdravko Tolimir*, Case No. IT-05-88/2-PT, Registry Submission Pursuant to Rule 33(B) of the Rules of Procedure and Evidence Regarding the Accused Tolimir's 13 July 2007 Submission on Appointment of Permanent Counsel, 18 July 2007, para.13.

1048 *Prosecutor v. Zdravko Tolimir*, Case No. IT-05-88/2-PT, Notification by the Deputy Registrar, 27 August 2007.

1049 *Prosecutor v. Zdravko Tolimir*, Case No. IT-05-88/2-PT, Registrar's Notification Regarding the Assignment of Legal Assistance to the Accused, 11 January 2008, para.2.

1050 *Prosecutor v. Zdravko Tolimir*, Case No. IT-05-88/2-PT, Accused's Submission Concerning the Appointment of Legal Advisors and the Need for the Court, Registry and Prosecution to Communicate with the Accused in the Serbian Language, as the Only Language he Understands, 03 March 2008 (filed: 05 March 2008), para.1; Registrar's Submission Regarding the Motions of the Accused Dated 13 February 2008 and 3 March 2008, 07 March 2008, para.5.

1051 *Prosecutor v. Zdravko Tolimir*, Case No. IT-05-88/2-PT, Status Conference, 12 March 2008, T.156-157.

1052 *Prosecutor v. Zdravko Tolimir*, Case No. IT-05-88/2-PT, Accused's Submission Concerning the Appointment of Legal Advisors and the Need for the Court, Registry and Prosecution to Communicate with the Accused in the Serbian Language, as the only Language he Understands, 03 March 2008 (filed: 05 March 2008), para.3.

1053 *Prosecutor v. Zdravko Tolimir*, Case No. IT-05-88/2-PT, Request for the Chamber to Allow Aleksandar Gajić, Legal Advisor to Zdravko Tolimir to be Present in the Courtroom, 12 February 2010 (filed: 16 February 2010); *Prosecutor v. Zdravko Tolimir*, Case No. IT-05-88/2-PT, Decision on Motion Requesting the Chamber to Allow the Accused's Legal Advisor to be Present in the Courtroom, 22 February 2010.

"to present legal arguments, make recommendations and raise objections in the case", as well as, under certain circumstances, "to appear in the courtroom, address other issues in court during trial, in particular, cross-examine or examine witnesses".[1054] The defendant submitted that this "legal aid" was not inconsistent with the exercise of his right to self-representation.[1055]

The prosecution objected to this defence request in light of the arguably "representational capacity substantively coextensive with that of appointed Counsel" requested by the accused.[1056] It submitted that concerns arising from the choice to self-represent did not justify such an expansion of the role of a legal associate.[1057]

The trial chamber granted the defence motion in part and allowed the legal advisor to address legal issues arising in the course of the proceedings after specific request by the accused, as well as administrative issues concerning the conduct of the proceedings.[1058] In the trial chamber's view, it "would be in the interests of justice" to grant the legal advisor a limited right of audience to address specific legal issues in light of his previous experience, despite the fact that he was not considered qualified to appear in court as defence counsel by the ICTY registry in terms of Rules 44 and 45 of the ICTY RPE.[1059] In addition, a specific limited right of audience was deemed

---

1054 *Prosecutor v. Zdravko Tolimir*, Case No. IT-05-88/2-T, Request to the Trial Chamber, 01 March 2010 (filed: 03 March 2010), para.1. *See also* Request to the Pre-trial Chamber for Leave to File of a Reply [sic] and Reply to the Prosecution's Response of 5 March 2010, 08 March 2010 (filed: 10 March 2010).

1055 *Prosecutor v. Zdravko Tolimir*, Case No. IT-05-88/2-T, Request to the Trial Chamber, 01 March 2010 (filed: 03 March 2010), para.4.

1056 *Prosecutor v. Zdravko Tolimir*, Case No. IT-05-88/2-T, Prosecution Response to Tolimir's Request to the Trial Chamber, 05 March 2010 (filed: 08 March 2010), para.4.

1057 *Prosecutor v. Zdravko Tolimir*, Case No. IT-05-88/2-T, Prosecution Response to Tolimir's Request to the Trial Chamber, 05 March 2010 (filed: 08 March 2010), para.5.

1058 *Prosecutor v. Zdravko Tolimir*, Case No. IT-05-88/2-T, Decision on Accused's Request to the Trial Chamber Concerning Assistance of his Legal Advisor, 28 April 2010 (Public redacted version issued on 27 May 2010. *See* Order Issuing a Public Redacted Version of the "Decision on Accused's Request to the Trial Chamber Concerning Assistance of his Legal Advisor", 27 May 2010), p.10.

1059 *Prosecutor v. Zdravko Tolimir*, Case No. IT-05-88/2-T, Decision on Accused's Request to the Trial Chamber Concerning Assistance of his Legal Advisor, 28 April 2010 (Public redacted version issued on 27 May 2010. *See* Order Issuing a Public Redacted Version of the "Decision on Accused's Request to the Trial Chamber Concerning Assistance of his Legal Advisor", 27 May 2010), para.24.

appropriate for purposes of dealing with matters arising from communication with the prosecution, such as "the scheduling of witnesses, the disclosure and delivery of materials between the parties, and other such exclusively administrative matters".[1060] Although the trial chamber adopted the view that a request for assistance in the examination of witness would not necessarily have to be denied merely because of the accused's choice to self-represent but rather would need to be assessed taking into account the specific circumstances of each case,[1061] it eventually reached the conclusion that assistance in the examination of witnesses "would stretch the boundaries of self-representation to an extent which the Chamber finds inconsistent with the principle of self-representation".[1062] The trial chamber took into account factors such as the potential impact on the integrity of the proceedings in case an inexperienced legal advisor not supervised by more experienced lead counsel would (cross-) examine witnesses.[1063] The bench clarified that it would not oppose a modified regime of participation of the accused in the proceedings in case he would wish to be assigned qualified defence counsel, but also that it would assign counsel even without any such wish if this were to be considered in the interests of justice.[1064]

1060 *Prosecutor v. Zdravko Tolimir*, Case No. IT-05-88/2-T, Decision on Accused's Request to the Trial Chamber Concerning Assistance of his Legal Advisor, 28 April 2010 (Public redacted version issued on 27 May 2010. *See* Order Issuing a Public Redacted Version of the "Decision on Accused's Request to the Trial Chamber Concerning Assistance of his Legal Advisor", 27 May 2010), para.25.

1061 *Prosecutor v. Zdravko Tolimir*, Case No. IT-05-88/2-T, Decision on Accused's Request to the Trial Chamber Concerning Assistance of his Legal Advisor, 28 April 2010 (Public redacted version issued on 27 May 2010. *See* Order Issuing a Public Redacted Version of the "Decision on Accused's Request to the Trial Chamber Concerning Assistance of his Legal Advisor", 27 May 2010), para.27.

1062 *Prosecutor v. Zdravko Tolimir*, Case No. IT-05-88/2-T, Decision on Accused's Request to the Trial Chamber Concerning Assistance of his Legal Advisor, 28 April 2010 (Public redacted version issued on 27 May 2010. *See* Order Issuing a Public Redacted Version of the "Decision on Accused's Request to the Trial Chamber Concerning Assistance of his Legal Advisor", 27 May 2010), para.31.

1063 *Prosecutor v. Zdravko Tolimir*, Case No. IT-05-88/2-T, Decision on Accused's Request to the Trial Chamber Concerning Assistance of his Legal Advisor, 28 April 2010 (Public redacted version issued on 27 May 2010. *See* Order Issuing a Public Redacted Version of the "Decision on Accused's Request to the Trial Chamber Concerning Assistance of his Legal Advisor", 27 May 2010), para.29-30.

1064 *Prosecutor v. Zdravko Tolimir*, Case No. IT-05-88/2-T, Decision on Accused's Request to the Trial Chamber Concerning Assistance of his Legal Advisor, 28

A review of the transcripts of the proceedings shows that the legal advisor in *Tolimir* made regular use of the limited right of audience and dealt with procedural and administrative issues, *e.g.* concerning tendering exhibits, scheduling issues or assisting with other technical matters in the course of cross-examination of witnesses by the accused.[1065] Upon specific request by the accused which was granted by the trial chamber, the legal advisor was in addition subsequently permitted to address legal arguments.[1066]

The trial chamber's approach in *Tolimir* appears to strike a careful balance between an acknowledgement of the need to provide a self-represented accused with the best possible assistance in order to ensure fair and expeditious proceedings on the one hand, and safeguarding the integrity of the proceed-

---

April 2010 (Public redacted version issued on 27 May 2010. *See* Order Issuing a Public Redacted Version of the "Decision on Accused's Request to the Trial Chamber Concerning Assistance of his Legal Advisor", 27 May 2010), para.32.

1065 *Prosecutor v. Zdravko Tolimir*, Case No. IT-05-88/2-T, Hearing, 03 May 2010, T.1503; Hearing, 17 May 2010, T.1906; Hearing, 18 May 2010, T.1969-1970; Hearing, 28 May 2010, T.2193; Hearing, 31 May 2010, T.2242, 2258; Hearing, 01 June 2010, T.2283-2284, 2357; Hearing, 16 June 2010, T.2810, 2834; Hearing, 17 June 2010, T.2893; Hearing, 06 July 2010, T.3549-3550; Hearing, 07 July 2010, T.3587, 3624; Hearing, 09 July 2010, T.3794; Hearing, 17 August 2010, T.4028-4029; Hearing, 19 August 2010, T.4121-4122; Hearing, 23 August 2010, T.4301-4302, 4311; Hearing, 31 August 2010, T.4632-4633, 4695; Hearing, 01 September 2010, T.4785-4788; Hearing, 02 September 2010, T.4854-4855, 4857, 4875; Hearing, 06 September 2010, T.4882; Hearing, 10 September 2010, T.5219, 5223; Hearing, 13 September 2010, T.5284; Hearing, 14 September 2010, T.5304-5305, 5344; Hearing, 15 September 2010, T.5392-5393, 5394, 5430-5432; Hearing, 16 September 2010, T.5492, 5551-5552; Hearing, 20 September 2010, T.5583, 5595, 5611, 5621-5622, 5638; Hearing, 21 September 2010, T.5682; Hearing, 23 September 2010, T.5800, 5823; Hearing, 28 September 2010, T.5911; Hearing, 29 September 2010, T.5981, 6010-6012, 6013; Hearing, 08 October 2010, T.6396, 6398; Hearing, 19 October 2010, T.6476-6477, 6511, 6536-6537; Hearing, 20 October 2010, T.6598-6600, 6605-6606, 6628; Hearing, 21 October 2010, T.6733; Hearing, 26 October 2010, T.6735; Hearing, 27 October 2010, T.6824-6826, 6843, 6845-6846, 6857, 6877; Hearing, 28 October 2010, T.6903, 6914, 6954, 6969-6971, 6976; Hearing, 29 October 2010, T.6985, 7017, 7027, 7063; Hearing, 01 November 2010, T.7123; Hearing, 04 November 2010, T.7316-7317, 7329-7332, 7334, 7344, 7348, 7353, 7359; Hearing, 08 November 2010, T.7389; Hearing, 11 November 2010, T.7672; Hearing, 15 November 2010, T.7700-7703, 7705-7706, 7710, 7713-7714; Hearing, 17 November 2010, T.7794; Hearing, 22 November 2010, T.7887-7888, 7898; Hearing, 24 November 2010, T.8083.

1066 *Prosecutor v. Zdravko Tolimir*, Case No. IT-05-88/2-T, Hearing, 19 August 2010, T.4158-4159.

ings and the nature of the decision to self-represent on the other. It is of note that the bench expressly referred to the possibility of ensuring the active participation of the accused in his case without however having to forego entirely the assistance of duly qualified counsel.[1067] This appears to approve of the idea that the right to self-representation and assistance by professional counsel do not necessarily have to be mutually exclusive. However, the trial chamber did not seize the opportunity to address the topic on a more general level.

In *Karadžić*, the accused considered a legal associate to be

> "an experienced legal advisor who can advise him on the quality and likelihood of success of pretrial [sic] motions, assist him in making submissions on complicated legal issues, and, if desired by the accused and permitted by the Trial Chamber, relieve him from time to time during the course of trial."[1068]

The trial chamber clarified the role to be played by the legal advisors of the accused in the course of trial in an order on the conduct of trial proceedings, stating that "[d]uring trial, the Accused's legal advisor, Mr. Peter Robinson, is permitted to be present in the courtroom and will have a right of audience limited to addressing the Trial Chamber on legal issues that arise during the proceedings".[1069] The bench made clear that this limited right of audience could only be exercised when specifically requested by the accused and granted by the trial chamber.[1070] The accused's second legal advisor, as well as a case manager, were permitted to be present in the courtroom in order

1067 *Prosecutor v. Zdravko Tolimir*, Case No. IT-05-88/2-T, Decision on Accused's Request to the Trial Chamber Concerning Assistance of his Legal Advisor, 28 April 2010 (Public redacted version issued on 27 May 2010. *See* Order Issuing a Public Redacted Version of the "Decision on Accused's Request to the Trial Chamber Concerning Assistance of his Legal Advisor", 27 May 2010), para.32: "[…] the Chamber informs the Accused that should he wish to reconsider the assignment of qualified counsel pursuant to the Rules, such assignment does not necessarily restrict his participation in the proceedings."

1068 *Prosecutor v. Radovan Karadžić*, Case No. IT-95-5/18-PT, Motion for Adequate Facilities and Equality of Arms: Legal Associates, 24 November 2008 (filed: 25 November 2008), para.28.

1069 *Prosecutor v. Radovan Karadžić*, Case No. IT-95-5/18-T, Order on the Procedure for the Conduct of Trial, 08 October 2009, para.T. *See also* discussion during Pre-trial Conference, 06 October 2009, T.470-478.

1070 *Prosecutor v. Radovan Karadžić*, Case No. IT-95-5/18-T, Order on the Procedure for the Conduct of Trial, 08 October 2009, para.U.

to assist with other matters, however without any right of audience.[1071] In addition, the trial chamber limited the maximum amount of legal advisors and/or case managers in the courtroom to two, unless otherwise specifically authorised.[1072]

Similar to the position adopted by the *Tolimir* trial chamber, the guidelines issued by the trial chamber adopt a reasonably pragmatic approach, offering the accused a maximum extent of professional legal and practical assistance in the course of court proceedings, while however being mindful of the defendant's *pro se* status.

With regard to the question which requirements could be set by the ICTY registry when acknowledging legal associates for purposes of the remuneration scheme, the appeals chamber stated in *Karadžić* that "[w]hile the provision of legal consultation would normally imply that a legal associate be either admitted to practice law or be a university professor of law, it does not *a priori* require that the legal associate possess the full expertise and experience required under Rule 45 of the Rules".[1073] This position indicates that the appeals chamber did not necessarily expect legal advisors of *pro se* defendants to fulfil the same qualification requirements – and consequently take the same responsibilities – as professional defence counsel.

A review of transcripts in *Karadžić* illustrates that the (significant) involvement of the legal advisor with a right of audience extended to a more legalistic level, *e.g.* addressing legal objections to the admission of evidence tendered by the prosecution or dealing with motions and responses filed by the defence team.[1074] On at least one occasion, the legal advisor also put

1071 *Prosecutor v. Radovan Karadžić*, Case No. IT-95-5/18-T, Order on the Procedure for the Conduct of Trial, 08 October 2009, para.V.

1072 *Prosecutor v. Radovan Karadžić*, Case No. IT-95-5/18-T, Order on the Procedure for the Conduct of Trial, 08 October 2009, para.W.

1073 *Prosecutor v. Radovan Karadžić*, Case No. IT-95-5/18-AR73.2, Decision on Interlocutory Appeal of the Trial Chamber's Decision on Adequate Facilities, 07 May 2009, para.17.

1074 *Prosecutor v. Radovan Karadžić*, Case No. IT-95-5/18-T, Hearing, 22 April 2010, T.1394-1395, 1450-1453, 1459, 1460-1461; Hearing, 23 April 2010, T.1493-1494, 1501-1502; Hearing, 27 April 2010, T.1744; Hearing, 28 April 2010, T.1751-1752, 1786-1787, 1839; Hearing, 05 May 2010, T.1849, 1852-1857, 1911; Hearing, 06 May 2010, T.1954-1955, 1996-1997, 2007-2008, 2034-2035; Hearing, 07 May 2010, T.2049-2052, 2055-2056; Hearing, 10 May 2010, T.2212; Hearing, 11 May 2010, T.2367, 2370; Hearing, 26 May 2010, T.2724-2725; Hearing, 31 May 2010, T.3039; Hearing, 01 June 2010, T.3149-3151; Hearing, 03 June 2010, T.3365; Hearing, 09 June 2010, T.3546; Hearing, 10 June 2010, T.3731-3733; Hearing,

15 June 2010, T.3739, 3742; Hearing, 21 June 2010, T.3905-3906, 3912-3913, 3923, 3934-3935, 3938-3940; Hearing, 30 June 2010, T.4402-4403, 4408-4410; Hearing, 01 July 2010, T.4434, 4460-4461, 4477-4478, 4488, 4506, 4516-4517; Hearing, 05 July 2010, T.4564, 4591, 4637-4638, 4641-4642, 4650; Hearing, 06 July 2010, T.4661, 4676-4677, 4704-4705; Hearing, 15 July 2010, T.5177, 5212, 5230; Hearing, 16 July 2010, T.5285-5286, 5317; Hearing, 19 July 2010, T.5496, 5498, 5502-5503; Hearing, 17 August 2010, T.5826; Hearing, 18 August 2010, T.5942-5943; Hearing, 20 August 2010, T.6039, 6100-6104; Hearing, 06 September 2010, T.6238-6239; Hearing, 13 September 2010, T.6589-6592, 6625-6628, 6631; Hearing, 14 September 2010, T.6694-6695; Hearing, 15 September 2010, T.6814; Hearing, 27 September 2010, T.6935, 6946; Hearing, 05 October 2010, T.7233-7235, 7239-7240, 7284; Hearing, 07 October 2010, T.7411-7412; Hearing, 08 October 2010, T.7593; Hearing, 11 October 2010, T.7614-7615, 7670-7671; Hearing, 12 October 2010, T.7739, 7776; Hearing, 14 October 2010, T.7935-7938, 7948; Rule 54 *bis* Hearing, 15 October 2010, T.7964-7967, 7970-7971, 7984-7987; Hearing, 15 October 2010, T.7992-7994; Hearing, 19 October 2010, T.8144, 8167-8168; Hearing, 20 October 2010, T.8216, 8246-8247, 8260, 8264-8265; Hearing, 26 October 2010, T.8287, 8382-8383; Hearing, 27 October 2010, T.8386, 8402-8405, 8409, 8416, 8452-8454; Hearing, 28 October 2010, T.8527-8528, 8556-8557; Hearing, 29 October 2010, T.8651-8652, 8659-8660, 8661-8662; Hearing, 01 November 2010, T.8753-8754; Hearing, 04 November 2010, T.9030-9034, 9110; Hearing, 02 February 2011, T.11179-11180; Hearing, 03 February 2011, T.11254; Hearing, 08 February 2011, T.11293-11294, 11377-11378; Hearing, 09 February 2011, T.11383-11385, 11391, 11397-11398, 11426; Hearing, 10 February 2011, T.11569; Hearing, 14 February 2011, T.11738, 11816-11817, 11819-11820, 11833; Hearing, 15 February 2011, T.11834-11838, 11894, 11906, 11913, 11914, 11919; Hearing, 16 February 2011, T.11975, 12049; Hearing, 17 February 2012, T.12053-12057, 12126-12128; Hearing, 22 February 2011, T.12145, 12171, 12191-12192, 12198; Hearing, 23 February 2011, T.12218; Hearing, 24 February 2011, T.12300-12302, 12361-12362, 12376, 12379-12381; Hearing, 25 February 2011, T.12474-12475; Hearing, 28 February 2011, T.12478-12480; Hearing, 01 March 2011, T.12611, 12643-12644, 12668-12669; Hearing, 02 March 2011, T.12794, 12802-12804, 12809-12810, 12813-12815; Hearing, 03 March 2012, T.12839, 12927, 12930, 12932; Rule 54 *bis* Hearing, 10 May 2011, T.13867, 13873-13877; Hearing, 31 May 2011, T.13880-13881, 13971; Hearing 01 June 2011, T.14010; Hearing, 03 June 2011, T.14190-14196, 14200-14201, 14204; Hearing, 14 June 2011, T.14639-14640; Hearing, 17 June 2011, T.14818-14820, 14877-14878, 14881, 14907; Hearing, 20 June 2011, T.14934, 14967, 14969-14970; Hearing, 21 June 2011, T.15033-15034, 15072-15073; Hearing, 22 June 2011, T.15158, 15202, 15204; Hearing, 23 June 2011, T.15257, 15279-15280, 15285; Hearing, 24 June 2011, T.15411, 15449-15451; Hearing, 28 June 2011, T.15495-15496, 15512-15513, 15515, 15550, 15571; Hearing, 29 June 2011, T.15574-15575, 15683; Hearing, 30 June 2011, T.15693; Hearing, 01 July 2011, T.15827-15828, 15830-15831, 15838; Hearing, 04 July 2011, T.15941; Hearing, 06 July 2011, T.16245-16247; Hearing, 13 July 2011, T.16459, 16463-16464;

Hearing, 14 July 2011, T.16596, 16602-16605, 16620, 16628-16633, 16636, 16638-16639; Hearing, 15 July 2011, T.16379; Hearing, 19 July 2011, T.16873, 16893-16894; Hearing, 20 July 2011, T.16989-16990; Hearing, 21 July 2011, T.17109-17110; Hearing, 16 August 2011, T.17199, 17203-17204, 17212-17213, 17295-17296; Hearing, 18 August 2011, T.17438-17439; Hearing, 19 August 2011, T.17486-17487, 17497-17498, 17576-17577; Hearing, 22 August 2011, T.17578-17579; Hearing, 24 August 2011, T.17782-17786, 17832; Hearing, 31 August 2011, T.18128; Hearing, 05 September 2011, T.18336-18342; Hearing, 06 September 2011, T.18465, 18485; Hearing, 07 September 2011, T.18513-18514; Hearing, 08 September 2011, T.18565-18566, 18568-18569, 18639; Hearing, 13 September 2011, T.18687-18688, 18710-18711; Hearing, 15 September 2011, T.18840-18841, 18844, 18847, 18887, 18898-18901; Hearing, 16 September 2011, T.19028-19029; Hearing, 19 September 2011, T.19133-19134, 19141-19142, 19148-19149; Hearing, 20 September 2011, T.19195, 19223-19226, 19228-19229; Hearing, 22 September 2011, T.19421; Hearing, 27 September 2011, T.19522; Hearing, 30 September 2011, T.19665, 19726-19727; Hearing, 20 October 2011, T.20302-30304; Hearing, 26 October 2011, T.20364-20365, 20367-20369, 20373-20374, 20376-20377, 20396; Hearing, 28 October 2011, T.20516-20517, 20555, 20615; Hearing, 31 October 2011, T.20620-20621; Hearing, 01 November 2011, T.20716-20720, 20728; Hearing 02 November 2011, T.20764-20767, 20804, 20835-20836; Hearing, 22 November 2011, T.21698-21699; Hearing, 23 November 2011, T.21846; Hearing, 24 November 2011, T.21892; Hearing, 28 November 2011, T.22001-22002, 22012, 22028; Hearing, 29 November 2011, T.22068-22069, 22076, 22079-22080; Hearing, 30 November 2011, T.22158; Hearing, 07 December 2011, T.22437-22439; Hearing, 11 January 2012, T.22732; Hearing, 13 January 2012, T.22992; Hearing, 24 January 2012, T.23448; Hearing, 25 January 2012, T.23618-23619; Hearing, 26 January 2012, T.23657-23658; Hearing, 27 January 2012, T.23754, 23785-23786; Hearing, 30 January 2012, T.23839; Hearing, 08 February 2012, T.24293-24294, 24331-24332, 24339-24341; Hearing, 09 February 2012, T.24440-24442, 24444-24447; Hearing, 15 February 2012, T.24793; Hearing, 16 February 2012, T.24897-24902; Hearing, 21 February 2012, T.24946-24947, 24951, 24953-24955, 24999-25000, 25004-25006, 25008; Hearing, 22 February 2012, T.25026-25027, 25048-25049; Hearing, 23 February 2012, T.25136, 25149-25150, 25170-25172, 25179; Hearing, 24 February 2012, T.25181; Hearing, 27 February 2012, T.25313-25315, 25323-25323, 25327, 25358-25359; Hearing, 28 February 2012, T.25414-25415, 25417-25418; Hearing, 01 March 2012, T.25590, 25622-25623, 25654-25655, 25668; Hearing, 06 March 2012, T.25806, 25812-25814, 25816-25817; Hearing, 07 March 2012, T.25941-25942, 25954-25957; Hearing, 12 March 2012, T.26095; Hearing, 14 March 2012, T.26313; Hearing, 15 March 2012, T.26321-26323, 26378-26380, 26384; Hearing, 20 March 2012, T.26414-26415, 26418, 26420, 26431-26432; Hearing, 21 March 2012, T.26562-26564, 26568-26569, 26578-26583, 26588; Hearing, 26 March 2012, T.26811, 26836; Hearing, 28 March 2012, T.27050, 27058, 27059, 27061; Hearing, 10 April 2012, T.27220-27221, 27230-27232, 27237-27238; Hearing, 11 April 2012, T.27369-27370; Hearing, 17 April 2012, T.27499-27501; Hearing,

questions to a witness in cross-examination relating to the subject matter of a motion potentially to be filed by the defence.[1075] This assistance thus appears to be less of an administrative nature, as in *Tolimir*, rather than provision of specific legal advice to the accused. The extensive involvement of the legal associate indicates that the trial chamber heavily relied on the legal advisor's role and influence, and – despite its initial position – often addressed him without being so requested by the accused to be able to deal with matters more swiftly.[1076]

Yet, it appeared in the course of the trial proceedings that the accused did not necessarily pay heed to advice given by his legal advisors with regard to his personal trial management.[1077] At times, it even seemed as if there might be open dispute between the accused and his lead legal associate.[1078] Notwithstanding, the accused and his legal advisor divided tasks in the context of the Rule 98*bis* submission after the close of the prosecution case: while the defendant presented arguments concerning the majority of counts in the indictment,[1079] his legal advisor took charge of presenting the oral motion for acquittal with regard to counts 1 (genocide in municipalities in 1992) and 11 (taking hostages) of the indictment.[1080] The fact that the trial

18 April 2012, T.27532-27533, 27553, 27557-27558, 27608-27609, 27621; Hearing, 20 April 2012, T.27752, 27797; Hearing, 23 April 2012, T.27846; Hearing, 25 April 2012, T.28068-28069, 28071, 28076-28077, 28113-28114; Hearing, 26 April 2012, T.28137-28138; Hearing, 01 May 2012, T.28231; Hearing, 02 May 2012, T.28323, 28372, 28383, 28413; Hearing, 03 May 2012, T.28502.

1075 *Prosecutor v. Radovan Karadžić*, Case No. IT-95-5/18-T, Hearing, 27 October 2010, T.8452-8453. *See also* Hearing, 10 November 2011, T.21243-21246. However, see also Hearing, 07 March 2012, T.25955-25956.

1076 *See*, however, specific request of the defence for a right of audience during an appeal hearing: *Prosecutor v. Radovan Karadžić*, Case No. IT-95-5/18-AR98bis.1, Respondent's Brief, 05 November 2012, para.317.

1077 *Prosecutor v. Radovan Karadžić*, Case No. IT-95-5/18-T, Hearing, 01 March 2011, T.12643-12644; Hearing, 09 November 2011, T.21123; Hearing, 18 November 2011, T.21633.

1078 *Prosecutor v. Radovan Karadžić*, Case No. IT-95-5/18-T, Hearing, 18 November 2011, T.21633.

1079 *Prosecutor v. Radovan Karadžić*, Case No. IT-95-5/18-T, Rule 98 *bis* Hearing, 11 June 2012, T.28580-28618. *See also* T.28580-28581: "First of all, I would like to pay tribute to our learned colleagues from the Prosecution because they made a huge effort to make some kind of indictment out of nothing."

1080 *Prosecutor v. Radovan Karadžić*, Case No. IT-95-5/18-T, Rule 98 *bis* Hearing, 11 June 2012, T.28569-28580, T.28619-28626. *See also Prosecutor v. Radovan*

chamber refrained from commenting on this significant task assumed by the accused's legal advisor at an important stage of the proceedings is indicative of an acceptance on its part of the important role in fact played by the advisor in the proceedings.[1081]

Of note to illustrate that the *Karadžić* trial chamber did not categorically countenance whichever assistance demanded by the accused is a request submitted by the defence for interns of the team to be present in the courtroom, in order to assist with cross-examination of witnesses, as well as a reward for interns working for free on the defence case.[1082] Prefacing a written defence request, the presiding judge did not seem convinced that the demand was justified, in light of the number of defence team members allowed to be present in the courtroom pursuant to the initial order of the bench, and the status of the defendant as self-represented accused.[1083] The remark of the presiding judge on behalf of the trial chamber indicates that the bench adopted the view that as self-represented accused and in light of the guidelines issued by the chamber, the defendant should essentially be responsible for his defence in the courtroom, rather than delegating responsibility for certain aspects to defence team members.

The defence filed an official request to modify the previous guidelines, arguing that the "modification would enhance Dr. Karadzic's ability to provide references to transcripts and other material during his cross examination, and would also reward the Legal Interns for their dedicated *pro bono* assistance to his case".[1084] It submitted that interns would be better placed in the courtroom than case managers, as envisaged by the guidelines.[1085]

Karadžić, Case No. IT-95-5/18-AR98bis.1, Respondent's Brief, 05 November 2012, para.317.

1081 *See, e.g.*, also remark of presiding judge at Hearing, 17 June 2011, T.14901: "The Accused: [Interpretation]: This is, again, leading and inaccurate. I mean, it's leading, and we'll prove that it is incorrect. Judge Kwon: You pre-empted Mr. Robinson's role. [...]".

1082 *Prosecutor v. Radovan Karadžić*, Case No. IT-95-5/18-T, Hearing, 22 April 2010, T.1460-1461.

1083 *Prosecutor v. Radovan Karadžić*, Case No. IT-95-5/18-T, Hearing, 23 April 2010, T.1493-1494, 1520-1521.

1084 *Prosecutor v. Radovan Karadžić*, Case No. IT-95-5/18-T, Request for Authorization for Legal Interns to be Present in the Courtroom, 26 April 2010, para.3.

1085 *Prosecutor v. Radovan Karadžić*, Case No. IT-95-5/18-T, Request for Authorization for Legal Interns to be Present in the Courtroom, 26 April 2010, para.10.

The prosecution did not object to the request under the caveat that any measures implemented to ensure confidentiality would not be jeopardised.[1086]

The trial chamber granted the request of the defence in part, allowing one intern to be present in the courtroom without any right of audience to assist the accused, however only as replacement of either one legal advisor or the case manager.[1087] According to the trial chamber, in formulating the initial order on the conduct of the proceedings,[1088] "it gave due consideration to the amount of assistance that the Accused, as a self-represented accused, would need in the courtroom during the proceedings" and "concluded that two people, either two legal advisors or a legal advisor and a case manager, in addition to the Accused himself, would be sufficient".[1089] The trial chamber took issue with the submission of the defence that presence in the courtroom would be a reward for the interns, stating that "[t]hese are serious criminal proceedings" and that "[t]he Accused may find other means by which to acknowledge the work of the defence interns" since "internal defence management issues are not the concern of the Chamber".[1090] Therefore, it allowed presence of an intern only as replacement of, but not in addition to, the legal advisor or case manager.[1091] The trial chamber did however

---

1086 *Prosecutor v. Radovan Karadžić*, Case No. IT-95-5/18-T, Prosecution's Response to Karadžić's Request for Legal Interns to be Present in the Courtroom, 27 April 2010. *See also* Leave to Reply: Request for Authorization for Legal Interns to be Present in the Courtroom, 28 April 2010, informing the trial chamber that defence interns are in fact required to sign an undertaking of confidentiality.

1087 *Prosecutor v. Radovan Karadžić*, Case No. IT-95-5/18-T, Decision on Accused's Request for Authorisation for Legal Interns to be Present in the Courtroom, 05 May 2010.

1088 *Prosecutor v. Radovan Karadžić*, Case No. IT-95-5/18-PT, Order on the Procedure for the Conduct of Trial, 08 October 2009, para.T-W.

1089 *Prosecutor v. Radovan Karadžić*, Case No. IT-95-5/18-T, Decision on Accused's Request for Authorisation for Legal Interns to be Present in the Courtroom, 05 May 2010, para.6.

1090 *Prosecutor v. Radovan Karadžić*, Case No. IT-95-5/18-T, Decision on Accused's Request for Authorisation for Legal Interns to be Present in the Courtroom, 05 May 2010, para.7.

1091 *Prosecutor v. Radovan Karadžić*, Case No. IT-95-5/18-T, Decision on Accused's Request for Authorisation for Legal Interns to be Present in the Courtroom, 05 May 2010, para.7.

leave open the possibility for the accused to apply for the presence of an intern in addition to the usual defence team members on a case-by-case basis.[1092]

II. Privileged communications with legal advisors

The accused in *Šešelj* requested to be given the opportunity to form an "expert team" in order to assist him with his defence,[1093] and demanded recognition by the ICTY registry of no less than 22 members of that team.[1094] The defendant submitted a new request for registration of legal advisors and the possibility of privileged communications with them one year later, in which he argued that in light of the fact that these advisors were not his counsel, they would not have to fulfil the requirements of Rule 44 of the ICTY RPE in order to be registered.[1095]

The trial chamber appeared not to be convinced by the accused's arguments and considered that any restrictions on privileged communications of the accused, including access to confidential materials, were "entirely reasonable and justified", in particular considering the need to protect victims and witnesses, as well as the integrity of the proceedings.[1096]

Subsequently in *Šešelj*, the subject matter of privileged communications of the accused with legal associates resurfaced due to the alleged intimidation of protected witnesses by these advisors: according to the ICTY registry, it appeared that the defendant abused his privileged communication facilities by, *inter alia*, disclosing confidential information or communicating with

---

1092 *Prosecutor v. Radovan Karadžić*, Case No. IT-95-5/18-T, Decision on Accused's Request for Authorisation for Legal Interns to be Present in the Courtroom, 05 May 2010, para.9.

1093 *Prosecutor v. Vojislav Šešelj*, Case No. IT-03-67-PT, Motion by the Accused for Normalisation of Conditions for Preparing a Defence, 26 October 2004 (filed: 09 November 2004), p.3-5.

1094 *Prosecutor v. Vojislav Šešelj*, Case No. IT-03-67-PT, Motion by the Accused for Normalisation of Conditions for Preparing a Defence, 26 October 2004 (filed: 09 November 2004), p.10.

1095 *Prosecutor v. Vojislav Šešelj*, Case No. IT-03-67-PT, Submission No. 115, 24 October 2005 (filed: 01 November 2005), p.1.

1096 *Prosecutor v. Vojislav Šešelj*, Case No. IT-03-67-PT, Decision on Submission Number 115, 16 June 2006, p.3.

unauthorised persons.[1097] The ICTY registry withdrew authorisation for privileged contact for two legal associates,[1098] and subsequently suspended payment of expenses to the associates for travel undertaken in order to gain privileged access to the accused.[1099] The decisions taken by the ICTY registry were upheld by the ICTY president.[1100] The trial chamber, seised of an oral request from the defendant to re-establish the status of two legal advisors in order to enable privileged communications,[1101] held that the refusal to re-establish the privileged status of the legal associates did not infringe the accused's right to a fair trial, but also that, nevertheless, their travel expenses at the time of presentation of the defence case should be covered in order to enable them to assist the accused.[1102]

Thereafter, the accused requested re-establishment of the privileged status of one legal advisor, including access to confidential information, threatening that otherwise he would not present a defence case.[1103] The trial chamber, however, rejected the defendant's request, considering that he had not presented any arguments which would justify reconsideration of the earlier decision, in particular in light of the fact that the legal associate in question

---

1097 *Prosecutor v. Vojislav Šešelj*, Case No. IT-03-67-T, Registry Submission Pursuant to Rule 33(B) Regarding the Accused's Submission No. 425, 23 September 2009, para.11, 13-14.

1098 *Prosecutor v. Vojislav Šešelj*, Case No. IT-03-67-T, Registry Submission Pursuant to Rule 33(B) Regarding the Trial Chamber's Decision on Monitoring Vojislav Šešelj's Communications, 01 December 2008, para.9.

1099 *Prosecutor v. Vojislav Šešelj*, Case No. IT-03-67-T, Registry Submission Pursuant to Rule 33(B) Regarding the Viewing of Video Material by Vojislav Šešelj's Legal Associates, 29 June 2009, para.4; Registry Submission Pursuant to Rule 33(B) Regarding the Accused's Submission No. 425, 23 September 2009, para.19-20, 32-33, 35. *See also* Submission No. 425, 11 September 2009 (filed: 15 September 2009).

1100 *Prosecutor v. Vojislav Šešelj*, Case No. IT-03-67-T, Decision on Vojislav Šešelj's Request for Review of Registrar's Decision of 10 September 2009, 21 October 2009, para.21, 25.

1101 *Prosecutor v. Vojislav Šešelj*, Case No. IT-03-67-T, Hearing, 12 January 2010, T.14830-14831.

1102 *Procureur c/ Vojislav Šešelj*, Affaire n° IT-03-67-T, Décision Relative à la Requête Orale de l'Accusé Aux Fins de Rétablissement de MM. Zoran Krasić et Slavko Jerković en Qualité de Collaborateurs Privilégiés, 10 février 2010, para.16.

1103 *Procureur c/ Vojislav Šešelj*, Affaire n° IT-03-67-T, Audience de la Règle 98 bis Jugement, 05 mai 2011, T.16991 (French transcript page) : « Si Zoran Krasic ne devient pas sur décision de la Chambre égal à tous les autres participants présents ici, je ne présenterai pas de défense. »

would still be in a position to assist the accused in the course of public hearings during the defence case.[1104] With regard to another legal associate against whom disciplinary proceedings had been initiated, the trial chamber rejected the accused's request for an immediate suspension of these proceedings[1105] on the basis that the existence of such a procedure did not infringe upon the defendant's right to a fair trial.[1106] In the contrary, the trial chamber rather found that the existence of such proceedings would contribute to the maintenance of an irreproachable conduct of members of any defence team, which above all was in the interests of the accused.[1107]

On the topic of privileged communications of self-represented accused with legal advisors, the ICTY registry submitted in the course of the *Krajišnik* appeal proceedings that the facilities offered to the appellant included recognition of up to three persons as legal associates, with whom he could have privileged communications; access to privileged telephone and facsimile line to enable the appellant to communicate with legal associates in privileged manner; as well as ability to send and receive documentation stored digitally on CDs and DVDs with legal associates, in a privileged manner.[1108] In order to be granted privileged communication with legal associates, these associates had to be recognised by the ICTY registry, *i.e.* they needed to satisfy the specific qualification standards set for defence counsel as *e.g.* in Rule 44 of the ICTY RPE.[1109]

1104 *Procureur c/ Vojislav Šešelj*, Affaire n° IT-03-67-T, Décision Consolidée Relative aux Requêtes Orales de l'Accusé en Relation avec la Présentation de sa Défense, 09 juin 2011, para.14-16.

1105 *Procureur c/ Vojislav Šešelj*, Affaire n° IT-03-67-T, Audience de la Règle 98 bis Jugement, 05 mai 2011, T.16991 (French transcript page).

1106 *Procureur c/ Vojislav Šešelj*, Affaire n° IT-03-67-T, Décision Consolidée Relative aux Requêtes Orales de l'Accusé en Relation avec la Présentation de sa Défense, 09 juin 2011, para.25.

1107 *Procureur c/ Vojislav Šešelj*, Affaire n° IT-03-67-T, Décision Consolidée Relative aux Requêtes Orales de l'Accusé en Relation avec la Présentation de sa Défense, 09 juin 2011, para.25.

1108 *Prosecutor v. Momčilo Krajišnik*, Case No. IT-00-39-A, Registry Submission on Momčilo Krajišnik's Request to Reverse the Decision of the Registry of 7 June 2007, 19 July 2007, para.21, 31.

1109 *Cf. Prosecutor v. Momčilo Krajišnik*, Case No. IT-00-39-A, Registry Submission on Momčilo Krajišnik's Request to Reverse the Decision of the Registry of 7 June 2007, 19 July 2007, para.22-23. *See also Prosecutor v. Vojislav Šešelj*, Case No. IT-03-67-PT, Decision on Appeal Against Decision Denying Permission for Legal Representatives to Visit the Detainee, 25 May 2006, para.6.

The appeals chamber found the requirements of the ICTY registry for designated legal associates to be reasonable.[1110] It also confirmed the ICTY registry's approach regarding privileged communications as "salutary practice", since in theory the basis for any such privilege was removed where an accused chose to self-represent and "accordingly has no entitlement to privileged communications".[1111] It appears from practice and jurisprudence that any privileged communication facilities have been granted on a courtesy basis, however, not as of right, to *pro se* defendants.[1112] This is based on a strict reading of the notion of lawyer-client privilege, which would not, as such, be applicable to accused that are not represented by counsel but are in fact conducting their defence in person.[1113]

The interest in protecting confidential information and preserving the overall integrity of international proceedings appears to justify such measures and leaves room to allow the extension of any privilege only in a monitored and limited manner. However, the issue goes further with regard to the question whether such privileged facilities could be invoked by *pro se* defendants as of right. As long as there is no guarantee for self-represented accused to be able to communicate in a privileged manner with at least some legal associates assisting in the preparation of the defence, it can be claimed that there is equally no guarantee that the right to adequate facilities in order to prepare the defence case is protected. It can be argued that the choice to conduct one's own defence would bring with it such disadvantages. Yet, as long as the associates in question fulfil such requirements as are established for other defence counsel practising before international criminal tribunals – thereby presumably addressing any accountability questions that may arise with regard to the protection of confidential information –, the reasons for withholding such a possibility are not necessarily clear.

Of interest in this context are the remarks in the fundamental dissent to the appeals chamber decision in *Krajišnik*. In light of the fact that the "de-

---

1110 *Prosecutor v. Momčilo Krajišnik*, Case No. IT-00-39-A, Decision on Krajišnik Request and Prosecution Motion, 11 September 2007, para.37.

1111 *Prosecutor v. Momčilo Krajišnik*, Case No. IT-00-39-A, Decision on Krajišnik Request and Prosecution Motion, 11 September 2007, para.33, para.33 fn.93.

1112 *Prosecutor v. Vojislav Šešelj*, Case No. IT-03-67-T, Registry Submission Pursuant to Rule 33(B) Regarding the Accused's Submission No. 425, 23 September 2009, para.26.

1113 *Prosecutor v. Vojislav Šešelj*, Case No. IT-03-67-T, Registry Submission Pursuant to Rule 33(B) Regarding the Accused's Submission No. 425, 23 September 2009, para.25.

cision neglects to establish how, for instance, the Appellant will be permitted to communicate with outside lawyers or non-lawyers", it expressed the concern "that the Appellant will be allowed to have unsupervised communications with individuals about whom the International Tribunal has no knowledge".[1114] It was questioned "whether this concept of undercover counsel is reconcilable with the fundamental principle of a public hearing".[1115]

This view raises the matter of the concept of public proceedings and whether discussion of this principle may encompass, and if so, to what extent, the composition of a defence team, in particular in proceedings with self-represented accused. It is to be questioned whether this concept would in fact be endangered in case a *pro se* defendant appears alone before court, but is assisted by numerous legal advisors who are heavily involved in the preparation of the case. Even though this approach might be open for discussion from a public policy point of view, it may not raise as problematic concerns as it appears at first sight.

In the framework of ICTY jurisprudence and practice, accused will have the opportunity for privileged communications merely with a limited and supervised number of legal associates who have been recognised by the ICTY registry. Only recognised advisors will have access to confidential information concerning the case, and a defendant sharing confidential information with persons other than the recognised legal advisors may be subject to contempt proceedings.[1116] In case there are still concerns about the passing of information to unauthorised persons by a self-represented accused, communications which do not fall in the category of privileged communications

1114 *Prosecutor v. Momčilo Krajišnik*, Case No. IT-00-39-A, Decision on Momčilo Krajišnik's Request to Self-Represent, on Counsel's Motions in Relation to Appointment of *Amicus Curiae*, and on the Prosecution Motion of 16 February 2007, Fundamentally Dissenting Opinion of Judge Schomburg on the Right to Self-Representation, 11 May 2007, para.78.

1115 *Prosecutor v. Momčilo Krajišnik*, Case No. IT-00-39-A, Decision on Momčilo Krajišnik's Request to Self-Represent, on Counsel's Motions in Relation to Appointment of *Amicus Curiae*, and on the Prosecution Motion of 16 February 2007, Fundamentally Dissenting Opinion of Judge Schomburg on the Right to Self-Representation, 11 May 2007, para.78.

1116 *Cf. Prosecutor v. Vojislav Šešelj*, Case No. IT-03-67-PT, Decision on Submission Number 115, 16 June 2006; *Prosecutor v. Radovan Karadžić*, Case No. IT-95-5/18-PT, Decision on Accused Request for Judicial Review of the Registry Decision on the Assignment of Mr. Marko Sladojević as Legal Associate, 20 April 2009, para.15.

may be subject to monitoring by the relevant authority, as is the case for all detainees.[1117] The only difficulty that might be encountered in this context is the issue of enforcement of such confidentiality agreements.[1118] In light of the fact that information which is not confidential should be available to the public in any event, it appears difficult to find a valid basis for refusing people to offer (*pro bono*) assistance to defendants who conduct their defence in person on the basis of information accessible to the public.[1119] Financial constraints will not be an argument against such assistance since in general financial aid will be provided only to a limited number of assistants to a self-represented accused,[1120] number which is determined according to a strict scheme which takes into account the financial situation of the defendant, the complexity of the case, as well as other factors. Similarly, the open policies adopted by the ICTY registry with regard to the provision of legal aid to indigent self-represented accused[1121] will ensure further transparency at least with regard to recognised legal teams assisting *pro se* defendants. Bearing in mind that self-represented accused usually will require as much professional assistance as possible in order to present an effective and efficient defence case, objections on the basis of the concept of public proceedings against the number and work of legal associates may have to be balanced

---

1117 *See* ICTY, Rules Governing the Detention of Persons Awaiting Trial or Appeal Before the Tribunal or Otherwise Detained on Authority of the Tribunal (IT/38/Rev. 9), as amended on 21 July 2005, Rules 58-65; United Nations Detention Unit Regulations to Govern the Supervision of Visits to and Communications With Detainees (IT/98/Rev. 4), as amended August 2009; ICTR, Rules Covering the Detention of Persons Awaiting Trial or Appeal Before the Tribunal or Otherwise Detained on the Authority of the Tribunal, 05 June 1998, Articles 58-65; SCSL, Rules Governing the Detention of Persons Awaiting Trial or Appeal before the Special Court for Sierra Leone or Otherwise Detained on the Authority of the Special Court for Sierra Leone ("Rules of Detention"), as amended on 14 May 2005, Rules 40(A), 41(B), 44(A), (D), 46, 47, 55(A); ECCC, Rules Governing the Detention of Persons Awaiting Trial or Appeal before the Extraordinary Chambers in Cambodia ("Detention Facility Rules"), 17 December 2008, Rules 9, 14, 30(7)-(13).

1118 Patricia M. Wald, *Tyrants on Trial. Keeping Order in the Courtroom* (New York: Open Society Justice Institute) 2009, p.53.

1119 *Cf.* in this regard submission by *amicus curiae* in *Milošević*: *Prosecutor v. Slobodan Milošević*, Case No. IT-02-54-T, Hearing, 10 April 2002, T.2791.

1120 Remuneration Scheme for Persons Assisting Indigent Self-Represented Accused, 01 April 2010, Rev. 2, para.2, 3.

1121 *See* public information on the legal aid scheme of the ICTY available at http://www.icty.org/sid/163 (last accessed 17 November 2012).

carefully against any perceived advantages for all participants. In this regard, the impact on the concept of public proceedings is arguably rather minor insofar as it will be obvious to any reasonable observer that the scope and magnitude of international criminal proceedings make it impossible for self-represented accused to prepare and present their case without any assistance and professional legal advice.

Besides, as is evident from the preceding discussion, even *pro se* defendants themselves now openly recognise the importance of such professional assistance in the preparation of their case. The scope of the part played by legal associates which is in part explicitly provided for and in part openly condoned by chambers is similarly a clear signal that judges in international criminal proceedings have come to recognise that the overall goal in cases with self-represented accused should be that a defendant receives the best and as much support as possible in order to prepare and present an effective defence case – even though he or she opted for exercising the right to self-representation. This does not mean, however, that an accused having made that choice is placed in a position of being able to simply pick and choose the best aspects of both representation by counsel and self-representation. Rather, there are clear limitations put into place which leave no doubt that a self-represented accused is supposed to and in fact does act as his or her own defence counsel. This necessarily entails certain restrictions on the role played by legal associates above all in their contact with the court. Yet, the reasonably balanced approach of taking advantage of the professional expertise of such associates as defence counsel whenever it might further the fair and expeditious conduct of the proceedings ensures that accused receive the assistance required while still appreciating the fact that they took the conscious decision of acting as their own defence counsel.

E. The accused choosing to self-represent and their motivations

I. General views on potential motives of *pro se* defendants

The exercise of the right to self-representation largely depends on the attitude by the accused choosing to present his or her defence in person. Therefore, in order to put the practical repercussions on the proceedings as discussed above into context, this dissertation will briefly examine the reasons for which defendants in international criminal proceedings may decide to take on this burden. Bearing in mind the potential motivations advanced in general discussions or by the accused themselves may assist in assessing the actual and potential implications of the right to self-representation as currently exercised, as well as the necessity to modify the approach towards a personal defence in international criminal proceedings.

Considering that the motives of accused for choosing to self-represent in the first place are likely to equally inspire the defendant's conduct in the subsequent course of the proceedings, they may inform judicial considerations on limiting the right to self-representation on the basis of obstructive behaviour of the accused.[1122] Therefore, a discussion on the motivations to conduct one's defence in person is in order at this juncture which connects the initial recognition and exercise of a right to self-representation in international criminal proceedings with potential restrictions of that right at a later stage.

On a general level, it has been noted previously that the system of international criminal tribunals currently does not allow for an accused who is represented by counsel to address the judges outside the constraints of an unsworn statement or testimony under oath in his or her own case. Therefore, it appears intelligible why defendants may wish to have a somewhat more elaborate standing in presenting their case to international criminal tribunals.[1123]

Both similarities and specific differences in the potential and alleged reasons which motivate accused to conduct their defence in person can be found in proceedings with *pro se* defendants. It has to be borne in mind that despite the link between the right to self-representation before international criminal tribunals and delays, interruptions as well as disruptions of the proceedings, there are different examples of more cooperative accused which appear to fall outside a commonly known pattern of obstruction. In light of these divergences, it appears that the manner in which proceedings unfold will eventually above all depend on the cooperation – or lack thereof – of the accused in question. This willingness to collaborate by the defendant may in part be connected to the manner in which accused may attempt to

---

1122 *See, e.g., Prosecutor v. Vojislav Šešelj*, Case No. IT-03-67-PT, Decision on Assignment of Counsel, 21 August 2006, para.29: "The Chamber considers that statements and publications of the Accused before his arrival in The Hague may be examined in order to understand his behaviour while in custody and to assess his intentions and his likely conduct at trial."

1123 Wolfgang Schomburg, Development of Human Rights Before International Criminal Tribunals. A European Perspective, 17(2) *Croatian Annual of Criminal Law and Practice* 909 (2010), at 920.

implement the ideas which formed the basis for their decision to conduct their defence in person in the beginning.

There is some indication that self-represented accused are above all not convinced that any professional counsel would be capable of presenting a defence which would in their view be adequate.[1124] At the same time, accused may simply try to "correct" the record by showing which crimes, in their view, were committed by opposing parties in order to be blamed on them.[1125] It has been opined that self-represented defendants want to delay proceedings; use proceedings for their own gains; and "use self-representation in an attempt to criticize or embarrass the ICTY".[1126] Defendants may have very distinct intentions to appear – in every sense of the word – alone in the courtroom.[1127] In that regard, it has been submitted that motives which inspire in particular (former) political leaders to opt for the right to self-representation include the

> "desire to speak on their own behalf, a mistrust of others to represent their understanding of events, the wish to utilize the forensic trial process as a political podium from which to attack the judicial process and the political powers and

---

1124 Nina H.B. Jørgensen, The Right of the Accused to Self-Representation Before International Criminal Tribunals, 98 *The American Journal of International Law* 711 (2004), at 711; Patricia M. Wald, *Tyrants on Trial. Keeping Order in the Courtroom* (New York: Open Society Justice Institute) 2009, p.37; Nancy Amoury Combs, Legitimizing International Criminal Justice: The Importance of Process Control, 33 *Michigan Journal of International Law* 321 (2012), at 374-376.

1125 Mark Lewis, The Trial of Radovan Karadzic: The Accused Takes up his Own Defense, 01 November 2012, available at http://world.time.com/2012/11/01/the-trial-of-radovan-karadzic-the-accused-takes-up-his-own-defense/#ixzz2B3FabTJV (last accessed 02 November 2012): "[…] He has now begun his bid to prove that Bosnian Muslims shelled and shot at their own people during the siege of Sarajevo from 1992 to 1995. […] The tactic of pushing the blame for war crimes onto Muslims and painting forced deportations as an unfortunate side effect of civil war is evident in the latest in an avalanche of recent correspondence from the Karadzic camp."

1126 Nicole L. Camier, Controlling the Wrath of Self-Representation: The ICTY's Crucial Trial of Radovan Karadzic, 44 *Valparaiso University Law Review* 957 (2010), at 988-989.

1127 Michael P. Scharf, The Legacy of the Milosevic Trial, 37 *New England Law Review* 915 (2003), at 918; Michael P. Scharf/Christopher M. Rassi, Do Former Leaders have an International Right to Self-Representation in War Crimes Trials?, 20 *Ohio State Journal on Dispute Resolution* 3 (2005), at 4-6; Marko Milanović, The Arrest and Impending Trial of Radovan Karadžić, 58 *International and Comparative Law Quarterly* 212 (2009), at 217, 218.

> forces which reduced them from positions of power and leadership to detention and trial."[1128]

Looking at the manner in which self-represented accused conduct (cross-) examinations or their defence in general, it appears to be a common denominator that the defendants are not necessarily challenging the indictments in their substance, but rather resort to justify any actions, whether in particular charged or not, with political necessities or actions in self-defence in an attempt to achieve the best results for their people.[1129] Indeed, it is a recurrent scheme of *pro se* defendants to allege their peoples' right to defend themselves against attacks from opposing parties,[1130] without however addressing the question how this was to be considered as viable justification for any alleged crimes.

One of the factors motivating accused to conduct their defence in person has been considered to be their desire to address their own views to the international arena.[1131] In the words of former ICTY Judge Wald:

> "[o]n a psychological level, these leaders have strong egos and are used to controlling those around them; they have confidence in their talents to continue that control even after arrest."[1132]

1128 Gideon Boas, Self-Representation Before the ICTY. A Case for Reform, 9 *Journal of International Criminal Justice* 53 (2011), at 54. *See also* Mirjan Damaška, Reflections on Fairness in International Criminal Justice, 10 *Journal of International Criminal Justice* 611 (2012), at 617: "If defendants were routinely permitted to mount their own defence, charismatic leaders in the role of defendants could easily use trials as the stage in propagating causes harmful to the promotion of human rights culture, or in manipulating trials for some other reasons [fn. omitted]. Even their skilfully orchestrated questions on cross-examination could have this detrimental effect."

1129 *Cf.* Patricia M. Wald, *Tyrants on Trial. Keeping Order in the Courtroom* (New York: Open Society Justice Institute) 2009, p.10, 12, 37.

1130 *See e.g. Prosecutor v. Slobodan Milošević*, Case No. IT-02-54-T, Defence Opening Statement, 14 February 2002, T.253-254; Defence Opening Statement, 15 February 2002, T.352-353, 409; Hearing, 04 February 2003, T.15552-15556; Hearing, 16 December 2003, T.30546-30548; Hearing, 28 January 2004, T.31651; *Prosecutor v. Radovan Karadžić*, Case No. IT-95-5/18-T, Defence Opening Statement, 01 March 2010, T.814-816; Hearing, 08 October 2010, T.7559-7561; Hearing, 28 October 2010, T.8499-8500.

1131 Göran Sluiter, Karadžić on Trial. Two Procedural Problems, 6 *Journal of International Criminal Justice* 617 (2008), at 618.

1132 Patricia M. Wald, *Tyrants on Trial. Keeping Order in the Courtroom* (New York: Open Society Justice Institute) 2009, p.37. *See also* Mikhail Wladimiroff, Former

II. Motivations expressed by self-represented accused

Some accused justified their choice of self-representation at least in part with the idea that they were on the ground at the relevant time and thus know best about the facts to be adjudicated.[1133] While the contribution of defendants to factual matters in the proceedings can indeed be significant, this justification does not exclude models of active participation by the accused which would allow for the factual knowledge and expertise to be shared without compelling a defendant into the decision to self-represent. Moreover, it is to be noted that of the five accused who acted *pro se* at some stage in their proceedings before the ICTY, two – Slobodan Milošević and Vojislav Šešelj – themselves graduated in law.[1134]

Slobodan Milošević left no doubt from the very beginning that he did not recognise the ICTY and therefore would not need any counsel assigned to represent his interests before it.[1135] Commentators saw the accused in this case as clearly pursuing a political objective and a general – not with his charges related – agenda considering the way in which he was running his own trial.[1136] The defendant himself stated that he considered his trial to be a political one, and that this was the reason why he could not be replaced by counsel in conducting his defence.[1137] For the accused, the proceedings were

---

Heads of State on Trial, 38 *Cornell International Law Journal* 949 (2005), at 965-966.

1133 *See e.g. Prosecutor v. Vojislav Šešelj*, Case No. IT-03-67-PT, Request of Dr Vojislav Šešelj for the Revocation of the Decision to Assign Standby Counsel (Submission No. 125), 03 January 2006 (filed: 16 January 2006), p.7; Hearing, 05 May 2011, T.17002; *Prosecutor v. Radovan Karadžić*, Case No. IT-95-5/18-PT, Status Conference, 17 September 2008 T.46; Status Conference, 19 January 2009, T.93; Status Conference, 08 September 2009, T.459; Submission on the Commencement of Trial, 21 October 2009, p.4; Hearing, 09 June 2010, T.3534.

1134 Nina H.B. Jørgensen, The Right of the Accused to Self-Representation Before International Criminal Tribunals, 98 *The American Journal of International Law* 711 (2004), at 711.

1135 *Prosecutor v. Slobodan Milošević*, Case No. IT-99-37-I, Initial Appearance, 03 July 2001, T.2. *See also Prosecutor v. Slobodan Milošević*, Case No. IT-02-54-T, Hearing, 10 April 2002, T.2806; Hearing, 11 November 2002, T.12837.

1136 *Cf.* Gideon Boas, Moving on From Milošević, 75 *European Lawyer* 54 (2008), at 55; Tom Dannenbaum, The Milošević Trial: Lessons for the Conduct of International Criminal Proceedings (Review of Gideon Boas), 33 *Yale Journal of International Law* 513 (2008), at 514-515.

1137 *See e.g. Prosecutor v. Slobodan Milošević*, Case No. IT-02-54-T, Hearing, 11 November 2002, T.12835.

a "farce" in which he could only take part by telling what he considered to be the truth.[1138] For him, the truth about the events in the Balkans had to be told.[1139] Given the considerable attention given to the proceedings at least in the beginning by not only the media but more importantly by a significant amount of the public in the former Yugoslavia,[1140] the scene was set for "Milosevic's frequent courtroom grandstanding".[1141] Comparisons were drawn between the courtroom behaviour of Slobodan Milošević and Saddam Hussein, the latter of whom was considered to apparently have learned from the way in which the former ran his proceedings.[1142]

Of note is also the resolve of Slobodan Milošević to proceed *pro se* despite the obvious negative effects on his own health, as can be seen from his statement that "at no price whatsoever would I leave the fight I'm fighting here and from this political process – trial".[1143]

Vojislav Šešelj equally made clear from the start that he would "destroy" the ICTY and allegedly at least in the beginning used the proceedings as political platform *inter alia* for his election campaigns.[1144] He repeatedly claimed that he had surrendered to the ICTY in order to "beat" or "vanquish"

1138 *Prosecutor v. Slobodan Milošević*, Case No. IT-02-54-T, Pre-trial Conference, 25 July 2002, T.8632-8633. *See also* Hearing, 01 September 2004, T.32327.

1139 *See e.g. Prosecutor v. Slobodan Milošević*, Case No. IT-99-37-AR73/IT-01-50-AR73/IT-01-51-AR73, Interlocutory Appeal Hearing, 30 January 2002, T.352/213/180; *Prosecutor v. Slobodan Milošević*, Case No. IT-02-54-AR73.7, Appeals Hearing, 21 October 2004, T.53.

1140 Bojan Toncic, Serbia: Milosevic Trial Grips Nation, BCR Issue 318, 14 February 2002, available at http://iwpr.net/report-news/serbia-milosevic-trial-grips-nation (last accessed 17 November 2012); Michael P. Scharf, The Legacy of the Milosevic Trial, 37 *New England Law Review* 915 (2003), at 930-931.

1141 Human Rights Watch, *The Balkans: Weighing the Evidence. Lessons from the Milosevic Trial*, Volume 18, No.10(D), December 2006, p.1.

1142 Jerrold M. Post/Lara K. Panis, Tyranny on Trial: Personality and Courtroom Conduct of Defendants Slobodan Milošević and Saddam Hussein, 38 *Cornell Journal of International Law* 823 (2005), at 829-833.

1143 *Prosecutor v. Slobodan Milošević*, Case No. IT-02-54-T, Hearing, 11 November 2002, T.12835.

1144 *Cf. Prosecutor v. Vojislav Šešelj*, Case No. IT-03-67-PT, Prosecution's Motion for Order Appointing Counsel to Assist Vojislav Šešelj With His Defence, 28 February 2003, para.9 and fn.18; Decision on the Prosecution's Motion for Order Appointing Counsel to Assist Vojislav Šešelj with his Defence, 09 May 2003, para.22 and fn.46.

it.[1145] While the defendant did state that he intended to reveal the truth about the events in former Yugoslavia, he equally remarked that he would do so "in the interest of Serbia and Serbian national interests".[1146] In this context, the accused even expressed his regret that the death sentence was not foreseen at the ICTY, since otherwise he could "proudly, with dignity, upright as my friend Saddam Hussein [...] put a final seal on my ideology. It would become immortal".[1147] In a similar vein, the defendant claimed that he was not interested in the outcome of his trial proceedings, but rather that he would "win in the eyes of the public" and "come out of this process with glory".[1148] The accused further appeared to be convinced that he would be best positioned to present his own defence since, according to his own assessment, he "never met a better lawyer than I am in my whole life".[1149] The defendant underscored on numerous occasions his opinion that as a law professor and being directly concerned, he was himself best suited to conduct his defence.[1150]

An additional factor to be taken into account is the fact that the accused in *Šešelj* voluntarily surrendered to the ICTY upon issuance of the indictment

---

1145 *Prosecutor v. Vojislav Šešelj*, Case No. IT-03-67-PT, Status Conference, 05 June 2007, T.1214; Status Conference, 17 August 2007, T.1361.

1146 *Prosecutor v. Vojislav Šešelj*, Case No. IT-03-67-PT, Request of the Accused for Trial Chamber II to Revoke the Decision to Assign Standby Counsel (Submission No. 84), 07 March 2005 (filed: 06 April 2005), para.1.1.

1147 *Prosecutor v. Vojislav Šešelj*, Case No. IT-03-67-T, Statement of the Accused, 08 November 2007, T.1946.

1148 *Prosecutor v. Vojislav Šešelj*, Case No. IT-03-67-PT, Status Conference, 17 August 2007, T.1400. *See also* Status Conference, 23 October 2007, T.1619.

1149 *Prosecutor v. Vojislav Šešelj*, Case No. IT-03-67-PT, Status Conference, 25 March 2003, T.66.

1150 *Prosecutor v. Vojislav Šešelj*, Case No. IT-03-67-PT, Defence Motion for Provisional Release, 14 June 2004 (filed: 24 June 2004), para.2, 12, 18; Request of the Accused to Revoke the Ruling of the Trial Chamber to Appoint Standby Counsel (Submission No. 81), 04 March 2005 (filed: 22 March 2005), p.4; Request of the Accused for Trial Chamber II to Revoke the Ruling to Assign Standby Counsel (Submission No. 82), 05 March 2005 (filed: 06 April 2005), p.4-6: "... So, God has given him brilliant powers of reasoning. And instead of verifying these superior powers of the accused, Trial Chamber II of the International Tribunal raises itself above God, scorns God's will and assigns him standby counsel. What is too much is too much."; Request of the Accused for Trial Chamber II to Revoke the Decision to Assign Standby Counsel (Submission No. 84), 07 March 2005 (filed: 06 April 2005), p.9.

against him,[1151] the underlying reasons for which one can only speculate about. In the prosecution's view, the accused did so motivated "by his acute sense of self-publicity, by his determination to undermine the work of this Tribunal and by his belief that the evidence against him would not be sufficient",[1152] as well as "by carefully calculated self-interest".[1153]

Radovan Karadžić appeared to adopt a reasoning similar to that of Slobodan Milošević, when he remarked during his initial appearance that he would defend himself before the ICTY like against a natural catastrophe.[1154] According to the defendant, he chose to present his defence in person since "the factual situation is so complicated that it can only be understood and presented by someone who had actually participated in it from the first day to the last".[1155] In a subsequent attempt to set out his defence theory, the accused appeared to suggest that in his view, he needed "to prove who wanted the war in the first place and how the war happened".[1156] The accused asserted on several occasions that he would use his proceedings to correct the record of events that had been established by the ICTY up to that point and that this would involve correction of the conviction of some former accused before the court.[1157] As put by the accused:

1151 *Prosecutor v. Vojislav Šešelj*, Case No. IT-03-67-PT, Order for Detention on Remand, 26 February 2003, p.2.

1152 *Prosecutor v. Vojislav Šešelj*, Case No. IT-03-67-PT, Prosecution's Response to "Defence Motion for Provisional Release", 07 July 2004, para.15.

1153 *Prosecutor v. Vojislav Šešelj*, Case No. IT-03-67-PT, Prosecution's Response to "Defence Motion for Provisional Release", 07 July 2004, para.16.

1154 *Prosecutor v. Radovan Karadžić*, Case No. IT-95-5/18-I, Initial Appearance, 31 July 2008, T.20: "Regardless of what I think about this institution, with all due respect to you personally, I will defend myself before this institution as I would defend myself before any natural catastrophe, to which I also deny the right to attack me."

1155 *Prosecutor v. Radovan Karadžić*, Case No. IT-95-5/18-PT, Submission on the Commencement of Trial, 21 October 2009, p.4.

1156 *Prosecutor v. Radovan Karadžić*, Case No. IT-95-5/18-T, Hearing, 01 November 2011, T.20685.

1157 *See e.g. Prosecutor v. Radovan Karadžić*, Case No. IT-95-5/18-PT, Status Conference, 17 September 2008, T.43; Status Conference, 23 July 2009, T.389-390; *Prosecutor v. Radovan Karadžić*, Case No. IT-95-5/18-T, Hearing, 03 November 2009, T.705; Hearing, 19 May 2010, T.2380; Hearing, 08 February 2011, T.11295. *See also Prosecutor v. Radovan Karadžić*, Case No. IT-95-5/18-T, Response to Prosecution Motion for Extension of Rule 68 Deadline, 07 December 2010, para.4; Hearing, 24 August 2011, T.17809.

> "[…] if we are going to go to trial, then there are going to be reviews of other trials where innocent men were convicted. I will be able to prove that they were convicted as innocent men as I defend myself here in these proceedings."[1158]

The trial chamber took these remarks as occasion to remind the accused that it was his task only to challenge the evidence presented by the prosecution and to concentrate on the specific facts of his own case, but not to attempt to retry anything that had been dealt with in the course of other trials before the tribunal.[1159] However, the accused reiterated his approach to the defence case and selection of defence witnesses as being based on his clear position that he would challenge everything:[1160]

> "Indeed, as Commander in Chief of the army and civilian leader of the police, Dr. Karadzic does not have the luxury of trying to deflect blame for the crimes to other organs, as most of the accused at the Tribunal have done. […] Dr. Karadzic's defence requires a frontal attack on the prosecution's case […]".[1161]

1158 *Prosecutor v. Radovan Karadžić*, Case No. IT-95-5/18-T, Defence Opening Statement, 02 March 2010, T.992-993.

1159 *Prosecutor v. Radovan Karadžić*, Case No. IT-95-5/18-PT, Status Conference, 23 July 2009, T.390; *Prosecutor v. Radovan Karadžić*, Case No. IT-95-5/18-T, Hearing, 03 November 2009, T.703; Decision on Appointment of Counsel and Order on Further Trial Proceedings, 05 November 2009, para.23.

1160 *Prosecutor v. Radovan Karadžić*, Case No. IT-95-5/18-PT, Status Conference, 02 April 2009, T.180: "[…] Have you not considered whether there are elements in there that don't really require to be challenged? […] For the time being, I only have in mind the weather; that I'm not going to challenge, but we'll see how things evolve over time. If it's sunny, I'm not going to challenge that. I will agree that it was sunny, yes."

1161 *Prosecutor v. Radovan Karadžić*, Case No. IT-95-5/18-AR73.10, Appeal from Decision on Duration of Defence Case, 11 October 2012 (filed: 12 October 2012), para.43-45.

According to the accused, he equally wanted the truth about the conflict to be established[1162] and considered not to be defending himself, but rather "the people over there who have suffered".[1163] According to the accused:

> "Instead of being accused for the events in our civil war, I should have been rewarded for all the good things I've done; [...] As time passes, this truth will be stronger and stronger and the accusations and the propaganda, the lies and hatred, will get weaker and weaker.[1164] [...] Gentlemen, the truth is on our side and it will only grow stronger. We did everything in our power to avoid the war and to minimise the consequences and the damages. There is no statute of limitations that will run out on that and lies are subject to statute of limitations and we will live to see it."[1165]

On the other hand, some accused might see no other possibility than deciding to conduct their defence in person when they are not assigned the legal associates which they had selected as defence counsel. To be mentioned in this regard is Momčilo Krajišnik who, when he initially requested to proceed *pro se* during the trial proceedings, indicated that his choice was a fallback position rather than firm conviction to exercise his right to self-representation.[1166]

In a similar vein, Zdravko Tolimir during his initial appearance informed the court that he would represent himself during the initial stages of the

---

1162 *Prosecutor v. Radovan Karadžić*, Case No. IT-95-5/18-AR73.5, Appeal of Decision on Commencement of Trial, 25 September 2009, para.2, 85; Reply Brief: Appeal of Decision on Commencement of Trial, 12 October 2009, para.38, 40. *See also Prosecutor v. Radovan Karadžić*, Case No. IT-95-5/18-T, Letter to Bosnia, 30 October 2012, p.3: "[...] I wish to ask you about your instructions to Bosnian Muslims to depart from Trebinje to make it look like the Bosnian Serbs were conducting ethnic cleansing [...] This is important to my defence because such tactics of blaming the Serbs for acts of the Muslims have spilled over from the war to the courtroom. I am now being charged with crimes that the Bosnian Muslims themselves committed in order to blame the Serbs and obtain international intervention. I need your testimony to clarify these matters for my Trial Chamber."

1163 *Prosecutor v. Radovan Karadžić*, Case No. IT-95-5/18-PT, Status Conference, 17 September 2008, T.43.

1164 *Prosecutor v. Radovan Karadžić*, Case No. IT-95-5/18-T, Defence Rule 84*bis* Statement, 16 October 2012, T.28849-28850.

1165 *Prosecutor v. Radovan Karadžić*, Case No. IT-95-5/18-T, Defence Rule 84*bis* Statement, 16 October 2012, T.28881.

1166 *Cf. Prosecutor v. Momčilo Krajišnik*, Case No. IT-00-39-T, Hearing, 25 May 2005, T.13399; Procedural Hearing, 26 May 2005, T.13420.

proceedings until counsel was assigned.[1167] The accused reiterated this choice at a further appearance,[1168] while however indicating that he was merely acting on his own because the ICTY registry did not accept the lawyer he requested to have appointed as his defence counsel.[1169] In light of the accused's remarks that he was merely defending himself pending assignment of counsel of his choice, the pre-trial judge went at great lengths to make clear to the defendant which consequences his choice would have and thus should not be taken lightly.[1170] Prompted by the accused's reiteration of his position that he "did not elect to defend [himself] because [he] wanted to do so but because the Registry wanted to impose counsel", the pre-trial judge once again inquired with him whether he did indeed consider everything his choice would entail.[1171] At a later stage, the accused appeared to indicate that he was the only person to know the facts of interest to the proceedings, and that he wished the truth to be established.[1172]

To be recalled is the initial situation in *Krajišnik*, where the accused equally had chosen a counsel not accepted by the ICTY registry and thus elected to present his defence in person. However, his request was denied at that point in time. Given that the accused in *Tolimir* upon further inquiry

---

1167 *Prosecutor v. Zdravko Tolimir*, Case No. IT-05-88/2-I, Initial Appearance, 04 June 2007, T.2. *See also* Submission on the Prosecution Request to Question the Accused, 06 July 2007 (filed: 12 July 2007), para.4.

1168 *Prosecutor v. Zdravko Tolimir*, Case No. IT-05-88/2-I, Further Appearance, 03 July 2007, T.21.

1169 *Prosecutor v. Zdravko Tolimir*, Case No. IT-05-88/2-I, Further Appearance, 03 July 2007, T.22-23, 33-34, 49. *See also* Submission by the Accused for Assistance of the Trial Chamber on Appointment of Permanent Counsel, 06 July 2007 (filed: 13 July 2007); Submission by the Accused to the Registrar for Leave to Conduct his Own Defence or to Appoint Counsel of his Own Choosing Pursuant to Article 21.4(d), and Rule 45(F) and Amended Rule 62(C) of the Rules, 06 August 2007 (filed: 10 August 2007).

1170 *Prosecutor v. Zdravko Tolimir*, Case No. IT-05-88/2-PT, Status Conference, 14 September 2007, T.54-57.

1171 *Prosecutor v. Zdravko Tolimir*, Case No. IT-05-88/2-PT, Status Conference, 14 September 2007, T.58.

1172 *Prosecutor v. Zdravko Tolimir*, Case No. IT-05-88/2-PT, Submission of the Accused to the Appeals and Pre-trial Chambers to Dismiss the Legally Unfounded Prosecution Motion Requesting Imposition of Counsel for the Accused Who is Conducting his own Defence, and Request that the Prosecution Withdraw its Motion, 06 May 2008 (filed: 19 May 2008), p.9; Response to the Prosecution's Motion Requesting the Appointment of Permanent Counsel for the Accused Tolimir, 02 June 2008 (filed: 05 June 2008), para.31.

did confirm his choice of self-representation, and further taking into account that he had voiced this choice from the beginning of the pre-trial proceedings, and not at some stage in the middle of the trial proceedings like Momčilo Krajišnik, the situations of the two accused in the end might not have been exactly comparable.

The examples outlined above illustrate that in general the motives prompting accused to conduct their defence in person are as varied as the personalities of the defendants. At the same time, however, there appears to be a certain similarity in argument specifically when considering the views expressed by accused who – except for one – used to be more or less high-level politicians at the time of the pertinent events. The specific motives for demanding a right to self-representation as presented by the defendants themselves provide indication as to why the proceedings thus far have been replete with complications.

A modified approach to a right to defend oneself in person would arguably render the running of international criminal proceedings less dependent on these motivations and thus on the whims of their subjects.

F. Preliminary observations

The second chapter of this dissertation has revealed that the right to self-representation on the international criminal level is not an issue easily ignored.

The judicial interpretation of the general right to self-representation leaves no doubt as to the general acknowledgement that a defendant in international criminal proceedings should be given the opportunity to present his or her own defence. However, the standards governing the practical exercise of the right to self-representation are not as uniformly established as – at first sight – the right itself. While the initial approach taken in the proceedings against Slobodan Milošević appeared to be straight-forward, practice showed itself to be more complex. The difference with regard to the exercise of the right to self-representation in the trial or appeals phase of a case is only a starting point. A multitude of practical issues related to the management of proceedings which impact both on the rights of accused and of other participants in proceedings is bound to follow. The intricacies in question include the possibility of self-incrimination by an accused presenting his or her defence; the issue of lack of experience in legal matters and managing criminal proceedings; potential language barriers in case the defendant does not fully understand and/or speak the working language(s) of the tribunal before which he or she is tried, probability which might only be increased before the ICC; as well as the manner in which resources are allocated to and used by the accused.

Even if a *pro se* defendant is assisted by professional legal advisors, the extent of their influence on the proceedings remains uncertain and will fluctuate from case to case. Considering that the actual motives of self-represented accused to present their defence in person invites speculation rather than certain assessment, the role to be played by legal associates will be equally varied. Thus, in order to define its limits it is necessary to consider decisions of chambers and submissions by participants, above all the defence, bearing in mind the specific circumstances of each case. While on the one hand this provides for the flexibility which is required to deal with newly arising issues, it creates on the other hand certain insecurity. This effect might be enhanced by the fact that the role of legal advisors will entirely depend on the attitude exhibited by the defendant concerned and the practical exercise of the right to self-representation. In turn, this may lead to the proceedings becoming dependant on the cooperation and good will of an accused who, through personal involvement and stalling techniques potentially recommended by professional defence counsel acting as legal associates, will be in a position to torpedo the conduct of the proceedings at any time.

Despite several years of experience with cases involving *pro se* defendants especially before the ICTY, inconsistencies and contradictions in litigations which are directly related to the exercise of the right to defend oneself and the status of the accused remain. As will be seen in the following chapter, those divergences are even more accentuated in the context of potential restrictions of the right to self-representation. Consequently, it will be crucial for any future cases involving *pro se* defendants, in particular before the ICC, to first become aware of these inconsistencies in order to then be in a position to overcome such issues by rectifying current flaws and adopting new solutions.

CHAPTER THREE. Restrictions on the exercise of the right to self-representation

A. Factors that may be considered when restricting self-representation

The preceding chapter has outlined under which conditions and to which extent the right to self-representation is recognised before international criminal tribunals, as well as the actual and potential repercussions of its exercise on the proceedings.

Against this background, it is equally significant to examine the circumstances in which this practical exercise of the right to self-represent may be restricted or revoked. A significant amount of jurisprudence has been generated evolving around questions of whether, how, and pursuant to which conditions counsel may be assigned to self-represented accused. At the same time, however, decisions issued in this context do not necessarily and coherently clarify the matters at stake. This section will attempt to highlight the problems and respective solutions considered in particular in proceedings before the ICTY in order to analyse the potential ramifications on current and future international criminal procedure.

One of the subject matters giving rise to discussion is the fact that any imposition or assignment of defence counsel is likely to occur against the expressed will of the accused. As outlined before, the ICTY appeals chamber underlined the presumptive nature of the right to self-representation as an "indispensable cornerstone of justice".[1173] However, it equally found that while indisputable, the right to self-representation was not absolute and thus may be subject to limitations when certain conditions are met.[1174]

1173 *Prosecutor v. Slobodan Milošević*, Case No. IT-02-54-AR73.7, Decision on Interlocutory Appeal of the Trial Chamber's Decision on the Assignment of Counsel, 01 November 2004, para.11. *See also Prosecutor v. Vojislav Šešelj*, Case No. IT-03-67-AR73.3, Decision on Appeal Against the Trial Chamber's Decision on Assignment of Counsel, 20 October 2006, para.11.

1174 *Prosecutor v. Slobodan Milošević*, Case No. IT-02-54-AR73.7, Decision on Interlocutory Appeal of the Trial Chamber's Decision on the Assignment of Counsel, 01 November 2004, para.12-18; *Prosecutor v. Vojislav Šešelj*, Case No. IT-03-67-AR73.3, Decision on Appeal Against the Trial Chamber's Decision on Assignment of Counsel, 20 October 2006, para.8. *See also* for the application of these principles

In order to legitimately impose restrictions on the exercise of the right to self-representation, years of pertinent jurisprudence have established five successive steps that may be followed by chambers in their assessment.[1175] These factors include: (1) the accused acting in an obstructionist fashion, namely disruptive behaviour that substantially and persistently obstructs the proper and expeditious conduct of trial;[1176] (2) a prior warning clearly stating that if such behaviour persists counsel will be assigned, a warning which must be explicit in explaining the conduct in question and specifying the consequences;[1177] (3) the application by the chamber concerned of the "clean slate principle", *i.e.* the need to establish additional obstructionist behaviour subsequent to the warning;[1178] (4) the observance of the proportionality principle, so that the restriction will only be acceptable if it is suitable, necessary, and its degree and scope remain in a reasonable relationship to the en-

---

Prosecutor v. Radovan Karadžić, Case No. IT-95-5/18-T, Decision on Appointment of Counsel and Order on Further Trial Proceedings, 05 November 2009, para.15-16, 21-24.

1175 For the application of these conditions *see e.g. Procureur c/ Vojislav Šešelj*, Affaire n° IT-03-67-T, Version Publique de la « Décision Consolidée Relative à l'Imposition du Conseil, l'Ajournement et la Requête de l'Accusation sur les Heures Supplémentaires Avec en Annexe l'Opinion Individuelle du Juge Antonetti Président de la Chambre », 24 novembre 2009, para.53-57.

1176 *Prosecutor v. Slobodan Milošević*, Case No. IT-02-54-AR73.7, Decision on Interlocutory Appeal of the Trial Chamber's Decision on the Assignment of Counsel, 01 November 2004, para.13. *See also Prosecutor v. Vojislav Šešelj*, Case No. IT-03-67-AR73.3, Decision on Appeal Against the Trial Chamber's Decision on Assignment of Counsel, 20 October 2006, para.20; *Prosecutor v. Radovan Karadžić*, Case No. IT-95-5/18-T, Decision on Appointment of Counsel and Order on Further Trial Proceedings, 05 November 2009, para.15, 21.

1177 *Prosecutor v. Vojislav Šešelj*, Case No. IT-03-67-AR73.3, Decision on Appeal Against the Trial Chamber's Decision on Assignment of Counsel, 20 October 2006, para.26. *See also Prosecutor v. Radovan Karadžić*, Case No. IT-95-5/18-T, Decision on Appointment of Counsel and Order on Further Trial Proceedings, 05 November 2009, para.15, 22.

1178 *Prosecutor v. Vojislav Šešelj*, Case No. IT-03-67-AR73.3, Decision on Appeal Against the Trial Chamber's Decision on Assignment of Counsel, 20 October 2006, para.26; *Prosecutor v. Vojislav Šešelj*, Case No. IT-03-67-AR73.4, Decision on Appeal Against the Trial Chamber's Decision (No.2) on Assignment of Counsel, 08 December 2006, para.27; *Procureur c/ Vojislav Šešelj*, Affaire n° IT-03-67-T, Version Publique de la « Décision Consolidée Relative à l'Imposition d'un Conseil, l'Ajournement, et la Requête de l'Accusation sur les Heures Supplémentaires Avec en Annexe l'Opinion Individuelle du Juge Antonetti Président de la Chambre », 24 novembre 2009, para.55.

visaged target, and if it is the least intrusive instrument;[1179] and finally (5) the obligation to ensure that the accused is heard on the matter.[1180]

Yet, practice has revealed that even if it is determined that these cumulative conditions have been fulfilled, and counsel is assigned or appointed in some role, further problems may ensue relating to the actual procedure to be applied when choosing a counsel that is to be assigned or appointed to a defendant's case.[1181]

The discussion in this chapter will not exclusively be concerned with the imposition of counsel upon an accused in order for counsel to represent the latter's interests, *i.e.* situations in which the right to self-representation is in fact rescinded. Rather, this chapter will analyse the conditions under which the right has been and can be restricted without however being revoked completely.

To set the scene for further discussion, the five successive and cumulative factors mentioned above are to be considered. Not all of these aspects are consistently or explicitly referred to in decisions germane to the analysis. Therefore, only the most prevalent and contentious subject matters will be analysed in further detail below.

1179 *Prosecutor v. Slobodan Milošević*, Case No. IT-02-54-AR73.7, Decision on Interlocutory Appeal of the Trial Chamber's Decision on the Assignment of Counsel, 01 November 2004, para.17-18. *See also Procureur c/ Vojislav Šešelj*, Affaire n° IT-03-67-T, Version Publique de la « Décision Consolidée Relative à l'Imposition d'un Conseil, l'Ajournement, et la Requête de l'Accusation sur les Heures Supplémentaires Avec en Annexe l'Opinion Individuelle du Juge Antonetti Président de la Chambre », 24 novembre 2009, para.77 (referring to *Prosecutor v. Limaj et al.*, Case No. IT-03-66-AR65, Decision on Fatmir Limaj's Request for Provisional Release, 31 October 2003, para.13); *Prosecutor v. Radovan Karadžić*, Case No. IT-95-5/18-T, Decision on Appointment of Counsel and Order on Further Trial Proceedings, 05 November 2009, para.16, 25.

1180 *Prosecutor v. Vojislav Šešelj*, Case No. IT-03-67-AR73.3, Decision on Appeal Against the Trial Chamber's Decision on Assignment of Counsel, 20 October 2006, para.52 fn.136. *See also Prosecutor v. Radovan Karadžić*, Case No. IT-95-5/18-T, Hearing, 03 November 2009 (*cf.* T.674: "This is an administrative hearing to discuss the manner in which the trial will proceed."); Decision on Appointment of Counsel and Order on Further Trial Proceedings, 05 November 2009, para.22.

1181 *See* arguments by the defence in *Prosecutor v. Radovan Karadžić*, Case No. IT-95-5/18-T, Motion to Vacate Appointment of Richard Harvey, 04 December 2009; and *Prosecutor v. Radovan Karadžić*, Case No. IT-95-5/18-AR73.6, Appeal from Decision on Motion to Vacate Appointment of Richard Harvey, 19 January 2010.

I. Obstruction of the proceedings

The first criterion – substantial and persistent obstruction or disruption of the proceedings through behaviour of the accused – appears to prompt the most problematic questions. This is plausible insofar as establishment of obstructionist behaviour will eventually be the trigger for imposing restrictions on the exercise of the right to self-representation.

Thus far, this particular aspect has been considered to encompass a number of divergent circumstances, including both intentional and unintentional disruption of the proceedings. Specifically, the full panoply of topics spans from ill-health of the accused, over more or less clearly disruptive behaviour to the merely theoretical potential impact of the exercise of the right to self-representation on future proceedings in general. At the same time, the benchmark to be reached in order to establish "substantial and persistent" obstruction of the proceedings has been set at rather different levels.

Therefore, given that jurisprudence and practice suggest that the criteria are not as clear-cut as they seem at first sight,[1182] it will have to be examined which conditions for the assignment of counsel are in fact applicable. For example, Slobodan Milošević's situation would not necessarily fall within the parameters set out above, as he – if one does not take into account his tendency to conduct lengthy, sometimes irrelevant, cross-examinations – did not act in a fashion as obstructive as it could be observed throughout the entire proceedings of Vojislav Šešelj. In a similar vein, the threshold to appoint counsel in *Karadžić* – albeit without touching the exercise of his right to self-representation – does not seem to have been as high as the one applied in *Šešelj*. Considering on the other hand the decision in *Norman* before the SCSL, the accused did not even have the opportunity to obstruct or disrupt the proceedings even if he had wanted to do so, given that his request to proceed *pro se* was aborted already in the beginning.

Obvious obstruction by an accused is still one of the more unambiguous factors which can eventually lead to curtailment of the exercise of the right to self-representation. However, the limit up to which disruptions may still be acceptable to a chamber, and beyond which restrictions are likely to be imposed, can vary considerably. At least it seems as if *not* acting in a disruptive manner will not be able to guarantee an accused any advantages compared

1182 *See* in this regard Rachel K. Jones, Untangling the Right to Self-Representation in the International Criminal Tribunal for the Former Yugoslavia, 43 *Georgia Law Review* 1285 (2009), at 1313-1316.

to obstructive defendants, as he or she then simply had "not behaved in a manner other than that expected of both a counsel and an accused person".[1183]

The divergence in the approaches to restricting the right to self-representation provoke the question if they can be reconciled or how they might impact on future proceedings for example before the ICC. Specific and properly defined standards are necessary to avoid procedural insecurity when it comes to limit a right supposedly as fundamental as the right to self-representation. Yet, a consistent approach followed too rigidly is not always the best option. As pointed out by the appeals chamber in *Karadžić*, a

> "more fluid and individualized approach to the appointment of standby counsel in cases of self-representation is amply justified by the fact that the reasons for and specific parameters of each appointment will vary considerably."[1184]

With flexibility standing against insecurity, the question arises which approach should be adopted in future proceedings, in particular before the ICC. It has been suggested that if ICC judges consider the defendant's right to a fair trial threatened by an ineffective defence due to the accused's self-representation, a solution well established before international criminal tribunals would be the appointment of standby counsel.[1185] This leads back to the discussion of whether an accused, by opting for self-representation, is in a position to knowingly and validly waive his right to a fair trial. However, this proposal does not solve the issue of the thresholds to be applied, not the least since the concept of an "ineffective defence" is not any less tenuous. In order to be able to further assess which steps should be taken in future proceedings, it is therefore necessary to first examine which factors were in fact determinative for limiting the right to self-representation in past trials.

1183 *Prosecutor v. Radovan Karadžić*, Case No. IT-95-5/18-T, Decision on Appointment of Counsel and Order of Further Trial Proceedings, 05 November 2009, para.21.

1184 *Prosecutor v. Radovan Karadžić*, Case No. IT-95-5/18-AR73.6, Decision on Radovan Karadžić's Appeal from Decision on Motion to Vacate Appointment of Richard Harvey, 12 February 2010, para.35.

1185 William A. Schabas, *An Introduction to the International Criminal Court* (Cambridge: Cambridge University Press) 3rd edition 2007, p.291.

1. Unintentional obstruction

a. The case of Slobodan Milošević

In *Milošević*, the trial chamber decided to assign counsel to the accused at the end of the prosecution case in light of the continuous negative impact of the defendant's state of health on the conduct of the proceedings.[1186] The trial chamber examined the history of the accused's health and the repercussions of the proceedings on his health and *vice versa*.[1187] The judges reached the conclusion that in case the accused continued to conduct his defence in person, his health would be further jeopardised, and even his life put at risk, or the proceedings would have to be interrupted in the future depending on the state of health of the defendant.[1188] According to the trial chamber, this situation endangered the integrity of the proceedings, so that "[n]o court, mindful of its duty to ensure a fair and expeditious trial and its inherent responsibility to preserve the integrity of the proceedings, could countenance this".[1189] It is important to note that the trial chamber based its decision solely on the concern to ensure a fair and expeditious trial for the accused, taking due account of the defendant's well-being,[1190] rather than any alleged intentional disruption of the proceedings by potential non-adherence to the medical regime by the accused.[1191]

Presenting arguments on behalf of the defendant – albeit without any instructions from the latter –, assigned counsel submitted before the appeals chamber:

1186 *Prosecutor v. Slobodan Milošević*, Case No. IT-02-54-T, Oral Ruling, 02 September 2004, T.32357-32359; Order on the Modalities to be Followed by Court Assigned Counsel, 03 September 2004; Reasons for Decision on Assignment of Defence Counsel, 22 September 2004.

1187 *Prosecutor v. Slobodan Milošević*, Case No. IT-02-54-T, Reasons for Decision on Assignment of Defence Counsel, 22 September 2004, para.52-62.

1188 *Prosecutor v. Slobodan Milošević*, Case No. IT-02-54-T, Reasons for Decision on Assignment of Defence Counsel, 22 September 2004, para.63.

1189 *Prosecutor v. Slobodan Milošević*, Case No. IT-02-54-T, Reasons for Decision on Assignment of Defence Counsel, 22 September 2004, para.65.

1190 *Prosecutor v. Slobodan Milošević*, Case No. IT-02-54-T, Reasons for Decision on Assignment of Defence Counsel, 22 September 2004, para.66.

1191 *Prosecutor v. Slobodan Milošević*, Case No. IT-02-54-T, Reasons for Decision on Assignment of Defence Counsel, 22 September 2004, para.67.

> "The Trial Chamber looked at an overarching principle, but in terms of building constructions, if you take out a brick of an arch, the arch falls down. And this is more than one brick. This is half the arch. This is so fundamental to the structure of the fairness of the trial that to view those rights as not being constituent parts of a fair trial that have to be respected, which is why they have been enshrined in the Statute, they cannot be ignored, and they determine whether what has taken place is fair or not."[1192]

Counsel further argued that there could be no balancing of rights that formed part of an overall right to a fair trial, as the right to self-representation was one of the minimum guarantees to be safeguarded.[1193] Problems with regard to work against the will of and without instructions from the accused were additionally highlighted.[1194]

The prosecution discussed in detail the various possibilities that could be envisaged in order to allow the proceedings to continue while taking due account of the accused's state of health. It adopted the view that this could only be achieved by imposition of counsel who fully represented the interests of the accused.[1195] The prosecution considered this solution to be warranted not only in light of the ill-health of the defendant, but also in light of his previous conduct, which, in its view, was "just short of obstructionism".[1196] Yet, the prosecution clarified that it did not seek the actual removal of the accused's right to self-represent, but rather an important restriction in his exercise of that right, which would still provide for the participation of the accused in the presentation of the defence case.[1197]

1192 *Prosecutor v. Slobodan Milošević*, Case No. IT-02-54-AR73.7, Appeals Hearing, 21 October 2004, T.19.

1193 *Prosecutor v. Slobodan Milošević*, Case No. IT-02-54-AR73.7, Appeals Hearing, 21 October 2004, T.21.

1194 *Prosecutor v. Slobodan Milošević*, Case No. IT-02-54-AR73.7, Appeals Hearing, 21 October 2004, T.20, 26-31.

1195 *Prosecutor v. Slobodan Milošević*, Case No. IT-02-54-T, Prosecution Submissions in Response to the Trial Chamber's 19 July 2004 "Further Order on Future Conduct of the Trial", 26 July 2004, para.5, 33, 35.

1196 *Prosecutor v. Slobodan Milošević*, Case No. IT-02-54-T, Prosecution Submissions in Response to the Trial Chamber's 19 July 2004 "Further Order on Future Conduct of the Trial", 26 July 2004, para.29.

1197 *Prosecutor v. Slobodan Milošević*, Case No. IT-02-54-T, Prosecution Submissions in Response to the Trial Chamber's 19 July 2004 "Further Order on Future Conduct of the Trial", 26 July 2004, para.41, 46.

In deciding on the appeal against the assignment of counsel, the appeals chamber established the conditions under which the right to self-representation could be restricted:

> "It must further be decided whether the right may be curtailed on the grounds that a defendant's *self-representation is substantially and persistently obstructing the proper and expeditious conduct of his trial.* The Appeals Chamber believes that, under the appropriate circumstances, the Trial Chamber may restrict the right on those grounds."[1198]

The appeals chamber found guidance in setting this standard in the possibility of restricting the equally fundamental right of being tried in one's presence, as outlined in Rule 80(B) of the ICTY RPE,[1199] stating that

> "[i]f a defendant's right to be present for his trial – which, to reiterate, is listed in the same string of rights and indeed in the same *clause* as the right to self-representation – may thus be restricted on the basis of substantial trial disruption, the Appeals Chamber sees no reason to treat the right to self-representation any differently."[1200]

More importantly, the appeals chamber considered such limitations to be possible even in cases of unintentional disruption, as would be the case with a defendant's ill-health impacting the proceedings.[1201]

While the appeals chamber upheld the trial chamber's general decision to assign counsel,[1202] it did not agree with the modalities of the assign-

1198 *Prosecutor v. Slobodan Milošević*, Case No. IT-02-54-AR73.7, Decision on Interlocutory Appeal of the Trial Chamber's Decision on the Assignment of Defence Counsel, 01 November 2004, para.13 (emphasis added).

1199 Rule 80 of the ICTY RPE reads: "The Trial Chamber may order the removal of an accused from the courtroom and continue the proceedings in the absence of the accused if the accused has persisted in disruptive conduct following a warning that such conduct may warrant the removal of the accused from the courtroom."

1200 *Prosecutor v. Slobodan Milošević*, Case No. IT-02-54-AR73.7, Decision on Interlocutory Appeal of the Trial Chamber's Decision on the Assignment of Defence Counsel, 01 November 2004, para.13 (emphasis in the original).

1201 *Prosecutor v. Slobodan Milošević*, Case No. IT-02-54-AR73.7, Decision on Interlocutory Appeal of the Trial Chamber's Decision on the Assignment of Defence Counsel, 01 November 2004, para.14: "But it cannot be that the only kind of disruption legitimately cognizable by a Trial Chamber is the intentional variety."

1202 *Prosecutor v. Slobodan Milošević*, Case No. IT-02-54-AR73.7, Decision on Interlocutory Appeal of the Trial Chamber's Decision on the Assignment of Defence Counsel, 01 November 2004, para.15.

ment,[1203] considering that the possibility for the accused to continue to participate in the trial proceedings had been limited too excessively under basic proportionality considerations.[1204] The mode of participation envisaged by the appeals chamber very much resembled a more active form of standby counsel, who would take over the defence of the accused only in case the latter would be considered unfit to proceed due to his health.[1205] Indeed, the appeals chamber itself considered that as regards the question of representation by counsel or accused, "[t]o a lay observer, [...] the difference may well be imperceptible".[1206]

The appeals chamber failed to outline the way in which it envisaged the model suggested for *Milošević* to be implemented in practice.[1207] Any workable arrangement would presume that the accused is willing to cooperate with assigned counsel. In light of the fact that counsel will in general be imposed upon a defendant against the latter's will, it appears unlikely that the accused in question will prove his or her readiness for cooperation. The model may be feasible in cases in which a defendant showed his or her cooperative attitude by selecting a counsel to step in as defence attorney if the accused turns out to be ill-suited to conduct his or her own defence. However, bearing in mind the basis upon which accused in general opt to represent themselves, this scenario seems more than unlikely.[1208] This indicates that

---

1203 *See Prosecutor v. Slobodan Milošević*, Case No. IT-02-54-T, Order on the Modalities to be Followed by Court Assigned Counsel, 03 September 2004.

1204 *Prosecutor v. Slobodan Milošević*, Case No. IT-02-54-AR73.7, Decision on Interlocutory Appeal of the Trial Chamber's Decision on the Assignment of Defence Counsel, 01 November 2004, para.16-18.

1205 *Prosecutor v. Slobodan Milošević*, Case No. IT-02-54-AR73.7, Decision on Interlocutory Appeal of the Trial Chamber's Decision on the Assignment of Defence Counsel, 01 November 2004, para.19-20.

1206 *Prosecutor v. Slobodan Milošević*, Case No. IT-02-54-AR73.7, Decision on Interlocutory Appeal of the Trial Chamber's Decision on the Assignment of Defence Counsel, 01 November 2004, para.20.

1207 *See* Göran Sluiter, 'Fairness and Interests of Justice'. Illusive Concepts in the *Milošević* Case, 3 *Journal of International Criminal Justice* 9 (2005), at 15-16; Mirjan Damaška, Assignment of Counsel and Perceptions of Fairness, 3 *Journal of International Criminal Justice* 3 (2005), at 8.

1208 *See e.g. Prosecutor v. Vojislav Šešelj*, Case No. IT-03-67-PT, Decision by Registrar, 05 September 2003, assigning standby counsel; and Decision by Deputy Registrar, 16 February 2004, replacing standby counsel; *Prosecutor v. Radovan Karadžić*, Case No. IT-95-5/18-AR73.8, Appeal from Order on the Trial Schedule, 10 June 2010, para.16. *See also* Nina H.B. Jørgensen, The Right of the Accused to Self-the conduct of the proceedings will – again – depend on the cooperation and good will of a single person, the accused.

Further complications might arise in light of the fact that any continuation of the proceedings in the absence of an accused who is unwilling to collaborate with assigned counsel are also contingent on the cooperation of witnesses: for instance, when the trial chamber in *Milošević* decided to proceed with the cross-examination of a witness by the prosecution despite the health-related absence of the defendant from court,[1209] the witness refused to answer any questions as long as the accused was not present.[1210] The witness eventually completed his testimony as soon as the defendant was again capable of attending the proceedings,[1211] but was subsequently convicted for contempt of court.[1212] A further witness refused to appear before the court for the duration of the absence of the accused.[1213] There were further instances when witnesses refused to testify in case counsel was assigned against the accused's wishes in the course of the proceedings, or were reluctant to cooperate with assigned counsel in the course of their testimony.[1214]

Representation Before International Criminal Tribunals, 98 *The American Journal of International Law* 711 (2004), at 721.

1209 *Prosecutor v. Slobodan Milošević*, Case No. IT-02-54-T, Hearing, 19 April 2005, T.38577-38591.

1210 *Prosecutor v. Slobodan Milošević*, Case No. IT-02-54-T, Hearing, 19 April 2005, T.38591-38597, 38606; Hearing, 20 April 2005, T.38616.

1211 *Prosecutor v. Slobodan Milošević*, Case No. IT-02-54-T, Hearing, 25 April 2005, T.38649-38719.

1212 *Prosecutor v. Slobodan Milošević*, Case No. IT-02-54-R77.4, Contempt Proceedings Against Kosta Bulatović, Order on Contempt Concerning Witness Kosta Bulatović, 20 April 2005; Rule 77 Hearing, 06 May 2005; Decision on Contempt of the Tribunal, 13 May 2005; Decision on Interlocutory Appeal on Kosta Bulatović Contempt Proceedings, 29 August 2005. *See also Prosecutor v. Slobodan Milošević*, Case No. IT-02-54-T, Hearing, 20 April 2005, T.38616-38617.

1213 *Prosecutor v. Slobodan Milošević*, Case No. IT-02-54-T, Hearing, 20 April 2005, T.38611-38612.

1214 *See Prosecutor v. Slobodan Milošević*, Case No. IT-02-54-T, Hearing, 09 September 2004, T.32721-32724; *Prosecutor v. Slobodan Milošević*, Case No. IT-02-54-AR73.7, Appeals Hearing, 21 October 2004, T.7.

b. Impact of the accused's state of health in other proceedings

Equally to be considered in the context of unintentional disruption of proceedings is the impact of the defendant's state of health in *Tolimir*: the accused protested against any inference from previous medical conditions that he would not be able to conduct his defence in person[1215] and considered the conduct by the ICTY registry in this context to be designed to exert pressure on the ICTY in order to revoke his right to self-representation.[1216] Yet, the trial chamber dismissed the accused's allegation that his rights had been violated and ordered the ICTY registry to keep it informed about the defendant's state of health.[1217]

In order to monitor the accused's health, a regime was established under which guards would check on the defendant every 30 minutes, including during nighttime.[1218] The accused complained about this procedure as depriving him of sleep and in consequence preventing him from adequately preparing for the proceedings.[1219] An alternative was proposed that would

---

1215 *Prosecutor v. Zdravko Tolimir*, Case No. IT-05-88/2-PT, Submission by the Accused for the Violation of the Guaranteed and Discretionary Rights and Freedoms of Detained Persons Awaiting Trial Before the International Tribunal, 17 August 2007 (filed: 23 August 2007), para.6; Submission by the Accused Concerning the Violation of the Guaranteed and Discretionary Rights and Freedoms of Detained Persons Awaiting Trial Before the International Tribunal, 23 August 2007 (filed: 28 August 2007), para.10; The Accused's Submission to the Registrar and the Pretrial Chamber to Review the Facts and Reasons for the Violation of Guaranteed and Discretionary Rights of the Accused Before the International Tribunal, 07 September 2007 (filed: 14 September 2007).

1216 *Prosecutor v. Zdravko Tolimir*, Case No. IT-05-88/2-PT, Submission of the Accused to the Tribunal Concerning the Deception of the Public and the Disturbance to my Family Caused by False Statements Made by the Registry and the Political and Media Pressures it has exerted on the Tribunal, 08 October 2007 (filed: 09 October 2007), para.5.

1217 *Prosecutor v. Zdravko Tolimir*, Case No. IT-05-88/2-PT, Decision on Tolimir's Submission on Violation of his Rights Submitted on 7 September 2007, 10 October 2007, p.3-4.

1218 *Prosecutor v. Zdravko Tolimir*, Case No. IT-05-88/2-PT, Submission by the Accused Concerning the Protection of his Discretionary and Guaranteed Rights and a Violation of Rights, 13 August 2008 (filed: 21 August 2008), para.4. *See also* Decision on Tolimir's Submission on Violation of his Rights Submitted on 7 September 2007, 10 October 2007, p.3 fn.14; Registrar's Submission on the Accused's Motion Dated 16 November 2007, 07 December 2007, para.10.

1219 *Prosecutor v. Zdravko Tolimir*, Case No. IT-05-88/2-PT, Urgent Request from Zdravko Tolimir on Conditions of Detention Because of Deprivation of Sleep, 08

monitor the accused's state of health by way of an electronic device, measure which the defendant rejected for reasons of faith,[1220] and out of fear of manipulation.[1221] The trial chamber suggested that the monitoring could be suspended if the accused was to take the prescribed medication, which, however, he also refused.[1222] The defendant persisted in his demand to stop the monitoring, arguing *inter alia* that the deprivation of sleep might impact on his ability to stand trial and present his defence in person.[1223]

Although the trial chamber determined that the accused's choice to conduct his own defence did not necessarily entail any further rights compared to defendants represented by counsel and that the additional burden of preparation formed part of that choice, it did consider that it might affect his ability to exercise his right to self-representation.[1224] Therefore, it concerned itself with the accused's state of health and recognised his right to refuse medical

---

December 2008 (filed: 09 December 2008), p.11-16. *See also* Status Conference, 30 July 2008, T.199; Status Conference, 31 October 2008, T.227-228; Status Conference, 27 February 2009, T.245-246; Registry Submission Pursuant to Rule 33 (B) Concerning the Accused's Medical Monitoring, 08 June 2009, p.3; Status Conference, 25 June 2009, T.259-260, 267-269; Status Conference, 22 October 2009, T.288-290; Status Conference, 16 December 2009, T.310-311.

1220 *Prosecutor v. Zdravko Tolimir*, Case No. IT-05-88/2-PT, Status Conference, 25 June 2009, T.260-264; Submission Concerning Deprivation of Sleep and the Fitting of Microchips to the Body of the Accused, 10 July 2009 (filed: 16 July 2009), para.1-5.

1221 *Prosecutor v. Zdravko Tolimir*, Case No. IT-05-88/2-PT, Status Conference, 25 June 2009, T.266.

1222 *Prosecutor v. Zdravko Tolimir*, Case No. IT-05-88/2-PT, Status Conference, 22 October 2009, T.286-287, 290-294.

1223 *Prosecutor v. Zdravko Tolimir*, Case No. IT-05-88/2-T, Zdravko Tolimir's Submission Concerning the Possible Trial Schedule for June, 10 May 2010 (filed: 13 May 2010), para.3; Hearing, 27 May 2010, T.2044-2045.

1224 *Prosecutor v. Zdravko Tolimir*, Case No. IT-05-88/2-T, Order Regarding the Nightly Monitoring of the Accused, 25 August 2010 (Public redacted version filed on 27 August 2010. *See* Notice of Filing of Public Redacted Version of the "Order Regarding the Nightly Monitoring of the Accused", 27 August 2010.), para.17.

treatment.[1225] While the defendant exercised this right[1226] and the monitoring was discontinued accordingly,[1227] the health of the accused appeared to change and prompt action soon after.[1228]

Of note in this regard is the separate opinion of one of the trial judges who expressed the view that while in general it was the accused's choice whether to accept a particular medical treatment, this could not be condoned in case any refusal on the part of the defendant would endanger the latter's health and thus jeopardise the conduct of the proceedings: in the judge's opinion, in order for justice to be done, an accused was under an obligation to remain alive and in good health.[1229] A similar position appears to have been taken by the prosecution in the proceedings against Slobodan Milošević, when it requested that his smoking privileges in detention be restricted in light of the fact that his smoking habit impacted on his health and thus on the conduct of the trial proceedings in general.[1230]

1225 *Prosecutor v. Zdravko Tolimir*, Case No. IT-05-88/2-T, Order Regarding the Nightly Monitoring of the Accused, 25 August 2010 (Public redacted version filed on 27 August 2010. *See* Notice of Filing of Public Redacted Version of the "Order Regarding the Nightly Monitoring of the Accused", 27 August 2010.), para.23, 28-29.

1226 *Prosecutor v. Zdravko Tolimir*, Case No. IT-05-88/2-T, Statement in Accordance with the Trial Chamber Decision of 25 August 2010, 31 August 2010 (filed: 01 September 2010).

1227 *Prosecutor v. Zdravko Tolimir*, Case No. IT-05-88/2-T, Second Registry Submission Pursuant to Rule 33(B) Concerning the Order Regarding the Nightly Monitoring of the Accused, 03 September 2010. *See also* Urgent Registry Submission Pursuant to Rule 33(B) Concerning the Order Regarding the Nightly Monitoring of the Accused, 30 August 2010; Decision on Urgent Registry Submission Pursuant to Rule 33(B) Concerning the Order Regarding the Nightly Monitoring of the Accused, 01 September 2010.

1228 *Prosecutor v. Zdravko Tolimir*, Case No. IT-05-88/2-T, Hearing, 19 October 2010, T.6477-6480; Registry Submission Pursuant to Rule 33(B) Concerning the Accused's Statements on 19 October 2010, 22 October 2010.

1229 *Prosecutor v. Zdravko Tolimir*, Case No. IT-05-88/2-T, Order Regarding the Nightly Monitoring of the Accused, 25 August 2010 (Public redacted version filed on 27 August 2010. *See* Notice of Filing of Public Redacted Version of the "Order Regarding the Nightly Monitoring of the Accused", 27 August 2010.), Judge Antoine Mindua's Separate and Concurring Opinion on the Order Regarding the Nightly Monitoring of the Accused, para.3.

1230 *Prosecutor v. Slobodan Milošević*, Case No. IT-02-54-T, Prosecution's Submission on the Implications of the Accused's Recurring Ill-Health and the Future Conduct of the Case – Corrected Version, 30 September 2003, para.33-34.

It has to be questioned whether the direction of the sort of opinion expressed by a member of the bench in *Tolimir* could not be a slippery slope. Considering for example the hypothesis of a defendant starting a hunger strike while in custody, extreme views may imply that the accused could be submitted to force feeding already at a stage when the good health – but not yet the life – of the detainee was in danger. However, as mentioned below, it is the expressed opinion of the World Medical Association[1231] and established human rights jurisprudence that force feeding in detention can violate the rights of the person involved and could amount to inhumane and degrading treatment or even torture, if no particular medical necessity in order to prevent lethal consequences has been shown.[1232] While this reasoning regards the balance of state obligations under human rights conventions, *i.e.* to protect the right to life as well as to physical integrity, the question remains whether an alleged need to see international justice be done can weigh as factor in any such balance.

Further to be discussed is the argument presented by the accused in *Karadžić* concerning the repercussions of the trial schedule on his health. While initially referring to his health as a factor that should be considered when determining the pace of trial proceedings,[1233] the defendant eventually filed a submission including a confidential medical report in which he argued that the increase of the schedule to five sitting days per week would jeopardise his health.[1234] The accused explicitly referred to *Milošević*, case in which the defendant eventually died of a heart attack and the trial could not be

---

1231 WMA Declaration of Malta on Hunger Strikers, as revised on 14 October 2006, para.21.

1232 *Nevmerzhitsky v. Ukraine*, Application no. 54825/00, Judgment, 12 October 2005, para.93-99. *See also A v. Germany*, Application no. 10565/83 (Commission), 1985; *Herczegfalvy v. Austria*, Application no. 10533/83, Judgment, 24 September 1992, para.79-84; *Ciorap v. Moldova*, Application no, 12066/02, Judgment, 19 September 2007, para.76-89.

1233 *See e.g. Prosecutor v. Radovan Karadžić*, Case No. IT-95-5/18-PT, Motion for Adequate Facilities and Equality of Arms: Legal Associates, 24 November 2008, para.21; *Prosecutor v. Radovan Karadžić*, Case No. IT-95-5/18-T, Submission on Trial Schedule, 20 May 2010, para.5; *Prosecutor v. Radovan Karadžić*, Case No. IT-95-5/18-AR73.8, Appeal from Order on the Trial Schedule, 10 June 2010, para.23.

1234 *Prosecutor v. Radovan Karadžić*, Case No. IT-95-5/18-T, Second Submission on Trial Schedule, 07 September 2010, para.3.

completed.[1235] Likewise, the defendant repeated his earlier argument that an increased sitting schedule would violate his right to adequate time and facilities to prepare his defence, since as self-represented accused, he would have to conduct all cross-examinations personally.[1236]

In its decision on the accused's second submission on the trial schedule, the trial chamber considered, taking into account the medical report, that increasing the sitting schedule to five days a week would not be detrimental to the accused's health.[1237] More importantly, the trial chamber considered the argument of the accused that he had to cross-examine all prosecution witnesses on his own whereas the prosecution would bring in new lawyers for their direct examinations to be "nonsensical", given that it was his choice to conduct his defence personally and that he could decide any time to be represented by counsel.[1238] The trial judges equally dismissed the argument that practical difficulties would arise from an increased hearing schedule.[1239] Yet, the bench determined that a four-day per week schedule with augmented sitting hours per day would equally serve the purpose of an expeditious trial, while at the same time giving the accused the possibility to use part of the non-sitting day to exercise to improve his health.[1240] The trial chamber did however reserve the possibility of increasing the schedule to five-day weeks

---

1235 *Prosecutor v. Radovan Karadžić*, Case No. IT-95-5/18-T, Second Submission on Trial Schedule, 07 September 2010, para.4. *Cf.* also Gideon Boas, Self-Representation Before the ICTY. A Case for Reform, 9 *Journal of International Criminal Justice* 53 (2011), at 61.

1236 *Prosecutor v. Radovan Karadžić*, Case No. IT-95-5/18-T, Second Submission on Trial Schedule, 07 September 2010, para.8-9. The prosecution opposed the submission: Prosecution's Response to Karadžić's Second Submission on Trial Schedule With Confidential Appendix A, 13 September 2010.

1237 *Prosecutor v. Radovan Karadžić*, Case No. IT-95-5/18-T, Decision on Accused's Second Submission on Trial Schedule, 23 September 2010 (made public by oral order of 27 September 2010), para.7.

1238 *Prosecutor v. Radovan Karadžić*, Case No. IT-95-5/18-T, Decision on Accused's Second Submission on Trial Schedule, 23 September 2010 (made public by oral order of 27 September 2010), para.8.

1239 *Prosecutor v. Radovan Karadžić*, Case No. IT-95-5/18-T, Decision on Accused's Second Submission on Trial Schedule, 23 September 2010 (made public by oral order of 27 September 2010), para.9.

1240 *Prosecutor v. Radovan Karadžić*, Case No. IT-95-5/18-T, Decision on Accused's Second Submission on Trial Schedule, 23 September 2010 (made public by oral order of 27 September 2010), para.10.

at any time.[1241] Yet, the matter surfaced again when one of the accused's legal advisors expressed his concerns with regard to the state of health of his client,[1242] and the defendant himself made remarks about him feeling too unwell to proceed with the cross-examination of a witness.[1243] The trial chamber suggested at that point that it could be considered whether, on an exceptional basis, the legal advisor could not proceed with cross-examining witnesses.[1244]

This decision of the trial chamber is of note insofar as it made abundantly clear that while the bench would continue to safeguard the interests of the accused, the latter at the same time should be aware that his choice to present his defence in person brought with it certain obligations and impediments to be borne by the defendant himself.

On a speculative note, the accused's reasoning on the one hand could be that the trial chamber would allow for considerable adjustments to the timing of the trial proceedings in order to accommodate the defendant's alleged health problems. On the other hand, the defendant should be aware that the same issue eventually led the trial and appeals chamber in *Milošević* to assign counsel even without any intentional obstruction by the accused. Although this indeed took place only at a rather late stage of the trial proceedings in *Milošević*, the accused in *Karadžić* cannot be certain, especially in light of the developments in the case law on restrictions to the right of self-representation, that the chambers would again adopt an equally lenient and accommodating approach in his case. This is even more probable when bearing in mind that both trial[1245] and appeals chamber[1246] considered the accused's concerns raised with regard to his health to be without merit. More importantly, the trial chamber explicitly referred to the various possibilities of

---

1241 *Prosecutor v. Radovan Karadžić*, Case No. IT-95-5/18-T, Decision on Accused's Second Submission on Trial Schedule, 23 September 2010 (made public by oral order of 27 September 2010), para.11.

1242 *Prosecutor v. Radovan Karadžić*, Case No. IT-95-5/18-T, Hearing, 30 September 2010, T.7199, 7202; Hearing, 14 October 2010, T.7935-7937.

1243 *Prosecutor v. Radovan Karadžić*, Case No. IT-95-5/18-T, Hearing, 15 October 2010, T.7989. *See also* Hearing, 14 October 2010, T.7931-7932.

1244 *Prosecutor v. Radovan Karadžić*, Case No. IT-95-5/18-T, Hearing, 14 October 2010, T.7935-7938.

1245 *Prosecutor v. Radovan Karadžić*, Case No. IT-95-5/18-T, Order on the Trial Schedule, 27 May 2010, para.7.

1246 *Prosecutor v. Radovan Karadžić*, Case No. IT-95-5/18-AR73.8, Decision on Appeal from Order on the Trial Schedule, 19 July 2010, para.12, fn.32.

presentation arrangements which could be considered if the schedule negatively impacted on the accused's health.[1247]

The practicality of any potential representation arrangements should be put to a test at a later stage of the proceedings: when the accused was unable to attend scheduled hearings due to illness, a number of court sittings were cancelled[1248] to allow the defendant to recover and subsequently resume his role in court. At the same time, however, the trial chamber considered possibilities to continue with the prosecution's presentation of evidence despite the accused's absence, including taking depositions pursuant to Rule 71 of the ICTY RPE.[1249]

Apart from his hunger strike that lasted for several weeks at the end of 2006, the health concerns of the accused in *Šešelj* were of a somewhat different nature: apart from the accused alleging "psychological" problems in view of the official attire worn by the judges in the courtroom,[1250] submissions dismissed as frivolous by the pre-trial judge,[1251] the defendant also exhibited physiological issues over the course of the proceedings. While at times it appeared that the accused raised his (ill-) health in order to support his claims of inability to prepare and of the inadequacy of conditions,[1252] at other times

---

1247 *Prosecutor v. Radovan Karadžić*, Case No. IT-95-5/18-T, Order on the Trial Schedule, 27 May 2010, para.7.

1248 *See e.g. Prosecutor v. Radovan Karadžić*, Case No. IT-95-5/18-T, Hearing, 05 December 2011, T.22435.

1249 *Prosecutor v. Radovan Karadžić*, Case No. IT-95-5/18-T, Hearing, 07 December 2011, T.22437-22439. *See*, however, Hearing, 08 December 2011, T.22443.

1250 *Prosecutor v. Vojislav Šešelj*, Case No. IT-03-67-PT, Status Conference, 26 February 2003, T.54-55; Status Conference, 03 July 2003, T.82-83, 106-107; Status Conference, 29 October 2003, T.149-150; Status Conference, 04 October 2004, T.298.

1251 *Prosecutor v. Vojislav Šešelj*, Case No. IT-03-67-PT, Status Conference, 03 July 2003, T.83.

1252 *Prosecutor v. Vojislav Šešelj*, Case No. IT-03-67-PT, Status Conference, 29 October 2003, T.149-151; Request by the Defendant to Change the Seat of the International Criminal Tribunal (Submission No. 90), 10 March 2005 (filed: 06 April 2005), p.5; Status Conference, 30 May 2005, T.352-353, 373-375; Request of the Accused for Trial Chamber II to Issue an Order for the Trial to Commence by 24 February 2006 or an Order to Abolish Detention, Dismiss the Indictment and Release Dr Vojislav Šešelj (Submission No. 116), 07 November 2005 (filed: 16 November 2005), p.3, 9; Submission Number 118, 11 November 2005 (filed: 16 November 2005); Motion for Trial Chamber I to Acquire a Complete Report on the Health of Professor Vojislav Šešelj (Submission No. 159), 19 May 2006 (filed: 22 June 2006), p.5-9; Status Conference, 19 May 2006, T.489-490, 494-495; *Prosecutor*

he seemed to be reluctant to be portrayed as not being in good health or unable to conduct his defence personally.[1253] The accused however did refer to health issues when arguing for a three day per week sitting schedule, instead of five as suggested by the prosecution.[1254] The trial chamber showed itself continuously concerned with the supervision of the accused's health and issued orders for repeated examination of his state of health.[1255] For example, the trial chamber ordered renewed expert medical examination of the accused in order to ascertain the defendant's state of health and its poten-

---

v. Vojislav Šešelj, Case No. IT-03-67-T, Status Conference, 29 October 2008, T.11294-11297; Submission of the Medical Opinion of a Team of Consultants Concerning the Current State of Health of Dr Vojislav Šešelj (Submission No. 418), 05 May 2009 (filed: 08 May 2009); Status Conference, 07 May 2009, T.14491-14495. *See also Prosecutor v. Vojislav Šešelj*, Case No. IT-03-67-PT, Status Conference, 04 July 2006, T.532; Status Conference, 03 November 2006, T.703-705.

1253 *Prosecutor v. Vojislav Šešelj*, Case No. IT-03-67-PT, Status Conference, 19 May 2006, T.504; *Prosecutor v. Vojislav Šešelj*, Case No. IT-03-67-T, Status Conference, 26 March 2009, T.14443-14444; Status Conference, 07 May 2009, T.14494; Administrative Hearing, 16 June 2009, T.14539-14542; Status Conference, 20 October 2009, T.14775-14776.

1254 *Prosecutor v. Vojislav Šešelj*, Case No. IT-03-67-PT, Status Conference, 19 May 2006, T.506; Status Conference, 08 November 2006, T.739-740. *See also Prosecutor v. Vojislav Šešelj*, Case No. IT-03-67-T, Status Conference, 29 October 2008, T.11300-11301.

1255 *Prosecutor v. Vojislav Šešelj*, Case No. IT-03-67-PT, Order to Registry and Commanding Officer of the United Nations Detention Unit, 11 July 2005; Status Conference, 26 September 2005, T.402-404; Status Conference, 24 January 2006, T.481-483; *Procureur c/ Vojislav Šešelj*, Affaire n° IT-03-67-PT, Ordonnance Portant Demande d'un Rapport Médical, 22 février 2007; *Prosecutor v. Vojislav Šešelj*, Case No. IT-03-67-PT, Status Conference, 04 April 2007, T.1012; *Prosecutor v. Vojislav Šešelj*, Case No. IT-03-67-T, Order for Medical Reports, 02 April 2009; Status Conference, 07 May 2009, T.14488-14490; *Procureur c/ Vojislav Šešelj*, Affaire n° IT-03-67-T, Ordonnance Relative Aux Rappors [sic] Médicaux, 13 mai 2009; *Prosecutor v. Vojislav Šešelj*, Case No. IT-03-67-T, Hearing, 07 July 2009, T.14561-14562; Status Conference, 20 October 2009, T.14773-14775; Administrative Hearing, 01 December 2010, T.16515-16516; Status Conference, 18 January 2011, T.16566-16567, 16603-16604; Administrative Hearing, 23 August 2011, T.17014-17018. *See also Prosecutor v. Vojislav Šešelj*, Case No. IT-03-67-T, Registry Submission Pursuant to Rule 33(B) Regarding the Trial Chamber's "Ordonnance Relative aux Observations du Greffe du 7 mai 2009", 08 May 2009; Registry Submission Pursuant to Rule 33(B) Regarding the Implementation of Medical Expert Recommendations, 03 November 2009.

tial impact on his participation in the proceedings.[1256] The ICTY registry for its part attempted to clarify issues raised by the accused with regard to his medical treatment and committed itself to the continued monitoring of the health of all accused in detention.[1257]

The review above shows that four of five accused who exercised their right to defend themselves at some stage of the proceedings had to deal with health problems allegedly or indeed impacting on their ability to prepare and present their defence case. Although one can only speculate whether any ill-health was caused or aggravated by the accused's self-representation, it does appear to affect their health status in a negative way, which might be due not only to long working hours, but also the stress of being on trial and having to prepare one's defence in detention. The emphasis of the trial chamber in *Karadžić* on the accused's choice to present his defence in person is of particular interest: the bench seemed to take the position that rather than overly accommodating potential health issues of the defendant, it would prefer him to hand over the preparation and presentation of his defence case to a professional attorney.

The outline also indicates that while some accused did in fact struggle with health problems, others appear to have used this argument merely to create further litigation potential and delays in the proceedings. Then, the distinction between unintentional disruption due to an accused's delicate state of health and intentional obstruction by a defendant exploiting any and all possibilities becomes blurred.

1256 *Prosecutor v. Vojislav Šešelj*, Case No. IT-03-67-T, Status Conference, 21 September 2010, T.16376-16378; *Procureur c/ Vojislav Šešelj*, Affaire n° IT-03-67-T, Ordonnance aux Fins de Faire Procéder à Une Nouvelle Expertise Médicale de Vojislav Šešelj, 19 octobre 2010 ; Ordonnance Portant Modification de l'Ordonnance aux Fins de Faire Procéder à Une Nouvelle Expertise Médicale de Vojislav Šešelj Enregistrée le 19 octobre 2010, 17 novembre 2010.

1257 *Prosecutor v. Vojislav Šešelj*, Case No. IT-03-67-T, Registry Submission Pursuant to Rule 33(B) Regarding Medical Issues Raised at the Administrative Hearing of 2 November 2010, 24 November 2010.

2. Intentional obstruction

a. The case of Vojislav Šešelj

A case in point for alleged intentional obstruction of the proceedings that is infamous for the obstructionist and disruptive behaviour of the accused are the *Šešelj* proceedings.

The pre-trial chamber in *Šešelj* considered it to be in the interests of justice to appoint standby counsel to the accused even before the start of the evidentiary phase of the proceedings.[1258] The judges considered the "attitude and actions" of the defendant to be "indicative of obstructionism"[1259] and found that he "increasingly demonstrat[ed] a tendency to act in an obstructionist fashion while at the same time revealing a need for legal assistance."[1260]

However, the pre-trial chamber clarified that the accused's right to self-representation was "left absolutely untouched" and that "standby counsel is not an *amicus curiae* but an assistant operating in the sphere of the Accused only".[1261] When seised of the decision by the accused at a later stage,[1262] the trial chamber denied the motion to re-examine the appointment of standby counsel as it was not satisfied of any change in circumstances which would justify revising the earlier decision, even though the trial chamber reiterated that the accused's right to defend himself had been left untouched by that appointment.[1263] A dissenting opinion argued that the imposition of standby

1258 *Prosecutor v. Vojislav Šešelj*, Case No. IT-03-67-PT, Decision on Prosecution's Motion for Order Appointing Counsel to Assist Vojislav Šešelj with his Defence, 09 May 2003, para.27.

1259 *Prosecutor v. Vojislav Šešelj*, Case No. IT-03-67-PT, Decision on Prosecution's Motion for Order Appointing Counsel to Assist Vojislav Šešelj with his Defence, 09 May 2003, para.26.

1260 *Prosecutor v. Vojislav Šešelj*, Case No. IT-03-67-PT, Decision on Prosecution's Motion for Order Appointing Counsel to Assist Vojislav Šešelj with his Defence, 09 May 2003, para.23.

1261 *Prosecutor v. Vojislav Šešelj*, Case No. IT-03-67-PT, Decision on Prosecution's Motion for Order Appointing Counsel to Assist Vojislav Šešelj with his Defence, 09 May 2003, para.28.

1262 *Prosecutor v. Vojislav Šešelj*, Case No. IT-03-67-PT, Request by the Accused to the Trial Chamber to Re-Examine Decision to Assign Stand-By Counsel to the Accused (Submission No. 45), 26 October 2004 (filed: 09 November 2004). *See also* Submission No. 57, 25 November 2004 (filed: 08 December 2004).

1263 *Prosecutor v. Vojislav Šešelj*, Case No. IT-03-67-PT, Decision on the Accused's Motion to Re-Examine the Decision to Assign Standby Counsel, 01 March 2005,

counsel should be revoked since up to that point the behaviour of the accused had not been so disruptive as to justify the appointment of standby counsel, and rather *amicus curiae* be assigned.[1264] The accused moved repeatedly for a review of the trial chamber's decision,[1265] motions which the trial chamber denied in light of the fact that it had already dealt with the matter.[1266]

One specific example which serves to illuminate the general attitude of the accused towards the proceedings relates to statements made by the defendants in the course of hearings. The trial chamber issued detailed guidelines at the beginning of the prosecution case which outlined the scope and nature of admissible questions as well as the manner in which (cross-) examinations should ideally be conducted.[1267] Despite these guidelines, the trial chamber later found itself compelled to order that any portions in transcripts and video recordings which may be harmful to the integrity of the proceedings, *e.g.* derogatory remarks of the accused about witnesses, be struck from the record.[1268] Similarly, the defendant was convicted in two cases,[1269] and indicted

---

p.4. *See also* Corrigendum to Decision on the Accused's Motion to Re-Examine the Decision to Assign Standby Counsel, 11 March 2005.

1264 *Prosecutor v. Vojislav Šešelj*, Case No. IT-03-67-PT, Decision on the Accused's Motion to Re-Examine the Decision to Assign Standby Counsel, 01 March 2005, Opinion Dissidente du Juge Antonetti, para.10, 12.

1265 *Prosecutor v. Vojislav Šešelj*, Case No. IT-03-67-PT, Request of the Accused to Revoke the Ruling of the Trial Chamber to Appoint Standby Counsel (Submission No. 81), 04 March 2005 (filed: 22 March 2005); Request of the Accused for Trial Chamber II to Revoke the Ruling to Assign Standby Counsel (Submission No. 82), 05 March 2005 (filed: 06 April 2005); Request of the Accused for Trial Chamber II to Revoke the Decision to Assign Standby Counsel (Submission No. 84), 07 March 2005 (filed: 06 April 2005); Request of Dr Vojislav Šešelj for the Revocation of the Decision to Assign Standby Counsel (Submission No. 125), 03 January 2006 (filed: 16 January 2006).

1266 *Prosecutor v. Vojislav Šešelj*, Case No. IT-03-67-PT, Decision on Request of the Accused to Revoke the Ruling of the Trial Chamber to Appoint Standby Counsel (Submissions Number 81, 82 and 84), 03 May 2005; Decision on Assignment of Counsel, 21 August 2006, para.3.

1267 *Procureur c/ Vojislav Šešelj*, Affaire n° IT-03-67-PT, Ordonnance Énonçant les Principes Directeurs Destinés à Régir la Présentation des Éléments de Preuve et le Comportement des Parties Pendant le Procès, 15 novembre 2007, para.17-28.

1268 *Procureur c/ Vojislav Šešelj*, Affaire n° IT-03-67-T, Ordonnance Aux Fins de Protéger l'Intégrité des Débats, 18 juin 2008.

1269 *Prosecutor v. Vojislav Šešelj*, Case No. IT-03-67-R77.2, Public Edited Version of "Judgement on Allegations of Contempt" Issued on 24 July 2009, 24 July 2009; upheld by the appeals chamber: *Prosecutor v. Vojislav Šešelj*, Case No. IT-03-67-R77.2-A, Judgement, 19 May 2010; *Prosecutor v. Vojislav Šešelj*, Case No. IT-in one additional case, for contempt of court in the context of alleged disclosure of confidential information by the defendant.[1270] The accused appeared to be determined to persist in his engagement of contempt proceedings.[1271]

Eventually, the trial chamber saw the time ripe to impose counsel to represent the defendant's interests in light of the continuous obstructive behaviour exhibited by the accused: it determined that the accused's statements made even before his surrender could be considered "in order to understand his behaviour while in custody and to assess his intentions and his likely conduct at trial".[1272] The trial chamber grouped the defendant's behaviour and attitude into categories such as obstructionist behaviour;[1273] deliberate

---

03-67-R77.3, Public Redacted Version of "Judgement" Issued on 31 October 2011, 31 October 2011, finding the accused guilty of one count of contempt of court and sentencing him to 18 months of imprisonment to be served concurrently with the sentence of 15 months imposed in the judgement of 24 July 2009.

1270 *Prosecutor v. Vojislav Šešelj*, Case No. IT-03-67-R77.4, Public Edited Version of "Decision on Failure to Remove Confidential Information from Public Website and Order in Lieu of Indictment" Issued on 9 May 2011, 24 May 2011.

1271 *Prosecutor v. Vojislav Šešelj*, Case No. IT-03-67-R77.3, Defence Closing Statement, 08 June 2011, T.380: "Now, there is a whole series of proceedings for court contempt, in which I intend to participate very actively, and I will do that in a very patient way. I might seem to you as a nervous person, but I can tell you that I am very thorough and very patient. Once one proceedings [sic] is completed, I'm going to create conditions for the next one. As soon as we finish the next one, I'm going to prepare myself for the next one and the next one, up to 10. That's what I decided. And it's not my problem; it is your problem, how you're going to get away from that. What are you going to do if all the aggregate sentences for contempt of court in my case reach 10 years?". *See also Prosecutor v. Vojislav Šešelj*, Case No. IT-03-67-R77.4, Initial Appearance, 06 July 2011, T.1: "Yes, I shall be representing myself also in all coming cases regarding contempt. I have planned another seven cases, another seven proceedings to take place for contempt of court, in addition to this one."

1272 *Prosecutor v. Vojislav Šešelj*, Case No. IT-03-67-PT, Decision on Assignment of Counsel, 21 August 2006, para.29.

1273 *Prosecutor v. Vojislav Šešelj*, Case No. IT-03-67-PT, Decision on Assignment of Counsel, 21 August 2006, para.34-40: "From the very beginning of the pre-trial proceedings, the Accused has raised irrelevant or specious matters amounting to obstructionist behaviour. […]".

disrespect for the rules;[1274] disruptive behaviour;[1275] as well as intimidation and slanderous comments in relation to witnesses.[1276] According to the bench, the general behaviour of the accused "compromises the dignity of the Tribunal and jeopardises the very foundations upon which its proper functioning is based".[1277]

The appeals chamber later confirmed the trial chamber's determination of circumstances which warranted restriction of the accused's right to self-representation.[1278] However, it overturned the imposition of counsel on procedural grounds.[1279] When the trial chamber considered this initial appeals chamber decision to reinstate the *status quo ante*, and again appointed standby counsel to the case,[1280] the defendant started a hunger strike.[1281]

1274 *Prosecutor v. Vojislav Šešelj*, Case No. IT-03-67-PT, Decision on Assignment of Counsel, 21 August 2006, para.41-54: "In almost all of his submissions, the Accused has shown a degree of unwillingness to follow rules set by the Tribunal or its organs. […] Many submissions, in addition to not complying with this Practice Direction, also contained offensive language or were described as 'offensive' in decisions and orders by the Tribunal. […] The Accused has made general statements on several occasions to the effect that he does not intend to follow the Rules, Practice Directions, or specific rulings of the judges or of the Chamber. […] Finally the Chamber notes with great concern that the Accused has sent to members of his expert team confidential documents […]".

1275 *Prosecutor v. Vojislav Šešelj*, Case No. IT-03-67-PT, Decision on Assignment of Counsel, 21 August 2006, para.55-62: "On 21 May 2003 the Accused filed a motion for disqualification of the previous bench based on the nationality and the religious affiliation of the three judges. The motion contained, among other inappropriate phrases, insults directed at the Presiding Judge […] The Chamber also notes instances of disruptive behaviour in Court on the part of the Accused during the pre-trial proceedings. In particular, the Accused has used offensive language towards the participants in these proceedings as well as against other individuals. […]".

1276 *Prosecutor v. Vojislav Šešelj*, Case No. IT-03-67-PT, Decision on Assignment of Counsel, 21 August 2006, para.63-65.

1277 *Prosecutor v. Vojislav Šešelj*, Case No. IT-03-67-PT, Decision on Assignment of Counsel, 21 August 2006, para.77.

1278 *Prosecutor v. Vojislav Šešelj*, Case No. IT-03-67-AR73.3, Decision on Appeal Against the Trial Chamber's Decision on Assignment of Counsel, 20 October 2006, para.21, 29, 51.

1279 *Prosecutor v. Vojislav Šešelj*, Case No. IT-03-67-AR73.3, Decision on Appeal Against the Trial Chamber's Decision on Assignment of Counsel, 20 October 2006, para.22, 26.

1280 *Prosecutor v. Vojislav Šešelj*, Case No. IT-03-67-PT, Order Concerning Appointment of Standby Counsel and Delayed Commencement of Trial, 25 October 2006.

1281 *Prosecutor v. Vojislav Šešelj*, Case No. IT-03-67-PT, Status Conference, 22 November 2006, T.777, 780-781; Professor Vojislav Šešelj's Decision to Refuse

In light of this and additional obstructive behaviour, including the accused's failure to attend a status conference due to his weakness caused by the hunger strike, the trial chamber decided to assign counsel to represent the defendant's interests.[1282] The appeals chamber in the second decision on the matter fully re-established the accused's right to self-represent.[1283] Subsequently, the pre-trial judge, who would later also be the presiding judge in the proceedings, left no doubt that in his opinion, no counsel or *amicus curiae* would be assigned to the accused.[1284] The defendant continued to conduct his defence in person several years later despite renewed attempts by the prosecution to have counsel imposed.[1285]

b. The case of Radovan Karadžić

In *Karadžić*, the accused reiterated his position that he had not been allowed sufficient time to adequately prepare when the case was declared ready for trial proceedings by the pre-trial judge.[1286] Consequently, the defendant requested to be granted an additional ten months to prepare for the trial pro-

---

Medical Treatment and Artificial Feeding While on Hunger Strike (Submission No. 223), 24 November 2006 (filed: 30 November 2006).

1282 *Prosecutor v. Vojislav Šešelj*, Case No. IT-03-67-T, Reasons for Decision (No. 2) on Assignment of Counsel, 27 November 2006, para.13-14.

1283 *Prosecutor v. Vojislav Šešelj*, Case No. IT-03-67-AR73.4, Decision on Appeal Against the Trial Chamber's Decision (No. 2) on Assignment of Counsel, 08 December 2006.

1284 *Prosecutor v. Vojislav Šešelj*, Case No. IT-03-67-PT, Status Conference, 13 March 2007, T.928; Status Conference, 27 September 2007, T.1521-1522.

1285 *Prosecutor v. Vojislav Šešelj*, Case No. IT-03-67-T, Oral Ruling, 20 October 2009, T.14751-14752; *Procureur c/ Vojislav Šešelj*, Affaire n° IT-03-67-T, Version Publique de la « Décision Consolidée Relative à l'Imposition d'un Conseil, l'Ajournement, et la Requête de l'Accusation sur les Heures Supplémentaires Avec en Annex l'Opinion Individuelle du Juge Antonetti Président de la Chambre », 24 novembre 2009, para.87.

1286 *Prosecutor v. Radovan Karadžić*, Case No. IT-95-5/18-PT, Status Conference, 20 August 2009, T.434; Status Conference, 08 September 2009, T.437.

ceedings.[1287] The trial chamber rejected the accused's arguments,[1288] decision which in essence was upheld by the appeals chamber.[1289]

In the following, the accused announced that he intended not to attend the hearing during which the prosecution was to give its opening statement or the proceedings in general until he deemed himself ready to do so.[1290] The trial chamber sent letters to the defendant, urging him to appear in the proceedings and notifying him of the potential consequences if he was indeed to boycott the beginning of the trial proceedings.[1291] Nonetheless, on the day the prosecution was scheduled to begin its opening statement, the defendant's stand in the courtroom remained empty.[1292] This caused the trial chamber to reiterate its demand to the accused to attend the proceedings and informed him again of the potential consequences should he continue to absent himself.[1293] In a hearing scheduled to discuss in which way to proceed, and attended by the defendant, the accused repeated his arguments concerning his readiness for trial as submitted before.[1294] Eventually, the trial chamber qualified the failure of the accused to appear, despite its repeated warnings, as behaviour that had "substantially and persistently obstructed the proper and expeditious conduct of his trial" and appointed counsel.[1295] Appointed

---

1287 *Prosecutor v. Radovan Karadžić*, Case No. IT-95-5/18-PT, Submission on Commencement of Trial, 03 September 2009, para.35.

1288 *Prosecutor v. Radovan Karadžić*, Case No. IT-95-5/18-PT, Status Conference, 08 September 2009, T.454-456.

1289 *Prosecutor v. Radovan Karadžić*, Case No. IT-95-5/18-AR73.5, Decision on Radovan Karadžić's Appeal of the Decision on Commencement of Trial, 13 October 2009.

1290 *Prosecutor v. Radovan Karadžić*, Case No. IT-95-5/18-PT, Submission on the Commencement of Trial, 21 October 2009, p.5. *See also* Response to Letter from the Chamber, 24 October 2009 (filed: 26 October 2009).

1291 *Prosecutor v. Radovan Karadžić*, Case No. IT-95-5/18-T, Decision on Appointment of Counsel and Order on Further Trial Proceedings, 05 November 2009, para.5-8.

1292 *Prosecutor v. Radovan Karadžić*, Case No. IT-95-5/18-T, Hearing, 26 October 2009, T.502.

1293 *Prosecutor v. Radovan Karadžić*, Case No. IT-95-5/18-T, Hearing, 26 October 2009, T.504; Hearing, 27 October 2009, T.510-511; Hearing, 02 November 2009, T.672-673.

1294 *Prosecutor v. Radovan Karadžić*, Case No. IT-95-5/18-T, Hearing, 03 November 2009, T.676-678.

1295 *Prosecutor v. Radovan Karadžić*, Case No. IT-95-5/18-T, Decision on Appointment of Counsel and Order on Further Trial Proceedings, 05 November 2009, para.21-25.

counsel was given approximately four months to familiarise him- or herself with the case and was to take over the defence at that time if – and only if – the accused would then still fail to attend the trial proceedings.[1296] The trial chamber left no doubt that the self-represented status of the defendant was not altered by this decision and that he was supposed to continue to prepare for trial and deal with daily matters.[1297] Certification to appeal the trial chamber's decision was denied,[1298] and appointed counsel was designated standby counsel at the beginning of the evidentiary phase of the proceedings.[1299]

In essence, this unfolding of events eventually did give the accused a total of 7.5 months of additional preparation time calculated from the point at which he filed his motion asking for another 10 months to prepare for the proceedings.[1300] At the same time, however, this course of action equally substantiated the trial chamber's determination to take control of the proceedings which were not to be subjected to the caprices of the defendant.

At first sight, the trial chamber's decisions are well-reasoned and unambiguous, taking into account settled jurisprudence and applicable procedure: following the issuance of a clear warning to the accused, the trial chamber reminded the defendant that counsel may be assigned to him and that the proceedings might continue in his absence if he chose to further obstruct the conduct of the proceedings.[1301] In addition, the trial chamber reflected on the proportionality of any sanction, given that it decided not to revoke the

---

1296 *Prosecutor v. Radovan Karadžić*, Case No. IT-95-5/18-T, Decision on Appointment of Counsel and Order on Further Trial Proceedings, 05 November 2009, para.25-26.

1297 *Prosecutor v. Radovan Karadžić*, Case No. IT-95-5/18-T, Decision on Appointment of Counsel and Order on Further Trial Proceedings, 05 November 2009, para.25, 27. *See also* Decision on Accused's Application for Certification to Appeal Decision on Appointment of Counsel and Order on Further Trial Proceedings, 23 November 2009, para.8.

1298 *Prosecutor v. Radovan Karadžić*, Case No. IT-95-5/18-T, Decision on Accused's Application for Certification to Appeal Decision on Appointment of Counsel and Order on Further Trial Proceedings, 23 November 2009.

1299 *Prosecutor v. Radovan Karadžić*, Case No. IT-95-5/18-T, Oral Decision, 13 April 2010, T.997-999; Decision on Designation of Standby Counsel, 15 April 2010.

1300 *Prosecutor v. Radovan Karadžić*, Case No. IT-95-5/18-PT, Submission on Commencement of Trial, 03 September 2009.

1301 *Prosecutor v. Radovan Karadžić*, Case No. IT-95-5/18-T, Hearing, 27 October 2009, T.510-511; Hearing, 02 November 2009, T.672-673. *See*, however, Hearing, 26 October 2009, T.504, which only conveys a warning of a rather general nature.

right of the accused to self-represent for the time being, while at the same time preparing for the eventuality of future lack of cooperation or good will on the part of the accused.

However, the level of obstruction which prompted the *Karadžić* trial chamber to consider imposition of counsel is significantly different from the standards adopted for example in the *Šešelj* proceedings. While the accused in *Šešelj* after years of consistent, substantial and supposedly intentional disruption of the proceedings continued to present his defence in person without even having been assigned standby counsel or only *amicus curiae*, the defendant in *Karadžić* had shown himself to be rather cooperative up to the point when he submitted that he was not ready to begin with the trial proceedings. It appears that for the trial chamber in *Karadžić*, the fact that the accused earlier in the proceedings had not "been at all rude or disrespectful to the Tribunal" did not mitigate the disruption of the proceedings considered to be significant and intentional, since, as the trial chamber noted, the accused "has not behaved in a manner other than that expected of both a counsel and an accused person".[1302] Although the appeals chamber made clear on several occasions that the determination of circumstances in which counsel is assigned to *pro se* defendants falls within the discretion of trial chambers,[1303] it may be questioned whether this meant to entail such striking discrepancies in the standards applied by the trial chambers.

1302 *Prosecutor v. Radovan Karadžić*, Case No. IT-95-5/18-T, Decision on Appointment of Counsel and Order on Further Trial Proceedings, 05 November 2009, para.21.

1303 *Prosecutor v. Slobodan Milošević,* Case No. IT-02-54-AR73.7, Decision on Interlocutory Appeal of the Trial Chamber's Decision on the Assignment of Defence Counsel, 01 November 2004, para.9. *See also Prosecutor v. Vojislav Šešelj*, Case No. IT-03-67-AR73.3, Decision on Appeal Against the Trial Chamber's Decision on Assignment of Counsel, 20 October 2006, para.20, agreeing with the consideration of the trial chamber in *Prosecutor v. Janković & Stanković*, Case No. IT-96-23/2-PT, Decision Following Registrar's Notification of Radovan Stanković's Request for Self-Representation, 19 August 2005, para.10.

II. Prior specific warning to the accused

In *Šešelj*, the appeals chamber was first to consider the requirement of an express warning to the accused when restricting his self-representation.[1304]

As a preliminary matter, the appeals chamber found that it was in a position to consider the appeal submission which had been lodged by the defendant in person rather than by counsel acting for the accused pursuant to the order of the trial chamber: referring to *Milošević* and the fact that the accused in these proceedings was equally permitted to participate personally in a similar situation, the appeals chamber determined that the trial chamber's decision "may not be interpreted so as to bar Šešelj's personal participation in the interlocutory appeal proceeding".[1305] At the same time, however, the appeals chamber determined that it was also validly seised of the appeal filed by counsel acting for the accused, considering that "assigned counsel may seek to appeal a Trial Chamber's decision to assign counsel out of the obligation to represent the accused's interests, even if the accused withholds consent or cooperation".[1306]

In order to determine the proper timing and nature of any warning to be issued to a *pro se* defendant as to the potential restriction of his or her right to self-representation, the appeals chamber sought guidance in the jurisprudence on Rule 80 of the ICTY RPE.[1307] Noting the fundamental nature of the right to self-representation,[1308] the appeals chamber held that any

> "warning with regard to possible assignment of counsel needs to be explicit, in the form of an oral or written statement to an accused explaining the disruptive

---

1304 *Prosecutor v. Vojislav Šešelj*, Case No. IT-03-67-AR73.3, Decision on Appeal Against the Trial Chamber's Decision on Assignment of Counsel, 20 October 2006, para.22.

1305 *Prosecutor v. Vojislav Šešelj*, Case No. IT-03-67-AR73.3, Decision on Appeal Against the Trial Chamber's Decision on Assignment of Counsel, 20 October 2006, para.10.

1306 *Prosecutor v. Vojislav Šešelj*, Case No. IT-03-67-AR73.3, Decision on Appeal Against the Trial Chamber's Decision on Assignment of Counsel, 20 October 2006, para.16, 17.

1307 *Prosecutor v. Vojislav Šešelj*, Case No. IT-03-67-AR73.3, Decision on Appeal Against the Trial Chamber's Decision on Assignment of Counsel, 20 October 2006, para.23-25.

1308 *Prosecutor v. Vojislav Šešelj*, Case No. IT-03-67-AR73.3, Decision on Appeal Against the Trial Chamber's Decision on Assignment of Counsel, 20 October 2006, para.23.

> behaviour and that, if it persists, the consequence will be restriction on the accused's right to self-representation."[1309]

The appeals chamber reviewed the discretionary exercise by the trial chamber, including whether it respected the principle of proportionality.[1310] It eventually overturned the trial chamber's decision to appoint counsel solely on the basis of lack of such warning.[1311]

The trial chamber for its part interpreted the decision by the appeals chamber to reinstate the *status quo ante* to its assignment of counsel and directly appointed standby counsel.[1312] The proceedings took a rather dramatic turn when the accused went on hunger strike in pursuance of, *inter alia*, his right to defend himself in person.[1313]

In contrast, the trial chamber in *Karadžić* considered to have duly warned the accused since he had received a number of warnings as to the consequences of his behaviour and in light of the fact that he was not only given opportunity to adequately adjust his conduct, but also given that the defendant was invited to himself suggest potential solutions for the situation at hand.[1314] The position of the trial chamber with regard to the propriety of these

1309 *Prosecutor v. Vojislav Šešelj*, Case No. IT-03-67-AR73.3, Decision on Appeal Against the Trial Chamber's Decision on Assignment of Counsel, 20 October 2006, para.26.

1310 *Prosecutor v. Vojislav Šešelj*, Case No. IT-03-67-AR73.3, Decision on Appeal Against the Trial Chamber's Decision on Assignment of Counsel, 20 October 2006, para.46-51.

1311 *Prosecutor v. Vojislav Šešelj*, Case No. IT-03-67-AR73.3, Decision on Appeal Against the Trial Chamber's Decision on Assignment of Counsel, 20 October 2006, para.52.

1312 *Prosecutor v. Vojislav Šešelj*, Case No. IT-03-67-PT, Order Concerning Appointment of Standby Counsel and Delayed Commencement of Trial, 25 October 2006.

1313 *Prosecutor v. Vojislav Šešelj*, Case No. IT-03-67-PT, Status Conference, 22 November 2006, T.777, 780-781; Professor Vojislav Šešelj's Decision to Refuse Medical Treatment and Artificial Feeding While on Hunger Strike, 24 November 2006 (filed: 30 November 2006).

1314 *Prosecutor v. Radovan Karadžić*, Case No. IT-95-5/18-T, Decision on Appointment of Counsel and Order of Further Trial Proceedings, 05 November 2009, para.22. *See also Prosecutor v. Radovan Karadžić*, Case No. IT-95-5/18-T, Decision on the Accused's Motion to Vacate Appointment of Richard Harvey, 23 December 2009, para.1.

warnings did not give rise to any criticism on the part of the appeals chamber.[1315]

III. "Clean slate" principle

Less than two months after the first appeals chamber decision in *Šešelj*, a second appeal was lodged against the subsequent trial chamber decision to assign counsel to the accused.[1316]

The appeals chamber in *Šešelj* in its second decision discussing the right of the accused to conduct his defence in person disapproved of the fact that the accused "was not given a clean slate by the Trial Chamber" after the earlier decision reinstating his right to self-representation.[1317] Notably, the appeals chamber found that, if it was to ignore the background to the trial chamber's decision, it would confirm the latter's prerogative to assign counsel in light of the accused's disruptive behaviour.[1318] However, it held that the defendant's right to self-represent had been "fully restored".[1319] According to the appeals chamber, the trial chamber had therefore abused its discretion in directly assigning standby counsel without first establishing additional obstructionist behaviour.[1320] Consequently, the appeals chamber reinstated the accused's right to self-representation a second time, explicitly instructed the trial chamber not to impose standby counsel unless the defen-

---

1315 *See Prosecutor v. Radovan Karadžić*, Case No. IT-95-5/18-AR73.6, Decision on Radovan Karadžić's Appeal from Decision on Motion to Vacate Appointment of Richard Harvey, 12 February 2010, para.5.

1316 *Prosecutor v. Vojislav Šešelj*, Case No. IT-03-67-T, Reasons for Decision (No. 2) on Assignment of Counsel, 27 November 2006.

1317 *Prosecutor v. Vojislav Šešelj*, Case No. IT-03-67-AR73.4, Decision on Appeal Against the Trial Chamber's Decision (No. 2) on Assignment of Counsel, 08 December 2006, para.24.

1318 *Prosecutor v. Vojislav Šešelj*, Case No. IT-03-67-AR73.4, Decision on Appeal Against the Trial Chamber's Decision (No. 2) on Assignment of Counsel, 08 December 2006, para.25.

1319 *Prosecutor v. Vojislav Šešelj*, Case No. IT-03-67-AR73.4, Decision on Appeal Against the Trial Chamber's Decision (No. 2) on Assignment of Counsel, 08 December 2006, para.26.

1320 *Prosecutor v. Vojislav Šešelj*, Case No. IT-03-67-AR73.4, Decision on Appeal Against the Trial Chamber's Decision (No. 2) on Assignment of Counsel, 08 December 2006, para.27.

dant again exhibited disruptive behaviour,[1321] and even set aside all proceedings conducted since the assignment of standby counsel.[1322]

When the prosecution at a later stage of the proceedings again attempted to have counsel assigned to the accused,[1323] the trial chamber rejected the request.[1324] On this and other occasions, the bench did not consider the requirements for imposition of counsel fulfilled, despite the conviction of the accused for contempt of court related to the disclosure of confidential information at a rather late stage of the trial proceedings.[1325]

Especially the second of the two decisions by the appeals chamber in *Šešelj* was highly contested in light of its background.[1326] The decisions have even been characterised as "being something of a theatre of the absurd".[1327]

1321 *Prosecutor v. Vojislav Šešelj*, Case No. IT-03-67-AR73.4, Decision on Appeal Against the Trial Chamber's Decision (No. 2) on Assignment of Counsel, 08 December 2006, para.28.

1322 *Prosecutor v. Vojislav Šešelj*, Case No. IT-03-67-AR73.4, Decision on Appeal Against the Trial Chamber's Decision (No. 2) on Assignment of Counsel, 08 December 2006, para.30.

1323 *Prosecutor v. Vojislav Šešelj*, Case No. IT-03-67-T, Prosecution's Motion to Terminate the Accused's Self-Representation, 28 July 2008.

1324 *Prosecutor v. Vojislav Šešelj*, Case No. IT-03-67-T, Oral Ruling, 20 October 2009, T.14751-14752; Version Publique de la « Décision Consolidée Relative à l'Imposition d'un Conseil, l'Ajournement, et la Requête de l'Accusation sur les Heures Supplémentaires Avec en Annex l'Opinion Individuelle du Juge Antonetti Président de la Chambre », 24 novembre 2009, para.87.

1325 *Procureur c/ Vojislav Šešelj*, Affaire n° IT-03-67-T, Version Publique de la « Décision Consolidée Relative à l'Imposition d'un Conseil, l'Ajournement, et la Requête de l'Accusation sur les Heures Supplémentaires Avec en Annex l'Opinion Individuelle du Juge Antonetti Président de la Chambre », 24 novembre 2009. *See also Prosecutor v. Vojislav Šešelj*, Case No. IT-03-67-T, Prosecution's Motion to Terminate the Accused's Self-Representation, 28 July 2008; *Procureur c/ Vojislav Šešelj*, Affaire n° IT-03-67-T, Version Expurgée de la "Version Expurgée de la 'Décision Relative à la Requête de l'Accusation aux Fins de Mettre Fin au Droit de l'Accusé à se Représenter Seul'" Enregistrée à Titre Confidentiel le 25 novembre 2008, 27 novembre 2008; *Prosecutor v. Vojislav Šešelj*, Case No. IT-03-67-T, Prosecution's Supplement to its Motion to Terminate the Accused's Self-Representation, 27 August 2009; Administrative Hearing, 20 October 2009, T.14751-14752.

1326 *See* Göran Sluiter, Compromising the Authority of International Criminal Justice. How Vojislav Šešelj Runs his Trial, 5 *Journal of International Criminal Justice* 529 (2007), at 533-536.

1327 Gideon Boas, Self-Representation Before the ICTY. A Case for Reform, 9 *Journal of International Criminal Justice* 53 (2011), at 64.

The appeals chamber itself acknowledged in its second decision that the first decision, interpreted by the trial chamber to reinstate the *status quo ante*, could have been clearer in expressing the complete restoration of the defendant's right to defend himself in person.[1328] Furthermore, the appeals chamber in its first decision overturned the trial chamber merely on procedural grounds, not however on the basis that the finding of obstructive behaviour on the part of the accused would have been incorrect.[1329] More importantly, the appeals chamber clearly stated that the trial chamber would be entitled to directly assign counsel following the appeals chamber decision should the accused continue his obstruction of the proceedings.[1330]

In light of this express warning to the defendant, it appears that the trial chamber merely took the necessary precautions by appointing standby counsel in order to have counsel familiar with the case in place should the eventuality of any assignment arise. It is not entirely clear from the first appeals chamber decision why such appointment of standby counsel – which in the past had been determined not to impact upon the right of the accused to self-represent[1331] – would have required a prior finding of additional obstructive behaviour by the defendant.

Additionally, while the accused had been acting in a distinctly obstructionist fashion throughout the proceedings, it is of even more significance that he decided to start a hunger strike after the October 2006 decision of the trial chamber to assign standby counsel which followed the first appeals chamber decision on the issue. This raised delicate questions for the ICTY to solve and, while decidedly not easy,[1332] the course the events took illustrates a succession of rather unfortunate decisions. Whichever position one

---

1328 *Prosecutor v. Vojislav Šešelj*, Case No. IT-03-67-AR73.4, Decision on Appeal Against the Trial Chamber's Decision (No. 2) on Assignment of Counsel, 08 December 2006, para.24.

1329 *See Prosecutor v. Vojislav Šešelj*, Case No. IT-03-67-AR73.3, Decision on Appeal Against the Trial Chamber's Decision on Assignment of Counsel, 20 October 2006, para.29.

1330 *Prosecutor v. Vojislav Šešelj*, Case No. IT-03-67-AR73.3, Decision on Appeal Against the Trial Chamber's Decision on Assignment of Counsel, 20 October 2006, para.52.

1331 *Prosecutor v. Vojislav Šešelj*, Case No. IT-03-67-PT, Decision on Prosecution's Motion for Order Appointing Counsel to Assist Vojislav Šešelj with his Defence, 09 May 2003, para.28.

1332 *Cf.* in this regard *Prosecutor v. Vojislav Šešelj*, Case No. IT-03-67-T, Urgent Order to the Dutch Authorities Regarding Health and Welfare of the Accused, 06 December 2006.

may take with regard to the choices made in this case, they surely did not contribute to an expeditious conduct of the trial which concluded its proceedings in March 2012, more than nine years after the surrender of the accused to the tribunal.[1333]

In light of the events in *Šešelj*, the detention unit of the ICTY prepared an information sheet for detainees deciding to enact in "voluntary protest fasts", providing details about the steps to be taken and the principles according to which detainees on hunger strike would be treated.[1334] These principles expressly include the Declaration of Malta of the World Medical Assembly[1335] which, *inter alia*, clarifies that force feeding is "never ethically acceptable".[1336]

The two decisions issued by the appeals chamber in *Šešelj* on the question of assignment of counsel to self-represented accused have the potential to significantly impact upon any future proceedings involving *pro se* defendants. Regarding the second appeals chamber decision, it has even been submitted that it might threaten the "crucial balance" to be struck between the right to self-representation and "the exercise of discretion by a trial chamber to limit that right where obstruction threatens the fairness of the trial or the interests of justice".[1337]

The fact that the appeals chamber in *Šešelj* eventually reinstated the accused's right to self-represent on two separate occasions has already been

---

1333 *See Prosecutor v. Vojislav Šešelj*, Case No. IT-03-67-T, Defence Closing Statement, 20 March 2012, T.17540.

1334 ICTY, Voluntary Protest Fasts – Information for Detainees, as revised 25 March 2009, available at: http://www.icty.org/x/file/Legal%20Library/Detention/voluntary_protest_fast-info_for_dets_rev_090325.pdf (last accessed 17 November 2012).

1335 WMA Declaration of Malta on Hunger Strikers, as revised on 14 October 2006, available at: http://www.wma.net/en/30publications/10policies/h31/index.html.pdf?print-media-type&footer-right=[page]/[toPage] (last accessed 17 November 2012).

1336 WMA Declaration of Malta on Hunger Strikers, as revised on 14 October 2006, Guidelines for the Management of Hunger Strikers, para.13. *See further* regarding the balance of interests at stake as considered before the ECtHR: *A v. Germany*, Application no. 10565/83 (Commission), 1985; *Herczegfalvy v. Austria*, Application no. 10533/83, Judgment, 24 September 1992, para.79-84; *Nevmerzhitsky v. Ukraine*, Application no. 54825/00, Judgment, 12 October 2005, para.93-99; *Ciorap v. Moldova*, Application no. 12066/02, Judgment, 19 September 2007, para.76-89.

1337 Gideon Boas, *The Milošević Trial: Lessons for the Conduct of Complex International Criminal Proceedings* (Cambridge: Cambridge University Press) 2007, p.235-236.

used as reason in order to underscore claims with regard to the position of the defence.[1338] Thus, it may have to be considered which implications the two appeals chamber decisions may have as a "model" for future proceedings with self-represented accused. Considering that the second decision of the appeals chamber in *Šešelj* was apparently taken against the background of the accused being on hunger strike, other defendants might refer to the perceived necessity of taking this rather extreme measure in order to be granted specific requests.[1339] The second decision of the appeals chamber lends itself to this sort of pressure used by self-represented accused even more in light of the fact that apart from the procedural grounds which led to the trial chamber's decisions being overturned, the appeals chamber seemed to agree with the trial judges' factual findings on the obstructionist and disruptive behaviour of the accused. After all, the appeals chamber explicitly warned the defendant already in its first decision that the trial chamber would be warranted to directly impose counsel should he persist in his disruptive behaviour.[1340] This leaves the impression that the accused was permitted to continue his defence in person despite the distinctly obstructive fashion in which he had behaved, merely because he decided to go on hunger strike in order to pressure the tribunal.

IV. Proportionality of the restriction and right to be heard

An additional matter to be considered in the context of restricting the exercise of the right to self-representation is the proportionality of any measure which may be imposed by trial chambers. This issue arose in the *Milošević* proceedings, when the appeals chamber modified the conditions set by the trial chamber under which assigned counsel should operate. A further concern

---

1338 *See e.g. Prosecutor v. Vojislav Šešelj*, Case No. IT-03-67-PT, Professor Vojislav Šešelj's Motion for a Decision by Trial Chamber III on Financing his Defence in Accordance with the Statute (Submission No. 294), 04 June 2007 (filed 14 June 2007), p.6, 8.

1339 *See e.g. Prosecutor v. Radovan Karadžić*, Case No. IT-95-5/18-AR73.6, Reply Brief 1: Appeal from Decision on Motion to Vacate Appointment of Richard Harvey, 01 February 2010, para.8.

1340 *Prosecutor v. Vojislav Šešelj*, Case No. IT-03-67-AR73.3, Decision on Appeal Against the Trial Chamber's Decision on Assignment of Counsel, 20 October 2006, para.52.

to be taken into account is the right of the accused to be heard on the matter, which however thus far did not give rise to any detailed discussions.[1341]

The appeals chamber in *Milošević* confirmed the trial chamber's general decision to assign counsel to the accused in light of his ill-health. However, the appeals chamber expressed doubts as to the proportionality of the imposed measure since in its view,

> "the Trial Chamber failed to recognize that any restrictions on Milošević's right to represent himself must be limited to the minimum extent necessary to protect the Tribunal's interest in assuring a reasonably expeditious trial. [...] a proportionality principle of this sort was clearly called for here."[1342]

The trial chamber in *Šešelj* similarly engaged in the assessment of proportionality of the potential imposition of counsel against the will of the accused. The bench concluded that this restrictive measure was not proportionate to the obstruction found to have been exhibited by the accused, given that the assignment of counsel would result in a delay of the proceedings of several months and above all affect the presentation of the defence case due to the stage at which the trial proceedings were at the time.[1343]

When appointing counsel to the accused in *Karadžić*, the trial chamber explicitly took into account the requirement that any restriction of the right to self-representation would need to be proportionate.[1344]

1341 *Cf. Prosecutor v. Vojislav Šešelj*, Case No. IT-03-67-AR73.3, Decision on Appeal Against the Trial Chamber's Decision on Assignment of Counsel, 20 October 2006, para.52 fn.136.

1342 *Prosecutor v. Slobodan Milošević*, Case No. IT-02-54-AR73.7, Decision on Interlocutory Appeal of the Trial Chamber's Decision on the Assignment of Defence Counsel, 01 November 2004, para.17-18.

1343 *Procureur c/ Vojislav Šešelj*, Affaire n° IT-03-67-T, Version Publique de la « Décision Consolidée Relative à l'Imposition d'un Conseil, l'Ajournement, et la Requête de l'Accusation sur les Heures Supplémentaires avec en Annexe l'Opinion Individuelle du Juge Antonetti Président de la Chambre », 24 novembre 2009, para.78-80.

1344 *Prosecutor v. Radovan Karadžić*, Case No. IT-95-5/18-T, Decision on Appointment of Counsel and Order on Further Trial Proceedings, 05 November 2009, para.16, 25.

V. Balance of interests

An analysis of the jurisprudence indicates that the criteria generally considered in the context of any potential restrictions of the right to self-representation stem from the balancing of interests at issue under the notion of a fair trial.

This balance does not form part of the strict proportionality test to be complied with when determining the nature and scope of any sanction to be imposed as discussed before. Rather, it impacts a chamber's discussion of whether the exercise of the right to self-representation should be restricted or revoked at all. Such a balance of interests is not one of the specific steps to be followed in the limitation of the right, but informs the more fundamental deliberation as to if, how, and to which extent the right to self-representation can and should be exercised. Even though there is some overlap in this discussion with the initial contemplation of fair trial issues when considering whether an accused's request to proceed *pro se* should be granted, this further balancing also comes into play when – subsequently – restrictions of the exercise of this right are to be justified.

The trial chamber in *Milošević* made clear that "[f]airness is [...] the overarching requirement of criminal proceedings",[1345] and opined that the "right to represent oneself must therefore yield when it is necessary to ensure that the trial is fair".[1346] Providing reasons for its decision to assign counsel to the accused, the bench reiterated its "fundamental duty [...] to ensure that the trial is fair and expeditious".[1347]

The balance of interests and its underlying motivations might be conducted slightly differently in cases where an accused is knowingly and intentionally engaging in obstructionist behaviour. In such cases, chambers appear to agree that the interest in protecting the integrity of proceedings should prevail if the defendant fails to improve his conduct even if given sufficient opportunity to do so. This will again be significantly different in cases of "uninten-

---

1345 *Prosecutor v. Slobodan Milošević*, Case No. IT-02-54-T, Reasons for Decision on Assignment of Defence Counsel, 22 September 2004, para.29. *See also Prosecutor v. Slobodan Milošević*, Case No. IT-02-54-T, Oral Ruling, 02 September 2004, T.32357-32359.

1346 *Prosecutor v. Slobodan Milošević*, Case No. IT-02-54-T, Reasons for Decision on Assignment of Defence Counsel, 22 September 2004, para.34.

1347 *Prosecutor v. Slobodan Milošević*, Case No. IT-02-54-T, Reasons for Decision on Assignment of Defence Counsel, 22 September 2004, para.65.

tional" obstruction such as the accused's ill-health. However, considering the *Milošević* proceedings, it may be questioned for which reasons the trial chamber did not consider the accused's behaviour to be obstructive[1348] to the extent to which he allegedly did not adhere to the prescribed medical regime,[1349] given that the defendant could arguably have intentionally and willingly influenced, at least to some extent, the impact of his ill-health on the conduct of the proceedings.

1. The right to expeditious proceedings

It is necessary to examine which factors have to be taken into account when this balance of interests is conducted, at the same time bearing in mind the heightened concern to protect the rights of accused in international criminal proceedings.[1350]

One of these interests is, as mentioned above, the concern to conduct proceedings not only fairly, but also expeditiously. This interest has to be balanced against the accused's right to present his or her case in person, exercise of which may negatively impact upon these concerns. In order to conduct such a balancing exercise, it has to be determined what is to be understood by an expeditious trial.[1351] The exact interpretation of this notion

---

1348 *Prosecutor v. Slobodan Milošević*, Case No. IT-02-54-T, Reasons for Decision on Assignment of Defence Counsel, 22 September 2004, para.67.

1349 *Prosecutor v. Slobodan Milošević*, Case No. IT-02-54-T, Reasons for Decision on Assignment of Defence Counsel, 22 September 2004, para.60-61. The accused contested this: *Prosecutor v. Slobodan Milošević*, Case No. IT-02-54-AR73.7, Appeals Hearing, 21 October 2004, T.13, 15, 81-82. *See also* Gideon Boas, *The Milošević Trial: Lessons for the Conduct of Complex International Criminal Proceedings* (Cambridge: Cambridge University Press) 2007, p.212.

1350 *Cf.* Joanne Williams, Slobodan Milosevic and the Guarantee of Self-Representation, 32 *Brooklyn Journal of International Law* 553 (2007), at 574-575. *See also* Salvatore Zappalà, The Rights of Victims v. the Rights of the Accused, 8 *Journal of International Criminal Justice* 137 (2010), at 144-145; Noah Weisbord/Matthew A. Smith, The Reason Behind the Rules: From Description to Normativity in International Criminal Procedure, 36 *North Carolina Journal of International Law and Commercial Regulation* 255 (2011), at 257-260.

1351 For three interests of accused protected by the right to an expeditious trial, *see* Hafida Lahiouel, The Right of the Accused to an Expeditious Trial, in: Richard May et al. (eds), *Essays on ICTY Procedure and Evidence. In Honour of Gabrielle Kirk McDonald* (The Hague: Kluwer Law International) 2001, p.197-213, at 198.

might be of specific importance if an accused expressly states that he or she would not disapprove of a lengthy trial, as long as they are given an opportunity to present their own views.[1352]

With regard to the *ad hoc* tribunals, the concept of expeditious trials proved to be sensitive insofar as accused readily argued that the completion strategy which regulated the gradual termination of the *ad hoc* tribunals unduly factored into chambers' decisions which were unfavourable for example regarding requested extensions of time or suspension of proceedings.[1353] However, if it is indeed the case – as one would hope – that financial or time constraints do not factor into the balance of any fair trial rights of the accused, it is to be questioned whether a defendant could voluntarily waive his or her right to an expeditious trial if found necessary to conduct their defence in person. While an accused would be the person most directly concerned by lengthy proceedings in light of the fact that he or she will usually spend the time of the proceedings in pre-trial detention, there are other participants

---

1352 *See e.g. Prosecutor v. Radovan Karadžić*, Case No. IT-95-5/18-T, Hearing, 04 November 2010, T.8990.

1353 *Cf.* filings by accused as well as frequent statements by judges or in decisions that completion strategy is not a factor to be taken into account with regard to fair trial rights of the accused: *Prosecutor v. Slobodan Milošević*, Case No. IT-02-54-AR73.4, Dissenting Opinion of Judge David Hunt on Admissibility of Evidence in Chief in the Form of Written Statements (Majority Decision given 30 September 2003), 21 October 2003, para.20-22; Separate Opinion of Judge Shahabuddeen Appended to Appeals Chamber's Decision Dated 30 September 2003 on Admissibility of Evidence-in-Chief in the Form of Written Statements, 31 October 2003, para.21; *Prosecutor v. Slobodan Milošević*, Case No. IT-02-54-AR73.7, Appeals Hearing, 21 October 2004, T.19; *Prosecutor v. Augustin Ngirabatware*, Case No. ICTR-99-54-T, Decision on Defence Motion to Vary Trial Date, 25 March 2009, para.21; *Prosecutor v. Augustin Ngirabatware*, Case No. ICTR-99-54-A, Decision on Augustin Ngirabatware's Appeal of Decisions Denying Motions to Vary Trial Date, 12 May 2009, para.31; *Prosecutor v. Radovan Karadžić*, Case No. IT-95-5/18-PT, Submission on Commencement of Trial, 03 September 2009, para.14; Motion for Leave to Reply and Reply: Motion for Binding Order to United States of America, 02 October 2009, para.4; *Prosecutor v. Radovan Karadžić*, Case No. IT-95-5/18-AR73.5, Reply Brief: Appeal of Decision on Commencement of Trial, 12 October 2009, para.39-40; *Prosecutor v. Radovan Karadžić*, Case No. IT-95-5/18-T, Submission on Trial Schedule, 20 May 2010, para.14; Order on the Trial Schedule, 27 May 2010, para.7. *See also*, however, *Prosecutor v. Vojislav Šešelj*, Case No. IT-03-67-PT, Prosecution Motion for Joinder (Partly Confidential), 01 June 2005, para.39; *Prosecutor v. Stanišić & Župljanin*, Case No. IT-08-91-PT, Stojan Zupljanin's Motion for Joinder With the Case of Radovan Karadzic, 02 December 2008, para.18-19.

and communities that might be interested in a speedy conclusion of a trial even if not purely out of budgetary considerations.[1354] Arguably, therefore, if the exercise of the right to self-representation as part of an overall fair trial guarantee unduly impacts upon the expeditious conduct of international criminal proceedings, the right to self-represent should yield if the right of accused to receive an adequate defence is sufficiently safeguarded by other means. Similar considerations as in the context of the question whether an accused can effectively waive the right to a fair trial by an informed decision to self-represent would apply.

However, at the same time doubts have been expressed as to the reliance of the trial chamber in *Milošević* on the concept of an expeditious trial in order to restrict the accused's right to self-representation.[1355] In this view, the trial chamber should have considered that it was for the accused to choose how to present his own defence, even if that occurred at the expense of his own health and of an effective defence.[1356] It was submitted that instead, the reasoning of the trial chamber should have been based on the broader notion of interests of justice, rather than the accused's right to a fair trial.[1357] This would allow restrictions of self-representation to achieve one of two goals: an expeditious trial and a certain average of defence.[1358] It was suggested that with regard to the second factor, any control by a trial chamber should be exercised on the basis of a standard of "minimum effectiveness and not one of full effectiveness".[1359] This argument was further developed several years later in light of the *Karadžić* proceedings as new addition to the gallery of self-represented defendants, in order to extend it to restrictions in view

1354 *See e.g.* for the STL: Rules of Procedure and Evidence (as of 25 November 2010). Explanatory Memorandum by the Tribunal's President, para.32.

1355 Göran Sluiter, 'Fairness and Interests of Justice'. Illusive Concepts in the *Milošević* Case, 3 *Journal of International Criminal Justice* 9 (2005), at 10.

1356 Göran Sluiter, 'Fairness and Interests of Justice'. Illusive Concepts in the *Milošević* Case, 3 *Journal of International Criminal Justice* 9 (2005), at 11: "There is nothing unfair about the manner in which Milošević was conducting his defence, including his choice of self-representation at the expense of his own health. No human-rights violation occurs if an individual of sound mind is offered all tools, but fails – of his own choice – to put up the most effective defence."

1357 Göran Sluiter, 'Fairness and Interests of Justice'. Illusive Concepts in the *Milošević* Case, 3 *Journal of International Criminal Justice* 9 (2005), at 11-12.

1358 Göran Sluiter, 'Fairness and Interests of Justice'. Illusive Concepts in the *Milošević* Case, 3 *Journal of International Criminal Justice* 9 (2005), at 12.

1359 Göran Sluiter, 'Fairness and Interests of Justice'. Illusive Concepts in the *Milošević* Case, 3 *Journal of International Criminal Justice* 9 (2005), at 14.

of disruptions by the accused or other abuse of the right to self-represent by the defendant.[1360]

The matter of expeditious proceedings might become of particular concern in case self-represented accused themselves raise the issue of the length of their trials. In *Šešelj*, the defendant raised the doctrine of abuse of process, arguing that his right to be tried without undue delay had been violated by the length of his detention and of the proceedings.[1361] The trial chamber rejected the accused's motions,[1362] without however discussing in detail any potential impact of the defendant acting *pro se* on the length of the proceedings,[1363] other than briefly referring to the position that the fact of an accused presenting his defence in person does not in and of itself justify any delays in the proceedings.[1364]

2. General fairness considerations

Yet, the opinion has been expressed that in case expeditiousness and fairness of international criminal proceedings have to be balanced against each other, expeditiousness would be an "important but less critical aspect of an international criminal trial".[1365]

1360 Göran Sluiter, Karadžić on Trial. Two Procedural Problems, 6 *Journal of International Criminal Justice* 617 (2008), at 619.

1361 *Prosecutor v. Vojislav Šešelj*, Case No. IT-03-67-T, Status Conference, 20 October 2009, T.14756-14764. *See also* Reply of Professor Vojislav Šešelj to the "Response to the Accused's Oral Motion for Termination of Proceedings Pursuant to the Abuse of Process Doctrine", 18 December 1009 (filed: 29 December 2009); Motion to Discontinue the Proceedings due to Flagrant Violation of the Right to a Trial Within a Reasonable Period in the Context of the Doctrine of Abuse of Process, 13 June 2011 (filed: 08 July 2011).

1362 *Procureur c/ Vojislav Šešelj*, Affaire n° IT-03-67-T, Décision Relative à la Requête Orale de l'Accusé pour Abus de Procédure, 10 février 2010.

1363 *Cf.* in this regard the position taken by the prosecution that "the length of the proceedings has also been impacted by the conduct of the Accused and the exercise of his self-representation": *Prosecutor v. Vojislav Šešelj*, Case No. IT-03-67-T, Prosecution's Response to the Accused's July 2011 Motion to Discontinue the Proceedings, 22 July 2011 (filed: 26 July 2011), para.3.

1364 *Procureur c/ Vojislav Šešelj*, Affaire n° IT-03-67-T, Décision Relative à la Requête de l'Accusé aux Fins de Mettre un Terme à son Procès, 29 septembre 2011, para.26.

1365 Gideon Boas, *The Milošević Trial: Lessons for the Conduct of Complex International Criminal Proceedings* (Cambridge: Cambridge University Press) 2007, p.215.

In a similar vein, the view has been adopted that the scope of the right to self-representation – and potential limitations which may have to be imposed on the exercise of this right – not only can, but sometimes have to be weighed against other elements which form part of the guarantee of a fair and expeditious trial, so that an "overall fairness" is preserved.[1366] According to this argument, restrictions are not so much caused by distinct, separate factors, but rather result from a balancing exercise of different interests at stake,[1367] and the threshold to be met for any limitations would be a danger of miscarriage of justice.[1368] It had been argued before in a comparable context that "the absolute right to a fair trial" may justify limitations of the right to self-representation.[1369]

In contrast, the decision to assign counsel to Slobodan Milošević has likewise been heavily criticised on the basis that it allegedly did not correspond with existing international law[1370] and that there could have been taken measures to provide for the accused's health issues falling short of actual imposition of counsel.[1371]

In a similar vein, the decision has been criticised on the grounds that the chamber should not have imposed counsel on Slobodan Milošević at all, and surely not on the basis of trying to ensure a fair and expeditious trial, given that in an adversarial system, both sides should be given opportunity to present their case in the manner chosen by them, with the ICTY "focusing on accuracy and upholding substantive and procedural rights" in order to

---

1366 Nina H.B. Jørgensen, The Problem of Self-Representation at International Criminal Tribunals. Striking a Balance Between Fairness and Effectiveness, 4 *Journal of International Criminal Justice* 64 (2006), at 69-70.

1367 Nina H.B. Jørgensen, The Problem of Self-Representation at International Criminal Tribunals. Striking a Balance Between Fairness and Effectiveness, 4 *Journal of International Criminal Justice* 64 (2006), at 75.

1368 Nina H.B. Jørgensen, The Problem of Self-Representation at International Criminal Tribunals. Striking a Balance Between Fairness and Effectiveness, 4 *Journal of International Criminal Justice* 64 (2006), at 71.

1369 Nina H.B. Jørgensen, The Right of the Accused to Self-Representation Before International Criminal Tribunals, 98 *The American Journal of International Law* 711 (2004), at 724.

1370 Milan Markovic, In the Interests of Justice?: A Critique of the ICTY Trial Court's Decision to Assign Counsel to Slobodan Milošević, 18 *Georgetown Journal of Legal Ethics* 947 (2005), at 950-953.

1371 Milan Markovic, In the Interests of Justice?: A Critique of the ICTY Trial Court's Decision to Assign Counsel to Slobodan Milošević, 18 *Georgetown Journal of Legal Ethics* 947 (2005), at 949.

"increase its legitimacy in the court of public opinion".[1372] It has been argued that imposition of counsel to *pro se* defendants could not be based on a more general notion of fairness and expeditiousness "because it reduces justice to a judicial afterthought".[1373]

Yet, there are equally arguments to the contrary, namely that precisely because of an accused's right to a fair trial he or she should have counsel imposed from the start. It has been stated in particular that during the *travaux préparatoires* of the ICCPR, there was initially no mention of a right to defend oneself in person.[1374] Eventually, at least part of this discussion might be superfluous at this point in time in light of the adoption of Rule 45*ter* for the ICTY RPE in November 2008, which explicitly provides for the appointment of counsel if it is in the interests of justice to do so. Thus, at least in the context of appointing counsel to fully represent the interests of an accused, it will merely have to be considered what might fall under the notion of "interests of justice", even though this will similarly require the balancing of the different interests at stake.[1375]

On a different but related note, it has been argued that outside observers could perceive the move of the trial chamber to assign counsel in *Milošević* to be unfair bearing in mind that it occurred at a time when the proceedings were about to move to the presentation of the defence, after the conclusion of the prosecution case.[1376] It is open to doubt whether this argument provides

---

1372 Constantinos Hotis, A 'Fair and Expeditious' Trial: A reappraisal of Slobodan Milošević's Right to Self-Representation Before the International Criminal Tribunal for the Former Yugoslavia, 6 *Chicago Journal of International Law* 775 (2006), at 787-789.

1373 Constantinos Hotis, A 'Fair and Expeditious' Trial: A reappraisal of Slobodan Milošević's Right to Self-Representation Before the International Criminal Tribunal for the Former Yugoslavia, 6 *Chicago Journal of International Law* 775 (2006), at 789.

1374 Michael P. Scharf/Christopher M. Rassi, Do Former Leaders have an International Right to Self-Representation in War Crimes Trials?, 20 *Ohio State Journal on Dispute Resolution* 3 (2005), at 11-12.

1375 *Cf. Prosecutor v. Vojislav Šešelj*, Case No. IT-03-67-PT, Decision on Prosecution's Motion for Order Appointing Counsel to Assist Vojislav Šešelj with his Defence, 09 May 2003, para.21. *See also* Philipp Ambach, Selbstvertretung im internationalen Strafprozess – Grundlagen, Kritik und ein Lösungsansatz für die prozessuale Handhabung in der Zukunft, 6 *Zeitschrift für Internationale Strafrechtsdogmatik* 286 (2009), at 295.

1376 Mirjan Damaška, Assignment of Counsel and Perceptions of Fairness, 3 *Journal of International Criminal Justice* 3 (2005), at 4, 7.

sufficient justification to deny any restriction of the right to self-represent. The view fails to detail why the alleged perception of outside observers should weigh so heavily in the balance of different interests of participants in the proceedings.

3. Further interests which may factor into the balance

It has been argued that the balancing exercise which has to be conducted should involve not merely the two concepts mentioned above, *i.e.* fairness and expeditiousness, but rather three, namely fairness, expeditiousness and "political reasonableness".[1377]

One might wonder whether in the course of a judicial balancing exercise, a factor openly "political" should indeed enter into the equation. Although, as mentioned before, there might indeed be a political component to trials with *pro se* defendants, it appears that a balancing exercise concerned with the safeguarding of accused's fair trial rights as well as with the integrity of the international criminal justice system should endeavour to detach itself from any political considerations as much as possible. This is all the more the case as any imposition of counsel for example based on the political motivations of a defendant to opt for self-representation which could be interpreted as "ideological censure of the accused"[1378] would be incompatible with the notion of impartiality to be respected before international criminal tribunals.

The question arises to which extent potential interests of the international community may also form part of the balance of interests. Certain obstructionist behaviour of defendants in international criminal trials may have the potential of jeopardising the integrity of international criminal proceedings in their entirety. This may eventually impact on the credibility of international criminal trials and the international criminal justice system in general and endanger the goals pronounced for international criminal proceedings.[1379]

1377 Tom Dannenbaum, The Milošević Trial: Lessons for the Conduct of International Criminal Proceedings (Review of Gideon Boas), 33 *Yale Journal of International Law* 513 (2008), at 515-516.

1378 Mario Chiavario, Some Considerations on Faces of Justice by a 'Non-Specialist', 6 *Journal of International Criminal Justice* 69 (2008), at 83.

1379 Qualifying some additional goals of international criminal justice as "aims of proceedings rather than aims of punishment": Mirjan Damaška, What is the Point

This leads to the question whether proceedings with *pro se* defendants are capable of contributing to the ambitions of international criminal justice, which include the aspiration of ascertainment of truth and establishing a reliable record of the events in the conflict.[1380] The aim of contributing to the establishment of a viable historical record may, to begin with, tend to conflict with the goal of international criminal proceedings to try individuals for alleged atrocities of a mass scale.[1381] This can be exacerbated in the context of proceedings with accused presenting their defence in person during which the style of the proceedings, *i.e.* the conduct of self-represented accused, rather than their content, *i.e.* the events, become the main matter of interest and focus of participants as well as the general public. By aggravating the potential conflict between individualised proceedings and the quest for a reasonable truthful record of events relevant to the charges under consideration, such proceedings with self-represented accused bear the potential of impacting on the integrity and credibility of international criminal proceedings.

Further factors that could be considered for a balance of interests in the context of analysing potential limitations to be imposed on the exercise of the right to self-representation may be interests of other participants to the proceedings, such as victim and witness communities.[1382] In particular in light of the increasing participation of victims in international criminal proceedings, with new structures provided for in the context of the ICC and other international criminal tribunals, the rights of the accused – including the right to self-representation considered as part of the right to a fair trial –

of International Criminal Justice?, 83 *Chicago-Kent Law Review* 329 (2008), at 331 fn.2.

1380 *Cf.* William A. Schabas, *An Introduction to the International Criminal Court* (Cambridge: Cambridge University Press) 3rd edition 2007, p.328; Jens David Ohlin, A Meta-Theory of International Criminal Procedure: Vindicating the Rule of Law, 14 *UCLA Journal of International Law and Foreign Affairs* 77 (2009), at 86, 95-97. However, outlining the problems with this goal: Mirjan Damaška, What is the Point of International Criminal Justice?, 83 *Chicago-Kent Law Review* 329 (2008), at 335-338, 340-342.

1381 Mirjan Damaška, What is the Point of International Criminal Justice?, 83 *Chicago-Kent Law Review* 329 (2008), at 332-333; Jenia Iontcheva Turner, Legal Ethics in International Criminal Defense, 10 *Chicago Journal of International Law* 685 (2010), at 693.

1382 Discussing the tension between procedural rights of the defence and victims' interests: Mirjan Damaška, What is the Point of International Criminal Justice?, 83 *Chicago-Kent Law Review* 329 (2008), at 333-334.

will have to be balanced against interests of participating victims.[1383] It has been indicated before that the right to a fair trial as arguably enjoyed by the prosecution may also be at stake.[1384]

The potentially sensitive situations which may arise in this context are well illustrated by reactions of victims and witnesses to being (cross-) examined by a self-represented accused, whom they may perceive as having played decisive roles in a conflict. It may be demanding to explain for example to victim witnesses that an accused is not only presumed innocent until proven guilty, but also that when conducting their defence in person, the defendants are entitled to question witnesses in an attempt to cast doubt on their credibility. Arguably, this scenario imposes a distinct burden on the judges to provide clarifications of the rights of self-represented accused as well as the procedures to be followed addressed to the witnesses.[1385] If specific trials are considered to be an opportunity for victims to present their stories and thereby contribute to the ascertainment of truth,[1386] these explanations may be of even higher importance. Even though a clear description may not be sufficient to alleviate the concerns of victim and witness communities, it is an important demonstration to all participants that the procedures before international criminal tribunals follow the highest standards. Thus, clarifications of this nature may also contribute to highlight the control of judges over the conduct of the proceedings, so that the content of the proceedings remains the main focus of events, rather than the actions of a self-represented accused inside and outside the courtroom.

It has been submitted that restrictions placed on the right to self-representation appear to be acknowledged in common law systems for the protection

---

1383 Mentioning the ensuing necessity to clearly define the extent and scope of victim participation: Salvatore Zappalà, The Rights of Victims v. the Rights of the Accused, 8 *Journal of International Criminal Justice* 137 (2010), at 139-140, 143-145. *See also* Jens David Ohlin, A Meta-Theory of International Criminal Procedure: Vindicating the Rule of Law, 14 *UCLA Journal of International Law and Foreign Affairs* 77 (2009), at 98.

1384 Arguing to the contrary, and stressing that "*only the accused has a right to a fair trial*": Salvatore Zappalà, The Rights of Victims v. the Rights of the Accused, 8 *Journal of International Criminal Justice* 137 (2010), at 149 (emphasis in the original).

1385 *See e.g. Prosecutor v. Radovan Karadžić*, Case No. IT-95-5/18-T, Hearing, 22 April 2010, T.1397-1398; Hearing, 16 December 2010, T.9997.

1386 Anna Maitland, Stalling Tactics or Due Process? The Karadzic Trial Resumes, 17 (3) *Human Rights Brief* 53 (2010).

of vulnerable witnesses, whereas civil law systems place an emphasis on the protection of the rights of the accused. According to this argument, it would then depend on whether civil or common law notions dominate the international criminal legal system in order to determine in which instances the right to self-representation should be restricted.[1387] This seems to be accurate when starting from the premise that the common law system tends to emphasise the individual rights – in particular with regard to freedom of choice – of an accused, whereas civil law systems rather see the need to protect that same accused against potential incursions into his rights from the side of the state. Yet, given that this dissertation deals with an international, or at least internationalised, context, it is questionable to which extent these "national" considerations are applicable to the cases at issue. Rather, it seems that in the international criminal context, even more interests are at stake and have to be balanced in the consideration of potential restrictions of self-representation, including defendants and their peer groups, victim communities, prosecution and court in particular, and international community in general.[1388] Thus, it might not be sufficient to merely draw from national considerations underlying limitations. In consequence, it has been argued that the right to self-representation as guaranteed for example by Article 21(4)(d) of the ICTY Statute has to be balanced against *e.g.* the interests enshrined in Article 20 of the ICTY Statute.[1389]

The discussions concerning potential restrictions of the right to self-representation and the balance of interests to be conducted in this context indicate that there is no unanimous position as to the elements and their respective weight encompassed in an overarching fair trial guarantee. The two broad positions adopted in the debate appear to be advocating either the imposition of counsel even against the will of the defendant in order to prevent the accused from forfeiting the possibility of conducting a professional and thus arguably more effective defence on the one side, or, quite to the contrary,

---

1387 Rachel K. Jones, Untangling the Right to Self-Representation in the International Criminal Tribunal for the Former Yugoslavia, 43 *Georgia Law Review* 1285 (2009), at 1298.

1388 *See* in this regard *Prosecutor v. Slobodan Milošević*, Case No. IT-02-54-T, Submission from the Office of the Prosecutor on the Future Conduct of the Case in the Light of the State of the Accused's Health and the Length and Complexity of the Case, 08 November 2002, para.26, referring to "concern for the public interest".

1389 Rachel K. Jones, Untangling the Right to Self-Representation in the International Criminal Tribunal for the Former Yugoslavia, 43 *Georgia Law Review* 1285 (2009), at 1300-1301.

the unconditional acceptance of the accused's decision to self-represent as expression of free will in light of the fact that the defendants will be in the best position to personally present the defence in their own case.

These divergent opinions raise the question which basis in fact underlies the balance of the different interests at stake. On the one side, there appears to be the notion of maximum autonomy of the accused which might even lead to an obviously ineffective, and thus potentially unfair, defence case presentation. On the other, the concept of greatest possible protection of an accused could be advocated which might override the expressed will of defendants at times if to an objective observer, it might be apparent that the accused by exercising his or her right to self-represent, would endanger not only his or her own health, but also his possibility of presenting an adequate defence.[1390]

As argued earlier in this dissertation, the main premise upon which to base any decisions regarding restrictions to be imposed on the right to self-representation should emphasise the need to present the accused with a possibility to present his or her case in a way the ensures his or her position as subject of the proceedings. In a similar vein, the review of the number and nature of factors which should be taken into account in the balance of interests which is necessarily to be conducted only serves to underscore the argument advanced in this dissertation that the right to defend oneself in person should in the future be interpreted and applied in a way which provides the accused with the opportunity to actively participate in their defence while at the same time avoiding the dangers of the exercise of the right to self-representation as could be seen thus far. This approach would on the one hand provide the accused with an opportunity to express their personal views in the case and contribute to the factual ascertainment of truth. On the other hand, it would safeguard the overall interests in fair and expeditious trials, as well as the integrity of international criminal proceedings.

By providing for this possibility which strikes a balance of the different factors involved already at the beginning, a viable option would be created

1390 *See* Mirjan Damaška, Assignment of Counsel and Perceptions of Fairness, 3 *Journal of International Criminal Justice* 3 (2005), at 5, arguing for an approach similar to the common law system; Michael Bohlander, 'A Fool for a Client' – Remarks on the Freedom of Choice and Assignment of Counsel at the International Criminal Tribunal for the Former Yugoslavia, 16 *Criminal Law Forum* 159 (2005), at 160.

which has the potential of significantly contributing to a well-balanced approach in future international criminal proceedings.

B. Nature and forms of restrictions

I. Imposition of counsel

Turning to the factual restriction of the exercise of the right to self-representation and the subject matter of imposition of counsel upon *pro se* defendants, it has been acknowledged by the ICTY appeals chamber that the determination of the particular circumstances in which such restrictions may occur falls within the discretion of trial chambers.

The appeals chamber found that the decision by a trial chamber to assign counsel is discretionary, deriving from the "organic familiarity with the day-to-day conduct of the parties and practical demands of the case".[1391] In its decision on the appeal against the trial chamber's decision on assignment of counsel in *Šešelj*,[1392] the appeals chamber adopted the same approach as in *Milošević*, stating, despite eventually reversing the trial chamber's decision to assign counsel,[1393] that

> "[w]hether the appropriate circumstances exist and what they are is a matter for the Trial Chamber to determine on a case by case basis when considering the particular facts of a case as a whole."[1394]

This view might even lead a trial chamber to reject an accused's request to conduct his defence in person from the very beginning of the proceedings.

1391 *Prosecutor v. Slobodan Milošević*, Case No. IT-02-54-AR73.7, Decision on Interlocutory Appeal of the Trial Chamber's Decision on the Assignment of Defence Counsel, 01 November 2004, para.9.

1392 *Prosecutor v. Vojislav Šešelj*, Case No. IT-03-67-AR73.3, Decision on Appeal Against the Trial Chamber's Decision on Assignment of Counsel, 20 October 2006, para.7. *See also Prosecutor v. Vojislav Šešelj*, Case No. IT-03-67-AR73.4, Decision on Appeal Against the Trial Chamber's Decision (No.2) on Assignment of Counsel, 08 December 2006, para.16.

1393 *Prosecutor v. Vojislav Šešelj*, Case No. IT-03-67-AR73.3, Decision on Appeal Against the Trial Chamber's Decision on Assignment of Counsel, 20 October 2006, para.52.

1394 *Prosecutor v. Vojislav Šešelj*, Case No. IT-03-67-AR73.3, Decision on Appeal Against the Trial Chamber's Decision on Assignment of Counsel, 20 October 2006, para.20.

As referred to *supra*, the trial chamber in *Janković & Stanković* considered that the right to self-representation might be limited in order to not endanger a fair trial: it adopted the view that such determination had to be made on a case-by-case basis, taking into account factors such as the ability of the accused to conduct his own defence, his attitude or behaviour,[1395] approach explicitly adopted by the appeals chamber in its *Šešelj* decision.[1396] The denial of the accused's request in *Janković & Stanković* was eventually based on the behaviour of the defendant which, in view of the chamber, "has been deliberately disrespectful and inappropriate to say the least".[1397]

While this approach is flexible and leaves considerable discretion to the respective trial chamber when it comes to the determination of factors potentially leading to the imposition of counsel, it creates on the other hand a situation where the threshold for such restriction is not necessarily clear. The reliance on divergent criteria by different trial chambers in separate cases invites confusion, even if in line with the appeals chamber jurisprudence. Considering subsequent appeals chamber jurisprudence, however, it appears that a certain margin of appreciation was deliberately provided for in order to enable trial judges to take due account of the specific circumstances of each case.

1. ICTY: Directive on the Assignment of Defence Counsel

The Directive on the Assignment of Defence Counsel[1398] issued by the ICTY registry is at first sight not directly applicable to the situation of self-represented accused. Yet, the guidelines will be analysed in more detail in light of the fact that some of the provisions were applied with regard to the question of a procedure that could be used for the appointment of counsel pursuant

1395 *Prosecutor v. Janković & Stanković*, Case No. IT-96-23/2-PT, Decision Following Registrar's Notification of Radovan Stanković's Request for Self-Representation, 19 August 2005, para.10.

1396 *Prosecutor v. Vojislav Šešelj*, Case No. IT-03-67-AR73.3, Decision on Appeal Against the Trial Chamber's Decision on Assignment of Counsel, 20 October 2006, para.20 fn.56.

1397 *Prosecutor v. Janković & Stanković*, Case No. IT-96-23/2-PT, Decision Following Registrar's Notification of Radovan Stanković's Request for Self-Representation, 19 August 2005, para.22, 23.

1398 Directive on the Assignment of Defence Counsel (Directive No. 1/94), as amended 29 June 2006 (IT/73/Rev. 11).

to a trial chamber order and the issue of potential choice of that counsel by an accused, as well as in the context of remuneration of legal associates of *pro se* defendants.

Based on Rule 45 of the ICTY RPE, the goal of the directive is to "provide legal assistance to indigent suspects or accused in the most efficient, economical and equitable manner".[1399] The detailed procedure to be followed in order for a suspect or an accused to be assigned counsel by the ICTY registry includes a thorough investigation by the ICTY registry into the means available to the accused and an assessment of his or her indigence.[1400] The burden of proof of indigence lies with the suspect or accused applying for assignment of counsel.[1401] This is important to note insofar as in case the applicant does not provide the information necessary to determine his or her indigence, it is open to the registrar to deny the request after due warning to the applicant.[1402] A decision is to be taken according to the information provided and depending on whether the suspect or accused might be able to cover part of the costs.[1403] If counsel is assigned, he or she will be chosen from the list prepared in accordance with Rule 45(B) of the ICTY RPE.[1404] The suspect or accused will be asked to select counsel from this list, although it will be for the ICTY registry to eventually decide whether the counsel chosen by the accused can indeed be assigned.[1405] Having fulfilled the prerequisites for assignment as laid down in the directive,[1406] assigned counsel will be paid according to the Defence Counsel Pre-trial or Trial Legal Aid

1399 Directive on the Assignment of Defence Counsel (Directive No. 1/94), as amended 29 June 2006 (IT/73/Rev. 11), Article 1(A).
1400 Directive on the Assignment of Defence Counsel (Directive No. 1/94), as amended 29 June 2006 (IT/73/Rev. 11), Articles 6(A)-(B), 7-10.
1401 Directive on the Assignment of Defence Counsel (Directive No. 1/94), as amended 29 June 2006 (IT/73/Rev. 11), Articles 8(A).
1402 Directive on the Assignment of Defence Counsel (Directive No. 1/94), as amended 29 June 2006 (IT/73/Rev. 11), Article 8(C).
1403 Directive on the Assignment of Defence Counsel (Directive No. 1/94), as amended 29 June 2006 (IT/73/Rev. 11), Article 11(A).
1404 Directive on the Assignment of Defence Counsel (Directive No. 1/94), as amended 29 June 2006 (IT/73/Rev. 11), Article 11(A)(i).
1405 Directive on the Assignment of Defence Counsel (Directive No. 1/94), as amended 29 June 2006 (IT/73/Rev. 11), Article 11(D).
1406 Directive on the Assignment of Defence Counsel (Directive No. 1/94), as amended 29 June 2006 (IT/73/Rev. 11), Article 14, 15.

Policies, respectively, depending on the stage of the proceedings.[1407] Pursuant to the directive, the suspect or accused concerned has means to challenge the decision of the registrar with regard to the assignment of counsel.[1408] The directive also provides for a dispute settlement mechanism, which seises different authorities of the ICTY of the dispute depending on the sum involved.[1409]

Similar directives exist at other international criminal tribunals to establish procedures according to which above all indigent accused can be provided with legal representation. At the ICTR, the pertinent directive includes a provision giving the registrar the possibility to assign counsel "in the interests of justice" in cases where the suspect or accused either requests assignment but fails to provide the necessary information, or does not obtain or request appointment of counsel or notify in writing of his or her decision to self-represent.[1410] This directive further contains a provision on the withdrawal of assignment in exceptional circumstances.[1411] Similar to the ICTR provision, the directive applicable before the Special Court for Sierra Leone provides for the possibility to assign counsel to a suspect or accused "in the interests of justice",[1412] as well as for withdrawal of counsel in exceptional circumstances.[1413] The relevant directive for the Special Tribunal for Lebanon deals more generally with defence counsel before the STL, whether chosen and paid for by the accused, or assigned to defendants upon proof of indigence.[1414] Under certain circumstances, in case the accused fails to elect representation or request assignment of counsel, the pre-trial judge will appoint counsel to the defendant, selecting from a list of three candidates provided by the head of the defence office.[1415]

1407 Directive on the Assignment of Defence Counsel (Directive No. 1/94), as amended 29 June 2006 (IT/73/Rev. 11), Article 23, 24.

1408 Directive on the Assignment of Defence Counsel (Directive No. 1/94), as amended 29 June 2006 (IT/73/Rev. 11), Article 13(B).

1409 Directive on the Assignment of Defence Counsel (Directive No. 1/94), as amended 29 June 2006 (IT/73/Rev. 11), Article 31.

1410 Directive on the Assignment of Defence Counsel, 14 March 2008, Article 10*bis*.

1411 Directive on the Assignment of Defence Counsel, 14 March 2008, Article 19.

1412 Directive on the Assignment of Counsel, 03 October 2003, Article 10.

1413 Directive on the Assignment of Counsel, 03 October 2003, Article 24.

1414 Directive on the Assignment of Defence Counsel, 20 March 2009 (as amended on 10 November 2010), Articles 6-7.

1415 Directive on the Assignment of Defence Counsel, 20 March 2009 (as amended on 10 November 2010), Article 24.

2. The case of Radovan Karadžić

The extent to which the ICTY Directive on the Assignment of Defence Counsel is applicable to the situation of self-represented accused, both with regard to the imposition of counsel and in the context of remuneration of legal advisors assisting *pro se* defendants, has been at issue in at least one case. Since there are no definite rules on the procedure to be applied when counsel is assigned by order of the trial chamber to an accused who is conducting his defence in person, eventually the appeals chamber had to determine the scope of applicability of the directive.

In *Karadžić*, the accused took issue with the procedure employed by the ICTY registry to appoint counsel upon order by the trial chamber, basing his arguments on a number of provisions of the directive. Ensuing submission of the parties triggered a discussion about the nature of a Rule 44 or 45 list (in this context referring to Rules 44 and 45 of the ICTY RPE[1416]), from which counsel might be selected. The appeals chamber eventually determined that a self-represented accused does not have a right to select counsel from any such list in case counsel's appointment had been ordered by a trial chamber as reaction to the defendant's behaviour.

a. Litigation

The defence motion to vacate the appointment of counsel selected by the ICTY registry submitted that the procedure applied in the selection process violated Article 21(4) of the ICTY Statute;[1417] appeals chamber jurisprudence;[1418] as well as certain provisions of the ICTY Directive on the Assignment of Defence Counsel.[1419] The accused argued that the ICTY registry

1416 Rule 45 ICTY RPE: "(A) Whenever the interests of justice so demand, counsel shall be assigned to suspects or accused who lack the means to remunerate such counsel. Such assignments shall be treated in accordance with the procedure established in a Directive set out by the Registrar and approved by the permanent Judges."

1417 *Prosecutor v. Radovan Karadžić*, Case No. IT-95-5/18-T, Motion to Vacate Appointment of Richard Harvey, 04 December 2009, para.6.

1418 *Prosecutor v. Radovan Karadžić*, Case No. IT-95-5/18-T, Motion to Vacate Appointment of Richard Harvey, 04 December 2009, para.7.

1419 *Prosecutor v. Radovan Karadžić*, Case No. IT-95-5/18-T, Motion to Vacate Appointment of Richard Harvey, 04 December 2009, para.17.

violated Articles 11(D) and 16(G) of the directive by not providing him with a list of counsel to select from and since he did not consent to counsel in question.[1420] He objected because selected counsel acted as defence counsel in another case which, according to the accused, raised doubts as to whether counsel "can attack Serbs in one trial and turn around and defend them in another".[1421] In a similar vein, the accused argued that the ICTY registry's interpretation of the conflict of interest provisions[1422] had deprived him of selecting counsel "familiar with the events in Bosnia and one who he could trust",[1423] even though submitting at the same time that the criteria applied eventually prevented him from choosing for example his legal advisor originating from the United States.[1424]

It was argued that the ICTY registry would have been obliged to provide the defendant with a Rule 45 list of counsel in order to select counsel for his own case.[1425] At the same time, the accused separately raised the issue of a "Rule 44 list"[1426] from which to select counsel as he was arguably entitled to, submitting that the ICTY registry was bound by the appeals chamber decision in *Šešelj* that referred to the alleged "Rule 44 list",[1427] since the appeals chamber would have decided accordingly had it envisaged that a divergent procedure could be adopted.[1428] The accused argued that his right to seek review of the ICTY registry's decision had been violated due to the refusal to let him select counsel.[1429] The two decisions referred to concerned

---

1420 *Prosecutor v. Radovan Karadžić*, Case No. IT-95-5/18-T, Motion to Vacate Appointment of Richard Harvey, 04 December 2009, para.8-16.

1421 *Prosecutor v. Radovan Karadžić*, Case No. IT-95-5/18-T, Motion to Vacate Appointment of Richard Harvey, 04 December 2009, para.15.

1422 *Prosecutor v. Radovan Karadžić*, Case No. IT-95-5/18-T, Reply Brief: Motion to Vacate Appointment of Richard Harvey, 18 December 2009, para.10-14.

1423 *Prosecutor v. Radovan Karadžić*, Case No. IT-95-5/18-T, Reply Brief: Motion to Vacate Appointment of Richard Harvey, 18 December 2009, para.15.

1424 *Prosecutor v. Radovan Karadžić*, Case No. IT-95-5/18-T, Reply Brief: Motion to Vacate Appointment of Richard Harvey, 18 December 2009, para.16-19.

1425 *Prosecutor v. Radovan Karadžić*, Case No. IT-95-5/18-T, Motion to Vacate Appointment of Richard Harvey, 04 December 2009, para.4, 10.

1426 *Prosecutor v. Radovan Karadžić*, Case No. IT-95-5/18-T, Reply Brief: Motion to Vacate Appointment of Richard Harvey, 18 December 2009, para.3.

1427 *Prosecutor v. Radovan Karadžić*, Case No. IT-95-5/18-T, Reply Brief: Motion to Vacate Appointment of Richard Harvey, 18 December 2009, para.4.

1428 *Prosecutor v. Radovan Karadžić*, Case No. IT-95-5/18-T, Reply Brief: Motion to Vacate Appointment of Richard Harvey, 18 December 2009, para.5.

1429 *Prosecutor v. Radovan Karadžić*, Case No. IT-95-5/18-T, Reply Brief: Motion to Vacate Appointment of Richard Harvey, 18 December 2009, para.8-9.

the assignment of counsel *upon request* of the defendant concerned. Similarly, the argument failed to outline how the alleged refusal to be given an opportunity to select counsel was linked to any potential violation of a right to have the ultimate decision reviewed.

In his appeal,[1430] the accused disagreed with the trial chamber's qualification of the portion at issue of the appeals chamber decision in *Šešelj* as *obiter*,[1431] arguing that both judges and prosecution erred in concluding that the *Šešelj* appeals chamber decision was limited to the particular context of that case,[1432] and submitting that the "right" granted to the accused in *Šešelj* went beyond ordinarily applicable minimum guarantees.[1433] According to the accused, the message would be clear so that in such case his only way to get to select standby counsel would be to go on hunger strike like the defendant in *Šešelj*.[1434] He argued that it was unreasonable and rewarded disruptive accused if they were allowed to choose standby counsel, while he was not given this possibility.[1435]

It was submitted that by ordering appointment of counsel, the trial chamber "signaled its intention" to override the choice of the accused to self-represent, so that he became an accused falling under Article 11(C)(ii) of the directive,

---

1430 *Prosecutor v. Radovan Karadžić*, Case No. IT-95-5/18-AR73.6, Appeal from Decision on Motion to Vacate Appointment of Richard Harvey, 19 January 2010. *See also Prosecutor v. Radovan Karadžić*, Case No. IT-95-5/18-T, Application for Certification to Appeal Decision Decision on Motion to Vacate Appointment of Richard Harvey, 29 December 2009; and Decision on Accused's Application for Certification to Appeal the Trial Chamber's Decision on Motion to Vacate Appointment of Richard Harvey, 13 January 2010.

1431 *Prosecutor v. Radovan Karadžić*, Case No. IT-95-5/18-AR73.6, Appeal from Decision on Motion to Vacate Appointment of Richard Harvey, 19 January 2010, para.34.

1432 *Prosecutor v. Radovan Karadžić*, Case No. IT-95-5/18-AR73.6, Reply Brief #1: Appeal from Decision on Motion to Vacate Appointment of Richard Harvey, 01 February 2010, para.3-5.

1433 *Prosecutor v. Radovan Karadžić*, Case No. IT-95-5/18-AR73.6, Reply Brief #1: Appeal from Decision on Motion to Vacate Appointment of Richard Harvey, 01 February 2010, para.6-7.

1434 *Prosecutor v. Radovan Karadžić*, Case No. IT-95-5/18-AR73.6, Reply Brief #1: Appeal from Decision on Motion to Vacate Appointment of Richard Harvey, 01 February 2010, para.8.

1435 *Prosecutor v. Radovan Karadžić*, Case No. IT-95-5/18-AR73.6, Appeal from Decision on Motion to Vacate Appointment of Richard Harvey, 19 January 2010, para.42-43.

who "failed to obtain or request the assignment of counsel".[1436] The defendant submitted that Article 11 of the directive was applicable to the imposition of counsel since it would not be logical to apply this provision in case a defendant refused or failed to comply with the procedure, "while refusing to allow a previously self-represented accused the same right".[1437]

The argument on the allegedly unavoidable hunger strike is severely flawed. The submission omits to mention that the appeals chamber itself limited the decision in *Šešelj* to the specific circumstances of the case which were indeed unique in light of the hunger strike of the accused in that case. Not only is the argument based on the assumption that the appeals chamber in *Šešelj* did in fact create a right to which other accused would be equally entitled, but can in fact be considered as blackmail by the defendant who submitted that he may have to embark on a hunger strike should he be denied any alleged right to select standby counsel.

Similarly, the defendant's argument on the origin of appointed counsel does not withstand further scrutiny. The ICTY registry left no doubt that not the nationality of any counsel on a selection list was determinative for the choice made, but rather considerations such as scheduling conflicts; potential conflicts of interests; and qualifications of counsel. In addition, the fact that the defendant's lead legal associate in the proceedings originated from the U.S., and thus from a major NATO member state, invalidates the implicit argument of the accused that he would not able to trust any counsel not hailing from the region of the former Yugoslavia.[1438] The accused's argument renders itself even more invalid in light of his own indication that he might have chosen his lead legal advisor as standby counsel had he not allegedly been prevented from doing so by the limited list provided.

Likewise, the accused failed to provide any further substantial basis for the argument as to the applicability of the entire ICTY Directive on the As-

---

1436 *Prosecutor v. Radovan Karadžić*, Case No. IT-95-5/18-AR73.6, Appeal from Decision on Motion to Vacate Appointment of Richard Harvey, 19 January 2010, para.69.

1437 *Prosecutor v. Radovan Karadžić*, Case No. IT-95-5/18-AR73.6, Appeal from Decision on Motion to Vacate Appointment of Richard Harvey, 19 January 2010, para.70.

1438 *See also Prosecutor v. Radovan Karadžić*, Case No. IT-95-5/18-T, Decision on the Accused's Motion to Vacate Appointment of Richard Harvey, 23 December 2009, para.42-43.

signment of Defence Counsel or selected provisions of it,[1439] or that the ICTY registry followed the procedure provided for in the directive in other cases.[1440] Even if assumed *arguendo* that the directive was applicable in its entirety to the situation at hand, it has to be borne in mind that the trial chamber's decision to appoint counsel did not modify in any way the *pro se* status of the accused.[1441] These circumstances do not create a situation in which the accused would fall under the definition of the directive according to which he "failed to obtain or request the assignment of counsel".[1442] The situation envisaged by the relevant provision is clearly concerned with suspects or accused who did not choose to conduct their defence in person, and thus does not, on its face, equal an accused unwilling or failing to choose counsel with a *pro se* defendant on whom counsel is imposed by order of a trial chamber.

The ICTY registry agreed that the issue at hand may impact on the accused's right to a fair trial,[1443] and recalled steps undertaken in the course of the proceedings in general and with regard to the selection of counsel in particular.[1444] It argued that rather than Rule 45 of the ICTY RPE concerning appointment of counsel upon request of indigent accused,[1445] or the direct-

---

1439 *Prosecutor v. Radovan Karadžić*, Case No. IT-95-5/18-AR73.6, Appeal from Decision on Motion to Vacate Appointment of Richard Harvey, 19 January 2010, para.62-77.

1440 *Prosecutor v. Radovan Karadžić*, Case No. IT-95-5/18-AR73.6, Appeal from Decision on Motion to Vacate Appointment of Richard Harvey, 19 January 2010, para.81.

1441 *See Prosecutor v. Radovan Karadžić*, Case No. IT-95-5/18-T, Decision on Appointment of Counsel and Order on Further Trial Proceedings, 05 November 2009, para.25-26.

1442 Directive on the Assignment of Defence Counsel (Directive No. 1/94), as amended 29 June 2006 (IT/73/Rev. 11), Article 11(C).

1443 *Prosecutor v. Radovan Karadžić*, Case No. IT-95-5/18-T, Registrar's Submission Pursuant to Rule 33(B) Regarding Radovan Karadžić's Motion to Vacate Appointment of Richard Harvey, 14 December 2009, para.24.

1444 *Prosecutor v. Radovan Karadžić*, Case No. IT-95-5/18-T, Registrar's Submission Pursuant to Rule 33(B) Regarding Radovan Karadžić's Motion to Vacate Appointment of Richard Harvey, 14 December 2009, para.6, 16, 17.

1445 *Prosecutor v. Radovan Karadžić*, Case No. IT-95-5/18-T, Registrar's Submission Pursuant to Rule 33(B) Regarding Radovan Karadžić's Motion to Vacate Appointment of Richard Harvey, 14 December 2009, para.41.

ive,[1446] Rule 44 of the ICTY RPE, additional jurisprudence and other considerations were applicable.[1447] It was pointed out that it would not be possible to appoint counsel from the Rule 45 List who had expressed concerns about a potential representation of uncooperative accused,[1448] and that the decision in *Šešelj* was interpreted to mean a list of counsel who satisfied the criteria established in Rule 44 of the ICTY RPE.[1449] It submitted that no established "Rule 44 list" existed and that the only official list, based on Rule 45(B) of the ICTY RPE, could merely be used as basis to further reduce a list of candidates eligible in the given circumstances.[1450] The ICTY registry agreed with the trial chamber's assessment that the directive would be directly applicable only to situations falling under Rule 45 of the ICTY RPE,[1451] and argued that a direct application of Article 16(G) of the directive would be unreasonable in the context of a *pro se* defendant.[1452]

It further agreed with the bench that a self-represented accused had no right to select appointed counsel,[1453] and submitted that the accused's asser-

---

1446 *Prosecutor v. Radovan Karadžić*, Case No. IT-95-5/18-T, Registrar's Submission Pursuant to Rule 33(B) Regarding Radovan Karadžić's Motion to Vacate Appointment of Richard Harvey, 14 December 2009, para.33.

1447 *Prosecutor v. Radovan Karadžić*, Case No. IT-95-5/18-T, Registrar's Submission Pursuant to Rule 33(B) Regarding Radovan Karadžić's Motion to Vacate Appointment of Richard Harvey, 14 December 2009, para.27.

1448 *Prosecutor v. Radovan Karadžić*, Case No. IT-95-5/18-T, Registrar's Submission Pursuant to Rule 33(B) Regarding Radovan Karadžić's Motion to Vacate Appointment of Richard Harvey, 14 December 2009, para.42.

1449 *Prosecutor v. Radovan Karadžić*, Case No. IT-95-5/18-T, Registrar's Submission Pursuant to Rule 33(B) Regarding Radovan Karadžić's Motion to Vacate Appointment of Richard Harvey, 14 December 2009, para.43, 44.

1450 *Prosecutor v. Radovan Karadžić*, Case No. IT-95-5/18-AR73.6, Registrar's Submission Pursuant to Rule 33 (B) Regarding Radovan Karadžić's Appeal from Decision on Motion to Vacate Appointment of Richard Harvey, 04 February 2010, para.23.

1451 *Prosecutor v. Radovan Karadžić*, Case No. IT-95-5/18-AR73.6, Registrar's Submission Pursuant to Rule 33 (B) Regarding Radovan Karadžić's Appeal from Decision on Motion to Vacate Appointment of Richard Harvey, 04 February 2010, para.18.

1452 *Prosecutor v. Radovan Karadžić*, Case No. IT-95-5/18-AR73.6, Registrar's Submission Pursuant to Rule 33 (B) Regarding Radovan Karadžić's Appeal from Decision on Motion to Vacate Appointment of Richard Harvey, 04 February 2010, para.19.

1453 *Prosecutor v. Radovan Karadžić*, Case No. IT-95-5/18-AR73.6, Registrar's Submission Pursuant to Rule 33 (B) Regarding Radovan Karadžić's Appeal from

tion that he might have opted for his legal advisor had he been on the list of counsel was without merit in light of the fact that the defendant had himself stated on previous occasions that he would not want to have his adviser as standby counsel.[1454] It asserted that this argument evidenced a misconception of the accused as to the scope of his rights as *pro se* defendant, given that he would not be entitled to legal aid under the official scheme in case standby counsel was assigned.[1455] According to the ICTY registry, the accused was given the opportunity to participate in the selection process "out of procedural fairness",[1456] and that the steps taken to identify counsel[1457] satisfied the test of proper exercise of its discretion.[1458] It contended that it would be unreasonable to require consent from an accused who had counsel appointed for the sole reason of exhibiting obstructionist behaviour to begin with,[1459] and that the provision of a list of counsel who could not be appointed for a number of reasons would have resulted in a waste of time and delayed the procedure.[1460] In the ICTY registry's view, it "would run counter to the spirit behind the establishment of the tribunal if it were to be accepted that

---

Decision on Motion to Vacate Appointment of Richard Harvey, 04 February 2010, para.24.

1454 *Prosecutor v. Radovan Karadžić*, Case No. IT-95-5/18-AR73.6, Registrar's Submission Pursuant to Rule 33 (B) Regarding Radovan Karadžić's Appeal from Decision on Motion to Vacate Appointment of Richard Harvey, 04 February 2010, para.29.

1455 *Prosecutor v. Radovan Karadžić*, Case No. IT-95-5/18-AR73.6, Registrar's Submission Pursuant to Rule 33 (B) Regarding Radovan Karadžić's Appeal from Decision on Motion to Vacate Appointment of Richard Harvey, 04 February 2010, para.30.

1456 *Prosecutor v. Radovan Karadžić*, Case No. IT-95-5/18-T, Registrar's Submission Pursuant to Rule 33(B) Regarding Radovan Karadžić's Motion to Vacate Appointment of Richard Harvey, 14 December 2009, para.30.

1457 *Prosecutor v. Radovan Karadžić*, Case No. IT-95-5/18-T, Registrar's Submission Pursuant to Rule 33(B) Regarding Radovan Karadžić's Motion to Vacate Appointment of Richard Harvey, 14 December 2009, para.45-49.

1458 *Prosecutor v. Radovan Karadžić*, Case No. IT-95-5/18-T, Registrar's Submission Pursuant to Rule 33(B) Regarding Radovan Karadžić's Motion to Vacate Appointment of Richard Harvey, 14 December 2009, para.50, 52.

1459 *Prosecutor v. Radovan Karadžić*, Case No. IT-95-5/18-T, Registrar's Submission Pursuant to Rule 33(B) Regarding Radovan Karadžić's Motion to Vacate Appointment of Richard Harvey, 14 December 2009, para.35.

1460 *Prosecutor v. Radovan Karadžić*, Case No. IT-95-5/18-T, Registrar's Submission Pursuant to Rule 33(B) Regarding Radovan Karadžić's Motion to Vacate Appointment of Richard Harvey, 14 December 2009, para.57.

an accused may only be properly represented by counsel of the same ethnic background".[1461]

It was suggested that the right enshrined in Article 21(4) of the ICTY Statute had not been violated since the choice provided therein had been made by the accused at the beginning of the proceedings by deciding to conduct his defence in person,[1462] while the appointment of counsel originated in the trial chamber's reaction to the defendant's obstructionist behaviour, and thus did not create a "cumulative and contemporaneous right to both self-representation and to choose counsel".[1463] It was submitted that the accused's right to self-representation had not been amended by the decision, therefore he continued to exercise this right, and thus he was not entitled, as of right, to select appointed counsel on the basis of Article 21(4) of the ICTY Statute.[1464]

It should be pointed out in this context that the ICTY registry did not unambiguously state the origin of its argument as to the subject matter of a list of counsel, as well as with regard to the inapplicability of Rule 45 of the ICTY RPE.[1465] Nor did the submission further explain how concerns expressed by counsel included on the Rule 45 list would prevent it from providing the entire list to the accused. If a defendant was to choose from that complete list, and counsel in question for whichever reason indeed voiced unwillingness to act as imposed counsel, the ICTY registry could simply ask for a replacement choice. It is not entirely clear whether this might collide with the "cabranking principle" arguably applicable to defence counsel before the ICTY, *i.e.* that a counsel selected by an accused should not from the

---

1461 *Prosecutor v. Radovan Karadžić*, Case No. IT-95-5/18-T, Registrar's Submission Pursuant to Rule 33(B) Regarding Radovan Karadžić's Motion to Vacate Appointment of Richard Harvey, 14 December 2009, para.53.

1462 *Prosecutor v. Radovan Karadžić*, Case No. IT-95-5/18-T, Registrar's Submission Pursuant to Rule 33(B) Regarding Radovan Karadžić's Motion to Vacate Appointment of Richard Harvey, 14 December 2009, para.29.

1463 *Prosecutor v. Radovan Karadžić*, Case No. IT-95-5/18-T, Registrar's Submission Pursuant to Rule 33(B) Regarding Radovan Karadžić's Motion to Vacate Appointment of Richard Harvey, 14 December 2009, para.30.

1464 *Prosecutor v. Radovan Karadžić*, Case No. IT-95-5/18-T, Registrar's Submission Pursuant to Rule 33(B) Regarding Radovan Karadžić's Motion to Vacate Appointment of Richard Harvey, 14 December 2009, para.31.

1465 *Prosecutor v. Radovan Karadžić*, Case No. IT-95-5/18-T, Registrar's Submission Pursuant to Rule 33(B) Regarding Radovan Karadžić's Motion to Vacate Appointment of Richard Harvey, 14 December 2009, para.41-42.

outset refuse to represent an accused's interests.[1466] However, the situation might be slightly different in situations of appointed counsel as any choice of a defendant would not be genuine in any event insofar as he or she has counsel imposed against his or her expressed choice to self-represent.

The prosecution adopted the view that an accused who received free legal assistance had no absolute right to select counsel, and that Article 11(D) of the directive was not applicable to the situation at stake.[1467] However, it did not provide any basis for the assertion that in light of the appointment of counsel against the will of the accused, the ICTY registry would be entitled "to exert more control over the selection process than is normal practice, in order to ensure the expeditious conduct of the trial".[1468] Comparable to the position of the ICTY registry, and with reference to an earlier decision in *Milošević*, the prosecution submitted that no consent could be required in the current situation, since otherwise the proceedings could be further obstructed by failure of the accused to cooperate.[1469] It did not consider the *Šešelj* decision to establish an "inviolable right to select standby counsel"[1470] and rather agreed with the trial chamber's assessment that the *Šešelj* appeals chamber decision was limited to the specific context of that case.[1471] The prosecution submitted that even if the appeals chamber was to find that the *Šešelj* decision was applicable, there were "cogent reasons in the interests

---

1466 Jarinde Temminck Tuinstra, Defending the Defenders. The Role of Defence Counsel in International Criminal Trials, 8 *Journal of International Criminal Justice* 463 (2010), at 469-470.

1467 *Prosecutor v. Radovan Karadžić*, Case No. IT-95-5/18-T, Prosecution Response to Karadžić's Motion to Vacate Appointment of Richard Harvey, 14 December 2009, para.3.

1468 *Prosecutor v. Radovan Karadžić*, Case No. IT-95-5/18-T, Prosecution Response to Karadžić's Motion to Vacate Appointment of Richard Harvey, 14 December 2009, para.4.

1469 *Prosecutor v. Radovan Karadžić*, Case No. IT-95-5/18-T, Prosecution Response to Karadžić's Motion to Vacate Appointment of Richard Harvey, 14 December 2009, para.5.

1470 *Prosecutor v. Radovan Karadžić*, Case No. IT-95-5/18-T, Prosecution Response to Karadžić's Motion to Vacate Appointment of Richard Harvey, 14 December 2009, para.6.

1471 *Prosecutor v. Radovan Karadžić*, Case No. IT-95-5/18-AR73.6, Prosecution's Response to Karadžić's Appeal from Decision on Motion to Vacate Appointment of Richard Harvey, 29 January 2010, para.16-17.

of justice to depart from it".[1472] The adoption of Rule 45*ter* of the ICTY RPE, without any reference to the directive, would be such a reason not to follow the procedure outlined in the *Šešelj* decision.[1473]

Further, the prosecution agreed with the trial chamber that Article 21(4)(b) and (d) of the ICTY Statute were inapplicable to the issue at hand[1474] since the minimum guarantees provided for had been safeguarded by giving the accused the opportunity to choose between self-representation and representation by counsel.[1475] It argued that the appointment of counsel did not change this situation,[1476] but should rather be seen as restriction of the right to self-representation.[1477] It was submitted that a "fundamental difference" existed between the voluntary choice to be represented by counsel and the imposition of counsel to a self-represented accused.[1478] In addition, it was argued that the directive tied in with Rule 45 of the ICTY RPE and thus also Article 21(4)(d) of the ICTY Statute, whereas the fact that Rule 45*ter* of the ICTY RPE did not refer to the directive would confirm the assertion that an order pursuant to Rule 45*ter* – as well as any "antecedent order" – did not implicate the rights enshrined in Article 21(4)(d) of the ICTY Statute.[1479] It was

1472 *Prosecutor v. Radovan Karadžić*, Case No. IT-95-5/18-AR73.6, Prosecution's Response to Karadžić's Appeal from Decision on Motion to Vacate Appointment of Richard Harvey, 29 January 2010, para.23.

1473 *Prosecutor v. Radovan Karadžić*, Case No. IT-95-5/18-AR73.6, Prosecution's Response to Karadžić's Appeal from Decision on Motion to Vacate Appointment of Richard Harvey, 29 January 2010, para.24-26.

1474 *Prosecutor v. Radovan Karadžić*, Case No. IT-95-5/18-AR73.6, Prosecution's Response to Karadžić's Appeal from Decision on Motion to Vacate Appointment of Richard Harvey, 29 January 2010, para.7.

1475 *Prosecutor v. Radovan Karadžić*, Case No. IT-95-5/18-AR73.6, Prosecution's Response to Karadžić's Appeal from Decision on Motion to Vacate Appointment of Richard Harvey, 29 January 2010, para.8.

1476 *Prosecutor v. Radovan Karadžić*, Case No. IT-95-5/18-AR73.6, Prosecution's Response to Karadžić's Appeal from Decision on Motion to Vacate Appointment of Richard Harvey, 29 January 2010, para.9, 10.

1477 *Prosecutor v. Radovan Karadžić*, Case No. IT-95-5/18-AR73.6, Prosecution's Response to Karadžić's Appeal from Decision on Motion to Vacate Appointment of Richard Harvey, 29 January 2010, para.11.

1478 *Prosecutor v. Radovan Karadžić*, Case No. IT-95-5/18-AR73.6, Prosecution's Response to Karadžić's Appeal from Decision on Motion to Vacate Appointment of Richard Harvey, 29 January 2010, para.12.

1479 *Prosecutor v. Radovan Karadžić*, Case No. IT-95-5/18-AR73.6, Prosecution's Response to Karadžić's Appeal from Decision on Motion to Vacate Appointment of Richard Harvey, 29 January 2010, para.12.

pointed out that even though Article 21(4)(d) of the ICTY Statute was arguably not applicable, the ICTY registry had adhered to it.[1480]

The trial chamber found Article 13(B) or other provisions of the directive not to be applicable[1481] and considered itself competent to entertain the issue in light of the fact that the matter would affect the fairness of trial.[1482] It rejected the argument that Article 21(4)(b) and (d) of the ICTY Statute had been violated,[1483] given that the accused decided to conduct his defence in person and continued to exercise this right,[1484] and that it was not its intention to signal that the accused would simultaneously be entitled to counsel of his own choosing.[1485] The trial chamber clarified that the decision to appoint counsel had been issued pursuant to Rule 54 of the ICTY RPE – rather than Rule 45*ter* – and that since the applicability of the directive in the case at hand was in doubt, the ICTY registry had no choice but to turn to its relevant provisions for guidance.[1486] While the bench rejected the ICTY registry's argument that it had not violated Article 11(D) of the directive even if it was applicable in its entirety,[1487] it did agree that a strict application of Article 16(G) of the directive would only lead to further obstruction of the proceed-

---

1480 *Prosecutor v. Radovan Karadžić*, Case No. IT-95-5/18-AR73.6, Prosecution's Response to Karadžić's Appeal from Decision on Motion to Vacate Appointment of Richard Harvey, 29 January 2010, para.13-15.

1481 *Prosecutor v. Radovan Karadžić*, Case No. IT-95-5/18-T, Decision on the Accused's Motion to Vacate Appointment of Richard Harvey, 23 December 2009, para.22.

1482 *Prosecutor v. Radovan Karadžić*, Case No. IT-95-5/18-T, Decision on the Accused's Motion to Vacate Appointment of Richard Harvey, 23 December 2009, para.23.

1483 *Prosecutor v. Radovan Karadžić*, Case No. IT-95-5/18-T, Decision on the Accused's Motion to Vacate Appointment of Richard Harvey, 23 December 2009, para.27, 28.

1484 *Prosecutor v. Radovan Karadžić*, Case No. IT-95-5/18-T, Decision on the Accused's Motion to Vacate Appointment of Richard Harvey, 23 December 2009, para.25.

1485 *Prosecutor v. Radovan Karadžić*, Case No. IT-95-5/18-T, Decision on the Accused's Motion to Vacate Appointment of Richard Harvey, 23 December 2009, para.26.

1486 *Prosecutor v. Radovan Karadžić*, Case No. IT-95-5/18-T, Decision on the Accused's Motion to Vacate Appointment of Richard Harvey, 23 December 2009, para.29, 30, 34.

1487 *Prosecutor v. Radovan Karadžić*, Case No. IT-95-5/18-T, Decision on the Accused's Motion to Vacate Appointment of Richard Harvey, 23 December 2009, para.31.

ings.[1488] By facilitating meetings of the accused with eligible counsel, the ICTY registry according to the bench even "went beyond" the purpose of providing the accused with a list of counsel.[1489]

More significantly, the trial chamber found that the *Šešelj* appeals chamber decision was very context-specific and could not be considered in isolation of that factual background.[1490] It expressed the view that despite the reference by the appeals chamber to a "Rule 44 list", no list of counsel existed but a "Rule 45 List" as provided for by the ICTY RPE.[1491] According to the trial chamber, it was "somewhat wanting" to assume a right of a self-represented accused to select counsel as precondition to the appointment of such counsel, even more so in cases where counsel had been appointed as a precautionary measure only.[1492]

Turning to the argument of the accused that had the list been prepared appropriately, he would have had the possibility to choose his "American legal advisor", the trial chamber clarified that by selecting his advisor, the accused would have deprived himself of resources for his own preparation in light of the fact that the *pro se* status of the defendant had not been altered by the appointment of counsel and since this counsel was to concentrate exclusively on the preparation for potential takeover of the defence in the future, rather than being concerned with the daily business of the proceedings.[1493] The trial chamber

---

1488 *Prosecutor v. Radovan Karadžić*, Case No. IT-95-5/18-T, Decision on the Accused's Motion to Vacate Appointment of Richard Harvey, 23 December 2009, para.32-34.

1489 *Prosecutor v. Radovan Karadžić*, Case No. IT-95-5/18-T, Decision on the Accused's Motion to Vacate Appointment of Richard Harvey, 23 December 2009, para.40. *See also* para.46.

1490 *Prosecutor v. Radovan Karadžić*, Case No. IT-95-5/18-T, Decision on the Accused's Motion to Vacate Appointment of Richard Harvey, 23 December 2009, para.35, 36, 38.

1491 *Prosecutor v. Radovan Karadžić*, Case No. IT-95-5/18-T, Decision on the Accused's Motion to Vacate Appointment of Richard Harvey, 23 December 2009, para.40.

1492 *Prosecutor v. Radovan Karadžić*, Case No. IT-95-5/18-T, Decision on the Accused's Motion to Vacate Appointment of Richard Harvey, 23 December 2009, para.38.

1493 *Prosecutor v. Radovan Karadžić*, Case No. IT-95-5/18-T, Decision on the Accused's Motion to Vacate Appointment of Richard Harvey, 23 December 2009, para.42.

> "[...] note[d] its view that the Accused's position that he does not (and will not) consent to Richard Harvey's appointment because the latter has represented Kosovo Albanians, has never represented Serbs, and has made statements that the Accused regards as critical of Serbs lacks any persuasive force and is, in fact, untenable. [...] Moreover, the Accused's argument that he should have been given an opportunity to choose a lawyer with whom he shares a common heritage, language, and trust, rather than a lawyer from a NATO country is, at best, suspicious: his senior legal adviser, Peter Robinson, comes from the United States of America, the country widely recognised as the leading NATO power. In addition, a number of his *pro bono* legal advisers also come from NATO countries."[1494]

The decision of the appeals chamber clarified a number of issues, *inter alia*, the question of the applicability of the ICTY Directive on the Assignment of Defence Counsel to self-represented accused; the issue of a right to select appointed (standby) counsel; and the question whether jurisprudence from other cases with self-represented accused can be used in the resolution of disputes in subsequent proceedings. The finding of the appeals chamber with regard to the latter is important insofar as it gives some indication on the approach to be taken with regard to precedents in the context of cases with self-represented accused.

Referring back to decisions in *Krajišnik* and *Milošević*, the appeals chamber reiterated that the rights guaranteed in Article 21(4)(d) of the ICTY Statute – self-representation *or* counsel of one's own choosing – were mutually exclusive.[1495] Therefore, in light of the fact that the accused had chosen to conduct his defence in person and elected to remain self-represented, he had no rights deriving from Article 21(4)(d) of the ICTY Statute with regard to a potential choice of counsel.[1496] In addition, the appeals chamber found that the trial chamber's decision to appoint counsel and potential ultimate decision to assign one was to be considered as restriction of the accused's right to self-representation, not as a potential recognition of a voluntary de-

1494 *Prosecutor v. Radovan Karadžić*, Case No. IT-95-5/18-T, Decision on the Accused's Motion to Vacate Appointment of Richard Harvey, 23 December 2009, para.43.

1495 *Prosecutor v. Radovan Karadžić*, Case No. IT-95-5/18-AR73.6, Decision on Radovan Karadžić's Appeal from Decision on Motion to Vacate Appointment of Richard Harvey, 12 February 2010, para.26.

1496 *Prosecutor v. Radovan Karadžić*, Case No. IT-95-5/18-AR73.6, Decision on Radovan Karadžić's Appeal from Decision on Motion to Vacate Appointment of Richard Harvey, 12 February 2010, para.26.

cision to cease that right.[1497] The appeals chamber held that the directive was not applicable to the case at hand, as it dealt with the assignment of counsel to indigent suspects or accused who wished to have counsel assigned rather than opting for self-representation.[1498] Yet, due to the lack of specific rules for situations such as the one at issue, it fell under the discretion of the ICTY registry to resort to comparable provisions like those in the directive, without rendering these provisions binding.[1499]

In the appeals chamber's view, the *Šešelj* decision had been "rendered in a unique factual and procedural context" and thus could not be considered to create rights going beyond those guaranteed in the ICTY Statute and RPE.[1500] More significantly:

> "The Appeals Chamber underscores that limitations of the right to self-representation are a rare occurrence, and that their details are necessarily context-specific. More particularly, the appointment of standby counsel is not subject to more formalized procedures designed to regularize the assignment of counsel to indigent suspects and accused who do not choose to self-represent. In assigning standby counsel, the Registrar or a Chamber may, but are not required to, make reference to procedures used in the assignment of counsel in other contexts. *This more fluid and individualized approach to the appointment of standby counsel in cases of self-representation is amply justified by the fact that the reasons for and specific parameters of each appointment will vary considerably.*"[1501]

1497 *Prosecutor v. Radovan Karadžić*, Case No. IT-95-5/18-AR73.6, Decision on Radovan Karadžić's Appeal from Decision on Motion to Vacate Appointment of Richard Harvey, 12 February 2010, para.27.

1498 *Prosecutor v. Radovan Karadžić*, Case No. IT-95-5/18-AR73.6, Decision on Radovan Karadžić's Appeal from Decision on Motion to Vacate Appointment of Richard Harvey, 12 February 2010, para.28.

1499 *Prosecutor v. Radovan Karadžić*, Case No. IT-95-5/18-AR73.6, Decision on Radovan Karadžić's Appeal from Decision on Motion to Vacate Appointment of Richard Harvey, 12 February 2010, para.29.

1500 *Prosecutor v. Radovan Karadžić*, Case No. IT-95-5/18-AR73.6, Decision on Radovan Karadžić's Appeal from Decision on Motion to Vacate Appointment of Richard Harvey, 12 February 2010, para.31-32.

1501 *Prosecutor v. Radovan Karadžić*, Case No. IT-95-5/18-AR73.6, Decision on Radovan Karadžić's Appeal from Decision on Motion to Vacate Appointment of Richard Harvey, 12 February 2010, para.35 (emphasis added).

b. Discussion

The extensive litigation on the issue of selecting a counsel appointed to a self-represented accused shows that no established procedure exists either for the specific case at hand, nor any more general framework that could be adapted to address concerns expressed by all parties on the matter. In addition, the manner in which some of the arguments in *Karadžić* were presented above all by the defence indicates that this matter seemed to be particularly emotionalised.[1502] Similarly, the length of the discussion as to which list based on what rule of the ICTY RPE might be at stake illustrates that the defendant – or his legal advisor(s) – was in fact convinced that he should not only be given the opportunity to select appointed counsel, but that he in fact would even have a right to do so.

The decision of the appeals chamber makes abundantly clear that any issues with regard to the appointment of counsel pursuant to an order of a trial chamber in response to distinct behaviour of a self-represented accused would have to be dealt with on a case-by-case basis. While this allows for the necessary flexibility to address the specific circumstances of each case, it also leaves all participants with a certain level of insecurity as to the procedure to be applied. At the same time, the approach by the ICTY registry with regard to selecting counsel as ordered by the trial chamber in *Karadžić* signals a certain readiness to adopt pragmatic solutions which are in everyone's interests.

There is no reasonable basis for the argument that a self-represented accused could select appointed counsel *as of right*.[1503] In light of the fact that the appointment of counsel is in fact a restriction of the right to self-representation and to be considered as sanction for previous obstructionist behaviour of the defendant, it would stretch the boundaries of diplomacy too far to grant that same accused the opportunity to contribute to the assignment

---

1502 *See also Prosecutor v. Radovan Karadžić*, Case No. IT-95-5/18-T, Application for Certification to Appeal Decision on Motion to Vacate Appointment of Richard Harvey, 29 December 2009, para.18: "The Trial Chamber should not force Dr. Karadzic into radicalizing his behaviour in order to obtain the rights he is entitled to, and that have been afforded to other accused at this Tribunal."

1503 *See*, however, arguing to the contrary that the language in the *Šešelj* appeals chamber decision indicates that the accused should have been allowed to choose appointed counsel: Nancy Amoury Combs, Legitimizing International Criminal Justice: The Importance of Process Control, 33 *Michigan Journal of International Law* 321 (2012), at 356.

of such counsel as of right. At the same time, however, it appears recommendable that a defendant is at least given the opportunity to participate in the process, bearing in mind the fact that at some point in the course of the proceedings, the situation may in fact arise that appointed counsel has to represent the interests of the accused. This may promote the willingness on the side of the defendant to cooperate with standby – and potentially assigned – counsel, thereby ensuring a more efficient procedure in case self-representation is revoked.

While some matters are still open for discussion even after extensive litigation, issues of wider import, such as the question of whether a self-represented accused might be entitled as of right to participate in the selection of an appointed or standby counsel, were sufficiently clarified as to be able to provide guidance for future proceedings. The positions adopted by virtually all participants other than the defendant are in line with the general approach to the guarantees in Article 21(4)(d) of the ICTY Statute – representation by counsel or self-representation – conservatively considered to be mutually exclusive. According to this position, the guaranteed rights are to be seen separately, so that once an accused has decided for either option, he or she is not in a position to claim the other right may have been violated. It is of interest to point out that a pre-trial chamber in *Šešelj* appeared to take the view that the wording of Article 21(4)(d) of the ICTY Statute would not exclude the possibility for a self-represented accused to have appointed counsel of his own choice.[1504]

Against the background of the more generally adopted position, it becomes obvious that the submission of the defendant in *Karadžić* on the role of appointed counsel within the defence team was based on a false premise. It appears the accused was under the misimpression that counsel was appointed in order to assist him in the preparation of his defence.[1505] However, as is clear from reading the initial decision on the appointment of counsel, the trial chamber in no way intended to amend the accused's self-represented

1504 *See Prosecutor v. Vojislav Šešelj*, Case No. IT-03-67-PT, Decision on Prosecution's Motion for Order to Appoint Counsel to Assist Vojislav Šešelj with his Defence, 09 May 2003, para.29.

1505 For a similar position, *see* submission of the prosecution in *Milošević*: *Prosecutor v. Slobodan Milošević*, Case No. IT-02-54-T, Pre-Defence Conference, 02 September 2003, T.25958.

status[1506] and envisaged appointed counsel to merely "prepare to represent" the defendant, having been appointed as sanction for the accused's obstructive behaviour.[1507] When bearing in mind this underlying rationale, it becomes obvious that the defendant's argument with which he almost threatened a new delay of proceedings if he chose to "dismiss" appointed counsel lacks any basis. The submission that any right to select standby counsel had been established which would only be granted to obstructionist accused whereas cooperation was penalised[1508] is similarly unjustified. The underlying reason for appointing counsel as well as the purpose of standby counsel – to prepare for the eventuality of representing the accused at a later stage – simply does not establish any basis for a right to select counsel.

This position does not change in light of the submission forwarded by the accused that since the trial chamber had signalled its "intention" to restrict his right to self-representation if necessary, he would automatically become a defendant represented by counsel if and as soon as standby counsel was in fact imposed,[1509] thereby replacing his right to self-representation by his right to be represented by counsel of his own choosing.[1510] Again, this argument is based on an incorrect assumption, in this case that imposition of standby counsel were to be considered the same as or equal to the right to be represented by counsel of one's own choosing enshrined in Article 21(4)(d) of the ICTY Statute. However, by its very nature, the imposition of appointed or standby counsel follows after the exercise of the accused's right to choose either representation by counsel or self-representation. If one follows the argument that once this choice has been made, the guarantees of the article have been safeguarded, there is no basis for the assertion that a right to select

---

1506 *Prosecutor v. Radovan Karadžić*, Case No. IT-95-5/18-T, Decision on Appointment of Counsel and Order on Further Trial Proceedings, 05 November 2009, para.25.

1507 *Prosecutor v. Radovan Karadžić*, Case No. IT-95-5/18-T, Decision on Appointment of Counsel and Order on Further Trial Proceedings, 05 November 2009, para.27-28.

1508 *Cf. Prosecutor v. Radovan Karadžić*, Case No. IT-95-5/18-AR73.6, Appeal from Decision on Motion to Vacate Appointment of Richard Harvey, 19 January 2010, para.42-43.

1509 *Prosecutor v. Radovan Karadžić*, Case No. IT-95-5/18-AR73.6, Appeal from Decision on Motion to Vacate Appointment of Richard Harvey, 19 January 2010, para.48.

1510 *Prosecutor v. Radovan Karadžić*, Case No. IT-95-5/18-AR73.6, Appeal from Decision on Motion to Vacate Appointment of Richard Harvey, 19 January 2010, para.47-48.

standby counsel is necessary to fulfil these guarantees. In line with this position, the appeals chamber left no doubt that the imposition of counsel in the course of the proceedings is not to be understood as recognition of a voluntary decision taken by the defendant to cease the exercise of his right to self-representation.[1511] Thus, the argument that Article 21(4) of the ICTY Statute would not make any distinction between accused electing to be represented by counsel of their own choice and accused having counsel imposed as sanction after them having chosen self-representation,[1512] stands without reason.

Another more general aspect clarified in the course of the litigation concerned the trial chamber specifically stating that its decision on the appointment of counsel was not based on Rule 45*ter*, but rather Rule 54 of the ICTY RPE.[1513] The trial chamber emphasised from the beginning that its decision did not affect the self-represented status of the accused who would "continue to represent himself".[1514] This is of note insofar as – similar to the issue of a right to select appointed counsel – the interpretation and application of Rules 45*ter* and 54 of the ICTY RPE in the context of appointment of counsel to self-represented accused had not been addressed previously.

1511 *Cf. Prosecutor v. Radovan Karadžić*, Case No. IT-95-5/18-AR73.6, Decision on Radovan Karadžić's Appeal from Decision on Motion to Vacate Appointment of Richard Harvey, 12 February 2010, para.27.

1512 *Prosecutor v. Radovan Karadžić*, Case No. IT-95-5/18-AR73.6, Appeal from Decision on Motion to Vacate Appointment of Richard Harvey, 19 January 2010, para.50, 51, 54.

1513 *See also Prosecutor v. Radovan Karadžić*, Case No. IT-95-5/18-T, Decision on Appointment of Counsel and Order on Further Trial Proceedings, 05 November 2009, para.28.

1514 *Prosecutor v. Radovan Karadžić*, Case No. IT-95-5/18-T, Decision on Appointment of Counsel and Order on Further Trial Proceedings, 05 November 2009, para.25. *See also* Decision on the Accused's Motion to Vacate Appointment of Richard Harvey, 23 December 2009, para.28, which reiterates: "[…] the manner in which the Registrar made his Decision, and the Decision itself, do not affect the Accused's continuing exercise of his right to self-representation"; and para.38, which reads in the relevant part: "[…] the counsel in question has been appointed simply to prepare himself to represent the interests of an accused sometime in the future, if that should be required". Note that the appeals chamber took this position as basis to find that the Directive on the Assignment of Defence Counsel was not applicable to the case at hand: *Prosecutor v. Radovan Karadžić*, Case No. IT-95-5/18-AR73.6, Decision on Radovan Karadžić's Appeal from Decision on Motion to Vacate Appointment of Richard Harvey, 12 February 2010, para.28.

While Rule 45*ter* was adopted for purposes of the ICTY only in November 2008,[1515] the ICTR incorporated a similar provision in Rule 45*quater* already in 2002,[1516] whereas for the ICC, the Regulations of the Court include a comparable provision after amendment.[1517] From a literal meaning, Rule 45*ter* of the ICTY RPE concerns the assignment – as opposed to mere appointment – of counsel who would thus directly take over the representation of the interests of the (then former) self-represented accused.[1518] In contrast, Rule 54 of the ICTY RPE is a general rule that vests a trial chamber with the competence to issue any orders that may be necessary for the preparation or conduct of trial.[1519]

The approach of the trial chamber in *Karadžić* to expressly specify the rule according to which it appointed counsel indicates that it distinguished between the two provisions. This leads to the conclusion that Rule 45*ter* of the ICTY RPE is to be seen separately of and complementary to established jurisprudence, and probably as codification of arguments previously based on more general notions such as the right to a fair trial, as had been suggested before in the context of Rule 45*quater* of the ICTR RPE.[1520] It is, however, to be doubted whether the adoption of this rule also signified any promotion of the case law through codification,[1521] considering Rule 45*ter* of the ICTY

1515 *Cf.* Mark Ellis, Self-Representation is a Privilege, Not a Right, 23 (42) *Lawyer* 6 (2009), who suggests that the amendment of the RPE happened "likely in anticipation of dealing with Karadzic [...]".

1516 *Cf.* Nina H.B. Jørgensen, The Right of the Accused to Self-Representation Before International Criminal Tribunals, 98 *The American Journal of International Law* 711 (2004), at 713.

1517 Regulation 76(1) of the ICC Regulations of the Court.

1518 Rule 45*ter* ICTY RPE provides: "The Trial Chamber may, if it decides that it is in the interests of justice, instruct the Registrar to assign a counsel to represent the interests of the accused."

1519 Rule 54 ICTY RPE reads: "At the request of either party or *proprio motu*, a Judge or a Trial Chamber may issue such orders, summonses, subpoenas, warrants and transfer orders as may be necessary for the purposes of an investigation or for the preparation or conduct of the trial."

1520 Nina H.B. Jørgensen, The Right of the Accused to Self-Representation Before International Criminal Tribunals, 98 *The American Journal of International Law* 711 (2004), at 713; Boris Petersdorf, *Eigenverteidigung und aufgedrängte Pflichtverteidigung im formellen Völkerstrafrecht* (Baden-Baden: Nomos Verlagsgesellschaft) 2010, p.57-58.

1521 Boris Petersdorf, *Eigenverteidigung und aufgedrängte Pflichtverteidigung im formellen Völkerstrafrecht* (Baden-Baden: Nomos Verlagsgesellschaft) 2010, p.58.

RPE is too general for such an import and also only deals with the rather specific issue of assignment of counsel, as opposed to appointment.

The interpretation of Rule 45*ter* of the ICTY RPE as applicable to situations where counsel is assigned to represent the interests of an accused suggests itself also in light of the review of the ICTY registry which argued that the accused "fail[ed] to recognise that in the instant case counsel is being appointed in preparation for possible future imposition".[1522] The trial chamber was even clearer when it explicitly stated that:

> "[...] while issued by the Trial Chamber and dealing with appointment of counsel, the Decision Appointing Counsel did not assign counsel pursuant to Rule 45*ter* to represent the interests of the Accused but was made pursuant to Rule 54 of the Rules."[1523]

This interpretation of a very limited scope of applicability of Rule 45*ter* of the ICTY RPE is further supported by the position adopted by the prosecution in *Šešelj* when it requested that counsel be assigned pursuant to Rule 45*ter* of the ICTY RPE in light of the accused's conviction for contempt of court.[1524]

Thus, it appears that Rule 45*ter* of the ICTY RPE will be resorted to in situations where it is in the interests of justice to impose counsel in order to directly and actively represent an accused's interests, limiting its application to circumstances in which the right to self-representation of the defendant is in fact revoked. In contrast, other measures that might have to be taken in order to restrict the exercise of the right to self-representation in the course of the proceedings without taking the ultimate step of revoking the right in its entirety appear to be appropriately based on provisions such as Rule 54 of the ICTY RPE, as well as pertinent jurisprudence and practice.

1522 *Prosecutor v. Radovan Karadžić*, Case No. IT-95-5/18-T, Registrar's Submission Pursuant to Rule 33(B) Regarding Radovan Karadžić's Motion to Vacate Appointment of Richard Harvey, 14 December 2009, para.42. *See also* para.43.

1523 *Prosecutor v. Radovan Karadžić*, Case No. IT-95-5/18-T, Decision on the Accused's Motion to Vacate Appointment of Richard Harvey, 23 December 2009, para.29.

1524 *Prosecutor v. Vojislav Šešelj*, Case No. IT-03-67-T, Prosecution's Supplement to its Motion to Terminate the Accused's Self-Representation, 27 August 2009, para.2, 12-15.

In conclusion, the determination by the appeals chamber concerning a "fluid and individualized approach to the appointment of standby counsel"[1525] could be seen as commendable insofar as it is indeed the case that the reasons for appointing counsel will be numerous, as can be seen from previous analysis of the different cases.

On the downside, the flexibility heralded by the appeals chamber is not conducive to the establishment of more certain legal standards in the context of assignment of counsel. This could be problematic in light of the fact that the background of counsel's appointment will vary and that designations thus far have not been interpreted consistently and the related mandates are not necessarily uniform.

Thus far, the litigation in *Karadžić* has been the first opportunity for discussing the procedure to be followed in case counsel is appointed to a self-represented accused. Even though it is unlikely that this matter will again arise in the context of proceedings before the ICTY, the extent of the litigation and the decision of the appeals chamber bear the potential of serving as guidelines for future comparable scenarios of appointment of counsel to *pro se* defendants before other international criminal tribunals.

II. The role of imposed counsel

1. Potential roles to be played by imposed counsel

Having discussed the situations in and procedures according to which counsel may be imposed on a self-represented accused, it has to be examined which nature such an assignment could have. Analysing the case law in this respect, it appears that depending on the degree of obstruction determined by the chamber concerned, and in keeping with the proportionality principle to be applied, different arrangements for assigned counsel are feasible. The concepts of assigned counsel, appointed counsel, and standby counsel will therefore be examined in more detail. While not at first sight falling within the parameters of assigned or appointed counsel, the notion and use of *amicus curiae* in cases with self-represented accused will be scrutinised in light of the mandate given to *amicus* in some cases.

1525 *Prosecutor v. Radovan Karadžić*, Case No. IT-95-5/18-AR73.6, Decision on Radovan Karadžić's Appeal from Decision on Motion to Vacate Appointment of Richard Harvey, 12 February 2010, para.35.

Taking first a brief look at national jurisprudence in this context, it seems that it quickly became apparent to domestic courts that the right given to accused to present their own case does not come without difficulties. To be mentioned is the case of *McKenzie* before the U.K. Court of Appeal, establishing the notion of a "McKenzie Friend".[1526] The court in this case reversed a lower court's decision on the basis that the judge had not allowed the defendant, who appeared without counsel, to have an assistant in court who would provide support.[1527] Having considered the length and complexity of the case in addition to the fact of lack of legal knowledge on the part of the defendant,[1528] the court, *inter alia* referring to a decision dating from 1831,[1529] held that "every party had the right to have a friend present in court beside him to assist by prompting, taking notes, and quietly giving advice".[1530]

Turning to the United States, Chief Justice Burger in his dissent in *Faretta* mentioned the possibility to use *amicus curiae* in trials with *pro se* defendants.[1531] While the majority in *Faretta* alluded to the concept of standby counsel merely in a footnote,[1532] several years later the U.S. Supreme Court would render a decision in which it expressly endorsed the concept of "standby counsel", even if this counsel participated against the accused's will.

In *McKaskle v. Wiggins*, a self-represented accused in a jury trial was assigned standby counsel by the trial judge.[1533] The defendant subsequently complained about undue interference of this counsel in his defence and

---

1526 *McKenzie v McKenzie* (Court of Appeal), [1971] P. 33, 12 June 1970.

1527 *McKenzie v McKenzie* (Court of Appeal), [1971] P. 33, 12 June 1970, at 33.

1528 *McKenzie v McKenzie* (Court of Appeal), [1971] P. 33, 12 June 1970, at 37, 42.

1529 *McKenzie v McKenzie* (Court of Appeal), [1971] P. 33, 12 June 1970, at 37-38, 41.

1530 *McKenzie v McKenzie* (Court of Appeal), [1971] P. 33, 12 June 1970, at 33.

1531 *Anthony Pasquall Faretta v. State of California* (U.S. Supreme Court), 422 U.S. 806, 30 June 1975, Dissenting Opinion Chief Justice Burger, joined by Justices Blackmun and Rehnquist, at 846 fn.7: "Some of the damage we can anticipate from a defendant's ill-advised insistence on conducting his own defense may be mitigated by appointing a qualified lawyer to sit in the case as the traditional 'friend of the court'. The Court does not foreclose this option."

1532 *Anthony Pasquall Faretta v. State of California* (U.S. Supreme Court), 422 U.S. 806, 30 June 1975, at 834 fn.46.

1533 *McKaskle v. Wiggins* (U.S. Supreme Court), 465 U.S. 168 (1984), 23 January 1984, at 171-172.

therefore violation of his right as recognised under *Faretta*.[1534] The U.S. Supreme Court found that the underlying reason to grant a right to self-representation, namely preservation of the defendant's dignity and autonomy, as well as presentation of his or her own defence, did not completely exclude the use of standby counsel.[1535] However, it was determined that the use of this concept required limits in order not to override the right to proceed *pro se*, namely that the accused should retain control over the presentation of his or her defence and that standby counsel, when participating without the accused's consent, should not undermine a jury's impression that the defendant was indeed self-represented.[1536] Appointment of standby counsel even against the accused's wishes was considered to be possible with a standby counsel who assisted in the context of routine matters and courtroom protocol.[1537] Justice White in his dissent rejected the conclusion of the majority and the two-pronged test upon which it was based, on the ground that the defendant's exercise of his *Faretta* right had been too much interfered with by standby counsel.[1538] It has been submitted that so far it is not entirely clear which actions may be taken by standby counsel in accordance with the U.S. Supreme Court decision, which potentially leads to a marginal distinction between an engaged standby counsel and socalled "hybrid representation".[1539]

Turning from examples found in the context of national jurisdictions to the international criminal legal system, it is striking that the appeals chamber and a number of trial chambers at the ICTY adopted different solutions in proceedings with self-represented accused when considering the role to be played by assigned or appointed counsel.

1534 *McKaskle v. Wiggins* (U.S. Supreme Court), 465 U.S. 168 (1984), 23 January 1984, at 171-173, 176.

1535 *McKaskle v. Wiggins* (U.S. Supreme Court), 465 U.S. 168 (1984), 23 January 1984, at 176-177.

1536 *McKaskle v. Wiggins* (U.S. Supreme Court), 465 U.S. 168 (1984), 23 January 1984, at 178. *See also* at 177: "We recognize, nonetheless, that the right to speak for oneself entails more than the opportunity to add one's voice to a cacophony of others."

1537 *McKaskle v. Wiggins* (U.S. Supreme Court), 465 U.S. 168 (1984), 23 January 1984, at 183-185.

1538 *McKaskle v. Wiggins* (U.S. Supreme Court), 465 U.S. 168 (1984), 23 January 1984, Dissenting Opinion Justice White, joined by Justices Brennan and Marshall, at 188-199.

1539 Nina H.B. Jørgensen, The Right of the Accused to Self-Representation Before International Criminal Tribunals, 98 *The American Journal of International Law* 711 (2004), at 717.

Thus far, jurisprudence illustrated the continuance of self-representation argued for by the accused even by hunger strike;[1540] the assignment of standby counsel;[1541] the designation of *amicus curiae*[1542] and later of counsel, albeit with a rather limited role;[1543] as well as the appointment of counsel, later designated standby counsel, to take over the representation of the accused in case of finding of further obstructive behaviour, without however touching the immediate exercise of the personal defence by the accused.[1544]

It will be analysed on which grounds the chambers based their reasoning to justify the respective solutions. In a similar vein, it will be addressed whether, bearing in mind the solutions adopted in international criminal proceedings up to this point, the right to self-representation and the right to be assisted by counsel in fact are – and should be – mutually exclusive, or whether some room might be left for more flexible approaches which take

---

1540 *Prosecutor v. Vojislav Šešelj*, Case No. IT-03-67-PT, Professor Vojislav Šešelj's Decision to Refuse Medical Treatment and Artificial Feeding While on Hunger Strike, 24 November 2006 (filed: 30 November 2006); *Prosecutor v. Vojislav Šešelj*, Case No. IT-03-67-AR73.4, Decision on Appeal Against the Trial Chamber's Decision (No.2) on Assignment of Counsel, 08 December 2006, para.28.

1541 *Prosecutor v. Vojislav Šešelj*, Case No. IT-03-67-PT, Decision on Prosecution's Motion for Order Appointing Counsel to Assist Vojislav Šešelj with his Defence, 09 May 2003, para.27, 30.

1542 *See e.g. Prosecutor v. Slobodan Milošević*, Case No. IT-99-37-PT, Order Inviting Designation of *Amicus Curiae*, 30 August 2001; *Prosecutor v. Slobodan Milošević*, Case No. IT-02-50-PT, Order Inviting Designation of *Amicus Curiae*, 30 October 2001; *Prosecutor v. Slobodan Milošević*, Case No. IT-02-51-PT, Order Inviting Designation of *Amicus Curiae*, 23 November 2001; *Prosecutor v. Slobodan Milošević*, Case No. IT-99-37-T, Order Concerning *Amici Curiae*, 11 January 2002; *Prosecutor v. Momčilo Krajišnik*, Case No. IT-00-39-A, Decision on Momčilo Krajišnik's Request to Self-Represent, on Counsel's Motion in Relation to Appointment of *Amicus Curiae*, and on the Prosecution Motion of 16 February 2007, 11 May 2007, para.18, 19.

1543 *Prosecutor v. Slobodan Milošević*, Case No. IT-02-54-T, Reasons for Decision on Assignment of Defence Counsel, 22 September 2004, para.69; *Prosecutor v. Slobodan Milošević*, Case No. IT-02-54-AR73.7, Decision on Interlocutory Appeal of the Trial Chamber's Decision on the Assignment of Defence Counsel, 01 November 2004, para.19-20.

1544 *Prosecutor v. Radovan Karadžić*, Case No. IT-95-5/18-T, Decision on Appointment of Counsel and Order on Further Trial Proceedings, 05 November 2009, para.25; Hearing, 13 April 2010, T.997-999; Decision on Designation of Standby Counsel, 15 April 2010.

into account the overarching right to a fair trial.[1545] One example to be mentioned in this regard is the decision of the *Norman* trial chamber at the SCSL, which considered that the right to self-representation could only be exercised with the assistance of counsel.[1546] The chamber examined the circumstances of the case[1547] and, more importantly, took into consideration the potential procedural difficulties.[1548] Eventually, the conduct – namely non-appearance – of the defendant led to the revocation of the right and imposition of counsel.[1549]

It has been mentioned before that, bending itself to the margin of discretion afforded to each trial chamber, the appeals chamber took the view that the appointment of standby counsel will very much depend on the particular facts of each case causing the assignment.[1550] The view expressed by the appeals chamber seems to indicate that a trial chamber and registry would enjoy a considerable margin of appreciation in the appointment of standby counsel.

This opinion, *i.e.* that different rules and related jurisprudence might be applicable in distinct situations, may be further supported by the position of the appeals chamber deciding on an interlocutory appeal in *Šešelj* which illustrates the bench's position that the notions of standby counsel and assigned counsel are to be distinguished: the appeals chamber clarified that "standby

---

1545 *Prosecutor v. Momčilo Krajišnik*, Case No. IT-00-39-A, Decision on Momčilo Krajišnik's Request to Self-Represent, on Counsel's Motion in Relation to Appointment of *Amicus Curiae*, and on the Prosecution Motion of 16 February 2007, Fundamentally Dissenting Opinion of Judge Schomburg on the Right to Self-Representation, 11 May 2007, para.2.

1546 *Prosecutor v. Samuel Hinga Norman et al.*, Case No. SCSL-04-14-T, Decision on the Application of Samuel Hinga Norman for Self-Representation Under Article 17(4)(d) of the Statute of the Special Court, 08 June 2004, para.32.

1547 *Prosecutor v. Samuel Hinga Norman et al.*, Case No. SCSL-04-14-T, Decision on the Application of Samuel Hinga Norman for Self-Representation Under Article 17(4)(d) of the Statute of the Special Court, 08 June 2004, para.13, 17.

1548 *Prosecutor v. Samuel Hinga Norman et al.*, Case No. SCSL-04-14-T, Decision on the Application of Samuel Hinga Norman for Self-Representation Under Article 17(4)(d) of the Statute of the Special Court, 08 June 2004, para.26.

1549 *Prosecutor v. Samuel Hinga Norman et al.*, Case No. SCSL-04-14-T, Ruling on the Issue of Non-Appearance of the First Accused Samuel Hinga Norman, the Second Accused Moinina Fofana, and the Third Accused, Allieu Kondewa at the Trial Proceedings, 01 October 2004, p.5-8.

1550 *Prosecutor v. Radovan Karadžić*, Case No. IT-95-5/18-AR73.6, Decision on Radovan Karadžić's Appeal from Decision on Motion to Vacate Appointment of Richard Harvey, 12 February 2010, para.35.

counsel is not assigned counsel", meaning that standby counsel would be limited in his or her participation in the trial.[1551] Despite the lack of any further elaboration in the context of this decision, the idea behind this position is presumably that an "assigned" counsel would be a counsel acting for an accused who used to conduct his defence in person previously, but whose exercise of the right was revoked, for example because of health issues or disruptive behaviour. Assigned counsel would thus act as defence counsel for the accused, who would not be able to conduct his own defence any more, either completely or in part.

In contrast, the appeals chamber's concept of standby counsel appears to be that such counsel would be appointed to a specific case with a self-represented accused, however enjoying rather limited opportunities to actually participate in the proceedings. The underlying idea in this case would be that standby counsel remains in the background, while at the same time being prepared to take over the preparation and presentation of the defence in court any time the bench would decide that the situation requires so. This concept would coincide with the approach taken by the trial chamber in *Karadžić*, which first tasked the ICTY registry to appoint counsel to prepare for trial in order to be ready to take over the defence for the accused in case this should be required,[1552] and then, at the beginning of the evidentiary phase a few months later, designated appointed counsel as standby counsel to the proceedings, specifying his role in the course of the trial.[1553]

2. Examples of implementation in practice

In practice, the ICTY has seen combinations of different approaches, *e.g.* in *Milošević*, with first *amici curiae* working in addition to the legal advisers of the accused in the background, and *amici* later being assigned as counsel; in *Krajišnik*, where the appeals chamber first appointed *amicus curiae*, in addition to assistance to the accused behind the scenes, as well as sub-

---

1551 *Prosecutor v. Vojislav Šešelj*, Case No. IT-03-67-AR73.4, Decision on Appeal Against the Trial Chamber's Decision (No.2) on Assignment of Counsel, 08 December 2006, para.24.

1552 *Prosecutor v. Radovan Karadžić*, Case No. IT-95-5/18-T, Decision on Appointment of Counsel and Order on Further Trial Proceedings, 05 November 2009, para.25.

1553 *Prosecutor v. Radovan Karadžić*, Case No. IT-95-5/18-T, Decision on Designation of Standby Counsel, 15 April 2010, para.8-9.

sequently permitting representation of the accused on the distinct issue of joint criminal enterprise;[1554] or in *Karadžić*, where the trial chamber not only accepted legal associates recognised by the ICTY registry to assist the accused, but later also appointed counsel who was then designated standby counsel which would be assigned to assume the preparation and presentation of the defence in case of further obstruction by the accused.[1555]

At an early stage in the *Milošević* proceedings, the chamber deemed it prudent to assign *amicus curiae* to the self-represented accused, outlining the tasks this would entail: while the chamber stressed that *amicus* was appointed to assist the bench, not the accused, counsel was nonetheless supposed to *e.g.* object to evidence, cross-examine witnesses or point out exculpatory evidence.[1556] This approach has been considered as attempt to ensure the participation of defence counsel in all but terms, raising "difficult ethical issues for counsel".[1557] Even though the accused did not approve of the assignment of *amici curiae* in the beginning, it appears that he eventually benefited from the assistance of the *amici*.[1558]

When the appeals chamber in *Milošević* subsequently had to decide on the appeal against the imposition of counsel upon the accused due to his ill-health,[1559] it did confirm the assignment, while however significantly modifying the mode of participation of that counsel in the presentation of

---

1554 *Cf.* with regard to what the author refers to as "hybrid representation" in domestic systems: Nina H.B. Jørgensen, The Right of the Accused to Self-Representation Before International Criminal Tribunals, 98 *The American Journal of International Law* 711 (2004), at 717.

1555 *Cf.* Wolfgang Schomburg, The Role of International Criminal Tribunals in Promoting Respect for Fair Trial Rights, 8 *Northwestern University Journal of International Human Rights* 1 (2009), at 50.

1556 *Prosecutor v. Slobodan Milošević*, Case No. IT-99-37-PT, Status Conference, 30 August 2001, T.7; Order Inviting Designation of *Amicus Curiae*, 30 August 2001, p.2; Order Concerning *Amici Curiae*, 11 January 2002.

1557 Daniel D. Ntanda Nsereko, Ethical Obligations of Counsel in Criminal Proceedings: Representing an Unwilling Client, 12 *Criminal Law Forum* 487 (2001), at 506.

1558 Steven Kay/Gillian Higgins, The Right of Self-Representation – The Lawyers in the Eye of the Storm, International Criminal Law Bureau 2010, p.2-3, available at http://www.internationallawbureau.com/blog/wp-content/uploads/2010/08/Lawyers-Self-representation-Kay-Higgins.pdf (last accessed 17 November 2012).

1559 *Prosecutor v. Slobodan Milošević*, Case No. IT-02-54-T, Oral Ruling, 02 September 2004, T.32357-32359; Reasons for Decision on Assignment of Defence Counsel, 22 September 2004. *See also Prosecutor v. Slobodan Milošević*, Case No. IT-02-54-AR73.7, Appeal Against the Trial Chamber's Decision on Assignment of Defence Counsel, 29 September 2004.

the defence.[1560] According to the appeals chamber, the accused should still be responsible for all crucial tasks usually associated with presenting one's defence, while counsel was expected to step in only if and when the health of the accused would prevent the latter from assuming his tasks as *de facto* defence counsel.[1561] The trial chamber subsequently took this disposition to confirm the rationale prompting it to assign counsel and considered that "the underlying obligation of counsel will be to continue to act in the best interests of the Accused [...]".[1562] According to the counsel concerned, the appeals chamber decision allowed for the "cooperative relationship" which had existed before between the accused and *amici curiae* to be re-established.[1563] The approach as envisaged by the appeals chamber has been characterised as "hybrid model", which was suggested to be the most appropriate form of representation for an accused such as Slobodan Milošević,[1564] while however recalling the hazards if the role of assigned counsel is not strictly defined.[1565]

When the appeals chamber in *Krajišnik* appointed *amicus curiae*, it set out the tasks associated with that appointment and clarified which status was not accorded to *amicus*: *amicus curiae* was expected "to assist the Appeals Chamber by arguing in favour of Mr. Krajišnik's interests", whereas he or she was "not requested to conduct any new factual investigations".[1566] The appeals chamber required *amicus* "to work independently from Mr.

1560 *See Prosecutor v. Slobodan Milošević*, Case No. IT-02-54-T, Order on the Modalities to be Followed by Court Assigned Counsel, 03 September 2004.

1561 *Prosecutor v. Slobodan Milošević*, Case No. IT-02-54-AR73.7, Decision on Interlocutory Appeal of the Trial Chamber's Decision on the Assignment of Defence Counsel, 01 November 2004, para.19-20: "[...] To a lay observer, who will see Milošević playing the principal courtroom role at the hearings, the difference may well be impercetible."

1562 *Prosecutor v. Slobodan Milošević*, Case No. IT-02-54-T, Decision on Assigned Counsel's Motion for Withdrawal, 07 December 2004, para.34.

1563 Steven Kay/Gillian Higgins, The Right of Self-Representation – The Lawyers in the Eye of the Storm, International Criminal Law Bureau 2010, p.4-5, available at http://www.internationallawbureau.com/blog/wp-content/uploads/2010/08/Lawyers-Self-representation-Kay-Higgins.pdf (last accessed 17 November 2012).

1564 Joanne Williams, Slobodan Milosevic and the Guarantee of Self-Representation, 32 *Brooklyn Journal of International Law* 553 (2007), at 600.

1565 Joanne Williams, Slobodan Milosevic and the Guarantee of Self-Representation, 32 *Brooklyn Journal of International Law* 553 (2007), at 601.

1566 *Prosecutor v. Momčilo Krajišnik*, Case No. IT-00-39-A, Decision on Momčilo Krajišnik's Request to Self-Represent, on Counsel's Motions in Relation to Appointment of *Amicus Curiae*, and on the Prosecution Motion of 16 February 2007, 11 May 2007, para.19.

Krajišnik", with the task being "to put forth grounds of appeal seeking reversal of convictions or reduction in sentence and to argue against grounds of appeal advanced by the Prosecution".[1567] At the same time, the appeals chamber clarified that *amicus curiae* would not be considered as party to the proceedings and therefore limited the extent to which it would potentially consider arguments submitted by *amicus curiae*.[1568]

When *amicus curiae* subsequently sought an extension of this particular mandate in order to file a specific ground of appeal, the appeals chamber declined the request with reference to its earlier decision, and held that *amicus* was not appointed with the same responsibilities as assumed by defence counsel, but rather in order to assist the bench to ensure the fairness of the appellate proceedings in light of the accused's choice to conduct his defence in person.[1569]

The trial chamber in *Karadžić* first decided to appoint counsel with the very limited mandate of preparing for the eventuality to take over the defence of the accused should the need arise.[1570] At the beginning of the evidentiary phase of the case, the trial chamber then proceeded to designate appointed counsel as "standby counsel" to the defendant, and outlined the tasks to be assumed by standby counsel more specifically, including continuing active preparation for the proceedings as well as the possibility of being requested to address the trial chamber on particular issues.[1571]

1567 *Prosecutor v. Momčilo Krajišnik*, Case No. IT-00-39-A, Decision on Momčilo Krajišnik's Request to Self-Represent, on Counsel's Motions in Relation to Appointment of *Amicus Curiae*, and on the Prosecution Motion of 16 February 2007, 11 May 2007, para.19.

1568 *Prosecutor v. Momčilo Krajišnik*, Case No. IT-00-39-A, Decision on Momčilo Krajišnik's Request to Self-Represent, on Counsel's Motions in Relation to Appointment of *Amicus Curiae*, and on the Prosecution Motion of 16 February 2007, 11 May 2007, para.20.

1569 *Prosecutor v. Momčilo Krajišnik*, Case No. IT-00-39-A, Decision on Motion of *Amicus Curiae* Regarding Appellate Ground of Ineffective Assistance of Counsel, 20 July 2007, para.8.

1570 *Prosecutor v. Radovan Karadžić*, Case No. IT-95-5/18-T, Decision on Appointment of Counsel and Order on Further Trial Proceedings, 05 November 2009, para.25, 26.

1571 *Prosecutor v. Radovan Karadžić*, Case No. IT-95-5/18-T, Decision on Designation of Standby Counsel, 15 April 2010, para.8-9: "In this capacity he will continue to be engaged in the proceedings and maintain the capacity to step in to represent the interests of the Accused should the Chamber determine that this is necessary. Until further order, Mr. Harvey's functions shall be as follows: (a) to receive copies of all court documents, filings, and disclosed materials generated by or sent

It is of note that in its written decision rendered two days after the start of the evidentiary phase,[1572] the trial chamber did not refer to Rule 45*ter* of the ICTY RPE in its disposition "designating" standby counsel: it determined, in light of Articles 20 and 21 of the ICTY Statute,[1573] as well as considering Rules 45*ter* and 80(B) of the ICTY RPE,[1574] that the behaviour monitored by the trial chamber up to that point in time did not for the time being warrant the assignment of counsel in order to represent the interests of the accused.[1575] However, pursuant to Rule 54 of the ICTY RPE,[1576] the trial chamber "designated" appointed counsel as standby counsel, in which capacity

> "he will continue to be engaged in the proceedings and maintain the capacity to step in to represent the interests of the Accused should the Chamber determine that this is necessary."[1577]

When the *Šešelj* pre-trial chamber appointed standby counsel, it equally outlined the tasks to be assumed by this counsel: it clearly envisaged an active assistance by counsel to the accused whenever so requested, while at the same time providing for the possibility of counsel to take over the

---

to the Accused; (b) to be present in the courtroom during the proceedings, assisted by one member of his team, should he consider it to be necessary [footnote 12: Should he be unable to attend any of the court proceedings, Mr. Harvey should inform the Chamber and may request that a member of his team attend in his absence]; (c) *to engage actively in ongoing substantive preparation of the case, in order to be prepared to put questions to witnesses on behalf of the Accused, or to represent his interests, at any time, should the Trial Chamber find this to be necessary*; and (d) to address the Chamber whenever so requested by the Chamber." (emphasis added).

1572 *Prosecutor v. Radovan Karadžić*, Case No. IT-95-5/18-T, Decision on Designation of Standby Counsel, 15 April 2010, para.5. *See also* Oral Ruling, 13 April 2010, T.997-999.

1573 *Prosecutor v. Radovan Karadžić*, Case No. IT-95-5/18-T, Decision on Designation of Standby Counsel, 15 April 2010, para.6.

1574 *Prosecutor v. Radovan Karadžić*, Case No. IT-95-5/18-T, Decision on Designation of Standby Counsel, 15 April 2010, para.7.

1575 *Prosecutor v. Radovan Karadžić*, Case No. IT-95-5/18-T, Decision on Designation of Standby Counsel, 15 April 2010, para.8.

1576 *Prosecutor v. Radovan Karadžić*, Case No. IT-95-5/18-T, Decision on Designation of Standby Counsel, 15 April 2010, para.10.

1577 *Prosecutor v. Radovan Karadžić*, Case No. IT-95-5/18-T, Decision on Designation of Standby Counsel, 15 April 2010, para.8.

presentation of the defence if the accused were to be removed from the courtroom according to Rule 80(B) of the ICTY RPE.[1578]

Comparing these tasks to the ones spelt out by the trial chamber in *Karadžić*,[1579] it appears that the trial chamber in *Šešelj* had in mind a much more cooperative relationship between accused and standby counsel than the trial chamber in *Karadžić*, which did not seem to envisage standby counsel as actual assistant to the defendant. This is indicated by the view adopted by the trial chamber in *Karadžić* when appointing counsel in order to prepare for the eventuality of taking over the presentation of the defence case,[1580] in an arrangement which the bench did not see to provide the accused with an addition to his defence team.[1581] Thus, it appears that the trial chamber considered "standby counsel" in the narrow sense of the term as a

---

1578 *Prosecutor v. Vojislav Šešelj*, Case No. IT-03-67-PT, Decision on Prosecution's Motion for Order Appointing Counsel to Assist Vojislav Šešelj with his Defence, 09 May 2003, para.30: "For the purposes of these proceedings, the role of standby counsel is strictly defined as follows: to assist the Accused in the preparation of his case during the pre-trial phase whenever so requested by the Accused; to assist the Accused in the preparation and presentation of his case at trial whenever so requested by the Accused; to receive copies of all court documents, filings and disclosed materials that are received by or sent to the Accused; to be present in the courtroom during the proceedings; *to be engaged actively in the substantive preparation of the case and to participate in the proceedings, in order always to be prepared to take over from the Accused at trial* (see below); to address the Court whenever so requested by the Accused or the Chamber; *to offer advice or make suggestions to the Accused as counsel sees fit, in particular on evidential and procedural issues*; as a protective measure in the event of abusive conduct by the Accused, to put questions to witnesses, in particular sensitive or protected witnesses, on behalf of the Accused if so ordered by the Trial Chamber, without depriving the Accused of his right to control the content of the examination [fn.56: Such a measure would be less intrusive than the alternative option of interrupting and discontinuing the examination of the Accused himself in the interests of justice.]; in exceptional circumstances to take over the defence from the Accused at trial should the Trial Chamber find, following a warning, that the Accused is engaging in disruptive conduct or conduct requiring his removal from the courtroom under Rule 80(B)." (italicised for emphasis).

1579 *Prosecutor v. Radovan Karadžić*, Case No. IT-95-5/18-T, Decision on Designation of Standby Counsel, 15 April 2010, para.9.

1580 *Prosecutor v. Radovan Karadžić*, Case No. IT-95-5/18-T, Decision on Appointment of Counsel and Order on Further Trial Proceedings, 05 November 2009, para.25-26.

1581 *Prosecutor v. Radovan Karadžić*, Case No. IT-95-5/18-T, Decision on the Accused's Motion for Postponement of Trial, 26 February 2010, para.48.

counsel who was indeed only to be activated in case it was determined to be necessary.

However, it should surface in *Šešelj* that the planned cooperation was apparently too much to ask for from the accused,[1582] fact which the defendant showed even more evidently after the appointment of standby counsel following the appeals chamber decision.[1583] However, at that point in time the trial chamber had already outlined a more limited role to be played by standby counsel which took into account that the accused was rather unlikely to cooperate.[1584]

3. Discussion

The view has been expressed that two distinct forms developing at international criminal tribunals in the context of the exercise of right to self-representation could be "qualified self-representation, with the accused representing his own case in conjunction with standby counsel", and "revoked self-representation, with court assigned counsel presenting the defence case without instructions".[1585]

Looking at the practical implications of the designation of standby counsel thus far, this opinion needs to be questioned. It does not appear that self-represented accused who have standby counsel appointed in any way cooper-

---

1582 *See Prosecutor v. Vojislav Šešelj*, Case No. IT-03-67-AR73.3, Decision on Appeal Against the Trial Chamber's Decision on Assignment of Counsel, 20 October 2006, para.50. *See also* Decision by Registrar, 05 September 2003, appointing standby counsel, and subsequently, Decision by Deputy Registrar, 16 February 2004, replacing first standby counsel.

1583 *Prosecutor v. Vojislav Šešelj*, Case No. IT-03-67-PT, Status Conference, 01 November 2006, T.627-629, where the accused refused to answer any question until the "spy", *i.e.* standby counsel, would be removed from the courtroom; T.632-633; and eventually T.635-636, with the accused himself being removed from the courtroom.

1584 *Prosecutor v. Vojislav Šešelj*, Case No. IT-03-67-PT, Order Concerning Appointment of Standby Counsel and Delayed Commencement of Trial, 25 October 2006, para.5(1); Status Conference, 01 November 2006, T.639-640.

1585 Nina H.B. Jørgensen, The Problem of Self-Representation at International Criminal Tribunals. Striking a Balance Between Fairness and Effectiveness, 4 *Journal of International Criminal Justice* 64 (2006), at 71.

ate with that counsel.[1586] Rather, given that such appointment is usually against the will of the accused, standby counsel might play a rather inactive role in the actual proceedings, with a self-represented accused relying on his legal associates when realising a need to present legal arguments. In addition, the concept of *amicus curiae*, used not only in *Milošević*, but also in *Krajišnik*, does, if at all, barely square with the first of the two categories. It seems that the discretion accorded to trial chambers in appointing counsel, as alluded to above, in addition furthers their creativity in establishing concepts of counsel's role in the proceedings. Unfortunately, this does not further the "consistency and clarity in the manner of appointment" asked for,[1587] which one indeed might think to be necessary in order for appointed counsel to know his or her exact role.[1588]

At the same time, it has been submitted that the mere appointment of standby counsel could serve to prevent defendants from obstructing the conduct of their trials.[1589] Indeed, appointing standby counsel from the start would send a clear signal to the *pro se* defendant that the possibility to conduct one's own defence also carries with it certain obligations and that the

---

1586 *See e.g.* in the case of Vojislav Šešelj: Nina H.B. Jørgensen, The Right of the Accused to Self-Representation Before International Criminal Tribunals, 98 *The American Journal of International Law* 711 (2004), at 721. *See also Prosecutor v. Vojislav Šešelj*, Case No. IT-03-67-PT, Decision by Registrar, 05 September 2003, assigning standby counsel; and Decision by Deputy Registrar, 16 February 2004, replacing standby counsel.

1587 Nina H.B. Jørgensen, The Problem of Self-Representation at International Criminal Tribunals. Striking a Balance Between Fairness and Effectiveness, 4 *Journal of International Criminal Justice* 64 (2006), at 72-73.

1588 *Cf.* in this regard the comment of appointed counsel, upon being designated standby counsel in *Karadžić*, and asked whether his role was now clear: "[…] that is most helpful and my team now knows about what the future holds in store. We've been on tender hooks until this moment." *Prosecutor v. Radovan Karadžić*, Case No. IT-05-5/18-T, Hearing, 13 April 2010, T.999.

1589 Michael P. Scharf, Chaos in the Courtroom: Controlling Disruptive Defendants and Contumacious Counsel in War Crimes Trials, 39 *Case Western Reserve Journal of International Law* 155 (2006-2007), at 167; Wolfgang Schomburg, Development of Human Rights Before International Criminal Tribunals. A European Perspective, 17(2) *Croatian Annual of Criminal Law and Practice* 909 (2010), at 922.

court will not allow for any disruptions to the proceedings in excess to those already caused by the accused's choice to self-represent in any event.[1590]

When assigning counsel, the trial chamber in *Milošević* for its part identified four possible concepts to be followed according to practice and the ICTY RPE, namely: (i) exclusive self-representation; (ii) exclusive legal representation; (iii) presentation of the defence case "in conjunction with counsel" according to a specific division of tasks; and (iv) self-representation in terms and appearance, while being assisted behind the scenes by legal advisors or associates.[1591]

Analysing these models, it appears that the first scenario should be a rare occurrence; especially international criminal tribunals thus far have not seen any indication that this had ever been attempted. The second model is linked to the right as enshrined in Article 21(4)(d) of the ICTY Statute and is of no further concern in the context of this dissertation. The third concept would come close to the solution as envisaged by the appeals chamber in *Krajišnik* when it granted the accused's request to be represented with regard to the issue of JCE, whereas the fourth model as outlined by the appeals chamber in *Milošević* appears to be the approach which thus far has been favoured by the accused who decided to exercise their right to self-representation before international criminal tribunals.

The review of the different positions adopted by trial and appeals chambers indicate a need to unambiguously define the tasks which should be assumed by appointed counsel, depending on their designation and role envisaged in the course of proceedings, even though it has also been submitted that the "special designation as standby counsel makes this mandate clear – to the defendant, the attorney, and the public".[1592]

Considering the divergent approaches of chambers in different cases, for example the standpoint adopted by the appeals chamber in *Milošević*, raises the question which difference the appeals chamber perceived between counsel assigned to the accused with the scope of assignment as outlined in its decision, *i.e.* a rather limited role of assistance, on the one hand, and the

---

1590 *See* Philipp Ambach, Selbstvertretung im internationalen Strafprozess – Grundlagen, Kritik und ein Lösungsansatz für die prozessuale Handhabung in der Zukunft, 6 *Zeitschrift für Internationale Strafrechtsdogmatik* 286 (2009), at 301 fn.147.

1591 *Prosecutor v. Slobodan Milošević*, Case No. IT-02-54-T, Reasons for Decision on Assignment of Defence Counsel, 22 September 2004, para.35.

1592 Jenia Iontcheva Turner, Legal Ethics in International Criminal Defense, 10 *Chicago Journal of International Law* 685 (2010), at 739.

role of a standby counsel which, comparably, in general will equally be expected to step in merely if and when determined necessary by the trial chamber concerned on the other. In contrast, standby counsel as appointed initially in *Šešelj* was to assume a significantly more active function than the designation would seem to indicate. The confusion and inconsistency calls for clarification for future proceedings with self-represented accused.

Analysing the different tasks which have been defined by trial and appeals chambers for divergent roles of appointed counsel, it appears that the picture of the role to be played by court-appointed counsel – independent of their official designation – is rather blurred.[1593] Appointed counsel seem to be well advised to explicitly request instructions on their expected role which are as detailed as possible and at the earliest time feasible upon their designation, in order to avoid any confusion that may arise in the context of the tasks to be assumed.

III. Potential ethical implications for imposed counsel

The imposition of counsel on a self-represented accused against the latter's will may also entail consequences for the counsel who are assigned to the defendant.

Considering relevant codes of professional conduct for counsel appearing before international criminal tribunals, it appears that they provide not only for independence of counsel and prohibit any actions which may further the impression that such independence is compromised,[1594] but also for performance in good faith of representation agreements, including a relationship of trust with the client.[1595] Defence counsel are under an obligation of diligence

---

1593 A general blur in designation and role appears to prevail at all levels: *see Prosecutor v. Radovan Karadžić*, Case No. IT-95-5/18-T, Status Conference, 03 September 2012, T.28776.

1594 Code of Professional Conduct for Counsel, ICC-ASP/4/Res.1, 02 December 2005, Article 6(2). Similar provisions can be found in: ICTR Code of Professional Conduct for Defence Counsel, 14 March 1998, Article 5; ICTY Code of Professional Conduct for Counsel Appearing Before the International Tribunal, IT/125 Rev. 3, 22 July 2009 (as amended), Article 10; Code of Professional Conduct for Counsel with the Right of Audience Before the Special Court for Sierra Leone, 13 May 2006 (as amended), Article 5(ii).

1595 Code of Professional Conduct for Counsel, ICC-ASP/4/Res.1, 02 December 2005, Article 14.

to act in the best interest of their clients,[1596] and subject to a duty of loyalty towards their clients.[1597] In case of an appointment or assignment as counsel, problems may ensue in light of obligations not to represent clients if such representation would go against, *inter alia*, the code of professional conduct.[1598] It is of interest to note that the SCSL code of conduct specifically provides for the scope of assignment in case counsel has been appointed as standby counsel or court-appointed counsel.[1599] It also specifies the conditions under which such appointed counsel might withdraw from the representation.[1600]

Regarding the discussion as to whether and to which extent a special relationship of trust and cooperation has to or should exist between defence counsel and client, it has to be noted that generally, the choice of one's own counsel can be subject to limitations, in particular with regard to counsel assigned by court and/or under a legal aid scheme.[1601] The European Court of Human Rights determined that while a relationship of trust between

---

1596 ICTR Code of Professional Conduct for Defence Counsel, 14 March 1998, Article 6; ICTY Code of Professional Conduct for Counsel Appearing Before the International Tribunal, IT/125 Rev. 3, 22 July 2009 (as amended), Article 11; Code of Professional Conduct for Counsel with the Right of Audience Before the Special Court for Sierra Leone, 13 May 2006 (as amended), Article 15(A).

1597 ICTR Code of Professional Conduct for Defence Counsel, 14 March 1998, Article 9(1); ICTY Code of Professional Conduct for Counsel Appearing Before the International Tribunal, IT/125 Rev. 3, 22 July 2009 (as amended), Articles 3(iv), 14(A).

1598 ICTY Code of Professional Conduct for Counsel Appearing Before the International Tribunal, IT/125 Rev. 3, 22 July 2009 (as amended), Article 9(A)(i).

1599 Code of Professional Conduct for Counsel with the Right of Audience Before the Special Court for Sierra Leone, 13 May 2006 (as amended), Article 14(B): "Where Defence Counsel has been appointed by a Judge or Chamber as stand-by counsel or court-appointed counsel, when representing a client such Defence Counsel shall: (i) prescribe the scope of representation to be provided; (ii) discuss with his client the conduct of the case, endeavour to obtain his instructions thereon and take account of views expressed by the client, while retaining the right to determine what course to follow; (iii) act throughout in the best interests of the client."

1600 Code of Professional Conduct for Counsel with the Right of Audience Before the Special Court for Sierra Leone, 13 May 2006 (as amended), Article 18(B): "Where Defence Counsel is appointed by a Judge or Chamber as Stand-by or Court-Appointed Counsel, representation may only be withdrawn or terminated with leave of a Judge or Chamber upon demonstration of good cause and where withdrawal or termination is in the interests of justice."

1601 *Prosecutor v. Vidoje Blagojević*, Case No. IT-02-60-T, Decision on Independent Counsel for Vidoje Blagojević's Motion to Instruct the Registrar to Appoint New Lead and Co-Counsel, 03 July 2003, para.117.

counsel and client was important, the right to choose one's counsel would necessarily be subject to limitations, *inter alia*, "where it is for the courts to decide whether the interests of justice require that the accused be defended by counsel appointed by them".[1602] While courts should take into account the wishes of the accused, such wishes could be discarded if this was in the interests of justice.[1603]

In order to illustrate the matters which may be at stake for counsel assigned to *pro se* defendants, the following section will briefly review relevant jurisprudence from international criminal tribunals which dealt either specifically with the question of choice of appointed counsel by self-represented accused, or more generally with the issue of trust between counsel and client and potential for replacement of counsel for lack of trust or in other "exceptional circumstances".

1. International Criminal Tribunal for the Former Yugoslavia

As becomes apparent when examining for example the filings of the accused and other participants in the *Karadžić* proceedings, problematic questions can arise in a situation in which counsel are appointed to defendants who do not approve of that assignment and thus counsel have to represent interests of accused potentially without any instructions from the defendant's part.[1604] In more recent proceedings, the ICTY registry expressed this concern in *Karadžić* when submitting that "the lawyers admitted to the Rule 45 list have not indicated their willingness to be imposed as counsel to an accused pursuant to Rule 45*ter* of the Rules" and that "some lawyers have expressed

---

1602 *Mayzit v. Russia*, Application no. 63378/00, Judgment, 06 July 2005, para.66, referring to *Croissant c. Allemagne*, Requête n° 13611/88, Arrêt, 25 septembre 1992, para.29. *See also Vitan c. Roumanie*, Requête n° 42084/02, Arrêt, 01 décembre 2008, para.59.

1603 *Mayzit v. Russia*, Application no. 63378/00, Judgment, 06 July 2005, para.66, referring to *Croissant c. Allemagne*, Requête n° 13611/88, Arrêt, 25 septembre 1992, para.29. *See also Vitan c. Roumanie*, Requête n° 42084/02, Arrêt, 01 décembre 2008, para.59.

1604 *Cf. Prosecutor v. Slobodan Milošević*, Case No. IT-02-54-T, Decision on Assigned Counsel's Motion for Withdrawal, 07 December 2004, para.22: "[…] assignment of counsel against the wishes of the accused is a developing area of law both in national and international jurisdictions".

concerns about representing accused without instructions".[1605] Consequently, in the registrar's view, they "would clearly not be able to appoint counsel against their will".[1606] Indications of the same concern were expressed during a status conference in *Karadžić* by counsel appointed by the ICTY registry upon order from the trial chamber, who stated to be "reluctant" to be present without the consent of the accused pending the decision on the appeal of the decision of counsel's appointment.[1607] However, the view has also been expressed that it was for the bench to control the proceedings, not for the accused, so that the potential (mental) impact any imposition of counsel might have on the defendant should not be considered as a factor.[1608]

The matter was raised in a critique of the trial chamber's decision in *Milošević* to assign counsel *inter alia* on the basis that the trial chamber did not take into account which problems could arise for counsel, also from an ethical point of view, if appointed to an unwilling "client".[1609] The dilemmas that assignment of counsel against the will of the accused entails became apparent in *Milošević*, when the defendant did not give counsel any instructions and criticised the latter's way of conducting examinations of defence

---

1605 *Prosecutor v. Radovan Karadžić*, Case No. IT-95-5/18-T, Registrar's Submission Pursuant to Rule 33(B) Regarding Radovan Karadžić's Motion to Vacate Appointment of Richard Harvey, 14 December 2009, para.42.

1606 *Prosecutor v. Radovan Karadžić*, Case No. IT-95-5/18-T, Registrar's Submission Pursuant to Rule 33(B) Regarding Radovan Karadžić's Motion to Vacate Appointment of Richard Harvey, 14 December 2009, para.42.

1607 *Prosecutor v. Radovan Karadžić*, Case No. IT-95-5/18-T, Status Conference, 28 January 2010, T.709-710.

1608 *Prosecutor v. Slobodan Milošević*, Case No. IT-02-54-AR73.7, Appeals Hearing, 21 October 2004, T.66: "But when Her Honour is concerned about the distress that would be caused to this accused by his having to deal with imposed counsel, I must ask this rhetorical question, but I hope it politely: Who is running this Court; the accused or the Judges who have been appointed to do so?".

1609 Göran Sluiter, 'Fairness and the Interests of Justice'. Illusive Concepts in the Milošević Case, 3 *Journal of International Criminal Law* 9 (2005), at 17.

witnesses.[1610] Assigned counsel addressed these difficulties in the course of an interlocutory appeal hearing.[1611]

In *Karadžić*, the accused foreshadowed his attitude with regard to the issue of standby counsel, and the ensuing stance towards cooperation with such standby counsel, early on in the proceedings: in a motion concerned with adequate facilities, the defendant submitted that

> "standby counsel and a self-represented accused have a built-in conflict of interest – the very nature of a standby counsel supposes that he will be willing to act contrary to the wishes of the accused by replacing him when the Trial Chamber deems it necessary."[1612]

In a similar vein, the defendant considered the appointment of standby counsel to be an indication of the trial chamber's determination "to force Dr. Karadzic into forfeiting his right to self-representation".[1613]

Vojislav Šešelj equally voiced fierce objections and allegations against standby counsel,[1614] which in one case led to standby counsel initiating domestic proceedings against the accused.[1615] With regard to the second standby counsel appointed to his case, the defendant initiated proceedings against

---

1610 *Prosecutor v. Slobodan Milošević*, Case No. IT-02-54-T, Hearing, 07 September 2004, T.32440-32441, 32470, 32504; Hearing, 08 September 2004, T.32560, 32579; Hearing, 09 September 2004, T.32632-32633, 32720; Hearing, 14 September 2004, T.32766-32767, 32803; Hearing, 12 October 2004, T.32962-32963; Hearing, 13 October 2004, T.33029-33030; Hearing, 19 October 2004, T.33124. *See also* Assigned Counsel's Motion for Withdrawal With Annex A, 08 November 2004, para.8, 10, 12, 19.

1611 *Prosecutor v. Slobodan Milošević*, Case No. IT-02-54-AR73.7, Appeals Hearing, 21 October 2004, T.26-27, 29-31.

1612 *Prosecutor v. Radovan Karadžić*, Case No. IT-95-5/18-PT, Motion for Adequate Facilities and Equality of Arms: Legal Associates, 24 November 2008, para.24. *See also* in this regard *Prosecutor v. Vojislav Šešelj*, Case No. IT-03-67-PT, Motion for Trial Chamber I to Acquire a Complete Report on the Health of Professor Vojislav Šešelj (Submission No. 159), 19 May 2006 (filed: 22 June 2006), p.4.

1613 *Prosecutor v. Radovan Karadžić*, Case No. IT-95-5/18-AR73.8, Appeal from Order on the Trial Schedule, 10 June 2010, para.16.

1614 *Cf. Prosecutor v. Vojislav Šešelj*, Case No. IT-03-67-AR73.3, Decision on Appeal Against the Trial Chamber's Decision on Assignment of Counsel, 20 October 2006, para.50.

1615 *Prosecutor v. Vojislav Šešelj*, Case No. IT-03-67-PT, Decision by Registrar, 05 September 2003, assigning standby counsel; and Decision by Deputy Registrar, 16 February 2004, replacing standby counsel.

that counsel in national courts.[1616] In light of the potential – and even likely – refusal of defendants to cooperate with standby counsel, such imposition has been characterised as "a cruel, almost abusive, assignment to limbo" and "nonsense".[1617]

Comparable issues arise in the context of assignment of *amicus curiae* who officially might not have to represent the interests of the accused, but *de facto* are assigned to argue in favour of the defendant's position. Thus, even though formally not defence counsel, *amicus* may find him- or herself in a situation in which arguments for the defence have to be presented without approval or instruction from the accused – thereby potentially creating an ethical conflict. In the ordinary sense of the term, *amicus curiae* can be invited by chambers to make submissions with regard to specific issues defined by the bench.[1618] The concept as such does neither include *amicus* appearing on a permanent basis before the court, nor arguing in favour of either party to the proceedings.[1619]

A separate concurring opinion to a decision on an interlocutory appeal brought by *amicus curiae* in *Milošević* adopted the position that *amicus curiae* is not a party to the proceedings, even though his or her mandate might have been extended in the particular case at hand.[1620] According to this view, before the ICTY, *amicus* was limited to the role of "a friend of the court, as distinguished from being a friend of the accused".[1621] It has been argued that the use of the concept of *amici curiae* could overcome some

---

1616 *Prosecutor v. Vojislav Šešelj*, Case No. IT-03-67-PT, Status Conference, 30 May 2005, T.366-367.

1617 Eugene Cerruti, Self-Representation in the International Arena: Removing a False Right to Spectacle, 40 *Georgetown Journal of International Law* 919 (2009), at 960-961.

1618 *See e.g.* Rule 74 of both ICTY and ICTR RPE; Rule 103 ICC RPE; Rule 74 SCSL RPE; Rule 131 STL RPE; Rule 33 ECCC IR.

1619 For an overview in the context of international tribunals, *see* Lance Bartholomeusz, The *Amicus Curiae* Before International Courts and Tribunals, 5 *Non-State Actors and International Law* 209 (2005), at 274-275, 278-280.

1620 *Prosecutor v. Slobodan Milošević*, Case No. IT-02-54-AR73.6, Decision on the Interlocutory Appeal by the *Amici Curiae* Against the Trial Chamber Order Concerning the Presentation and Preparation of the Defence Case, 20 January 2004, Separate Opinion of Judge Shahabuddeen, para.5-6.

1621 *Prosecutor v. Slobodan Milošević*, Case No. IT-02-54-AR73.6, Decision on the Interlocutory Appeal by the *Amici Curiae* Against the Trial Chamber Order Concerning the Presentation and Preparation of the Defence Case, 20 January 2004, Separate Opinion of Judge Shahabuddeen, para.15.

of the difficulties that might arise in case counsel is imposed and might have to act without instructions from the accused, given that *amici* would forward arguments for the defence without necessarily interfering with the potential strategy of the unwilling defendant.[1622] This was preferred over the option of for example standby or assigned counsel who, it was argued, could not represent an uncooperative and indeed unwilling accused without acting against professional ethics.[1623]

In contrast, however, the use of the concept in *Milošević* has also been heavily criticised as "fundamental mistake", since *amicus curiae* cannot work both as "pseudo-counsel for an accused" and as "pseudo-assistants to the bench".[1624] Their role played as envisaged by the trial chamber was characterised as an "anomaly" not in line with the usual understanding of the concept, although the underlying rationale for assigning some sort of counsel for the side of the defence was acknowledged.[1625] The use of the concept furthermore has been considered to blur the lines between the initial concept of *amicus curiae* (as *e.g.* envisaged in Rule 74 of the ICTY RPE) and actual parties to the proceedings,[1626] thereby also creating insecurity as

---

1622 Jarinde Temminck Tuinstra, Assisting an Accused to Represent Himself. Appointment of *Amici Curiae* as the Most Appropriate Option, (2006) *Journal of International Criminal Justice* 47, at 54.

1623 Jarinde Temminck Tuinstra, Assisting an Accused to Represent Himself. Appointment of *Amici Curiae* as the Most Appropriate Option, (2006) *Journal of International Criminal Justice* 47, at 57-58, 61-62.

1624 Wolfgang Schomburg, The Role of International Criminal Tribunals in Promoting Respect for Fair Trial Rights, 8 *Northwestern University Journal of International Human Rights* 1 (2009), at 54. *See also* Wolfgang Schomburg, Development of Human Rights Before International Criminal Tribunals. A European Perspective, 17(2) *Croatian Annual of Criminal Law and Practice* 909 (2010), at 921-922.

1625 Michael Bohlander, The Defence, in: Gideon Boas/William A. Schabas (eds), *International Criminal Law Developments in the Case Law of the ICTY* (Leiden/Bosten: Martinus Nijhoff Publishers) 2003, p.35-74, at 44-45.

1626 Lance Bartholomeusz, The *Amicus Curiae* Before International Courts and Tribunals, 5 *Non-State Actors and International Law* 209 (2005), at 248. *See also* Sarah Williams/Hannah Woolaver, The Role of the *Amicus curia* before International Criminal Tribunals, 6 *International Criminal Law Review* 151 (2006), at 166; Boris Petersdorf, *Eigenverteidigung und aufgedrängte Pflichtverteidigung im formellen Völkerstrafrecht* (Baden-Baden: Nomos Verlagsgesellschaft) 2010, p.200-202.

to the rules of conduct to be adhered to by *amici*.[1627] Using this model was characterised as introducing defence counsel for the accused "through the backdoor".[1628] In addition, the issue of uncooperative accused was raised in light of the potential harm caused to defendants if *amici*, not being aware of a defence strategy mounted by the accused, broach matters contrary to those expressed by the defendant.[1629] To be mentioned in this context are also the apparent difficulties in the beginning with regard to the role to be played by the *amici curiae* appointed in *Krajišnik*, with the appeals chamber having to define which kind of filings under which title could be received from the *amici*.[1630] It has therefore been argued that in light of the tasks in fact assumed by *amici*, the trial chamber should have assigned counsel if considered appropriate rather than taking the detour of appointing *amicus curiae*.[1631] This view illustrates why the role of *amicus curiae* assigned to assist a self-represented accused may raise similar or even the same ethical issues that may arise for imposed standby counsel or assigned counsel.

In addition to the objections voiced with regard to the use of models of standby counsel or *amicus curiae*, more specific concerns also arise in the context of potential conflicts of interests for counsel. Instructive as to the general stance adopted before the ICTY is *Blagojević & Jokić*, case in which the appeals chamber clarified that defence counsel has a duty to represent an accused even against the latter's will if such resistance from the defendant against his representation by that specific counsel is not justified.[1632] This

1627 Sarah Williams/Hannah Woolaver, The Role of the *Amicus curia* before International Criminal Tribunals, 6 *International Criminal Law Review* 151 (2006), at 164.

1628 Philipp Ambach, Selbstvertretung im internationalen Strafprozess – Grundlagen, Kritik und ein Lösungsansatz für die prozessuale Handhabung in der Zukunft, 6 *Zeitschrift für Internationale Strafrechtsdogmatik* 286 (2009), at 299.

1629 Philipp Ambach, Selbstvertretung im internationalen Strafprozess – Grundlagen, Kritik und ein Lösungsansatz für die prozessuale Handhabung in der Zukunft, 6 *Zeitschrift für Internationale Strafrechtsdogmatik* 286 (2009), at 300.

1630 *Prosecutor v. Momčilo Krajišnik*, IT-00-39-A, Decision on Krajišnik Request and Prosecution Motion, 11 September 2007, para.22, 47-50.

1631 Boris Petersdorf, *Eigenverteidigung und aufgedrängte Pflichtverteidigung im formellen Völkerstrafrecht* (Baden-Baden: Nomos Verlagsgesellschaft) 2010, p.202.

1632 *Prosecutor v. Vidoje Blagojević*, Case No. IT-02-60-AR73.4, Public and Redacted Reasons for Decision on Appeal by Vidoje Blagojević to Replace his Defence Team, 07 November 2003, para.54: "In circumstances such as this, where an Appellant unjustifiably resists legal representation from assigned Counsel, Counsel's

illustrates the distinction drawn by the appeals chamber between the guarantee of a fair trial and defence for the accused to be safeguarded by the ICTY on the one hand, and potential wishes of the accused with regard to the person representing the defendant's interests on the other. The impugned trial chamber decision clarified that it was not for an accused to "unilaterally destroy the trust" to counsel in the hope that counsel would be withdrawn.[1633] It found that there was no justification for the defendant's refusal to communicate with counsel, behaviour which in view of the trial chamber, "as a form of protest, is not permissible".[1634] In order to foster rebuilding of a trustful relationship between counsel and the accused, the trial chamber ordered the ICTY registry to assign an additional legal representative for a specific period of time and with particular tasks.[1635]

With regard to self-represented accused, the *Milošević* trial chamber determined that failure by the accused to cooperate with assigned counsel would not result in him being able to argue any injustice in the presentation of the defence case.[1636] This is of note insofar as it is similar to the notion found

---

professional obligations to continue to represent the accused remain. The Appeals Chamber is satisfied that Counsel in this case is committed to representing the Appellant, and that the Appellant will receive a fair trial with the assistance of his assigned Counsel. In dismissing the Appellant's appeal, the Appeals Chamber wishes to make it clear to the Appellant that he has now exhausted all avenues available to voice his objections that he has not been accorded that to which he has no justifiable reason to demand. The Tribunal will not entertain a demand by an Appellant for that to be granted to him to which he has established no entitlement." *See also Prosecutor v. Vojislav Šešelj*, Case No. IT-03-67-AR73.3, Decision on Appeal Against the Trial Chamber's Decision on Assignment of Counsel, 20 October 2006, para.45.

1633 *Prosecutor v. Vidoje Blagojević*, Case No. IT-02-60-T, Decision on Independent Counsel for Vidoje Blagojević's Motion to Instruct the Registrar to Appoint New Lead and Co-Counsel, 03 July 2003, para.100.

1634 *Prosecutor v. Vidoje Blagojević*, Case No. IT-02-60-T, Decision on Independent Counsel for Vidoje Blagojević's Motion to Instruct the Registrar to Appoint New Lead and Co-Counsel, 03 July 2003, para.110.

1635 *Prosecutor v. Vidoje Blagojević*, Case No. IT-02-60-T, Decision on Independent Counsel for Vidoje Blagojević's Motion to Instruct the Registrar to Appoint New Lead and Co-Counsel, 03 July 2003, para.114, p.48-49.

1636 *Prosecutor v. Slobodan Milošević*, Case No. IT-02-54-T, Reasons for Decision on Assignment of Defence Counsel, 22 September 2004, para.70: "Should the Accused fail to cooperate with counsel, the trial will nonetheless proceed. If such failure on the part of the Accused results in material which is actually relevant to the Accused's case not being present, then the Accused must bear responsibility for that and cannot plead injustice."

in *Faretta*, where the U.S. Supreme Court held that an accused having chosen to represent himself could later not appeal any conviction on the basis of ineffective defence.[1637] It is even more interesting when bearing in mind that at least two judges of the *Milošević* trial chamber adopted a rather different view only little more than one year earlier in the decision rejecting assignment of counsel which stated that having defence counsel act without instructions from the accused could amount to effectively depriving the accused of his or her right to a defence.[1638]

Afterwards, when assigned counsel sought to withdraw from the case, but were refused their request from the ICTY registry up to the ICTY president,[1639] they argued that in light of the continued non-cooperation by the accused, they would not be in a position to act in accordance with the code of conduct to be adhered to by counsel appearing before the ICTY and would be subjected to a conflict of interests.[1640] The trial chamber dismissed counsel's submissions, finding that

> "[w]hat is required of counsel is that they act in what they perceive to be the best interests of the Accused. [...] To hold otherwise would be to allow an accused to frustrate the statutory duty of the Trial Chamber to ensure that a trial

---

1637 *Cf. Anthony Pasquall Faretta v. State of California* (U.S. Supreme Court), 422 U.S. 806, 30 June 1975, at 834 fn.46.

1638 *Prosecutor v. Slobodan Milošević*, Case No. IT-02-54-T, Reasons for Decision on the Prosecution Motion Concerning Assignment of Counsel, 04 April 2003, para.24-25. Criticising the trial chamber's decision in, *inter alia*, this respect, *see* Michael Bohlander, 'A Fool for a Client' – Remarks on the Freedom of Choice and Assignment of Counsel at the International Criminal Tribunal for the Former Yugoslavia, 16 *Criminal Law Forum* 159 (2005), at 165.

1639 The issue of non-cooperation and related problems had been raised before: *see Prosecutor v. Slobodan Milošević*, Case No. IT-02-54-AR73.7, Appeal Against the Trial Chamber's Decision on Assignment of Defence Counsel, 29 September 2004, para.93. *See also* Steven Kay/Gillian Higgins, The Right of Self-Representation – The Lawyers in the Eye of the Storm, International Criminal Law Bureau 2010, p.4, available at http://www.internationallawbureau.com/blog/wp-content/uploads/2010/08/Lawyers-Self-representation-Kay-Higgins.pdf (last accessed 17 November 2012).

1640 *Prosecutor v. Slobodan Milošević*, Case No. IT-02-54-T, Assigned Counsel's Motion for Withdrawal With Annex A, 08 November 2004, para.34, 36, 38, 55. *See also Prosecutor v. Slobodan Milošević*, Case No. IT-02-54-T, Assigned Counsel's Request to the President Pursuant to Article 19(F) of the Directive on Assignment of Defence Counsel for a Review of the Deputy Registrar's Decision dated 14 December 2004 Refusing Assigned Counsel's Application to Withdraw With Attachment 1, 28 December 2004.

> is fair. […] When counsel is assigned and acts in accordance with a court order, the obligations inherent in the normal counsel-client relationship must be modified to the extent necessary to give effect to the order appointing counsel."[1641]

In the trial chamber's view, assigning counsel against an accused's will could not be seen to put pressure on that assigned counsel so as to endanger his or her integrity.[1642] The judges reiterated that

> "[t]he requirement that the trial be fair and that it be concluded in a sufficiently expeditious manner cannot be frustrated by the Accused's refusal to communicate with or instruct counsel lawfully assigned to him."[1643]

Subsequently, the appeals chamber clarified in *Šešelj* that the defendant's refusal to communicate or cooperate with assigned counsel could be no reason to jeopardise the fair and expeditious nature of the proceedings.[1644]

The president of the ICTY seised to review the decision of the ICTY registry to deny withdrawal of counsel essentially agreed with the registrar's conclusion, finding that any other decision would have rendered the appeals chamber decision on assignment of counsel "nugatory".[1645] The president concluded by encouraging assigned counsel to recognise that "[r]epresenting criminal defendants is not an easy task" and advised that it would be good to

> "recognize that fact, to realize the breadth of activities that they can carry out even in the absence of Milošević's cooperation, and to continue making the best professional efforts on his behalf that are possible under the circumstances."[1646]

1641 *Prosecutor v. Slobodan Milošević*, Case No. IT-02-54-T, Decision on Assigned Counsel's Motion for Withdrawal, 07 December 2004, para.19.

1642 *Prosecutor v. Slobodan Milošević*, Case No. IT-02-54-T, Decision on Assigned Counsel's Motion for Withdrawal, 07 December 2004, para.23.

1643 *Prosecutor v. Slobodan Milošević*, Case No. IT-02-54-T, Decision on Assigned Counsel's Motion for Withdrawal, 07 December 2004, para.33. *See also Prosecutor v. Vojislav Šešelj*, Case No. IT-03-67-AR73.3, Decision on Appeal Against the Trial Chamber's Decision on Assignment of Counsel, 20 October 2006, para.45.

1644 *Prosecutor v. Vojislav Šešelj*, Case No. IT-03-67-AR73.3, Decision on Appeal Against the Trial Chamber's Decision on Assignment of Counsel, 20 October 2006, para.45.

1645 *Prosecutor v. Slobodan Milošević*, Case No. IT-02-54-T, Decision Affirming the Registrar's Denial of Assigned Counsel's Application to Withdraw, 07 February 2005, para.10.

1646 *Prosecutor v. Slobodan Milošević*, Case No. IT-02-54-T, Decision Affirming the Registrar's Denial of Assigned Counsel's Application to Withdraw, 07 February 2005, para.13.

To be mentioned is an incident that took place during a status conference in *Šešelj* when the accused was removed from the courtroom given his refusal to answer any questions or productively participate in the status conference with standby counsel present in the courtroom.[1647] Standby counsel suggested that a status conference could be held with the accused, but not standby counsel present in order to address the issues at stake.[1648] However, this idea was rejected by at least one of the judges who left no doubt that it was not for the accused to determine which course the proceedings should take.[1649]

It has been argued in this context that any ethical obligations regarding uncooperative accused should not give rise to problems in light of the fact that any defence tasks should be fulfilled according to objective standards bearing in mind the circumstances of the case at hand.[1650] In such situations, uncooperative accused were not much dissimilar to indifferent ones, with the latter case not giving rise to potential conflict of interests either.[1651] In a similar vein, it has been argued that the appointment of standby counsel in case a defendant intends to boycott the proceedings with instructions to the defence lawyer would strike a sensible balance between different perceptions of the nature of the attorney-accused relationship.[1652]

1647 *Prosecutor v. Vojislav Šešelj*, Case No. IT-03-67-PT, Status Conference, 01 November 2006, T.627-636.

1648 *Prosecutor v. Vojislav Šešelj*, Case No. IT-03-67-PT, Status Conference, 01 November 2006, T.655.

1649 *Prosecutor v. Vojislav Šešelj*, Case No. IT-03-67-PT, Status Conference, 01 November 2006, T.656: "[…] Judge Robinson: Can I say I would not be in a position to accept that course. The procedures here are not to be determined by the accused. […] What would be slighted in my view, would not be you but the dignity and prestige of the Chamber, of the Tribunal, were that course to be followed."

1650 Philipp Ambach, Selbstvertretung im internationalen Strafprozess – Grundlagen, Kritik und ein Lösungsansatz für die prozessuale Handhabung in der Zukunft, 6 *Zeitschrift für Internationale Strafrechtsdogmatik* 286 (2009), at 299.

1651 Philipp Ambach, Selbstvertretung im internationalen Strafprozess – Grundlagen, Kritik und ein Lösungsansatz für die prozessuale Handhabung in der Zukunft, 6 *Zeitschrift für Internationale Strafrechtsdogmatik* 286 (2009), at 299-300.

1652 Jenia Iontcheva Turner, Legal Ethics in International Criminal Defense, 10 *Chicago Journal of International Law* 685 (2010), at 740.

2. International Criminal Tribunal for Rwanda

At the ICTR, trial chambers have taken different views on the necessity of a relationship of trust and sufficient communication between an accused and his defence counsel. An examination of the ICTR provisions and the related jurisprudence on the assignment of counsel may shed some light on the discussions even though they have not been interpreted and applied in the context of proceedings with self-represented accused.

Rule 44*bis* of the ICTR RPE provides for duty counsel to be available to the ICTR.[1653] In addition, Rule 45(H) of the ICTR RPE provides for the replacement of assigned counsel upon request of a suspect, accused or his counsel.[1654] Furthermore, Rule 45(I) of the ICTR RPE seeks to prevent counsel from withdrawing from a case in the course of the proceedings.[1655]

Albeit not in the context of self-represented accused, the ICTR had to interpret the meaning of "exceptional circumstances" as provided for in an older version of Article 19 of the Directive on Assignment of Defence

1653 Rule 44*bis* ICTR RPE: "(A) A list of duty counsel who speak one or both working languages of the Tribunal and have indicated their willingness to be assigned pursuant to this Rule shall be kept by the Registrar. (B) Duty counsel shall fulfil the requirements of Rule 44, and shall be situated within reasonable proximity to the Detention Facility and the Seat of the Tribunal. (C) The Registrar shall at all time ensure that duty counsel will be available to attend the Detention Facility in the event of being summoned. (D) If an accused, or suspect transferred under Rule 40 *bis*, is unrepresented at any time after being transferred to the Tribunal, the Registrar shall as soon as practicable summon duty counsel to represent the accused or suspect until counsel is engaged by the accused or suspect, or assigned under Rule 45. (E) In providing initial legal advice and assistance to a suspect transferred under Rule 40 bis, duty counsel shall advise the suspect of his or her rights including the rights including referred to in Rule 55 (A)."

1654 Rule 45(H) ICTR RPE: "Under exceptional circumstances, at the request of the suspect or accused or his counsel, the Chamber may instruct the Registrar to replace an assigned counsel, upon good cause being shown and after having been satisfied that the request is not designed to delay the proceedings."

1655 Rule 45(I) ICTR RPE: "It is understood that Counsel will represent the accused and conduct the case to finality. Failure to do so, absent just cause approved by the Chamber, may result in forfeiture of fees in whole or in part. In such circumstances the Chamber may make an order accordingly. Counsel shall only be permitted to withdraw from the case to which he has been assigned in the most exceptional circumstances."

Counsel at the time[1656] in light of several defendants' requests for replacement of assigned counsel due to lack of trust: in *Akayesu*, the trial chamber held on the facts of the case that the alleged lack of confidence in the ability of counsel to present the accused's case did indeed amount to such exceptional circumstances and granted the defendant's request to replace counsel, without however specifying what the alleged "inappropriate behaviour" entailed.[1657] The trial chamber in *Bagosora* followed this approach and considered the failure of assigned counsel to communicate with his client about the case in fact created a lack of trust on the part of the accused amounting to exceptional circumstances in the sense of the directive warranting replacement of assigned counsel.[1658] In contrast, the trial chamber did not find exceptional circumstances to be established in *Ntakirutimana*, where the accused, in view of the trial chamber, wanted to have specific counsel appointed, rather than remedy an actual lack of trust with assigned counsel. The trial chamber also clarified that an indigent accused provided with legal assistance free of charge could not always ask for counsel of his or her own choice.[1659]

The trial chamber in *Ntahobali* considered that a "breakdown in communication and trust between the Accused and his defence team [...] constitutes exceptional circumstances within the ambit of Rule 45(H) of the Rules".[1660] The bench adopted the view that a "proper relationship of communication and trust" needed to be established in order "to ensure an effective defence and for smooth proceedings in relation to the Tribunal as a whole".[1661] Since the accused expressed his willingness to represent himself pending assignment of new counsel of his choice, the trial chamber found that the request was

---

1656 The current version of the Directive on the Assignment of Defence Counsel, 14 March 2008, reads in Article 19(A)(i) as follows: "The Registrar may (i) In exceptional circumstances, at the request of the accused, or his Counsel, withdraw the assignment of Counsel; [...]".

1657 *Procureur c. Jean-Paul Akayesu*, Affaire n° ICTR-96-4-T, Décision Faisant Suite à une Demande de l'Accusé de Changement d'Avocat Commis d'Office, 20 novembre 1996.

1658 *Prosecutor v. Théoneste Bagosora*, Case No. ICTR-96-7-T, Decision on the Request by the Accused for Change of Assigned Counsel, 26 June 1997.

1659 *Prosecutor v. Gérard Ntakirutimana*, Case No. ICTR-96-10-T & ICTR-96-17-T, Decision on the Motions of the Accused for Replacement of Assigned Counsel / Corr., 11 June 1997.

1660 *Prosecutor v. Nyiramasuhuko & Ntahobali*, Case No. ICTR-97-21-T, Decision on Ntahobali's Motion for Withdrawal of Counsel, 22 June 2001, para.14.

1661 *Prosecutor v. Nyiramasuhuko & Ntahobali*, Case No. ICTR-97-21-T, Decision on Ntahobali's Motion for Withdrawal of Counsel, 22 June 2001, para.14.

not designed to delay the proceedings and thus granted it.[1662] However, the trial chamber decided *proprio motu*, in light of the seriousness of the charges brought against the accused and given concerns about the defendant personally cross-examining rape victims, to appoint a duty counsel pursuant to Rule 44*bis* (D) of the ICTR RPE "so as to ensure that the Accused is assisted in the conduct of his defence".[1663] Despite its reliance on the necessity of a proper counsel-client relationship, the trial chamber clarified that counsel is independent in his or her exercise of professional judgement, and that although it needs "to be assured that a Counsel properly conducts an accused's defence and protects the latter's lawful interest during trial, but also has to verify that the accused does not abuse this right".[1664] Furthermore, "[w]hile counsel should take full instructions about facts surrounding the case, this does not imply that Counsel have to consult with the accused whenever any step in his defence is taken by the Counsel".[1665]

The trial chamber in *Barayagwiza* interpreted the same rules, but reached a different conclusion: the accused argued that his fair trial rights would be violated if he was to be present during his proceedings and represented by defence counsel,[1666] and therefore instructed defence counsel not to act on his behalf.[1667] Defence counsel remained passive in the hearings and filed a motion to withdraw from their mandate.[1668] The trial chamber considered that rather than amounting to exceptional circumstances within the meaning of Rule 45(I) of the ICTR RPE, the arguments had to be considered as obstructionist.[1669] More explicitly, the trial chamber determined that

---

1662 *Prosecutor v. Nyiramasuhuko & Ntahobali*, Case No. ICTR-97-21-T, Decision on Ntahobali's Motion for Withdrawal of Counsel, 22 June 2001, para.19.

1663 *Prosecutor v. Nyiramasuhuko & Ntahobali*, Case No. ICTR-97-21-T, Decision on Ntahobali's Motion for Withdrawal of Counsel, 22 June 2001, para.20.

1664 *Prosecutor v. Nyiramasuhuko & Ntahobali*, Case No. ICTR-97-21-T, Decision on Ntahobali's Motion for Withdrawal of Counsel, 22 June 2001, para.22.

1665 *Prosecutor v. Nyiramasuhuko & Ntahobali*, Case No. ICTR-97-21-T, Decision on Ntahobali's Motion for Withdrawal of Counsel, 22 June 2001, para.23.

1666 *Prosecutor v. Jean-Bosco Barayagwiza*, Case No. ICTR-97-19-T, Decision on Defence Counsel Motion to Withdraw, 02 November 2000, para.5-6.

1667 *Prosecutor v. Jean-Bosco Barayagwiza*, Case No. ICTR-97-19-T, Decision on Defence Counsel Motion to Withdraw, 02 November 2000, para.11-12.

1668 *Prosecutor v. Jean-Bosco Barayagwiza*, Case No. ICTR-97-19-T, Decision on Defence Counsel Motion to Withdraw, 02 November 2000, para.17.

1669 *Prosecutor v. Jean-Bosco Barayagwiza*, Case No. ICTR-97-19-T, Decision on Defence Counsel Motion to Withdraw, 02 November 2000, para.16.

> "[…] Counsel are under an obligation to mount an active defence in the best interest of the Accused. It should further be noted that Counsel is assigned, not appointed. In the view of the Chamber, this does not only entail obligations towards the client, but also implies that he represents the interests of the Tribunal to ensure that the Accused receives a fair trial. The aim is to obtain efficient representation and adversarial proceedings."[1670]

Therefore, in the circumstances of the case, counsel could not simply follow instructions by the accused not to represent him.[1671]

In his separate and concurring opinion, Judge Gunawardana went a step further and considered the appropriate solution to the case at hand to be the appointment of standby counsel.[1672] Judge Gunawardana interpreted the notion of Article 20(4)(d) of the ICTR Statute, "to have legal assistance assigned to him or her, in any case where the interests of justice so require", to encompass such an assignment.[1673]

When subsequently new counsel were assigned to the accused by the trial chamber,[1674] the appeals chamber upheld this decision, stating that in light of Article 19(1) of the ICTR Statute, a trial chamber was entitled to assign counsel against the accused's will if the latter had waived his right to be present at and participate in the proceedings.[1675]

The propriety of the decision has been questioned on the ground that trust was needed for representation, and that "[t]here is clearly no trust or confidence in a case of forced representation".[1676] It has been questioned how counsel were supposed to present a defence in the best interests of an accused

---

1670 *Prosecutor v. Jean-Bosco Barayagwiza*, Case No. ICTR-97-19-T, Decision on Defence Counsel Motion to Withdraw, 02 November 2000, para.21.

1671 *Prosecutor v. Jean-Bosco Barayagwiza*, Case No. ICTR-97-19-T, Decision on Defence Counsel Motion to Withdraw, 02 November 2000, para.24.

1672 *Prosecutor v. Jean-Bosco Barayagwiza*, Case No. ICTR-97-19-T, Decision on Defence Counsel Motion to Withdraw, 02 November 2000, Concurring and Separate Opinion of Judge Gunawardana.

1673 *Prosecutor v. Jean-Bosco Barayagwiza*, Case No. ICTR-97-19-T, Decision on Defence Counsel Motion to Withdraw, 02 November 2000, Concurring and Separate Opinion of Judge Gunawardana.

1674 *Prosecutor v. Ferdinand Nahimana et al.*, Case No. ICTR-99-52-A, Judgement, 28 November 2007, para.122.

1675 *Prosecutor v. Ferdinand Nahimana et al.*, Case No. ICTR-99-52-A, Judgement, 28 November 2007, para.127.

1676 Daniel D. Ntanda Nsereko, Ethical Obligations of Counsel in Criminal Proceedings: Representing an Unwilling Client, 12 *Criminal Law Forum* 487 (2001), at 504.

without any instructions from the latter.[1677] The argument has been made that in case of outright refusal to cooperate on the part of the accused, a defence attorney's sole possibility would be to withdraw save for violation of applicable ethical codes.[1678]

3. Discussion

It has to be questioned whether the rather harsh approach of chambers at different international criminal tribunals with regard to the necessity of a relationship of trust between counsel and accused is viable. Although it is understandable that the judges in their decisions also have to take into account the need for smooth and effective proceedings, keeping in mind the interests of the international community, it should be asked whether a proper relationship between accused and counsel should not be one of the most basic rights to be accorded to defendants in international criminal trials. Especially when – at least in theory – they assume most responsibilities during trial due to their choice of self-representation, *pro se* defendants might have an even greater need for legal associates in the background whom they can trust in their work and advice. At the same time, however, it has to be kept in mind that the standard for a trustful relationship between counsel and client is arguably higher in cases in which the accused in fact chose to be represented by professional counsel rather than having counsel assigned against his or her will as sanction for previous obstructionist behaviour.

One could resolve the issue by distinguishing between legal advisors who remain in the background, paid for by the accused (subsidised by financial aid if required) and not appearing in court on the one hand, and potentially assigned or standby counsel desired by the bench to be present in court during proceedings and to be prepared to take over the defence of a self-represented accused when the chamber sees it fit on the other. While the first might well be a person with a special relationship with the accused, the latter could be a person who might be of second choice for the accused personally, but be more capable of not only effectively representing the defendant's interests before an international criminal tribunal due probably to his or her familiarity

1677 Daniel D. Ntanda Nsereko, Ethical Obligations of Counsel in Criminal Proceedings: Representing an Unwilling Client, 12 *Criminal Law Forum* 487 (2001), at 505.

1678 Jenia Iontcheva Turner, Legal Ethics in International Criminal Defense, 10 *Chicago Journal of International Law* 685 (2010), at 738-739.

with international criminal proceedings, but in addition be a first choice for being able to safeguard the interests of the international community in uniting a guarantee for a fair trial and being compatible with the requirements set for counsel appearing before the pertinent international criminal tribunal. This divergence can *e.g.* be illustrated by the situation in *Tolimir*, in which the ICTY registry did not consider the first choice of the accused of defence counsel to fulfil the requirements set by the ICTY registry for counsel funded by the ICTY.[1679]

A further factor to be taken into account is that an accused willing to obstruct the proceedings could otherwise use his refusal to communicate with assigned counsel to cause significant delays, thereby jeopardising the fair and expeditious conduct of the trial. This position also appears to be the underlying reasoning for decisions such as the one rendered by the trial chamber in *Milošević* as referred to above.[1680] However, as the submission in *Milošević* by assigned counsel made abundantly clear,[1681] defence counsel will have difficulties in presenting a defence which is indeed in the interests of an accused who refuses to even only communicate with counsel. In order to remedy such potential conflict, one could imagine a more active role to be played by trial chambers who take it on to actively engage in the proceedings also when it comes to examining the defence case and, *e.g.*, to make suggestions with regard to witnesses to be called or call witnesses on behalf of the court. Given that this option is usually already provided for in any event,[1682] this should not come as much of a new addition to the role of the bench.

1679 *Prosecutor v. Zdravko Tolimir*, Case No. IT-05-88/2-PT, Registry Submission Pursuant to Rule 33(B) of the Rules of Procedure and Evidence Regarding the Accused Tolimir's 13 July 2007 Submission on Appointment of Permanent Counsel, 18 July 2007, para.13.

1680 *Prosecutor v. Slobodan Milošević*, Case No. IT-02-54-T, Reasons for Decision on Assignment of Defence Counsel, 22 September 2004, para.70.

1681 *Prosecutor v. Slobodan Milošević*, Case No. IT-02-54-T, Assigned Counsel's Motion for Withdrawal With Annex A, 08 November 2004, para.34, 36, 38, 55.

1682 Rule 98 of both ICTY and ICTR RPE reads: "A Trial Chamber may order either party to produce additional evidence. It may *proprio motu* summon witnesses and order their attendance."; Rule 165 of the STL RPE provides: "After hearing the Parties, the Trial Chamber may, *proprio motu* or at the request of a Party, order either Party or a victim participating in the proceedings to produce additional evidence. It may, after hearing the Parties, *proprio motu* summon witnesses and order their attendance."

C. Preliminary observations

The preceding chapter has demonstrated that the framework for restrictions of the right to self-representation at first sight appears to be more consolidated than the exercise of the right to conduct the defence in person as such. It is generally acknowledged that specific steps need to be taken and factors considered in order to determine whether and to which extent the exercise of the right to self-representation may be restricted.

Yet, a closer look reveals that similar general concepts are used in rather different ways depending on the circumstances of each case at hand. In particular, the nature and scope of obstructive behaviour that might eventually trigger restrictions of the right to defend oneself in person has seen divergent interpretations in practice. In addition, the nature of any restriction, above all the role to be played by an appointed counsel, is not necessarily consistent despite a similarity in the terms which are used to designate such roles.

The ambiguity surrounding the scope of appointed counsel's mandate may lead self-represented accused to reject any cooperation with appointed counsel from the outset. This may give rise to further complications, in particular if the tasks to be assumed – and above all those not to be assumed – by appointed counsel remain unspecified. A more clearly defined structure regarding the role of appointed counsel, as well as consequences emanating from such appointment for both accused and imposed counsel can forestall further complications.

While such a structure would assist in a transitional period, it is argued that an established framework addressing first and foremost the active participation of an accused in international criminal proceedings would ensure that matters concerned with the potential restrictions of such participation may be resolved more easily.

As will be outlined in the last chapter of this dissertation, international criminal tribunals seised of requests for exercise of the right to self-representation in the future, especially the ICC, should consider the possibility of establishing a regime which provides for mandatory representation by counsel while at the same time giving defendants the opportunity to actively participate in the presentation of their defence case if they so wish. While such a model would safeguard an accused's right to conduct the defence in person, it would at the same time provide the opportunity to overcome issues with the practical exercise of the right to self-representation as outlined in this dissertation.

CHAPTER FOUR. Suggestions for future interpretations of the right to defend oneself in person

A. Conclusion: Lessons to be learned

This dissertation illustrates an attempt to provide an extensive, even though not exhaustive, account of the developments of the right to self-representation before international criminal tribunals from its initial recognition to the latest progresses dealing with procedural matters arising in the course of proceedings with *pro se* defendants. Primarily based on an analysis of the relevant jurisprudence which interprets and applies the underlying provisions, this dissertation outlines the potential and practical repercussions of the exercise of the right to self-representation, and demonstrates the difficulties trial and appeals chambers at different international criminal tribunals face when trying to accommodate the desire of accused to contribute their share to the conduct of the proceedings, and the necessity to safeguard fair trial rights and the integrity of the international criminal justice system at the same time.

Having seen the manner in which the right to self-representation has been interpreted, applied and exercised before international criminal tribunals, it is argued that the right to defend oneself in person should be given a new meaning which does not necessarily draw exclusively from national or regional interpretations of the right, but rather is adjusted to the specific requirements of international criminal proceedings.

The review of the pertinent jurisprudence which formed the main part of this dissertation has shown that the initial recognition of the right to self-representation apparently failed to take into account the practical implications any exercise of this right would have on the conduct of international criminal proceedings. In the course of several years, different trial and appeals chambers at a number of international criminal tribunals saw themselves confronted with the repercussions which the desire of accused to present their defence in person has on the proceedings. This required the judges to address matters initially on an *ad hoc* basis in order to safeguard the accused's right to fair and expeditious proceedings, as well as to protect the interests of other participants and the international community more generally. While this approach provided the flexibility which is necessary to adequately balance the interests at stake in light of the particular circumstances of each case, it equally led to inconsistencies in the jurisprudence. At the same time, it appears trial and appeals chambers may have failed to reconsider decisions adopted earlier, even though it had become apparent in the meantime that the positions initially adopted might not be apposite to deal with the questions at hand.

It can be concluded that after years of generating jurisprudence on the interpretation and application of the right to self-representation, the established body of case law can be used as point of reference in order to deal with a variety of situations that potentially arise in the proceedings with *pro se* defendants. While the jurisprudence adopts specific lines of argument which are generally followed by the majority of chambers, the case law still leaves sufficient room to provide for flexible solutions which are tailored to the specific circumstances of the matter at hand. Such flexibility allows for the possibility to adjust and improve decisions and solutions which may not adequately deal with the latest developments at international criminal institutions like the ICC. This presupposes an adequate familiarity of ICC judges with the existing body of law and practice created by the *ad hoc* tribunals in order to be able to address flaws and use the material in the best possible way.

It is argued that in order to provide for a fresh start in the context of the exercise of the right to defend oneself in person, the body of jurisprudence which deals with this right has to be carefully assessed and, as necessary, reviewed and reconsidered in order to provide for international criminal proceedings which safeguard the accused's interest to actively participate in the proceedings without endangering the fundamental right to a fair and expeditious trial. This is required in light of the situations which have arisen thus far in proceedings with *pro se* defendants, clearly indicating that a right to self-representation as interpreted before the *ad hoc* tribunals cannot feasibly be exercised in the context of international criminal proceedings.

At the same time, it will be necessary for judges in future international criminal proceedings that see themselves confronted with self-represented accused to reconsider the approach of the heavy reliance on national or regional interpretations of the right to defend oneself in person. As argued in this dissertation, the international criminal legal system will have to accept its existence as cosmos of its own accord, which may draw from experience in national and regional jurisdictions, without however losing sight of its genuine international and independent character. Acknowledging the significance and influence of general principles as derived from comparative law exercises, it has been argued that "now is the time for international criminal law to unchain itself from these constraints".[1683]

B. Potential room for active participation by accused in the proceedings

Turning to the more concrete subject matter as to how chambers should deal with requests of accused to exercise the right to defend oneself in person in the future, it may be asked in which way the ICC should deal with the existing jurisprudence on the issue and which lessons will have to be drawn in order to avoid recurrence of negative implications of the right to defend oneself in person.

The ICC, as a fairly new institution independent of the *ad hoc* tribunals, will be in a position to take the opportunity to revise the legacy of the ICTY and ICTR which, as illustrated in the course of this dissertation, may be seen as dealing with the issue of the right to self-representation and its practical implications for international criminal proceedings only in a rather unsatisfactory manner.

Considering the procedural framework of international criminal tribunals, it has to be taken into account that the procedural structures of the *ad hoc* tribunals, at least initially, were based on primarily adversarial models of law,[1684] or at least incorporated notions of both civil and common law systems.[1685] Bearing in mind years of jurisprudence and practice which de-

---

1683 Gideon Boas, *The Milošević Trial: Lessons for the Conduct of Complex International Criminal Proceedings* (Cambridge: Cambridge University Press) 2007, p.287.

1684 *E.g. Prosecutor v. Slobodan Milošević*, Oral Ruling, 18 December 2002, T.14574; Reasons for Decision on the Prosecution Motion Concerning Assignment of Counsel, 04 April 2003, para.8, 20. *See also* Michael Bohlander, 'A Fool for a Client' – Remarks on the Freedom of Choice and Assignment of Counsel at the International Criminal Tribunal for the Former Yugoslavia, 16 *Criminal Law Forum* 159 (2005), at 159; Mirjan Damaška, Assignment of Counsel and Perceptions of Fairness, 3 *Journal of International Criminal Justice* 3 (2005), at 5.

1685 *See e.g.* Rachel K. Jones, Untangling the Right to Self-Representation in the International Criminal Tribunal for the Former Yugoslavia, 43 *Georgia Law Review* 1285 (2009), at 1318, considering the ICTY to be a "true hybrid tribunal"; Michael P. Scharf/Christopher M. Rassi, Do Former Leaders have an International Right to Self-Representation in War Crimes Trials?, 20 *Ohio State Journal on Dispute Resolution* 3 (2005), at 15, 21, qualifying *inter alia* the ICTY as "sui generis, representing a blending of the common law and civil law approaches".

veloped the international criminal legal system up to the adoption of the ICC Rome Statute, it can be argued that the way forward for international criminal proceedings takes into account notions of both systems alike without however leaning primarily to one side or the other. A concrete example for this approach can be found in Article 54(1)(a) of the Rome Statute,[1686] which imposes the duty upon the prosecutor to investigate both incriminating and exonerating circumstances.[1687] Taking it one step further, it has been argued that the ICC model is one of a kind which takes the procedural structure of international criminal law on a new level away from merely drawing from the experience of national systems,[1688] and that "taken as a whole", the ICC's procedural system is "truly unique".[1689]

In such a setting which can be seen as at least hybrid in nature, it should be difficult to object to the ICC and other international criminal tribunals adopting a new approach to the interpretation and exercise of the right to defend oneself in person, including any potential restrictions of this right, which is tailored to the particular circumstances of international criminal proceedings.[1690]

Considering the overall implications of granting the right to self-representation in international criminal proceedings and in light of the problems analysed above arising from the exercise of this right, it will be necessary for future international criminal proceedings to resort to more innovative

---

1686 Article 54(1)(a) Rome Statute: "The Prosecutor shall: (a) In order to establish the truth, extend the investigation to cover all facts and evidence relevant to an assessment of whether there is criminal responsibility under this Statute, and, in doing so, investigate incriminating and exonerating circumstances equally; [...]".

1687 *Cf.* Althea Alexis, The Convergence of the Common Law and Inquisitorial Systems in International Criminal Law, in: Emmanuel Decaux *et al.* (eds), *From Human Rights to International Criminal Law: Studies in Honour of an African Jurist, the Late Judge Lairy Kama* (Leiden/Boston: Martinus Nijhoff Publishers) 2007, p.461-481, at 478-479; Fatou Bensouda, The ICC Statute – An Insider's Perspective on a Sui Generis System for Global Justice, 36 *North Carolina Journal of International Law and Commercial Regulation* 277 (2011), at 280.

1688 *See* Eugene Cerruti, Self-Representation in the International Arena: Removing a False Right to Spectacle, 40 *Georgetown Journal of International Law* 919 (2009), at 968-969.

1689 Claus Kreß, The Procedural Law of the International Criminal Court in Outline: Anatomy of a Unique Compromise, 1 *Journal of International Criminal Justice* 603 (2003), at 605.

1690 *Cf.* with regard to the ICTY: Mirjan Damaška, Assignment of Counsel and Perceptions of Fairness, 3 *Journal of International Criminal Justice* 3 (2005), at 6.

measures which allow accused to actively participate in their own case, while at the same time safeguarding the overarching fair trial right of defendants, as well as other interests involved. The possibility of permitting such measures has been alluded to early on in the jurisprudence on the matter,[1691] as well as practised in some cases,[1692] and one could imagine that especially

1691 *Prosecutor v. Slobodan Milošević*, Case No. IT-02-54-T, Order on the Modalities to be Followed by Court Assigned Counsel, 03 September 2004, p.3; Reasons for Decision on Assignment of Defence Counsel, 22 September 2004, para.36, 69. *See also Prosecutor v. Slobodan Milošević*, Case No. IT-02-54-T, Submission from the Office of the Prosecutor on the Future Conduct of the Case in the Light of the State of the Accused's Health and the Length and Complexity of the Case, 08 November 2002, para.21; Prosecution Submissions in Response to the Trial Chamber's 19 July 2004 "Further Order on Future Conduct of the Trial", 26 July 2004, para.41, 46; Attachment "B" to Prosecution Submissions in Response to the Trial Chamber's 19 July 2004 "Further Order on Future Conduct of the Trial", 26 July 2004, para.10, 12; *Prosecutor v. Vojislav Šešelj*, Case No. IT-03-67-PT, Prosecution's Motion for Order Appointing Counsel to Assist Vojislav Šešelj With His Defence, 28 February 2003, para.14; Status Conference, 14 September 2006, T.605-606; *Prosecutor v. Radovan Karadžić*, Case No. IT-95-5/18-PT, Status Conference, 17 September 2008, T.42, 44: "[…] There is precedent in this Tribunal for an accused person to participate actively in the presentation of his own defence, even where he has counsel also actively conducting the case in conjunction with him. […] So there is no absolute choice, simple, absolute choice, between being there on your own, trying to do everything in court on your own, and being represented in court by someone else and having to remain silent; there are other options."; Decision on the Accused's Request that All Materials, Including Transcripts, be Disclosed to him in Serbian and Cyrillic Script, 25 September 2008, para.14; Decision on Accused Motion for Adequate Facilities and Equality of Arms: Legal Associates, 28 January 2009, para.36; *Prosecutor v. Zdravko Tolimir*, Case No. IT-05-88/2-T, Decision on Accused's Request to the Trial Chamber Concerning Assistance of his Legal Advisor, 28 April 2010 (Public redacted version issued on 27 May 2010. *See* Order Issuing a Public Redacted Version of the "Decision on Accused's Request to the Trial Chamber Concerning Assistance of his Legal Advisor", 27 May 2010), para.32.

1692 *Cf. Prosecutor v. Momčilo Krajišnik*, Case No. IT-00-39-T, Reasons for Oral Decision Denying Mr Krajišnik's Request to Proceed Unrepresented by Counsel, 18 August 2005, para.34; *Prosecutor v. Momčilo Krajišnik*, Case No. IT-00-39-A, Judgement, 17 March 2009, para.119. *See also Prosecutor v. Prlić et al.*, Case No. IT-04-74-T, Revised Version of the Decision Adopting Guidelines on Conduct of Trial Proceedings, 28 April 2006, p.6, II.c), allowing for accused to put additional questions to witnesses after cross-examination by their counsel in exceptional circumstances and upon authorisation of the chamber. *Procureur c/ Prlić et consorts*, Affaire n° IT-04-74-T, Décision Portant sur les Modalités de l'Interrogatoire des Témoins, 10 mai 2007, para.8-12; and in particular Opinion Individuelle du

chambers at the ICC may be willing to draw from previous experiences and adopt more creative solutions. Such a deviation could be justified on the basis of considering that the right forming part of the fair trial guarantee in fact recognised on an international level, as alluded to in the first chapter of this dissertation, is to be seen as a right to a personal defence in a more encompassing sense, rather than as a right to self-representation as interpreted and applied in international criminal proceedings up to this point. This would provide future international criminal proceedings, in particular before the ICC, with the necessary flexibility to address the question of how to ensure that the accused remain the subject of their own proceedings. Of particular interest in this context is Regulation 74(2) of the ICC Regulations of the Court,[1693] which implies that an accused, if so authorised by the chamber, may be permitted to participate in the proceedings *alongside* his or her counsel – in circumstances other than under Article 67(1)(h) of the Rome Statute.[1694] This provision presents judges with a concrete basis to authorise the active participation of defendants in their case if considered appropriate, without the accused having to conduct his or her entire defence case in person. It will have to be addressed, however, how this provision might be applicable to accused not found to be entitled to legal aid, given that it refers explicitly only to those with such an entitlement.

Unless this flexible approach is taken, it might be difficult to argue any significant deviation from the existing jurisprudence considering the extent to which the ICTY in particular formed the development of international criminal law in general and of a right to self-representation more specifically, as there are no other bodies of international criminal jurisprudence the ICC could justifiably rely on in trying to find solutions. Yet, the ICC is an inde-

---

Juge Jean-Claude Antonetti, Président de la Chambre de Première Instance, Concernant la Décision Certifiant l'Appel de la Décision Portant sur les Modalités de l'Interrogatoire des Témoins, 28 juin 2007. The trial chamber's decision was confirmed on appeal: *Prosecutor v. Prlić et al.*, Case No. IT-04-74-AR73.5, Decision on Praljak's Appeal of the Trial Chamber's 10 May 2007 Decision on the Mode of Interrogating Witnesses, 24 August 2007 (filed: 26 August 2007).

1693 Regulation 74(2) reads: "Whenever represented by defence counsel, the person entitled to legal assistance shall, subject to article 67, paragraph 1 (h), act before the Court through his or her counsel, *unless otherwise authorised by the Chamber*." (emphasis added).

1694 Article 67(1)(h) provides: "1. In the determination of any charge, the accused shall be entitled […] to the following minimum guarantees, in full equality: […] (h) To make an unsworn oral or written statement in his or her defence […]".

pendent judicial body which can arguably go back to the relevant national and international jurisprudence and doctrine and come to different conclusions taking into account the underlying consideration of the accused's role in the proceedings, which in the concerned chamber's view would suit the specificities of the Court better. As regards the issue of the right to self-representation in particular, one could for example imagine that the ICC takes into account the critics of the U.S. Supreme Court decision in *Faretta*, together with the potential for abuses of the right to self-representation that surfaced in the context of international criminal proceedings, and concludes that such a right to self-representation would need to be handled far more restrictively in proceedings before it.

This would balance the factors of international instruments widely recognising the possibility to present one's own defence in person on the one hand, with the different interpretations of the defendant's role in their own trials in diverse national jurisdictions on the other.

One should also take into account the differences inherent in the proceedings before the ICC. To be mentioned in this context is the important emphasis on victim participation. Therefore, victims' rights are added to the rights that need to be balanced in cases with self-represented accused. Especially if accused originate from systems where self-representation is not practised at the level of serious crimes, and if the proceedings involve a significant amount of represented victims, a bench could argue restriction of self-representation to pay heed to victims' rights.

On the other hand, the international jurisprudence thus far has left no doubt that the right to self-representation is to be considered as "cornerstone" right comparable to other fair trial rights. The relevant provision in the Rome Statute mirrors the language of other statutes and international human rights provisions, thus making it more difficult to argue in favour of a new regime governing the exercise of the right to self-representation. In light of the considerations above, it seems unlikely that the ICC will make a complete turnaround in a first case with a self-represented accused. Rather, it might argue for a more restrictive interpretation of the right, taking into account the legacy of other international criminal tribunals as a whole. This argument might be justified more easily by taking the position of the fair trial right to be guaranteed as a right to a personal defence, rather than to full-fledged self-representation as practised – at least at first sight – especially before the *ad hoc* tribunals.

A deviation from established practices in international criminal procedure will necessitate suggestions for a potential approach to be adopted in future international criminal trials. At the outset, if an accused harbours the idea of presenting his or her defence in person before an international criminal tribunal, a detailed explanation should be provided as to the possible models that might be envisaged for such a personal defence. Bearing in mind the precedent in particular of trials at the ICTY, this might also encompass a justification as to a changed position adopted with regard to a right to complete self-representation. The defendant should be made aware that even though he or she might not act as their own defence counsel, this will not necessarily preclude a personal and active participation in the proceedings.

Even more importantly, a change in approach will not come in a vacuum, but will have some support in previous cases during which judges were faced with the necessity to balance an accused's wish to participate in the proceedings with other exigencies of trial rights and management. Examples from more recent developments indicate that the need to deviate from the initial stringent recognition of a right to self-representation has been recognised.

For example, the developments in the *Karadžić* proceedings may eventually provide useful examples of implementation in practice when the necessity arises to justify a change in approach: while recognising the defendant's asserted right to self-representation, the trial chamber in this case was fast in having his legal associates recognised;[1695] granted these advisors limited rights of audience in the trial proceedings; and swiftly appointed standby counsel in a clear signal to the accused that he should not take his *pro se* status for granted.[1696] This indicates a more stringent control of the proceedings by the trial chamber, as demanded for example in the wake of the *Milošević* trial.[1697] It also demonstrates that the trial chamber may have been willing to recognise that an accused could be authorised to actively participate in the proceedings,[1698] while at the same time being wary of the implicit

---

1695 *See Prosecutor v. Radovan Karadžić*, Case No. IT-95-5/18-PT, Motion for Adequate Facilities and Equality of Arms: Legal Associates, 24 November 2008 (filed: 25 November 2008), Annex B; Decision on Accused Request for Judicial Review of the Registry Decision on the Assignment of Mr. Marko Sladojević as Legal Associate, 20 April 2009.

1696 *See* Philipp Ambach, Selbstvertretung im internationalen Strafprozess – Grundlagen, Kritik und ein Lösungsansatz für die prozessuale Handhabung in der Zukunft, 6 *Zeitschrift für Internationale Strafrechtsdogmatik* 286 (2009), at 301 fn.147.

1697 *Cf.* Gideon Boas, Moving on From Milošević, 75 *European Lawyer* 54 (2008), at 55.

1698 *See* in particular remark of the presiding judge at the start of the defence case: *Prosecutor v. Radovan Karadžić*, Case No. IT-95-5/18-T, Pre-Defence Conference,

risks for the defendant in the presentation of his case or other participants interested in a fair, and equally expeditious, trial.

The STL RPE expressly provide for the possibility of accused to make relevant statements to the trial chamber at any time during the proceedings.[1699] However, even more significant for purposes of this argument is the meaning which has been given to the right to defend oneself in person before the STL, as outlined by the STL President:

> "In light of recent unfortunate experiences at the ICTY, [...] the drafters of the RPE thought it necessary to construe the right of the accused in Article 16 'to defend himself or herself in person' as the right of the accused to ask questions, call witnesses or examine or cross-examine witnesses either himself or – whenever required by the interests of justice – with the assistance of defence counsel (of the accused's own choosing or assigned by the Tribunal). *Such assistance does not necessarily preclude an otherwise active role by the accused throughout the proceedings*. Indeed, the complexity of international criminal proceedings is such that it is almost inconceivable that an accused, in order to fully ensure his defence, will not need the assistance of experienced defence counsel."[1700]

This is an approach of potentially significant impact on the interpretation of the right to defend oneself in person in future proceedings before international criminal proceedings. It specifically acknowledges the import of the existing jurisprudence and clarifies that this body of case law is at the heart of an obviously felt need for modification. While this interpretation does not go as far as demanding representation by counsel in all cases, it at least leaves the door open to new models of active participation of accused in their own proceedings. Even though this interpretation has not been – and is unlikely to be – tested in practice, it provides some indication of possible future interpretations of the right to defend oneself in person.

Even more instructive – and in this case tested in practice – is the approach taken in the *Prlić* proceedings before the ICTY which could serve as a model for future cases. Of particular interest is the practice that was adopted

---

15 October 2012, T.28827: "[...] As a self-represented accused, Mr. Karadzic, you've been an active participant in this trial for over two years now [...]".

1699 Rule 144 of the STL RPE reads: "(A) The accused may make statements to the Trial Chamber at any stage of the proceedings, provided such statements are relevant to the case at issue."; Rule 147 STL RPE provides: "(C) The accused may make a final statement on matters relevant to the trial."

1700 Rules of Procedure and Evidence (as of 25 November 2010). Explanatory Memorandum by the Tribunal's President, para.32 (emphasis added).

at the beginning of the evidentiary phase, when the trial chamber allowed the accused to put additional questions to witnesses upon authorisation by the bench.[1701] Some of the defendants made extensive use of this possibility and in general put supplementary questions in the course of cross-examination of prosecution witnesses, and even broached procedural and other objections similar to what would be raised by defence counsel.[1702]

At a later point in *Prlić*, however, this scheme was modified in order to avoid waste of time by legally untrained accused asking irrelevant questions.[1703] Interestingly enough, even though the appeals chamber upheld the trial chamber's restriction, it did not question or even discuss the submission that there is a "right of the Appellant to participate directly in the proceedings alongside his counsel".[1704] While this should largely be due to the fact that

---

1701 *Prosecutor v. Prlić et al.*, Case No. IT-04-74-T, Revised Version of the Decision Adopting Guidelines on Conduct of Trial Proceedings, 28 April 2006, p.6, II.c).

1702 *See e.g. Prosecutor v. Prlić et al.*, Case No. IT-04-74-T, Hearing, 05 May 2006, T.1431-1436; Hearing, 09 May 2006, T.1621-1642; Hearing, 25 May 2006, T.2610-2612, 2662-2668; Hearing, 31 May 2006, T.2979-2987, 2988-2995; Hearing, 03 July 2006, T.4233-4234, 4253-4254, 4258-4260, 4311; Hearing, 04 July 2006, T.4338, 4354, 4359, 4376, 4383-4384, 4442-4464; Hearing, 05 July 2006, T.4470-4506, 4534-4535, 4629; Hearing, 06 November 2006, T.9542-9546, 9608, 9624; Hearing, 14 December 2006, T.11759-11796; Hearing, 24 January 2007, T.12821-12848, 12854-12862, 12869-12872, 12886; Hearing, 15 February 2007, T.14162-14163, 14166, 14201-14202, 14231-14232, 14238-14265; Hearing, 19 February 2007, T.14267-14297, 14304, 14365; Hearing, 19 March 2007, T.15868-15870, 15915-15933; Hearing, 21 March 2007, T.16067-16068, 16091-16092, 16128-16130; Hearing, 27 March 2007, T.16385-16396, 16417-16418, 16426-16428; Hearing, 28 March 2007, T.16520-16522, 16532-16545; Hearing, 29 March 2007, T.16549-16559, 16581-16583, 16627-16638; Hearing, 02 April 2007, T.16647, 16700-16701; Hearing, 16 April 2007, T.17097-17128; Hearing, 02 May 2007, T.17891-17892, 17892-17930. The accused Praljak gave an opening statement: *see* Accused Praljak Opening Statement, 27 April 2006, T.911-991; 04 May 2009, T.39450-39482, and testified as witness in his own case for an extensive period: *see* Hearings from 04 May 2009 to 10 September 2009, T.39483-44698. The accused Petković also testified as witness in his own case: *see* Hearings from 11 February 2010 to 11 March 2010, T.49280-50867. The accused Prlić provided an unsworn statement pursuant to Rule 84*bis* of the ICTY RPE: *see* Hearing, 05 May 2008, T.27457-27546; 06 May 2008, T.27547-27577.

1703 *Procureur c/ Prlić et consorts*, Affaire n° IT-04-74-T, Décision Portant sur les Modalités de l'Interrogatoire des Témoins, 10 mai 2007, para.10-11.

1704 *Prosecutor v. Prlić et al.*, Case No. IT-04-74-AR73.5, Decision on Praljak's Appeal of the Trial Chamber's 10 May 2007 Decision on the Mode of Interrogating Witnesses, 24 August 2007 (filed: 26 August 2007), para.11.

the appeals chamber deferred to a discretionary decision by the trial chamber on the conduct of trial, it is nevertheless interesting that the appeals chamber did not seem to find it necessary to refute or even discuss the submission that such a *right* indeed exists. This does not seem to entirely match with the view adopted in earlier cases with self-represented accused that the right to self-representation and the right to counsel of choice are mutually exclusive.

Subsequently, in the course of discussions of the guidelines for the presentation of the defence case,[1705] the presiding judge dissented from a majority decision by expressing the view that the previous guidelines should be revised so as to provide for the participation of the accused, considering *inter alia* that a defendant would have the right to put questions to witnesses at any stage of the proceedings.[1706] An appeal against the majority decision of the trial chamber which restricted the possibility to cross-examine for the accused to events in which he took part or with regard to matters about which he had a specific knowledge at the time of the events charged in the indictment[1707] was granted in part by the appeals chamber. In the appeals chamber's view, it had been acknowledged previously that an accused could be permitted, under exceptional circumstances, to participate in the examination of

1705 *Procureur c/ Prlić et consorts*, Affaire n° IT-04-74-T, Décision Portant Adoption des Lignes Directrices Pour la Présentation des Éléments de Preuve à Décharge, 24 avril 2008, para.3.

1706 *Procureur c/ Prlić et consorts*, Affaire n° IT-04-74-T, Opinion Dissidente du Président, Jean-Claude Antonetti sur la Décision Portant sur une Demande de Réexamen Présentée par la Défense Praljak, 26 juin 2008, p.2 : « [...] il en a le droit en vertu de l'Article 21 du Statut qui dispose qu'il a le droit 'à interroger' ou 'faire interroger'. Si les mots ont un sens, il convient de conclure qu'il peut en **personne** poser ses questions ou bien s'il a un avocat, le faire interroger par celui-ci [...] En quatrième lieu, l'accusé Praljak a indiqué qu'il témoignerait lui-même sur les faits reprochés. Cette prise de position implique une participation personnelle au procès, l'accusé ne se contenant pas de garder le silence. » (emphasis in the original).

1707 *Procureur c/ Prlić et consorts*, Affaire n° IT-04-74-T, Décision Portant sur une Demande de Réexamen Présentée par la Défense Praljak, 26 juin 2008, p.5 : « Attendu que la Chambre estime que lesdites 'compétences spécifiques' font référence aux compétences exercées par un Accusé au moment des faits allégués et par l'exercice desquelles il est mis en cause par l'Acte de l'accusation modifié du 11 juin 2008 [...] ».

witnesses, even though he was represented by counsel.[1708] According to the appeals chamber, the clarification given by the trial chamber of the term "specific expertise" ("*compétences spécifiques*") was too inflexible to be able to adequately address future requests for participation by the accused and thus could potentially lead to a violation of the defendant's right under Article 21 of the ICTY Statute.[1709] Going even further, the appeals chamber considered that the guidelines issued by the trial chamber were not restricted to events in which the accused took part or relating to matters of which he had specific expertise, but that they left room for interventions by the defendant in other situations.[1710] When another accused in the case requested leave to examine witnesses in the course of the defence case, the trial chamber referred back to its initial guidelines and subsequent decisions thereon, which already accorded the possibility to do so to each accused in the proceedings on an exceptional basis.[1711] The trial chamber further clarified that at the same time, in light of the accused being represented by counsel, solely defence counsel were authorised to intervene in the proceedings, cross-examine witnesses in a primary role or raise objections during hearings.[1712] However, the bench did provide the accused with the opportunity to participate in the closing arguments of their respective defence for a limited amount of time.[1713]

Compared to the previous decisions and practice adopted by the *Prlić* trial chamber, and especially bearing in mind the extent of the latest appeals chamber decision on this issue, the later position of the trial chamber appears

1708 *Prosecutor v. Prlić et al.*, Case No. IT-04-74-AR73.11, Decision on Slobodan Praljak's Appeal of the Trial Chamber's Decision on the Direct Examination of Witnesses dated 26 June 2008, 11 September 2008, para.19.

1709 *Prosecutor v. Prlić et al.*, Case No. IT-04-74-AR73.11, Decision on Slobodan Praljak's Appeal of the Trial Chamber's Decision on the Direct Examination of Witnesses dated 26 June 2008, 11 September 2008, para.21.

1710 *Prosecutor v. Prlić et al.*, Case No. IT-04-74-AR73.11, Decision on Slobodan Praljak's Appeal of the Trial Chamber's Decision on the Direct Examination of Witnesses dated 26 June 2008, 11 September 2008, para.22.

1711 *Procureur c/ Prlić et consorts*, Affaire n° IT-04-74-T, Ordonnance Portant Sur les Modalités de l'Intervention de l'Accusé Prlić en Audience, 15 juillet 2009, p.4-6.

1712 *Procureur c/ Prlić et consorts*, Affaire n° IT-04-74-T, Ordonnance Portant Sur les Modalités de l'Intervention de l'Accusé Prlić en Audience, 15 juillet 2009, p.4, 6.

1713 *Procureur c/ Prlić et consorts*, Affaire n° IT-04-74-T, Ordonnance Portant Calendrier (Mémoires en Clôture, Réquisitoire et Plaidoiries Finales), 01 novembre 2010, p.8 para.6.

to signify a certain retraction of the previously adopted more liberal approach towards the active participation of the accused. Nonetheless, the opportunity for the defendants to participate to a certain limited extent, *e.g.* in the presentation of the closing arguments, still illustrates a compromise model which strikes a balance between the wishes of accused to contribute to the proceedings and the necessity to ensure a smooth development of the case.

A review of the transcripts in the *Prlić* proceedings indicates that the accused did indeed take the opportunity to actively participate in their case apart from testifying as witnesses or giving an unsworn statement. The review equally shows that a model of active participation such as the one adopted by the *Prlić* trial chamber necessitates a firm management of the proceedings by the trial chamber in order to keep the case on track. Yet, the judges seemed to be divided on the question of the extent to which accused should in fact be allowed to participate.[1714]

Notwithstanding the trial chamber's intention to restrict the scope of participation by the accused, the cross-examination by defendants continued largely in the same manner as before, with at least one of the accused taking on most of the cross-examination time allocated to his defence team.[1715]

1714 *Procureur c/ Prlić et consorts*, Affaire n° IT-04-74-T, Opinion Individuelle du Juge Jean-Claude Antonetti, Président de la Chambre de Première Instance, Concernant la Décision Certifiant l'Appel de la Décision Portant sur les Modalités de l'Interrogatoire des Témoins, 28 juin 2007; *Prosecutor v. Prlić et al.*, Case No. IT-04-74-T, Hearing, 24 September 2008, T.32699; Hearing 13 January 2009, T.35265, 35268-35269; Hearing, 01 March 2010, T.50197-50198.

1715 *See e.g. Prosecutor v. Prlić et al.*, Case No. IT-04-74-T, Hearing, 14 May 2007, T.18304-18306; Hearing, 24 May 2007, T.19066-19069, 19070-19141, 19162; Hearing, 30 May 2007, T.19325-19356; Hearing, 21 June 2007, T.20274-20346; Hearing, 28 August 2007, T.21748-21753, 21753-21768; Hearing, 30 August 2007, T.21787-21788, 21831-21840, 21841-21888; Hearing, 25 September 2007, T.22739-22745, 21745-21772; Hearing, 04 October 2007, T.23197-23221; Hearing, 27 November 2007, T.25177-25181, 25181-25196; Hearing, 28 January 2008, T.26872-26873; Hearing, 08 May 2008, T.27806-27818; Hearing, 14 May 2008, T.27979-27985; Hearing, 27 May 2008, T.28645-28651, 28652-28653, 28682-28687; Hearing, 09 June 2008, T.29244-29250; Hearing, 24 September 2008, T.32681-32682, 32698-32699, 32743-32744; Hearing, 30 October 2008, T.34055-34078; Hearing, 13 January 2009, T.35263-35270, 35321-35323; Hearing, 14 January 2009, T.35326-35327; Hearing, 09 February 2009, T.36551-36553; Hearing, 10 February 2009, T.36717-36720; Hearing, 18 February 2009, T.37098, 37170; Hearing, 19 February 2009, T.37188, 37190-37193, 37215-37218; Hearing, 09 March 2009, T.37861-37862; Hearing, 24 March 2009, T.38493-38494, 38524, 38531, 38534-38535, 38555-38557; Hearing, 25 March 2009, T.38568-38569,

Despite the unambiguous guidelines issued by the trial chamber, in some instances accused intervened in the proceedings without prior authorisation from the trial chamber, or with regard to matters which fell outside the scope of participation as determined in the guidelines. One accused intervened repeatedly and prompted the trial chamber to remind him of the guidelines; he eventually declared himself dissatisfied with the conduct of the proceedings and expressed his intention to discontinue his participation and absent himself from the hearings.[1716] The accused consequently did not attend the hearings until the completion of the defence case.

It has been pointed out before that giving an accused the possibility to speak more freely in international criminal proceedings could contribute to the ascertainment of the truth[1717] and would satisfy a defendant's desire to not entirely disappear behind professional counsel in proceedings which at the international level often have political connotations.[1718] Furthermore, the right to defend oneself in person has previously been interpreted as a right to actively participate in the proceedings,[1719] which could easily serve as basis for more innovative methods for direct participation of accused while however paying heed to the interests of justice. This would, on the one hand, provide defendants with an important opportunity to tell their side of the story and prevent them from becoming a mere object of the proceedings.[1720] On the other hand, it would permit such participation only to an

38577, 38636; Hearing, 03 December 2009, T.47747-47750; Hearing, 08 December 2009, T.47859-47860, 47860-47862; Hearing, 27 January 2010, T.49005-49018; Hearing, 01 March 2010, T.50116-50194.

1716 *Prosecutor v. Prlić et al.*, Case No. IT-04-74-T, Hearing, 01 March 2010, T.50194-50205.

1717 Claude Jorda/Jérôme de Hemptienne, Un Nouveau Statut pour l'Accusé dans la Procédure du Tribunal Pénal International pour l'ex-Yougoslavie, in: Richard May et al. (eds), *Essays on ICTY Procedure and Evidence. In Honour of Gabrielle Kirk McDonald* (The Hague: Kluwer Law International) 2001, p.215-229, at 224.

1718 Claude Jorda/Jérôme de Hemptienne, Un Nouveau Statut pour l'Accusé dans la Procédure du Tribunal Pénal International pour l'ex-Yougoslavie, in: Richard May et al. (eds), *Essays on ICTY Procedure and Evidence. In Honour of Gabrielle Kirk McDonald* (The Hague: Kluwer Law International) 2001, p.215-229, at 226.

1719 Wolfgang Schomburg, The Role of International Criminal Tribunals in Promoting Respect for Fair Trial Rights, 8 *Northwestern University Journal of International Human Rights* 1 (2009), at 61.

1720 *See Prosecutor v. Momčilo Krajišnik*, Case No. IT-00-39-A, Decision on Momčilo Krajišnik's Request to Self-Represent, on Counsel's Motion in Relation to Appointment of *Amicus Curiae*, and on the Prosecution Motion of 16 February 2007,

extent which still allows for trials to be conducted fairly and expeditiously, without hindrance by procedural complexities tackled by non-professionals.[1721] Going even further, it has been submitted that in light of the fact that the ICC imposes even stricter criteria on defence counsel to be admitted to appear before the Court, it would be strange to allow on the other side potentially unqualified accused to present their own defence.[1722] Such arguments may provide a valid basis for international criminal tribunals such as the ICC to adopt a position in future trials which protects the justified interest of defendants to participate in their trials alongside safeguarding further fair trial rights of accused and rights of other participants as well as more pragmatic issues of trial management.

There are a number of reasons why any modified forms of participation for accused, as suggested in this dissertation, might not be easily implemented. To begin with, jurisprudence in particular at the ICTY has placed great significance on the right to self-representation in its more extreme form, which may render it more difficult to achieve the acceptance and justification of a significant shift in the approach in practice. In addition, the attitude of accused who thus far insisted on conducting their defence in person and their approach to run the proceedings do not necessarily suggest that other defendants may in the future be willing to forego any perceived advantages which may have been granted to accused in proceedings before their time under the umbrella of a fair trial right which had been considered as fundamental.

However, the model which this dissertation suggests to adopt, *i.e.* providing accused with the possibility of active participation in their proceedings with mandatory representation by professional defence counsel, could adequately address these concerns. While on the one hand taking due account of the significance of the right to defend oneself in person and the potential desire of accused to contribute to the conduct of their proceedings, this approach at the same time ensures the adequate preparation and presentation of a defence case bearing in mind the right to a fair and expeditious trial of

---

Fundamentally Dissenting Opinion of Judge Schomburg on the Right to Self-Representation, 11 May 2007, para.3, 26.

1721 *See* Philipp Ambach, Selbstvertretung im internationalen Strafprozess – Grundlagen, Kritik und ein Lösungsansatz für die prozessuale Handhabung in der Zukunft, 6 *Zeitschrift für Internationale Strafrechtsdogmatik* 286 (2009), at 303.

1722 Michael P. Scharf/Christopher M. Rassi, Do Former Leaders have an International Right to Self-Representation in War Crimes Trials?, 20 *Ohio State Journal on Dispute Resolution* 3 (2005), at 27.

the accused, as well as taking into account the interests of other participants to the proceedings and the international community in general.

A concrete suggestion for proceedings in which accused voice the desire to actively participate in their defence could include the requirement for any defendant to be represented by professional defence counsel with several years of relevant experience in international criminal proceedings. The selection of defence counsel would then be the same as within established procedures in case an accused elects to be represented by counsel of his or her own choice. At the same time, it will be for the bench to decide on a case-by-case basis when to allow an accused to directly address issues in the courtroom, make statements to the judges or (cross-) examine witnesses. Concrete guidelines will then have to be established from the beginning of the proceedings in order to establish conditions under which a defendant may speak and situations in which any participation may be restricted. These guidelines should in general address the specific division of tasks between counsel and accused in order to avoid confusion and unnecessary and time-consuming discussions during trial. More specifically, such guidelines could include for example concrete indications as to when and with regard to which witnesses an accused may be permitted to conduct (cross-) examinations – whether supplementing counsel's examination or entirely without counsel. Similarly, it would be necessary to address the issue of whether for example procedural questions would fall exclusively within the provenance of professional defence counsel. Concrete sanctions should be foreseen for situations in which a defendant abuses the active participation opportunities accorded to him or her on a discretionary basis. Such sanctions could relate to not permitting the accused to (cross-) examine a specific witness, refrain from addressing the bench in the course of the proceedings, up to reverting to the old established model of having counsel representing the accused's interests in full, with the defendant being reduced to a more observing role.

Depending on the behaviour and specific knowledge of an accused, such participation would not only ensure the defendant feeling as actual subject of the proceedings, but could also contribute to the ascertainment of facts and determination of issues in order to give the judges the possibility to come to a verdict having in mind a picture of events as complete and multi-faceted as possible. In addition, this approach would adequately balance all interests involved: while the accused is given the opportunity to have his or her say, the fairness of the proceedings is enhanced by the presence and participation of professional defence counsel. In the same vein, concerns regarding the right to a fair trial enjoyed by the prosecution as well as potentially victims participating in the proceedings would be addressed by removing the pitfalls inherent in full-fledged self-representation, and ascertaining that the proceedings are indeed controlled by the bench.

It is to be hoped that the International Criminal Court, as jurisdiction which is most likely to have to deal with the right to self-representation in the future, will learn the lesson from the *ad hoc* tribunals. The ICC could provide accused with the possibility to address the court and actively participate in their proceedings without having to choose between self-representation as it could be seen before the *ad hoc* tribunals with all its dangers and pitfalls; taking the witness stand in order to testify under oath; or being left without any opportunity whatsoever to contribute to their proceedings and present their views on the case.

Then, international criminal tribunals would be in a position to fulfil not only the role of a guardian of the rights of accused in international criminal proceedings, but also their truth-seeking function and contribute to establishing factual records of the events they are concerned with in a reasonably objective manner. International criminal justice may then be able to advance its goals set as high in theory and so challenging to achieve in practice.

ANNEX. Summary (German)

Selbstverteidigung vor Internationalen Strafrechtstribunalen – Zusammenfassung (Abstract)

Erstes Kapitel. Hintergrund

A. Einleitung: Thema und Untersuchungsgang

Die Frage nach einem Recht auf Selbstverteidigung[1723] vor internationalen Strafrechtstribunalen stellt sich insbesondere in den letzten Jahren angesichts eines verstärkten Aufkommens dieser Thematik vor allem im Zusammenhang der Arbeit des Tribunals für Ex-Jugoslawien (ICTY).

Angesichts der Komplikationen welche durch die Ausübung eines Rechts auf Selbstverteidigung in der Praxis entstehen, erörtert die vorliegende Dissertation, inwieweit die gegenwärtig anerkannte Ausgestaltung eines solchen Rechts tatsächlich praktikabel ist. Im Anschluss an eine ausführliche Diskussion der relevanten Entscheidungen und Ansätze, welche hauptsächlich in der theoretischen und praktischen Arbeit des ICTY zum Tragen kommen, stellt die vorliegende Dissertation eine mögliche Alternative im Rahmen eines Rechts auf eine persönliche Verteidigung vor, welche die Interessen aller Verfahrensbeteiligten sowie anderweitig Interessierter in Betracht zieht und eine Alternative für die zukünftige Arbeit des Internationalen Strafgerichtshofes (IGStH) bieten kann.

1723 Der Begriff "Selbstverteidigung" wird im Folgenden in Ermangelung einer adäquaten deutschen Bezeichnung als Übersetzung des Begriffs „right to self-representation" oder „right to defend oneself in person" verwendet. Dabei ist zu beachten, dass dies lediglich eine Wortwahl in Anlehnung an die englische Bezeichnung der „self-representation" oder „*pro se* defence" darstellt, und im Zusammenhang der vorliegenden Arbeit nicht mit dem Rechtsbegriff der Selbstverteidigung im deutschen Strafrecht zu verwechseln ist.

B. Das Recht auf Selbstverteidigung in nationalen und regionalen Jurisdiktionen

Um eine Grundlage für die Diskussion des Rechts auf Selbstverteidigung vor internationalen Strafrechtstribunalen zu schaffen, erörtert die vorliegende Arbeit zunächst die Interpretation und Auslegung eines Rechts auf Selbstverteidigung in nationalen und regionalen Systemen.

I. Nationale Jurisdiktionen

1. Common law-Systeme: Das Beispiel von *Faretta v. California*

Für die Untersuchung in nationalen Strafverfahren greift die vorliegende Arbeit Beispiele heraus, welche auch für die folgende Diskussion des Rechts auf Selbstverteidigung vor internationalen Instanzen von Relevanz sind. Besonders zu nennen ist im Rahmen der *common law*-Rechtsprechung die Entscheidung des U.S. Supreme Court in *Faretta v. California*,[1724] da diese Entscheidung als Referenz für spätere Entscheidungen in internationalen Tribunalen dienen sollte. Allgemein kann festgestellt werden, dass – wenn auch sehr generalisiert – das Recht auf Selbstverteidigung in *common law*-Systemen von fundamentaler Bedeutung ist und als Verfahrensgrundrecht von Angeklagten im Strafverfahren ausgelegt wird. Die Entscheidungsfreiheit des Individuums wird gegen Eingriffe der Staatsgewalt, zum Beispiel durch Beiordnung eines Verteidigers gegen den Willen des Angeklagten, geschützt. Von Bedeutung ist hierbei, dass im Falle einer Vertretung durch Strafverteidiger für Angeklagte im Allgemeinen keine Möglichkeit besteht, im Laufe eines Verfahrens zu Wort zu kommen, es sei denn, sie treten unter Eid in den Zeugenstand, was auch zur Folge hat, dass sie durch die gegnerische Partei ins Kreuzverhör genommen werden können.

2. Civil law- / Andere Systeme: Kurzübersicht relevanter Gesetzestexte

In einer großen Anzahl von auf *civil law*-Ansätzen beruhenden Rechtssystemen kann festgestellt werden, dass das Recht auf Selbstverteidigung zwar

1724 *Anthony Pasquall Faretta v. State of California* (U.S. Supreme Court), 422 U.S. 806, 30 June 1975.

anerkannt, in der Regel aber auf niedrigere Instanzen oder tendentiell weniger komplexe Verfahren beschränkt ist. Aufgrund der potentiellen Relevanz in zukünftigen Verfahren insbesondere vor dem Internationalen Strafgerichtshof bietet die vorliegende Arbeit eine kurze Übersicht einiger ausgewählter Gesetzestexte von Vertragsstaaten des Römischen Statuts. Diese Untersuchung gibt Grund zu der – notwendigerweise generalisierten – Annahme, dass ein Recht auf Selbstverteidigung auf einem anderen Verständnis beruht als in *common law*-Systemen und damit seine Ausübung in der Praxis von geringerer Bedeutung ist. Im Gegensatz zu *common law*-Systemen gibt es dafür jedoch in der Regel für Angeklagte die Möglichkeit, ihre Ansichten im Laufe des Verfahrens darzulegen, ohne dafür in den Zeugenstand treten zu müssen.

II. Regionale Jurisdiktionen

1. Relevante Normen

Bestimmte Normen in Instrumenten wie dem Internationalen Pakt über Bürgerliche und Politische Rechte (IPbpR) oder der Europäischen Konvention für Menschenrecht (EMRK) bieten die Grundlage für relevante Rechtsprechung regionaler und internationaler Instanzen, welche sich mit dem Schutz von Menschenrechten befassen. Dabei bildete Artikel 14(3)(d) des IPbpR unter anderem die Basis für äquivalente Vorschriften in den Statuten der Internationalen Strafrechtstribunale für Ex-Jugoslawien und Ruanda.[1725] Von Interesse ist für die vorliegende Arbeit die Auslegung dieses Textes durch das Human Rights Committee, die sich im Laufe der Zeit von einem kategorischen[1726] zu einem eher pragmatischen Ansatz veränderte.[1727]

1725 Internationaler Pakt über Bürgerliche und Politische Rechte, GA Res. 2200A (XXI), 16 Dezember 1966 ("IPbpR"), Artikel 14(3)(d).

1726 Human Rights Committee, General Comment No. 13, 13 April 1984, para.11.

1727 Human Rights Committee, General Comment No. 32, CCPR/C/GC/32, 23 August 2007, para.37.

Auf regionaler Ebene sind Artikel 6(3)(c) EMRK,[1728] sowie Artikel 8(2)(d) AMRK[1729] zu nennen. Der Inter-Amerikanische Gerichtshof für Menschenrechte machte in einem Kommentar zur AMRK deutlich, dass die persönliche Verteidigung eines Angeklagten dann möglich ist, wenn dies auch im nationalen Gesetz vorgesehen ist.[1730] Darüber hinaus sei die Verteidigung durch einen Anwalt notwendig, wenn der Grundsatz eines fairen Verfahrens dies verlange.[1731] Weniger eindeutig in der Formulierung ist Artikel 7(1)(c) AfKMVR, der ausdrücklich nur das Recht auf einen Verteidiger schützt.[1732] Dies wurde sowohl als Anzeichen gesehen, dass wahrscheinlich auch ein Recht auf Selbstverteidigung zugestanden ist,[1733] wie auch als Garantie der Selbstverteidigung wie in anderen Menschenrechtsinstrumenten.[1734] Vergleichbar allgemein gehalten – wenn auch weniger im Hinblick auf strafrechtliche Verfahren – ist der Text der Charta der Grundrechte der Europäischen Union.[1735]

1728 Konvention zum Schutze der Menschenrechte und Grundfreiheiten in der Fassung des Protokolls Nr. 11, 04. November 1950 (EMRK), Artikel 6(3)(c).

1729 American Convention on Human Rights, O.A.S Treaty Series No. 36, 1144 U.N.T.S. 123, OEA/Ser.L.V/II.82 doc.6 rev. 1 at 25 (1992) (AMRK), Artikel 8(2)(d).

1730 Inter-American Court of Human Rights, Advisory Opinion OC-11/90, Exceptions to the Exhaustion of Domestic Remedies (Art. 46(1), 46(2)(a) and 46(2)(b) American Convention on Human Rights), 10 August 1990, para.25.

1731 Inter-American Court of Human Rights, Advisory Opinion OC-11/90, Exceptions to the Exhaustion of Domestic Remedies (Art. 46(1), 46(2)(a) and 46(2)(b) American Convention on Human Rights), 10 August 1990, para.26.

1732 African (Banjul) Charter on Human and Peoples' Rights, 1981, OAU Doc. CAB / LEG/67/3 rev. 5, 21 I.L.M 58 (1982) (AfKMVR), Artikel 7(1)(c).

1733 M. Cherif Bassiouni, Human Rights in the Context of Criminal Justice: Identifying International Procedural Protections and Equivalent Protections in National Constitutions, 3 *Duke Journal of Comparative and International Law* 235 (1993), S. 283.

1734 Valère Eteka Yemet, *La Charte Africaine des Droits de l'Homme et des Peuples* (Paris: L'Harmattan) 1996, S. 85. Weniger eindeutig in der Auslegung ist U. Oji Umozurike, *The African Charter on Human and Peoples' Rights* (The Hague / Boston / London: Martinus Nijhoff Publishers) 1997, S. 32.

1735 Charta der Grundrechte der Europäischen Union, 2000/C 364/1, 07. Dezember 2000, Artikel 47.

2. Human Rights Committee und Europäischer Gerichtshof für Menschenrechte

Relevante Entscheidungen des Human Rights Committee (HRC) und des Europäischen Gerichtshofes für Menschenrechte (EGMR) sind weitere Anzeichen dafür, dass es keinen globalen Konsens für die Auslegung und Ausübung des Rechts auf Selbstverteidigung gibt.

In *Hill v. Spanien* befand das HRC angesichts der Umstände des Falles auf eine Verletzung von Artikel 14(3)(d) IPbpR,[1736] ohne jedoch auf eine detailliertere Diskussion der Auslegung und Anwendung des Rechts einzugehen.[1737] Der EGMR entschied in *Croissant v. Deutschland*, dass § 140 StPO nicht gegen Artikel 6(3)(c) EMRK verstößt.[1738] Jedoch handelte es sich in diesem Fall nicht um die Verweigerung eines Rechts auf Selbstverteidigung, sondern vielmehr um die gerichtliche Bestellung eines zusätzlichen Verteidigers gegen den Willen des Angeklagten. Diese Auslegung wurde vom Gerichtshof beibehalten.[1739] Bereits zuvor hatte der EGMR Artikel 6(3)(c) EMRK dahingehend ausgelegt, dass diese Norm drei unterschiedliche Rechte umfasst, nämlich das Recht, sich selbst zu verteidigen, das Recht auf einen Verteidiger nach Wahl, und, unter gewissen Umständen, den Anspruch auf Rechtshilfe.[1740]

Besonders deutlich wird die Diskrepanz in der Rechtsprechung im Fall *Correia de Matos v. Portugal*, in dem EGMR und HRC aufgrund derselben Sachlage entgegengesetzte Entscheidung trafen.[1741]

1736 *Michael and Brian Hill v. Spain*, Human Rights Committee, Communication No. 526/1993, U.N. Doc. CCPR/C/59/D/526/1993, 02 April 1997, para.2.1-4.4, 14.2.

1737 Vgl. Michael P. Scharf/Christopher M. Rassi, Do Former Leaders have an International Right to Self-Representation in War Crimes Trials?, 20 *Ohio State Journal on Dispute Resolution* 3 (2005), S. 16-17.

1738 *Croissant c. Allemagne*, Requête n° 13611/88, Arrêt, 25 septembre 1992, para.27.

1739 *Lagerblom v. Sweden*, Application no. 26891/95, Judgment, 14 April 2003, para.50.

1740 *Pakelli c. Allemagne*, Requête n° 8398/78, Arrêt, 05 avril 1983, para.31.

1741 *Carlos Correia de Matos c. Portugal*, Requête n° 48188/99, Décision, 15 novembre 2001; *Carlos Correia de Matos c. Portugal*, Comité des droits de l'homme, Communication No. 1123/2002, U.N. Doc. CCPR/C/86/D/1123/2002, 26 mars 2006. *Siehe auch* Wolfgang Schomburg, Development of Human Rights Before International Criminal Tribunals. A European Perspective, 17(2) *Croatian Annual of Criminal Law and Practice* 909 (2010); Wolfgang Schomburg, Some Reflections on the Right to Self-Representation Before International Tribunals, 12 *ERA Forum* 189 (2011).

III. Einfluss nationaler und regionaler Auslegungen des Rechts auf Selbstverteidigung auf das internationale Strafrechtssystem

Die vorangehende Diskussion ist von Bedeutung, da internationale Strafrechtstribunale regelmäßig auf nationale und regionale Interpretationen und Praxis zurückgreifen, um die Normen für die Anwendung in internationalen Jurisdiktionen auszulegen.[1742] Vor allen Dingen in den Anfängen ist ein wiederholtes Aufgreifen der Entscheidungen z.B. in *Faretta*, *Hill* oder *Croissant* zu beobachten. Darüber hinaus gibt Artikel 21 des Römischen Statuts des IGStH ausdrücklich die Möglichkeit, auf nationale Normen Bezug zu nehmen, sollte sich dies als notwendig erweisen.[1743] Obwohl im Zusammenhang der vorliegenden Arbeit die Position vertreten wird, dass internationales (Prozess-)Strafrecht als unabhängiges System betrachtet werden sollte, das auf nationale und regionale Interpretationen lediglich als Inspiration zurückgreift, legt Artikel 21 des Römischen Statuts dennoch nahe, dass der Ansatz, welcher in nationalen und regionalen Instanzen verfolgt wird, auch in Zukunft von Bedeutung sein wird.

C. Zwischenbemerkung

Diese erste Übersicht zeigt, dass es keine einheitliche Position zu Auslegung oder Ausübung des Rechts auf Selbstverteidigung gibt. Von besonderer Bedeutung für die Diskussion in der vorliegenden Arbeit ist es, diese Differenz vor Augen zu behalten in dem Bewusstsein, dass Systeme mit unterschiedlichen Lösungsansätzen in Konsequenz auch Divergenzen in der aktiven Beteiligung von Angeklagten im Laufe eines Strafverfahrens aufweisen.

1742 Für eine allgemeine Übersicht, vgl. Gerhard Werle, *Principles of International Criminal Law* (The Hague: TMC Asser Press) 2nd edition 2009, para.135-182.

1743 Rome Statute for the International Criminal Court, A/CONF.183/9, 17 July 1998 ("Rome Statute", "ICC Statute"), Artikel 21(1)(c).

Zweites Kapitel. Das Recht auf Selbstverteidigung in internationalen Strafrechtsverfahren

A. Gesetzliche Vorschriften zum Recht auf Selbstverteidigung

Die relevanten Vorschriften für internationale Strafrechtstribunale spiegeln in der Regel die Texte von Menschenrechtsinstrumenten, insbesondere des IPbpR, wider.[1744] Von Bedeutung für die vorliegende Untersuchung sind: Artikel 21(4)(d) ICTY Statut[1745] und 20(4)(d) ICTR Statut;[1746] sowie Artikel 17(4)(d) SCSL Statut;[1747] Artikel 16(4)(d) des Statuts für das Special Tribunal for Lebanon (STL Statut);[1748] und Artikel 67(1)(d) des Römischen Statuts des IGStH.[1749]

Von Interesse für die Anwendung dieser Vorschriften sind außerdem einige prozessuale Regelungen internationaler Strafrechtstribunale, welche in der Regel oben genannte Normen weiter ausbauen und ergänzen. Zu nennen sind in diesem Zusammenhang Verfahrensregel 45(F)[1750] und 45*ter*[1751] der ICTY Rules of Procedure and Evidence (ICTY RPE), und mit gleicher Formulierung Verfahrensregel 45(F) und 45*quater* der ICTR Rules of Procedure and Evidence (ICTR RPE), sowie Verfahrensregel 21(4) der ICC Rules of

1744 Vgl. den direkten Bezug auf Artikel 14 IPbpR im Bericht des UN Generalsekretärs zum Entwurf des ICTY Statuts: Report of the Secretary-General Pursuant to Paragraph 2 of Security Council Resolution 808 (1993), S/25704, 03 May 1993, para.106.

1745 Updated Statute of the International Criminal Tribunal for the Former Yugoslavia (as amended 07 July 2009 by Resolution 1877) ("ICTY Statute"), Article 21(4)(d).

1746 Statute of the International Criminal Tribunal for Rwanda, 31 January 2010 (as amended) ("ICTR Statute"), Article 20(4)(d).

1747 Statute of the Special Court for Sierra Leone, annexed to the Agreement between the United Nations and the Government of Sierra Leone on the Establishment of a Special Court for Sierra Leone, 16 January 2002 ("SCSL Statute"), Article 17(4)(d).

1748 Statute of the Special Tribunal for Lebanon, S/RES/1757 (2007), Attachment, 30 May 2007 ("STL Statute"), Article 16(4)(d).

1749 Rome Statute, Article 67(1)(d).

1750 Rules of Procedure and Evidence, IT/32/Rev. 47, 28 August 2012 ("ICTY RPE"), Rule 45(F).

1751 Rule 45*ter* ICTY RPE.

Procedure and Evidence[1752] und Vorschrift 76(1) der Regulations of the Court des ICC.[1753]

B. *Gerichtliche Auslegung des Rechts auf Selbstverteidigung*

Ein Schwerpunkt der vorliegenden Dissertation liegt auf der Analyse relevanter Rechtsprechung an internationalen Strafrechtstribunalen. Die Rechtsprechung ist die reichhaltigste Quelle zur Analyse der praktischen Umsetzung des Rechts auf Selbstverteidigung und beansprucht aus diesem Grund den umfangreichsten Teil der vorliegenden Arbeit. Die praktische Ausübung des Rechts auf Selbstverteidigung tritt damit in den Fokus der Analyse und dient zur Verdeutlichung der Problemfelder, welche in zukünftigen Verfahren mit sich selbst verteidigenden Angeklagten besonders beachtet werden müssen.

I. Die anfängliche Anerkennung des Rechts auf Selbstverteidigung

1. Das Verfahren gegen *Slobodan Milošević*

Slobodan Milošević war der erste Angeklagte allgemein und vor dem ICTY, welcher das Recht, sich selbst zu verteidigen, beanspruchte. Milošević machte deutlich, dass er das Tribunal nicht anerkenne und aus diesem Grund keinen Verteidiger benötige.[1754] Zu Beginn des Verfahrens gab diese Haltung wenig Anlass zur Diskussion, obwohl die Kammer zwei rechtliche Berater des Angeklagten offiziell anerkannte[1755] und zusätzlich *amicus curiae* zur Unterstützung der Kammer bestellte.[1756]

1752 Rule 21(4) of the Rules of Procedure and Evidence, ICC-ASP/1/3, 10 September 2002.

1753 Regulation 76(1) of the Regulations of the Court, ICC-BD/01-03-11 (as amended), 02 November 2011.

1754 *Prosecutor v. Slobodan Milošević*, Case No. IT-99-37-I, Initial Appearance, 03 July 2001, T.2.

1755 *Prosecutor v. Slobodan Milošević*, Case No. IT-99-37-PT & IT-01-50-PT, Order, 15 November 2001, p.3; *Prosecutor v. Slobodan Milošević*, Case No. IT-02-54-T, Order, 16 April 2002, p.3.

1756 *Prosecutor v. Slobodan Milošević*, Case No. IT-99-37-PT, Status Conference, 30 August 2001, T.6-7; Order Inviting Designation of *Amicus Curiae*, 30 August

Eine kurze Übersicht akademischer Meinungen zum *Milošević*-Ansatz zeigt, dass unter anderem in Frage gestellt wurde, ob Angeklagten, welche zuvor hohe Führungspositionen bekleideten, grundsätzlich zugestanden werden sollte, sich selbst zu verteidigen.[1757] Darüber hinaus wurde argumentiert, dass anstatt des *amicus curiae* ein Verteidiger hätte bestellt werden sollen, um den notwendigerweise politischen Konnotationen des Verfahrens Rechnung zu tragen.[1758]

Nachdem der Gesundheitszustand des Angeklagten den Verfahrensablauf wiederholt und signifikant beeinträchtigte, bestellte die Kammer in *Milošević* einen Verteidiger, um weitere Verzögerungen und damit eine Gefährdung des Rechts des Angeklagten auf ein zügiges Verfahren zu verhindern.[1759] Die Rechtsmittelkammer machte deutlich, dass das Recht auf Selbstverteidigung zwar einen fundamentalen Status genießt, aber kein absolutes Recht darstellt, also unter gewissen Umständen auch eingeschränkt werden könnte.[1760]

2. Vom *Milošević*-Ansatz zu unterscheidende Ansätze

Für die vorliegende Arbeit ist es darüber hinaus von Bedeutung, andere Ansätze anzusprechen, welche von Kammern an internationalen Strafrechtstribunalen verfolgt wurden und das Recht, sich selbst zu verteidigen nicht

---

2001, p.2; Order Concerning *Amici Curiae*, 11 January 2002. *See also Prosecutor v. Slobodan Milošević*, Case No. IT-02-54-T, Reasons for the Decision on the Prosecution Motion Concerning Assignment of Counsel, 04 April 2003, para.3.

1757 Michael P. Scharf / Christopher M. Rassi, Do Former Leaders have an International Right to Self-Representation in War Crimes Trials?, 20 *Ohio State Journal on Dispute Resolution* 3 (2005), at 20-26.

1758 Tom Dannenbaum, The Milošević Trial: Lessons for the Conduct of International Criminal Proceedings (Review of Gideon Boas), 33 *Yale Journal of International Law* 513 (2008), at 515-516.

1759 *Prosecutor v. Slobodan Milošević*, Case No. IT-02-54-T, Oral Ruling, 02 September 2004, T.32357-32359; Order on the Modalities to be Followed by Court Assigned Counsel, 03 September 2004; Reasons for Decision on Assignment of Defence Counsel, 22 September 2004.

1760 *Prosecutor v. Slobodan Milošević*, Case No. IT-02-54-AR73.7 Decision on Interlocutory Appeal of the Trial Chamber's Decision on the Assignment of Defence Counsel, 01 November 2004.

zwangsläufig ermöglichten. Zu nennen sind in diesem Kontext die Entscheidungen in *Janković & Stanković* am ICTY[1761] und in *Norman* am SCSL.[1762]

II. Anerkennung des Rechts auf Selbstverteidigung in unterschiedlichen Verfahrensinstanzen

Es gibt mehrere Anzeichen dafür, dass dem Recht auf Selbstverteidigung je nach Stand des Verfahrens unterschiedliche Bedeutung zugedacht werden könnte. Zum Beispiel wurde in einer Entscheidung der Rechtsmittelinstanz in *Šešelj* angedeutet, dass die Schwelle für Einschränkungen des Rechts im Vorverfahren höher liegen würde als im Hauptverfahren.[1763] Ausführlicher zu diskutieren sind vor allem die relevanten Entscheidungen in *Krajišnik*, sowohl im Hauptverfahren als auch in der Berufungsinstanz.

1. Das Verfahren gegen Momčilo Krajišnik: Hauptverfahren

Im Laufe des Hauptverfahrens teilte Momčilo Krajišnik der Kammer seinen Entschluss mit, seine Verteidigung für den weiteren Verlauf des Verfahrens selbst zu übernehmen.[1764] Im Rahmen weiterer Diskussionen wurde deutlich, dass der Angeklagte dies weniger aus Überzeugung, als vielmehr aufgrund seiner Unzufriedenheit mit der Arbeit seiner Verteidiger auf sich nehmen wollte.[1765] Die Kammer beschloss, dem Angeklagten ein gewisses Fragerecht einzuräumen, wodurch er im Anschluss an seine Verteidiger an Zeugen

---

1761 *Prosecutor v. Janković & Stanković*, Case No. IT-96-23/2-PT, Decision Following Registrar's Notification of Radovan Stanković's Request for Self-Representation, 19 August 2005.

1762 *Prosecutor v. Samuel Hinga Norman et al.*, Case No. SCSL-04-14-T, Decision on the Application of Samuel Hinga Norman for Self-Representation Under Article 17(4)(d) of the Statute of the Special Court, 08 June 2004.

1763 *Prosecutor v. Vojislav Šešelj*, Case No. IT-03-67-AR73.3, Decision on Appeal Against the Trial Chamber's Decision on Assignment of Counsel, 20 October 2006, para.28.

1764 *Prosecutor v. Momčilo Krajišnik*, Case No. IT-00-39-T, Hearing, 25 May 2005, T.13399, T.13402, T.13405-13406.

1765 *Prosecutor v. Momčilo Krajišnik*, Case No. IT-00-39-T, Procedural Hearing, 26 May 2005, T.13418-13420.

weitere Fragen stellen konnte.[1766] Schließlich kamen die Richter jedoch zu dem Schluss, dass es dem Angeklagten an der nötigen Überzeugung fehlte, um die Entscheidung zur Selbstverteidigung informiert und bewusst treffen zu können, und gab aus diesem Grund dem Gesuch des Angeklagten nicht statt.[1767] Das Fragerecht des Angeklagten wurde jedoch im weiteren Verlauf verlängert.[1768]

2. Das Verfahren gegen *Momčilo Krajišnik*: Berufungsverfahren

Zu Beginn des Berufungsverfahrens wollte der Angeklagte erneut seine Verteidigung selbst übernehmen. In einer richtungweisenden und viel diskutierten Entscheidung befand die Berufungskammer, dass sich die Ausübung des Rechts auf Selbstverteidigung im Berufungsverfahren nicht wesentlich von der Ausübung im Hauptverfahren unterscheide und begründete damit ein Recht auf Selbstverteidigung auch im Berufungsverfahren.[1769]

Eine „fundamental" abweichende Meinung kritisierte den Ansatz der Mehrheit scharf und ließ keine Zweifel, dass das Recht auf Selbstverteidigung in der bis zu diesem Zeitpunkt bestehenden Form weder im Haupt- noch im Berufungsverfahren wünschens- oder empfehlenswert wäre.[1770]

1766 *Prosecutor v. Momčilo Krajišnik*, Case No. IT-00-39-T, Procedural Hearing, 26 May 2005, T.13439-13440.

1767 *Prosecutor v. Momčilo Krajišnik*, Case No. IT-00-39-T, Reasons for Oral Decision Denying Mr Krajišnik's Request to Proceed Unrepresented by Counsel, 08 June 2005.

1768 *Prosecutor v. Momčilo Krajišnik*, Case No. IT-00-39-T, Hearing, 28 September 2005, T.17205-17206.

1769 *Prosecutor v. Momčilo Krajišnik*, Case No. IT-00-39-A, Decision on Momčilo Krajišnik's Request to Self-Represent, on Counsel's Motion in Relation to Appointment of *Amicus Curiae*, and on the Prosecution Motion of 16 February 2007, 11 May 2007.

1770 *Prosecutor v. Momčilo Krajišnik*, Case No. IT-00-39-A, Decision on Momčilo Krajišnik's Request to Self-Represent, on Counsel's Motion in Relation to Appointment of *Amicus Curiae*, and on the Prosecution Motion of 16 February 2007, 11 May 2007, Fundamentally Dissenting Opinion of Judge Schomburg on the Right to Self-Representation.

3. Diskussion

Die im Zusammenhang der Diskussion in *Krajišnik* verdeutlichten unterschiedlichen Positionen illustrieren die Divergenz in Interpretation und Anwendung des Rechts auf Selbstverteidigung. In der vorliegenden Arbeit wird die Ansicht vertreten, dass die ursprüngliche Auslegung eines Rechts auf Selbstverteidigung den speziellen Umständen internationaler Strafprozesse ungenügend Rechnung trägt und daher in Zukunft entsprechend modifiziert werden sollte. Dabei geht es darum, den Angeklagten eine angemessene aktive Beteiligung am Verfahren zu ermöglichen, die nicht lediglich auf eine Zeugenaussage unter Eid beschränkt ist. Die Mehrheitsentscheidung der Berufungskammer scheint die Möglichkeit einer Revision der ursprünglichen Position nicht erkannt zu haben oder wollte sie nicht nutzen – in jedem Fall aber erscheint die Begründung eines Rechts auf Selbstverteidigung wie in dieser Entscheidung vorgesehen der Realität nicht angemessen.

III. Das Recht auf ein faires Verfahren und der Einfluss der Selbstverteidigung

Das Recht auf Selbstverteidigung ist Teil eines umfassenderen Rechts auf ein faires Verfahren. Die vorliegende Dissertation wirft die Frage auf, inwiefern das Recht auf Selbstverteidigung mit anderen Teilrechten in Abwägung zu stellen ist, um ein allgemein gerechtes Verfahren nicht zu gefährden. Dabei können auch die Interessen anderer Beteiligter an einem fairen Verfahren eine Rolle spielen. Angesichts der praktischen Erfahrung mit der Ausübung des Rechts auf Selbstverteidigung scheint eine modifizierte Ausgestaltung des Rechts auf eine persönliche Verteidigung angebracht, um das allgemein geltende Recht auf ein faires Verfahren nicht unnötig zu beeinträchtigen.

C. Mögliche und tatsächliche praktische Auswirkungen der Ausübung des Rechts auf Selbstverteidigung

Der überwiegende Teil der vorliegenden Dissertation beschäftigt sich mit den möglichen und tatsächlichen praktischen Auswirkungen der Ausübung des Rechts auf Selbstverteidigung auf die Durchführung internationaler Strafverfahren. Hauptsächliche Grundlage dafür bildet die Analyse relevanter

Verfahren, um den praktischen Aspekt zu betonen; einschlägige akademische Meinungen werden gegebenenfalls in Diskussionen weiter behandelt.

I. Negative Folgen der Entscheidung, sich selbst zu verteidigen

Bereits in *Milošević* ließ die Rechtsmittelkammer keinen Zweifel, dass ein Angeklagter etwaige negative Konsequenzen seiner Wahl zu akzeptieren hätte und sich nicht auf die Umstände seiner Selbstverteidigung berufen könnte.[1771] An anderer Stelle wurde die Ansicht vertreten, dass sich selbst verteidigende Angeklagte nach denselben Maßstäben wie professionelle Verteidiger behandelt werden würden und sich von ihrer Wahl, die Verteidigung persönlich durchzuführen, keine Vorteile erhoffen dürften.[1772] In der Praxis ist jedoch zu beobachten, dass selbst Angeklagte, welche selbst ein rechtswissenschaftliches Studium abgeschlossen haben – z. B. *Slobodan Milošević* und *Vojislav Šešelj* – zum Teil signifikanten Spielraum im Verfahrensverlauf genossen. Zumindest zu einem Großteil ist dies damit zu rechtfertigen, dass das Grundrecht des Angeklagten auf ein faires Verfahren in einer etwaigen Interessenabwägung zu bevorzugen ist.

II. Risiko der Selbstbezichtigung

Ein sich selbst verteidigender Angeklagter läuft im Verfahrensverlauf gerade während der Befragung von Zeugen ein nicht zu unterschätzendes Risiko, sich selbst zu belasten. Insbesondere im Rahmen von Kreuzverhören müssen Angeklagte ihre Verteidigungstheorie darlegen. Bereits in *Milošević* erachtete die Kammer im Hauptverfahren es deshalb für notwendig, den Angeklagten bezüglich seines Rechts zu schweigen zu belehren und warnte ihn, dass die Kammer sich die Möglichkeit vorbehielt, im Laufe des Verfahrens geäußerte sachbezogene Stellungnahmen des Angeklagten in der Urteilsfindung

---

1771 *Prosecutor v. Slobodan Milošević*, Case No. IT-02-54-AR73.6, Decision on Interlocutory Appeal by the *Amici Curiae* Against the Trial Chamber Order Concerning the Presentation and Preparation of the Defence Case, 20 January 2004, para.19.

1772 *Prosecutor v. Slobodan Milošević*, Case No. IT-02-54-T, Pre-Defence Conference, 02 September 2003, T.25959; *Prosecutor v. Zdravko Tolimir*, Case No. IT-05-88/2-T, Pre-Trial Conference, 25 February 2010, T.317-318.

zu berücksichtigen.[1773] In der Folge ersuchte die Anklage in *Karadžić* und *Tolimir* die jeweils zuständige Kammer, eine ähnliche Belehrung des Angeklagten vorzunehmen,[1774] jedoch mit unterschiedlichen Ergebnissen: während die Kammer in *Tolimir* eine zum *Milošević*-Verfahren wortgleiche Belehrung zu Beginn der Beweisaufnahme verlas,[1775] übernahm die Kammer in *Karadžić* die von der Anklage vorgeschlagene Belehrung nur zum Teil[1776] und machte darüber hinaus im Laufe des Verfahrens deutlich, dass sie sachbezogene Stellungnahmen des Angeklagten nicht in der Beweisaufnahme berücksichtigen würde.[1777]

III. Komplexe Verfahren und (mangelnde) rechtliche Kenntnisse

1. Nutzung des rechtlichen Rahmens durch sich selbst verteidigende Angeklagte

Die rechtliche und sachliche Komplexität internationaler Strafrechtsverfahren ist nicht zu leugnen.[1778] Wie in der vorliegenden Arbeit anhand konkreter Beispiele illustriert, kann jedoch insbesondere in späteren Verfahren festgestellt werden, dass sich selbst verteidigende Angeklagte den ihnen zur Verfügung stehenden rechtlichen Rahmen zunehmend zu nutzen verstehen. Es kann gefragt werden, ob sich dies unter Umständen in einem neu bewerteten

---

1773 *Prosecutor v. Slobodan Milošević*, Case No. IT-02-54-T, Order, 19 February 2002, Annex A (d).

1774 *Prosecutor v. Radovan Karadžić*, Case No. IT-95-5/18-T, Prosecution Motion for an Instruction Regarding the Admissibility of Submissions and Statements of the Accused, 23 February 2010; *Prosecutor v. Zdravko Tolimir*, Case No. IT-05-88/2-PT, Prosecution Motion for an Instruction Regarding the Admissibility of Submissions and Statements of the Accused, 23 February 2010.

1775 *Prosecutor v. Zdravko Tolimir*, Case No. IT-05-88/2-T, Pre-Trial Conference, 25 February 2010, T.322.

1776 *Prosecutor v. Radovan Karadžić*, Case No. IT-95-5/18-T, Hearing, 13 April 2010, T.999-1000.

1777 *Prosecutor v. Radovan Karadžić*, Case No. IT-95-5/18-T, Hearing, 13 April 2010, T.1084-1085; Hearing, 15 September 2010, T.6775; Hearing, 16 December 2010, T.10012; Hearing 18 January 2011, T.10470; Hearing, 10 February 2011, T.11562-11563.

1778 Vgl. Gideon Boas, Self-Representation Before the ICTY. A Case for Reform, 9 *Journal of International Criminal Justice* 53 (2011), at 79-81.

Verhältnis zwischen Angeklagten und Anwälten, welche ihnen als Rechtsberater zur Seite stehen, begründet.

2. Einfluss mangelnder rechtlicher Kenntnisse auf den Verfahrensablauf

Bereits im Laufe der Diskussion, ob die Ausübung des Rechts auf Selbstverteidigung zugelassen werden kann, spielen mangelnde rechtliche Kenntnisse des Angeklagten eine Rolle.[1779] Darüber hinaus gibt es Anzeichen dafür, dass der Einfluss dieses Kenntnismangels auf den Verfahrensablauf unter Umständen Ausmaße annehmen kann, welche die Kammer zu einer Einschränkung des Rechts auf Selbstverteidigung bewegen.[1780]

IV. Sprachliche Barrieren und ihr Einfluss auf das Recht auf Selbstverteidigung

1. *Ad hoc*-Tribunale

Nicht zu unterschätzen ist der Einfluss sprachlicher Barrieren auf die Ausübung des Rechts auf Selbstverteidigung. Aufgrund unterschiedlicher Regelungen werden *ad hoc*-Tribunale und IStGH im Folgenden getrennt betrachtet.

Bereits zu Beginn des Verfahrens in *Karadžić* verlangte der Angeklagte, dass ihm Dokumente von der Anklage lediglich auf Serbisch und in kyrilli-

---

1779 *Prosecutor v. Janković & Stanković*, Case No. IT-96-23/2-PT, Decision Following Registrar's Notification of Radovan Stanković's Request for Self-Representation, 19 August 2005, para.20; *Prosecutor v. Momčilo Krajišnik*, Case No. IT-00-39-T, Reasons for Oral Decision Denying Mr Krajišnik's Request to Proceed Unrepresented by Counsel, 18 August 2005, para.34.

1780 *Prosecutor v. Vojislav Šešelj*, Case No. IT-03-67-AR73.3, Decision on Appeal Against the Trial Chamber's Decision on Assignment of Counsel, 20 October 2006, para.23 fn.26; *Prosecutor v. Momčilo Krajišnik*, Case No. IT-00-39-A, Decision on Krajišnik Request and Prosecution Motion, 11 September 2007, para.41. Vgl. *Prosecutor v. Radovan Karadžić*, Case No. IT-95-5/18-PT, Decision on Accused Motion for Adequate Facilities and Equality of Arms: Legal Associates, 28 January 2009, para.31, 36; bestätigt in der Berufungsinstanz: *Prosecutor v. Radovan Karadžić*, Case No. IT-95-5/18-AR73.2, Decision on Interlocutory Appeal of the Trial Chamber's Decision on Adequate Facilities, 07 May 2009, para.13-14.

scher Schrift zugestellt werden.[1781] Auf Antrag der Anklage wurden jedoch für das Verfahren ausreichende englische Sprachkenntnisse des Anklagten festgestellt,[1782] wodurch sich der Umfang des zu übersetzenden Materials zumindest zu einem Teil verringerte.

Die Diskussionen in *Tolimir* und *Šešelj* gestalteten sich problematischer: beide Angeklagten bestanden darauf, sämtliche verfahrensrelevanten Materialien lediglich auf Serbisch und in kyrillischer Schrift zu erhalten; *Šešelj* verlangte darüber hinaus Papierform anstelle von elektronischer Bereitstellung, da er sich weigerte, für seine Vorbereitungen einen Computer zu verwenden.[1783] Diesem Ersuchen wurde zu einem Großteil von der zuletzt zuständigen Kammer im Vorverfahren stattgegeben.[1784] Die Diskussionen in *Tolimir* zogen sich hinsichtlich unterschiedlicher Aspekte über einen bedeutenden Zeitraum.[1785]

1781 *Prosecutor v. Radovan Karadžić*, Case No. IT-95-5/18-I, Appeal Against the Registry Decision to Provide Me with Transcripts in English Language Only, or as Audio Recordings, 15 August 2008 (filed: 19 August 2008). Vgl. auch *Prosecutor v. Radovan Karadžić*, Case No. IT-95-5/18-PT, Decision on the Accused's Request that all Materials, Including Transcripts, be Disclosed to Him in Serbian and Cyrillic Script, 25 September 2008.

1782 *Prosecutor v. Radovan Karadžić*, Case No. IT-95-5/18-PT, Decision on Prosecution Motion Seeking Determination that the Accused Understands English for the Purposes of the Statute and the Rules of Procedure and Evidence, 26 March 2009; bestätigt in der Berufungsinstanz: *Prosecutor v. Radovan Karadžić*, Case No. IT-95-5/18-AR73.3, Decision on Interlocutory Appeal of the Trial Chamber's decision on Prosecution Motion Seeking Determination that the Accused Understands English, 04 June 2009.

1783 Vgl. *Prosecutor v. Vojislav Šešelj*, Case No. IT-03-67-PT, Request of the Accused to Disclose Materials of the Prosecution in Written Form and in Serbian, 26 October 2004 (filed: 09 November 2004); Professor Vojislav Šešelj's Motion for Review of the Decision on Form of Disclosure Issued by Trial Chamber I on 4 July 2006, 11 May 2007 (filed: 17 May 2007).

1784 *Procureur c/ Vojislav Šešelj*, Affaire n° IT-03-67-PT, Décision Relative à la Requête 289 Concernant le Mode de Communication de Pièces, 07 juin 2007.

1785 Vgl. *Prosecutor v. Zdravko Tolimir*, Case No. IT-05-88/2-PT, Submission of the Accused for the Delivery of Documents and Transcripts of the Trial in a Language that He Reads and Writes, 08 July 2007, und schließlich *Prosecutor v. Zdravko Tolimir*, Case No. IT-05-88/2-T, Decision on Zdravko Tolimir's Request for Transcripts in a Language which he Understands, 27 August 2010.

2. Internationaler Strafgerichtshof

Obgleich diese Thematik vor dem IGStH bislang noch keine Rolle im Zusammenhang mit sich selbst verteidigenden Angeklagten spielte, sollte doch auf die unterschiedlichen Regelungen hingewiesen werden. Artikel 67(1)(a) des Römischen Statuts scheint einen höheren Standard des Sprachverständnisses vorauszusetzen, welcher über die Anforderungen des ICTY hinausgeht.[1786] Angesichts der potentiell breit gefächerten Zuständigkeit des IGStH und der damit verbundenen Sprachvielfalt könnte dies im Zusammenhang mit sich selbst verteidigenden Angeklagten unter Umständen zu einem signifikanten Ressourcenaufwand führen.

V. Angemessene Zeit und Ressourcen für sich selbst vertretende Angeklagte

Insbesondere die Zuteilung von Ressourcen – vor allem Zeit und finanzielle Mittel – für die Vorbereitung und Präsentation der Verteidigung führt in unterschiedlichen Fällen zu Diskussionen. Die Beantwortung dieser Fragen wird insbesondere durch das Recht des Angeklagten auf ein faires Verfahren beeinflusst, welches auch das Recht auf ein zügiges Verfahren und auf angemessen Ressourcen einschließt.

1. Angemessene Zeit

Die Frage nach der angemessenen Zeit nicht nur für die Vorbereitung auf das Verfahren, sondern auch im Laufe der Beweisaufnahme auf Zeugenbefragungen und ähnliches stellt sich insbesondere für sich selbstverteidigende Angeklagte. Allgemein scheint anerkannt, dass diese mehr Zeit als professionelle Verteidiger benötigen werden,[1787] und Kammern haben sich bislang

---

1786 Vgl. *Prosecutor v. Germain Katanga*, Case No. ICC-01/04-01/07, Judgment on the Appeal of Mr. Germain Katanga Against the Decision of Pre-Trial Chamber I entitled "Decision on the Defence Request Concerning Languages", 27 May 2008.

1787 Vgl. *Prosecutor v. Slobodan Milošević*, Case No. IT-02-54-AR73.6, Decision on the Interlocutory Appeal by the *Amici Curiae* Against the Trial Chamber Order Concerning the Presentation and Preparation of the Defence Case, 20 January 2004.

flexibel gezeigt, Fristverlängerungen und ähnliche Aufschübe zu gewähren.[1788] Insbesondere sahen Verfahren mit sich selbst verteidigenden Angeklagten häufig eine reduzierte Anzahl an Gerichtstagen pro Woche, um der erhöhten Belastung der Angeklagten Rechnung zu tragen und damit ausreichend Zeit für eine angemessene Vorbereitung zur Verfügung zu stellen.[1789]

2. Angemessene Ressourcen

Die adäquate Ausstattung von sich selbst verteidigenden Angeklagten ist in der Regel zumindest in technischer und logistischer Hinsicht selten Streitthema. Wenn es auch zu Komplikationen kommen kann, etwa wenn sich in einem überwiegend PC-basierten Verfahren der Angeklagte weigert, einen Computer und die damit einhergehenden Programme zum Verfahrensmanagement zu verwenden, gibt es angesichts der Ausstattung wie zum Beispiel zusätzliche Zellen in der Untersuchungshaftanstalt als Büroräume oder Möglichkeiten zum vertraulichen Austausch mit rechtlichen Beratern selten Grund zur Beschwerde. Schwierigkeiten birgt vielmehr grundsätzlich die Tatsache, dass die Angeklagten in der Regel für die Dauer des Verfahrens in Untersuchungshaft verbleiben, was Aufgaben, welche normalerweise von Verteidigern übernommen werden, für den Angeklagten erheblich einschränkt.[1790]

Wesentlich mehr Potential für Meinungsverschiedenheiten bietet die Frage der finanziellen Unterstützung von sich selbst verteidigenden Angeklagten. Für den Fall eines Angeklagten, welcher anwaltlich vertreten und dabei als unfähig eingestuft wird, die Kosten der Verteidigung selbst zu bestreiten, gibt es klare Richtlinien. Im Gegensatz dazu musste die Vorgehens-

---

1788 Vgl. z.B. *Prosecutor v. Radovan Karadžić*, Case No. IT-95-5/18-T, Decision on the Accused's Motion for Postponement of Trial, 26 February 2010; Decision on Accused's Motion for Suspension of Proceedings, 18 August 2010; *Prosecutor v. Zdravko Tolimir*, Case No. IT-05-88/2-T, Decision on the Accused's Information and Requests for the Trial Chamber 04 March 2010.

1789 Diskutiert werden in diesem Zusammenhang die Entwicklungen in *Karadžić* und *Tolimir*.

1790 Vgl. in diesem Kontext die Diskussionen in *Milošević* und *Šešelj*: *Prosecutor v. Slobodan Milošević*, Case No. IT-02-54-T, Decision on Accused's Application for Provisional release, 06 March 2002; *Prosecutor v. Vojislav Šešelj*, Case No. IT-03-67-PT, Decision on Defence Motion for Provisional Release, 23 July 2004.

weise für sich selbst verteidigende Angeklagte erst in der Praxis im Rahmen mehrerer Verfahren und Streitsachen von Kammern ausgearbeitet werden.

Krajišnik war das erste Verfahren, in welchem die Frage nach finanzieller Beihilfe für sich selbst verteidigende Angeklagte entschieden werden musste. In einer für folgende Verfahren wegweisenden Entscheidung befand die Berufungskammer, dass ein sich selbst verteidigender Angeklagter grundsätzlich Anspruch auf finanzielle Unterstützung erheben kann.[1791] Während die anfängliche Diskussion in *Šešelj* größtenteils parallel zu *Krajišnik* verlief, sollte die Diskussion zur finanziellen Unterstützung verdeutlichen, dass derartige Verfahren vor allem auch von der Kooperation des Angeklagten abhängen. Der Angeklagte weigerte sich mehrere Jahre lang, Informationen weiterzugeben, welche eine Bestimmung der Höhe der Unterstützung ermöglicht hätten. Kurz vor Beginn der Präsentation der Verteidigung bestimmte die Kammer daher *proprio motu*, dass der Angeklagte für den Rest des Verfahrens 50 Prozent der theoretisch maximal möglichen Beihilfe erhalten sollte.[1792]

Die genaue Ausgestaltung der finanziellen Unterstützung gab im Einzelfall weiterhin Anlass zur Diskussion. In *Karadžić* erhob der Angeklagte Anspruch auf finanzielle Beihilfe, und kritisierte dabei den Betrag, welcher seinen Beratern zugestanden wurde.[1793] Im weiteren Verlauf des Verfahrens erhob der Angeklagte erfolgreich Anspruch auf eine Erhöhung der zugestandenen Unterstützung sowohl für das Vorverfahren,[1794] als auch für das Hauptverfahren.[1795] Dahingegen wurde deutlich gemacht, dass die Entscheidung des

---

1791 *Prosecutor v. Momčilo Krajišnik*, Case No. IT-00-39-A, Decision on Krajišnik Request and Prosecution Motion, 11 September 2007, para.40-42.

1792 *Procureur c/ Vojislav Šešelj*, Affaire n° IT-03-67-T, Version Expurgée de la « Décision Relative au Financement de la Défense » Enregistrée le 29 octobre 2010, 02 novembre 2010 ; bestätigt in der Berufungsinstanz: *Prosecutor v. Vojislav Šešelj*, Case No. IT-03-67-R33B, Public Redacted Version of the "Decision on the Registry Submission Pursuant to Rule 33(B) Regarding the Trial Chamber's Decision on Financing the Defence" Rendered on 8 April 2011, 17 May 2011.

1793 *Prosecutor v. Radovan Karadžić*, Case No. IT-95-5/18-PT, Motion for Adequate Facilities and Equality of Arms: Legal Associates, 24 November 2008.

1794 *Prosecutor v. Radovan Karadžić*, Case No. IT-95-5/18-T, Appeal of OLAD Decision in Relation to Additional Pre-Trial Funds, 10 November 2009; and Decision on Appeal of OLAD Decision in Relation to Additional Pre-Trial Funds, 17 December 2009.

1795 *Prosecutor v. Radovan Karadžić*, Case No. IT-95-5/18-T, Request for Review of OLAD Decision on Trial Phase Remuneration, 14 January 2010; and Decision on

Präsidenten des ICTY bezüglich der finanziellen Unterstützung keinen direkten Einfluss auf die Entscheidung der Kammer hinsichtlich des Beginns des Hauptverfahrens ausübte.[1796]

3. Nutzung der Ressourcen durch sich selbst verteidigende Angeklagte

Die Rechtsprechung gibt gewisse Anhaltspunkte, unter welchen Umständen ein verschwenderischer Umgang mit Ressourcen kritisiert wird. Dabei handelt es sich insbesondere um Eingaben, welche nach Einschätzung der Kammer als unnötig oder willkürlich einzustufen waren und dies für den Angeklagten hätte ersichtlich sein müssen.[1797] Die gegebenenfalls ablehnende Haltung einer Kammer verschärft sich unter Umständen, falls ein Angeklagter derartige Eingaben macht, sich jedoch darüber hinaus über unzureichende Ressourcen beklagt.

Verzögerungen in Verfahren mit sich selbst verteidigenden Angeklagten werden in der Regel von einer Anzahl von Faktoren beeinflusst. Als konkretes

---

Request for Review of OLAD Decision on Trial Phase Remuneration, 19 February 2010.

1796 *Prosecutor v. Radovan Karadžić*, Case No. IT-95-5/18-T, Decision on Accused's Motion for Postponement of Trial, 26 February 2010; bestätigt in der Berufungsinstanz: *Prosecutor v. Radovan Karadžić*, Case No. IT-95-5/18-AR73.7, Decision on Appeal from Decision on Motion for Further Postponement of Trial, 31 March 2010.

1797 Vgl. z.B. *Prosecutor v. Vojislav Šešelj*, Case No. IT-03-67-PT, Status Conference, 03 July 2003, T.83; Decision on Motion Number 28, 19 December 2003; Decision on "Request of the Accused Asking President of the Tribunal Theodor Meron to Reverse the Decision of the Deputy Registrar Prohibiting Dr Vojislav Šešelj From Communicating with Anyone and Receiving Visits for at least 60 Days", 21 September 2005; *Prosecutor v. Vojislav Šešelj*, Case No. IT-03-67-AR72.1, Decision on Motion for Reconsideration of the "Decision on the Interlocutory Appeal Concerning Jurisdiction" Dated 31 August 2004, 15 June 2006; *Prosecutor v. Zdravko Tolimir*, Case No. IT-05-88/2-AR73.1, Decision on Interlocutory Appeal Against Oral Decision of the Pre-Trial Judge of 11 December 2007, 28 March 2008; *Prosecutor v. Zdravko Tolimir*, Case No. IT-05-88/2-T, Decision on the Accused's Submission of 18 August 2008, 02 September 2008; *Prosecutor v. Radovan Karadžić*, Case No. IT-95-5/18-PT, Decision on Motion to Exclude Testimony of War Correspondents, 20 May 2009; *Prosecutor v. Radovan Karadžić*, Case No. IT-95-5/18-T, Decision on Accused's Motion to Strike Scheduled Shelling Incident on Grounds of Collateral Estoppel, 31 March 2010; Decision on the Accused's Motion to Exclude Testimony of Aernout van Lynden, 17 May 2010.

Beispiel untersucht die vorliegende Dissertation von Angeklagten durchgeführte Zeugenbefragungen, welche oft durch repetitive, irrelevante oder argumentative Fragen zu weiteren Verzögerungen führen. In diesem Zusammenhang wird besonders deutlich, dass Kammern grundsätzlich willens sind, sich selbst verteidigenden Angeklagten aufgrund ihrer mangelnden Expertise zunächst einen gewissen Spielraum zuzugestehen. Gerade in *Milošević* jedoch nutzte der vorsitzende Richter häufig die Möglichkeit, Fragen des Angeklagten durch das Abschalten des Mikrofons zu beenden. In *Karadžić* sah sich die Kammer nach einer gewissen Anlaufzeit genötigt, dem Angeklagten strikte Zeitvorgaben für seine Zeugenbefragungen zu setzen, war jedoch bereit, bei angemessener Begründung diese Zeit entsprechend zu verlängern.

Vor allem in *Karadžić* wurde deutlich, welche Auswirkungen Verzögerungen im Verfahrensverlauf auf alle Beteiligten haben können.[1798] In diesem Verfahren mussten mindestens drei Zeugen, deren Aussagen für den Beginn der Beweisaufnahme angesetzt waren, zwei Mal vergeblich zum Sitz des ICTY reisen, bevor sie schließlich beim dritten Mal aussagen konnten.[1799] Die mentale Vorbereitung auf eine Aussage vor Gericht wirft vor allen Dingen bei Opferzeugen Fragen der Retraumatisierung auf, ein Effekt welcher durch die wiederholte Verzögerung der Aussage gegebenenfalls verstärkt werden kann.

D. *Die Rolle von Rechtsberatern für sich selbst verteidigende Angeklagte*

Die Rolle von Rechtsberatern für sich selbst verteidigende Angeklagte scheint sich insbesondere in späteren Verfahren insofern verändert zu haben, als rechtliche Berater häufiger auch im Gerichtssaal in Erscheinung treten und damit weniger ausschließlich im Hintergrund agieren. Während sich selbst verteidigende Angeklagte deutlich machten, dass sie ihre Berater lediglich als Unterstützung ansehen und selbst die Rolle des Verteidigers in eigener Sache einnehmen,[1800] ist doch zu beobachten, dass Berater eine wichtige

---

1798 Vgl. *Prosecutor v. Radovan Karadžić*, Case No. IT-95-5/18-T, Hearing, 31 May 2010, T.3065-3066.

1799 *Prosecutor v. Radovan Karadžić*, Case No. IT-95-5/18-T, Prosecution's Response to Application for Certification to Appeal and for Stay Pending Appeal of Decision on Commencement of Evidence, 01 March 2010, para.7-8.

1800 Vgl. *Prosecutor v. Zdravko Tolimir*, Case No. IT-05-88/2-PT, Accused's Submission Concerning the Appointment of Legal Advisors and the Need for the Court, Registry and the Prosecution to Communicate with the Accused in the Serbian

Rolle im Verfahrensverlauf spielen und zumindest bei manchen Angeklagten wesentlich mehr als lediglich Assistenten sind. Die konkrete Rolle der Berater scheint jedoch, wie einiges in Verfahren mit sich selbst verteidigenden Angeklagten, von den Vorstellungen des Angeklagten abzuhängen.

E. Die Entscheidung, sich selbst zu verteidigen und mögliche Motivationen

Über die möglichen Motive von Angeklagten, sich selbst verteidigen zu wollen, kann notwendigerweise nur spekuliert werden. Dennoch bietet die Analyse einiger Aussagen von Angeklagten und von deren Verhalten im Laufe der Verfahren gewisse Anhaltspunkte. Häufig wird die Absicht geäußert, die Chronik des relevanten Konflikts wie in Strafverfahren dargestellt zu „korrigieren" und damit zur Wahrheitsfindung beizutragen.[1801] Einige Angeklagte haben jedoch auch offen die politische Motivation ihrer Selbstverteidigung dargelegt.[1802] Grundsätzlich kann festgestellt werden, dass sich vor allem früher hochrangige Persönlichkeiten des Politik- und Armeeapparates für die Ausübung ihres Rechts auf Selbstverteidigung entscheiden.[1803]

Language, as the only Language he Understands, 03 March 2008 (filed: 05 March 2008); *Prosecutor v. Zdravko Tolimir*, Case No. IT-05-88/2-T, Request to the Trial Chamber, 01 March 2010 (filed: 03 March 2010).

1801 *Prosecutor v. Slobodan Milošević*, Case No. IT-99-37-AR73/IT-01-50-AR73/IT-01-51-AR73, Interlocutory Appeal Hearing, 30 January 2002, T.352/213/180; *Prosecutor v. Slobodan Milošević*, Case No. IT-02-54-AR73.7, Appeals Hearing, 21 October 2004, T.53; *Prosecutor v. Radovan Karadžić*, Case No. IT-95-5/18-PT, Status Conference, 17 September 2008, T.43; Status Conference, 23 July 2009, T.705; *Prosecutor v. Radovan Karadžić*, Case No. IT-95-5/18-T, Hearing, 03 November 2009, T.705; Hearing, 19 May 2010, T.2380; Hearing, 08 February 2011, T.11295.

1802 *Prosecutor v. Vojislav Šešelj*, Case No. IT-03-67-PT, Prosecution's Motion for Order Appointing Counsel to Assist Vojislav Šešelj With his Defence, 28 February 2003, para.8, fn.18; Decision on the Prosecution's Motion for Order Appointing Counsel to Assist Vojislav Šešelj with his Defence, 09 May 2003, para.22, fn.46.

1803 Vgl. Patricia M. Wald, *Tyrants in Trial. Keeping Order in the Courtroom* (New York: Open Society Justice Institute) 2009, p.10, 12, 37; Gideon Boas, Self-Representation Before the ICTY. A Case for Reform, 9 *Journal of International Criminal Justice* 53 (2011), at 54.

F. Zwischenbemerkung

Das zweite Kapitel der vorliegenden Arbeit verdeutlicht, welche Auswirkungen die Ausübung eines Rechts auf Selbstverteidigung auf den Verfahrensverlauf in internationalen Strafrechtstribunalen hat und haben kann. Die Selbstverteidigung der Angeklagten beeinflusst alle Bereiche des Verfahrens und um die Rechte des Angeklagten zu wahren, und dabei die Interessen anderer Verfahrensbeteiligter nicht außer Acht zu lassen, müssen signifikante Anpassungen vorgenommen werden. Die praktischen Folgen der Ausübung des Rechts auf Selbstverteidigung legen nahe, dass die gegenwärtig übliche Ausgestaltung für künftige Verfahren im Interesse aller kaum zu halten sein dürfte.

Drittes Kapitel. Beschränkungen der Ausübung des Rechts auf Selbstverteidigung

A. Faktoren, welche bei der Beschränkung von Selbstverteidigung in Betracht gezogen werden können

Im Laufe verschiedener Verfahren und nach Jahren praktischer Erfahrung mit sich selbst verteidigenden Angeklagten entwickelte die Rechtsprechung Kriterien, welche bei der potentiellen Beschränkung des Rechts auf Selbstverteidigung in Betracht gezogen werden.

I. Verfahrensbehinderndes Verhalten des Angeklagten

Das *Milošević*-Verfahren musste aufgrund des angegriffenen Gesundheitszustandes des Angeklagten wiederholt und zum Teil für längere Zeit unterbrochen werden. Die Kammer entschied sich letztlich zur Bestellung eines Verteidigers, um weiteren negativen Konsequenzen für die Gesundheit des Angeklagten, sowie zusätzlichen Verzögerungen des Verfahrens vorzubeugen.[1804] Die Kammer stützte die Entscheidung ausdrücklich auf den Gesundheitszustand des Angeklagten und dessen Einfluss auf den Verfahrensablauf, nicht jedoch auf etwaige bewusste Verfahrensbehinderung von Seiten des Angeklagten. Die Behinderung des Verfahrens aufgrund eines Zustands,

---

1804 *Prosecutor v. Slobodan Milošević*, Case No. IT-02-54-T, Reasons for Decision on Assignment of Defence Counsel, 22 September 2004.

welcher nicht zwangsläufig durch den Angeklagten beeinflusst werden konnte, wurde somit als ausreichend angesehen, das vormals als fundamental eingestufte Recht auf Selbstverteidigung signifikant einzuschränken. Von Bedeutung für folgende Verfahren war insbesondere der Standard, welcher von der Kammer in der Berufungsinstanz festgelegt wurde: das Recht auf Selbstverteidigung könnte beschränkt werden, falls die Ausübung des Rechts auf Selbstverteidigung den Verfahrensverlauf substantiell und anhaltend beeinträchtigt.[1805]

Im Gegensatz steht der scheinbar eindeutige Fall gewollter und bewusster Verfahrensbehinderung, welche ausschließlich vom Willen und der Einstellung des Angeklagten abhängt. Allerdings bestehen auch in diesem Zusammenhang divergierende Standards: der Angeklagte in *Šešelj* verteidigte sich nach acht Jahren in Haft, drei zusätzlichen unabhängigen Verfahren im Zusammenhang des Vorwurfs der Veröffentlichung vertraulicher Informationen,[1806] insgesamt offensichtlich gewollter und bewusster Verfahrensbehinderung, sowie zahlreichen Anträgen auf Bestellung eines Verteidigers durch die Anklage nicht nur nach wie vor selbst, sondern hatte auch erfolgreich gegen die Beistellung von „standby counsel“[1807] mit einem Hungerstreik protestiert.[1808] Dahingegen wurde in *Karadžić* bereits ein Verteidiger berufen, als der Angeklagte sich „lediglich“ weigerte, dem Beginn des Verfahrens

1805 *Prosecutor v. Slobodan Milošević*, Case No. IT-02-54-AR73.7, Decision on Interlocutory Appeal of the Trial Chamber's Decision on the Assignment of Defence Counsel, 01 November 2004.

1806 *Prosecutor v. Vojislav Šešelj*, Case No. IT-03-67-R77.2, Public Edited Version of "Judgement on Allegations of Contempt" Issued on 24 July 2009, 24 July 2009; bestätigt in der Berufungsinstanz: *Prosecutor v. Vojislav Šešelj*, Case No. IT-03-67-R77.2-A, Judgement, 19 May 2010. *Prosecutor v. Vojislav Šešelj*, Case No. IT-03-67-R77.3, Public Redacted Version of Second Decision on Prosecution's Motion Under Rule 77 Concerning Further Breaches of Protective Measures (Three Books) Issued on 03 February 2010, 04 February 2010; *Prosecutor v. Vojislav Šešelj*, Case No. IT-03-67-R77.4, Public Edited Version of "Decision of Failure to Remove Confidential Information From Public Website and Order in Lieu of Indictment" Issued on 9 May 2011, 24 May 2011.

1807 In Ermangelung einer adäquaten deutschen Übersetzung wird im folgenden der englische Ausdruck des "standby counsel" verwendet.

1808 Vgl. *Prosecutor v. Vojislav Šešelj*, Case No. IT-03-67-AR73.3, Decision on Appeal Against the Trial Chamber's Decision on Assignment of Counsel, 20 October 2006, und nur kurze Zeit später: *Prosecutor v. Vojislav Šešelj*, Case No. IT-03-67-AR73.4, Decision on Appeal Against the Trial Chamber's Decision (No. 2) on Assignment of Counsel, 08 December 2006.

beizuwohnen mit der Begründung, für die Beweisaufnahme nicht ausreichend vorbereitet zu sein.[1809]

II. Ausdrückliche Verwarnung des Angeklagten

Bevor das Recht auf Selbstverteidigung beschränkt oder entzogen wird, ist eine ausdrückliche Warnung notwendig: als in *Šešelj* die Kammer im Hauptverfahren zum ersten Mal einen Verteidiger bestellte, wurde diese Entscheidung in der Rechtmittelinstanz aufgehoben, da nach Ansicht der Rechtsmittelkammer keine entsprechende Warnung gegeben wurde. Die Notwendigkeit einer Warnung wurde in Anlehnung an Regel 80 der ICTY RPE entwickelt, welche vor dem Entfernen eines Angeklagten aus dem Gerichtssaal ebenfalls eine explizite Warnung vorsieht.[1810]

III. „Clean slate"-Prinzip

Ebenfalls in *Šešelj* kam erstmals das sogenannte „clean slate"-Prinzip zum Tragen: kurze Zeit nach der Entscheidung der Kammer in der Rechtsmittelinstanz, welche die Entscheidung der Kammer im Hauptverfahren aufhob, bestellte letztere erneut einen Verteidiger. Der Angeklagte begann daraufhin einen Hungerstreik und stellte die Einnahme notwendiger Medikamente ein.[1811] Die Rechtsmittelkammer hob die Entscheidung erneut auf, diesmal mit der Begründung, dass ein „standby counsel" direkt in Folge der ersten Entscheidung gegen die Bestellung eines Verteidigers bestellt worden war, ohne erneutes Fehlverhalten des Angeklagten ausdrücklich festzustellen.[1812]

1809 *Prosecutor v. Radovan Karadžić*, Case No. IT-95-5/18-T, Decision on Appointment of Counsel and Order on Further Trial Proceedings, 05 November 2009, para.21.

1810 *Prosecutor v. Vojislav Šešelj*, Case No. IT-03-67-AR73.3, Decision on Appeal Against the Trial Chamber's Decision on Assignment of Counsel, 20 October 2006.

1811 Vgl. *Prosecutor v. Vojislav Šešelj*, Case No. IT-03-67-T, Urgent Order to the Dutch Authorities Regarding Health and Welfare of the Accused, 06 December 2006.

1812 *Prosecutor v. Vojislav Šešelj*, Case No. IT-03-67-AR73.4, Decision on Appeal Against the Trial Chamber's Decision (No. 2) on Assignment of Counsel, 08 December 2006.

Beide Entscheidungen der Kammer in der Berufungsinstanz in *Šešelj* gaben Anlass zu ausführlichen Diskussionen und insbesondere zu Kritik.[1813]

IV. Verhältnismäßigkeit und das Recht, zur Sache gehört zu werden

Die Verhältnismäßigkeit einer Beschränkung stand in *Milošević* zur Diskussion. Als die Kammer aufgrund des Einflusses der Gesundheit des Angeklagten auf das Verfahren einen Verteidiger zur Seite stellte, gab sie diesem ein weitgehendes Mandat. Die Kammer in der Rechtsmittelinstanz bewertete das Ausmaß dieses Mandats jedoch als zu weitreichend verglichen mit dem Status des Rechts auf Selbstverteidigung und der Art der Verfahrensbehinderung.[1814] Dementsprechend wurde die Rolle des Verteidigers signifikant eingeschränkt, und das Verfahren mit dem sich selbst verteidigenden Angeklagten zum größten Teil wie zuvor weitergeführt.

Das Recht eines Angeklagten, zur Sache gehört zu werden, gab bislang wenig Anlass zur Diskussion,[1815] wohl da bislang in der Regel allen potentiell von Einschränkungen des Rechts auf Selbstverteidigung betroffenen Angeklagten ausreichend Gelegenheit gegeben wurde, sich zur Sache zu äußern.

V. Interessenabwägung

Wie bereits zuvor angedeutet, ist im Rahmen einer eventuellen Beschränkung des Rechts auf Selbstverteidigung eine Abwägung unterschiedlicher Interessen durchzuführen. Zum einen ist von Belang, dass dieses Recht Teil eines

---

1813 Z.B. Gideon Boas, *The Milošević Trial: Lessons for the Conduct of Complex International Criminal Proceedings* (Cambridge: Cambridge University Press) 2007, at 235-236; Göran Sluiter, Compromising the Authority of International Criminal Justice. How Vojislav Šešelj Runs his Trial, 5 *Journal of International Criminal Justice* 529 (2007), at 533-536; Gideon Boas, Self-Representation Before the ICTY. A Case for Reform, 9 *Journal of International Criminal Justice* 53 (2011), at 64.

1814 *Prosecutor v. Slobodan Milošević*, Case No. IT-02-54-AR73.7, Decision on Interlocutory Appeal of the Trial Chamber's Decision on the Assignment of Defence Counsel, 01 November 2004.

1815 Vgl. z.B. *Prosecutor v. Vojislav Šešelj*, Case No. IT-03-67-AR73.3, Decision on Appeal Against the Trial Chamber's Decision on Assignment of Counsel, 20 October 2006, para.52 fn.136.

allumfassenderen Rechts auf ein faires Verfahren darstellt. Darüber hinaus können auch die Interessen der Anklage auf ein faires Verfahren eine Rolle spielen, sowie die Interessen von Opfergemeinschaften und Zeugen, und schließlich das Interesse der internationalen Gemeinschaft an einem fairen und raschen Abschluss des Verfahrens, welches zur Wahrheitsfindung und idealerweise auch Konfliktlösung beiträgt.

B. Art und Ausgestaltung von Beschränkungen

I. Bestellung eines Verteidigers durch das Gericht

Obgleich nicht direkt auf Verfahren mit sich selbst verteidigenden Angeklagten anwendbar, kam die „ICTY Directive on the Assignment of Defence Counsel" („ICTY Richtlinie")[1816] in mindestens einem Verfahren zum Tragen und wird deshalb in der vorliegenden Arbeit erläutert. Diese Richtlinie legt das Verfahren zur Bestellung von Pflichtverteidigern fest, beschäftigt sich jedoch nicht mit der Auswahl von Verteidigern, welche aufgrund einer Entscheidung einer Kammer einem sich selbst verteidigenden Angeklagten beigestellt werden.

In *Karadžić* zeigte sich der Angeklagte mit der Wahl des von Seiten des Gerichts ausgewählten beigestellten Verteidigers unzufrieden, und stellte einen Antrag auf Aufhebung der Bestellung dieses Verteidigers. Er vertrat die Ansicht, ein Recht auf Wahl des beigeordneten Verteidigers zu genießen, sich unter anderem auf eine Entscheidung der Rechtsmittelkammer in *Šešelj* und Vorschriften der ICTY Richtlinie berufend.[1817] Die einzelnen Argumente der Verfahrensbeteiligten werden genauer betrachtet, da zum Teil wenig haltbare Positionen vertreten wurden und dieses Verfahren den bislang einzigen Anhaltspunkt bietet, wie derartige Streitsachen in künftigen Verfahren behandelt werden könnten.

1816 Directive on the Assignment of Defence Counsel (Directive No. 1/94), as amended 29 June 2006 (IT/73/Rev. 11).

1817 *Prosecutor v. Radovan Karadžić*, Case No. IT-95-5/18-T, Motion to Vacate Appointment of Richard Harvey, 04 December 2009.

II. Die Rolle des gerichtlich bestellten Verteidigers

Mögliche Rollen für gerichtlich bestellte Verteidiger reichen von *amicus curiae* über „standby counsel" bis zu Verteidigern, welche die Präsentation der Verteidigung des Angeklagten vollständig übernehmen. Mandate und Bezeichnungen wurden bislang jedoch nicht einheitlich gehandhabt, weshalb Beispiele aus der Praxis diskutiert werden.[1818]

Slobodan Milošević wurden bereits zu Beginn des Verfahrens *amici curiae* zur Seite gestellt, welche nach Vorstellung der Kammer zum fairen Ablauf des Verfahrens mit besonderer Berücksichtigung der Rechte des Angeklagten beitragen sollten.[1819] Die Rolle der *amici* änderte sich, als die Kammer beschloss, dem Angeklagten aufgrund seiner angegriffenen Gesundheit und der damit verbundenen Verfahrensbehinderung Verteidiger zur Seite zu stellen.[1820] Der von den Richtern zugestandene weite Spielraum wurde jedoch von der Rechtsmittelkammer signifikant eingeschränkt und das Mandat der Verteidiger dem eines „standby counsel" angeglichen.[1821]

Momčilo Krajišnik wurde im Berufungsverfahren ebenfalls *amicus curiae* zur Seite gestellt.[1822] Zusätzlich wurde dem Rechtsberater des Angeklagten

---

1818 Vgl. z.B. *Prosecutor v. Slobodan Milošević*, Case No. IT-02-54-PT, Order Inviting Designation of *Amicus Curiae*, 30 August 2001; *Prosecutor v. Vojislav Šešelj*, Case No. IT-03-67-PT, Decision on Prosecution's Motion for Order Appointing Counsel to Assist Vojislav Šešelj with his Defence, 09 May 2003; *Prosecutor v. Vojislav Šešelj*, Case No. IT-03-67-AR73.4, Decision on Appeal Against the Trial Chamber's Decision (No. 2) on Assignment of Counsel, 08 December 2006; *Prosecutor v. Momčilo Krajišnik*, Case No. IT-00-39-A, Decision on Momčilo Krajišnik's Request to Self-Represent, on Counsel's Motion in Relation to Appointment of *Amicus Curiae*, and on the Prosecution Motion of 16 February 2007, 11 May 2007; *Prosecutor v. Radovan Karadžić*, Case No. IT-95-5/18-T, Decision on Appointment of Counsel and Order on Further Trial Proceedings, 05 November 2009.

1819 *Prosecutor v. Slobodan Milošević*, Case No. IT-99-37-PT, Status Conference, 30 August 2001, T.7; Order Inviting designation of *Amicus Curiae*, 30 August 2001; Order Concerning *Amici Curiae*, 11 January 2002.

1820 *Prosecutor v. Slobodan Milošević*, Case No. IT-02-54-T, Oral Ruling, 02 September 2004, T.32357-32359; Reasons for Decision on Assignment of Defence Counsel, 22 September 2004.

1821 *Prosecutor v. Slobodan Milošević*, Case No. IT-02-54-AR73.7, Decision on Interlocutory Appeal of the Trial Chamber's Decision on the Assignment of Defence Counsel, 01 November 2004.

1822 *Prosecutor v. Momčilo Krajišnik*, Case No. IT-00-39-A, Decision on Momčilo Krajišnik's Request to Self-Represent, on Counsel's Motion in Relation to Appoint-

jedoch die Möglichkeit gegeben, sich zu einem bestimmten Punkt der Berufung einzubringen.[1823]

Bezeichnungen und Ausgestaltung der Rolle von beigeordneten Verteidigern sind wenig einheitlich. Ein Vergleich zum Beispiel der Mandate der „standby counsel" in den einzelnen Verfahren verdeutlicht, dass die Bezeichnung wenig einheitlich verwendet wird. Insgesamt sind sowohl Beiordnung von Verteidigern und ihre Mandate größtenteils von Fall zu Fall unterschiedlich. Dies gibt zum einen zwar die notwendige Flexibilität, um auf unterschiedliche Situationen und Konstellation reagieren zu können, zum anderen bringt dies auch eine gewisse Unsicherheit ob der Rolle beigeordneter Verteidiger mit sich.

III. Mögliche ethische Implikationen für gerichtlich bestellte Verteidiger

Im Rahmen der gerichtlichen Beiordnung von Verteidigern gegen den Willen eines sich selbst verteidigenden Angeklagten werden auch die potentiellen ethischen Komplikationen für die beigeordneten Verteidiger diskutiert.[1824] Es besteht die Gefahr, dass die Verteidiger mit der Kooperationsverweigerung eines Angeklagten umgehen müssen, welcher keine Anweisungen für die Gestaltung der Verteidigung geben und, je nach Mandat der Verteidiger, gegebenenfalls durch eigene Aktionen die Arbeit der Verteidiger sabotieren könnte.[1825] Jedoch wurde von Gerichtsseite verhältnismäßig einheitlich festgestellt, dass gerichtlich bestellte Verteidiger einen gewissen objektiven Standard der Verteidigung auch ohne Anweisungen des Angeklagten aufrecht erhalten können und darüber hinaus in erster Linie dem Gericht und der internationalen Strafjustiz verpflichtet sind.[1826]

---

ment of *Amicus Curiae*, and on the Prosecution Motion of 16 February 2007, 11 May 2007.

1823 *Prosecutor v. Momčilo Krajišnik*, Case No. IT-00-39-A, Decision on Momčilo Krajišnik's Motion to Reschedule Status Conference and Permit Alan Dershowitz to Appear, 28 February 2008.

1824 Vgl. *Prosecutor v. Slobodan Milošević*, Case No. IT-02-54-T, Decision on Assigned Counsel's Motion for Withdrawal, 07 December 2004, para.22.

1825 Vgl. Göran Sluiter, 'Fairness and the Interests of Justice'. Illusive Concepts in the Milošević Case, 3 *Journal of International Criminal Justice* 9 (2005), at 17.

1826 Vgl. *Prosecutor v. Vidoje Blagojević*, Case No. IT-02-60-AR73.4, Public and Redacted Reasons for Decision on Appeal by Vidoje Blagojević to Replace his Defence Team, 07 November 2003, para.54; *Prosecutor v. Slobodan Milošević*,

Am ICTR beschäftigten Kammern sich mit der Frage, welches Vertrauensverhältnis zwischen Verteidigern und Angeklagten als angemessen gesehen werden kann, um eine angemessene Verteidigung noch zu ermöglichen.[1827]

C. Zwischenergebnis

Das dritte Kapitel der vorliegenden Dissertation versucht anhand praktischer Beispiele zu verdeutlichen, welche Auswirkungen die Ausübung des Rechts auf Selbstverteidigung auf den Verfahrensverlauf vor internationalen Strafrechtstribunalen haben kann. Die Untersuchung zeigt auch, dass die Behandlung etwaiger Probleme von Fall zu Fall unterschiedlich ist und damit zwar Flexibilität, jedoch auch Divergenzen erzeugt.

Viertes Kapitel. Vorschläge für zukünftige Interpretationen eines Rechts auf persönliche Verteidigung im Strafverfahren

A. Fazit

Die vorliegende Dissertation legt dar, dass die Ausübung eines Rechts auf Selbstverteidigung im aktuell existierenden Ausmaß in künftigen Verfahren an internationalen Strafrechtstribunalen nicht mehr durchführbar ist. Aufgrund des überwiegend negativen Einflusses auf den Verfahrensverlauf und die Rechte des Angeklagten ist die Beibehaltung der bisherigen Gestaltung nicht mehr zu rechtfertigen.

Case No. IT-02-54-T, Decision on Assigned Counsel's Motion for Withdrawal, 07 December 2004, para.23; *Prosecutor v. Vojislav Šešelj*, Case No. IT-03-67-AR73.3, Decision on Appeal Against the Trial Chamber's Decision on Assignment of Counsel, 20 October 2006.

1827 *Procureur c. Jean-Paul Akayesu*, Affaire No. ICTR-96-4-T, Décision Faisant Suite à une Demande de l'Accusé de Changement d'Avocat Commis d'Office, 20 novembre 1996 ; *Prosecutor v. Théoneste Bagosora*, Case No. ICTR-96-7-T, Decision on the Request by the Accused for Change of Assigned Counsel, 26 June 1997; *Prosecutor v. Gérard Ntakirutimana*, Case No. ICTR-96-10-T & ICTR-96-17-T, Decision on the Motions of the Accused for Replacement of Assigned Counsel / Corr., 11 June 1997; *Prosecutor v. Jean-Bosco Barayagwiza*, Case No. ICTR-97-19-T, Decision on Defence Counsel Motion to Withdraw, 02 November 2000; *Prosecutor v. Nyiramasuhuko & Ntahobali*, Case No. ICTR-97-21-T, Decision on Ntahobali's Motion for Withdrawal of Counsel, 22 June 2001.

B. *Möglichkeiten für eine aktive Beteiligung von Angeklagten im Strafverfahren*

In der vorliegenden Dissertation wird argumentiert, dass ein Recht auf eine persönliche Verteidigung an die Stelle des bislang praktizierten Rechts auf Selbstverteidigung treten sollte. In diesem Rahmen kann Angeklagten die Möglichkeit zur aktiven Beteiligung gegeben werden und können gleichzeitig die Interessen aller Beteiligten – einschließlich des Angeklagten – gewahrt werden. Dadurch bleibt der Angeklagte Subjekt des Verfahrens während zur gleichen Zeit auch anderen Interessen der internationalen Strafjustiz Rechnung getragen werden kann.

Bibliography

A. Doctrine

Alexis, Althea: The Convergence of the Common Law and Inquisitorial Systems in International Criminal Law, in: Emmanuel Decaux *et al.* (eds), *From Human Rights to International Criminal Law: Studies in Honour of an African Jurist, the Late Judge Lairy Kama* (Leiden / Boston: Martinus Nijhoff Publishers) 2007, p.461-481

Ambach, Philipp: Selbstvertretung im internationalen Strafprozess – Grundlagen, Kritik und ein Lösungsansatz für die prozessuale Handhabung in der Zukunft, 6 *Zeitschrift für Internationale Strafrechtsdogmatik* 286 (2009)

Ambos, Kai: International criminal procedure: "adversarial", "inquisitorial" or mixed?, 3 *International Criminal Law Review* 1 (2003)

Bantekas, Ilias: Reflections on Some Sources and Methods of International Criminal and Humanitarian Law, 6 *International Criminal Law Review* 121 (2006)

Bartholomeusz, Lance: The *Amicus Curiae* Before International Courts and Tribunals, 5 *Non-State Actors and International Law* 209 (2005)

Bassiouni, M. Cherif: Human Rights in the Context of Criminal Justice: Identifying International Procedural Protections and Equivalent Protections in National Constitutions, 3 *Duke Journal of Comparative and International Law* 235 (1993)

Bassiouni, M. Cherif / Manikas, Peter: *The Law of the International Criminal Tribunal for the Former Yugoslavia* (New York: Transnational Publishers, Inc.) 1996

Bassiouni, M. Cherif: International Recognition of Victims' Rights, 6 *Human Rights Law Review* 203 (2006)

Belgrade Centre for Human Rights: *Human Rights in Serbia and Montenegro 2005. Legal Provisions, Practice and Awareness in the State Union of Serbia and Montenegro Compared to International Human Rights Standards* (Belgrade: The Belgrade Centre for Human Rights) 2006

Belgrade Centre for Human Rights: *Human Rights in Serbia 2006. Legal Provisions and Practice Compared to International Human Rights Standards* (Belgrade: The Belgrade Centre for Human Rights) 2007

Bensouda, Fatou: The ICC Statute – An Insider's Perspective on a Sui Generis System for Global Justice, 36 *North Carolina Journal of International Law and Commercial Regulation* 277 (2011)

Beresford, Stuart / Lahiouel, Hafida: The Right to be Defended in Person or Through Legal Assistance and the International Criminal Court, 13 *Leiden Journal of International Law* 949 (2000)

Boas, Gideon: The Right to Self-Representation in International and Domestic Criminal Law – Limitations and Qualifications on that Right, in: Hirad Abtahi / Gideon Boas (eds), *The Dynamics of International Criminal Justice. Essays in Honour of Sir Richard May* (Leiden / Boston: Martinus Nijhoff Publishers) 2006, p.39-93

Boas, Gideon: *The Milošević Trial: Lessons for the Conduct of Complex International Criminal Proceedings* (Cambridge: Cambridge University Press) 2007

Boas, Gideon: Moving on From Milošević, 75 *European Lawyer* 54 (2008)

Boas, Gideon: Self-Representation Before the ICTY. A Case for Reform, 9 *Journal of International Criminal Justice* 53 (2011)

Bohlander, Michael: The Defence, in: Gideon Boas / William A. Schabas (eds), *International Criminal Law Developments in the Case Law of the ICTY* (Leiden / Bosten: Martinus Nijhoff Publishers) 2003, p.35-74

Bohlander, Michael: 'A Fool for a Client' – Remarks on the Freedom of Choice and Assignment of Counsel at the International Criminal Tribunal for the Former Yugoslavia, 16 *Criminal Law Forum* 159 (2005)

Bonomy, Iain: The Reality of Conducting a War Crimes Trial, 5 *Journal of International Criminal Justice* 348 (2007)

Camier, Nicole L.: Controlling the Wrath of Self-Representation: The ICTY's Crucial Trial of Radovan Karadzic, 44 *Valparaiso University Law Review* 957 (2010)

Carter, Shawn A.: The Pro Se Dilemma: Can Too Many Rights Make a Wrong?, 62 *Louisiana Law Review* 1299 (2002)

Cassese, Antonio: Reflections on International Criminal Justice, 6(1) *The Modern Law Review* 1 (1998)

Cassese, Antonio: The Influence of the European Court of Human Rights on International Criminal Tribunals – Some Methodological Remarks, in: Morten Bergsmo (ed.), *Human Rights and Criminal Justice for the Downtrodden. Essays in Honour of Asbjørn Eide* (Leiden / Boston: Martinus Nijhoff Publishers) 2003, p.19-52

Chiavario, Mario: Some Considerations on Faces of Justice by a 'Non-Specialist', 6 *Journal of International Criminal Justice* 69 (2008)

Cerruti, Eugene: Self-Representation in the International Arena: Removing a False Right to Spectacle, 40 *Georgetown Journal of International Law* 919 (2009)

Combs, Nancy Amoury: Legitimizing International Criminal Justice: The Importance of Process Control, 33 *Michigan Journal of International Law* 321 (2012)

Croquet, Nicolas A.J.: The International Criminal Court and the Treatment of Defence Rights: A Mirror of the European Court of Human Rights' Jurisprudence, 11 *Human Rights Law Review* 91 (2011)

Croquet, Nicolas A.J.: The Right to Self-Representation under the European Convention on Human Rights: What Role for the Limitation Analysis?, 3 *European Human Rights Law Review* 292 (2012)

Damaška, Mirjan: *The Faces of Justice and State Authority. A Comparative Approach to the Legal Process* (New Haven / London: Yale University Press) 1986

Damaška, Mirjan: Assignment of Counsel and Perceptions of Fairness, 3 *Journal of International Criminal Justice* 3 (2005)

Damaška, Mirjan: What is the Point of International Criminal Justice?, 83 *Chicago-Kent Law Review* 329 (2008)

Damaška, Mirjan: The Competing Visions of Fairness: The Basic Choice for International Criminal Tribunals, 36 *North Carolina Journal of International Law and Commercial Regulation* 365 (2011)

Damaška, Mirjan: Reflections on Fairness in International Criminal Justice, 10 *Journal of International Criminal Justice* 611 (2012)

Danieli, Yael: Massive Trauma and the Healing Role of Restorative Justice, in: Carla Ferstman / Mariana Goetz / Alan Stephens (eds), *Reparations for Victims of Genocide, War Crimes and Crimes Against Humanity. Systems in Place and Systems in the Making* (Leiden / Boston: Martinus Nijhoff Publishers) 2009, p.41-77

Dannenbaum, Tom: The Milošević Trial: Lessons for the Conduct of International Criminal Proceedings (Review of Gideon Boas), 33 *Yale Journal of International Law* 513 (2008)

Decker, John F.: The Sixth Amendment Right to Shoot Oneself in the Foot: An Assessment of the Guarantee of Self-Representation Twenty Years After Faretta, 6 *Seton Hall Constitutional Law Journal* 483 (1996)

Delmas-Marty, Mireille: The Contribution of Comparative Law to a Pluralist Conception of International Criminal Law, 1 *Journal of International Criminal Justice* 13 (2003)

Dembour, Marie-Bénédicte / Haslam, Emily: Silencing Hearing? Victim-Witnesses at War-Crimes Trials, 15 *European Journal of International Law* 151 (2004)

Dworkin, Gerald: Entry on Paternalism in: Stanford Encyclopaedia of Philosophy, available at http://plato.stanford.edu/entries/paternalism/ (last accessed 17 November 2012).

Ellis, Mark S.: The Evolution of Defense Counsel Appearing Before the International Criminal Tribunal for the Former Yugoslavia, 37 *New England Law Review* 949 (2003)

Ellis, Mark: Self-Representation is a Privilege, Not a Right, 23 (42) *Lawyer* 6 (2009)

Emmerson, Ben / Ashworth, Andrew: *Human Rights and Criminal Justice* (London: Sweet & Maxwell) 1st edition 2001

Findlay, Mark / McLean, Clare: Emerging International Criminal Justice, 18(3) *Current Issues in Criminal Justice* 457 (2007)

Finegan, Sharon: Pro Se Criminal Trials and the Merging of Inquisitorial and Adversarial Systems of Justice, 58 *Catholic University Law Review* 445 (2009)

Fletcher, Laurel E. / Weinstein, Harvey M.: Violence and Social Repair: Rethinking the Contribution of Justice to Reconciliation, 24 *Human Rights Quarterly* 573 (2002)

Foster, Jacob: The Use of Foreign Law in Constitutional Interpretation: Lessons from South Africa, 45 *University of San Francisco Law Review* 79 (2010)

Friman, Håkan: Chapter IV. Rights of Persons Suspected or Accused of a Crime, in: Roy S. Lee (ed.), *The International Criminal Court. The Making of the Rome Statute. Issues, Negotiations, Results* (The Hague / London / Boston: Kluwer Law International) 2002, p.247-262

Gaede, Karsten: *Fairness als Teilhabe – Das Recht auf konkrete und wirksame Teilhabe durch Verteidigung gemäß Art. 6 EMRK* (Berlin: Duncker & Humblot GmbH) 2007

Goldschmidt, Jona: Judicial Assistance to Self-Represented Litigants: Lessons from the Canadian Experience, 17 *Michigan State Journal of International Law* 601 (2008-2009)

Grande, Elisabetta: Italian Criminal Justice: Borrowing and Resistance, 48 *American Journal of Comparative Law* 227 (2000)

Greenawalt, Alexander K.A.: The Pluralism of International Criminal Law, 86 *Indiana Law Journal* 1063 (2011)

Hashimoto, Erica J.: Defending the Right of Self-Representation: An Empirical Look at the Pro Se Felony Defendant, 85 *North Carolina Law Review* 423 (2007)

Hashimoto, Erica J.: Resurrecting Autonomy: The Criminal Defendant's Right to Control the Case, 90 *Boston University Law Review* 1147 (2010)

Heller, Kevin Jon: A Poisoned Chalice: The Substantive and Procedural Defects of the Iraqi High Tribunal, 39 *Case Western Reserve Journal of International Law* 261 (2007)

Hotis, Constantinos: A 'Fair and Expeditious' Trial: A Reappraisal of Slobodan Milosevic's Right to Self-Representation Before the International Criminal Tribunal for the Former Yugoslavia, 6 *Chicago Journal of International Law* 775 (2006)

Howard, Joshua L.: Hybrid Representation and Standby Counsel: Let's Clear the Air for the Attorneys of South Carolina, 52 *South Carolina Law Review* 851 (2001)

Human Rights Watch, *The Balkans: Weighing the Evidence. Lessons from the Milosevic Trial*, Volume 18, No.10(D), December 2006

Jones, Rachel K.: Untangling the Right to Self-Representation in the International Criminal Tribunal for the Former Yugoslavia, 43 *Georgia Law Review* 1285 (2009)

Jorda, Claude / de Hemptienne, Jérôme: Un Nouveau Statut pour l'Accusé dans la Procédure du Tribunal Pénal International pour l'ex-Yougoslavie, in: Richard May et al. (eds), *Essays on ICTY Procedure and Evidence. In Honour of Gabrielle Kirk McDonald* (The Hague: Kluwer Law International) 2001, p.215-229

Jørgensen, Nina H.B.: The Right of the Accused to Self-Representation Before International Criminal Tribunals, 98 *The American Journal of International Law* 711 (2004)

Jørgensen, Nina H.B.: The Problem of Self-Representation at International Criminal Tribunals. Striking a Balance Between Fairness and Effectiveness, 4 *Journal of International Criminal Justice* 64 (2006)

Jouet, Mugambi: Reconciling the Conflicting Rights of Victims and Defendants at the International Criminal Court, 26 *Saint Louis University Public Law Review* 249 (2007)

Kay, Steven / Higgins, Gillian: The Right of Self-Representation – The Lawyers in the Eye of the Storm, International Criminal Law Bureau 2010, available at http://www.internationallawbureau.com/blog/wp-content/uploads/2010/08/Lawyers-Self-Representation-Kay-Higgins.pdf (last accessed 17 November 2012)

Kim, Kensie: Mixed Systems in Legal Origin Analysis, 83 *Southern California Law Review* 693 (2010)

Koskenniemi, Martti: Between Impunity and Show Trials, 6 *Max Planck Yearbook of United Nations Law* 1 (2002)

Kreß, Claus: Witnesses in Proceedings Before the International Criminal Court: An Analysis in the Light of Comparative Criminal Procedure, in: Horst Fischer / Claus Kreß / Sascha Rolf Lüder (eds), *International and National Prosecution of Crimes Under International Law. Current Developments* (Berlin: Berlin Verlag Arno Spitz GmbH) 2001, p.309-383

Kreß, Claus: The Procedural Law of the International Criminal Court in Outline: Anatomy of a Unique Compromise, 1 *Journal of International Criminal Justice* 603 (2003)

Lahiouel, Hafida: The Right of the Accused to an Expeditious Trial, in: Richard May *et al.* (eds), *Essays on ICTY Procedure and Evidence. In Honour of Gabrielle Kirk McDonald* (The Hague: Kluwer Law International) 2001, p.197-213

Lewis, Mark: The Trial of Radovan Karadzic: The Accused Takes up his Own Defense, 01 November 2012, available at http://world.time.com/2012/11/01/the-trial-of-radovan-karadzic-the-accused-takes-up-his-own-defense/#ixzz2B3FabTJV (last accessed 02 November 2012)

Linton, Suzannah: Putting Cambodia's Extraordinary Chambers Into Context, 11 *Singapore Yearbook of International Law*195 (2007)

Livingstone Allen, Sarah: Faretta: Self-Representation, or Legal-Misrepresentation?, 90 *Iowa Law Review* 1553 (2005)

Lombardi, Gregory P.: Legitimacy and the Expanding Power of the ICTY, 37 *New England Law Review* 887 (2003)

Maitland, Anna: Stalling Tactics or Due Process? The Karadzic Trial Resumes, 17 (3) *Human Rights Brief* 53 (2010)

Mancuso, Salvatore: The New African Law: Beyond the Difference Between Common Law and Civil Law, 14 *Annual Survey of International and Comparative Law* 39 (2008)

Markovic, Milan: In the Interests of Justice?: A Critique of the ICTY Trial Court's Decision to Assign Counsel to Slobodan Milošević, 18 *Georgetown Journal of Legal Ethics* 947 (2005)

McAuliffe deGuzman, Margaret: Article 21, in: Otto Triffterer (ed.), *Commentary on the Rome Statute of the International Criminal Court. Observers' Notes, Article by Article* (Munich: Verlag C.H. Beck) 2nd edition 2008, p.701-712

McGonigle, Brianne N.: Bridging the Divides in International Criminal Proceedings: An Examination into the Victim Participation Endeavor of the International Criminal Court, 21 *Florida Journal of International Law* 93 (2009)

Mégret, Frédéric: Beyond "Fairness": Understanding the Determinants of International Criminal Procedure, 14 *UCLA Journal of International Law and Foreign Affairs* 37 (2009)

Mettraux, G. / Cengic, A.: The Role of a Defence Office – Some Lessons from Recent and not so Recent War Crimes Precedents, in: Michael Bohlander (ed.), *International Criminal Justice. A Critical Analysis of Institutions and Procedures* (London: Cameron May Ltd) 2007, p.391-428

Mettraux, Guénaël: Foreword, 8 *Journal of International Criminal Justice* 75 (2010)

Milanović, Marko: The Arrest and Impending Trial of Radovan Karadžić, 58 *International and Comparative Law Quarterly* 212 (2009)

Mundis, Daryl A.: From 'Common Law' Towards 'Civil Law': The Evolution of the ICTY Rules of Procedure and Evidence, 14 *Leiden Journal of International Law* 367 (2001)

Nikas, Luke: Rethinking the Use of Foreign Law and Public Consensus: The U.S. Supreme Court's Inconsistent Methods for Defining Constitutional Rights, 13 *Lewis & Clark Law Review* 1007 (2009)

Ntanda Nsereko, Daniel D.: Ethical Obligations of Counsel in Criminal Proceedings: Representing an Unwilling Client, 12 *Criminal Law Forum* 487 (2001)

Ohlin, Jens David: A Meta-Theory of International Criminal Procedure: Vindicating the Rule of Law, 14 *UCLA Journal of International Law and Foreign Affairs* 77 (2009)

Pellet, Alain: Chapter 25. Applicable Law, in: Antonio Cassese / Paola Gaeta / John R.W.D. Jones (eds), *The Rome Statute of the International Criminal Court: A Commentary (Volume II)* (Oxford: Oxford University Press) 2002, p.1051-1084

Petersdorf, Boris: *Eigenverteidigung und aufgedrängte Pflichtverteidigung im formellen Völkerstrafrecht* (Baden-Baden: Nomos Verlagsgesellschaft) 2010

Petit, Robert / Ahmed, Anees: A Review of the Jurisprudence of the Khmer Rouge Tribunal, 8 *Northwestern University Journal of International Human Rights* 165 (2010)

Pizzi, William T. / Marafioti, Luca: The New Italian Code of Criminal Procedure: The Difficulties of Building an Adversarial System on a Civil Law Foundation, 17 *Yale Journal of International Law* 1 (1992)

Post, Jerrold M. / Panis, Lara K.: Tyranny on Trial: Personality and Courtroom Conduct of Defendants Slobodan Milošević and Saddam Hussein, 38 *Cornell Journal of International Law* 823 (2005)

Richards, Jaime Kristine: Shots, Shoes, and Self-Representation: Indiana v. Edwards and the New Limitation on the Sixth Amendment Right of Self-Representation, 60 *Mercer Law Review* 1509 (2009)

Robinson, Patrick L.: Ensuring Fair and Expeditious Trials at the International Criminal Tribunal for the Former Yugoslavia, 11 *European Journal of International Law* 569 (2000)

Robinson, Patrick L.: Rough Edges in the Alignment of Legal Systems in the Proceedings at the ICTY, 3 *Journal of International Criminal Justice* 1037 (2005)

Robinson, Patrick L.: Fair but Expeditious Trials, in: Hirad Abtahi / Gideon Boas (eds), *The Dynamics of International Criminal Justice. Essays in Honour of Sir Richard May* (Leiden / Boston: Martinus Nijhoff Publishers) 2006, p.169-192

Sabelli, Martin / Leyton, Stacey: Train Wrecks and Freeway Crashes: An Argument for Fairness and Against Self Representation in the Criminal Justice System, 91 *Journal of Criminal Law and Criminology* 161 (2000)

Saunders, Cheryl: The Use and Misuse of Comparative Constitutional Law, 13 *Indiana Journal of Global Legal Studies* 37 (2006)

Schabas, William A.: *The UN International Criminal Tribunals. The Former Yugoslavia, Rwanda and Sierra Leone* (Cambridge: Cambridge University Press) 2006

Schabas, William A.: *An Introduction to the International Criminal Court* (Cambridge: Cambridge University Press) 3rd edition 2007

Schabas, William A.: Article 67, in: Otto Triffterer (ed.), *Commentary on the Rome Statute of the International Criminal Court. Observers' Notes, Article by Article* (Munich: Verlag C.H. Beck) 2nd edition 2008, p.1247-1274

Scharf, Michael P.: The Legacy of the Milosevic Trial, 37 *New England Law Review* 915 (2003)

Scharf, Michael P.: Is It International Enough? A Critique of the Iraqi Special Tribunal in Light of the Goals of International Criminal Justice, 2 *Journal of International Criminal Justice* 330 (2004)

Scharf, Michael P. / Rassi, Christopher M.: Do Former Leaders have an International Right to Self-Representation in War Crimes Trials?, 20 *Ohio State Journal on Dispute Resolution* 3 (2005)

Scharf, Michael P.: Chaos in the Courtroom: Controlling Disruptive Defendants and Contumacious Counsel in War Crimes Trials, 39 *Case Western Reserve Journal of International Law* 155 (2006-2007)

Schomburg, Wolfgang / Wild, Tobias: The Defence Rights in the Practice of the International Criminal Tribunals, 4 *ERA Forum* 533 (2004)

Schomburg, Wolfgang: The Role of International Criminal Tribunals in Promoting Respect for Fair Trial Rights, 8 *Northwestern University Journal of International Human Rights* 1 (2009)

Schomburg, Wolfgang: Development of Human Rights Before International Criminal Tribunals. A European Perspective, 17(2) *Croatian Annual of Criminal Law and Practice* 909 (2010)

Schomburg, Wolfgang: Some Reflections on the Right to Self-Representation Before International Tribunals, 12 *ERA Forum* 189 (2011)

Scoccia, Danny: In Defence of Hard Paternalism, 27(4) *Law & Philosophy* 351 (2008)

Sitarama, Ganesh: The Use and Abuse of Foreign Law in Constitutional Interpretation, 32 *Harvard Journal of Law and Public Policy* 653 (2009)

Skilbeck, Rupert: Frankenstein's Monster. Creating a New International Procedure, 8 *Journal of International Criminal Justice* 451 (2010)

Sluiter, Göran: 'Fairness and the Interests of Justice'. Illusive Concepts in the *Milošević* Case, 3 *Journal of International Criminal Justice* 9 (2003)

Sluiter, Göran: Compromising the Authority of International Criminal Justice. How Vojislav Šešelj Runs his Trial, 5 *Journal of International Criminal Justice* 529 (2007)

Sluiter, Göran: Karadžić on Trial. Two Procedural Problems, 6 *Journal of International Criminal Justice* 617 (2008)

Snukals, Beverly W. / Sturtevant Jr., Glen H.: Pro Se Litigation: Best Practices from a Judge's Perspective, 42 *University of Richmond Law Review* 93 (2007)

Swart, Bert: Damaska and the Faces of International Criminal Justice, 6 *Journal of International Criminal Justice* 87 (2008)

Tochilovsky, Vladimir: Legal Systems and Cultures in the International Criminal Court: The Experience from the International Criminal Tribunal for the Former Yugoslavia, in: Horst Fischer / Claus Kreß / Sascha Rolf Lüder (eds), *International and National Prosecution of Crimes Under International Law. Current Developments* (Berlin: Berlin Verlag Arno Spitz GmbH) 2001, p.627-644

Tolbert, David / Swinnen, Frederick: The Protection of, and Assistance to, Witnesses at the ICTY, in: Hirad Abtahi / Gideon Boas (eds), *The Dynamics of International Criminal Justice. Essays in Honour of Sir Richard May* (Leiden / Boston: Martinus Nijhoff Publishers) 2006, p.193-229

Toncic, Bojan: Serbia: Milosevic Trial Grips Nation, BCR Issue 318, 14 February 2002, available at http://iwpr.net/report-news/serbia-milosevic-trial-grips-nation (last accessed 17 November 2012)

Trechsel, Stefan: *Human Rights in Criminal Proceedings* (Oxford: Oxford University Press) 2005

Tuinstra, Jarinde Temminck: Assisting an Accused to Represent Himself. Appointment of *Amici Curiae* as the Most Appropriate Option, (2006) *Journal of International Criminal Justice* 47

Tuinstra, Jarinde Temminck: Defending the Defenders. The Role of Defence Counsel in International Criminal Trials, 8 *Journal of International Criminal Justice* 463 (2010)

Turner, Jenia Iontcheva: Legal Ethics in International Criminal Defense, 10 *Chicago Journal of International Law* 685 (2010)

Umozurike, U. Oji: *The African Charter on Human and Peoples' Rights* (The Hague / Boston / London: Martinus Nijhoff Publishers) 1997

Wald, Patricia M.: *Tyrants on Trial. Keeping Order in the Courtroom* (New York: Open Society Justice Institute) 2009

Weisbord, Noah / Smith, Matthew A.: The Reason Behind the Rules: From Description to Normativity in International Criminal Procedure, 36 *North Carolina Journal of International Law and Commercial Regulation* 255 (2011)

Werle, Gerhard: *Principles of International Criminal Law* (The Hague: TMC Asser Press) 2nd edition 2009

Whiting, Alex: In International Criminal Prosecutions, Justice Delayed can be Justice Delivered, 50 *Harvard International Law Journal* 323 (2009)

Williams, Joanne: Slobodan Milosevic and the Guarantee of Self-Representation, 32 *Brooklyn Journal of International Law* 553 (2007)

Williams, Sarah / Woolaver, Hannah: The Role of the *Amicus curia* before International Criminal Tribunals, 6 *International Criminal Law Review* 151 (2006)

Wladimiroff, Mikhail: Former Heads of State on Trial, 38 *Cornell International Law Journal* 949 (2005)

Yemet, Valère Eteka: *La Charte Africaine des Droits de l'Homme et des Peuples* (Paris: L'Harmattan) 1996

Zahar, Alexander: Legal Aid, Self-Representation, and the Crisis at the Hague Tribunal, 19 *Criminal Law Forum* 241 (2008)

Zappalà, Salvatore: *Human Rights in International Criminal Proceedings* (Oxford: Oxford University Press) 2005

Zappalà, Salvatore: The Rights of Victims v. the Rights of the Accused, 8 *Journal of International Criminal Justice* 137 (2010)

B. *Table of cases*

Extraordinary Chambers in the Courts of Cambodia

Case File No. 002/19-09-2007-ECCC/OCIJ (PTC 03), C22/I/61, Co-Prosecutor's Response to an Application for Reconsideration of the Pre-Trial Chamber's Decision Regarding a Civil Party's Right of Audience, 17 July 2008

Case File No. 002/19-09-2007-ECCC/OCIJ (PTC 03), C22/I/68, Decision on Application for Reconsideration of Civil Party's Right to Address Pre-Trial Chamber in Person, 28 August 2008

International Criminal Court

Prosecutor v. Germain Katanga

Case No. ICC-01/04-01/07, Defence Document in Support of Appeal Against "Decision on the Defence Request Concerning Languages", 31 January 2008 (filed: 01 February 2008)

Case No. ICC-01/04-01/07, Judgment on the Appeal of Mr. Germain Katanga Against the Decision of Pre-Trial Chamber I entitled "Decision on the Defence Request Concerning Languages", 27 May 2008

Procureur c. Thomas Lubanga Dyilo

Affaire n° ICC-01/04-01/06, Décision sur la Demande d'Autorisation d'Appel de la Défense Relative à la Transmission des Demandes de Participation des Victimes, 06 novembre 2006

Situation in Uganda

No. ICC-02/04-01/05, Decision on Prosecutor's Application for Leave to Appeal in part Pre-Trial Chamber II's Decision on the Prosecutor's Applications for Warrants of Arrest under Article 58, 19 August 2005

No. ICC-02/04-01/05, Decision on Prosecutor's Applications for Leave to Appeal dated the 15th day of March and to Suspend or Stay Consideration of Leave to Appeal dated the 11th day of May 2006, 10 July 2006

International Criminal Tribunal for Rwanda

Procureur c. Jean-Paul Akayesu / Prosecutor v. Jean-Paul Akayesu

Affaire n° ICTR-96-4-T, Décision Faisant Suite à une Demande de l'Accusé de Changement d'Avocat Commis d'Office, 20 novembre 1996

Case No. ICTR-96-4-A, Judgement, 01 June 2001

Prosecutor v. Théoneste Bagosora

Case No. ICTR-96-7-T, Decision on the Request by the Accused for Change of Assigned Counsel, 26 June 1997

Prosecutor v. Jean-Bosco Barayagwiza

Case No. ICTR-97-19-T, Decision on Defence Counsel Motion to Withdraw, 02 November 2000

Prosecutor v. Jean Kambanda

Case No. ICTR-97-23-A, Judgement, 19 October 2000

Prosecutor v. Karemera et al.

Case No. ICTR-98-44-T, Decision on Joseph Nzirorera's Eleventh Notice of Rule 68 Violation and Motion for Stay of Proceedings, 11 September 2008

Case No. ICTR-98-44-T, Decision on Joseph Nzirorera's 13th, 14th, and 15th Notices of Rule 68 Violation and Motions for Remedial Measures: ZF, Michel Bakuzakundi, and Tharcisse Renzaho, 18 February 2009

Case No. ICTR-98-44-T, Decision on Joseph Nzirorera's 12th Notice of Rule 68 Violation, 26 March 2009

Case No. ICTR-98-44-T, Decision on Joseph Nzirorera's 23rd Notice of Rule 66 Violation and Motion for Remedial and Punitive Measures: Witness ALG, 30 March 2009

Case No. ICTR-98-44-T, Decision on Joseph Nzirorera's 21st Notice of Rule 66 Violation and Motion for Remedial and Punitive Measures: Théophile Urikumwenimana, 22 April 2009

Procureur c. Mika Muhimana

Affaire n° ICTR-95-1-B-I, Décision Relative à la Requête de la Défense aux Fins de Traduction des Documents de l'Accusation et des Actes de Procédure en Kinyarwanda, Langue de l'Accusé, et en Français, Langue de son Conseil, 06 novembre 2001

Prosecutor v. Ferdinand Nahimana et al.

Case No. ICTR-99-52-A, Judgement, 28 November 2007

Prosecutor v. Augustin Ngirabatware

Case No. ICTR-99-54-T, Decision on Defence Motion to Vacate Trial Date of 4 May 2009, 25 February 2009

Case No. ICTR-99-54-T, Decision on Defence Motion to Vary Trial Date, 25 March 2009

Case No. ICTR-99-54-A, Decision on Augustin Ngirabatware's Appeal of Decisions Denying Motions to Vary Trial Date, 12 May 2009

Prosecutor v. Gérard Ntakirutimana

Case No. ICTR-96-10-T & ICTR-96-17-T, Decision on the Motions of the Accused for Replacement of Assigned Counsel / Corr., 11 June 1997

Prosecutor v. Nyiramasuhuko & Ntahobali

Case No. ICTR-97-21-T, Decision on Ntahobali's Motion for Withdrawal of Counsel, 22 June 2001

Procureur c. Vincent Rutaganira

Affaire n° ICTR-95-1C-P, Décision Relative à la Requête aux Fins de Transmission des Documents en Versions Française et Kinyarwanda, 06 décembre 2004

International Criminal Tribunal for the Former Yugoslavia

Prosecutor v. Zlatko Aleksovski

Case No. IT-95-14/1-AR73, Decision on Prosecutor's Appeal on Admissibility of Evidence, 16 February 1999

Prosecutor v. Blagojević & Jokić

Case No. IT-02-60-T, Decision on Independent Counsel for Vidoje Blagojević's Motion to Instruct the Registrar to Appoint New Lead and Co-Counsel, 03 July 2003

Prosecutor v. Vidoje Blagojević

Case No. IT-02-60-AR73.4, Public and Redacted Reasons for Decision on Appeal by Vidoje Blagojević to Replace his Defence Team, 07 November 2003

Prosecutor v. Delalić et al.

Case No. IT-96-21-T, Decision on Defence Application for Forwarding the Documents in the Language of the Accused, 25 September 1996

Case No. IT-96-21-A, Appeals Judgement, 20 February 2001

Prosecutor v. Dražen Erdemović

Case No. IT-96-22-A, Judgement, 07 October 1997, Separate and Dissenting Opinion of Judge Cassese

Prosecutor v. Anto Furundžija

Case No. IT-95-17/1-T, Judgement, 10 December 1998

Prosecutor v. Janković & Stanković

Case No. IT-96-23/2-PT, Registrar's Notification Pursuant to Rule 33(B) of the Rules of Procedure and Evidence Regarding Radovan Stanković's Legal Representation, 31 May 2005

Case No. IT-96-23/2-PT, Decision Following Registrar's Notification of Radovan Stanković's Request for Self-Representation, 19 August 2005

Prosecutor v. Radovan Karadžić

Case No. IT-95-5/18-PT, Registry Submission Pursuant to Rule 33(B) Regarding the Accused's Representation and the Transmission of Court Documents, 06 August 2008

Case No. IT-95-5/18-I, Appeal Against the Registry Decision to Provide Me with Transcripts in English Language Only, or as Audio Recordings, 15 August 2008 (filed: 19 August 2008)

Case No. IT-95-5/18-PT, Submission of the Deputy Registrar Pursuant to Rule 33(B) Regarding Appeal by Mr. Karadžić of 19 August 2008, 27 August 2008

Case No. IT-95-5/18-PT, Prosecution's Response to Karadžić's Submission Regarding the Registry's Provision of Transcripts in the English Language, 02 September 2008

Case No. IT-95-5/18-PT, Decision on the Accused's Request that All Materials, Including Transcripts, be Disclosed to him in Serbian and Cyrillic Script, 25 September 2008

Case No. IT-95-5/18-PT, Motion for Adequate Facilities and Equality of Arms: Legal Associates, 24 November 2008 (filed: 25 November 2008)

Case No. IT-95-5/18-PT, Decision on Accused Motion for Adequate Facilities and Equality of Arms: Legal Associates, 28 January 2009

Case No. IT-95-5/18-PT, Prosecution Motion Seeking a Determination that the Accused Understands English for the Purposes of the Statute and the Rules of Procedure and Evidence, 17 February 2009

Case No. IT-95-5/18-AR73.2, Appeal of the Trial Chamber's Decision on Adequate Facilities, 02 March 2009 (filed: 05 March 2009)

Case No. IT-95-5/18-AR73.2, Prosecution's Response to Karadžić's Appeal of the Trial Chamber's Decision on Adequate Facilities, 13 March 2009

Case No. IT-95-5/18-PT, Response to Prosecution Motion Seeking Determination that the Accused Understands English, 20 March 2009

Case No. IT-95-5/18-PT, Decision on Prosecution Motion Seeking Determination that the Accused Understands English for the Purposes of the Statute and the Rules of Procedure and Evidence, 26 March 2009

Case No. IT-95-5/18-AR73.2, Registrar's Submission Pursuant to Rule 33 (B) Regarding Radovan Karadžić's Appeal of the Trial Chamber's Decision on Adequate Facilities, 30 March 2009

Case No. IT-95-5/18-PT, Decision on Accused Request for Judicial Review of the Registry Decision on the Assignment of Mr. Marko Sladojević as Legal Associate, 20 April 2009

Case No. IT-95-5/18-PT, Appeal of the Trial Chamber's Decision on Languages, 29 April 2009

Case No. IT-95-5/18-AR73.2, Decision on Interlocutory Appeal of the Trial Chamber's Decision on Adequate Facilities, 07 May 2009
Case No. IT-95-5/18-PT, Prosecution Response to Karadžić's Appeal of Trial Chamber's Decision on Languages, 11 May 2009
Case No. IT-95-5/18-PT, Decision on Motion to Exclude Testimony of War Correspondents, 20 May 2009
Case No. IT-95-5/18-AR73.3, Decision on Interlocutory Appeal of the Trial Chamber's Decision on Prosecution Motion Seeking Determination that the Accused Understands English, 04 June 2009
Case No. IT-95-5/18-PT, Motion for Binding Order: Government of Norway, 08 July 2009
Case No. IT-95-5/18-PT, Motion for Binding Order: Government of Belgium, 20 July 2009
Case No. IT-95-5/18-PT, Motion for Binding Order to NATO, 22 July 2009
Case No. IT-95-5/18-PT, Motion for Binding Order: Government of Austria, 03 August 2009
Case No. IT-95-5/18-PT, Motion for Binding Order: Government of Italy, 03 August 2009
Case No. IT-95-5/18-PT, Motion for Binding Order: Government of Bangladesh, 05 August 2009
Case No. IT-95-5/18-PT, Motion for Binding Order: Government of Malta, 05 August 2009
Case No. IT-95-5/18-PT, Motion for Binding Order: Government of Malaysia, 03 August 2009 (filed: 10 August 2009)
Case No. IT-95-5/18-PT, Motion for Binding Order: Government of Pakistan, 10 August 2009
Case No. IT-95-5/18-PT, Withdrawal of Motion for Binding Order to NATO, 10 August 2009
Case No. IT-95-5/18-PT, Motion for Binding Order: Government of Germany, 12 August 2009
Case No. IT-95-5/18-PT, Motion for Binding Order: Government of Poland, 12 August 2009
Case No. IT-95-5/18-PT, Motion for Binding Order: Government of Egypt, 14 August 2009
Case No. IT-95-5/18-PT, Motion for Binding Order: Government of Jordan, 14 August 2009
Case No. IT-95-5/18-PT, Motion for Binding Order: Government of Turkey, 24 August 2009
Case No. IT-95-5/18-PT, Motion for Binding Order: Government of France, 24 August 2009
Case No. IT-95-5/18-PT, Withdrawal of Motion for Binding Order to Bangladesh, 24 August 2009
Case No. IT-95-5/18-PT, Motion for Binding Order: Government of Iran, 26 August 2009

Case No. IT-95-5/18-PT, Motion for Binding Order: Government of Bosnia, 31 August 2009

Case No. IT-95-5/18-PT, Motion for Binding Order: Government of Denmark, 02 September 2009

Case No. IT-95-5/18-PT, Submission on Commencement of Trial, 03 September 2009

Case No. IT-95-5/18-PT, Motion for Binding Order: Government of Sweden, 04 September 2009

Case No. IT-95-5/18-PT, Withdrawal of Motion for Binding Order: Government of Jordan, 04 September 2009

Case No. IT-95-5/18-PT, Motion for Binding Order: Government of Croatia, 11 September 2009

Case No. IT-95-5/18-PT, Motion for Binding Order: Government of The Netherlands, 11 September 2009

Case No. IT-95-5/18-PT, Motion for Binding Order: Government of the United Kingdom, 11 September 2009

Case No. IT-95-5/18-PT, Motion for Binding Order: Government of the United States of America, 11 September 2009

Case No. IT-95-5/18-PT, Withdrawal of Motion for Binding Order: Government of Malta, 22 September 2009

Case No. IT-95-5/18-PT, Answer to the Request for Motion for a Binding Order to be Issued to the Government of the Federal Republic of Germany for the Production of Documents Pursuant to Rule 54bis, 25 September 2009

Case No. IT-95-5/18-AR73.5, Appeal of Decision on Commencement of Trial, 25 September 2009

Case No. IT-95-5/18-PT, Motion for Binding Order: Government of Greece, 28 September 2009

Case No. IT-95-5/18-PT, Submissions on Trial Procedure, 28 September 2009

Case No. IT-95-5/18-PT, Withdrawal of Motion for Binding Order: Government of Malaysia, 28 September 2009

Case No. IT-95-5/18-PT, Withdrawal of Motion for Binding Order: Government of Sweden, 30 September 2009

Case No. IT-95-5/18-PT, Motion for Leave to Reply and Reply: Motion for Binding Order to United States of America, 02 October 2009

Case No. IT-95-5/18-T, Order on the Procedure for the Conduct of Trial, 08 October 2009

Case No. IT-95-5/18-AR73.5, Reply Brief: Appeal of Decision on Commencement of Trial, 12 October 2009

Case No. IT-95-5/18-AR73.5, Decision on Radovan Karadžić's Appeal of the Decision on Commencement of Trial, 13 October 2009

Case No. IT-95-5/18-PT, Withdrawal of Motion for Binding Order: Government of the United Kingdom, 14 October 2009

Case No. IT-95-5/18-PT, Submission on the Commencement of Trial, 21 October 2009

Case No. IT-95-5/18-PT, Withdrawal of Motion for Binding Order: Government of Denmark, 21 October 2009

Case No. IT-95-5/18-PT, Response to Letter from the Chamber, 24 October 2009 (filed: 26 October 2009)

Case No. IT-95-5/18-T, Letter to Presiding Judge, 02 November 2009

Case No. IT-95-5/18-T, Withdrawal of Motion for Binding Order: Government of Egypt, 02 November 2009

Case No. IT-95-5/18-T, Withdrawal of Motion for Binding Order: Government of Greece, 02 November 2009

Case No. IT-95-5/18-T, Withdrawal of Motion for Binding Order: Government of Turkey, 02 November 2009

Case No. IT-95-5/18-T, Withdrawal of Motion for Binding Order: Government of Austria, 04 November 2009

Case No. IT-95-5/18-T, Decision on Appointment of Counsel and Order on Further Trial Proceedings, 05 November 2009

Case No. IT-95-5/18-T, Appeal of OLAD Decision in Relation to Additional Pre-Trial Funds, 10 November 2009

Case No. IT-95-5/18-T, Decision on Accused's Application for Certification to Appeal Decision on Appointment of Counsel and Order on Further Trial Proceedings, 23 November 2009

Case No. IT-95-5/18-T, Withdrawal of Motion for Binding Order: Government of Belgium, 30 November 2009

Case No. IT-95-5/18-T, Withdrawal of Motion for Binding Order: Government of Norway, 30 November 2009

Case No. IT-95-5/18-T, Withdrawal of Motion for Binding Order: Government of Poland, 01 December 2009

Case No. IT-95-5/18-T, Motion to Vacate Appointment of Richard Harvey, 04 December 2009

Case No. IT-95-5/18-T, Prosecution Response to Karadžić's Motion to Vacate Appointment of Richard Harvey, 14 December 2009

Case No. IT-95-5/18-T, Registrar's Submission Pursuant to Rule 33(B) Regarding Radovan Karadžić's Motion to Vacate Appointment of Richard Harvey, 14 December 2009

Case No. IT-95-5/18-T, Decision on Appeal of OLAD Decision in Relation to Additional Pre-Trial Funds, 17 December 2009

Case No. IT-95-5/18-T, Reply Brief: Motion to Vacate Appointment of Richard Harvey, 18 December 2009

Case No. IT-95-5/18-T, Decision on the Accused's Motion to Vacate Appointment of Richard Harvey, 23 December 2009

Case No. IT-95-5/18-T, Application for Certification to Appeal Decision on Motion to Vacate Appointment of Richard Harvey, 29 December 2009

Case No. IT-95-5/18-T, Request for Review of OLAD Decision on Trial Phase Remuneration, 14 January 2010

Case No. IT-95-5/18-AR73.6, Appeal from Decision on Motion to Vacate Appointment of Richard Harvey, 19 January 2010

Case No. IT-95-5/18-T, Withdrawal of Motion for Binding Order: Government of Pakistan, 27 January 2010

Case No. IT-95-5/18-AR73.6, Prosecution's Response to Karadžić's Appeal from Decision on Motion to Vacate Appointment of Richard Harvey, 29 January 2010

Case No. IT-95-5/18-T, Motion for Postponement of Trial, 01 February 2010

Case No. IT-95-5/18-AR73.6, Reply Brief #1: Appeal from Decision on Motion to Vacate Appointment of Richard Harvey, 01 February 2010

Case No. IT-95-5/18-T, Prosecution's Response to Karadžić's Motion for Postponement of Trial, 03 February 2010

Case No. IT-95-5/18-AR73.6, Registrar's Submission Pursuant to Rule 33 (B) Regarding Radovan Karadžić's Appeal from Decision on Motion to Vacate Appointment of Richard Harvey, 04 February 2010

Case No. IT-95-5/18-T, Prosecution's Further Response to Karadžić's Motion for Postponement of Trial Pursuant to Trial Chamber's Order of 03 February 2010 with Confidential Appendices A-F, 09 February 2010

Case No. IT-95-5/18-AR73.6, Decision on Radovan Karadžić's Appeal from Decision on Motion to Vacate Appointment of Richard Harvey, 12 February 2010

Case No. IT-95-5/18-T, Submission Pursuant to Trial Chamber's Order Setting Deadlines for Further Submissions, 22 February 2010

Case No. IT-95-5/18-T, Supplemental Submission on Motion for Postponement of Trial Following President's Decision, 22 February 2010

Case No. IT-95-5/18-T, Prosecution Motion for an Instruction Regarding the Admissibility of Submissions and Statements of the Accused, 23 February 2010

Case No. IT-95-5/18-T, Decision on Accused's Motion for Postponement of Trial, 26 February 2010

Case No. IT-95-5/18-T, Application for Certification to Appeal and for Stay Pending Appeal of Decision on Commencement of Evidence, 01 March 2010

Case No. IT-95-5/18-T, Prosecution's Response to Application for Certification to Appeal and for Stay Pending Appeal of Decision on Commencement of Evidence, 01 March 2010

Case No. IT-95-5/18-T, Oral Decision, 02 March 2010, T.993-995

Case No. IT-95-5/18-T, Motion to Strike Allegation G9 on Grounds of Collateral Estoppel, 04 March 2010

Case No. IT-95-5/18-AR73.7, Appeal from Decision on Commencement of Evidence, 09 March 2010

Case No. IT-95-5/18-AR73.7, Prosecution Response to Karadžić's Appeal of Decision on Postponement of Trial, 17 March 2010

Case No. IT-95-5/18-T, Withdrawal of Motion for Binding Order: Government of Italy, 19 March 2010

Case No. IT-95-5/18-T, Decision on Accused's Motion to Strike Scheduled Shelling Incident on Grounds of Collateral Estoppel, 31 March 2010

Case No. IT-95-5/18-AR73.7, Decision on Appeal from Decision on Motion for Further Postponement of Trial, 31 March 2010

Case No. IT-95-5/18-T, Motion for Stay of Proceedings: Violation of Burden of Proof and Presumption of Innocence, 01 April 2010

Case No. IT-95-5/18-T, Decision on Motion for Stay of Proceedings, 08 April 2010

Case No. IT-95-5/18-T, Oral Decision, 13 April 2010, T.997-999

Case No. IT-95-5/18-T, Withdrawal of Motion for Binding Order: Government of The Netherlands, 13 April 2010

Case No. IT-95-5/18-T, Decision on Designation of Standby Counsel, 15 April 2010

Case No. IT-95-5/18-T, Request for Authorization for Legal Interns to be Present in the Courtroom, 26 April 2010

Case No. IT-95-5/18-T, Prosecution's Response to Karadžić's Request for Legal Interns to be Present in the Courtroom, 27 April 2010

Case No. IT-95-5/18-T, Leave to Reply: Request for Authorization for Legal Interns to be Present in the Courtroom, 28 April 2010

Case No. IT-95-5/18-T, Decision on Accused's Request for Authorisation for Legal Interns to be Present in the Courtroom, 05 May 2010

Case No. IT-95-5/18-T, Motion to Exclude Testimony of Aernout van Lynden, 14 May 2010

Case No. IT-95-5/18-T, Second Motion for Finding of Disclosure Violation and Remedial Measures, 14 May 2010

Case No. IT-95-5/18-T, Decision on the Accused's Motion to Exclude Testimony of Aernout van Lynden, 17 May 2010

Case No. IT-95-5/18-T, Prosecution's Response to Accused's Motion to Exclude Testimony of Aernout van Lynden, 17 May 2010

Case No. IT-95-5/18-T, Submission on Trial Schedule, 20 May 2010

Case No. IT-95-5/18-T, Order on the Trial Schedule, 27 May 2010

Case No. IT-95-5/18-T, Application for Certification to Appeal Order on Trial Schedule and For Stay Pending Appeal, 31 May 2010

Case No. IT-95-5/18-T, Decision on Accused's Application for Certification to Appeal the Trial Chamber's Order on Trial Schedule and for Stay, 04 June 2010

Case No. IT-95-5/18-AR73.8, Appeal from Order on the Trial Schedule, 10 June 2010

Case No. IT-95-5/18-AR73.8, Prosecution Response to Karadžić's Appeal of Order on Trial Schedule, 21 June 2010

Case No. IT-95-5/18-AR73.8, Decision on Appeal from Order on the Trial Schedule, 19 July 2010

Case No. IT-95-5/18-T, Motion for Binding Order: Government of Belgium, 16 August 2010 (filed: 17 August 2010)

Case No. IT-95-5/18-T, Decision on Accused's Motion for Suspension of Proceedings, 18 August 2010

Case No. IT-95-5/18-T, Second Submission on Trial Schedule, 07 September 2010

Case No. IT-95-5/18-T, Withdrawal of Second Motion for Binding Order: Government of Belgium, 10 September 2010

Case No. IT-95-5/18-T, Oral Ruling, 13 September 2010, T.6592-6594

Case No. IT-95-5/18-T, Prosecution's Response to Karadžić's Second Submission on Trial Schedule With Confidential Appendix A, 13 September 2010

Case No. IT-95-5/18-T, Decision on Accused's Second Submission on Trial Schedule, 23 September 2010 (made public by oral order of 27 September 2010)

Case No. IT-95-5/18-T, Decision on Accused's Seventeenth Motion for Finding of Disclosure Violation and for Remedial Measures, 29 September 2010

Case No. IT-95-5/18-T, Twentieth Motion for Finding of Disclosure Violation and for Remedial Measures, 05 October 2010

Case No. IT-95-5/18-T, Submission on Site Visit, 06 October 2010 (made public by subsequent order of the trial chamber: Order Lifting Confidentiality of Decision on Site Visit and Related Pleadings, 24 May 2011)

Case No. IT-95-5/18-T, Twenty-Second Motion for Finding of Disclosure Violation and for Remedial Measures, 07 October 2010

Case No. IT-95-5/18-T, Prosecution's Consolidated Response to Karadžić's Eighteenth and Nineteenth Motions for Finding of Disclosure Violation and for Remedial Measures, 11 October 2010

Case No. IT-95-5/18-T, Twenty-Third Motion for Finding of Disclosure Violation and for Remedial Measures, 12 October 2010

Case No. IT-95-5/18-T, Twenty-Fourth Motion for Finding of Disclosure Violation and for Remedial Measures, 13 October 2010

Case No. IT-95-5/18-T, Motion for Binding Order: European Union, 19 October 2010

Case No. IT-95-5/18-T, Withdrawal of Twenty-Third Motion for Finding of Disclosure Violation and for Remedial Measures, 27 October 2010

Case No. IT-95-5/18-T, Withdrawal of Twenty-Fifth Motion for Finding of Disclosure Violation and for Remedial Measures, 29 October 2010

Case No. IT-95-5/18-T, Motion for Binding Order: Government of Venezuela, 01 November 2010

Case No. IT-95-5/18-T, Motion for Binding Order: United Nations, 01 November 2010

Case No. IT-95-5/18-T, Decision on Accused's Eighteenth to Twenty-First Disclosure Violation Motions, 02 November 2010

Case No. IT-95-5/18-T, Oral Ruling, 03 November 2010, T.8906-8909

Case No. IT-95-5/18-T, Decision on Accused's Twenty-Second, Twenty-Fourth and Twenty-Sixth Disclosure Violation Motions, 11 November 2010

Case No. IT-95-5/18-T, Order on Submissions for a Site Visit, 15 November 2010 (made public by subsequent order of the trial chamber: Order Lifting Confidentiality of Decision on Site Visit and Related Pleadings, 24 May 2011)

Case No. IT-95-5/18-T, Motion for Finding of Disclosure Violation and for Remedial Measures #17 bis, 25 November 2010

Case No. IT-95-5/18-T, Motion for Binding Order: United Nations and NATO, 29 November 2010

Case No. IT-95-5/18-T, Prosecution Request for Reconsideration of Trial Chamber's 11 November 2010 Decision, 01 December 2010

Case No. IT-95-5/18-T, Order in Relation to Exhibits Marked for Identification Pending English Translation, 06 December 2010

Case No. IT-95-5/18-T, Response to Prosecution Motion for Extension of Rule 68 Deadline, 07 December 2010

Case No. IT-95-5/18-T, Second Motion for Binding Order: Government of Iran, 07 December 2010

Case No. IT-95-5/18-T, Second Motion for Binding Order: United States of America, 07 December 2010

Case No. IT-95-5/18-T, Decision on Prosecution's Request for Reconsideration of Trial Chamber's 11 November 2010 Decision, 10 December 2010

Case No. IT-95-5/18-T, Second Submission on Site Visit, 13 December 2010 (made public by subsequent order of the trial chamber: Order Lifting Confidentiality of Decision on Site Visit and Related Pleadings, 24 May 2011)

Case No. IT-95-5/18-T, Withdrawal of Motion for Binding Order: Government of Canada, 06 January 2011

Case No. IT-95-5/18-T, Registry Submission Pursuant to Rule 33(B) on the Presence of the Accused During a Potential Site Visit, 14 January 2011 (made public by subsequent order of the trial chamber: Order Lifting Confidentiality of Decision on Site Visit and Related Pleadings, 24 May 2011)

Case No. IT-95-5/18-T, Motion for Binding Order: United Arab Emirates, 18 January 2011

Case No. IT-95-5/18-T, Motion for Binding Order: Saudi Arabia, 18 January 2011

Case No. IT-95-5/18-T, Third Motion for Binding Order: United States of America, 24 January 2011

Case No. IT-95-5/18-T, Motion for Fourth Suspension of the Proceedings, 02 February 2011

Case No. IT-95-5/18-T, Withdrawal of Thirty Fourth Disclosure Violation Motion, 07 February 2011

Case No. IT-95-5/18-T, Prosecution's Response to Karadžić's Motion for Fourth Suspension of Proceedings, 08 February 2011

Case No. IT-95-5/18-T, Oral Ruling, 10 February 2011, T.11474-11476

Case No. IT-95-5/18-T, Decision on the Accused's Thirty-Second, Thirty-Third, Thirty-Fifth and Thirty-Sixth Disclosure Violation Motions, 24 February 2011

Case No. IT-95-5/18-T, Withdrawal of Motion for Binding Order: European Union, 24 February 2011

Case No. IT-95-5/18-T, Forty-Third for Finding of Disclosure Violation and for Remedial Measures (February 2011), 02 March 2011

Case No. IT-95-5/18-T, Forty-Fourth for Finding of Disclosure Violation and for Admission of Statement of Rajko Koprivica Pursuant to Rule 92 Quater, 08 March 2011

Case No. IT-95-5/18-T, Motion for Fifth Suspension of the Proceedings, 08 March 2011

Case No. IT-95-5/18-T, Forty-Fifth Motion for Finding of Disclosure Violation and for Remedial Measures (Batch 576), 16 March 2011

Case No. IT-95-5/18-T, Decision on Accused's Motion for Fifth Suspension of the Proceedings, 17 March 2011

Case No. IT-95-5/18-T, Forty-Sixth Motion for Finding of Disclosure Violation and for Sanctions: March 2011 – 66(A)(ii), 05 April 2011

Case No. IT-95-5/18-T, Withdrawal of Second Motion for Binding Order: Government of Denmark, 05 April 2011

Case No. IT-95-5/18-T, Third Motion for Binding Order: Government of Bosnia, 05 April 2011

Case No. IT-95-5/18-T, Decision on Accused's Forty-Third to Forty-Fifth Disclosure Violation Motions, 08 April 2011

Case No. IT-95-5/18-T, Withdrawal of Second Motion for Binding Order: Government of Bosnia, 11 April 2011

Case No. IT-95-5/18-T, Fourth Motion for Binding Order: United States of America, 12 April 2011

Case No. IT-95-5/18-T, Forty-Seventh Motion for finding of Disclosure Violation and for Further Suspension of Proceedings (March 2011 – Rule 68), 19 April 2011

Case No. IT-95-5/18-T, Response of the United States of America to the Trial Chamber's 13 April 2011 "Invitation to the United States of America", 28 April 2011

Case No. IT-95-5/18-T, Forty-Eighth Motion for Finding of Disclosure Violation and for Sanctions (April 2011), 02 May 2011

Case No. IT-95-5/18-T, Withdrawal of Fourth Motion for Binding Order: United States of America, 02 May 2011

Case No. IT-95-5/18-T, Order Lifting Confidentiality of Decision on Site Visit and Related Pleadings, 24 May 2011

Case No. IT-95-5/18-T, Annexes to Fiftieth Motion for Finding of Disclosure Violation and Motion for Seventh Suspension of Proceedings, 03 June 2011

Case No. IT-95-5/18-T, Memorandum in Support of Fiftieth Motion for Finding of Disclosure Violation and Motion for Seventh Suspension of Proceedings, 06 June 2011

Case No. IT-95-5/18-T, Fourth Motion for Binding Order: Government of Bosnia, 07 June 2011

Case No. IT-95-5/18-T, Decision on Accused's Forty-Ninth and Fiftieth Disclosure Violation Motions, 30 June 2011

Case No. IT-95-5/18-T, Prosecution's Disclosure Report, 27 July 2011 (filed: 28 July 2011)

Case No. IT-95-5/18-T, Fifty-Sixth Motion for Finding of Disclosure Violation and for Sanctions: Witness KDZ029, 18 August 2011

Case No. IT-95-5/18-T, Request for Review of Decision on Defence Team Funding, 22 August 2011

Case No. IT-95-5/18-T, Registrar's Submission Pursuant to Rule 33(B) Regarding Radovan Karadžić's Request for Review of Decision on Defence Team Funding, 05 September 2011

Case No. IT-95-5/18-T, Reply Brief: Request for Review of Decision on Defence Team Funding, 08 September 2011

Case No. IT-95-5/18-T, Memorandum in Support of Sixtieth Motion for Finding of Disclosure Violation (Ivo Atlija), 21 December 2011

Case No. IT-95-5/18-T, Motion for Interviews of Prosecution Witnesses or an Order Requiring Prosecution to Proof their Witnesses by Telephone, 31 October 2011

Case No. IT-95-5/18-T, Motion for Reconsideration of Decision on Ninth Suspension of Proceedings: Witness KDZ456, 31 October 2011

Case No. IT-95-5/18-T, Registrar's Submission Pursuant to Rule 33(B) of the Rules Regarding Radovan Karadžić's Motion for Interviews of Prosecution Witnesses or an Order Requiring Prosecution to Proof their Witnesses by Telephone, 31 October 2011

Case No. IT-95-5/18-T, Motion for Suspension of Proceedings Prior to Srebrenica Evidence, 11 November 2011

Case No. IT-95-5/18-T, Supplemental Submission: Motion for Suspension of Proceedings Prior to Srebrenica Evidence, 18 November 2011

Case No. IT-95-5/18-T, Decision on Accused's Motion for Suspension of Proceedings Prior to Start of Srebrenica Evidence, 22 November 2011

Case No. IT-95-5/18-T, Request for Review of Decision on Office Space, 20 December 2011

Case No. IT-95-5/18-T, Decision on Request for Review of Decision on Defence Team Funding, 31 January 2012

Case No. IT-95-5/18-T, Decision on the Request for Review of Decision on Office Space, 10 February 2012

Case No. IT-95-5/18-T, Decision on Second Site Visit, 10 February 2012 (made public by subsequent order of the trial chamber: Order Lifting Confidentiality of Decision on Second Site Visit and Related Pleadings, 04 July 2012)

Case No. IT-95-5/18-T, Motion for Trial Sessions to be held in the Former Yugoslavia, 07 May 2012

Case No. IT-95-5/18-T, Scheduling Order on Close of the Prosecution Case, Rule 98 bis Submissions, and Start of the Defence Case, 26 April 2012

Case No. IT-95-5/18-T, Decision on Accused's Motion for Trial Sessions to be Conducted in the Former Yugoslavia and for Invitation to Governments of Bosnia and Herzegovina, Republika Srpska, and Serbia, 04 July 2012

Case No. IT-95-5/18-T, Order Lifting Confidentiality of Decision on Second Site Visit and Related Pleadings, 04 July 2012

Case No. IT-95-5/18-T, Motion for New Trial for Disclosure Violations, 13 August 2012

Case No. IT-95-5/18-T, Defence Submission Pursuant to Rule 65 ter and Related Motions, 27 August 2012

Case No. IT-95-5/18-T, Decision on Time Allocated to the Accused for the Presentation of his Case, 19 September 2012

Case No. IT-95-5/18-T, Addendum to Order in Relation to Accused's Notice of Request of Protective Measures for Witnesses Issued on 8 October 2012, 09 October 2012

Case No. IT-95-5/18-T, Decision of the Registrar, 10 October 2012 (filed: 11 October 2012)

Case No. IT-95-5/18-AR73.10, Appeal from Decision on Duration of Defence Case, 11 October 2012 (filed: 12 October 2012)

Case No. IT-95-5/18-T, 74th Motion for Finding of Disclosure Violation: Demurenko Material, 22 October 2012

Case No. IT-95-5/18-AR98bis.1, Respondent's Brief, 05 November 2012

Prosecutor v. Momčilo Krajišnik

Case No. IT-00-39-T, Prosecution's Submissions on Self-Representation, 31 May 2005

Case No. IT-00-39-T, Registrar's Notification Pursuant to Rule 33(B) of the Rules of Procedure and Evidence Regarding Momčilo Krajišnik's Legal Representation, 31 May 2005

Case No. IT-00-39-T, Registrar's Submission Pursuant to Rule 33(B) of the Rules of Procedure and Evidence Regarding the Resources that Can be Made Available to Momčilo Krajišnik if He is to Represent Himself, 03 June 2005

Case No. IT-00-39-T, Defence Submissions: Summary of Current Position on Self-Representation by Mr Krajišnik, 08 June 2005

Case No. IT-00-39-T, Oral Decision, 22 July 2005, T.17048

Case No. IT-00-39-T, Reasons for Oral Decision Denying Mr. Krajišnik's Request to Proceed Unrepresented by Counsel, 18 August 2005

Case No. IT-00-39-A, Decision on Momčilo Krajišnik's Request to Self-Represent, on Counsel's Motion in Relation to Appointment of Amicus Curiae, and on the Prosecution Motion of 16 February 2007, 11 May 2007

Case No. IT-00-39-A, Request to Provide Conditions to Work and to Reverse the Decision of the Registry of 07 June 2007, 10 June 2007 (filed: 18 June 2007)

Case No. IT-00-39-A, Registry Submission on Momčilo Krajišnik's Request to Reverse the Decision of the Registry of 7 June 2007, 19 July 2007

Case No. IT-00-39-A, Decision on Motion of Amicus Curiae Regarding Appellate Ground of Ineffective Assistance of Counsel, 20 July 2007

Case No. IT-00-39-A, Decision on Krajišnik Request and on Prosecution Motion, 11 September 2007

Case No. IT-00-39-A, Decision on Momčilo Krajišnik's Motion to Reschedule Status Conference and Permit Alan Dershowitz to Appear, 28 February 2008

Case No. IT-00-39-A, Prosecution Motion for Clarification and Reconsideration of the Appeal Chamber's "Decision on Momčilo Krajišnik's Motion to Reschedule Status Conference and Permit Alan Dershowitz to Appear", 29 February 2008

Case No. IT-00-39-A, Decision on Prosecution's Motion for Clarification and Reconsideration of the Decision of 28 February 2008, 11 March 2008

Case No. IT-00-39-A, Public and Redacted Amicus Curiae's Reply to the Prosecution's Response to Amicus Curiae's Appellate Brief, 24 June 2008

Case No. IT-00-39-A, Judgement, 17 March 2009

Prosecutor v. Kvočka et al.

Case No. IT-98-30/1-AR73.5, Decision on Interlocutory Appeal by the Accused Zoran Žigić Against the Decision of Trial Chamber I dated 5 December 2000, 25 May 2001

Prosecutor v. Limaj et al.

Case No. IT-03-66-AR65, Decision on Fatmir Limaj's Request for Provisional Release, 31 October 2003

Prosecutor v. Slobodan Milošević

Case No. IT-99-37-PT, Order Inviting Designation of Amicus Curiae, 30 August 2001

Case No. IT-02-50-PT, Order Inviting Designation of Amicus Curiae, 30 October 2001

Case No. IT-99-37-PT & IT-01-50-PT, Order, 15 November 2001

Case No. IT-02-51-PT, Order Inviting Designation of Amicus Curiae, 23 November 2001

Case No. IT-99-37-PT, Order Concerning Amici Curiae, 11 January 2002

Case No. IT-02-54-T, Order, 19 February 2002

Case No. IT-02-54-T, Brief on the Provision of Adequate Facilities to Allow the Accused to Prepare his Defence, 05 March 2002 (filed: 06 March 2002)

Case No. IT-02-54-T, Amici Curiae Brief on Issues of Cross-Examination by the Accused in Person Including the 'Tu Quoque' Principle, 05 March 2002 (filed: 06 March 2002)

Case No. IT-02-54-T, Decision on Accused's Application for Provisional Release, 06 March 2002

Case No. IT-02-54-T, Prosecution's Brief Concerning the Scope of Cross-Examination and the "Tu Quoque" Defence, 06 March 2002

Case No. IT-02-54-T, Registry Report on Practical Facilities Available to Accused, 18 March 2002 (filed: 19 March 2002)

Case No. IT-02-54-T, Order, 16 April 2002

Case No. IT-02-54-T, Oral Ruling, 24 April 2002, T.3737-3740

Case No. IT-02-54-T, Submission from the Office of the Prosecutor on the Future Conduct of the Case in the Light of the State of the Accused's Health and the Length and Complexity of the Case, 08 November 2002

Case No. IT-02-54-T, Oral Ruling, 18 December 2002, T.14574

Case No. IT-02-54-T, Reasons for the Decision on the Prosecution Motion Concerning Assignment of Counsel, 04 April 2003

Case No. IT-02-54-T, Amici Curiae Submission in Response to the Order of the Trial Chamber Concerning the Implications of the Accused's Health Dated 24 September 2003, 27 September 2003

Case No. IT-02-54-T, Prosecution's Submission on the Implications of the Accused's Recurring Ill-Health and the Future Conduct of the Case – Corrected Version, 30 September 2003

Case No. IT-02-54-T, Order of Further Instruction to the Amici Curiae, 06 October 2003

Case No. IT-02-54-AR73.4, Dissenting Opinion of Judge David Hunt on Admissibility of Evidence in Chief in the Form of Written Statements (Majority Decision given 30 September 2003), 21 October 2003

Case No. IT-02-54-AR73.4, Separate Opinion of Judge Shahabuddeen Appended to Appeals Chamber's Decision Dated 30 September 2003 on Admissibility of Evidence-in-Chief in the Form of Written Statements, 31 October 2003

Case No. IT-02-54-AR73.6, Decision on the Interlocutory Appeal by the Amici Curiae Against the Trial Chamber Order Concerning the Presentation and Preparation of the Defence Case, 20 January 2004

Case No. IT-02-54-T, Prosecution Submissions in Response to the Trial Chamber's 19 July 2004 "Further Order on Future Conduct of the Trial", 26 July 2004

Case No. IT-02-54-T, Oral Ruling, 02 September 2004, T.32357-32359

Case No. IT-02-54-T, Order on the Modalities to be Followed by Court Assigned Counsel, 03 September 2004

Case No. IT-02-54-T, Reasons for Decision on Assignment of Defence Counsel, 22 September 2004

Case No. IT-02-54-AR73.7, Appeal Against the Trial Chamber's Decision on Assignment of Defence Counsel, 29 September 2004

Case No. IT-02-54-AR73.7, Decision on Interlocutory Appeal of the Trial Chamber's Decision on the Assignment of Defence Counsel, 01 November 2004

Case No. IT-02-54-T, Assigned Counsel's Motion for Withdrawal With Annex A, 08 November 2004

Case No. IT-02-54-T, Decision on Assigned Counsel's Motion for Withdrawal, 07 December 2004

Case No. IT-02-54-T, Assigned Counsel's Request to the President Pursuant to Article 19(F) of the Directive on Assignment of Defence Counsel for a Review of the Deputy Registrar's Decision dated 14 December 2004 Refusing Assigned Counsel's Application to Withdraw With Attachment 1, 28 December 2004

Case No. IT-02-54-T, Decision Affirming the Registrar's Denial of Assigned Counsel's Application to Withdraw, 07 February 2005

Case No. IT-02-54-T, Order on Contempt Concerning Witness Kosta Bulatović, 20 April 2005

Case No. IT-02-54-R77.4, Contempt Proceedings Against Kosta Bulatović, Decision on Contempt of the Tribunal, 13 May 2005

Case No. IT-02-54-A-R77.4, Contempt Proceedings Against Kosta Bulatović, Decision on Interlocutory Appeal on Kosta Bulatović Contempt Proceedings, 29 August 2005

Case No. IT-02-54-T, Decision in Relation to Severance, Extension of Time and Rest, 12 December 2005

Prosecutor v. Prlić et al. / Procureur c/ Prlić et consorts

Case No. IT-04-74-T, Revised Version of the Decision Adopting Guidelines on Conduct of Trial Proceedings, 28 April 2006

Affaire n° IT-04-74-T, Décision Portant sur les Modalités de l'Interrogatoire des Témoins, 10 mai 2007

Affaire n° IT-04-74-T, Opinion Individuelle du Juge Jean-Claude Antonetti, Président de la Chambre de Première Instance, Concernant la Décision Certifiant l'Appel de la Décision Portant sur les Modalités de l'Interrogatoire des Témoins, 28 juin 2007

Case No. IT-04-74-AR73.5, Decision on Praljak's Appeal of the Trial Chamber's 10 May 2007 Decision on the Mode of Interrogating Witnesses, 24 August 2007 (filed: 26 August 2007)

Affaire n° IT-04-74-T, Décision Portant Adoption des Lignes Directrices Pour la Présentation des Éléments de Preuve à Décharge, 24 avril 2008

Affaire n° IT-04-74-T, Décision Portant sur une Demande de Réexamen Présentée par la Défense Praljak, 26 juin 2008

Affaire n° IT-04-74-T, Opinion Dissidente du Président, Jean-Claude Antonetti sur la Décision Portant sur une Demande de Réexamen Présentée par la Défense Praljak, 26 juin 2008

Case No. IT-04-74-AR73.11, Decision on Slobodan Praljak's Appeal of the Trial Chamber's Decision on the Direct Examination of Witnesses Dated 26 June 2008, 11 September 2008

Affaire n° IT-04-74-T, Ordonnance Portant Sur les Modalités de l'Intervention de l'Accusé Prlić en Audience, 15 juillet 2009

Affaire n° IT-04-74-T, Ordonnance Portant Calendrier (Mémoires en Clôture, Réquisitoire et Plaidoiries Finales), 01 novembre 2010

Prosecutor v. Vojislav Šešelj / Procureur c/ Vojislav Šešelj

Case No. IT-03-67-PT, Notification (re defence matters), 25 February 2003 (filed: 26 February 2003)

Case No. IT-03-67-PT, Order for Detention on Remand, 26 February 2003

Case No. IT-03-67-PT, Prosecution's Motion for Order Appointing Counsel to Assist Vojislav Šešelj With His Defence, 28 February 2003

Case No. IT-03-67-PT, Order on Translation of Documents, 06 March 2003

Case No. IT-03-67-PT, Decision on Prosecution's Motion for Order Appointing Counsel to Assist Vojislav Šešelj with His Defence, 09 May 2003

Case No. IT-03-67-PT, Decision on Motion for Disqualification, 10 June 2003 (filed: 11 June 2003)

Case No. IT-03-67-PT, Decision by Registrar, 05 September 2003

Case No. IT-03-67-PT, Decision on Motion Number 28, 19 December 2003 (filed: 22 December 2003)

Case No. IT-03-67-PT, Decision by Deputy Registrar, 16 February 2004

Case No. IT-03-67-PT, Motion No.30, 27 January 2004 (filed: 26 March 2004)

Case No. IT-03-67-PT, Defence Motion for Provisional Release, 14 June 2004 (filed: 24 June 2004)

Case No. IT-03-67-PT, Prosecution's Response to "Defence Motion for Provisional Release", 07 July 2004 (filed: 20 July 2004)

Case No. IT-03-67-PT, Decision on Defence Motion for Provisional Release, 23 July 2004 (filed: 28 July 2004)

Case No. IT-03-67-PT, Submission No.48, 03 November 2004 (filed: 05 November 2004)

Case No. IT-03-67-PT, Motion by the Accused for Normalisation of Conditions for Preparing a Defence, 26 October 2004 (filed: 09 November 2004)

Case No. IT-03-67-PT, Request of the Accused to Disclose Materials of the Prosecution in Written Form and in Serbian (Submission No. 43), 26 October 2004 (filed: 09 November 2004)

Case No. IT-03-67-PT, Request by the Accused to the Trial Chamber to Re-Examine Decision to Assign Stand-By Counsel to the Accused (Submission No. 45), 26 October 2004 (filed: 09 November 2004)

Case No. IT-03-67-PT, Prosecution's Response to Accused's Request for Disclosure of Materials in Written Form and in Serbian, 23 November 2004

Case No. IT-03-67-PT, Submission No.59, 29 November 2004 (filed: 02 December 2004)

Case No. IT-03-67-PT, Submission No.57, 25 November 2004 (filed: 08 December 2004)

Case No. IT-03-67-PT, Submission No.63, 08 December 2004 (filed: 30 December 2004)

Case No. IT-03-67-PT, Submission No.66, 15 December 2004 (filed: 05 January 2005)

Case No. IT-03-67-PT, Submission No.67, 15 December 2004 (filed: 05 January 2005)

Case No. IT-03-67-PT, Decision on the Accused's Motion to Re-Examine the Decision to Assign Standby Counsel, 01 March 2005

Case No. IT-03-67-PT, Decision on the Accused's Motion to Re-Examine the Decision to Assign Standby Counsel, 01 March 2005, Opinion Dissidente du Juge Antonetti

Case No. IT-03-67-PT, Corrigendum to Decision on the Accused's Motion to Re-Examine the Decision to Assign Standby Counsel, 11 March 2005

Case No. IT-03-67-PT, Request of the Accused to Revoke the Ruling of the Trial Chamber to Appoint Standby Counsel (Submission No. 81), 04 March 2005 (filed: 22 March 2005)

Case No. IT-03-67-PT, Request of the Accused for Trial Chamber II to Revoke the Ruling to Assign Standby Counsel (Submission No. 82), 05 March 2005 (filed: 06 April 2005)

Case No. IT-03-67-PT, Request of the Accused for Trial Chamber II to Revoke the Decision to Assign Standby Counsel (Submission No. 84), 07 March 2005 (filed: 06 April 2005)

Case No. IT-03-67-PT, Request by the Defendant to Change the Seat of the International Criminal Tribunal (Submission No. 90), 10 March 2005 (filed: 06 April 2005)

Case No. IT-03-67-PT, Decision on Request of the Accused to Revoke the Ruling of the Trial Chamber to Appoint Standby Counsel (Submissions Number 81, 82 and 84), 03 May 2005

Case No. IT-03-67-PT, Prosecution Motion for Joinder (Partly Confidential), 01 June 2005

Case No. IT-03-67-PT, Order to Registry and Commanding Officer of the United Nations Detention Unit, 11 July 2005

Case No. IT-03-67-PT, Submission No.99, 25 July 2005 (filed: 03 August 2005)

Case No. IT-03-67-PT, Decision on "Request of the Accused Asking President of the Tribunal Theodor Meron to Reverse the Decision of the Deputy Registrar Prohibiting Dr Vojislav Šešelj From Communicating With Anyone and Receiving Visits for at least 60 Days", 21 September 2005

Case No. IT-03-67-PT, Submission No.115, 24 October 2005 (filed: 01 November 2005)

Case No. IT-03-67-PT, Request of the Accused for Trial Chamber II to Issue an Order for the Trial to Commence by 24 February 2006 or an Order to Abolish Detention, Dismiss the Indictment and Release Dr Vojislav Šešelj (Submission No. 116), 07 November 2005 (filed: 16 November 2005)

Case No. IT-03-67-PT, Submission Number 118, 11 November 2005 (filed: 16 November 2005)

Case No. IT-03-67-PT, Request of Dr Vojislav Šešelj for the Issuing of an Order to Approve the Payment of Expenses for Preparation of his Defence (Submission No. 124), 03 January 2006 (filed: 16 January 2006)

Case No. IT-03-67-PT, Request of Dr Vojislav Šešelj for the Revocation of the Decision to Assign Standby Counsel (Submission No. 125), 03 January 2006 (filed: 16 January 2006)

Case No. IT-03-67-PT, Decision on Appeal Against Decision Denying Permission for Legal Representatives to Visit the Detainee, 25 May 2006

Case No. IT-03-67-PT, Registry Submission Pursuant to Rule 33(B) on the Facilities and Services that May be Available to Vojišlav [sic] Šešelj to Conduct his Defence, 08 June 2006

Case No. IT-03-67-AR72.1, Decision on Motion for Reconsideration of the "Decision on the Interlocutory Appeal Concerning Jurisdiction" Dated 31 August 2004, 15 June 2006

Case No. IT-03-67-PT, Decision on Submission Number 115, 16 June 2006

Case No. IT-03-67-PT, Decision on Filing of Motions, 19 June 2006

Case No. IT-03-67-PT, Motion for Trial Chamber I to Acquire a Complete Report on the Health of Professor Vojislav Šešelj (Submission No. 159), 19 May 2006 (filed: 22 June 2006)

Case No. IT-03-67-PT, Decision on Form of Disclosure, 04 July 2006

Case No. IT-03-67-PT, Decision on Assignment of Counsel, 21 August 2006

Case No. IT-03-67-PT, Registrar's Submission Pursuant to the Trial Chamber's Request for Further Information on the Request by Vojislav Šešelj for Payment of Expenses for the Preparation of his Defence, 21 September 2006

Case No. IT-03-67-AR73.3, Decision on Appeal Against the Trial Chamber's Decision on Assignment of Counsel, 20 October 2006

Case No. IT-03-67-PT, Order Concerning Appointment of Standby Counsel and Delayed Commencement of Trial, 25 October 2006

Case No. IT-03-67-PT, Prosecution Motion for Medical Examination of the Accused and for Consideration of Assignment of Counsel, 16 November 2006

Case No. IT-03-67-PT, Professor Vojislav Šešelj's Decision to Refuse Medical Treatment and Artificial Feeding While on Hunger Strike (Submission No. 223), 24 November 2006 (filed: 30 November 2006)

Case No. IT-03-67-T, Reasons for Decision (No. 2) on Assignment of Counsel, 27 November 2006

Case No. IT-03-67-T, Urgent Order to the Dutch Authorities Regarding Health and Welfare of the Accused, 06 December 2006

Case No. IT-03-67-AR73.4, Decision on Appeal Against the Trial Chamber's Decision (No.2) on Assignment of Counsel, 08 December 2006

Case No. IT-03-67-PT, Interlocutory Appeal by Professor Vojislav Šešelj Against the Decision on Form of Disclosure Issued by Trial Chamber I on 4 July 2006, 01 February 2007 (filed: 14 February 2007)

Affaire n° IT-03-67-PT, Ordonnance Portant Demande d'un Rapport Médical, 22 février 2007

Case No. IT-03-67-AR73.5, Decision on Vojislav Šešelj's Interlocutory Appeal Against the Trial Chamber's Decision on Form of Disclosure, 17 April 2007

Case No. IT-03-67-PT, Professor Vojislav Šešelj's Motion for Review of the Decision on Form of Disclosure Issued by Trial Chamber I on 4 July 2006 (Submission No. 289), 11 May 2007 (filed: 17 May 2007)

Case No. IT-03-67-PT, Professor Vojislav Šešelj's Motion for a Decision by Trial Chamber III on Financing his Defence in Accordance with the Statute (Submission No. 294), 04 June 2007 (filed: 14 June 2007)

Affaire n° IT-03-67-PT, Décision Relative à la Requête 289 Concernant le Mode de Communication de Pièces, 07 juin 2007

Case No. IT-03-67-PT, Prosecution's Response to the Accused's Motion for a Decision by Trial Chamber III on Financing his Defence in Accordance with the Statute (Number 294), 28 June 2007

Case No. IT-03-67-PT, Registry Submission Pursuant to Rule 33(B) of the Rules Regarding Vojislav Šešelj's Motion for a Decision by the Trial Chamber on Financing his Defence, 29 June 2007

Affaire n° IT-03-67-PT, Décision Relative au Financement de la Défense de l'Accusé, 30 juillet 2007

Affaire n° IT-03-67-PT, Décision Relative à la Mise En Œuvre du Financement de la Défense, 30 octobre 2007

Affaire n° IT-03-67-PT, Ordonnance Énonçant les Principes Directeurs Destinés à Régir la Présentation des Éléments de Preuve et le Comportement des Parties Pendant le Procès, 15 novembre 2007

Affaire n° IT-03-67-T, Ordonnance Aux Fins de Protéger l'Intégrité des Débats, 18 juin 2008

Case No. IT-03-67-T, Prosecution's Motion to Terminate the Accused's Self-Representation, 28 July 2008

Affaire n° IT-03-67-T, Version Expurgée de la « Version Expurgée de la 'Décision Relative à la Requête de l'Accusation aux Fins de Mettre Fin au Droit de l'Accusé à se Représenter Seul' » Enregistrée à Titre Confidentiel le 25 novembre 2008, 27 novembre 2008

Case No. IT-03-67-T, Registry Submission Pursuant to Rule 33(B) Regarding the Trial Chamber's Decision on Monitoring Vojislav Šešelj's Communications, 01 December 2008

Case No. IT-03-67-T, Request for the Trial Chamber to Secure the Financing of Professor Vojislav Šešelj's Defence (Submission No. 411), 15 January 2009 (filed: 03 February 2009)

Case No. IT-03-67-T, Registry Third Submission Pursuant to Rule 33(B) of the Rules Regarding the Financing of the Accused's Defence, 16 March 2009

Case No. IT-03-67-T, Order for Medical Reports, 02 April 2009

Affaire n° IT-03-67-T, Décision Relative au Financement de la Défense de l'Accusé, 23 avril 2009

Case No. IT-03-67-T, Submission of the Medical Opinion of a Team of Consultants Concerning the Current State of Health of Dr Vojislav Šešelj (Submission No. 418), 05 May 2009 (filed: 08 May 2009)

Case No. IT-03-67-T, Registry Submission Pursuant to Rule 33(B) Regarding the Trial Chamber's "Ordonnance Relative aux Observations du Greffe du 7 mai 2009", 08 May 2009

Affaire n° IT-03-67-T, Ordonnance Relative Aux Rappors [sic] Médicaux, 13 mai 2009

Case No. IT-03-67-T, Registry Submission Pursuant to Rule 33(B) Regarding the Viewing of Video Material by Vojislav Šešelj's Legal Associates, 29 June 2009

Case No. IT-03-67-R77.2, Public Edited Version of "Judgement on Allegations of Contempt" Issued on 24 July 2009, 24 July 2009

Case No. IT-03-67-T, Prosecution's Supplement to its Motion to Terminate the Accused's Self-Representation, 27 August 2009

Case No. IT-03-67-T, Submission No. 425, 11 September 2009 (filed: 15 September 2009)

Case No. IT-03-67-T, Registry Submission Pursuant to Rule 33(B) Regarding the Accused's Submission No. 425, 23 September 2009

Case No. IT-03-67-T, Oral Ruling, 20 October 2009, T.14751

Case No. IT-03-67-T, Decision on Vojislav Šešelj's Request for Review of Registrar's Decision of 10 September 2009, 21 October 2009

Case No. IT-03-67-T, Registry Submission Pursuant to Rule 33(B) Regarding the Implementation of Medical Expert Recommendations, 03 November 2009

Affaire n° IT-03-67-T, Version Publique de la « Décision Consolidée Relative à l'Imposition d'un Conseil, l'Ajournement, et la Requête de l'Accusation sur les Heures Supplémentaires Avec en Annexe l'Opinion Individuelle du Juge Antonetti Président de la Chambre », 24 novembre 2009

Case No. IT-03-67-R77.2-A, Decision on Motion for Disqualification of Judges Fausto Pocar and Theodor Meron From the Appeals Proceedings, 02 December 2009

Case No. IT-03-67-T, Reply of Professor Vojislav Šešelj to the "Response to the Accused's Oral Motion for Termination of Proceedings Pursuant to the Abuse of Process Doctrine", 18 December 2009 (filed: 29 December 2009)

Affaire n° IT-03-67-T, Décision Relative à la Requête Orale de l'Accusé Aux Fins de Rétablissement de MM. Zoran Krasić et Slavko Jerković en Qualité de Collaborateurs Privilégiés, 10 février 2010

Case No. IT-03-67-R77.2-A, Judgement, 19 May 2010

Case No. IT-03-67-T, Registry Submission Pursuant to Rule 33(B) of the Rules Regarding the Registry's Indigency Investigation of the Accused Vojislav Šešelj, 25 June 2010

Case No. IT-03-67-T, Decision of the Deputy Registrar, 05 July 2010

Affaire n° IT-03-67-T, Ordonnance aux Fins de Faire Procéder à Une Nouvelle Expertise Médicale de Vojislav Šešelj, 19 octobre 2010

Affaire n° IT-03-67-T, Version Expurgée de la « Décision Relative au Financement de la Défense » Enregistrée le 29 octobre 2010, 02 novembre 2010

Case No. IT-03-67-R33B, Registry Submission Pursuant to Rule 33(B) Following the Trial Chamber's Decision on Financing of Defence Dated 29 October 2010, 18 November 2010

Case No. IT-03-67-T, Registry Submission Pursuant to Rule 33(B) Regarding Medical Issues Raised at the Administrative Hearing of 2 November 2010, 24 November 2010

Affaire n° IT-03-67-T, Ordonnance Portant Modification de l'Ordonnance Portant Calendrier Enregistrée le 24 mars 2011, 14 avril 2011

Case No. IT-03-67-R33B, Public Redacted Version of the "Decision on the Registry Submission Pursuant to Rule 33(B) Regarding the Trial Chamber's Decision on Financing the Defence" Rendered on 8 April 2011, 17 May 2011

Case No. IT-03-67-R77.4, Public Edited Version of "Decision on Failure to Remove Confidential Information from Public Website and Order in Lieu of Indictment" Issued on 9 May 2011, 24 May 2011

Affaire n° IT-03-67-T, Décision Consolidée Relative aux Requêtes Orales de l'Accusé en Relation avec la Présentation de sa Défense, 09 juin 2011

Affaire n° IT-03-67-T, Opinion Individuelle Concordante du Président de la Chambre Relative à la Décision Consolidée de la Chambre Relative aux Requêtes Orales de l'Accusé en Relation avec la Présentation de sa Défense, 09 juin 2011

Case No. IT-03-67-T, Motion to Discontinue the Proceedings due to Flagrant Violation of the Right to a Trial Within a Reasonable Period in the Context of the Doctrine of Abuse of Process, 13 June 2011 (filed: 08 July 2011)

Case No. IT-03-67-T, Registry Submission Pursuant to Rule 33(B) Further to the Decision on Financing of the Defence, 21 June 2011 (filed: 22 June 2011)

Case No. IT-03-67-R77.4, Registry Submission Pursuant to Rule 33(B) Regarding the Application of the Decision on Financing, 11 July 2011 (filed: 12 July 2011)

Case No. IT-03-67-T, Prosecution's Response to the Accused's July 2011 Motion to Discontinue the Proceedings, 22 July 2011 (filed: 26 July 2011)

Affaire n° IT-03-67-T, Décision Relative à la Requête de l'Accusé aux Fins de Mettre un Terme à son Procès, 29 septembre 2011

Case No. IT-03-67-R77.3, Public Redacted Version of "Judgement" Issued on 31 October 2011, 31 October 2011

Prosecutor v. Stanišić & Župljanin

Case No. IT-08-91-PT, Stojan Zupljanin's Motion for Joinder With the Case of Radovan Karadzic, 02 December 2008

Prosecutor v. Zdravko Tolimir

Case No. IT-05-88/2-PT, Submission of the Accused for the Delivery of Documents and Transcripts of the Trial in a Script and Language that He Reads and Writes, 08 July 2007 (filed: 10 July 2007)

Case No. IT-05-88/2-PT, Submission on the Prosecution Request to Question the Accused, 06 July 2007 (filed: 12 July 2007)

Case No. IT-05-88/2-PT, Submission by the Accused for Assistance of the Trial Chamber on Appointment of Permanent Counsel, 06 July 2007 (filed: 13 July 2007)

Case No. IT-05-88/2-PT, Prosecution's Response to Submission of Zdravko Tolimir Dated 08 July 2007, 13 July 2007

Case No. IT-05-88/2-PT, Registry Submission Pursuant to Rule 33(B) of the Rules of Procedure and Evidence Regarding the Accused Tolimir's 13 July 2007 Submission on Appointment of Permanent Counsel, 18 July 2007

Case No. IT-05-88/2-PT, Registrar's Submission on "Submission of the Accused for Delivery of Documents and Transcripts of the Trial in a Script and Language that he Reads and Writes", 18 July 2007

Case No. IT-05-88/2-PT, Decision on Submission of Tolimir Requesting Translation of Documents and Transcripts, 20 July 2007

Case No. IT-05-88/2-PT, Decision on Motion by the Accused for Review of the Registry's Decision of 29 June 2007, 20 July 2007

Case No. IT-05-88/2-PT, Submission of the Accused to the Registrar Requesting the Delivery of Files and Documents in Written Form, in the Cyrillic Script and the Serbian Language, which are in Official Use in the Country of the Accused, 02 August 2007 (filed: 10 August 2007)

Case No. IT-05-88/2-PT, Submission by the Accused to the Registrar for Leave to Conduct his Own Defence or to Appoint Counsel of his Own Choosing Pursuant to Article 21.4(d), and Rule 45(F) and Amended Rule 62(C) of the Rules, 06 August 2007 (filed: 10 August 2007)

Case No. IT-05-88/2-PT, Submission by the Accused for the Violation of the Guaranteed and Discretionary Rights and Freedoms of Detained Persons Awaiting Trial Before the International Tribunal, 17 August 2007 (filed: 23 August 2007)

Case No. IT-05-88/2-PT, Submission by the Accused Concerning the Violation of the Guaranteed and Discretionary Rights and Freedoms of Detained Persons Awaiting Trial Before the International Tribunal, 23 August 2007 (filed: 28 August 2007)

Case No. IT-05-88/2-PT, Notification, 27 August 2007

Case No. IT-05-88/2-PT, The Accused's Submission to the Registrar and the Pre-Trial Chamber Concerning Status Issues and the Financing of his Defence in Accordance with Article 21 of the Statute of the International Criminal Tribunal for the Former Yugoslavia, 04 September 2007 (filed: 07 September 2007)

Case No. IT-05-88/2-PT, The Accused's Submission to the Registrar and the Pre-Trial Chamber to Review the Facts and Reasons for the Violation of Guaranteed and Discretionary Rights of the Accused Before the International Tribunal, 07 September 2007 (filed: 14 September 2007)

Case No. IT-05-88/2-PT, The Accused's Motion to the Pre-Trial Chamber to Suspend the Decision on the Filing of Preliminary Motions until the Abduction of the Accused is Resolved, the Prosecution Material Disclosed, and the Decision Made on the Motion by the Accused Concerning the Financing of his Defence in Accordance with Article 21 of the Statute of the International Criminal Tribunal for the Former Yugoslavia, 25 September 2007 (filed: 27 September 2007)

Case No. IT-05-88/2-PT, Registrar's Submission on the Accused's Motion Dated 25 September 2007, 03 October 2007

Case No. IT-05-88/2-PT, Submission of the Accused to the Tribunal Concerning the Deception of the Public and the Disturbance to my Family Caused by False Statements Made by the Registry and the Political and Media Pressures it has Exerted on the Tribunal, 08 October 2007 (filed: 09 October 2007)

Case No. IT-05-88/2-PT, Decision on Tolimir's Submission on Violation of his Rights Submitted on 07 September 2007, 10 October 2007

Case No. IT-05-88/2-PT, Prosecution's Response to Submission by the Accused Dated 25 September 2007, With Appendix, 10 October 2007

Case No. IT-05-88/2-PT, Decision on Motion for Suspension of Time Limit for Filing of Preliminary Motions, 18 October 2007

Case No. IT-05-88/2-PT, Submission by the Accused to the Registrar and the Pre-Trial Chamber for Leave to Appoint a Legal Advisor and Defence Team, 10 October 2007 (filed: 23 October 2007)

Case No. IT-05-88/2-PT, Motion to the Pre-Trial Chamber and the Registrar Concerning Assistance in Appointing a Legal Advisor, Disclosure of Material in a Language the Accused Understands and Notification of Special Defence on the Charges in the Indictment, 16 November 2007 (filed: 20 November 2007)

Case No. IT-05-88/2-PT, Prosecution Response to the Accused's 16 November 2007 Motion, 04 December 2007

Case No. IT-05-88/2-PT, Registrar's Submission on the Accused's Motion Dated 16 November 2007, 07 December 2007

Case No. IT-05-88/2-PT, Submission of the Accused to the Tribunal Concerning the Need for Communication Between the Trial Chamber, Prosecution and Registry With the Accused in his Mother Tongue, Serbian, and Using the Cyrillic Alphabet, which he can Understand, 07 December 2007 (filed: 13 December 2007)

Case No. IT-05-88/2-PT, Oral Ruling, 11 December 2007, T.113-117

Case No. IT-05-88/2-PT, Submission of the Accused to the Presiding Judge of Pre-Trial Chamber II for Leave to File an Appeal Against the Oral Ruling of the Pre-Trial Judge Ordering Communication Between the Accused and the International Tribunal and Disclosure of Material Supporting the Indictment in a Language, Script and Form that the Accused does not Understand, 17 December 2007 (filed: 19 December 2007)

Case No. IT-05-88/2-PT, Prosecution's Response to the Accused's Request for Certification of the Pre-Trial Judge's Oral Decision of 11 December 2007, 28 December 2007

Case No. IT-05-88/2-PT, The Accused's Submission to the Pre-Trial Chamber, Registrar and Prosecution Concerning Disregard by the Tribunal for the Fundamental Rights and Actual Wishes of the Accused Regarding Communication and Appointment of the Accused's Legal Counsel, 03 January 2008 (filed: 10 January 2008)

Case No. IT-05-88/2-PT, The Accused's Submission to the Registrar and the Pre-Trial Chamber Concerning the Submission to the Accused of Documents in a Language and Script the he does not Speak, Read, Write or Understand, 07 January 2008 (filed: 10 January 2008)

Case No. IT-05-88/2-PT, Registrar's Notification Regarding the Assignment of Legal Assistance to the Accused, 11 January 2008

Case No. IT-05-88/2-PT, Decision on Accused's Submission Dated 07 December 2007 and Decision on Certification to Appeal, 15 January 2008

Case No. IT-05-88/2-PT, Decision on Motion for Certification to Appeal the 11 December Oral Decision, 15 January 2008

Case No. IT-05-88/2-PT, Submission of the Accused to the Pre-Trial Chamber, the Registrar and the Prosecutor Concerning the Need for Communication with the Accused in a Language and Script that he Understands, 23 January 2008 (filed: 25 January 2008)

Case No. IT-05-88/2-AR73.1, Appeal by the Accused to the Presiding Judge of Chamber II Against the Verbal Ruling of the Pre-Trial Judge Ordering Communication Between the Accused and the International Tribunal and the Obligation to Accept Material Accompanying the Indictment in a Language, Script and Form that the Accused does not Understand, 25 January 2008 (filed: 31 January 2008)

Case No. IT-05-88/2-PT, Submission of the Accused to the Trial Chamber, Registrar and Prosecutor for Delivery of Documents in a Language which the Accused does not Understand, 31 January 2008 (filed: 05 February 2008)

Case No. IT-05-88/2-PT, Submission of the Accused to the Pre-Trial Chamber, the Registrar and Prosecutor on the Return of Documents which the Accused does not Understand and the Request that all Communication and Correspondence be carried out in the Serbian Language and Script which the Accused Solely Understands, 01 February 2008 (filed: 05 February 2008)

Case No. IT-05-88/2-PT, Accused's Submission Concerning the Appointment of Legal Advisors and the Need for the Court, Registry and the Prosecution to Communicate with the Accused in the Serbian Language, As the Only Language he Understands, 03 March 2008 (filed: 05 March 2008)

Case No. IT-05-88/2-PT, Registrar's Submission Regarding the Motions of the Accused Dated 13 February 2008 and 03 March 2008, 07 March 2008

Case No. IT-05-88/2-AR73.1, Decision on Interlocutory Appeal Against Oral Decision of the Pre-Trial Judge of 11 December 2007, 28 March 2008

Case No. IT-05-88/2-PT, Submission by the Accused to the Trial Chamber, Registry and Prosecution on Depriving the Accused of his Guaranteed Rights, on Creating Conditions for Normal Communication with the Accused and his Legal Advisors, and on Proper Conduct of the Proceedings, 26 March 2008 (filed: 03 April 2008)

Case No. IT-05-88/2-PT, Submission by the Accused to the President of the Tribunal, the Registrar and the Pre-Trial Chamber, with the Request that the "Decision on Interlocutory Appeal against Oral Decision of the Pre-Trial Judge of 11 December 2007" be submitted to him in Serbian, the only Language he Understands, 10 April 2008 (filed: 15 April 2008)

Case No. IT-05-88/2-PT, Accused's Motion to the President of the Tribunal and Members of the Appeals Chamber to Exercise their Discretionary Powers and Reconsider their Decision on the Appeal Against the Interlocutory Appeal Against the Oral Decision of the Pre-Trial Judge of 11 December 2007, 16 April 2008 (filed: 18 April 2008)

Case No. IT-05-88/2-PT, Submission of the Accused to the Prosecuting Attorney, the Office of the Prosecutor, the Registry and the Pre-Trial Chamber with Request that all Materials from the Indictment be Submitted to him in a Language he that Understands, 21 April 2008 (filed: 25 April 2008)

Case No. IT-05-88/2-PT, Prosecution's Motion Requesting Appointment of Permanent Counsel for Accused Tolimir, 29 April 2008

Case No. IT-05-88/2-PT, Submission of the Accused to the Appeals and Pre-Trial Chambers to Dismiss the Legally Unfounded Prosecution Motion Requesting Imposition of Counsel for the Accused Who is Conducting his own Defence, and Request that the Prosecution Withdraw its Motion, 06 May 2008 (filed: 19 May 2008)

Case No. IT-05-88/2-PT, Supplement to the Accused Zdravko Tolimir's Motion to the President of the Tribunal and Members of the Appeals Chamber to Review their Decision on the Appeal Against the Decision of the Pre-Trial Judge of 11 December 2007, 30 May 2008 (filed: 04 June 2008)

Case No. IT-05-88/2-PT, Response to the Prosecution's Motion Requesting the Appointment of Permanent Counsel for the Accused Tolimir, 02 June 2008 (filed: 05 June 2008)

Case No. IT-05-88/2-PT, Response by the Accused Zdravko Tolimir to the Question of the Pre-Trial Judge Regarding Receipt of Audio and Video Material, 05 June 2008 (filed: 10 June 2008)

Case No. IT-05-88/2-AR73.1, Decision on Zdravko Tolimir's Request for Reconsideration of the Appeals Chamber's Decision of 28 March 2008, 18 June 2008

Case No. IT-05-88/2-PT, Statements in Accordance with the Decision of the Pre-Trial Judge of 30 June 2008 Concerning Disclosure, 30 June 2008 (filed: 01 July 2008)

Case No. IT-05-88/2-PT, Submission of the Accused to the Registrar of the Tribunal and the Pre-Trial Chamber Pursuant to the Order of the Pre-Trial Judge dated 30 June 2008 on Disclosure, 04 July 2008 (filed: 09 July 2008)

Case No. IT-05-88/2-PT, Prosecution Submission Regarding 30 July 2008 Status Conference, 25 July 2008

Case No. IT-05-88/2-PT, Response to the Prosecutor's Submission of 25 July 2008, 28 July 2008 (filed: 29 July 2008)

Case No. IT-05-88/2-PT, Submission by the Accused Concerning the Protection of his Discretionary and Guaranteed Rights and a Violation of Rights, 13 August 2008 (filed: 21 August 2008)

Case No. IT-05-88/2-T, Decision on the Accused's Submission of 18 August 2008, 02 September 2008

Case No. IT-05-88/2-PT, Urgent Request from Zdravko Tolimir on Conditions of Detention Because of Deprivation of Sleep, 08 December 2008 (filed: 09 December 2008)

Case No. IT-05-88/2-PT, Motion of the Accused for the Pre-Trial Chamber and Registrar of the Tribunal to Create Minimum Conditions for the Preparation of his Defence, 06 February 2009 (filed: 10 February 2009)

Case No. IT-05-88/2-PT, Registry Submission Pursuant to Rule 33(B) Concerning the Accused's Medical Monitoring, 08 June 2009

Case No. IT-05-88/2-PT, Notification, 23 June 2009

Case No. IT-05-88/2-PT, Submission Concerning Deprivation of Sleep and the Fitting of Microchips to the Body of the Accused, 10 July 2009 (filed: 16 July 2009)

Case No. IT-05-88/2-PT, Notification, 19 October 2009

Case No. IT-05-88/2-PT, Request for the Chamber to Allow Aleksandar Gajić, Legal Advisor to Zdravko Tolimir to be Present in the Courtroom, 12 February 2010 (filed: 16 February 2010)

Case No. IT-05-88/2-PT, Decision on Motion Requesting the Chamber to Allow the Accused's Legal Advisor to be Present in the Courtroom, 22 February 2010

Case No. IT-05-88/2-PT, Prosecution Motion for an Instruction Regarding the Admissibility of Submissions and Statements of the Accused, 23 February 2010

Case No. IT-05-88/2-T, Request to the Trial Chamber, 01 March 2010 (filed: 03 March 2010)

Case No. IT-05-88/2-T, Decision on the Accused's Information and Requests for the Trial Chamber, 04 March 2010

Case No. IT-05-88/2-T, Prosecution Response to Tolimir's Request to the Trial Chamber, 05 March 2010

Case No. IT-05-88/2-T, Request to the Pre-Trial Chamber for Leave to File of a Reply and Reply to the Prosecution's Response of 5 March 2010, 08 March 2010 (filed: 10 March 2010)

Case No. IT-05-88/2-T, Decision on Accused's Request to the Trial Chamber Concerning Assistance of his Legal Advisor, 28 April 2010 (Public redacted version issued on 27 May 2010. See Order Issuing a Public Redacted Version of the "Decision on Accused's Request to the Trial Chamber Concerning Assistance of his Legal Advisor", 27 May 2010)

Case No. IT-05-88/2-T, Zdravko Tolimir's Submission Concerning the Possible Trial Schedule for June, 10 May 2010 (filed: 13 May 2010)

Case No. IT-05-88/2-T, Decision on Zdravko Tolimir's Submission Concerning the Possible Trial Schedule for June, 26 May 2010

Case No. IT-05-88/2-T, Zdravko Tolimir's Request for Transcripts in a Language which he Understands, 09 July 2010 (filed: 12 July 2010)

Case No. IT-05-88/2-T, Prosecution's Response to Zdravko Tolimir's Request for Transcripts in a Language which he Understands, 23 July 2010

Case No. IT-05-88/2-T, Reply to the Responses of the Registrar and the Prosecutor and a Request Regarding the Trial Schedule, 11 August 2010 (filed: 13 August 2010)

Case No. IT-05-88/2-T, Decision on Accused's Motion for Suspension of Proceedings, 18 August 2010

Case No. IT-05-88/2-T, Order Regarding the Nightly Monitoring of the Accused, 25 August 2010 (Public redacted version filed on 27 August 2010. See Notice of Filing of Public Redacted Version of the "Order Regarding the Nightly Monitoring of the Accused", 27 August 2010.)

Case No. IT-05-88/2-T, Decision on Zdravko Tolimir's Request for Transcripts in a Language which he Understands, 27 August 2010

Case No. IT-05-88/2-T, Urgent Registry Submission Pursuant to Rule 33(B) Concerning the Order Regarding the Nightly Monitoring of the Accused, 30 August 2010

Case No. IT-05-88/2-T, Statement in Accordance with the Trial Chamber Decision of 25 August 2010, 31 August 2010 (filed: 01 September 2010)

Case No. IT-05-88/2-T, Decision on Urgent Registry Submission Pursuant to Rule 33(B) Concerning the Order Regarding the Nightly Monitoring of the Accused, 01 September 2010

Case No. IT-05-88/2-T, Second Registry Submission Pursuant to Rule 33(B) Concerning the Order Regarding the Nightly Monitoring of the Accused, 03 September 2010

Case No. IT-05-88/2-T, Registry Submission Pursuant to Rule 33(B) Concerning the Accused's Statements on 19 October 2010, 22 October 2010

Special Court for Sierra Leone

Prosecutor v. Samuel Hinga Norman et al.

Case No. SCSL-04-14-T, Decision on the Application of Samuel Hinga Norman for Self Representation Under Article 17(4)(d) of the Statute of the Special Court, 08 June 2004

Case No. SCSL-04-14-T, Ruling on the Issue of Non-Appearance of the First Accused Samuel Hinga Norman, the Second Accused Moinina Fofana, and the Third Accused, Allieu Kondewa at the Trial Proceedings, 01 October 2004

Prosecutor v. Issa Hassan Sesay et al.

Case No. SCSL-04-15-T, Gbao – Decision on Application to Withdraw Counsel, 06 July 2004

Case No. SCSL-04-15-AR73, Gbao – Decision on Appeal Against Decision on Withdrawal of Counsel, 23 November 2004

Prosecutor v. Charles Ghankay Taylor

Case No. SCSL-03-01-PT, Decision on Urgent and Public Defence Motion Requesting Leave for Charles Ghankay Taylor to Give an Un-Sworn Statement from the Dock, 29 May 2007

Human Rights Committee

Michael and Brian Hill v. Spain, Communication No. 526/1993, U.N. Doc. CCPR/C/59/D/526/1993, 02 April 1997

Carlos Correia de Matos c. Portugal, Communication No. 1123/2002, U.N. Doc. CCPR/C/86/D/1123/2002, 26 mars 2006

Concepción Sánchez González v. Spain, Communication No. 1005/2001, U.N. Doc. CCPR/C/74/D/1005/2001, 21 March 2002

Marina Torregrosa Lafuente et al. v. Spain, Communication No. 866/1999, U.N. Doc. CCPR/C/72/D/866/1999, 16 July 2001

European Court of Human Rights

A v. Germany, Application no. 10565/83 (Commission), 1985

Belziuk v. Poland, Application no. 23103/93, Judgment, 25 March 1998

Carlos Correia de Matos c. Portugal, Requête n° 48188/99, Décision partielle, 14 septembre 2000

Carlos Correia de Matos c. Portugal, Requête n° 48188/99, Décision, 15 novembre 2001

Ciorap v. Moldova, Application no. 12066/02, Judgment, 19 September 2007

Croissant c. Allemagne, Requête n° 13611/88, Arrêt, 25 septembre 1992

Dombo Beheer B.V. v. The Netherlands, Application no. 14448/88, Judgement, 27 October 1993

Galstyan v. Armenia, Application no. 26986/03, Judgment, 15 February 2008

Grigoryevskikh v. Russia, Application no. 22/03, Judgment, 09 July 2009

Güveç v. Turkey, Application no. 70337/01, Judgment, 20 April 2009

Herczegfalvy v. Austria, Application no. 10533/83, Judgment, 24 September 1992

Kremzow v. Austria, Application no. 12350/86, Judgment, 21 September 1993

Lagerblom v. Sweden, Application no. 26891/95, Judgment, 14 April 2003

Mayzit v. Russia, Application no. 63378/00, Judgment, 06 July 2005

Melin v. France, Application no. 12914/87, Judgement, 22 June 1993

Moiseyev v. Russia, Application no. 62936/00, Judgment, 06 April 2009

Monnell and Morris v. United Kingdom, Application no. 9562/81 & 9819/82, Judgment, 02 March 1987

Nevmerzhitsky v. Ukraine, Application no. 54825/00, Judgment, 12 October 2005

Padalov c. Bulgarie, Requête n° 54784/00, Arrêt, 10 novembre 2006

Pakelli c. Allemagne, Requête n° 8398/78, Arrêt, 05 avril 1983
Sakhnovskiy v. Russia [GC], Application no. 21272/03, Judgment, 02 November 2010
Sejdovic v. Italy [GC], Application no. 56581/00, Judgment, 01 March 2006
Shulepov v. Russia, Application no. 15435/03, Judgment, 01 December 2008
Seyithan Demir v. Turkey, Application no. 25381/02, Judgment, 28 October 2009
Talat Tunç c. Turquie, Requête n° 32432/96, Arrêt, 27 juin 2007
Timergaliyev v. Russia, Application no. 40631/02, Judgment, 14 January 2009
Tripodi v. Italy, Application no. 13743/88, Judgment, 22 February 1994
Vitan c. Roumanie, Requête n° 42084/02, Arrêt, 01 décembre 2008
X. v. Austria, Application no. 7138/75 (Commission), Decision, 05 July 1977
Zana v. Turkey [GC], Application no. 18954/91, Judgment, 25 November 1997

United Kingdom

R. v Desmond Francis Lyons, (1979) 68 Cr. App. R. 104, 10-11 July 1978
McKenzie v McKenzie (Court of Appeal), [1971] P. 33, 12 June 1970
R. v Ernest Isaac Woodward, (1944) 29 Cr. App. R. 159, 08 December 1943

United States

Adams v. U.S. ex rel. McCann (U.S. Supreme Court), 317 U.S. 269, 21 December 1942
Carter v. People of State of Illinois (U.S. Supreme Court), 329 U.S. 173, 09 December 1946
Anthony Pasquall Faretta v. State of California (U.S. Supreme Court), 422 U.S. 806, 30 June 1975
Godinez v. Moran (U.S. Supreme Court), 509 U.S. 389, 24 June 1993
Indiana v. Ahmad Edwards (U.S. Supreme Court), 554 U.S. 164, 19 June 2008
Martinez v. Court of Appeal of California, Fourth Appellate District (U.S. Supreme Court), 528 U.S. 152 (2000), 12 January 2000
Warren McCleskey v. Walter D. Zant (U.S. Supreme Court), 499 U.S. 467, 16 April 1991
McKaskle v. Wiggins (U.S. Supreme Court), 465 U.S. 168 (1984), 23 January 1984
Powell et al. v. State of Alabama (U.S. Supreme Court), 287 U.S. 45, 07 November 1932
Price v. Johnston (U.S. Supreme Court), 334 U.S. 266, 24 May 1948
Jay Printz v. Richard Mack (U.S. Supreme Court), 521 U.S. 898, 27 June 1997
Donald P. Roper v. Christopher Simmons (U.S. Supreme Court), 543 U.S. 551, 01 March 2005
United States of America v. Kashani Farhad (U.S. Court of Appeals Ninth Circuit), 190 F.3d 1097, 13 September 1999
United States of America v. William Stewart McDowell (U.S. Court of Appeals Sixth Circuit), 814 F.2d 245, 16 March 1987
United States of America v. Rigoberto Moya-Gomez (U.S. Court of Appeals Seventh Circuit), 860 F.2d 706, 30 September 1988

Schriften zum Internationalen und Europäischen Strafrecht

Herausgegeben von

Prof. Dr. Martin Heger, Humboldt-Universität zu Berlin
Prof. Dr. Florian Jeßberger, Universität Hamburg
Prof. Dr. Frank Neubacher, M.A., Universität zu Köln
Prof. Dr. Helmut Satzger, LMU München
Prof. Dr. Gerhard Werle, Humboldt-Universität zu Berlin

Veröffentlichungen:

Zehn Jahre Völkerstrafgesetzbuch
Bilanz und Perspektiven eines „deutschen Völkerstrafrechts“
Herausgegeben von Prof. Dr. Florian Jeßberger und Julia Geneuss, LL.M. (NYU)
2013, 306 S., brosch., 79,– €, SBN 978-3-8487-0279-4
(Schriften zum Internationalen und Europäischen Strafrecht, Bd. 1)

Europäische Strafrechtsprinzipien
Ein Beitrag zur systematischen Fortentwicklung übergreifender Grundlagen
Von Dr. Andreas B. Schaut
2012, 344 S., brosch., 89,– €, ISBN 978-3-8329-7968-3
(Schriften zum Internationalen und Europäischen Strafrecht, Bd. 2)

Referral of Cases from International to National Criminal Jurisdictions
Transferring Cases from the ICTY and the ICTR to National Jurisdictions
Von RAin Dr. Lena Lindemann
2013, 300 S., brosch., 78,– €, ISBN 978-3-8329-7742-9
(Schriften zum Internationalen und Europäischen Strafrecht, Bd. 3)

Notwehr und Notstand im deutsch-türkischen Rechtsvergleich
Unter Berücksichtigung französischer und italienischer Rechtstraditionen
Von Dr. Özdem Özaydın
2013, 278 S., brosch., 72,– €, ISBN 978-3-8329-7771-9
(Schriften zum Internationalen und Europäischen Strafrecht, Bd. 4)

Turkey and the International Criminal Court
A Substantive Criminal Law Analysis in the Context of the Principle of Complementarity
Von Dr. Ali Emrah Bozbayındır
2013, 168 S., brosch., 42,– €, ISBN 978-3-8487-0346-3
(Schriften zum Internationalen und Europäischen Strafrecht, Bd. 5)

Die Bedeutung des Europäischen Strafrechts und sein Einfluss in Georgien
Von Dr. Bachana Jishkariani
2013, 286 S., brosch., 76,– €, ISBN 978-3-8487-0344-9
(Schriften zum Internationalen und Europäischen Strafrecht, Bd. 6)

Völkerrechtsverbrechen und Verfolgungsermessen
§ 153f StPO im System völkerrechtlicher Strafrechtspflege
Von Dr. Julia Geneuss, LL.M. (NYU)
2013, 364 S., brosch., 95,– €, ISBN 978-3-8487-0354-8
(Schriften zum Internationalen und Europäischen Strafrecht, Bd. 7)

Strafrechtliche Legislativkompetenzen der Europäischen Union
Eine Gegenüberstellung der Kompetenzlage vor und nach dem Vertrag von Lissabon
Von Dr. Fabian Dorra
2013, 312 S., brosch., 79,– €, ISBN 978-3-8487-0445-3
(Schriften zum Internationalen und Europäischen Strafrecht, Bd. 8)

Strafrecht und Terrorismusbekämpfung
Eine vergleichende Untersuchung der Bekämpfung terroristischer Vorbereitungsverhandlungen in Deutschland, Großbritannien und Spanien
Von Dr. Anneke Petzsche
2013, 494 S., brosch., 109,– €, ISBN 978-3-8487-0806-2
(Schriften zum Internationalen und Europäischen Strafrecht, Bd. 9)

Witness Preparation in International and Domestic Criminal Proceedings
Von Dr. Kai Oliver Schüttpelz
2014, 220 S., brosch., 59,– €, ISBN 978-3-8487-0778-2
(Schriften zum Internationalen und Europäischen Strafrecht, Bd. 10)

Self-Representation Before International Criminal Tribunals
Von Dr. Sarah Raveling
2014, 468 S., brosch., 109,– €, ISBN 978-3-8487-0875-8
(Schriften zum Internationalen und Europäischen Strafrecht, Bd. 11)

Binnendissonanzen im AT
Die Vorfeld- und Beteiligungsstrafbarkeit nach dem StGB im Spannungsfeld zwischen europäischen Vorgaben und deutscher Strafrechtsdogmatik
Von Dr. Julia Brons
2014, 606 S., brosch., 134,– €, ISBN 978-3-8487-1121-5
(Schriften zum Internationalen und Europäischen Strafrecht, Bd. 12)